Gatekeepers of the Arab Past

The publisher gratefully acknowledges the generous support of the Humanities Endowment Fund of the University of California Press Foundation.

. . .

The publisher also acknowledges the generous contribution to this book provided by the Cooperative Society at the University of Texas, Austin.

Gatekeepers of the Arab Past

Historians and History Writing in Twentieth-Century Egypt

Yoav Di-Capua

UNIVERSITY OF CALIFORNIA PRESS

Berkeley Los Angeles London

University of California Press, one of the most distinguished university presses in the United States, enriches lives around the world by advancing scholarship in the humanities, social sciences, and natural sciences. Its activities are supported by the UC Press Foundation and by philanthropic contributions from individuals and institutions. For more information, visit www.ucpress.edu.

University of California Press
Berkeley and Los Angeles, California

University of California Press, Ltd.
London, England

Library of Congress Cataloging-in-Publication Data

Di-Capua, Yoav, 1970–.
Gatekeepers of the Arab past : historians and history writing in twentieth-century Egypt / Yoav Di-Capua.
p. cm.
Includes bibliographical references and index.
ISBN 978-0-520-25732-0 (cloth : alk. paper)
ISBN 978-0-520-25733-7 (pbk. : alk. paper)
1. Historiography—Egypt. 2. Egypt—Historiography. 3. Nationalism—Egypt. 4. Historians—Egypt. 5. Egypt—History—20th century. I. Title.
DT107.824.D53 2009
907.2'062—dc22 2009006143

Manufactured in the United States of America

18 17 16 15 14 13 12 11 10 09
11 10 9 8 7 6 5 4 3 2 1

The paper used in this publication meets the minimum requirements of ANSI/NISO Z39.48–1992 (R 1997) *(Permanence of Paper).*

To Shula and Dario Di-Capua

CONTENTS

List of Illustrations *ix*
List of Tables *xi*
Acknowledgments *xiii*
List of Abbreviations *xv*

Introduction *1*

1. Historicizing Ottoman Egypt: 1890–1906 *19*
2. Talking History: 1906–1920 *66*
3. The ʿĀbdīn House of Records: The 1920s *91*
4. Competing for History: 1930–1952 *141*
5. Ghurbāl's School: 1930–1952 *186*
6. Partisan Historiography: The 1940s and Beyond *219*
7. Demonstrating History: The 1950s *248*
8. Controlling History: The 1960s *282*
9. Authoritarian Pluralism: 1970–2000 *311*

Conclusion *337*

Bibliography *345*
Index *371*

ILLUSTRATIONS

1. Concluding page of Amīn b. Ḥasan al-Ḥalawānī's treatise *Nabsh al-hadhayān*, 1889. *42*
2. Cover page of Georges Douin's *Navarin*. *120*
3. Gabriel Hanotaux (1853–1944). *124*
4. Allegory as political power. *236*

TABLES

1. Published Source Material from the ʿĀbdīn Project *118*
2. Number of History Books Published in Arabic on Modern Egypt *145*
3. Selected Nationalist and Royalist Publications *182*
4. The First Generation of Academic History Students, 1934–1952 *192*
5. Geographical Focus of Ph.D. Dissertations and M.A. Theses on Modern History, 1925–1954 *204*
6. Temporal Focus of Ph.D. Dissertations and M.A. Theses, 1925–1954 *205*
7. Selective Publications on Saʿd Zaghlūl to 1952 *227*

ACKNOWLEDGMENTS

From its origins in convoluted seminar papers, through a slightly more organized dissertation, and, finally, into a somewhat coherent book, this academic process would not have been successfully completed without the extremely generous support of two institutions: Princeton University, where I was a graduate student, and the University of Texas at Austin, where I currently work. In particular, I wish to acknowledge the Co-operative Society at the University of Texas, for awarding me a subvention grant, and the American Philosophical Society, which supported the last stages of research and writing.

In addition, three individuals deserve special acknowledgment: Khaled Fahmy, of New York University, served as my de facto adviser throughout this project and demonstrated an exceptional ability to listen and instruct. He dedicated dozens of hours to conversations on Egyptian historiography and other intellectual and more earthly concerns. He carefully read and commented on the entire manuscript, and I profited immensely from his remarkable sensitivity to the deeds and thoughts of past generations. It is only rarely that one encounters a teacher with whom one reaches a profound level of understanding. It makes a better learning process and, more important, a valuable human experience. I deeply thank him for that.

At Princeton, Robert Tignor supervised my work during the years 1999 to 2004. I thank Professor Tignor for balancing my enthusiasm with his rich perspective and experience. He taught me to express my ideas in a more careful, accurate, and clear fashion. This was always followed by rigorous and insightful criticism. Despite his myriad other commitments, he worked with such great speed and devotion that he made me feel as though I were his only student. Working with him was a real pleasure and a wonderful lesson for life.

Back home, Israel Gershoni was the one who, during the 1990s, first introduced me to Arab intellectual history. His passion for scholarship and dedication to his students serve for me as a model. Especially today, as the gap between scholarship and the real world of Middle East politics exponentially widens, his optimism and belief in the virtue of historical studies are an inspiration.

In the very final stages of bringing this manuscript to light, I immensely benefited from readers' reports from Roger Owen, of Harvard University; Bob Vitalis, of the University of Pennsylvania; Nancy Gallagher, of the University of California, Santa Barbara; and another reader, anonymous, though meticulous and committed. Rather than responding with the usual page and a half criticism on the run, all four paid careful attention to small details as well as to the overall line of argumentation. I am genuinely grateful for the profound impact their comments have had on the shape of this research.

Alongside these mentors, a group of close friends, colleagues, and teachers took the time to read, converse, and share their impressions and ideas with me, and their comments have made this work stronger. These are Zur Shalev, Cyrus Schayegh, Yumna Masarwa, Will Hanley, Ori Lev, Louisa Shea, and Bruce Fudge. The late Lara Moore kindly introduced me to archival science. I thank Samah Selim for the opportunity to read and discuss with her a host of Arabic novels. Arthur Goldschmidt vividly shared with me his memories from Cairo of the 1960s. Many years ago Avraham Yinon taught me Arabic. I thank him for that. Mostly, I am particularly indebted to my wife, Stephennie Mulder. Although sadly, these days we men can no longer convince our wives to "type our manuscripts," I am fortunate indeed to have in Stephennie a true friend and intellectual partner. I thank her for many hours of careful reading, sympathetic corrections to my "Henglish," and for thinking this project through with me.

My parents, Shula and Dario, contemporaries of the people I study, deserve special acknowledgment. Always prioritizing education, they afforded me the luxury of scholarship. I feel fortunate and grateful to have them at my side. My brother, Noam, always reminded me of my other abiding interest, by sharing with me several bird-watching trips.

A close community of dear technocratic and skeptical friends, who neither share academic scholarship with me nor believe in its value , supported me despite their misguided convictions. Whether in Geneva, Jerusalem, Rome, Tel Aviv, or London, their lack of understanding and qualified love were a constant source of encouragement.

Finally, I wish to assure the reader that even during this postmodern age—which, to many established historians in my field, appears as the worst possible historiographical era—this book is based on a true story.

ABBREVIATIONS

AUC	American University in Cairo
EHS	Egyptian Historical Society (until 1952 was known as the Royal Historical Society of Egypt)
EI^2	*Encyclopaedia of Islam,* 2nd ed. (Leiden: E. J. Brill, 1960–)
EMNL	Egyptian Movement for National Liberation
IJMES	*International Journal of Middle East Studies*
MTM	*Al-Majalla al-tārākhiyya al-miṣriyya*
RGS	Royal Geographical Society
SOAS	School of Oriental and African Studies
UAR	United Arab Republic

Introduction

In 2004, Ra'ūf 'Abbās, one of Egypt's leading historians, published his autobiography. This memoir, ostensibly a pedestrian intellectual autobiography of a retired history professor, proved instead to be a frontal assault on Egypt's entire historiographical establishment. The author spared no one: neither the stars of Egypt's academic elite nor the lowliest graduate student escaped the lashing of his pen. Over the course of 336 crowded pages, he accused his colleagues of poor academic standards, plagiarism, intellectual shallowness, ethical violations, political partisanship, and collaboration with the state's security services. His many anecdotes ranged from the selling of academic degrees to rich Saudi students to the plagiarizing of foreign books by Egyptian professors. The state, which for the past half century had refused to deposit its records in the public archive, was to blame as well.[1] Yet, scandalous as his memoir was, 'Abbās revealed nothing new. In fact, he merely scratched the surface of a seemingly chronic debate that had begun soon after World War I and had already exploded one hot summer two decades previously.

Cairo, August 1987. After a long process of preparation, the conference "Commitment and Objectivity in Contemporary Egyptian Historiography" was ready to begin. In Egypt, history writing had long been a sensitive issue, but the organizers' plan to engage directly with questions of politicization, censorship, and official state-guided projects of history rewriting charged this event with the

1. Ra'ūf 'Abbās, *Mashaynāhā khutān: Sīra dhātiya* (Cairo: Dār al-hilāl, 2004), pp. 133, 146, 205, 221–247, 236, 253, 257–258, 265, 270–272.

excitement reserved for the first crossing of a forbidden boundary. The role of Aḥmad ʿAbdallāh—who had led the January 1972 student uprising—as historian, co-organizer, and mediator assured the participants that, this time, slogans and taboos would not be respected. A sense of expectation was in the air. The press coverage was extensive; foreign bodies attended and helped finance the conference, and political circles evinced interest as well.[2] Concerned for their reputation, some historians chose to boycott it.[3] To those who participated, it was clear that the four-day symposium was not only a rare academic occurrence but also an exceptional public event. Years of relative silence, on one hand, and aggressive accusations of distortion and falsification of history, on the other, were about to be substituted with meaningful discussion.

The published conference proceedings prove that the expectation and excitement were justified.[4] Indeed, taboos, slogans, and old habits of silence were ignored, and some sensational declarations made headlines.[5] Though there was no official government representation, representatives of nearly every other imaginable institution and school of thought, attended the event, along with numerous individuals: Marxists who had served time in jail, committed historians of national parties, those who had participated in orchestrated projects of history rewriting, Islamists (who had begun writing modern history only recently), amateur journalists, and numerous party-unaffiliated academics and independent historians, who wrote history for history's sake alone. Members of at least three generations of history writers presented their perspectives. All disciplines—social, economic, political, intellectual, and legal history—were properly represented. They talked about almost everything: the impact of colonialism on modern historiography; the role of party-affiliated historiography; professional versus amateur writing; the influence of the press; the dysfunctional historiographical infrastructure; the corrupting influence of state-power; and, of course, the meaning of objectivity and impartiality in history writing.[6]

However, the exchange at the conference was far from peaceful and harmoni-

2. An estimated seventy-five newspapers and journals covered the conference. Jamāl Salīm, "Al-Tashhīr bi-zuʿamāʾ Miṣr," *Rūz al-Yūsuf,* September 14, 1987, pp. 24–27; ʿĀṭif Muṣṭafa, "Zuʿamāʾ Miṣr bayna al-ḥaqīqa al-tārīkhiyya wa-l-tashhīr al-siyāsī," *Al-Hilāl,* October 1987, pp. 156–161; Yūsuf al-Quʿayd, "Sanawāt mā qabla al-thawra," *Al-Muṣawwar,* December 18, 1987, pp. 59–61.

3. Yūsuf al-Quʿayd and ʿAbd al-Raḥmān al-Badrī, "Fawdat al-tārīkh fī Miṣr," *Al-Muṣawwar,* September 11, 1987, p. 15.

4. Aḥmad ʿAbdallāh, ed., *Tārīkh Miṣr bayna al-manhaj al-ʿilmī wa-l-ṣirāʿ al-ḥizbī* (Cairo: Dār shuhdī li-l-nashr, 1988).

5. For example, Huda ʿAbd al-Nāṣir, a professor of political science and the daughter of Gamal ʿAbd al-Nasser, denied the rumors that her father kept a detailed diary. *Rūz al-Yūsuf,* September 14, 1987, p. 3.

6. Ibid., pp. 5–14.

ous. Disagreeing on most subjects, including such basic matters as the appropriate terms of discussion, Egypt's leading historians, affiliated with various schools of thought, were immediately at odds with one another. Visibly concerned, one historian dramatically warned that if Egypt were ever going to be able to function as a national community, its historians must find common ground.[7] This palpable sense of historiographical crisis assisted in channeling the discussion. Thus, two main concerns guided the discussants at the conference: *What is the history of modern Egyptian historiography, and which kind of history writing would best serve the collective needs of the Egyptian people?* The articulation of these questions has had a lasting impact, for they have come to dominate Egyptian public and professional discussion on historiography in the years since. The aim of this work is to attempt to provide an answer to the first.

• • •

Modern history as Egyptians read, write, think, and know it today is of fairly recent origins. It was forged as a comprehensive system of knowledge, in fact as a new idea, only at the very end of the Ottoman era. As a system of thought, it served as a necessary prerequisite for the existence of modernity itself. Similar to eighteenth-century Europe, in which the modern idea of history constituted the essence of the Enlightenment/modernity effort, the Egyptian project of modernity and nationalism, the Nahḍa, was also dependent on history for its own successful realization.

The reason for the interconnectedness of history and modernity is related to the structure of modernity in general and to the perception of time in particular. Until the early modern period, mythical, theological, and biological chronological frames taught humans that the future could bring nothing fundamentally new. Understood from a theological point of view, the nature of individuals, society, and humanity in general was destined to remain the same until the arrival of the Day of Judgment.[8] Modernity rejected these assumptions and, by using the power of science and technology, directed itself toward the future as a realm of operation and conquest. In contrast with premodern attempts to conceptualize human experience, for modernity "the future should be a horizon of planning, not only of days, weeks or even years, but of the long-term . . . changes."[9] A significant component of this vision was the idea of progress: the sense of constant development into the future. During the nineteenth century, progress had come to be accepted as a universal object of human endeavor—that is, not merely the

7. al-Quʿayd and al-Badrī, "Fawdat al-tārīkh fī Miṣr," p. 13.

8. Reinhart Koselleck, *The Practice of Conceptual History: Timing History, Spacing Concepts*, translated by Todd Samuel Presner et al. (Stanford, CA: Stanford University Press, 2002), p. 111.

9. Ibid., p. 120.

progress of individual fields, such as the arts and sciences, but the general progress of history itself.[10] Thereafter, the entire intellectual foundation of any project of modernity, European, Egyptian, or other, was designed and constructed as one of historical progress.[11] With progress serving as the temporal motor of modernity, various chronological frames, and the forms of writing that represented them (annals and chronicles), fell short of accounting for the new experiences modernity had to offer. Deemed obsolete, these were replaced by modern historical narration, which, for the first time, divided the past into neat categories of periods and eras and gave them names.

Thus, if in the past theology had justified the ways of God to man, showing how man got to where he was and why, modernity replaced theology with "a more persuasive (and more rational) donor of meaning and direction: namely, *history*."[12] Thus, with the increasing secularization of thought, history's task was to justify the validity of the modern enterprise and provide it with firm credentials. Since it illustrated why and how modernity is the ultimate culmination of human progress, it also acquired the power to legitimize and underpin any intellectual and ideological position.[13] Put simply, it became impossible to conceive of and execute modernity without historical thought. Regardless of the forum in which one chose to operate—political, economic, social, or other—if it aspired to be modern, it must be based on history.[14]

Although grossly oversimplified, this framework for how modernity and history became interdependent over a period of two hundred years is precisely what makes the questions Egyptian historians asked in August 1987 more than a mere preoccupation with the history of their own practice. Indeed, Egypt had its own very specific experience with the modern idea of history, as will be shown below, and, for this reason, in the final analysis the 1987 conference was about how Egypt forged, justified, and explained its own particular modernity. Thus, by offering a critical analysis of the way the modern category of historical knowledge was acculturated and naturalized in Egypt, we actually study the way history was used in order to institute various Egyptian projects of modernity, from colonial domination, through partial independence, to authoritarian rule. This is the deeper meaning behind the question Egyptian historians posed and the reason it is worthy of special scholarly attention.

10. Ibid., pp. 229–230.

11. Ibid., p. 93.

12. Beverley Southgate, *Postmodernism in History: Fear or Freedom?* (London: Routledge, 2003), p. 30

13. Ibid., p. 29.

14. This understanding of modernity and history is based on the German school of "conceptual history" *(Begriffsgeschichte).* See also John Zammito, "Koselleck's Philosophy of Historical Time(s) and the Practice of History," *History and Theory* 43, no. 1 (2004): pp. 124–135.

. . .

The story of how modern Egyptian nationalism utilized Egypt's many pasts (Pharaonic, Greco-Roman, Arab, Islamic) has been told often and well.[15] However, utilizing the past and studying it critically are two different things. Indeed, none of the intellectuals who harnessed Egypt's multiple pasts for the sake of nation building had actually studied the history of that appropriated past. And so, the aim of this book, in contrast with metaphysical appropriation, is to examine the thought and practice of modern Egyptian historiography. In doing so, I turn to a systematic investigation of the means by which Egyptians made sense of their modern past. Particularly, this book is about the career of the modern idea of history in Egypt. Accepting as a vantage point the theoretical premise that this modern idea of history is philosophically different from previous systems of historical representation, such as the Islamic chronicle, I trace how this idea was naturalized in Egypt during the previous century. Like using a modern machine, putting an idea to work prescribes the adoption of certain modes of operation and ways of reasoning.

Thus, examining the questions Egyptian historians articulated in order to establish historical findings exposes a certain explanatory reasoning. An analysis of the various debates on the real histories that Egypt needs illustrates how the mechanisms of normative reasoning (plans for what *ought* to be) work. Similarly, discussion of the accessibility and availability of historical records explains the organizational reasoning of modern historiography. And finally, by finding out why Egyptians decided to practice modern history in the first place, we examine the justificatory reasoning of this new discipline. Thus, by studying the thought and practice of modern Egyptian historiography, this work identifies and analyzes these diverse ways of reasoning and configures them into a more general understanding of the structure and operating logic of modern Egyptian historiography.

Modern Egyptian historiography has already been the subject of several fine studies in both English and Arabic. Beginning in the late 1950s and ending with another detailed study in 2003, a series of scholars have identified the most influential historians and books, classified them into schools and trends of thought, and marked their political, social, and institutional associations.[16] By doing so, they introduced order into the field and articulated a set of relevant questions

15. Israel Gershoni and James Jankowski, *Egypt, Islam and the Arabs: The Search for Egyptian Nationhood, 1900–1930* (New York: Oxford University Press, 1986); Donald Reid, *Whose Pharaohs? Archeology, Museums and Egyptian National Identity from Napoleon to World War I* (Berkeley: University of California Press, 2002).

16. Anthony Gorman, *Historians, State and Politics in Twentieth Century Egypt: Contesting the Nation* (London: Routledge-Curzon, 2003).

and common terms of discussion. Put differently, they set the criteria for what constitutes modern Egyptian historiography and identified some of the things that we need to know about it.

Notwithstanding the many merits of their endeavor, previous students of Egyptian historiography, both Western and local, approached the subject from the same problematic angle: they neglected to critically examine history as a new category of knowledge and as a new system of thought. Consequently, they "bought into" their protagonists' agenda and therefore took at face value an entire methodological, theoretical, and thematic apparatus that profoundly shaped their own research and findings. Most problematic, they tried to understand modern Egyptian historiography using a convention that was itself a product of the phenomenon they were trying to understand. Therefore, despite these scholars' important contribution to the advancement of knowledge of Egypt, their scholarship has been caught in a kind of cycle of self-definition that could not tell the modern nation-state from the means of its historical representation and investigation.

Certainly, any attempt to critically analyze an object by willfully accepting its inherent premises and logic of operation is a futile effort whose horizons of innovation are philosophically limited. Hence, in this book I take issue with the axiomatic acceptance of the terms that modern Egyptian historiography created in order to forge Egypt as an object of investigation. As the chapters that follow will demonstrate in detail, there was nothing natural or neutral about the emergence of modern Egyptian historiography and its association with the culture of nationalism. It is not a coincidence that modern history emerged with the modern nation. A brief survey of the literature will illustrate this analytical fault.

The study of early modern historiography (1800–1900) began with the pioneering work of Jamāl al-Dīn al-Shayyāl (1958). Western historians, notably Jack Crabbs, followed suit.[17] Despite writing in different times and places, both al-Shayyāl and Crabbs grasped modern historiography in similar developmental terms. According to them, during the Ottoman occupation of Egypt, between 1517 and 1798, when the French began their occupation, history writing in Egypt was completely dead.[18] In that sense, the chronicler ʿAbd al-Raḥmān al-Jabartī (d. 1825/26) was the final link in an outstanding intellectual pedigree of Islamic chroniclers who, although skipping the Ottoman era, stretched all the way back

17. Jamāl al-Dīn al-Shayyāl, *Al-Tārīkh wa-l-muʾarrikhūn fī Miṣr fī-l-qarn al-tāsiʿ ʿashar* (Cairo: Maktabat al-nahḍa al-miṣriyya, 1958); Jack Crabbs, *The Writing of History in Nineteenth-Century Egypt: A Study in National Transformation* (Cairo: American University in Cairo Press, 1984).

18. As we shall see, this particular argument was originally made during the 1920s. Al-Shayyāl, Crabbs, and most other scholars uncritically accepted it.

to sixteenth- and fifteenth-century chroniclers Ibn Iyās and al-Maqrīzī.[19] By reviving interest in history, al-Jabartī put an end to this silence. With his mysterious death, the classical tradition of Islamic historiography came to an end as well. However, in view of the alleged historiographical emptiness of the Ottoman era, al-Jabartī was seen as more than simply the continuer of a remarkable tradition: he was the reviver, or even the reinventor, of the Islamic historical institution after a long period of inactivity. Historian David Ayalon, among the first to substantiate this perception, called the phenomenon "the enigma of al-Jabartī."[20] With this as the accepted vantage point, the basic premise for the analysis of Egypt's early modern history writing was that it was created on top of nothing.

Once in operation, the framework for the development of the modern historiographical tradition during the nineteenth century continued along this line of reasoning. Al-Shayyāl and Crabbs agreed that what they were dealing with was a straightforward, linear transformation from traditional forms of writing to modern ones. With this guiding logic, they built their story along the following lines: from chronicle to a modern narrative, from mere description to analysis, from a flowery language of rhymed prose *(sajʿ)* to economical journalistic writing, from fragmentation of reason to ordered causality, and from bias to objectivity.[21]

This process was illustrated by a series of great thinkers and their texts, beginning with Rifāʿa al-Ṭahṭāwī and his disciples, who marked the beginning of Western impact on local writing, continuing with the encyclopedist ʿAlī Mubārak Pasha, who revived the genre of the *khiṭaṭ,* to the neo-chroniclers Mikhāʾīl Shārūbīm and Ismāʿīl Sarhank, who began to provide complex explanations for historical events, and including the nationalist historians Muṣṭafa Kāmil and Muḥammad Farīd, who let ideology shape their historical understanding, and the Syrian-Egyptian émigré Jurjī Zaydān, who popularized and refined the modern style of writing by giving it a contemporary European touch. The last and final stage in this developmental process was the emergence of the "professional and objective" academic historian Muḥammad Ṣabrī, who symbolized Egypt's crossing of the threshold of professionalism.[22] After a century of experimentation, 1920 was the year modern historiography was alleged to have appeared in a mature form.

19. al-Shayyāl, *Al-Tārīkh wa-l-muʾarrikhūn,* pp. 10–47. See also Gamal el-Din el-Shayyal, "Some Aspects of Intellectual and Social Life in Eighteenth-Century Egypt," in P. M. Holt, ed., *Political and Social Change in Modern Egypt* (London: Oxford University Press, 1968), pp. 117–132.

20. David Ayalon, "The Historian al-Jabartī," in Bernard Lewis and P. M. Holt, eds., *Historians of the Middle East* (London: Oxford University Press, 1962), p. 391.

21. Crabbs, *The Writing of History in Nineteenth-Century Egypt,* pp. 13–26.

22. The work of Ṣabrī is discussed below. Ibid., pp. 199–209.

In hindsight, for al-Shayyāl and Crabbs, this gradual substitution of an Islamic historiography with a modern one was an obvious and perfectly natural process that they intended to celebrate rather than to explain.[23] As Crabbs put it: "Interpretation, analysis and judgment are now considered the *sine qua non* of good historical writing, and these characteristics will form our basis for determining the 'modernity' of nineteenth-century Egyptian historiography."[24] Concomitantly, the writers of these pioneering works studied early modern Egyptian historiography in terms of what it ought to be (liberal, progressive, modern, and, in short, European) rather than in terms of what it was and what it could be.[25]

Consequently, the study of nineteenth-century historiography had not yet answered a basic question: Why modern history? What was the reason that Egyptian scholars abandoned a glorious tradition of Islamic historiography (written in the form of chronicles and *khiṭaṭ*) and replaced it with a new intellectual product (the modern narrative) that had little to do with Egypt's own experience? If we choose to view Egyptian history writing critically, a series of more specific questions should follow: What does it actually mean to move from a premodern historiographical regime to a modern one (i.e., what is the difference between a chronicle and a modern narrative)? What constitutes a specifically historical "sense" or meaning? Which intellectual mechanisms assisted in creating this

23. al-Shayyāl, *Al-Tārīkh wa-l-mu'arrikhūn*, pp. 195–209; Crabbs, *The Writing of History in Nineteenth-Century Egypt*, pp. 185, 199, 200–201.

24. Crabbs, *The Writing of History in Nineteenth-Century Egypt*, p. 15.

25. In recent years some of the assumptions on which al-Shayyāl and Crabbs based their analysis have been refuted, not through questioning the intellectual foundations of their knowledge, but by means of direct historical investigation of the intellectual realities prevailing in eighteenth-century Egypt. These refuting studies present a group of historical works, many in manuscript form, that were available to al-Jabartī and were even used by him. With the "mythical enigma" of al-Jabartī uncovered, it becomes clear that, though he was an exceptional historian, his writings—*and by implication early modern historiography in general*—were not created ex nihilo. Nelly Hanna, "The Chronicles of Ottoman Egypt: History or Entertainment?" in Hugh Kennedy, ed., *The Historiography of Islamic Egypt, c. 950–1800* (Leiden, the Netherlands: E. J. Brill, 2001), pp. 237–250; Daniel Crecelius, "Al-Jabartī's *'Ajā'īb al-Athār fī-l-Tarājim wa-l-Akhbār* and the Arabic Histories of Ottoman Egypt in the Eighteenth Century," in Kennedy, ed., *The Historiography of Islamic Egypt*, pp. 233–234. More generally, scholars such as Peter Gran, Kenneth Cuno, and Nelly Hanna have attempted to refute the "wasteland thesis" by identifying the roots of modernity, capitalism, and civil society. Their excellent works, however, fall short of systematically exposing the historiographical logic that created and maintained the wasteland thesis for the better part of the twentieth century. Peter Gran, "Modern Trends in Egyptian Historiography: A Review Article," *International Journal of Middle East Studies* 9, no. 3 (August 1978): 367–371; Kenneth Cuno, "Muhammad 'Ali and the Decline and Revival Thesis in Modern Egyptian History," in Ra'ūf 'Abbās, ed., *Iṣlāḥ am taḥdīth? Miṣr fī 'aṣr Muḥammad 'Alī* (Cairo: al-Majlīs al-a'la li-l-thaqāfa, al-jam'iyya al-miṣriyya li-l-dirāsāt al-tārīkhiyya, 2000), 93–119; Nelly Hanna, *In Praise of Books: A Cultural History of Cairo's Middle Class, Sixteenth to the Eighteenth Century* (Syracuse, NY: Syracuse University Press, 2003).

sense? Which concepts of time formed Egypt's Islamic and modern historical cultures? And, more generally, what gave Egyptian historiography its unity and direction?

While students of nineteenth-century historiography automatically accepted the concept of the modernity of history, scholars of the twentieth century added the nation to this convention. Youssef Choueiri, Ibrāhīm 'Abd al-Mun'im al-Jumay'ī, and Anthony Gorman moved onward to study the entire course of twentieth-century historiography.[26] With a host of more specific studies supplementing their work, they begin their investigation in 1920, right where Crabbs had ended. Like the attendees of the August 1987 conference, they also wanted to know why historical writing had become so politicized and to gain an understanding of the reasons for continuous state involvement in history writing. In search of answers, they paid much attention to party politics, state power, national identity, and minority histories. They were also sensitive to the issue of shifts in historical representation.[27]

However, much of what they were dealing with resulted from the bond between the modern idea of history and nationalism. In fact, at a certain point—which they failed to identify—history writing took the modern nation-state as its ultimate subject of investigation. Thereafter, most studies on modern Egypt became biographies of an autonomous, singular, and self-referential nation. Undoubtedly, the absolute meaninglessness of modern Egyptian history without the nation served as the invitation for national political parties to fill the gap and suggest their own histories. By far, this was the most significant intellectual development since the association of modernity and history during the nineteenth century. Thus, to understand the causes for the politicization of history writing, we must delve deeply into the meaning, mechanisms, and structures of the modern idea of history and criticize its convenient association with nationalism.

On a more specific level of analysis, modernity also prescribed certain types of organizational and explanatory reasoning, which then created patterns of professionalization and institutional involvement in the writing of history. Two examples illustrate the importance of studying these hitherto unaccounted-for connections. The first concerns the concepts that constitute modern historical thought; the other relates to how a newly created institution, the archive, shaped historical thought and practice.

26. Youssef Choueiri, *Arab History and the Nation-State: A Study in Modern Arab Historiography 1820–1980* (London: Routledge, 1989); 'Abd al-Mun'im Ibrāhīm al-Jumay'ī, *Itijāhāt al-kitāba al-tārīkhiyya fi tārīkh Miṣr al-ḥadīth wa-l-mu'āṣir* (Cairo: 'Ayn li-l-dirāsāt wa-l-buḥūth al-insāniyya wa-l-ijtimā'iyya, 1994); Gorman, *Historians, State and Politics in Twentieth Century Egypt.*

27. Thomas Mayer, *The Changing Past: Egyptian Historiography of the Urabi Revolt, 1882–1983* (Gainesville: University Press of Florida, 1988).

By and large, though concepts such as objectivity, science, and methodology were commonly used by Egyptian historians, scholars of the field systematically refrained from analyzing their meaning. As a result, in the twentieth century, a major historiographical division between academic and nonacademic historians remains unexplained. Why were academic historians so profoundly at odds with what they called "amateur and politicized writers"? What was "professional" and unpolitical about academic writing, and how was it different from other forms of writing? In order to answer these questions, we need to examine these academic notions of objectivity and science in the context of modern cultural competition.[28]

The modern institution of the archive and its working order should also be subjected to critical analysis. Until recently, such an examination was not considered to be the task of studies on historiography. Rather than seeing the archive as part of a unified historiographical process, scholars focused only on the external manifestations and general character of such institutions, describing them as "political" or "colonial."[29] Given that historical thought did not progress from one book to another or from one historian to another, scholarly attention should be directed to the archives and libraries that did play a dominant role in creating the architecture of historical knowledge. Thus, by critically examining the structure of the first so-called public research archive in ʿĀbdīn, we learn what sort of histories could be imagined from the way the archive classified and organized historical evidence. Given that the majority of the historical studies that were based on ʿĀbdīn's source material dealt with how Muḥammad ʿAlī created modern Egypt, it is crucial to examine how the structure and working procedures of this institution influenced scholarship.

In sum, by taking for granted the theoretical nexus among modernity, nationalism, and history, scholars examined modern Egyptian historiography using the same terms that this system created in order to fulfill its own task: the forging of modern Egyptian nationhood. Not coincidentally, the story that Egyptian and foreign historians provided for the building of the nation (from medieval decadence to modern progression and from colonial control to independence) was the very one that scholars of historiography provided for explaining and describing modern Egyptian historiography. During this circular process, they viewed terms such as *history, nationalism, colonialism, progress,* and *modernity* as fixed, sealed boxes, carrying universal meaning. Hence, the basic question

28. Other concepts such as reform and decline also await explanation. A study of these concepts would illustrate how each school of thought within Egyptian historiography—academic, colonial, Marxist, or popular-nationalist—used these concepts in accordance with the different ways they defined what constitutes historical change.

29. Gorman, *Historians, State and Politics in Twentieth Century Egypt,* pp. 15–22.

of which assumptions guided historians from the public sphere to the sources, and back, remains unaddressed—and with it, the concerns of the August 1987 conference.

• • •

The main argument of this study is that the modern idea of history is a form of thought and a habit of mind that arrived in Egypt in the late nineteenth century, bringing with them specific institutions and modes of reasoning. With time, they created their own particular logic of operation that was equipped with new tools for historical intelligibility that were—and still are—intimately linked to both modernity and nationalism. This argument refers to two different temporal orders. The first relates to the articulation of the modern idea of history, which stretches from roughly 1890 until the 1980s and beyond, when an era of historiographical self-examination began. The second frame relates to how this new idea shaped historical knowledge about modern Egypt.[30] Thus, with rare exceptions, it was widely accepted that modern Egyptian history began sometime during the late eighteenth century. Considering this framework, I deal in this study with how modern Egyptian historiography (from 1890 onward) conceptualized the actual history of modern Egypt (from 1798/1805 to the present).[31]

In the first chapter I argue that, beginning in 1890, a series of conceptual changes occurred in three central dimensions of reality: *time, space,* and *subjectivity.* These changes led to the gradual historicization of the Egyptian worldview. At the very core of this process was the realization that in order to get a grip on current affairs one needs to know their histories as part of a general process of development. Once historicization—this automatic extrapolation of the past to the future—was acknowledged as a more modern form of thinking, an entire genre of historical writing, namely, the chronicle, was considered to be out of touch with reality and hence obsolete. Consequently, writers such as Ismāʿīl Sarhank began to compose historical compositions that were in part modern and yet continued the premodern Islamic tradition. Thus, when dealing with the contemporary era, these hybrid compositions had a single subject that progressively developed over time and a well-defined space that framed this subject. In that sense these were modern compositions. However, when dealing with the premodern era, these works adhered to the ideal of recording all possible events

30. I have decided to study closely only historical texts that deal with modern Egypt (rather than Pharaonic, Greco-Roman, Islamic, and Ottoman histories), because they are more relevant for the making of Egyptian modernity. Nonetheless, I refer to other periods quite widely.

31. The construction "1798/1805" signifies the years that are used interchangeably to mark the beginning of the modern era, 1798 being the year of the French invasion and 1805 being the year that Muḥammad ʿAlī took power.

(natural disasters, social events, and marvelous deeds) in all places and in accordance to a standard temporal order of days, weeks, or years. In that sense, they were more like premodern works. Over time, slowly but surely, the historicized modern narrative emerged triumphant, and the chronicles disappeared.

Following these conceptual changes and heavily influenced by colonial ideas about science and modernity, Egyptian historiography took the nation as its ultimate subject of inquiry, defined its geography apart from the Ottoman political body, and marked the persistent development of this entity into the future. More than being an abstract idea that operated only at an arcane level of conceptualization, the 1905 centennial celebration of Muḥammad ʿAlī's accession to power marked the birth of modern Egyptian nationhood. Thereafter, a powerful historical paradigm, which viewed Muḥammad ʿAlī as the founder of a modern nation on top of a corrupt Ottoman order, was put in place. Throughout this study, this paradigm is referred to as the "founder paradigm/thesis."

Chapter 2 covers the era that stretches from the beginning of the twentieth century to the 1919 nationalist revolution. This allegedly incoherent era, which was neither fully Ottoman nor entirely nationalist, witnessed the apex of a powerful process of de-Ottomanization, during which the outdated Egyptian-Ottoman elite was Arabized and Egyptianized. The main argument I make in this chapter is that this process was propelled forward by a series of linguistic and semantic constructs that created a strong theoretical dependency among nationalism, modernity, and history writing. Aiming toward building an elaborate system of political modernity, a full-fledged semantic field created the theoretical infrastructure of this system and conditioned what could be thought and apprehended at any given time. Thus, this semantic field organized ideas about authority, sovereignty, public and private spheres of political action, jurisdictional structures, citizenship, and other crucial aspects of political modernity. Structurally biased against monarchic rule, colonial domination, and Ottomanism in general, it automatically privileged a republican order of popular sovereignty. By doing so it nourished the activity and grounded the legitimacy of Egypt's growing popular political parties, such as the Wafd and the National Party.

Literally pushed out of history, King Fu'ād responded by launching the most extensive historiographical project ever seen in the region, beginning in 1920. Chapter 3 tells its story. The project lasted more than twenty-five years and involved a host of foreign archivists, philologists, and historians (among them: Eugenio Griffini, Jean Deny, Angelo Sammarco, and Pierre Crabitès). It also brought about the establishment of the first "public archive," in Fu'ād's own palace at ʿĀbdīn, and published close to eighty heavy tomes on modern Egyptian history. Undeniably colonial in essence, the royal project introduced to Egyptian historiography three complementary elements. First, substantiating the "founder paradigm," it set the criteria for what constituted "proper historical knowledge" with regard to modern Egypt. Then, it disseminated the assumption that, both physically and epistemologically, there could be no valid historical evidence outside the archive (which systematically excluded Ottoman and subaltern pasts).[32] Finally, it introduced the concepts of scientific objectivity and expert authority.

During the 1930s, three historiographical trends competed for hegemony: nascent academia, royal historiography, and the popular-nationalist tradition. In chapters 4 and 5 I examine the power balance among these schools and the opposing modes of historical comprehension they advocated. Greatly influenced by the royal project, academic historian Muḥammad Shafīq Ghurbāl and his many disciples accepted the royal working assumption, according to which European reason should guide Egypt along the road to modernity. In accordance with this position, academia borrowed the working methodology of archive-based history and a European ideology of professionalism, which claimed to be scientific, objective, and politically impartial. Objecting to any form of political commitment, only academic circles developed a strong ethical code of operation.

In contrast, the main task of Egypt's foremost nationalist historian, ʿAbd al-Raḥmān al-Rāfiʿī, was to refute the massive project of royal historiography and free the nation's history from colonial and royal control. As the stubborn leader of the National Party, al-Rāfiʿī fiercely denied Europe's right to guide Egypt toward modernity and reason. In a series of lengthy works (which have since become classics), al-Rāfiʿī wove Egypt's modern history around the political agenda of the National Party. Chapter 4 shows how royal historiography (written in French, Italian, and English) strove to undermine al-Rāfiʿī's credibility and refute his arguments. Examining the bulk of scholarship on modern Egypt as it was created between the late 1920s to the early 1950s, as well as a host of historiographical debates, chapter 4 illustrates how each historiographical position was tied to a different vision of Egyptian modernity.

By asking why and how Egyptian historiography became such a political business, I examine the phenomenon of political partisanship in history writing in chapter 6. Going beyond the impact of mundane acts of censorship, imprisonment, and overt political pressures, I argue that the main reason for politicized writing evolved not necessarily from these political realities but from the structure of modern historical knowledge itself. Specifically, it draws attention to

32. The practices of this archive were a major reason for the proliferation of the myth that modern scholarship invented itself from nothing after 1798, as well as the fiction of a historiographical wasteland between 1516 and 1798. Accepting the objectivity and the universal value of the ʿĀbdīn archive is one of the characteristics of previous writers on the subject, who, as argued above, uncritically subscribed to the existing terms of discussion.

the fact that many works of history were national allegories. Time and again, we find that political parties and their leaders saw themselves not only as mere representatives but also as actual embodiments of the nation. Hence, writing the history of political leaders such as Saʿd Zaghlūl (for the Wafd) and Muṣṭafa Kāmil (for the National Party) was synonymous with writing the nation's history. Concomitantly, historical criticism of these leaders was deemed a frontal political attack on the party, the nation, patriotism, and sometimes even on historical truth itself. Such forms of allegorical writing were prolific. Tracing this phenomenon as far ahead as the late 1980s in this chapter, I pin down the reasons and mechanisms for this kind of politicization of history writing. Another aspect of partisanship concerned the emergence of Marxist scholarship, which, though thematically and methodologically innovative, was motivated by a philosophy of political engagement. Both of these phenomena ran against the professional creed of academia and were instrumental in normalizing politicization as a natural and inevitable aspect of history writing.

Commencing in July 1952 and continuing with the October 1956 nationalization of the Suez Canal, the long struggle for independence began realizing its goals. Naturally, this accomplishment was accompanied by the demand to rethink modern history in a fashion that would explain these staggering achievements and show the way toward modernity and, with it, complete intellectual and cultural liberation. Existing histories, most notably the royal project and academic writings, were viewed as the creators and perpetuators of Egypt's modern misery and not as the much-anticipated solution to it.

Chapters 7 and 8 cover these high hopes for a new history, the new modern experience they promised, and ultimately the successive disappointments of the 1960s and the collapse of the socialist historiographical order. Two main arguments form this chapter. First, during the 1950s, Egyptian historiography took a self-congratulatory and metahistorical turn that, to some degree, detached it from the study of the past and from the value of historical truthfulness. During this phase, the previously marginalized national epic of al-Rāfiʿī was officially embraced but was, in actual practice, reduced to a few revolutionary turning points in history (1801, 1805, 1882, 1919) that (inexplicably) led directly to the 1952 Revolution. Compatible Pan-Arab histories were written as well. Accepted as the official vision of history, the national epic exempted historians from actually studying the past critically and inevitably undermined the value of historical truthfulness. During the same period, Ghurbāl's academic school was shunted away from mainstream cultural life. Considered to be colonial, elitist, and reactionary, academics began a long struggle aimed at defending their professional credibility and ethical convictions. Represented by social historian Aḥmad ʿIzzat ʿAbd al-Karīm, Ghurbāl's disciple and heir, this school struggled against socialist historian Muḥammad Anīs and his state-supported group. The era ended without any definitive success for either of these groups.

Finding that the existing histories of Egypt's modern and recent experience were useful as identity codifiers but were unable to nourish a constructive modernization effort, the state embraced socialism. With it came a radical Marxist interpretation of modern Egyptian history and a compellingly neat theoretical structure. Hence, after the 1961 socialist turn, Marxist historians, traditionally persecuted and brutally suppressed, now provided Egypt with the philosophical means to redefine its past, correct the present, and shape the future. In an unprecedented way, Egypt's political agenda was entirely fashioned on the insights and structure of a Marxist philosophy of history. Believing in the existence of historical laws of development, the Marxists argued that by studying the patterns and laws of the past they could scientifically plan for the future. Thus, Marxist historical scholarship and central planning became a standard aspect of Egypt's domestic policy. Essentially utopian in its belief in the human ability to master and control history, the Marxist-socialist promise to predict the future by studying the past eventually failed. Afterward, the third generation of academic historians combined the methodology and ethical commitment of Ghurbāl's school with the thematic concerns, social sensitivity, and creativity of Marxist-socialist scholarship. Since the 1970s, these writers have figured strongly in the public arena.

In the last three decades of the century, the life of the mind in Egypt functioned under the paradoxical purview of an authoritarian yet pluralistic regime. While more freedom of expression and association existed in comparison to Nasserist Egypt, the relative liberalization of public life strengthened, rather than weakened, authoritarianism. In chapter 9, I evaluate the impact of this paradox on the historiographical marketplace and argue that it is the main cause for what Egyptian intellectuals termed "a crisis of historical consciousness." Both Sadat and Mubarak forged a system of authoritarian pluralism in which previously marginalized groups, such as the Muslim Brotherhood, were invited to write and publish extensively. In a matter of a few years the historiographical marketplace was flooded with contradictory accounts. Since no state archive existed in which to verify claims and counterclaims about, for instance, the "true" nature of Nasserism, textual hierarchy collapsed. Furthermore, as a result of the pressures on educational infrastructure and the politicization of university campuses, the academic historical community lost its hard-won professional authority, and its public status declined. In search of a creative perspective from which to approach this crisis of historical consciousness, the 1987 conference, and those that followed it, raised the following questions: *What is the history of modern Egyptian historiography? And which kind of history writing would best serve the collective needs of the Egyptian people?*

• • •

Syrian philosopher Sadik Jallal al-Azm has recently mentioned that in a relatively short span of time the Arabs intensely experimented with a host of modern forces, "such as capitalism, nationalism, colonialism, secularism, liberalism, populism, socialism, communism, Marxism, modernism, developmentalism, evolutionism, the idea of progress, scientific knowledge [and] applied technology (both civil and military)."[33]

The modern category of historical knowledge played a central role in comprehending, articulating, translating, explaining, and disseminating the above-mentioned projects into the Egyptian mental environment. As such this knowledge illustrates the explanatory potential of intellectual history that approaches the Arab modern experience from the perspective of systems of intelligibility. This book, therefore, joins a few other studies that offer a comprehensive analysis of specific categories of knowledge and their respective literary genres. Whether they are anthropology and ethnography, cartography with the map, fiction writing with the novel, literary criticism and the critical essay, or sociology and history with the argumentative book format, such elaborate intellectual systems and their means of expression are sensitive to the dilemmas and paradoxes that are associated with the experience of indigenous modernity.[34]

Indeed, the main issue at stake is to account for the Arab experience of modernity from a global perspective. This is a classic task for the intellectual history of the Middle East, a sometimes troubled discipline, yet the only one that is organically designed to deal with abstractions. In recent decades the intellectual history of the Arab world fell from favor and is increasingly seen as elitist, indifferent to the real experience of disenfranchised "subalterns," and, worse, methodologically and theoretically uninspiring. The reasons for this grim state of affairs lie

33. Sadik Jallal al-Azm, "Western Historical Thinking from Arabian Perspective," in Jören Rüsen, ed., *Western Historical Thinking: An Intercultural Debate* (New York: Berghahn, 2002), pp. 121–122.

34. See, for instance: Prasenjit Duara, *Rescuing History from the Nation: Questioning Narratives of Modern China* (Chicago: University of Chicago Press, 1995). For the Middle East, see: James McDougall, "Colonial Words: Nationalism, Islam, and Languages of History in Algeria," unpublished Ph.D. thesis, Oxford University, 2002; Omnia ElShakry, "The Great Social Laboratory: Reformers and Utopians in Twentieth Century Egypt," unpublished Ph.D. dissertation, Princeton University, 2001); Marwa Elshakry, "Darwin's Legacy in the Arab East: Science, Religion and Politics, 1870–1914," unpublished Ph.D. dissertation, Princeton University, 2003; and Wilson Jacob, "Working Out Egypt: Masculinity and Subject Formation between Colonial Modernity and Nationalism, 1870–1940," unpublished Ph.D. dissertation, New York University, 2005.

well beyond the scope of this discussion.[35] However, it is possible to postulate that the decline of intellectual history occurred as a result of the two increasingly irrelevant conventions through which Middle East intellectual history had been traditionally narrated, namely, Islamic reform/modernism and the optimistic secular and liberal progression of the Nahḍa. Though both of these conventions had some pathbreaking and undeniable scholarly achievements, on some basic level they were irrevocably linked to the *"what went right/wrong"* interpretative mode. With the coming of postmodernism and the increasing sensitivity to the existence of indigenous modernities and to some of its traumatic features, the *what went right/wrong* perspective was rendered obsolete. Indeed, the old intellectual history was blind to and largely indifferent to the nuanced ambiguities and paradoxes of modernity and the way in which they shaped the psychological experience of everyday life.[36]

And so, whether we study literary criticism or economic thought, the task of intellectual history in the present is to critically examine the modern Arab condition from the perspective of its exclusive philosophical relation with a global intellectual tradition. As scholars all over the world begin to speak of the emergence of a global historiographical practice, the desire to understand the intellectual traditions of non-Western societies and the various itineraries of text and thought is gaining momentum.[37] *Western Historical Thinking: An Intercultural Debate,* a recent collection by eminent scholars such as Jören Rüsen and Peter Burke, has done so with relation to the discipline of history. These scholars raised one of the most pressing intellectual concerns of our time: To what degree may we say that the European/Western model of making sense of the past is universal? With this question in mind, could countries such as Indonesia, Kenya, Peru, China, and Egypt simply import the European historiographical model in a fashion that would satisfy their cultural and political needs, or is history writing culturally bound? Of great relevance are related concerns such as what should non-Western societies do, and what have they done so far, with their centuries old historiographical traditions? Perhaps because

35. From an initial exploration of the history of intellectual history, primarily that of Egypt, see Israel Gershoni, "The Theory of Crisis and the Crisis in a Theory: Intellectual History in Twentieth-Century Middle Eastern Studies," in Israel Gershoni, Amy Singer, and Y. Hakan Erdem, eds., *Middle East Historiographies: Narrating the Twentieth Century* (Seattle: Washington University Press, 2006), pp. 131–182.

36. For a new understanding of middle-class Levantine modernity, see Keith David Watenpaugh, *Being Modern in the Middle East: Revolution, Nationalism, Colonialism, and the Arab Middle Class* (Princeton, NJ: Princeton University Press, 2006).

37. Dipesh Chakrabarty, "A Global and Multicultural 'Discipline' of History?" *History and Theory* 45, no. 1 (2006): pp. 101–109.

of the increasing body of less menacing postmodern literature, more scholars evince interest in how history is being written and used, that is, with questions of method and theory, practice and thought. Drawing on these new interpretational possibilities, I analyze in this book the Egyptian experience of modernity with relation to the foremost medium through which it was articulated: history. Put in this global context, I aim to show how a non-European country "thinks with history."

1

Historicizing Ottoman Egypt

1890–1906

THE COMING OF HISTORY

At the close of the nineteenth century, Egypt was a place marked by rapid intellectual, political, economic, and cultural changes. It was an extremely dynamic era. None of the changes that occurred in the period can be explained by a single ideology (nationalism, Pan-Islamism, constitutionalism) or a fixed set of abstract intellectual agendas (positivism, Darwinism, Spenserism), and it is very important to acknowledge the diversity of thought that is to be found in the thinking of this period. If dynamism was a sign of the era, it necessarily meant that intellectual horizons were wide open for the absorption, modification, and implementation of new ideas and ideologies. To be sure, in late nineteenth-century Egypt there was no poverty of expectations.

But Egypt of that era was not an autonomous unit, as it was still an integral member of the intellectual and cultural order, if not of the political regime, of the Ottoman Empire. And as much as the above is true for Egypt, it is especially valid for the rest of the Arab provinces of the empire. All over the Ottoman Empire these were times of change. The foundation of civil and technical institutions, coupled with an increased educational effort on the part of Christian missionaries, challenged the old categories of knowledge. Europe was indeed close. New styles of reasoning were made available. The revolution in the technology of the written word, the unprecedented flourishing of private newspapers, and a host of other forms of artistic writing were coupled with the growing power of a new stratum of urban literates.[1] Ideas arrived from just about anywhere in the

1. Şerif Mardin, *The Genesis of Young Ottoman Thought: A Study in the Modernization of Turkish Political Ideas* (Syracuse, NY: Syracuse University Press, 2000).

Mediterranean basin and far beyond it: Istanbul, Paris, Beirut, London, Baghdad, Rome, Jaffa, Damascus, and even the Indian subcontinent. An informed group of literates gathered to discuss these ideas in private salons, coffee houses, and voluntary associations, as well as in less innocent gatherings, such as political clubs. The new media gave rise to new forms of protest that soon developed into a form of political consciousness. The modern Ottoman/Arab intellectual was born.

For the better part of that century and especially since the reign of Khedive Ismāʿīl, Egypt was where these trends came to focus. Increased efforts in the field of urban planning resulted in the creation of new Cairo, soon called "Paris along the Nile." This renewed city was by no means the summa of Egypt's historical components. The opposite is true. It was a city whose French architectural language corresponded with a past that was not at all Egyptian. This irrelevant past was promulgated in stone and spirit. The new buildings, boulevards, and squares were supported by a set of policies that were designed to alter the urban habits of its inhabitants. The Cairo project was only partly successful. Despite its beauty, along with the khedive's other modernizing projects it was to cost him his throne.

This era was also a period in which Egypt's sensitive, finely tuned ethnic, religious, and social equilibrium was reconsidered. In ways both tacit and clearly manifest, this balance was conditioned by the power politics of the Orient and the competition for political and economic hegemony. By and large, the rapidly growing Greek, Italian, Maltese, Jewish, French, and British communities created for themselves a privileged position as protected agents of modernity. Many were after easy money and effortless profits. Many were successful. Others had nothing to do with modernity and by their simple skills had managed to make themselves only slightly less poor than the Egyptians they lived among.[2]

Following the green revolution in cotton production of the late 1860s and the Hamidian autocracy in greater Syria, a large and newly arrived community of Christian Syrians established itself in Egypt's ever-developing urban centers.[3] They brought with them an essentially secular outlook, a daring intellectual curiosity, and a remarkable drive for public activity. The prolific novelist, pioneer journalist, and experimental historian Jurjī Zaydān was among them and was one of the foremost representatives of this group. In most of his work, he spoke of and for the Syrian Christian community. Zaydān's life could easily be read as a continuous drive for acknowledgment and acceptance by the Egyptian Muslim majority. At the same time, deserting Beirut, the journalistic entrepreneurs Fāris

2. See Juan Cole, *Colonialism and Revolution in the Middle East* (Princeton, NJ: Princeton University Press, 1993), pp. 190–212.

3. On the "boom years," see Michael Reimer, *Colonial Bridgehead: Government and Society in Alexandria, Egypt 1807–1882* (Cairo: AUC Press, 1997), pp. 107–122.

Nimr and Yaʿqūb Ṣarrūf reestablished their journal, *Al-Muqtaṭaf*, in Cairo. There, they acted as the high priests of science, useful knowledge, and moral improvement. Their secular reason knew no bounds for its designs. These were indeed the high days of the Nahḍa, the modernistic renaissance of the Arab East. However, even the outstanding success of the Lebanese community fell short of satisfying the desire to belong.

The meteoric rise of the Syrians ignited the sensitivities of the already diverse urban population. Social and political inequalities became a subject for debate. Communal strife became more common. Many of the violent acts were framed by a growing, yet vague, anti-imperialist and anti-foreign sentiment. Consequently, the definition of who was a foreigner was set in place.[4] Subsequently, this newly defined group of foreigners became concerned with public security, and the Egyptian intelligentsia became increasingly preoccupied with what brought the inhabitants of the Nile Valley together as a functioning political community.[5] The audacious vision of at least one frustrated social and professional group resulted in an explosive situation in the summer of 1881. Mobility, ethnic rivalry, and division of state power were in question. A year later, when the dust settled, the Urabists found themselves on the island of Ceylon. While in exile, they had much time to reflect and write. Maḥmūd Sāmī al-Bārūdī, an innovative neoclassical poet, brought this genre to new heights. Maḥmūd Fahmī, better known as al-Muhandis, experimented with a combination of universal and contemporary Egyptian history.

The British gradually, yet firmly, established themselves as the new rulers of the Nile Valley. Soon enough, soldiers, bureaucrats, investors, bankers, merchants, adventurers, and opportunists flooded the country. Many of them were of middle-class origins or lower, in search of an upward mobility denied them back home. They were after fame and fortune. Like elsewhere in the British Empire, in return for their services many were offered the possibility to have decent careers and perhaps become a "sir" or a "lord" or perhaps just rich. Inasmuch as the colonial system corresponded with a fixed catalog of imperial interests, it also functioned as a code of conduct and a way of life. The life of Sir Evelyn Baring, whose successes brought him the title Lord Cromer, epitomized the classic experience of British colonialism in Egypt. Hence, quite ironically, rather than Egypt being dependent on the colonialists, on many levels it was the other way around.[6] Like the Urabists, quite early on, the British too began writing apologetically

4. Will Hanley, "Foreignness and Localness in Alexandria, 1880–1914," unpublished Ph.D. dissertation, Princeton University, 2007.

5. Reimer, *Colonial Bridgehead*, pp. 171–182.

6. Trevor Mostyn, *Egypt's Belle Époque Cairo 1869–1952* (London: Quartet Books, 1989), pp. 129–141.

for their politics in Egypt. Significant parts of that writing were in the form of historylike books.[7]

Even though from a practical point of view the British occupation brought 365 years of Ottoman rule (1517–1882) to an end, Egypt's future, still under Ottoman suzerainty, might still have developed in several directions other than a narrowly defined anti-colonial nationalism. And indeed, for a while it actually did. Regardless of the myriad of possible explanations one chooses to account for the revolutionary events of 1881–82, one thing is certain: European imperialism did not stifle the political imagination. On the contrary, it opened a new realm of theoretical possibilities for the organization of public life. Gradually, the future became something to engage with in a new ideological form. As the century drew to a close, a growing number of literate individuals started to reconsider their commitment to Turkish-Ottoman culture. They began to mold this object called "Egypt." The British efforts to "capture" Egypt in numbers, through statistics partly showed them the way.

A gallery of unconventional personalities encapsulates the spirit of the era. The Armenian cabinet minister and three-time premier Nūbār Pasha embodies the aspirations of an upper class of bureaucrats, which put its trust in the forces of European progress. Nūbār, a classic product of the Egyptian ruling house's longstanding, uncertain affiliation with Europe, tacitly favored close cooperation with Britain while fiercely denying it actually took place. An agent of accelerated and radical modernization, he was involved in the establishment of the Mixed Courts and personally supervised the development of several extremely impressive projects ranging from railway construction to the digging of the Suez Canal. Along with many other members of his class, he became somewhat too rich from such enterprises. In 1899 he died in Paris.[8]

Nūbār's contemporary, ʿAbdallāh al-Nadīm, nicknamed the "orator of the revolution," was a ship's carpenter, a poet, a journalist, and an experienced manufacturer of anti-colonial dissent, opposition, and patriotic solidarity. Coming from humble rural origins, he knew only Arabic to Nūbār's eleven languages. While Nūbār studied at the pasha's expense in Paris, al-Nadīm's father was conscripted to the same benefactor's army. Al-Nadīm never hid his reservations about Europe's growing involvement and called for an anti-imperialist alliance of the East. Al-Nadīm cultivated an active lifestyle: he spent much of his time moving from one place to another after getting short, angry notices from local

7. The first in such a series of accounts was Sir Alfred Milner's *England in Egypt* (London: E. Arnold, 1899).

8. Robert Hunter, "Self-Image and Historical Truth: Nubar Pasha and the Making of Modern Egypt," *Middle Eastern Studies* 23, no. 3 (July 1987): pp. 363–375; Arthur Goldschmidt, *A Biographical Dictionary of Modern Egypt* (Boulder, CO: Lynne Rienner Publishers, 2000), pp. 157–158.

authorities to move on. To be sure, his proximity in mind and spirit to the great agitator of the era, Jamāl al-Dīn al-Afghānī, did not help him to find security.[9] In 1896, at forty-one, he died while in exile in Istanbul.

And then there was the eminent shaykh Muḥammmad ʿAbduh: a maverick Islamic thinker, a mufti, a *mujtahid,* and a teacher who, despite grave consequences, never lost an opportunity to make his opinions public. Involved in almost every meaningful aspect of public life, he was among the few to experience two quintessentially different worlds: that of the Egyptian village and that of the European metropolis of Paris.

ʿAbduh readily acknowledged that during the course of the nineteenth century, standard religious authority had dwindled. It had become difficult to see what the contribution of the Islamic tradition to the modern era could possibly be. The cultural dilemma of how to salvage the Islamic "deposit of knowledge or truth, originating with a past authority and handed down with a religious community," troubled several Islamic societies around the world, most notably that on the Indian subcontinent.[10] However, under the intellectual leadership of ʿAbduh, one of the most resourceful and innovative movements of Islamic reformism anywhere assumed the burden of trying to creatively modify tradition and at the same time retain Islamic authenticity. This was and remained a gigantic cultural challenge.

Like al-Afghānī before him, ʿAbduh's point of departure was essentially modern, very contemporary, and thus compatible with the worldview of the emerging middle-class *effendiyya* (see below). He accepted the Western cultural consensus that the main unit for historical analysis is civilization and that reform should influence the trajectory of civilization. Like other members of this generation, he subscribed to the view that Islamic civilization is in a dismal state of decline and paralysis. However, he rejected the alleged incompatibility between Islam and science and called for a new approach to the *sunna,* the goal of which was to appropriate the driving force behind the success of Western civilization, namely, rationality.

The process of rethinking the tradition was based on a return to the unadulterated *sunna* of the Prophet. Later termed *salafiyya,* this philosophy maintained that the original *sunna* was subjected to centuries of blind and distorting imitation *(taqlīd),* which ultimately brought about the present state of decline. Identifying *taqlīd* as the cause of decline and prescribing rational investigation, or *ijtihād,* as a cure were a rather modern reading of Islamic history and legal thought. Thus, though *taqlīd* was a classic doctrinal concept that meant unjustified legal conformity, during the nineteen century its meaning was altered "into

9. Goldschmidt, *A Biographical Dictionary of Modern Egypt,* pp. 146–147; P.C. Sadgrove, "Al-Nadīm Sayyid ʿAbdallāh," *EI²*, 7, p. 852a.

10. Daniel Brown, *Rethinking Tradition in Modern Islamic Thought* (Cambridge: Cambridge University Press, 1999), pp. 1–2 and elsewhere.

a broad designation for cultural and intellectual stagnation and unwillingness to experiment with ideas."[11] Striving for the development of a rational method, as the linchpin of *ijtihād,* ʿAbduh's next move was to make, so to speak, more "room" for reason by engaging with theological rationalism and reformulating the concept of *tawḥīd.*

Tawḥīd (literally, "making one") is a non-Koranic term that historically was used in theological debates regarding the nature of divine unity and is intimately tied to the position of the ninth-century theological school of the Muʿtazila.[12] Although from the tenth and eleventh century, rationalist Muʿtazilite theology had waned, replaced by an Ashʿarite orthodoxy, ʿAbduh purposely decided to revisit the now-unpopular school of Muʿtazilite thought, although never openly claming to be a Muʿtazilite himself.[13] Thus, writing his seminal 1897 work *Risālat al-tawḥīd* (Epistle of Divine Unity), ʿAbduh emphasized the role of free will and reason and thus "effectively, though subtly, modified some key positions in the formerly dominant Ashʿarī position."[14] His notion of unity as *tawḥīd* rejected the possibility of a "conflict between reason and revelation as . . . otherwise God would have created rationality in vain." Indeed, "ʿAbduh goes on to place *tawḥīd* squarely at the center of the prophet Muḥammad's mission."[15]

The accumulated impact of ʿAbduh's thought had several outcomes. First, he relegitimized the expansive usage of rational tools and thus strengthened the prevalent reformist notion of *ijtihād.* Second, answering Western critics, he refuted the alleged inherent incompatibility of Islamic revelation and reason, thus temporarily solving a prevalent cultural dilemma that had weighed heavily on the shoulders of indigenous reformists.[16] Third, he made a case for the plural-

11. Bernard Weiss, "Taqlīd," in *The Oxford Encyclopedia of the Modern Islamic World* (Oxford: Oxford University Press, 1995), pp. 187–189. For a critical view of this formulation, see Wael Hallaq, "Was the Gate of Ijtihād Closed?" *International Journal of Middle East Studies* 16, no. 1 (1984): pp. 3–41.

12. The Muʿtazila, which was identified with a rational approach to questions of doctrine, embraced *tawḥīd* as its primary principle and called for a nonliteral interpretation of the Koran using rational tools, which were collectively known as *qiyās.* Many of the differences between the Muʿtazila and their opponents came to focus in the question of whether the Koran was created or eternal.

13. When the conservative shaykh ʿUlaysh of al-Azhar challenged ʿAbduh, asking "if he had given up Ashʿarite teaching to follow the Muʿtazilite," ʿAbduh replied, "If I give up blind acceptance *(taqlīd)* of Ashʿarite doctrine, why should I take up blind acceptance of the Muʿtazila?" Quoted in Richard Martin, Mark Woodward, and Dwi Atmaja, *Defenders of Reason in Islam: Muʿtazilism from Medieval School to Modern Symbol* (Oxford: One World, 1997), p. 130.

14. Tamara Sonn, "Tawḥīd," in *The Oxford Encyclopedia of the Modern Islamic World,* p. 194.

15. Ibid., p. 195.

16. Albert Hourani, *Arabic Thought in the Liberal Age, 1798–1939* (Cambridge: Cambridge University Press, 1993), pp. 130–192.

ity of religious interpretation, and, finally, he positioned the Islamic reformist movement in Egypt at the intellectual forefront of Islamic reformism in general and even as the point of departure for twentieth-century neo-Muʿtazilism. Indeed, so much was bold and modern in ʿAbduh's thought that it is likely that many elements of it would have been entirely lost even on an audacious reformer such as the Yemenite Muḥammad Ibn ʿAlī al-Shawkānī (d. 1832).

Because ʿAbduh's agenda was highly relevant, it attracted a rich gallery of public figures from other Arab lands and from across the cultural spectrum. And so, alongside young secularists such as Qāsim Amīn (1863–1908), Aḥmad Luṭfī al-Sayyid (1872–1963), and Saʿd Zaghlūl (1857–1927), there were also the young Rashīd Riḍā (1865–1935), who arrived in Egypt in 1897, the Syrian circle of Jamāl al-Dīn al-Qāsimī (1886–1914), language reformer ʿAbd al-Qādir al-Maghribī (1867–1956), and many more.[17] Crystallizing during the 1890s, ʿAbduh's circle replaced the incoherent politics of dissent-cum-reform that had characterized the previous generation of al-Afghānī and al-Nadīm with a philosophically driven worldview. The circle's politics of cultural synthesis and coexistence also functioned as an alternative to the individualism of the Nahḍa's "stars," such as Zaydān, and, more generally, to the Syrian Christian circle, which was not committed to Islamic authenticity. It also gained ʿAbduh the personal appreciation of Lord Cromer, who considered the thinker an exemplary innovator and, in private correspondence, regarded his circle as "*bona fide* Mohamedan reformers."[18] In 1905 ʿAbduh died prematurely at the age of fifty-four, and his cultural coalition slowly began to disintegrate.

On the social level, the new protobourgeois class of journalists, doctors, lawyers, teachers, bureaucrats, and technicians known as the *effendiyya* assumed greater public influence and began to vie for even more. Beginning in the 1880s, this new middle class gradually drifted away from the Ottoman world and into the bosom of colonial modernity, which complemented its skills and worldview. *Effendis* gradually replaced Turkish with Arabic and supplemented it with French, Italian, or English. The *nahḍawī*-inspired *effendiyya* did not simply embrace change as an abstract accumulative process but articulated the desirable form and direction of this change by developing an expansive notion of reform. With their specific schemes for reform, the *effendis* assumed that by changing the lives of peasants, who were the majority of Egypt's inhabitants, and, to a lesser

17. On Syrian reformism and ties to Egypt, see David Commins, *Islamic Reform: Politics and Social Change in Late Ottoman Syria* (Oxford: Oxford University Press, 1990)

18. Afaf Lutfi al-Sayyid Marsot, *Egypt and Cromer: A Study in Anglo-Egyptian Relations* (London: John Murray, 1968), p. 176.

degree, the lives of the new urban working class, they would also reform their civilization.[19] Whatever discussion took place on one level or another in literary salons, learned societies, welfare organizations, the burgeoning media, political clubs, colonial offices, Masonic lodges, and secret societies, it was driven by a social philosophy of progress whose mantra was reform, and it gradually replaced civilization with nation.

But all the while, other Egyptians were also a factor: Egypt's rank and file—ordinary people who left little, if any, written testimony behind them, people whose lives were one long struggle for survival. Over the years, these individuals became increasingly important, not because of something they thought, wrote, said, or initiated, but simply because they had become the condemned objects of history. The intellectual dynamism of this era produced more and more ideas, blueprints, and tangible projects of how to mold, change, reorient, and otherwise fundamentally alter the lives of this faction for the benefit of the common good. This sort of thinking, rather than the *courbaj* (a whip with five thongs, made out of hippopotamus hide), whose usage declined sharply in this period, now affected rural Egyptians—a sort of thinking that, despite its goodwill, only rarely changed their lives for the better.[20]

On a different social front, women did not wait for the intellectual Qāsim Amīn and his like to tell them that they should be modern and emancipated. Already years beforehand, feminist pioneers such as Zaynab Fawwāz and Hind Nawāfil took up the pen and daringly created new spheres of action. Taking their destinies into their own hands, they sought to reformulate their social environment in search of wider possibilities and greater equality. A key weapon in their arsenal was the "salon," an urban intellectual generator of the first rate. Yet, the limits remained. As colonial rule established itself, women had to cope not only with the biases of their own society but also with those of the British. This double paternalism hampered their success but was never able to strangle it.[21]

Parallel to women's activism, the emergence of an activist political camp whose main goal was the immediate British evacuation of Egypt and the Sudan occurred in the late 1890s. Headed by the young Muṣṭafa Kāmil (1874–1908), a French-educated lawyer, this group also included Muḥammad Farīd (1868–1919) and Shaykh ʿAbd al-ʿAzīz Jawīsh (1872–1929) and was a magnet for young educated Muslims. Espousing an ideological mélange that mixed Pan-Islamism with

19. Michael Gasper, "Civilizing Peasants: The Public Sphere, Islamic Reform and the Generation of Political Modernity in Egypt, 1875–1919," unpublished Ph.D. dissertation, New York University, 2004.

20. Khaled Fahmy, "The Police and the People in Nineteenth-Century Egypt," *Die Welt des Islam* 39, no. 3 (1999): pp. 340–377.

21. Beth Baron, *The Women's Awakening in Egypt: Culture, Society and the Press* (New Haven, CT: Yale University Press, 1994).

a distinctive nationalism, Muṣṭafa Kāmil sought the patronage of the nationalist-minded khedive ʿAbbās Ḥilmī II, who since his appointment in 1892 had been a thorn in the side of the British.[22]

Along with the Ottoman sultan Abdülhamid, the khedive extended material, political, and moral support to the group. Thus, in 1895 he was instrumental in the establishment of a secret group, the Society for the Revival of the Nation, which later was a springboard for the establishment of Kāmil's strong National Party. The khedive also supported the daily newspaper *Al-Muʾayyad,* which, under the leadership of Shaykh ʿAlī Yūsuf (1863–1913), became the mouthpiece of the palace-Kāmil coalition.[23] At the same time it was also an alternative for pro-British Syrian media, such as *Al-Muqaṭṭam.*

Making periodic contributions to *al-Muʾayyad* and, after 1900, to his own aggressive organ *Al-Liwāʾ,* Muṣṭafa Kāmil had a gift for the politics of scandal. As his actions following the 1906 Dinshaway incident illustrate, he was highly skillful in utilizing local as well as international public opinion in his struggle against occupation. Somewhat naively, however, he opted for French support against the British and was wholly disappointed at the 1904 *entente cordiale,* when the two powers traded French freedom to act in Morocco for the continuation of British rule in Egypt. This event also signaled a fallout between Kāmil and ʿAbbās Ḥilmī II, who now sought rapprochement with Britain. Kāmil's circle always contended that physical liberation from the British and constant opposition to them on all matters were preconditions for cultural and national revival. This course of action positioned this camp, and even the khedive, in opposition to ʿAbduh and his followers. As the khedive later recorded, ʿAbduh was "a man of remarkable intelligence, but a pusillanimous character. He was devoted to England" and had "unfortunate links with the occupiers."[24]

By deed and thought, all of these 1890s reformers, dissidents, idealists, dreamers, and liberators contributed to an environment that ultimately gave birth to the

22. In 1893 ʿAbbās Ḥilmī II tried to replace his prime minister and introduce other changes to his cabinet without prior British consent. This led to his first head-on confrontation with Cromer, which he lost. A year later, while visiting the border with Sudan, the khedive criticized the military preparedness and performance of the Egyptian army under the leadership of the British colonel Herbert Kitchener. Though initially Kitchener offered his resignation, Cromer had the khedive reverse his criticism. As the events of August 1914 would later prove, Kitchener never forgot this episode, nor did he forgive the khedive. For a vivid account of the "rebellious khedive," see Jacques Berque, *Egypt: Imperialism and Revolution* (London: Faber and Faber, 1972), pp. 163–169; and Lutfi al-Sayyid Marsot, *Egypt and Cromer* (1968), pp. 98–136.

23. After 1906, when the Kāmil-palace coalition disintegrated, ʿAlī Yūsuf and *Al-Muʾayyad* remained loyal to the khedive.

24. ʿAbbās Ḥilmi II, *The Last Khedive of Egypt: Memoirs of Abbas Hilmi II,* translated by Amira Sonbol (Reading, UK: Ithaca Press 1998), pp. 91, 180.

rise of modern historical consciousness and historical writing. Yet, what exactly happened in this era that afforded this historiographical change? Was there any definitive agent of literary change? Does calling it "nationalist," as some scholars have suggested, really account for modern history?[25] Does the much broader concept of Nahḍa successfully reflect this trend?[26] Was it purely a matter of class struggle and the formation of a working class?[27] Was it economic transformation in an impending global era?[28] Or was modern writing an imposition of a colonial mode of thought?[29] Though it was surely, in part, about all of these things, none of them, taken alone, is specific enough to account for the birth of a new type of thinking.

Indeed, an attempt to find a single explanatory conceptual frame for these disparate movements presents certain problems. Rather than being a durable analytical tool, a holistic approach to history is usually merely provocative. Nevertheless, if one attempts to frame this era by a single grand concept and requires that concept to have verifiable explanatory power, the model that rises to the task is that of historicism. This model demands some elucidation, however. As with other nineteenth-century terms that at first enjoyed semantic clarity, the word *historicism* has become obscure and could now mean (too) many things in a postmodern era. Philosophers of history identify three principal meanings for the term. First, *historicism* is identified with the historiographical outlook and practice of nineteenth-century scholarship in the humanities (specifically that which is affiliated with Leopold Von Ranke). Second, in another sense, during the early years of the twentieth century in Europe, *historicism* represented the moral relativism and loss of faith in the values of modern Western culture (usually used with reference to the "crisis of historicism.") Third, more recently, the concept of historicism has been employed in order to urge the recognition of the historical and cultural specificity of ideas (usually dubbed "the new historicism").[30] And if

25. Alexander Schölch, *Egypt for the Egyptians! The Socio-political Crisis in Egypt 1878–1882* (London: Ithaca Press, 1981), pp. 135–226; Charles Wendell, *The Evolution of the Egyptian National Image* (Berkeley: University of California Press, 1972), pp. 162–200.

26. Anwar 'Abd al-Malik, *Nahḍat Miṣr* (Cairo: al-Hay'a al-miṣriyya al-'āmma li-l-kitāb, 1983), especially parts 1 and 2.

27. Joel Beinin and Zachary Lockman, *Workers on the Nile: Nationalism, Islam and the Egyptian Working Class, 1882–1954* (Princeton, NJ: Princeton University Press, 1987), pp. 23–82. See especially 'Alī Barakāt, *Taṭawwur al-milkīyya al-zirā'iyya fī Miṣr, 1813–1914, wa athruhu 'ala al-ḥaraka al-siyāsiyya* (Cairo: Dār al-thaqāfa al-jadīda, 1977), pp. 149–282.

28. Roger Owen, *The Middle East in the World Economy, 1800–1914* (London: I. B. Tauris, 1993), pp. 122–152, 216–243.

29. Timothy Mitchell, *Colonizing Egypt* (Berkeley: University of California Press, 1991).

30. Georg Iggers, "Historicism: The History and Meaning of the Term," *Journal of the History of Ideas* 56, no. 1 (1995): pp. 129–152.

we leave philosophers of history aside and ask students of comparative literature what historicism is, their answer will be immensely more complicated.[31]

So, without burdening ourselves too much with the enormous literature on the subject, I will use *historicism* in a rather simple sense: "Historicism is the supposition that an adequate understanding of human reality can be gained only through considering it in terms of the place which it secured for itself, and the role which it played, within a historical process of development."[32] As yet, there is no well-defined theory of historicism but only a certain vision or an attitude toward history, which Carl Schorske has referred to as "thinking *with* history." For Schorske, "'Thinking *with* history' . . . implies the utilization of elements of the past in the cultural construction of the present and future."[33] More than anything else, Schorske thought of history in terms of an elementary intellectual and mental habit. Historian Anouar Abdel-Malek proposed a vision of late nineteenth-century Egypt as a period in which historical consciousness was born. Though his concept lacked any analytical power, he clearly observed the phenomenon of historicism becoming a normative practice.[34] But how did this concept establish itself in Egypt?

Indeed, for late nineteenth-century Egyptian men and women, historicism was a new language, a sort of an epistemic umbrella that imposed and conditioned certain modes of reasoning. Thus, from a practical point of view, historicist thought achieved three things. It prescribed the viewing of things in terms of their final outcome; it encouraged the search for the roots of any given phenomenon; and it assumed that history is a changing stream governed by secular reason. (The concept of "rise and decline" was one popular way to explain historical change.) More than anything else, however, historicism sought to understand the past from the point of view of the final outcome of progress: that is, the *future.* As such, historicism accounts for many of the above-mentioned ideologies, ideas, and collective aspirations, including, but not limited to, nationalism. It conditioned them and was simultaneously reformulated by them once they became operative. Evidently, the nature of this relationship was a two-way traffic.

As the thinking of the literate urban class was gradually historicized, historicism was being standardized and customized to create its own particularly

31. For a particularly convoluted intellectual ancestry of historicism, see Paul Hamilton, *Historicism,* the New Critical Idiom Series (London: Routledge, 1996).

32. Maurice Mandelbaum, *History, Man, and Reason; A Study in Nineteenth-Century Thought* (Baltimore: Johns Hopkins University Press, 1971), p. 41.

33. Carl E. Schorske, *Thinking with History* (Princeton, NJ.: Princeton University Press, 1998), p. 3.

34. 'Abd al-Malik, *Nahḍat Miṣr,* pp. 215–248.

Egyptian lexicon. By the end of the century, historicism became a new way of making sense of things, a new way of knowing, and a privileged mode of meaning making. Viewed in light of early nineteenth-century thought, this sort of understanding formed the essence of the historicist divide.

Focusing on the 1890s, I propose in this chapter that historicism enabled the gradual appearance of modern history as a new literary genre and that modern history was substituted for previous forms of historical knowledge. As part of this process, historicism created a powerful view of modern Egypt. How did it happen? Operating at the very abstract level, historicism brought about a change in the understanding of three dimensions of reality: *time*, *space*, and *subjectivity*. The implications of such shifts were, indeed, enormous, for these three modified dimensions completely reformulated history writing. More or less gone was the monumental chronicle. Gone, too, was even the *khiṭaṭ*, the vast cultural-geographical survey that is endemic to the Egyptian literary tradition. Deemed "medieval," these forms of writing, and indeed modes of thinking, gradually became obsolete, leaving behind them an enormous cultural space. Instead, historicism privileged the short, modern narrative in the form of an article or a book.

However, this process was slightly more complicated and less straightforward than is usually assumed. Reading through the literature of the 1890s, one is almost immediately struck by its heterogeneous—or for lack of a better word, hybrid—nature, that is, by the contrast between what historical works were *meant* to be and what they actually *were*. For example, the historical chronicle of the era is not yet a concise and modern history book, but, at the same time, it is also quite different from the classic medieval chronicles. The same is true with regard to historical novels, which, in the eyes of many, are hardly considered worthy of the title novel. Since this "imperfect" literature does not fall neatly into common categorizations, it needs to be studied on its own terms in its own intellectual environment. Such an approach will enable us to look deep into the formation process of the genre of modern history. More specifically, I focus on a significant element in this process: a certain paradigmatic view according to which Muḥammad ʿAlī created modern Egypt.

Finally, before we turn to discuss how this historiographical shift came about, it is important to acknowledge the elitist nature of this enterprise, one that was carried out by a small class of intellectuals and their enthusiastic *effendi* collaborators. Hence, not all of the texts discussed here were influential in themselves. While some were canonized by subsequent generations, most were probably not so important in their day and were soon forgotten. Yet, notwithstanding their past status, they do reflect the broader intellectual trends of the time and illustrate how the end result of this intellectual process was the emergence of modern historical consciousness.

A CURIOUS DEBATE

In May 1902 (in observance of the date in the Hijri calendar) and again in May 1905 (for the Gregorian one), an unusual ceremony took place in Egypt's main cities.[35] In what seems to be an innovation of political culture, Egypt's ruling family celebrated the centennial anniversary of Muḥammad 'Alī's inauguration as viceroy of Egypt. Already in April 1905 a special committee was formed in order to plan for that year's event.[36] The hands of its members were full. They declared the event a national holiday and a day off work.[37] The Cairo tram company was asked to change its schedule. On the banks of the Nile, a special area was designated to contain the expected large crowds. Cabins were installed for the respected spectators who were willing to pay two hundred piasters. All others were charged a flat fee of ten piasters a ticket. Tickets sold rapidly. All income was designated for charity. In the neighboring 'Abd al-'Azīz theater, a new play was performed: *Muḥammad 'Alī.* A huge musical parade and fireworks were scheduled for the day.[38] Passionate speeches were delivered.[39] Similar celebrations were also held in Alexandria, al-Fayyūm, and other cities.[40] *Al-Ahrām*'s headline declared: "The Commemoration of Muḥammad 'Alī or Egypt's National Holiday."[41] This was, in fact, Egypt's first significant celebration of a national holiday.

In the weeks and days that preceded the celebrations, prominent figures published learned articles about Muḥammad 'Alī's legacy. Never before had so much history been published and celebrated in such a short span of time, even in the aftermath of the 'Urābī revolt. Writers said that Muḥammad 'Alī had revived Egypt, saved it from decline, and put it on the same track as that of progressive nations.[42] They said he was nominated by the people to rule Egypt.[43] They celebrated his commercial, industrial, and agricultural development projects. They spoke about the creation of infrastructure.[44] They called him "the founder of the

35. Kenneth Cuno was the first to point to the broader historiographical significance of the following debate. In part, he based his understanding on an elusive colloquium paper by Sayyid 'Ashmāwī. Cuno, "Muhammad 'Ali and the Decline and Revival Thesis in Modern Egyptian History."

36. *Al-Ahrām,* April 12, 1905, p. 1.

37. Ibid., May 12, 1905, p. 2.

38. Ibid., p. 2.

39. Ibid., May 15, 1905, p. 1.

40. Ibid., p. 2.

41. Ibid., April 12, 1905, p. 1.

42. Ibid., May 12, 1905, p. 1.

43. Writers mentioned Shaykh 'Umar Makram as responsible for the act of nomination. *Al-Ahrām,* May 12, 1905, p. 1; *Al-Ahrām,* May 15, 1905, p. 1.

44. Ibid., May 12, 1905, p. 1.

royal family,"[45] "the founder of the Egyptian emirate *(imāra),*" and the "founder and reviver of the Egyptian lands *(diyār).*"[46]

However, what they meant to say, and indeed would say later on, was that Muḥammad ʿAlī was the *founder of modern Egypt.*[47] During this period, the Ottoman Empire and its ruling sultan were not even mentioned. The ceremonial court rituals that once symbolized Egypt's essential bond to the sultans in Istanbul seemed to have been irreversibly erased from memory.

Already in February 1901, during the heyday of his alliance with ʿAbbās Ḥilmī, Muṣṭafa Kāmil called in *Al-Liwāʾ* for the celebration of this anniversary as a national holiday. Now, standing before an audience of thirty-five hundred men and women gathered in Alexandria, he gave an unusually passionate speech in which he posed a series of rhetorical questions:[48] "How did he [Muḥammad ʿAlī] lead Egypt? How did he save her from oblivion? How did he remove her from the world of darkness into that of light, how did he conquer, strike and emerge triumphant. . . . How did he exterminate the oppressors and unite the country under one flag?"[49] He knew the answer: with the help of the Egyptian nation, which entrusted its affairs to his skillful hands (452). Who could ignore or deny all of these achievements, wondered Muṣṭafa Kāmil (454)?

The one person who could was Shaykh Muḥammad ʿAbduh, who, as we have seen, had his own ideas about history and Islamic authenticity. In spite of the apparently genuine general excitement and the extensive press coverage, ʿAbduh stubbornly refused to be impressed. He had several important reservations. The contested issue was Muḥammad ʿAlī's legacy. Going against the stream of panegyric speeches and laudatory newspaper articles, ʿAbduh called into question the entire perception of Egypt's experience under Muḥammad ʿAlī. ʿAbduh's writings soon sparked the first historiographical debate of twentieth-century Egypt.

45. Ibid., May 1, 1905, p. 1.

46. Ibid., April 12, 1905, p. 1. Already in 1840 the French had created a medal of Muḥammad ʿAlī, also dubbing him *muḥyī al-dawla al-miṣriyya.* Gaston Wiet, *Mohammed Ali et les beaux-arts* (Cairo: Société royale d'études historiques, 1950), p. 329. The use of such titles had many medieval precedents and would have been familiar to the inhabitants of Cairo. This is particularly true of the designation "reviver" (*muḥyī*), which was first used by the heroic medieval military general, and founder of the Ayyubid dynasty, Saladin, in his inscription on the western gate of the Citadel. There, he is designated the Reviver of the Empire of the Commander of the Faithful *(muḥyī dawlat amīr al-muʾminīn).* Nasser Rabbat, *The Citadel of Cairo* (Leiden, the Netherlands: E. J. Brill, 1995), p. 71.

47. According to the historian ʿAbd al-Raḥmān al-Rāfiʿī and ʿAshmāwī, the title "the founder of modern Egypt" first appeared in an Alexandria-based newspaper *(The Reform)* and only later in the *Egyptian Gazette.* Cuno, "Muhammad ʿAli and the Decline and Revival Thesis in Modern Egyptian History," pp. 93–111; ʿAbd al-Raḥmān al-Rāfiʿī, *Muṣṭafa Kāmil: Bāʿith al-ḥaraka al-waṭaniyya* (Cairo: Maktabat al-nahḍa al-miṣriyya, 1939), p. 158.

48. al-Rāfiʿī, *Muṣṭafa Kāmil: Bāʿith al-ḥaraka al-waṭaniyya,* pp. 158–160.

49. Ibid., pp. 451–452.

"Only God knows," exclaimed ʿAbduh after reading the newspapers, "what the great deal of talk on Muḥammad ʿAlī is all about."[50] Simply put, this talk was about what came to be acknowledged as the unique contribution of the pasha to the modernization of Egypt. In the June 1, 1902, issue of *Al-Hilāl,* editor Jurjī Zaydān argued that through a series of administrative, military, agriculture, commercial, industrial, and educational reforms, Muḥammad ʿAlī had changed the course of Islamic history and opened an entirely new and progressive era. This edifice was built on top of the ruins of a crumbling and corrupt Ottoman-Mamluk order.[51] In 1905, two more detailed and inclusive versions of this story appeared for the Gregorian date of the anniversary. From that point onward, this historical perception of Muḥammad ʿAlī as the maker of the modern Egyptian nation prevailed.[52]

Precisely a week later, ʿAbduh's riposte to Zaydān appeared in *Al-Manār.* Though the article was anonymously signed "historian," ʿAbduh's authorship has been posthumously established.[53] His perspective was original. Through a series of questions that seem as if they were taken from a seminar in a modern university a century later, ʿAbduh effectively challenged the entire "founder paradigm": What was the condition of Egypt before the pasha's ascendance to the governorship? What would Egypt's reality look like if he had never taken power? What was the price paid by Egypt's rank and file for the pasha's policies? To whose benefit did the reforms play out? And finally, did the life of Egyptians improve or worsen following his rule?[54] One by one ʿAbduh answered these questions.

According to him, following popular opposition, the French expedition departed, and Egyptians expected some sort of a civil approach to public affairs *(an yashruqa nūr madaniyya . . .),* but Muḥammad ʿAlī did not idly wait for the fulfillment of that expectation (178). Instead, he established himself as a sole ruler, promoted corrupt people, and joined all the Egyptian villages into one huge estate governed by his house (179). ʿAbduh acknowledged Muḥammad ʿAlī's establishment of industry but contended that he never considered the poor working conditions of the workers (181–182). He perfected irrigation but did so mainly in

50. Muḥammad ʿAbduh, "Āthār Muḥammad ʿAlī fī Miṣr," *Al-Manār* 5, no. 5 (June 7, 1902): p. 175.

51. Though the text is not signed, its language and a reference to one of his works clarify that the writer is Jurjī Zaydān: "Muḥammad ʿAlī Bāsha," *Al-Hilāl,* June 1902, pp. 517–541.

52. "Tārīkh Muḥammad ʿAlī Bāshā," *Al-Muqtaṭaf,* June 1905, pp. 553–554, July, pp. 521–532, August, pp. 637–647, September, pp. 717–720, October, pp. 797–808, November, pp. 901–909, December, pp. 943–953, January 1906, pp. 15–18. See also Zaydān's "al-Yūbīl al-miʾaīnī li-taʾssīs al-arīka al-khadīwiyya," *Al-Hilāl,* May 1905, pp. 443–449.

53. See Muḥammad ʿAbduh, *Al-Aʿmāl al-kāmila li-l-imām Muḥammad ʿAbduh,* ed. Muḥammad ʿImāra (Beirut: al-Muʾassasa al-ʿarabiyya li-l-dirāsāt wa-l-nashr, 1972), vol. 1, pp. 721–728.

54. ʿAbduh, "Āthār Muḥammad ʿAlī," pp. 175–183.

order to water his own estates. He introduced medicine to Egypt but primarily for the sake of the army and in order to discover the criminal soldiers who defected from service (180). He indeed sent students to Europe but controlled them even while they were abroad. These students, maintained ʿAbduh, were nothing but machines with no control over what they produced (181). He invested in culture, but all the translated books were locked in a closet and were never publicly distributed (181). Had he ever thought about reforming the Arabic and Turkish languages? (180). Had he ever thought of consulting the citizens and establishing a just constitutional government? He built a strong army, but did Egyptians really enjoy being part of this army, were they proud of it, were they happy to be drafted and go to war? (180).

ʿAbduh's categorical answer was no. The soldiers defected. They knew that they could depart from the army only when they were dead. None of the soldiers was thinking of his army or navy in patriotic terms, as "their army." The Egyptian soldiers detested the army, which did not even promote them (182). In order to secure his independent position vis-à-vis the Sublime Porte, Muḥammad ʿAlī promoted foreign intruders *(dukhalāʾ)* who enjoyed rights that were denied to Egyptians. Thus, the nationalist *(waṭanī)* became a stranger in his own home, unsure of his decisions (179–180). Concluding his attack, ʿAbduh argued that Muḥammad ʿAlī was indeed a courageous soldier, agriculturist, and industrialist, but as far as Egypt was concerned, he simply conquered it. The true life of Egypt was put to death under his reign (183).

Two weeks later as the debate grew stronger, ʿAbduh published another article in which he dealt with the entire legacy of Muḥammad ʿAlī's dynasty and directly refuted Kāmil's speech. Now, the whole course of nineteenth-century Egyptian history was put up for debate. According to ʿAbduh, both socially and politically, Muḥammad ʿAlī's legacy was the most important issue for consideration *(umm al-masāʾil)*.[55] In refutation of Kāmil's premise, ʿAbduh argued that if Muḥammad ʿAlī was such a great ruler, why had all of his achievements evaporated after his death? How come the Egyptian political community itself had deteriorated to such a low point? (232–233). Who had ruined the industrial achievements that Muṣṭafa Kāmil was so proud of? If he was right in arguing that Muḥammad ʿAlī had molded Egypt into one united nation *(waṭanan wāḥidan li umma wāḥida)* and propagated the spirit of patriotism *(maḥabat al-waṭan),* where were all of these qualities to be found now? (234).

According to Muṣṭafa Kāmil, Muḥammad ʿAlī's rule was based on three principles: (a) protection of the state from foreign assault, (b) promotion of Egyptians

55. Muḥammad ʿAbduh, "A aḥyāhā Muḥammad ʿAlī wa amātahā khalafuhu?" *Al-Manār* 5, no. 6 (June 22, 1902): p. 232.

to self-rule, and (c) avoidance of debt. Obviously, concluded ʿAbduh, his successors had not followed these guidelines. The khedive Ismāʿīl took billions in loans,[56] while Tawfīq ignored the plea of the soldiers for justice and brought about the British occupation.[57] At that point, the debate touched on the sensitive issue of the ʿUrābī revolt, following which ʿAbduh had been imprisoned. On the basis of his historical analysis, he attacked Muṣṭafa Kāmil, who regarded the revolt as nothing but dangerous political chaos *(fitna)*. Next, ʿAbduh took on the impotence and submission of the current khedive, ʿAbbās Ḥilmī II, who at this point was still Muṣṭafa Kāmil's chief protector (235). Nothing, it seemed, could escape ʿAbduh's wrath.

But what really made ʿAbduh so angry? What prompted him to insult the pasha as ignoramus who could not read or write? (236). Obviously, this was not the first time that Muḥammad ʿAlī's legacy had come under fire. A contemporary of the pasha, the eminent chronicler ʿAbd al-Raḥmān al-Jabartī, was the first to make public similar concerns. In fact, much of ʿAbduh's knowledge of this era was based on al-Jabartī's account. ʿAbduh must have also come across the work of Aḥmad al-Rajabī (d. 1827 or 1829), the man hired by the pasha to refute al-Jabartī's accusations.[58] He must have known that the previous debate ended with a ban on the publication and distribution of al-Jabartī's account and a systematic destruction of all existing copies. (The ban was finally lifted only in 1878.) He must have known that by going against the ruling family he was also putting himself in danger. Besides, if al-Jabartī and al-Rajabī had already conducted this debate back in the 1820s, why was it important to bring it up again? Was there something different this time? Did the centennial celebrations mark any meaningful shift in Egypt's political or cultural orientation? Was there something behind the celebration that justified such an unusual reaction on ʿAbduh's part? In hindsight, had ʿAbduh really put his finger on some major turning point?

The answer to all of these questions is yes. Something major was indeed at stake, and this something was quintessentially different from the exchange of the 1820s or any other nineteenth-century historiographical debate. However, in order to understand the impending shift properly, we need to go back in time to consider some traits of late nineteenth-century Egyptian historiography.

56. One can only imagine the revisionist contents of ʿAbduh's book on the Ismāʿīl era. Unfortunately, save for two incomplete drafts, this work was lost. Gamal el-Din el-Shayyal, *A History of Egyptian Historiography in the Nineteenth Century* (Alexandria: University of Alexandria Press, 1962), pp. 68–69. For the surviving drafts see ʿAbduh, *Al-Aʿmāl al-kāmila*, pp. 401–411.

57. ʿAbduh, "A aḥyāhā Muḥammad ʿAlī," pp. 234–235.

58. For an excellent introduction to al-Rajabī's response to al-Jabartī, see Khalīl bin Aḥmad al-Rajabī, *Tārīkh al-wazīr Muḥammad ʿAlī Bāshā* (Cairo: al-Āfāq al-ʿarabiyya, 1997), pp. 7–54.

THREE QUESTIONS ABOUT LATE NINETEENTH-CENTURY HISTORIOGRAPHY

The genre of modern history writing experienced a long and unsure path of development, which reached its zenith only in the 1930s. Until then, some promising experiments failed. Other, initially questionable, paths proved viable and showed continuation with much success. However, in Egypt, as elsewhere in the Ottoman Empire, modern history writing first had to take into account the histories that were already there. A substantial encounter between new and old forms of history writing occurred as late as the 1890s. Only by that time can we identify a considerable body of historical literature that tried to fuse these two different traditions. Since in the first stages of this encounter, none of these writing forms achieved prominence, the final literary result was of a fluid nature. Perhaps for this reason, previous scholarship has entirely overlooked this phenomenon. As mentioned in the introduction, al-Shayyāl and Crabbs studied nineteenth-century Egyptian historiography only as a straightforward story of transition, during which history writing could be either "modern" or "traditional" but certainly not both.

Historiographically speaking, this third, combined category meant that abstract description was not necessarily substituted with penetrating analysis; the flowery language of *saj*ʿ did not entirely vanish to clear the way for a concrete journalistic tone; tight causal explanations coexisted with loose forms of argumentation; and finally, both state documents and popular folklore served as building materials for the historiography of this era. In most cases, all of these features appeared in the very same work. As was the case with the Arabic novel, a certain instability was the hallmark of the developing genre.[59]

How, then, can we analyze this literature, and what can we learn from it? In the following lines I propose to focus on three questions that every Egyptian history writer, whether consciously or not, has had to grapple with: First, how does one tell history? Second, what is its subject? And finally, where does it take place? To answer these questions is to explore the impact of historicism on three crucial historiographical dimensions: *time, subjectivity,* and *space*. Such an investigation will give substance and meaning to my argument that the main feature of the historiography of the 1890s is its hybrid nature. In addition—and highly relevant to our general concern here—these perceptual changes facilitated the creation of a powerful model under which Egypt's modern historical experience was organized. The curious debate cited above could not have taken place without the gradual transcendence of these three dimensions.

59. I thank Samah Selim for pointing out these similarities.

How Does One Tell History?

Time is structured through narration. Thus, a shift from a chronicle to a modern narrative is, first and foremost, a profound change in the historian's perception of historical time. Awareness of time was not new to Islamic historians when this shift occurred. Already in the fifteenth century, these historians contended that "the object of history is man and time."[60] Thus, there is no need to take the reader on a tour of Islamic historiography during the eighteenth and nineteenth centuries in order to make the point that the fashion in which historians have chosen to tell their stories underwent a fundamental change in the late 1800s. Slowly but surely, historians shifted from a fragmented chronicle, bound by the day-by-day or year-by-year unfolding of time, to an internally structured narrative that formed into a more or less coherent plot. Thus, such a change is an indication for a shift in the historian's understanding of the speed and direction of human development (hence, time). Let us turn to look more closely at how the narrative structures time.

Modern narratives are premised on the conception of history as a continuous and progressive process (though not necessarily a linear one).[61] This concept is of recent origin. "It came into being in the wake of increasing secularization and the concomitant rise of scientific inquiry; and it was preceded by mythological and theological conceptions which discounted the significance of chronological (i.e. linear) time for an understanding of the past."[62] Originally, this process was endemic to the West. It reached a point of culmination during the nineteenth century and gradually penetrated the Ottoman Empire as well.

A good place to locate such changes in Egypt is in Zaydān's 1889 pioneering account *Tārīkh Miṣr al-ḥadīth* (A Modern History of Egypt).[63] Because of Zaydān's broad modernistic agenda, my discussion of his book will go beyond the immediate concern of this section (notions of historical time) to discuss some

60. Franz Rosenthal, *A History of Muslim Historiography* (Leiden, the Netherlands: E. J. Brill, 1952), p. 205.

61. Eviatar Zerubavel, *Time Maps: Collective Memory and Social Shape of the Past* (Chicago: University of Chicago Press, 2003).

62. Sigfried Kracauer, "Time and History," *History and Theory*, Beiheft 6 (1966): p. 65.

63. An alternative place to start this historiographical inquiry could have been Salīm al-Naqqāsh's 1884 *Miṣr li-l-miṣriyyīn* (Egypt for the Egyptians). However, since the first four volumes that dealt with the reign of Muḥammad ʿAlī and his successors were either lost, or deliberately destroyed, or perhaps never written, we are left with only five volumes that discuss contemporary events from 1882 until shortly before the author's death in 1884. Thus, because of its crippled status, it is useful mainly as a record of contemporary events. Undoubtedly, al-Naqqāsh undertook one of the most impressive projects since the beginning of the century. Crabbs, *The Writing of History in Nineteenth-Century Egypt*, pp. 188–190.

aspects of the book's reception. Such a discussion will also serve as a general introduction to the historiography of the era, its structure, and its concerns.

Thematically, *Tārīkh Miṣr al-ḥadīth* covered the history of Egypt from the time of the pharaohs to the present. By and large, the organizing principle was the succession of rulers and dynasties. The word *modern* in the title referred to history and not to Egypt. Hence, Zaydān was aware that he was experimenting with a new genre. In fact, he did his best to present Egyptian history in an entirely new format. He used short journalistic-style sentences with no *saj'*. As an author he seemed to have been emotionally detached from the story of Egypt. No praises and panegyrics to past and present rulers accompanied the text. The role of religion, let alone that of God, was entirely overlooked.

Likewise, no marvelous deeds *('ajā'ib)* were recorded. He used new Orientalist scholarship extensively in his reflections on Islamic history and refused to use the Koran and *ḥadīth* (a prophetic tradition) as historical sources.[64] For some, the design of the book came as a great shock: pictures, maps, illustrations, drawings, and even tables and an index accompanied the text. Zaydān's visualization of history would reach new levels of popularity in his future journalistic project, *Al-Hilāl*. Thus, this history book was a mere dress rehearsal for his plunge deep into the world of literary journalism.

Zaydān's introduction to the book was somewhat different from what one might expect of that time. Rather than opening with a paean for Almighty God, Zaydān praised science. He regarded history as the most useful of all critical sciences. He deemed it a helpful tool for reflecting on public affairs. He associated history with the interests of the common people *('amma)* as well as with those of the elite *(khāṣṣa)*. He argued that his work was composed in accordance with strict criteria of rational scrutiny and judgment *(aḥkām 'aqliyya)* and hoped that it would be distributed to schools around the country.[65] In Zaydān's mind, history had a mission, and he intended to carry it out with as much scientific precision as he possibly could. In short, it was a classic historicist manifesto on the power of history to guide and direct human affairs. To be sure, it was the first time that such an agenda was put forward in detail in Egypt, even if, as we shall now see, the final result did not follow the outline of this agenda.

A very short while after its publication, the book reached the hands of Amīn al-Ḥalawānī, a resident of the Arabian Peninsula, historian, linguist, astronomer, and a man of letters, though, admittedly, of rather mediocre achievements.[66]

64. Lewis Beier Ware, "Jurjī Zaydān: The Role of a Popular History in the Formation of a New Arab World-View," unpublished Ph.D. dissertation, Princeton University, 1973, p. 163.

65. Jurjī Zaydān, *Tārīkh Miṣr al-ḥadīth* (Cairo: Maṭba'at al-muqtaṭaf, 1889), pp. 1–5.

66. Amīn b. Ḥasan al-Ḥalawānī, *Nabsh al-hadhayān min tārīkh Jurjī Zaydān* (1889; Medina, Saudi Arabia: Maktabat ibn al-qiyām, 1989), pp. 15–17; Khayr al-dīin Ziriklī, *Al-A'lām, qāmūs*

He read it in the midst of a journey to India. Apparently, al-Ḥalawānī was so shocked that he immediately—in spite of the great inconvenience of writing while being away from his bountiful and famous library[67]—composed a riposte and published it while in India. He titled it *Nabsh al-hadhayān min tārīkh Jurjī Zaydān* (Excavating for Nonsense in the History of Jurjī Zaydān). Al-Ḥalawānī sternly objected to Zaydān's visualization of history and went as far as arguing that some of the pictures were mere fakes.[68] But there was something more to it, aside from matters of form. As one student observed, "Al-Ḥalawānī's book was a not-too-cleverly disguised attack on Christian qualifications to write Islamic history."[69] He despised Zaydān's cultural circles, whose domestication of European knowledge, he believed, was encroaching on the faith of Islam.[70] No doubt, he identified this whole project as a sort of *bid'a* and, indeed, with much vanity, nicknamed himself *muḥyī al-sunna wa mumīt al-bid'a* (the reviver of the right path and the exterminator of heretical innovation).[71]

In his book, al-Ḥalawānī listed 101 mistakes of various kinds in Zaydān's heretical innovation *Tārīkh Miṣr al-ḥadīth,* ranging from transliteration, translation, and spelling mistakes to wholesale historical inaccuracies. Supposedly, many of these mistakes originated in the Western sources of the Orientalists. Furthermore, al-Ḥalawānī's book was written in the ornate style of "*al-radd 'ala*" (refutation of), which was a common form of traditional religious polemics, entirely in opposition to Zaydān's light modernistic tone.

The story could have ended here if not for the unexpected meeting of Zaydān's Christian colleague, Ilyās Ṣāliḥ, and al-Ḥalawānī, who accidentally met in Cairo in 1890. Ṣāliḥ approached al-Ḥalawānī, saying that word had reached him about his new book. Al-Ḥalawānī confirmed the rumor. Ṣāliḥ inquired if the author would send him a copy. Al-Ḥalawānī agreed. Ṣāliḥ said he was interested in getting to the bottom of things so that historical truth *(ḥaqiqa tārīkhiyya)* could be revealed. Al-Ḥalawānī said that this was indeed a worthy and indispensable cause. Ṣāliḥ proceeded more aggressively and hinted at al-Ḥalawānī's hostility toward Zaydān and the Syrian-Christian community more generally. At that point, al-Ḥalawānī's face was said to have changed color.[72] Yet, in spite of the tension, an aura of respectability was maintained. Then, Ṣāliḥ proposed

---

tarājim li-ashhar al-rijāl wa-l-nisā' min al-'arab wa-l-musta'ribīn wa-l-mustashriqīn (Beirut: Dār al-'ilm li-l-malāyīn, 1986), vol. 2, pp. 15–16.

67. Shortly before his death in 1898, he sold the library to a Dutch Orientalist from Leiden. Al-Ḥalawānī, *Nabsh al-hadhayān,* pp. 15–17.

68. Ibid., p. 33.

69. Ware, "Jurjī Zaydān," p. 196.

70. al-Ḥalawānī, *Nabsh al-hadhayān,* pp. 35–37.

71. Ibid., p. 31.

72. Jurjī Zaydān, *Radd rannān 'ala nabsh al-hadhayān* (Cairo: Maṭba'at al-ta'līf, 1891), p. 3.

the unthinkable: "It would be lovely if you would register your opposition and criticism in one of the daily newspapers, and I will respond to it for the benefit of the public."[73] Al-Ḥalawānī, visibly shocked, promised to consider the offer. The meeting is said to have ended. To no one's surprise, the promised public debate in a journalistic arena, believed by al-Ḥalawānī to be already controlled by the Syrian-Christians, never took place.

In fact, it was some time before Ṣāliḥ got hold of al-Ḥalawānī's treatise. Paraphrasing al-Ḥalawānī's title, Ṣāliḥ wrote to a friend, "When I learned of his nonsense *(al-hadhayān)* I requested a copy of it so I could examine his excavation *(nabsh),* but he did not send me one."[74] Eventually, Zaydān too got hold of al-Ḥalawānī's text and went on to publish an amused and witty response: *Radd rannān ʿala nabsh al-hadhayān* (An Echoing Riposte to the Excavating of Nonsense).[75] Zaydān identified two sections in al-Ḥalawānī's work. The first, he claimed, was about mere slander and defamation. The second was a purported critical examination of Zaydān's work. Zaydān, a new émigré himself, was extremely sensitive to comments against Syrian-Christians. Nevertheless, he moved quickly to the critical part, addressing in turn the 101 alleged mistakes listed by al-Ḥalawānī. Zaydān admitted to making only five spelling mistakes but immediately brushed them off as irrelevant mishaps of a writer who composed his entire book in only two stressful years. The rest of the "mistakes" were simply references that were based on European scholarship, which, in the eyes of al-Ḥalawānī, were entirely unacceptable. In any case, Zaydān said he found even more mistakes in al-Ḥalawānī's treatise of merely thirty pages. Mostly, Zaydān wrote, he was concerned not with such nitpicking but with the ability to reveal historical truth and believed that, whatever that truth might consist of, such revelation was a feasible project.[76] Concluding the debate, he blamed al-Ḥalawānī for using his spelling mistakes as an excuse for slander and self-aggrandizement.[77]

73. Ibid., p. 4.

74. Ibid., p. 3.

75. The authorship of *Radd rannān* calls for clarification, as this text is not known to be Zaydān's book. Lewis Beier Ware ascribes the book to Zaydān even though it does not appear in any available catalog as Zaydān's work. He also cites an untraceable 1891 edition by Zaydān's publishing house, Dār al-hilāl. The only available copy of *Radd rannān* lists Ilyās Ṣāliḥ as the author and Maṭbaʿat al-taʾlīf as the publisher. Ilyās Ṣāliḥ also signed the text. If one reads through this treatise, however, it is clear that Zaydān is indeed the author, as he writes in a first-person voice about his responses to al-Ḥalawānī's accusations. At the end of the text there is also a small signature by Zaydān. It seems, therefore, that Ilyās Ṣāliḥ wrote only the introduction, in which he tells about his encounter with al-Ḥalawānī. Matti Moosa also ascribes the text to Zaydān, though he failed to identify al-Ḥalawānī as the author of *Nabsh al-hadhayān*. Matti Moosa, *The Origins of Modern Arabic Fiction* (Boulder, CO: Lynne Rienner Publishers, 1997), p. 217; Ware, "Jurjī Zaydān," p. 196.

76. Zaydān, *Radd rannān,* p. 7.

77. Ibid., p. 32.

This forgotten episode is of some importance, since it was the first encounter between Zaydān's pioneering attempts at historical representation and the opposition they met. This debate also set the tone for future condemnations of Zaydān's histories, all of which specifically came from the circles of Rashīd Riḍā and ʿAbduh. Quite interestingly, al-Ḥalawānī did not object to any particular aspect of Zaydān's work but denied the entire project altogether as a piece of invalid historical knowledge. He reacted mainly to form and not to content and meaning. Thus, however shocked al-Ḥalawānī was by Zaydān's writings, he failed to notice that while in form Zaydān's work was indeed innovative, in substance he narrated history in a way that was not entirely unfamiliar to Islamic historiography. In hindsight, it was an exchange between two scholars who shared so little that their entire debate acquired a certain comic dimension, in fact, right to its end. While traveling in Lebanon, al-Ḥalawānī—*muḥyī al-sunna wa mumīt al-bidʿa*—was misidentified as a Western spy and killed on the spot.[78]

Returning to a discussion of Zaydān's work and the issue of Islamic historiographical continuity, I find it worth pointing out that despite this episode with al-Ḥalawānī and contrary to his claims, the *Tārīkh Miṣr* was a complex composition that combined three forms of writing—annals, chronicles, and modern narratives. This complexity was especially pronounced with regard to Zaydān's perception of time. According to the standard historiographical interpretation, because annalists are contemporaries of the facts they record, they are unable to include reflections on what happened later. Likewise, they rarely take into account what happened earlier. In other words, their work lacks the powerful tool of retrospective analysis (viewing things in terms of what caused them). This is why annalists usually compose factographical accounts, which are formed of multiple unrelated stories, always broken by the annalists' chosen time unit of description (day, week, month, etc.). Especially when written in a modern era, such accounts, having been separated from their organic medieval cultural context, which relied heavily on a network of genres and subgenres, such as *ṭabaqāt, tarājim,* poetry, and the *khiṭaṭ,* seem to carry little value in terms of continuity, coherence, and meaning.[79] Significant parts of Zaydān's writing lacked retrospective analysis.[80]

On the other hand, parts of Zaydān's oeuvre resemble the kind of work carried out by chroniclers such as al-Jabartī. Like chroniclers, Zaydān used his

78. al-Ziriklī, *Al-Aʿlām,* vol. 2, p. 16, fn. 1. In his chapter on Zaydān, Matti Moosa has confused the identity of al-Ḥalawānī with a later critic and thus missed the point of the debate. Moosa, *The Origins of Modern Arabic Fiction,* p. 217.

79. Jerzy Topolski, "Historical Narrative: Towards a Coherent Structure," *History and Theory* 26, no. 4 (December 1987): pp. 77–78.

80. See Zaydān's discussion of the Mamluk era, in which history begins anew with each sultan's accession to power: *Tārīkh Miṣr al-ḥadīth,* pp. 27–37.

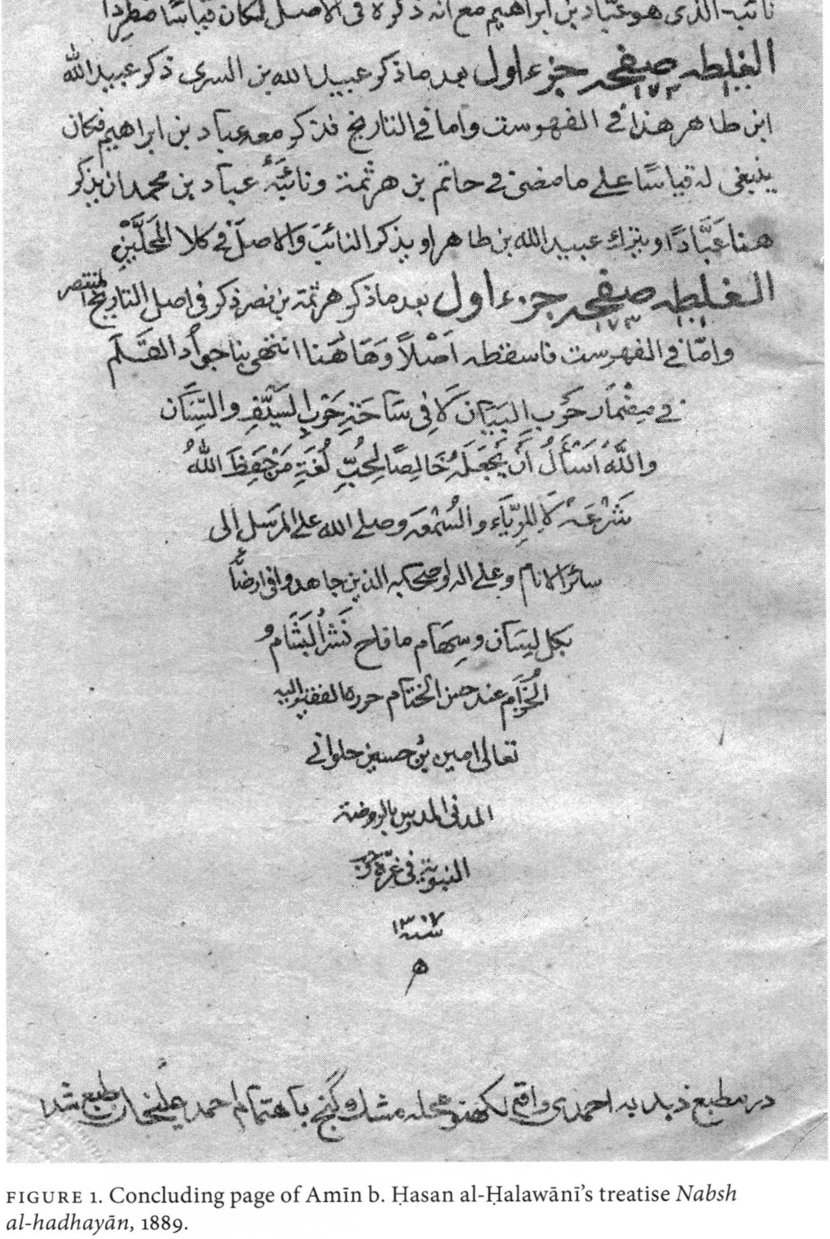

٣١

نائب- الذی هو عبّاد بن ابراهیم مع انه ذکره فی الاصل لکان قیاسًا مُطّرِدًا

الغلطه صفحه ۱۷۳ جزء اول بعد ما ذکر عبید الله بن السری ذکر عبید الله

ابن طاهر هذا فی الفهرست واما فی التاریخ فذکر معه عباد بن ابراهیم فکان

ینبغی له قیاسًا علی ما مضی فی حاتم بن هرثمة ونائبه عباد بن محمد ان یذکر

هنا عبّادًا او یترك عبید الله بن طاهر او یذکر النائب والاصل فی کلا المحلّین

الغلطه صفحه ۱۷۷ جزء اول بعد ما ذکر هرثمة بن نصر ذکر فی اصل التاریخ المنتصر

واما فی الفهرست فاسقطه اصلاً وها هنا انتهی بنا جواد القلم

فی مضمار حرب البیان لا فی ساحة حرب السیف والسنان

والله اسأل ان یجعله خالصًا لحب لغة من حفظ الله

شرعه لا للریاء والسمعة وصلی الله علی المرسل الی

سائر الانام وعلی آله وصحبه الذین جاهدوا واوضحوا

بکل لسان وسهام ما فاح نشر البشام و

الخزام عند حسن الختام حرره الفقیر الیه

تعالی امین بن حسن حلوانی

المدنی المدرس بالروضة

النبویة فی غرة

سنة ۱۳۰۷

هـ

در مطبع ذبدة احمدی واقع لکهنؤ محله مشك گنج باهتمام احمد علیخان طبع شد

FIGURE 1. Concluding page of Amīn b. Ḥasan al-Ḥalawānī's treatise *Nabsh al-hadhayān*, 1889.

knowledge of what had already occurred (retrospective point of view) in order to reflect on his subject. Consequently, he could offer sequences of sentences that were connected not only chronologically (as the annalists do) but also by causal/conditional relationship. The result is that a certain "description of the past becomes more complete, more dense, and comes closer to reality with its internal interconnections."[81]

Furthermore, when discussing recent historical events, Zaydān activated his retrospective point of view in addition to his understanding of the aftermath of the events (perspective). Perspective view increased Zaydān's capacity to conceptualize and, by extension, his ability to link scattered events into a coherent causal story.[82] Nonetheless, it is important to note that the lion's share of this work is free of such perspective and clearly falls within the previous two categories (annals and chronicles).

Finally, in spite of Zaydān's modernistic rhetoric, which had so infuriated al-Ḥalawānī and his like, his book treated time in a way not dissimilar to that of al-Jabartī and only slightly different from that of al-Ṭahṭāwī. In the final analysis, *Tārīkh Miṣr al-ḥadīth* was organized according to the succession of dynasties and rulers, and not according to a more comprehensive notion of an era or a period of time. Seriality (monotonous recording), rather than temporality (a coherent sense of a period), was the dominant sense of time. More than anything else, Zaydān's first modern history book was a mélange of stylistic choices with the appearance of an overstated modern surface.

In 1892 Muḥammad Diyāb ʿAbd al-Ḥakam, an official in the Ministry of Education, published his *Khulāṣat tārīkh Miṣr al-qadīm wa-l-ḥadīth* (A Concise History of Ancient and Modern Egypt). As promised by its title, it was indeed a very short and descriptive account of Egyptian life in the Nile Valley. It owed much to Zaydān's history by replicating its economical style of writing as well as its visual format. Likewise, it did not form one continuous narrative, as the time framework was fragmented and lacked the linkage of cause and effect.[83] Although he, too, used the term *modern,* Diyāb, like Zaydān, did not formulate a sense of what constitutes a "period" in history, nor did he reflect on how to differentiate among different periods. Like the previous writer, he favored a serial flow of time.

In 1894, marine officer Ismāʿīl Sarhank began the publication of his monumental *Ḥaqāʾiq al-akhbār ʿan duwal al-biḥār* (True Narrations of Maritime Nations). It was modeled on the classic chronicle and covered human and Egyptian history

81. Topolski, "Historical Narrative," pp. 79–80. See Zaydān's discussion of the 1798 French expedition: *Tārīkh Miṣr al-ḥadīth,* pp. 148–153.

82. See Zaydān's description of the ʿUrābī affair: ibid., pp. 282–318.

83. See his discussion of the ʿUrābī revolt: Muḥammad ʿAbd al-Ḥakam Diyāb, *Khulāṣat tārīkh Miṣr al-qadīm wa-l-ḥadīth* (Cairo: al-Maṭbaʿa al-amīriyya bi bulāq, 1892), pp. 102–110.

from the country's creation to its present in three thick tomes.[84] Though the work looks and reads exactly like a sixteenth-century chronicle, the section that deals with the nineteenth century was heavily influenced by modern writing. This section includes detailed causal explanations and plenty of source material, personally collected by the author and attached in the form of footnotes.[85] The result was a relatively coherent text that sought to explain particular problems (such as the financial difficulties under Khedive Ismāʿīl).[86] For the first time in Egyptian history writing, this author also provided a vague sense that the nineteenth century was somehow different from previous times, though he did not develop this issue. Sarhank's account is yet another example of a hybrid work in which the author thinks and writes differently about different eras. Most probably influenced by Salīm al-Naqqāsh's *Miṣr li-l-miṣriyyīn,* Sarhank dealt with contemporary issues in a narrative form and with more distant events in the form of chronicle.[87]

The same could also be said with regard to Maḥmūd Fahmī, who, in 1894–95, while in exile with his fellow Urabists, wrote *Al-Baḥr al-zākhir fī tārīkh al-ʿālam wa akhbār al-awāʾil wa-l-awākhir* (The Bottomless Sea on the Events of World History). This nominally bottomless account of human history purported to cover the entire course of humanity from the beginning of time to the present. It paid much attention to the history of the great European nations and was based on European textbooks found on the island of Ceylon.[88] Obviously, Fahmī had the model of the medieval chronicler al-Ṭabarī's universal history in mind. When dealing with Egypt's recent experience and especially with the ʿUrābī revolt, the author's account came closer to a concise and coherent statement, an attempt at justifying his rebellious act.[89] It read almost as a statement given in court. (Legal language was also a product of this era.) Likewise, it was concise and causal. In the end however, Fahmī's composition lacked any sense of historical progress through time; indeed, it proudly declared itself to have followed Ibn Khaldūn's cyclical notion of time.[90]

In 1898, state official Mikhāʾīl Shārūbīm published another inclusive chronicle modestly titled *al-Kāfī fī tārīkh Miṣr al-qadīm wa-l-ḥadīth* (A Definitive History of

84. The last volume was finally published only in 1923.

85. Ismāʿīl Sarhank, *Ḥaqāʾiq al-akhbār ʿan duwal al-biḥār* (Cairo: al-Maṭbaʿa al-amīriyya būlāq, 1896), vol. 2, pp. 366–440.

86. Ibid., pp. 354–366.

87. See the protocols of Aḥmad ʿUrābī's dramatic investigation in court: al-Naqqāsh, *Miṣr li-l-miṣriyyīn,* vol. 7, pp. 5–25.

88. Crabbs, *The Writing of History in Nineteenth-Century Egypt,* p. 132.

89. Maḥmūd Fahmī, *Al-Baḥr al-zākhir fī tārīkh al-ʿālam wa akhbār al-awāʾil wa-l-awākhir* (Cairo: al-Maṭbaʿa al-kubra al-amīriyya bi būlāq, 1894–95), vol. 1, pp. 203–284.

90. Crabbs, *The Writing of History in Nineteenth-Century Egypt,* p. 132; Fahmī, *Al-Baḥr al-zākhir fī tārīkh,* vol. 1, pp. 1–9. On cyclical time, see discussion below.

Ancient and Modern Egypt). It was a well-documented account but was by no means definitive. Like Sarhank before him, Shārūbīm also had access to state documents, which he used in order to narrate Egypt's recent experience. As had been the case with Sarhank's work, the contemporary part was as not as fragmented as the rest of the book. It, too, seemed to borrow much from al-Naqqāsh. Though Shārūbīm's title suggests a history of two different eras (ancient and modern), the text did not render any meaning to this suggestion. Thus, what Shārūbīm's notion of an era was or when the ancient period ends and the modern one begins are not clear.

Reflecting on this great series of chronicles, one is reminded of the words of Albert Hourani, speaking on Lebanese historiography in the same period: "There has been a tradition among Lebanese historians to base their work simply upon what previous historians have written, and in particular upon the four or five major chronicles."[91] This, of course, was a heritage from another era. As noted by Chase Robinson, "Many in the traditionalist culture of medieval Islam did not [write their work from scratch], choosing instead to epitomize, continue, update, or otherwise improve pre-existing works."[92] Apparently, this practice persisted into the nineteenth century. Thus, even the eminent ʿAbd al-Raḥmān al-Jabartī continued it while systematically concealing his sources.[93] In the 1890s, this practice was modified. Egyptian historians followed it only with regard to the remote past. Contemporary events were given new titles (usually using the word *modern*) and presented with greater clarity, transparency, and above all with new source material, which was often attached to the text.

Nonetheless, despite such modifications, by the end of this decade the tradition of such chronicles was further marginalized. Muḥammad Farīd and Muṣṭafa Kāmil concluded this period with short accounts of Ottoman and regional history. Especially groundbreaking was *Al-Shams al-mushriqa* (The Rising Sun), Kāmil's 1904 history of Japan. In fact, Kāmil's book was the first to employ a linear and progressive notion of time. Japan's history had a goal, and Kāmil traced its progress from the mid-nineteenth century to the present. Clearly, this notion of time was deeply committed to the idea of progress. As such, it presented a temporally consecutive account of Japanese transformation in the modern era. In opposition to other books reviewed thus far, *Al-Shams al-mushriqa* was a study written entirely from a perspective point of view. This perspective increased Kāmil's capacity for conceptualization and, by extension, his ability to link scattered events into a coherent story. He did so by carefully selecting the facts, deciding

91. Albert Hourani, "Historians of Lebanon," in Holt and Lewis, eds., *Historians of the Middle East*, p. 244.

92. Chase Robinson, *Islamic Historiography* (Cambridge: Cambridge University Press, 2003), p. 177.

93. Crecelius, "Al-Jabartī's *ʿAjāʾīb al-Athār fī-l-Tarājim wa-l-Akhbār,*" p. 223.

on their hierarchization, and linking them by great causal chains of events into meaningful and coherent processes that stretched right into the promised future of Japan as a modernized nation.

Even though Kāmil's book was not about Egypt per se, it was written in the context of the Japanese-Russian war, which had fully captured the Arab, Iranian, and, especially, the Egyptian imagination.[94] As Kāmil put it, "I believe that the history of Japan teaches the Eastern nations important lessons."[95] This purely historicist reasoning, according to which history is a tool for uncovering the laws of progress, framed much of Kāmil's activity, political and otherwise.

In sum, the previous pages have treated the perception of time in two senses: first, in the sense of periodization and, second, in the sense of a historical continuum as part of a process of development. I have demonstrated that historians, in order to form a unified notion of time, have developed and employed tools of perception, such as retrospective and perspective. From a theoretical point of view, however, these two senses (periodization and continuum) are intimately linked. Thus, whereas in a chronicle time is a mere *seriality,* in a modern narrative time is experienced as *temporality,* in other words, as an element that has the function of inauguration, transition, and termination of processes. Both elements are meaningful because they manifest the structures and aim of historical stories and render them coherent.[96] By the end of the nineteenth century, history began to be written from the point of view of the future, in which "the keyword is Progress, History is understood as process, and Time itself as moving to an end (progression)."[97] I will return to this issue in greater detail in the conclusion to this chapter. Meanwhile, in terms of praxis, most of the works we have looked at presented a rather hybrid form of these two senses of time. There were still multiple valid options of how to tell a story.

What Is the Subject of History?

What is the subject of the works written by Ismā'īl Sarhank or Mikhā'īl Shārūbīm? Do they have a subject? Should they have one? The last decade of the nineteenth century showed a greater degree of preoccupation with these questions than was shown earlier and a movement toward histories that tell only one story,

94. See, for instance, "Ta'ākhur miṣr wa taqaddum al-yābān," *Al-Ahrām* (June 29, 1905): p. 1.

95. Muṣṭafa Kāmil, *Al-Shams al-mushriqa,* vol. 2 of *Al-Mu'alafāt al-kāmila li Muṣṭafa Kāmil Bāshā* (Cairo: al-'Arabī, 2001), p. 19.

96. Hayden White, "The Rule of Narrativity: Symbolic Discourse and the Experience of Time," *University of Ottawa Quarterly* 55, no. 4 (1985): p. 294.

97. François Hartog, "Time, History and the Writing of History: The *Order* of Time," in Rolf Torstendahl and Irmline Veit-Brause, eds., *History-Making: The Intellectual and Social Formation of a Discipline* (Stockholm: Kungl. Vitterhets Historie och Antikvitets Akademien, 1996), p. 96.

focused on one evolving and changing subject. Chronicles, by their very nature, are accounts that tend to treat all facts as equal and, as long as they happened in a certain time unit, present them in any order. Thus, a chronicle is a domain in which virtually everything is possible. With the exception of their writing on the contemporary era, all three main chronicles of the 1890s (Sarhank's, Shārūbīm's, and Fahmī's) lacked any definitive sense of subject.

Other works pretended to have a subject. Supposedly, Zaydān's *Tārīkh Miṣr al-ḥadīth* was about Egypt. In reality, however, it continued an old tradition in which the subject of Egypt was not defined, nor was it dominant or changing. The reader of Zaydān has only a vague sense of what constitutes the subject of Egypt, aside from the fact that the unrelated events he wrote of happened to take place in the Nile Valley. Consequently, works such as those of Zaydān and Muḥammad Diyāb read as a "who's who" of the Nile Valley. Again, their history is a domain in which everything is possible.

In 1890, government official and future national activist Muḥammad Farīd published *Kitāb al-bahja al-tawfīqiyya fī tārīkh mu'āssis al-'ā'ila al-khudaywiyya* (The Grandeur Most Divine in the Account of the Founder of the Khedival Line). Farīd's book was a sort of biography of Muḥammad 'Alī *(mu'āssis al-diyār al-miṣriyya),* in which his career and some aspects of material development were intimately linked.[98] In many ways, it was a work of laudatory dynastic history with a certain patriotic flavor.[99] However, this book projected a sense that change/reforms *(iṣlāḥāt)* and the man who engendered them are the subject matters of history.[100] Farīd broke from previous ways of writing in which almost every sequence of events through time became the concern of the historian (for example, floods and epidemics). Yet, he did not think that if change occurred then a certain entity was necessarily changing. Muḥammad 'Alī was not yet a metaphor for the evolving Egyptian nation as the ultimate subject of history.

Muṣṭafa Kāmil, in contrast, chose a well-defined subject for his histories, even if on some occasions a loose notion of time failed to account for their process of becoming. In his *Al-Mas'ala al-sharqiyya* (The Eastern Question), Kāmil focused on the question of foreign relationships as a complex web of interests, developing across time.[101] The subject of his book *Al-Shams al-mushriqa* was the modernization process of the nation-state of Japan. This book was the first time that change was linked to the process of modernity, which was represented only by

98. Muḥammad Farīd, *Kitāb al-bahja al-tawfīqiyya fī tārīkh mu'āssis al-'ā'ila al-khudaywiyya* (Cairo: al-Maṭba'a al-amīriyya, 1890), p. 2.

99. See his usage of the term *waṭan:* ibid., pp. 3, 183.

100. Ibid., pp. 183–196.

101. Kāmil's book was based on primary source materials collected in Europe. Al-Rāfi'ī, *Muṣṭafa Kāmil,* p. 44.

the nation-state. It had one subject, one story, and, as we have already seen, one notion of linear time.

Thus, it seems that by 1905, the ideas that history had a particular subject and that it was the task of the historian to trace this subject across time and account for its development had begun to gain currency.

Where Does History Take Place?

Where does history happen? Is there a specific place in which historical events occur? What shape does it have? Does it change? If so, what is history's role in that process? No matter where we choose to begin and end our Egyptian spatial inquiry, the last third of the nineteenth century will form an important chapter in it. During 1888–89, ʿAlī Mubārak Pasha, a civil engineer and senior state official, began the publication of his twenty-volume monumental survey, *Al-Khiṭaṭ al-tawfīqiyya al-jadīda.* The *khiṭaṭ* was a literary genre endemic to the Islamic tradition. Though originating in Baghdad like the bulk of the Islamic historiographic tradition, it later spread to Cairo, where it was naturalized and further developed. There, under al-Maqrīzī (d. 1442), it reached a point of culmination.[102] The *khiṭaṭ* formed a unique literary genre, because it powerfully synchronized notions of people, landscape, history, and culture and ordered them alphabetically. It was not merely a work of geography or topography, nor was it a chronicle. Far more inclusive, the *khiṭaṭ* was a mélange of religious and other, more earthly concerns that, joined together, created an intimate, yet highly informative, portrayal of human spatial experience through time.[103]

In Arabic, the word *khiṭṭa* conveys the sense of an outline or a free-form, loose sketch.[104] What is "sketched" or outlined in the literary genre derived from this meaning is a space or an area in which human lives and landscapes coalesce. In the literature of the *khiṭaṭ,* human beings and the events of their lives are always tied to a particular locality. Viewed otherwise, the word *khiṭṭa* conveys exactly the opposite sense: that of the rough, suspiciously straight, well-demarcated, and heavily guarded modern political border *(ḥadd).* ʿAlī Mubārak wrote in a period in which the modern border had already made its appearance on the geopolitical landscape of Europe and beyond. Yet, despite his long sojourn in France, where he was no doubt exposed to the full operating logic of French territorial claims, he consciously chose a different notion of landscape that corresponded with the region's cultural heritage.

102. Ayman Fuad Sayyid, "L'évolution de la composition du genre de khiṭaṭ en Égypte musulmane," in Kennedy, ed., *The Historiography of Islamic Egypt,* pp. 77–92.

103. For a discussion of some of these traits, see Samir Saul, "Ali Moubarak, un historien égyptien et son oeuvre," *Storia della Storiographia* 5 (1984): pp. 77–85.

104. See Claude Cahen, "Khiṭaṭ," *EI*^{2}, vol. 5, p. 22b.

Interestingly, ʿAlī Mubārak's rejection of the European territorial concept was paralleled in his rejection of the work of Muḥammad Amīn Fikrī, who, in 1878, had published one of the first books on Egyptian geography. Influenced by his academic experience in France (especially in the field of geography), Fikrī purported to have written a book on national geography. Like history books from this era, however, the result was quite incoherent, as it tried to satisfy the demands of modern geography and at the same time to invoke older, more intimate notions of geographical knowledge.[105] Though this book was a reminder that more than one geographical perception of Egypt was at play, ʿAlī Mubārak did not follow Fikrī's model.[106]

ʿAlī Mubārak's work raises a basic question, namely, What geographical perceptions of Egypt existed in this period? In truth, Hellenic, Roman, pre-Islamic, Arab-Islamic, European renaissance, and modern visions of Egyptian geography coexisted simultaneously.[107] One thing is sure, however; the geographic entity of Miṣr, in the sense used by ʿAlī Mubārak and the majority of the Egyptian population (but not by Muḥammad Amīn Fikrī), was first and foremost Cairo and "its country, meaning the hinterland of towns and villages that supported it, politically and materially. This meaning was also invoked with the phrases such as 'the Cairo region' and 'Cairo country.'"[108] This spatial notion was typical of the Ottoman-Egyptian worldview of the time, even as it was undergoing a profound change. In Ottoman times, provinces and hinterlands were named after the capitals to which they were administratively, economically, and culturally attached. Whether the proper terms were Bilād, Quṭur, or something else, such designations were the hallmarks of an Ottoman and pre-Ottoman order and, during the next century, would go on to acquire radically new meanings.[109] As mentioned above, even during the centennial celebrations, the old Ottoman meaning of "Miṣr" according to which Muḥammad ʿAlī was "the founder of the Egyptian emirate *(imāra)*" and the "founder and reviver of the Egyptian lands *(diyār)*" was still pub-

105. Muḥammad Amīn Fikrī, *Jughrāfīyat Miṣr* (Cairo: Maṭbaʿat wādī al-Nīl, 1878), pp. 1–4.

106. Nonetheless, ʿAlī Mubārak was fully aware of new modes of investigating and writing in the geographical, historical, and natural sciences and even criticized their neglect by the contemporary Islamic curriculum. Reimer, *Colonial Bridgehead,* p. 8

107. This question is deserving of a separate study. For multicultural visions of the Nile Valley alone, see Haggai Erlich and Israel Gershoni, eds., *The Nile: Histories, Culture, Myths* (Boulder, CO: Lynne Rienner Publishers, 2000), especially pp. 71–76, 105–119, and 121–127.

108. Timothy Mitchell, *Rule of Experts: Egypt, Techno-politics, Modernity* (Berkeley: University of California Press, 2002), pp. 180–181.

109. One of these new meanings occurred in the Nasserist political lexicon, which designated *quṭriyya* as a negative emphasis on local/regional interests at the expense of the Arab nation as a whole.

licly used.[110] Likewise, ʿAbduh's official title expressed the same notion: *muftī al-diyār al-miṣriyya.*

ʿAlī Mubārak continued this venerable literary-spatial tradition. The first six volumes of his work focused on Cairo. One volume was dedicated to Alexandria, and the rest, to a detailed description of entire villages and towns alphabetically arranged. Canals, dams, mosques, Ṣūfī orders, and even the Nilometer were carefully accounted for. Biographies and local histories were juxtaposed with the descriptions of landscape.[111] Even though the author himself "made his career" in Paris and then in the glamorous Cairo of Ismāʿīl, his own biography appeared next to the history of his village Birinbāl (Daqahliyya Province).[112] The same language was used to describe both the new designs of Cairo and the most remote village under its sphere of influence. Quite remarkably, not even a single map appeared in this work. A map, let alone a modern one, was in opposition to Mubārak's cosmographic notion, one that came straight from the stock of the Islamic literary tradition. While from the medieval period maps had certainly been a part of the Islamic geographical tradition, they were entirely foreign to the spatial-literary tradition of the *khiṭaṭ*. This was Miṣr, and its character and boundaries were best known through words, not alien charts.

But during the last decades of the nineteenth century, this notion of space was seriously challenged. In the wake of increasing European domination of Africa, lines were drawn all over and around Egypt. The Cairo–Cape Town and Dakar-Djibouti lines were only metaphorical, of course, but the European expedition to "mark and rule" deep into the heart of Africa was part of Egypt's immediate experience. For instance, already in 1873, Khedive Ismāʿīl had financed British explorer Samuel Baker in order to conquer the equator (whatever that may have meant) and to establish a strong military presence there.[113] However, much to the dismay of Egyptian nationalists, the first article of the 1899 Sudan agreement between "Egypt" and England, or, as they saw it, between Būṭrus Ghālī and Cromer, clearly defined Sudan as a distinct entity, which de facto, though not de jure, separated it from Egypt and formed Egypt's southern border.[114] The 1904 crisis between England and France and the 1906 border dispute between England (theoretically on behalf of Egypt) and the Ottomans were two tangible precursors of the impending post–World War I order.

110. Nonetheless, this meaning was already marginal and entirely vanished a short while afterward. *Al-Ahrām*, April 12, 1905, p. 1.

111. See, for example, his entry on Dimyāṭ: ʿAlī Mubārak, *Al-Khiṭaṭ al-tawfīqiyya al-jadīda li-Miṣr al-qāhira* (Cairo: al-Hay'a al-miṣriyya al-ʿāmma l-il-kitāb, 1994), vol. 11, pp. 93–142.

112. Ibid., pp. 102–160.

113. Naʿūm Shuqayr, *Tārīkh al-Sūdān* (Beirut: Dār al-jīl, 1981), p. 251.

114. For the Arabic text of the agreement, see al-Rāfiʿī, *Muṣṭafa Kāmil*, pp. 132–135.

By 1905, the once unbounded kingdom of Muḥammad ʿAlī took the familiar shape of Egypt without the Sudan, almost exactly as we know it today. Gone were the huge desert frontiers with their ambiguous political status. Bit by bit, the vast overlapping domains were marked. As the twentieth century progressed, each piece of land gradually came under direct political sovereignty. No marginal areas were allowed. The entire desert was claimed. People and tribes were squeezed into well-defined geographical categories. Mapping, not merely as a representation of reality, but as the political tool that shaped it, became a ubiquitous technology.

What was the role of history in all of that? Quite simply, Egyptian history writers conveyed the sense that the new geopolitical body of Egypt had always been there.[115] They encouraged Egyptians to think of their community in a new spatiotemporal fashion. Egypt, though an entirely new entity, was simply projected as far back as the Pharaonic past. To be sure, there was an abundance of sources (including archaeological ones) to make the point. Zaydān's visual history, equipped with a modern map, fulfilled precisely this function.[116] None of the chronicles discussed above echoed ʿAlī Mubārak's notion of Egypt. Indeed, this sort of writing suddenly seemed backward and obsolete.[117] Egypt was now thought of as one geographical unit, and not merely as "greater Cairo." The old category of geographical knowledge began to be displaced. History, once loosely committed to a vague sense of territory, was now taking place in an arbitrarily marked geographical space called Egypt, clearly defined and with no quotation marks.

Thus it was that by the end of the nineteenth century, historicism had generated and modified temporal and spatial notions. It also emphasized the interconnectedness of all three notions. A change in one would necessarily lead to a change in the two others as well. The former categories of historical and geographical knowledge were destabilized and displaced. The transition was slow and, at first, unsure. For almost two decades, a plethora of stylistically unstable histories were published. Many, tragically enough, tried to satisfy two irreconcilable worlds. These "imperfect histories," as one historian chose to call them,[118] were permanently pushed aside during the 1930s. The imperfect historiography of

115. My discussion is inspired by the similar case of Siam: Thongchai Winichakul, *Siam Mapped: A History of the Geo-body of a Nation* (Honolulu: University of Hawaii Press, 1994), especially chapter 7.

116. See especially the 1911 edition of Zaydān's *Tārīkh Miṣr al-ḥadīth.*

117. However, later in the twentieth century, Muḥammad Kurd ʿAlī published *Khiṭaṭ al-shām*, 6 vols. (Damascus: al-Maṭbaʿa al-ḥadītha, 1925–28).

118. Ann Rigney, *Imperfect Histories: The Elusive Past and the Legacy of Romantic Historicism* (Ithaca, NY: Cornell University Press, 2001).

this era was just the first stage in the appearance of the modern genre of history writing. Yet, regardless of the era's seeming incoherence, it is a critical one, for its historiographical production reveals to us the basic notions that made the historiographical change possible in the first place. The fingerprints of historicism were everywhere. Indeed, in terms of extent, historicism was now to be found in newspapers, journals, and, above all, historical novels. In whatever medium Egyptians chose in order to think and write about the past, historicism had simply become too powerful to ignore.

HOW TO PROMOTE HISTORICAL MINDEDNESS?

Muṣṭafa Kāmil's speech at the centennial commemoration was an astonishing celebration of the moral value of history. In it, he encouraged his audience to embrace the study of the past as a means to repair their collective future:

> What is the lethal drug that the nation has taken with such a pleasure? What is the disastrous misfortune of the country that befell its inhabitants while they (passively) continue to gaze at it? How come this beloved nation forgot that it was she who conquered, subjugated, stroked, and emerged triumphant . . . ? Obviously, the reason for this disastrous state of affairs is the neglect of civil education (tarbiyya waṭaniyya) and the erasure of instructive history to the mind and spirit. . . . History, History! This is the common school for all classes of the nation. This is the instructor that will acculturate the glorious prince, the celebrated minister, the erudite scholar, the student, and the ordinary poor man.[119]

In this remarkable speech, the eternally moralizing Kāmil encouraged the gathered crowds to become historically minded and historically informed, that is, to be aware of the meaningful relationship between the past and the present and to utilize that relationship for the benefit of the future by exploring and developing it. That such a speech would be delivered in such a public context demonstrates the degree to which historical mindedness had penetrated the popular imagination. Muṣṭafa Kāmil was not the only one who discovered the power of history in an increasingly changing age. Historical mindedness was engendered by multiple oral and written means. History writing per se, as discussed above, was only one of them and, in fact, was perhaps the least important agent of historicist thought. The press, which was a growing sector, European works, which were now increasingly translated, and especially the historical novel *(riwāya tārīkhiyya),* which enjoyed popularity, functioned as the most important and vital agents of historical mindedness.

The role of both the press and translations of foreign literature have already

119. al-Rāfiʿī, *Muṣṭafa Kāmil,* pp. 459–460.

been discussed at length elsewhere.[120] Those other studies concluded that popular journals *(Al-Muqtaṭaf* and *Al-Hilāl)* and translated books, such as those written by Samuel Smiles, Edmond Demolins, and Gustave Le Bon, were a major force for the propagation in Arabic of European ideas such as Darwinism, Spencerism, and Victorian positivism.[121] In his grand manifesto of indigenous rehabilitation and colonial self-justification, *England in Egypt,* British administrator Alfred Milner put some of these ideas to work. This intellectual influence was a classic manifestation of nineteenth-century confidence in the ability, and the moral necessity, to shape, reform, and order the human condition on all fronts of life. All of these ideas were historicist in the sense that they acknowledged the human condition as part of a historical process of progress in which the future is malleable. In Egypt, as in other parts of the Ottoman Empire, the language and assumptions of historicism gradually began to sink in.

Building on these previous discussions regarding the agents and products of historicism, I examine in this section the historical novel as one of the most important media for historicist thought. Again, Zaydān played a leading role in shaping and propagating this genre. From 1891 to his death in 1914, Zaydān published no fewer than twenty-one historical novels.[122] His sources of inspiration were the works of Smiles, Demolins, the classic historical novels of Dumas, both *père* and *fils,* and Walter Scott.[123] In 1885, while visiting the library of the British Museum, he eagerly devoured these works.[124] He must have also been influenced by the earlier experiments of several Lebanese writers, such as Salīm al-Bustānī.[125]

120. See Albert Hourani, *Arabic Thought in the Liberal Age,* pp. 245–259; Nadia Farag, "Al-Muqtataf 1876–1900: A Study of the Influences of Victorian Thought on Modern Arabic Thought," unpublished Ph.D. thesis, Oxford University, 1969; and Ami Ayalon, *The Press in the Arab Middle East: A History* (New York: Oxford University Press, 1995), pp. 28–49.

121. For a popular journal article about science with a reference to the deeds of Muḥammad ʿAlī, see "Al-ʿIlm wa khayr al-bilād," *Al-Muqtaṭaf,* February 1, 1887, pp. 270–274. In 1880, Samuel Smiles's *Self-Help* was translated by Yaʿqūb Ṣarrūf as *Sirr al-najāḥ;* for a discussion of this, see Elshakry, "Darwin's Legacy in the Arab East," pp. 107–114; Mitchell, *Colonizing Egypt,* pp. 108–109; and Afaf Lutfi al-Sayyid-Marsot, *Egypt and Cromer* (New York: Frederick A. Praeger, 1969), pp. 152–153. In 1899 Aḥmad Fatḥī Zaghlūl translated Demolins's *A quoi tient la supériorité des Anglo-Saxons* as *Sirr taqaddum al-inklis;* see Elshakry, "Darwin's Legacy in the Arab East," pp. 107–114; and Mitchell, *Colonizing Egypt,* pp. 110–111. Le Bon's works on the psychology of the crowds and the history of Islam were available in translation into Arabic before World War I; see Mitchell, *Colonizing Egypt,* pp. 122–127. For the rise of Social Darwinism, see ElShakry, "The Great Social Laboratory"; and Elshakry, "Darwin's Legacy in the Arab East."

122. See a list in Thomas Philipp, *Ğurğī Zaidān: His Life and Thought* (Beirut: Franz Steiner Verlag, 1979), pp. 235–236, 238–239.

123. Regarding the works of Demolins, see ibid., pp. 11–14, 164.

124. Ware, "Jurjī Zaydān," pp. 65–66, 210.

125. Moosa, *The Origins of Modern Arabic Fiction,* pp. 157–183.

He began serializing the novels in *Al-Hilāl* even while he was conducting research and writing them. Readership reacted to them, and, if necessary, corresponding changes were introduced to the final printed edition.[126] Zaydān's impressive literary output covered the whole course of pre-Arab, Arab, Islamic, and Egyptian history to the present. Even though each novel dealt with a particular period of history, together they created a sense of historical continuity. At the same time, Zaydān was writing real history books, such as *Tārīkh al-tamaddun al-islāmī* (History of Islamic Civilization, published 1901–6).

This impressive literary output did not go unnoticed. The technical aspects of Zaydān's career are more than well known to us. However, in most cases the discussion of his work also ends there. Thus far, historians and students of Arabic literature have had an ambiguous, if not a dismissive, view of Zaydān the novelist. On the one hand, they argue, "There can be little doubt that he played an important role as an educator and popularizer . . . opening up new areas of cultural and historical interest."[127] The historian Albert Hourani writes, "It was Jurji Zaydan who did more than any other to create a consciousness of the Arab past, by his histories and still more by his series of historical novels."[128] On the other hand, "Zaydān's novels . . . strike the modern critic, both stylistically and thematically, as almost *unbearably pedestrian*" (my emphasis).[129]

The most obvious and disappointing example of this perspective on Zaydān appears in the detailed composition of Matti Moosa. For an entire chapter, Moosa meticulously describes the plot of each of Zaydān's novels, only to tell us in the end that "though Zaydan may not be considered a great novelist in some world sense, he revolutionized the Arab novel and paved the way for future novelists, whether they were inspired by historical themes or not."[130] Also, Moosa was consistently apologetic about Zaydān's not having written them or his history books in a mature European style.[131] Like other students of Arabic literature, Moosa leaves us with the impression that Zaydān was a great popularizer of some (always vague and unspecified) concoction of fiction and historical reality.

Consequently, while Zaydān is praised for his superstructural cultural role, his novels remain poorly studied. The practical outcome of this attitude has been that the novels of Zaydān were deemed not worth pursuing very far. Even Zaydān's excellent biographer, Thomas Philipp, dedicated only a page and a half

126. Ware, "Jurjī Zaydān," pp. 208–209.

127. Paul Starkey, "Egyptian History in the Modern Egyptian Novel," in Kennedy, ed., *The Historiography of Islamic Egypt*, p. 252

128. Hourani, *Arabic Thought in the Liberal Age*, p. 277.

129. Starkey, "Egyptian History in the Modern Egyptian Novel," p. 253.

130. Moosa, *The Origins of Modern Arabic Fiction*, p. 213.

131. Ibid., pp. 213, 217.

out of a total of 249 pages to a discussion of his historical novels. Thus, most of those who studied Zaydān, including Ṭaha Badr, worked more or less within this evasive convention.[132] And so, what remains to be answered is: By what mechanism did Zaydān come to be acknowledged for his unique contribution as educator, popularizer, and shaper of Arab historical consciousness? How did these "pedestrian" novels manage to play such a pivotal role? What does it mean to popularize; is it only a matter of sheer quantity?

From the admittedly limited perspective of historiography, I reconsider Zaydān's ambiguous position in this section. In order to address these issues, let us examine two of his novels that dealt with Egypt's history in the eighteenth and nineteenth centuries: *Al-Mamlūk al-shārid* (The Fugitive Mamluk, 1891–92) and *Istibdād al-mamālīk* (The Tyranny of the Mamluks, 1892–93). In brief, *Istibdād al-mamālīk* takes place during the reign of ʿAlī Bey al-Kabīr and his fellow Mamluks some years before the French invasion. The plot revolves around the dispersion of ʿAbd al-Raḥmān's family under the oppression, exploitation, extraction, and violence of the Mamluks and the family's final reunification after years of suffering. ʿAbd al-Raḥmān, a prominent and wealthy merchant from Cairo, is driven to poverty by Mamluk exploitation. They steal his merchandise, exploit him, draft his only child into the army, accept money and his own conscription in return for his son's release, but violate the agreement by drafting them both.[133] ʿAbd al-Raḥmān defects from the army, his son, Ḥasan, disappears, and Sālima, the mother, is evicted from their house. The once happy family disintegrates, causing great agony. Zaydān's description of their misery at the hands of the Mamluks is detailed. Finally, with the decline of Mamluk power and the restoration of Ottoman power, the family reunites and is able to regain its wealth and happiness. Quite remarkably, the personal happiness and destiny of all the protagonists is entirely dependent on the outcome of real historical events, such as a siege on Acre.[134]

The second novel, *Al-Mamlūk al-shārid,* narrates the story of a Mamluk prince who managed to escape the notorious 1811 citadel massacre, in which Muḥmmad ʿAlī treacherously dispensed with the core of Mamluk leadership (hence the title "The Fugitive Mamluk"). In the novel, which is based on a dubiously "true" story,

132. Acknowledging the ambiguous position of scholarship, Paul Starkey called for the reevaluation of his work; see Starkey, "Egyptian History in the Modern Egyptian Novel," pp. 253, 262. See also Philipp, *Ǧurǧī Zaidān,* pp. 235–236; Ṭaha Badr, *Taṭawwūr al-riwāya al-ʿarabiyya al-ḥadītha* (Cairo: Dār al-maʿārif, 1963), pp. 89–115; and Roger Allen, *The Arabic Novel* (Syracuse, NY: Syracuse University Press, 1995), pp. 25–28.

133. See, for instance, Jurjī Zaydān, *Istibdād al-mamālīk* (Cairo: Dār al-hilāl, 1965), pp. 8–9, 15, 19–20, 54–55.

134. See ibid., pp. 54–58.

or at least a common popular tale, the penniless Mamluk escaped to Lebanon. Years after his escape, he encounters Egyptian armies under the leadership of Muḥmmad ʿAlī's son, Ibrāhīm. He joins them, pardoned by the viceroy, and, of course, reunites with his family. Zaydān's scenes are based on real historical events of the Egyptian occupation of Syria in the 1830s. These events are narrated retrospectively from the viewpoints of his protagonists.

In my point of departure, I, like previous scholars, take into account Zaydān's occupation as both a novelist and a historian.[135] Novels are usually limited to fiction; historical works, to reality. Thus, I am not the first to make the point that the popularity of Zaydān's novels has something to do with the mix of these two spheres and the tension between them. However, this is far from being a complete explanation of his success, as it falls short of accounting for what was so compelling about his blurring of fiction and reality.

Historical novels operate on the border between fiction and reality. This location is a vital condition for their very existence. The illusion of dealing with reality creates a sense of truthfulness that reinforces the epistemological status of the novel. This intoxicatingly ambiguous position allows the historical novel to report history (truth, reality) and at the same time to manipulate its meaning by recasting the historical stage (fiction). Especially in the case of Zaydān, who wrote novels, history books, and articles on the very same topics, the line between fiction and reality was deliberately kept blurred.[136] This is why it is not surprising to find that in the context of his strictly historical debate with ʿAbduh, amazingly enough Zaydān referred the reader to his novel *Al-Mamlūk al-shārid* as an authoritative historical source for learning about Mamluk tyranny.[137] Quite remarkable is Zaydān's decision to footnote some of his early novels, thus reinforcing their factuality and his (alleged) commitment to report, in whatever medium, what he took to be historical truth.[138] Nevertheless, Moosa's argument that "Zaydan saw fiction as subservient to history, and not vice versa" and that his main concern was "to relate history as it really was" is both inaccurate and naive.[139] Though there is absolutely no doubt that in Zaydān's mind fiction was a realm that *should* be committed to reality, in practice, he continually confused the two realms. Indeed, this is precisely what gave his novels their persuasive

135. Badr, *Taṭawwūr al-riwāya*, pp. 90–91; Moosa, *The Origins of Modern Arabic Fiction*, pp. 197–218.

136. Badr, *Taṭawwūr al-riwāya*, pp. 90–92.

137. Jurjī Zaydān, "Muḥammad ʿAlī Bāshā," *Al-Hilāl*, June 1902, p. 524.

138. See Jurjī Zaydān, *Ghadat karbalā'* (Beirut: Dār maktabāt al-ḥayā, 1969), pp. 11, 173, 180–182, 200–201; Ware, "Jurjī Zaydān," p. 217; and Starkey, "Egyptian History in the Modern Egyptian Novel," pp. 254, 260.

139. Moosa, *The Origins of Modern Arabic Fiction*, p. 198.

power, for, in them, historical facts could be managed and enhanced in ways unimaginable in other genres. Otherwise, his readers could have read chronicles. His own testimony of commitment to "facts" and "history as it really was" should not mislead us. As we have seen and will see again, writers in this period provided extremely sophisticated statements about the nature and purpose of their work. However, time and again, the final result did not live up to the expectation raised by their manifestos.[140] By blurring reality and fiction, Zaydān was able to explore several levels of historical meaning that at the time were largely neglected. He could provide the reader with a clear sense of "Mamluk tyranny," which, as opposed to what Moosa would have liked us to believe, is far from being a "historical fact." No other historical genre in this period had this capacity for malleability.

On another level, Zaydān proposed new solutions to some concerns of late nineteenth-century historiography. His exploration resulted in a modified sense of *time* and *subjectivity* that encouraged his readership to "think with history" and even showed them how to do so. It is here that we should search for another reason for his tremendous impact.

To begin with, though in literary terms Zaydān's characters are somehow shallow, they do a remarkable job of illustrating the vicissitudes of the individual buffeted by history. As Georg Lukács has noted: "What matters therefore in the historical novel is not the retelling of great historical events but the poetic awakening of the people who figured in those events."[141] Indeed, Zaydān's novels are about self-experienced history. The protagonists are not merely the products of history but also its designers. For Zaydān, human beings are a creation of themselves and of their own actions in history. The impression of a natural or a divine occurrence as a shaping force in history was never considered. Amīn Bek, ʿAbd al-Raḥmān, and other protagonists are fully historicized individuals with a rather well-developed sense of their place in the world. One would not be able to imagine Muḥammad ʿAlī, shallow or not, as a metaphor for the awakening Egyptian nation or to imagine the later literature on the 1919 Revolution without the careful groundwork of these novels.

Another characteristic of Zaydān's novels is their predictive determinism. As in the novels of Walter Scott, "the happy-ever-after ending suggests a closed, morally stable universe from which all conflict has been expunged."[142] Such a hermetically closed and secured environment allowed Zaydān to convey the sense that history in general has an optimizing quality and that the future is a

140. See also a discussion of Amīn Sāmī's work in chapter 2.

141. Georg Lukács, *The Historical Novel*, translated by Hannah and Stanley Mitchell from *A történelmi regény* (Lincoln: University of Nebraska Press, 1983), p. 42.

142. Rigney, *Imperfect Histories*, p. 29.

promising territory. Ironically, when Zaydān ended the first serialized version of *Al-Mamlūk al-shārid* with the tragic death of Saʿīd, the fugitive's loyal and beloved assistant, readers and critics alike protested, and Zaydān was forced to change the novel's end.[143]

Another important aspect of Zaydān's novels is their moralizing quality. Zaydān understood fairly well that stories are a bottomless reservoir of values. In his novels a constant struggle occurs between "good" and "bad," which are correspondingly represented by hero/heroine and villain. Fictional characters are projected back into historical reality. The Mamluks, for instance, are usually depicted as corrupt and oppressive. Muḥammad ʿAlī, in contrast, represented benevolence and progress.[144] Even the 1811 massacre, which was indeed a horrific act, is presented in the novel as the outcome of historical necessity. Time and again, the various protagonists explain that this act was inevitable, since the Mamluks objected to the modernization of the army *(al-niẓām ʿaskarī al-ḥadīth)* and the forces of progress that Muḥammad ʿAlī introduced (145–146). At one point, Amīn Bek, the fugitive Mamluk who was the sole survivor of the massacre, justified or at least understood the historical causes of the massacre. Years later he applied the lessons from the massacre to the Ottomans, who understood that in order to modernize their army they should follow the example of Muḥammad ʿAlī (235).

It is often mentioned that Zaydān's novels illustrate a struggle in the past between two moral extremes.[145] Since these two sides represent two conflicting sets of values, the reader is left with a clear sense of what injustice, oppression, and dedication "really" look like. Thus, Zaydān successfully historicized values such as loyalty, love, dedication, persistence, and, especially, self-reliance and self-realization. We learn that these values are "to be found" in the past and that only through historical thinking (i.e., the projection of the future back into the past) do they become fully accessible as real lessons for life. Indeed, they serve as a sort of modern and popular "mirror for princes."

Finally, the most basic legacy of Zaydān's novels is that Arabs could now think of history, and of reality in general, in terms of developmental tendencies governed by a rational causal mechanism.[146] Zaydān illustrated that all historical events are part of a single linear sequence of time. Furthermore, Zaydān's novels had a critical influence on what counts as a historical era. His progressive per-

143. "Ta'līf al-riwāyāt wa intiqādihā," *Al-Muqtāṭaf,* February 1, 1892, pp. 245–249; Ware, "Jurjī Zaydān," p. 209.

144. Jurjī Zaydān, *Al-Mamlūk al-shārid* (Cairo: Dār al-hilāl, 1965), pp. 47–48, 92–106, 132, 147.

145. On morality, see Thomas Philipp, "Approaches to History in the Work of Jurji Zaydan," *Asian and African Studies* 9, no. 1 (1973): pp. 83–84.

146. For historical novels and the concept of time, see Richard Humphrey, *The Historical Novel as Philosophy of History* (Leeds: Institute for German Studies, 1986), p. 14.

ception of time is demarcated by various eras, which, while acknowledging the uniqueness of the past as distinct from the present, emphasized the overarching connectedness of different epochs. Thus, this emphasis helped the readership in answering the questions, What was it like to live back then? How did these eras feel to the people living in them? And how are they related to us?

As we have seen, with regard to the Mamluks and Muḥammad ʿAlī, Zaydān's sense of "a period" was one that was clearly distinguishable from those in the past and those in the future. Zaydān's approach to these periods, presented as polarities, fashioned the mental organization of the past. As such, even though readers might not know much about the actuality of Mamluk history (facts), after reading some of these novels they would view eighteenth-century Mamluk rule as a coherently "bad" era (interpretation/fiction). Considering the state of history writing in this era, the creation of a sense of historical periods with clear causal relationships to other periods is an important conceptual marker, even if these periods were not yet given specific names. Hence, Zaydān's novels represent a preliminary attempt at a modern reorganization of historical time (periodization).

Here, I have challenged the scholarly habit of uncritically enshrining Zaydān in the literary-historiographical canon, where he has been left to languish. Perhaps this state of affairs has less to do with Zaydān's disorienting message than it has to do with the common conventions about what the modern novel should and should not be. In the final analysis, though it may be true that Zaydān was not a great scholar or an original thinker and thus has often been characterized as an eclectic, if ambitious, synthesizer of half-baked ideas, his true contribution was in his remarkable ability to put all of the above to work under the label of "history." In the hands of Zaydān, historical novels became an arena where all aspects of human life were properly historicized. This is precisely where the common observation with respect to Zaydān's iconic status may be substantiated. His novels promoted historical mindedness, and through them, we may trace how "thinking with history" has become an essential tool for modern life.[147]

CONCLUSION

Studying the Islamic literary tradition in the late 1800s, literary critic Sabry Hafez was intrigued by the question, How do new literary genres emerge in a particular culture at a specific time, and why? Focusing specifically on the rise of the Arabic

147. The genre of the historical novel, however, did not die with Zaydān. It continued to flourish in the hands of other historical novelists, such as the great poet Muṣṭafa Luṭfī al-Manfalūṭī, who freely plagiarized/Arabized whatever foreign novel he could put his hands on and, later, by Muḥmmad Farīd Abū al-Ḥadīd.

short story, Hafez's general answer was that novel ways of rationalization and perception are fundamental to the emergence of new genres.[148] By analyzing the acculturation process of historicism in an Ottoman-Egyptian environment, I have illustrated in this chapter how a new conceptual tool was instrumental for the emergence of a new genre.

As we have seen, this was not a clear-cut process, as much of the historical writing discussed above was of an unstable character. Once belonging to a specific Ottoman-Egyptian cultural and intellectual sphere, under the pressure of historicism, the literatures of the 1890s were forced to relocate. However, as one skeptical observer has commented, "Take any exercise in social mapping and this is the hybrids that are missing. Take most models and arrangements of multiculturalism and it is hybrids that are not counted, not accommodated, so what?"[149] Did Crabbs and al-Shayyāl really miss something? In the period under discussion, this fluid literature was not the margins of a hegemonic intellectual phenomenon but the core of it. Studying this literature is not yet another exercise in the reflection of the neglected intellectual periphery of the canon. Quite the contrary, it is a direct look into the formation of the modern Arab historiographical canon itself. There were no other histories. And thus, returning to our initial point of departure, by studying this "imperfect" and "pedestrian" literature, we can begin to understand the significance of the curious debate around the centennial celebrations. Let us return now to this debate.

Obviously, the tensions concerning the centennial celebrations reached far beyond anything purely personal. Though much love had never been lost between the various parties and their respective communities, cleavages obscure the point that this debate should be seen in the context of a political community that knew it had reached an important crossroads. The various exchanges illustrate the degree to which abstract ideas, which had once appeared only in esoteric texts, now acquired significant public presence and thus ushered in the impending triumph of the modern regime of historicity.

This new order took the shape of a powerful framework for the intellectual organization of Egypt's entire historical experience—the "founder paradigm."[150] By this I mean *a set of predetermined assumptions that condition the questions Egyptian historians ask, the kind of evidence they look at, and the way in which*

148. Sabry Hafez, *The Genesis of Arabic Narrative Discourse: A Study in the Sociology of Modern Arabic Literature* (London: Saqi Books, 1993), pp. 17–36.

149. Jan Nederveen Pieterse, "Hybridity, So What? The Anti-hybridity Backlash and the Riddles of Recognition," *Theory, Culture and Society* 18, nos. 2–3 (2001): p. 220.

150. See again Cuno, "Muhammad 'Ali and the Decline and Revival Thesis in Modern Egyptian History," pp. 93–119. For "modern regime of historicity," see Hartog, "Time, History and the Writing of History," p. 96.

they order the two to make sense out of the past.[151] The founder paradigm can do all of the above and thus brings the historian a great distance in terms of organizing information into a coherent argument. It also has given historicism a distinctively Egyptian face. On the basis of what we already know, an analysis of the three historical dimensions of historicism and, especially, of the relationship among them will illustrate how the paradigm works.

Time: The founder paradigm employs several levels of meaning with regard to time, such as continuity and periodization. By implication, history is grasped as a progressive temporal order, which locates facts within great causal chains of events.[152] Concomitantly, history is seen and judged from the future vantage point of its eventual success. Thus, the present is no longer an extension, an expansion, or simply a repetition of the past. Rather, it is the future's point of beginning "as an open, un-built site never visited before, but a place reachable and constructible."[153] This discovery of the future is, perhaps, one of the most fascinating perceptional shifts that occurred in late nineteenth-century Egypt. The founder paradigm was the most suitable medium to capture and act on this discovery.

Thus, the founder thesis marked the "rise" of an independent Egyptian community (the rush toward the newly discovered future) and the "decline" of the Ottoman order (all that would hamper the rush). It necessarily meant that Egypt was divorcing itself from its Ottoman past, a past that did not lend itself to representation according to the new model described here. Furthermore, it prescribed that the most important temporal events of nineteenth-century Egypt were the various military campaigns and the way a series of state-imposed reforms were planned and executed. Slowly but surely, the founder paradigm detached the nineteenth century from the rest of Egypt's historical experience, reduced the medieval era to nothing, and insisted on the uniqueness of the modern era. Soon, two opposing temporal regimes would emerge.[154]

Subjectivity: A student of Chinese historiography has observed that "modern

151. I borrowed this definition from Beth Evert, "Paradigm," in Robert Audi, ed., *The Cambridge Dictionary of Philosophy* (Cambridge: Cambridge University Press, 1999), pp. 641–642.

152. The founder paradigm assumes that Egyptian history is a linear process and not a cyclical one. In a cyclical process, the beginning and the ending points are the same. Linearity, in contrast, assumes that the end of the process is more valuable than the point of beginning. Mandelbaum, *History, Man, and Reason*, pp. 43–44.

153. Therborn Göran, "Routes to/through Modernity," in Mike Featherston, Scott Lash, and Roland Robertson, eds., *Global Modernities* (London: Sage Publications, 1995), p. 126.

154. 'Abduh was highly skeptical about this sort of understanding. By pointing to the price paid by Egypt's rank and file, the objects of development, he questioned the moral aspect of progress. By discrediting Muḥammad 'Alī's successors as failures, he sought to illustrate that they brought progress to a halt or that progress had never occurred in the first place.

history is meaningless without a subject—that which remains even as it changes."[155] When Muṣṭafa Kāmil, Zaydān, or even Alfred Milner and Lord Cromer celebrated reforms as means (and signs) of modernity, they had a certain notion that something was *developing*. History, in other words, must have a subject on which that development can be charted. The true subject of development is not merely a series of abstract changes but a certain entity. Any change in agriculture, industry, and economy is necessarily an expression of the development of this entity. This is how Egypt was forged as the true and ultimate subject of history. Consequently, because Egypt became the subject of history, the reforms of Muḥammad ʿAlī were grasped as the means by which we can measure the nation's development. From that point onward, the pasha's reforms became an important issue that dominated, and to a certain extent continues to dominate, the historiography of the era (Western and Arab alike).

Space: To see a thing is to see it against a certain background. If the subject matter of history is Egypt, it could be experienced only if a certain setting extends around and behind it. This background setting is the politically defined space of Egypt. Those who initiated the celebrations and governed the land of Egypt understood, even if only on a very basic level, that this setting is not merely an Ottoman province but a nation-state called Egypt.[156]

Now, with these three notions put in place, they should be viewed as a whole. And when all three are jointly projected, an image of Egypt begins to appear: a modern nation-state in which people and territory were synchronized in a movement toward the future. This synchronization is what forged Egypt as an independent historiographical unit. Though I have discussed these three elements separately, the founder paradigm prescribed their coalescence. Thus, change and reforms were signs of the emerging nation as the subject of history, but simultaneously they also measured time by serving as indicators for the nation's progression. Such interconnectedness illustrates "the close association between the idea of progress and the nation," which comes into focus in the understating of "the nation as progress and History as the progress of the nation."[157]

However, since events do not (simply) offer themselves as stories, the task of the founder paradigm was to resolve this impasse.[158] It did so by creating a system of relevance that dictated what the object of historical knowledge was, what questions to ask, what evidence to look for, and how to order these concerns into a meaningful story about the past. Everything that did not fall within this cat-

155. Duara, *Rescuing History from the Nation*, p. 27.

156. See also Mitchell, *Rule of Experts*, pp. 180–181.

157. Hartog, "Time, History and the Writing of History," p. 12

158. This is the basic insight of Hayden White's entire historiographical project. See Ann Rigney, "Narrativity and Historical Representation," *Poetics Today* 12, no. 3 (Autumn 1991): p. 598.

egory was effectively ignored as "medieval" or "uninteresting, unintelligible, or otherwise unworthy of attention."[159] This is how the Gordian knot between history and emergence of the nation-state was tied.[160] Even though in 1902 the title "the founder of modern Egypt" was not yet in use when referring to the pasha,[161] Zaydān's writings and some of Kāmil's actions had already put the historical and mental substances of this title in their right place.[162]

This new historical understanding also enabled literate Egyptians to join the march of nations by asking a classic European nineteenth-century question: *From whence do we come, and where are we going?* Whereas for Islamic historiography (which viewed history as a catalog of events ordered from the past to the present) the first part of this question is by no means a novelty, the second part (which views the entire process from the future) surely is. The ground was now prepared for the search for and the celebration of the nation's origins, and the history of this quest, which stretches as far back as the Pharaonic era, is already well known to us.[163]

From the perspective of this book, historicism, which perceives societies as organic entities that are connected by objective and independent bonds, was exclusively harnessed for the cause of distinctive territorial nationalism. This link was to remain in place for decades to come. Nevertheless, having said that, I do not wish to overemphasize the coherence and maturity of the founder paradigm.[164] In 1905, many important questions were left open while others were not yet asked—for example: What was the role of the people in the modernization process? Was it Muḥammad ʿAlī who started modernization? What were his sources of inspiration? What role did foreigners play in this process? Was 1798 a historical turning point? And who benefited the most from the establishment of modern Egypt? In addition, certain conceptual developments, with regard to language, for example, needed to take place before national modern historiography could achieve cultural prominence. In fact, in 1905 not even a single book focused on the founder paradigm as a full-fledged interpretation of modern history. One should remember that, in the final analysis, the majority of Egyptians still considered themselves to be Ottoman subjects. Furthermore, it is entirely unclear to

159. See the relevant discussion in Rigney, *Imperfect Histories*, p. 68.

160. Nicholas Dirks, "History as a Sign of the Modern," *Public Culture* 2, no. 2 (Spring 1990): p. 25.

161. During the 1890s, Muḥammad ʿAlī was referred to as the "founder of the khedival dynasty." See *Al-Hilāl*, April 1892, p. 337.

162. See, for instance, *Al-Hilāl*, April 1892, pp. 337–353, May 1892, pp. 385–401; and *Al-Hilāl*, May 1897, p. 641. See again Zaydān, *Al-Mamlūk al-shārid*, pp. 98–106, 132, 147.

163. Israel Gershoni and James Jankowski, *Egypt, Islam and the Arabs: The Search for Egyptian Nationhood, 1900–1930* (New York: Oxford University Press, 1986).

164. As we shall see, the founder paradigm would undergo considerable development before it appeared as a truly hegemonic framework for historical investigation.

what degree the implications of these developments were comprehensible even to those who toiled for their realization.

To be sure, what ʿAbduh understood in the years of 1902 and 1905 is that if he lost this debate, an iron curtain of denial and ignorance would descend on Egypt's pre-1805 past, a curtain that would condemn Egypt's Islamic and Ottoman heritage to oblivion. Already in 1897, in a private conversation with Rashīd Riḍā, ʿAbduh condemned anti-Ottoman sentiments and dismissed the thesis of Ottoman decline.[165] He passed away only a short while after the centennial debate, without ever knowing how right he would be. For people such as Zaydān, for royalists, and even for colonialists such as Cromer, this paradigm was a positive sign of promising progress. For a fourth group, probably the majority, the consequences of it may not have been fully clear yet. Ironically, Muṣṭafa Kāmil, the man who envisioned this holiday and worked hard to turn it into a reality, continued to regard himself as "an Ottoman Egyptian" *(miṣrī ʿuthmānī)*.[166] Thus, he did not yet grasp, or for political reasons could not admit, the fundamental incompatibility between a territorial and ethnic Egyptian entity and the Ottoman order, in which territory and ethnicity do not overlap.

This chapter began with the assumption that even after 1882, Egypt might still have developed in other directions than the nationalist one. It concludes by saying that in 1906 Egypt's direction was clearly established. Though since the 1880s Egyptian society had made great progress in turning ideas into political themes, political themes into convictions, and convictions into commitments, nationalist commitments were not yet fully translated into a unified (political) action, and a certain ambiguity was a sign of these times.

The 1906 Dinshaway incident, however, assisted in eradicating this vagueness and ushered in an era of unified political action. The incident famously started as a pedestrian pigeon-shooting event, during which a group of British soldiers unknowingly encroached on the means of livelihood of Dinshaway villagers, who, in response, defended their interests and seriously injured the British. Already feeling the mounting pressure of hostile popular forces, the British were inclined to read such events not as simple criminal acts but as opposition to British rule. They thus reacted swiftly and harshly. For this purpose they convened the Special Tribunal, a body whose sole task was to bypass the limitations of the Egyptian Criminal Code. Since its establishment in 1895, this tribunal had never been in session. Agitated by the trial, during which fifty-two of the accused were given thirty minutes to present their case and then severely punished, a new political generation was formed, which took matters into its own hands.[167]

165. ʿAbduh, *Al-Aʿmāl al-kāmila*, pp. 732–733.

166. Crabbs, *The Writing of History in Nineteenth-Century Egypt*, p. 153.

167. Lutfi al-Sayyid Marsot, *Egypt and Cromer* (1969), pp. 169–173.

The manner of the court, the severity of the sentences, the gruesome public executions that followed, and the imperial display of indifference were not all that accompanied this entire affair. Another aspect, and one of the most troubling from a strictly internal perspective, was the instrumental role played by Būṭrus Ghālī (an interim minister of justice), Aḥmad Fatḥī Zaghlūl (president of the Native Courts), and Ibrāhīm Ḥilbāwī (public prosecutor) in bringing about this perceived miscarriage of justice. Were Egypt's best and brightest siding with the occupiers against their fellow countrymen?

Many believed that this was indeed the case, and in subsequent years all three men were to pay some public price. One, Būṭrus Ghālī, would pay with his life. With the post-Dinshaway expansion of the political scene and with a new generation of *effendis,* who were committed to political activism with more dedication than ever before, came a qualitative turn. Namely, the embryonic semantic field of the 1890s, which spoke for political modernity, matured in a fashion that facilitated complex historical thinking. Then, as we shall see in chapter 2, history became increasingly entangled with specific political projects.

2

Talking History

1906–1920

By 1920, modern historical thought had reached a certain point of maturity. My aim in this chapter is to explain this process. With improved accessibility to new types of knowledge and completely new forms of intellectual organization, the perceptual tools of educated people were modified, at first quite slowly, but by 1919, quite decisively. Though it is yet too early to speak of a genre of modern history, the development of new linguistic resources, in fact an entire semantic field, was the crucial and final element that brought the historicization process to a mature point. The association between history writing on the one hand and a more developed political lexicon than that of the 1890s on the other hand formed the ultimate standard for public relevancy.[1] Equipped with new concepts and a new literary structure, modern history became a formidable tool for political legitimacy. It was also the primary abstract tool for making things modern and, ultimately, for determining what is, and is not, "modern" and "Egyptian." An analysis of historical thought during this era illustrates that it provided a tremendous advantage to popular parties and posed a huge challenge to monarchic authority. Before we turn to see why this was the case, a few words are in order about the radical transformation of Egyptian politics during this era.

After Dinshaway, British rule was past its apogee. Despite concrete achievements in the fields of administration, hydraulics, commerce, public health, and infrastructure, following the Dinshaway debacle the colonial momentum of the 1880s and 1890s lost much of its strength. Cromer himself was sick and tired, as

1. For the political lexicon of previous decades, see Gasper, "Civilizing Peasants."

the "system of one man-rule which he created was not only an inefficient method of directing Egyptian affairs but also one that placed a near impossible burden on his own shoulders."[2] That year, he left Egypt under a barrage of criticism, and an unexpected economic slump further frustrated the British project. Along with this loss of impetus, an end also came to the timidity of the nationalist opposition of earlier times. Though the political demands remained more or less the same, revolving around constitutionalism and independence, the means of fulfilling them changed radically.

One notable change was that the post-Dinshaway generation began organizing itself into political parties, secret associations, and grassroots organizations. In a relatively short span of time, no fewer than six new political parties came into existence. Most of them, such as Ḥizb al-Nubalā' (Party of Nobles, 1908), al-Ḥizb al-Dusturī (the Constitutional Party, 1910), al-Ḥizb al-Miṣrī (The Egyptian Party, 1908), and Ḥizb al-'Ummāl (the Workers Party, 1909), represented ad hoc issues and small publics. Their life span was thus quite limited. But alongside these marginal parties, two major rival political blocs emerged. For the next half century, they would have a critical and lasting effect on the Egyptian political scene. The first was Kāmil's National Party, which was established in 1907. It had an Islamic and ultranationalist profile. The second was the Umma Party, founded at the same time and headed by some of 'Abduh's followers, such as Aḥmad Luṭfī al-Sayyid, the intellectual star and editor of their newspaper *Al-Jarīda*. Compared with the National Party, they were considered moderate. Cromer's successors had to navigate their policies in this new political terrain.

Eldon Gorst (1907–1911) was Cromer's hand-picked successor and had served under him since the 1880s. Realizing that the political ground was shifting, Gorst deserted Cromer's autocratic ways and sought rapprochement with and the accommodation of oppositional forces. In his words, "I wanted to render our rule more sympathetic to the Egyptians in general and to the *Muhammedans in particular* by restoring good feeling between the Anglo-Egyptian officials and the natives of the country."[3] While Gorst successfully approached Khedive 'Abbās Ḥilmī II—still the symbolic sovereign of the Egyptian-Ottoman province—and secured his cooperation, he was less successful with moderate party leaders and even less so with radical nationalists.

Most opposition came from a host of overt and covert popular organizations that were associated with the National Party and Kāmil. Their worldview was radical, their politics zealous. Presiding over grassroots activism, they considered

2. Roger Owen, *Lord Cromer: Victorian Imperialist Edwardian Proconsul* (Oxford: Oxford University Press, 2004), p. 327.

3. Quoted in Robert L. Tignor, *Modernization and British Colonial Rule in Egypt, 1882–1914* (Princeton, NJ: Princeton University Press, 1966), p. 292.

the Egyptian government, headed by figures such as Ḥusayn Fakhrī, Būṭrus Ghālī, and Sa'd Zaghlūl, to be tyrannical and oppressive. The fact that the government was presided over by the British and was not guided by a constitution rendered it illegitimate. With virtually no place at all for lawful opposition and no proper representation, the conflict took place in the streets. Even after Kāmil's early death in 1908, his followers regularly took to the streets, organizing a demonstration or a strike. Public speechmaking and a compatible form of vociferous journalism brought the message to new, urban crowds. The prevalent belief in the government's illegitimacy and the inability to influence the political course of affairs resulted in violent talk. When National Party member Shaykh Jawīsh wrote an article in which he praised political murder in India and when other justifications for political violence proliferated, the British and the government knew they should act.[4]

The official response to the often chauvinist mood of the times was the 1909 Press Law. As a reenactment of the original 1881 Press Law, it allowed the government to censor, completely shut down, and persecute the editors and writers of several popular organs.[5] The reenactment of the Press Law coincided with the British request to extend the Suez Canal concession an additional half century. Seen at the time as the "mother of all questions," the request prompted people to action. A common slogan of the time was "Men of the Waṭanī Party to save the canal."[6] With the alleged illegitimacy of the government in mind and with violent language all around, the nationalists viewed "saving" the canal as a call to arms. The 1908 success of the Committee of Union and Progress (CUP) in deposing Abdülhamid served as an example of how much young patriots could accomplish.

In February 1910, Ibrāhīm Wardānī, an unsuccessful pharmacist and a member of the secret post-Dinshaway "Mutual Brotherhood Society," pulled the trigger of his revolver and killed Premier Būṭrus Ghālī. Given the atmosphere, Ghālī embodied all that was wrong: he had signed the 1899 Sudan Agreement, presided over the Dinshaway trial, reinstated the notorious Press Law, and supported the British request for extending the Suez concession. For the country's political elite, the murder came as a shock, as it not only exposed the seething underworld of the ultranationalists but also testified to the elite's lack of control over the masses. Ghālī's Copt membership complicated matters even more.[7] With the threat of

4. Malak Badrawi, *Political Violence in Egypt 1910–1924: Secret Societies, Plots and Assassinations* (Richmond, UK: Curzon Press, 2000), p. 30, 32, 46.

5. For this reason many activists left for Switzerland, where, after a mere year of residency, they were granted citizenship and hence protection from prosecution back home.

6. Badrawi, *Political Violence in Egypt,* p. 12.

7. Already in 1908, Jawīsh wrote that "the Copts should be kicked to death." Tignor, *Modernization and British Colonial Rule in Egypt,* p. 310; Berque, *Egypt,* p. 206.

mounting sectarian tensions, the government revisited the penal code and issued a series of so-called Exceptional Laws, which further restricted freedom of speech and association.[8] These new measures specifically targeted the National Party.

By 1910 the country was in need of leadership, but the khedive was unable to provide it. For he was caught again, as he had been many times before, in the crossfire between the British and the nationalists. Furthermore, as the one who had originally recommended Ghālī to Gorst, he was considered somewhat responsible for the nationalist setback of the past two years. Worse still, his persistent support of Abdülhamid and his rejection of the CUP—whose policy toward Egypt he considered "insane demagogy and megalomania"—portrayed him in a reactionary light.[9] His endorsement of the Press Law could only strengthen this view. 'Abbās Ḥilmī II was still a constitutionalist, but he was no longer the dynamic and unconventional khedive he once was. As far as the nationalists were concerned, the khedive, the government, and the British had collaborated against Egypt. Much to his dismay, this was a common view, and he knew it.[10]

In 1911 Gorst suddenly died. With his tenure largely seen as a failure, his departure ushered in the revival of unilateralism and strong-arm policies. Herbert Kitchener, commander in chief of India, took up where Cromer had left off. In crude colonial terms, his job was to pacify the country and improve its economy. These were two missions in which Gorst had obviously failed. Certainly Kitchener did not seek rapprochement with the ultranationalists, and in a relatively short span of time the National Party chairman Muḥammad Farīd and other key figures, such as Shaykh Jawīsh, were sent into permanent exile. The inevitable outcome of this situation was the strengthening of the Jarīda-Umma group, which operated from within the government and thus had regular access to state power.

Kitchener's attitude toward the palace was equally aggressive. Since the 1894 Frontiers incident, the Khedive had been his nemesis. Cognizant of the change, the khedive tried to resume his anti-British nationalist activity. Though the khedive's nationalist credentials were by now rather worn and his connections largely ineffective, Kitchener still sought an opportunity to depose him. Following the outbreak of World War I, he refused to allow the khedive's return to Egypt from his summer vacation in Istanbul. In December, 'Abbās Ḥilmī II was officially deposed.

In his place, Prince Ḥusayn Kāmil, the khedive's uncle and the eldest living

8. The three new laws targeted demonstrations, strikes, and political conspiracy. They also allowed the exile of whoever was designated a criminal. See Arthur Goldschmidt and Robert Johnston, ed., *Historical Dictionary of Egypt* (Lanham, MD: Scarecrow Press, 2003), p. 144.

9. Hilmi II, *The Last Khedive of Egypt*, p. 99.

10. Ibid., p. 126; Badrawi, *Political Violence in Egypt*, p. 80.

prince of the royal house, was offered the sultanate. The new sultan had no ambition of his own and was politically insignificant. In December 1914, Egypt was made a protectorate, and the British presence there assumed a permanent character. The suzerainty of the Ottomans was terminated. The law of the land became a martial one. With the Ottoman framework rendered obsolete, the Jarīda-Umma group offered an alternative secular vision that borrowed only the modern and universal side of ʿAbduh's teaching and divorced its Islamic side. Divided into secular and Islamic camps, ʿAbduh's followers parted ways, and Rashīd Riḍā and Aḥmad Luṭfī al-Sayyid became adversaries.[11]

As the war ended, the Jarīda-Umma group quickly transformed itself into a popular diplomatic delegation, or *wafd,* then used the generic term as the name of its party. Framed as a broad coalition of politically interested parties, the Wafd spoke on behalf of the nation and requested unconditional independence. Over the next several years, it would set the country on a course of gradual liberation. The palace, now in the firm hands of the resourceful king Aḥmad Fu'ād, sought to regain the monarchic authority, which had been lost during the past decade. He thus found himself in competition with the mainstream nationalism of the Wafd.

With all of these critical vicissitudes of power and with a certain inconclusive political orientation, this era saw a meaningful change in all spheres of life. Most significant was the proliferation of a de-Ottomanization process on the one hand and the increased nationalization of the mind on the other—two sides of the same coin. Indeed, the fifteen years that elapsed from the beginning of the twentieth century to World War I constitute a peculiar transitional period. The Ottoman order, especially the social and cultural one, was not yet entirely gone, and the new nationalist era was not yet firmly established. Even though the direction of change was clear, Egypt was partly an independent nation-state, partly a colony, and partly Ottoman. This peculiarity has often meant that students of nationalism have instinctively "hurried" through this era until they reach the solid national ground of the 1919 Revolution.[12] Ottomanists, however, generally steer clear of it entirely, remaining instead in the familiar and warm bosom of the previous century. A third approach has been to view this era as part of a "long nineteenth century," but few contemporary researchers have adopted this distinctive option.[13]

11. Hourani, *Arabic Thought in the Liberal Age,* pp. 193–221.

12. Even devoted students of Egyptian nationalism have been quite abbreviated when dealing with this era. Gershoni and Jankowski, *Egypt, Islam and the Arabs,* pp. 3–20.

13. See, for instance, Ehud Toledano, "Social and Economic Change in the 'Long Nineteenth Century,'" in M. W. Daly, ed., *The Cambridge History of Egypt* (Cambridge: Cambridge University Press, 1998), vol. 2, pp. 252–284.

COMING TO TERMS WITH POLITICAL MODERNITY

What de-Ottomanized pre-1919 Egypt? As we have already seen, the modest beginnings of the de-Ottomanization process are discernable as early as the 1890s. As time went by, however, these forces were augmented, reaching a zenith, and a certain level of abstraction, during the actual political collapse of the empire. In this section I seek to clarify what exactly we should study when we talk about de-Ottomanization of pre-1919 Egypt and why it was politically and historiographically relevant.

Ehud Toledano rightly dates the de-Ottomanization process, an active endeavor of collective amnesia, as a predominantly pre-1919 phenomenon. According to him, de-Ottomanization was characterized by a dual sociocultural change in which the once-hegemonic Turcophone elite strove to remold its cultural orientation by entirely Egyptianizing or Arabizing it.[14] Forgetting their Ottomanness was a conscious mechanism of survival in an increasingly nationalist age.[15] Textually however, Toledano bases his argument on post-1919 references. Thus, he relies on the writing of the eminent national historian ʿAbd al-Raḥmān al-Rāfiʿī, who began writing nationalist history only in 1928. Certainly, al-Rāfiʿī embodies a classic anti-Ottoman tendency, but rather than initiating this process, he only concluded it. The same is also true for Toledano's other agents of de-Ottomanization: the fate of the Ottoman archives and the initiation of official royal historiography (two important concerns, which I will discuss in the next two chapters).[16] Thus, if all pertinent historiographical evidence appears later than 1919, how then was Egyptian culture de-Ottomanized?[17]

A significant part of the answer may be found in the creation of a political lexicon, one that was relevant to the real-life process of nation-state building and to the political radicalization described above. But such a lexicon is a complex

14. He writes: "By the last quarter of the nineteenth century the elite became more Egyptian-Ottoman than Ottoman-Egyptian, paving the way for the emergence of an Egyptian elite in the first quarter of the twentieth century, which could boast an Ottoman-Egyptian ancestry, but had a fully developed Egyptian national identity." Ehud Toledano, "Forgetting Egypt's Ottoman Past," in Jayne Warner, ed., *Cultural Horizons: A Festschrift in Honor of Talat S. Halman* (Syracuse, NY: Syracuse University Press, 2001), p. 153.

15. Ibid., p. 152.

16. Ibid., pp. 153–160.

17. Referring to this question, Toledano's argument that "until World War I, Arab historiography, including that in Egypt, was quite positive about the Ottoman past" is inaccurate. Toledano based his claim on Rifaat Ali Abou-El-Haj, who also provides no historiographical source material to support such an argument. Toledano, "Forgetting Egypt's Ottoman Past," p. 152; Rifaat Ali Abou-El-Haj, "The Social Uses of the Past: Recent Arab Historiography of Ottoman Rule," *IJMES* 14, no. 2 (1982): pp. 185–201.

subject to trace historically. Linguistic possibilities develop or lapse into disuse; old meanings fade or are enriched. One word may simultaneously signify several meanings. Nevertheless, the ability to form coherent concepts out of this linguistic forest is a critical political tool and a requirement for modern political action. As we shall now see, long before World War I, new linguistic resources had secured the nation and the people as the ultimate subjects of history and, by implication, suppressed the imperial Ottoman frame of identity. The study of Egypt's emerging semantic field substantiates Toledano's general argument and explains how pre-1919 Egyptian culture was de-Ottomanized.

By tracing the specific biography of each old, modified, or new word, Ami Ayalon has painstakingly constructed a detailed picture of nineteenth-century linguistic change in the Arab East.[18] Among many other developments, the expansion of political journalism and the literary energies of the Nahḍa facilitated this change. As noted by Ghisaline Alleaume, the Egyptian journalistic scene was vibrant, heterogeneous, flexible, and especially keen to any form of historical argumentation.[19] Particularly during the last two decades of that century, newspapers and journals made a significant contribution to the expansion of an Arabic political vocabulary. But there were also other media. Perhaps the most famous case for preoccupation with language was that of Shaykh al-Marṣafī's *Risālat al-kalim al-thmān* (Treatise on Eight Words). This text was published a month after the beginning of the 'Urābī revolt, likely as a form of response to it.[20] For the first time, the book paid close attention to eight important words, in fact, political concepts *(nation, homeland, government, justice, oppression, politics, liberty,* and *education).* Al-Marṣafī was also the person who is believed to have coined the name Nahḍa.[21]

However, despite the relatively harmonious cooperation of al-Marṣafī's political language and 'Urābī's actions, these words were not yet part of an alternative course for political organization. The modern meaning of government, with its attendant structures, principles, and values, needed more time to develop. This reality frustrated Lord Cromer, who in 1906 complained that he had never read in the national press a "single, accurate, well-argued or useful article on such matters as finance, education or the working of the judicial system."[22] After his retirement, he retrospectively elaborated on this issue, adding, "The words

18. Ami Ayalon, *Language and Change in the Arab Middle East* (New York: Oxford University Press, 1987).

19. Ghisaline Alleaume, "L'Égypte et son histoire: Actualité et controversés première partie: La presse et l'histoire," *Bulletin du CEDEJ* 20, no. 2 (1986): pp. 9–34.

20. Mitchell, *Colonizing Egypt*, pp. 131–138.

21. Elshakry, "Darwin's Legacy in the Arab East," p. 202.

22. Quoted in Tignor, *Modernization and British Colonial Rule in Egypt*, p. 271.

absolute monarchy, limited monarchy, republic, parliamentary government, federal council, and other of a like nature, when applied to the government of any country, will readily convey to an educated European a general idea of how the government of the particular country in question is conducted. But the political dictionary may be ransacked in vain for any terse description of the government of Egypt."[23] Unfair as these words may be, Cromer referred mainly to the 1890s. As mentioned above, by 1906 al-Marṣafī's eight words had been greatly enriched in meaning and were entertained as part of a semantic field which offered several political courses of action.

Analyzing this very same phenomenon in the context of nation-building in the Middle East, Sami Zubaida has argued, "Alongside state forms there developed a whole complex of political models, vocabularies, organizations and techniques which have established and animated what I call a political field of organization, mobilization, agitation and struggle. The vocabularies of this field are those of nation, nationality and nationalism, of popular sovereignty, democracy, liberty, legality and representation, of political parties and parliamentary institutions."[24] What Zubaida has called a political field is explained here through the proliferation of modern semantics. The creativity and cultural energy that Egyptian intellectuals invested in the creation of such a semantic universe were absolutely remarkable. Against the social backdrop of the bureaucratization and professionalization of the middle class, several on-the-ground processes breathe life into this field: political competition between the Jarīda-Umma group and the National Party, the anti-colonial struggle, and labor politics. The writings of Aḥmad Luṭfī al-Sayyid show how the fixed meanings of the late nineteenth-century political vocabulary were transformed into a multilayered language whose logic was both modern and nationalist. The following concepts and principles were extracted from Luṭfī al-Sayyid's writings: the propagation of literacy, the underlining of the shared culture and language, the acceptance of the state as the only legitimate body politic that represents all community members, the need for a rationalized legal system, a measurable economy, the concealing of class, ethnic, and religious diversities, and a strong commitment to the idea of popular sovereignty. Through a prolific career of journalistic and other writings, Luṭfī al-Sayyid enriched and, in fact, defined the boundaries of this semantic field, which elaborated the basic structures of political modernity. Rationalization, organization of ideas about authority, distinguishing between the public and private spheres of operation, and substantiating the idea of citizenship are examples of such structures. Appearing in

23. Evelyn Baring Cromer, *Modern Egypt* (New York: Macmillan, 1908), vol. 2, pp. 261–262.

24. Sami Zubaida, *Islam, the People and the State: Essays on Political Ideas and Movements in the Middle East* (London: Routledge, 1989), pp. 145–146.

Luṭfī al-Sayyid's writings before 1919, such ideas could be found in virtually any daily newspaper from this period.[25]

These principles and values were proliferated primarily through political journalism, and many even served as the cornerstones of concrete collective projects. A few examples for such enterprises come to mind: the establishment of the embryonic Cairo University in 1907–8 by a coalition of diverse public figures and Zaghlūl's actions to promote public education and the improvised night schools of the National Party. These projects indicated the universal importance that the Egyptian elite ascribed to literacy and education.[26] Of unique importance in this regard was Cairo's law school, which trained an entire tier of bureaucrats and public leaders whose language and actions were geared toward political modernity. Thus, through such institutions and with the critical help of journalism, words that were hitherto associated with an Ottoman political imagination, such as *government,* could now invoke the following associations: domination, obedience, legislation, jurisdiction, public opinion, freedom of opinion, rights, and popular representation.

Considering these new conceptual resources, it is no small wonder that speechmaking became one of the most prolific public activities of the time and was practiced by secondary school students and mature political leaders alike. Traces of these new meanings may be found in a random assortment of political slogans collected from the rallies and demonstrations of the period—for instance: "Down with the press law," "The government is unjust," "Down with the tyrants," "This is the habitual practice of tyrants," "Long live justice," and "Long live freedom."[27] Indeed, the debate and struggle over the application of the 1909 Press Law illustrate how these concepts were put to work on behalf of a concrete political worldview. Similar things can also be said about working-class activism, for example, the unionization of tramway workers and cigarette workers. So new was this conceptual world that on some occasions, as in the case of the words *strike* and *union,* new terms in Arabic needed to be coined.[28]

25. Originally published in December 1909, Aḥmad Luṭfī al-Sayyid, "Iṭlabū al-ḥuriya, iṭlabū al-istiqlāl," in his *Al-Muntakhabāt* (Cairo: Dār al-nashr al-ḥadīth, 1937), vol. 1, pp. 180–182; originally published in September 1911, "Aḥmad 'Urābī," ibid., pp. 252–256; originally published in January 1912, "Al-Ḥaraka al-nisā'iyya fī Miṣr," ibid., pp. 268–271; originally published in February 1912, "Ma'radunā al-ṣinā'ī wa-l-zirā'ī," ibid., pp. 272–275; originally published in May 1912, "Al-Ḥuriyya," ibid., pp. 296–298; "Ḥuriyyat al-ra'y," pp. 299–302. See also his *Al-Muntakhabāt* (Cairo: Maṭba'at al-muqtaṭaf, 1945), vol. 2, pp. 57–100.

26. Establishing the university was a joint venture by figures such as Muḥammad 'Abduh, Muṣṭafa Kāmil, Sa'd Zaghlūl, and even Jurjī Zaydān. See Donald Reid, *Cairo University and the Making of Modern Egypt* (Cambridge: Cambridge University Press, 1990), pp. 27–67.

27. Badrawi, *Political Violence in Egypt,* p. 5.

28. Beinin and Lockman, *Workers on the Nile,* pp. 48–82.

Since the anti-colonial struggle was the subject of much of this activity, by default, it also had dramatic implications for both the Egyptian monarchy and Ottoman identity. Several techniques were employed by the nationalists in order to enhance the reception of this new language. One ubiquitous method was to create concepts, give them names, and arrange them hierarchically.[29] Usually, this arrangement took the form of pairs. Each pair consisted of concept and anti-concept. Pertaining to the question of de-Ottomanization, the following organization was a powerful tool in that process: "modern" *(ḥadīth)* versus "old" *(qadīm)* and "modern age" *('aṣr ḥadīth)* versus "Ottoman age" *('aṣr 'uthmānī)*. By polarizing these concepts and impregnating them with meaning, Egyptian culture treated Ottomanism precisely the same way that sixteenth-century Europe contrasted "renaissance" with "medievalism" and "Hellenes" with "barbarians." Once this form of arrangement gained currency, these pairs could be easily separated from their original conditions of emergence and their former concrete historical context.[30] This is why there was a decreasing interest in Ottoman and Mamluk history. For nationalized intellectuals, the words *Ottomans* and *Mamluks* invoked nothing but the association of an unmodern and backward system of rule. It is remarkable to think that only twenty years or so beforehand, these words had meant something entirely different.

Likewise, the impact of the semantic field on the political status of the Egyptian monarchy was dramatic. As briefly mentioned above, Khedive 'Abbās Ḥilmī II could not find his proper place within the politics of the time and shifted his alliances periodically in pursuit of short-term tactical gain. By his own admission, he profoundly mistrusted the Jarīda-Umma group and loathed the post-1908 National Party. He wrote that Farīd was an "inexperienced shepherd of a flock that lack cohesion" and considered Jawīsh a fanatic and an undisciplined charlatan.[31] As far as he was concerned, if the National Party radicals triumphed or even if the moderate nationalists had their way, the royal prerogative will be severely limited. The khedive was right. Some indication for the lowering of monarchic status was present in the language of the era, which was essentially republican. Thus, common conceptual pairs and counterpairs were: "king" versus "people," "popular sovereignty" versus "authoritarianism," "monarchy" versus "republic," "independence" versus "colonialism," and "constitutions and Parliament" versus "autocracy."[32] Clearly, these conceptual pairs fortified the claim of the nation "as

29. The following discussion was inspired by Reinhart Koselleck, *Futures Past: On the Semantics of Historical Time,* trans. Keith Tribe (Cambridge, MA: MIT Press, 1985), pp. 159ff.

30. Ibid., pp. 163–164.

31. Hilmi II, *The Last Khedive of Egypt,* pp. 101, 130–131, 141.

32. Tellingly, one the first articles to be published after the fall on the monarchy in July 1952 was titled "The Constitution Defeated the King." *Rūz al-yūsuf,* August 4, 1952, pp. 22–23.

the newly realized sovereign subject of history embodying a moral and political force that has overcome dynasties and aristocracies . . . who, historically speaking, represent only themselves."[33] Quite alarmingly, it also implied that the basis for national life was made up only of popular political parties, elections, and Parliament.[34] Evidently, then, this new field provided the Egyptian public the capacity for political reasoning and thus conditioned what could be thought and apprehended at any given time.

Posing an immediate threat to the symbolic space of royal authority, this new environment was hardly compatible with the monarchy. There was no better indication of this than the repeated attempts by radical nationalists to assassinate both the khedive and Ḥusayn Kāmil. In July 1914, a short while before his deposition, the khedive was lightly wounded when an Egyptian student in Istanbul shot him. Two similar attempts involving revolvers and bombs were carried out in Egypt in April and July 1915, these times against his successor.[35] Though both the khedive and the prince survived, the meaning of these actions was quite clear to the third monarch of the century, Sultan Fu'ād. Evidently, the monarchy had to play by rules it could not change and had little power to shape.

Indeed, from that point until its demise in July 1952, Egypt's royal house operated in the face of strong ideological criticism. The criticism used language as a weapon and drew straight from this rich linguistic arsenal. The monarchy was greatly disadvantaged by its incompatibility with this new linguistic field, especially when the growing state bureaucracy, and more broadly the *effendiyya*, operated from within its logic. Since the monarchy no longer provided bureaucrats with their means of livelihood, they were free to develop different values and aspirations. Consequently, there was no symbiotic relationship between the monarchy and the bureaucrats. How to make powerful government officials loyal to the monarchy instead of to their superiors in politics was a major challenge, especially when some bureaucrats were also popular political activists.[36] As a result of such troubling circumstances, in 1920 King Fu'ād launched a massive historiographical project that aimed, among other things, to create an alternative historical consciousness that would convincingly settle the apparent contradiction between the idea of the nation/people and that of the dynasty. In addition,

33. Duara, *Rescuing History,* p. 4.

34. Though written in 1929, the statement of the prominent intellectual and politician Muḥammad Ḥusayn Haykal illustrates the point: "The birth and death of kings, their accession to the throne, their disposition, and their conquests and wars are not the basis for the life of nations." Quoted in Israel Gershoni, "Imagining and Reimagining the Past: The Use of History by Egyptian Nationalist Writers, 1919–1952," *History and Memory* 4, no. 2 (1992): p. 17.

35. For the full story of all three attempts in the context of national politics, see Badrawi, *Political Violence in Egypt,* pp. 113–133.

36. The brothers Zaghlūl are a case in point.

it also aimed at strengthening the bond with the nationalized bureaucracy. This strategy is commonly known today as "official nationalism."[37]

As far as historiography was concerned, this field was also a precondition for any historical narrative of the nation. At the same time, however, modern history was the only literary form that could meaningfully relate to the semantic field by deliberate structural design. In that sense, history and the new language of political modernity complemented each other. Since supporters of the popular parties created and nourished this linguistic environment, it automatically legitimized them. They spoke and wrote in this language. Therefore, they had little need for the writing of history books that would establish their credentials, and we are consequently left with almost no modern history books from this period. Quite obviously, it was clear to every newspaper reader (or listener) what the National Party and, later on, the Wafd were trying to do. In contrast, it became obvious to the monarchy that, as opposed to previous times, modern historical consciousness was "not only the outcome of political representation but also its necessary condition."[38] Hence, it needed to begin writing history.

In sum, by matching meanings to forms, Egyptian intellectuals and activists created a rich semantic universe that literally "came to terms" with political modernity, at the expense of the monarchy and Ottoman identity. This was the single most important intellectual development that occurred between 1900 to 1920. Not only did it de-Ottomanize Egyptian culture; it also set the rules for political action and the politics of historical representation with which the rules were associated. Historiographically, this new lexicon and its succinct prose rendered obsolete the rhetorical quality that was once demanded of historians.

ABOUT BYGONES AND NOT QUITE BYGONES

In the 1890s, history writing was an avocation for former state officials, politically ambitious individuals, men of letters, some journalists, and amateurs from various walks of life. All were men.[39] Especially prolific was the group of former state officials. They held administrative positions and played a central public role. Many started writing at retirement (Sarhank, Shārūbīm), only after a lifelong effort to amass a private collection of documents and records. Through

37. The term was coined by Benedict Anderson, *Imagined Communities,* 2nd ed. (1983; London: Verso, 1991), p. 110.

38. Dirks, "History as a Sign of the Modern," p. 25.

39. In 1894, feminist activist Zaynab Fawwāz declared, "History, which is the best of all sciences, is largely dominated by men. Not a single one of those male historians has dedicated a single chapter in which to discuss women who represent half of human kind." Quoted in Gorman, *Historians, State and Politics in Twentieth Century Egypt,* p. 104.

their networks and connections, they gained access to documents and private testimonies, relying as well on their own memories. No other historians had access to such a wealth of sources. The data were not shared. In a way, they practically monopolized historical source material. With a great deal of time, enough money, and especially the right network of connections, they dedicated their final years to writing. By all accounts, they were leisure-class historians. However, whether their source of cultural authority was their participation in the political process or, as in Zaydān's case, the writings of the European Orientalists (for Islamic history) and of colonial officials (for the modern era), they all faced the same task: discerning how to cope with the challenge of historicism.

Requiem to a Glorious Career

Historiographical influence is not the first thing that comes to mind when thinking of Cromer's legacy in Egypt. Nonetheless, in hindsight, his 1908 book, *Modern Egypt,* was a historiographical landmark.[40] Though it was a work of imperial justification and not a history book proper, it almost instantly influenced Egyptian intellectuals and continued to do so for the next four decades. Part of the book's appeal was Cromer's claim to represent scientific accuracy and truth.[41] He did so by alluding to the universal truthfulness of archival documentation and by providing a stream of statistics and calculations that used scientific credibility in order to create the impression of truthfulness.[42] His sources were inaccessible to Egyptians. As Cromer himself suggested, his motivation for writing was the fear that in "a semi-civilized country like Egypt," the safeguards to historical truth hardly existed. "It sometimes happens," wrote Cromer, "that, as time goes on, the measure of fiction increases, whilst that of fact tends to evaporate."[43] Obviously, he thought that Egypt's case lay safely in the realm of fiction, myth, and half truths. By writing the history of Egypt, Cromer sought to demonstrate the power invested in a scientific approach to historical reality. Among many others, Zaydān was truly impressed.

With greater coherency than ever before, Cromer brought history, modernity, and the nation-state together. He did so mainly by transforming the sense of historical change into the powerful concept of reform as the ultimate means for achieving mature modernity. As I argued in chapter 1, though during the 1890s reform was a ubiquitous concept, it was not yet functioning as a full-fledged principle for organizing nineteenth-century Egyptian history. By writing of reform

40. Much of the book was drafted years before its publication, largely during the 1890s.

41. Cromer, *Modern Egypt,* vol. 1, pp. 1–3.

42. Ibid., vol. 1, pp. 1–3, and vol. 2, pp. 304–310.

43. Ibid., vol. 1, pp. 2–3.

in the Egyptian historical context, Cromer fused three crucial elements: history, modernity, and Egypt. While previous writers such as Muḥammad Farīd and even Zaydān had difficulties determining what "change" was and which changes were worthy of attention, Cromer mastered both concerns. Indeed, the message of much of the second volume was a call for reforms on all possible fronts of life, ranging from the moral to the material.[44] Thus, Cromer's pivotal historiographical contribution was his suggestion that the experience of modernity is opened up only with the discovery of history itself, in which the nation-state is at once its own subject and object.

Always finely tuned to changes in his cultural and political environment, Zaydān decided to act on Cromer's insights. In 1911 he reissued a revised edition of his 1889 classic, *Tārīkh Miṣr al-ḥadīth.* It was a heavily modified version in which the section on nineteenth-century Egypt was entirely rewritten. In many ways, the differences between these two editions encapsulated the historiographical distance covered by Egyptian intellectuals since the 1890s. Zaydān's point of departure, in his attempt to improve his old historical agenda, is by now familiar: "When Muḥammad ʿAlī seized Egypt, it was in a state of commercial, agricultural, and cultural decay. His task was to reform it."[45] *Reform (iṣlāḥ)* became a key term and was affiliated with the greater phenomenon of the Nahḍa as a megaplan for national reform. Heavily influenced by Cromer, Milner, and others, Zaydān subscribed to the "statistical turn" and heavily quoted Cromer's calculations.[46] After two and a half decades of British presence, local intellectuals had embraced the habit of measuring and quantifying Egypt's progress. The amount of land reclaimed, the number of new institutions formed, the status of the state-budget balance, the number of miles of railways laid—such were the issues foremost in the minds of these reformers.[47] Obviously, the ability to forge Egypt as an economic, calculable entity went hand in hand with the development of the corresponding geographical, linguistic, and literary dimensions discussed here.[48]

However, in spite of Zaydān's awareness and efforts, he seems to have reached his intellectual limits in this book. With the advent of de-Ottomanization, he no longer appeared in harmony with this process. Thus, as a Christian, Zaydān quietly advocated a very particular—Nahḍa-oriented—interpretation of nationalism, which highlighted the role of all Arabs as the subject of Islamic history. For him, the *waṭan* was not necessarily Egypt but also, and sometimes exclusively,

44. Ibid., vol. 2, pp. 397–542.
45. Zaydān, *Tārīkh Miṣr al-ḥadīth* (1911), p. 174.
46. Ibid., pp. 174–194, 210–213, 329, 344–347.
47. Ibid., pp. 202–227, 343–346.
48. On statistics, see Mitchell, *Rule of Experts,* pp. 80–119.

Syria, Palestine, and Iraq.[49] Put differently, Zaydān's entire historiographical project had a strong Ottoman flavor attached to it. Indeed, in 1908, immediately after the Young Turks revolution, Zaydān optimistically wrote to a friend, commending him for his decision to begin learning Turkish: "It is the language of our government; after the gloom of tyranny has been disappeared, after knowledge has prevailed over ignorance and after the constitution has been proclaimed, our time has come to demonstrate to the other nations that we are a living nation who knows to gather and to unite, and that we help our government with our tongues, pens and words."[50]

In addition, Zaydān's writing had a problem of focus. His extremely wide scope of interests included Islamic history, modern history, and literature and, as such, did not join neatly into a coherent national narrative. Furthermore, if the value of a modern historical work lies above all in its capacity to point beyond itself as representation of the past in the future, Zaydān's work was unable to do this as efficiently as the nationalists expected. Thus, shortly before his death he wrote to his son, summing up his long and prolific career:

> All this [criticism] does not interest me either. But it weakens my determination to exert myself in the service of this nation the history of which was lying dead. I brought it back to life and I indeed say without boasting it was I who revived Arab literature by what I wrote and by the influence my book had upon the envious feelings of the writers, inducing them to compete. Before the appearance of *al-Hilāl* nobody mentioned the history of Islam. Those who composed works about it copied only from ancient authors. Today they begin to write in a reflective and explanatory matter. All this they got from my work.[51]

It was true. "They" indeed got much of "this" from his work. But they also wanted more, and they wanted it to be different. But whoever these people were, they would have to wait.

The Indian Summer of the Chronicle

Literary extinction, that is, the complete disappearance of a genre, is a rare phenomenon. It occurs in environments that go through a fundamental process of cultural reorientation. In such times of complete reshuffling of the mind and

49. For Zaydān's unfocused notion of nationalism, see Thomas Philipp, "Language, History and Arab National Consciousness in the Thought of Jurjī Zaydān (1861–1914)," *IJMES* 4, no. 1 (1973): pp. 3–22.

50. Jurjī Zaydān, *The Autobiography of Jurji Zaidan*, trans. and ed. Thomas Philipp (Washington DC: Three Continents Press, 1990), p. 78.

51. Originally this passage was written in reference to the attack by Rashīd Riḍā's circles. Ibid., p. 85.

spirit, societies are more prone to leave behind some extra cultural baggage. Egypt of this era was such a place, and, after the demise of the *khiṭaṭ* genre, the chronicle was supposed to be deemed the next redundant weight. However, awkwardly enough, the chronicle persisted. The very same genre that began to change during the 1890s and was expected to disappear soon afterward was still, in the first few decades of the early twentieth century, alive and kicking—so much so that work on two new chronicles was underway. One of them would become a classic. Curiously, in 1919, by the time of its publication, that chronicle seemed to be in such dissonance with its environment that a scholar such as Crabbs could simply ignore the original context and discuss it along with the work of ʿAlī Mubārak Pasha, written half a century beforehand.[52] But despite such omissions, bygones were not yet bygones. What was the cultural weight of these new chronicles? Which social and cultural milieux supported these projects? And why, despite its continued success, did the genre finally fade?

A biographical profile of four leisured historians before 1919 shows a deep commitment to the cultural world of the Ottoman Empire. Amīn Sāmī (1857–1941), Aḥmad Shafīq (1860–1940), Prince ʿUmar Ṭūsūn (1872–1944), and Fahmī Kallīnī (1860–1954) were members of the third generation of the Egyptian-Ottoman elite. They were polyglot and educated men who were oriented toward imperial Istanbul and Europe alike. Turkish and Arabic were their first tongues; French was their second. They saw the world through imperial and monarchic eyes. Concomitantly, most of them were royal employees or simply members of the royal family (e.g., Prince ʿUmar Ṭūsūn). Whereas the generation of their parents needed to compromise its Turcophone orientation and blend it with a distinctive Egyptian quality, their generation was asked to add a strong national flavor to it.[53] All of them chose to do so by "nationalizing" the monarchy and assisting, as best as they could, in concealing its incompatibility with the idea of the nation and its semantic resources. Let us take a look at the work of two of these figures.

Amīn Sāmī and Aḥmad Shafīq were the two stubborn history writers who continued the tradition of chronicles well into the 1930s. Though their writing had much in common, it was the work of Amīn Sāmī that left a long-lasting impression. An engineer by education, Amīn Sāmī held several official positions in the education system as director of the teacher-training school Dār al-ʿulūm and of the khedival Nāṣiriyya school.[54] After independence he was personally nominated by King Fu'ād as a senate member and remained in public life as

52. Crabbs, *The Writing of History in Nineteenth-Century Egypt,* pp. 119–125.

53. On their parents' generation, see Toledano, "Social and Economic Change in the 'Long Nineteenth Century,'" pp. 264–266.

54. al-Ziriklī, *Al-Aʿlām,* vol. 2, p. 17; Amīn Sāmī, "Lammā kuntu muʿalimān," *Al-Hilāl,* April 1937, pp. 610–612.

late as 1928.[55] In 1916 he started publishing *Taqwīm al-Nīl* (Almanac of the Nile). The three-volume work took a quarter of a century to write and twenty years to publish (1916–36), but it was immediately canonized as a literary monument for the Nile Valley.[56]

Taqwīm al-Nīl was an extremely ambitious project. It looked like a chronicle, but at the same time it functioned as an unprecedented reservoir of primary source material that was not available anywhere else. The author found many of his sources in European archives at a time when hardly any scholar was able to make sense of such material.[57] This was one of the main reasons for its canonization. *Taqwīm al-Nīl* covered Egyptian history from A.D. 622 to the end of the Ismāʿīl era in three volumes (the third volume alone, however, was composed of three parts: 1848–63, 1863–72, and 1872–79) and had an appendix that focused on the history of the Nile's civil engineering (bridges, canals, barrages, etc.) to 1915. In the words of Crabbs, "It was a highly heterogeneous mélange of materials ranging from the technical to historical to the poetical."[58]

The endless stream of information included detailed statistics of population growth, cotton prices, accounts of geography, cloud patterns, rain belts, the state of bridges and canals, and, of course, precious information about the cyclical flow of the Nile.[59] In many ways, it was an attempt to fuse the *khiṭaṭ* genre with the statistical turn of the British colonial administration. It had no single subject, no sense of "Egypt" as a distinct geographical entity, and it tended to treat time as an endless flow of days, weeks, and months in the rhythm of the Nile's flow itself. Likewise, it did not distinguish between the Ottoman and the modern Egyptian periods.

Its historical part aimed, among other things, to position the monarchy at the heart of Egypt's recent historical experience. It reads as an apologia for what, by that time, was acknowledged as the dynasty's weak historical performance and misdeeds (especially with regard to the reigns of Saʿīd and Ismāʿīl).[60] Sāmī respected and protected the dynasty's reputation and readily manipulated the original documents he consulted in *Dār al-maḥfūẓāt*. Thus, he deliberately omitted the words of Muḥammad ʿAlī, who depicted the Egyptian people as "wild

55. The constitution allowed Fu'ād to nominate two-fifths of the senators. Sāmī also contributed regularly to Egypt's newspapers and periodicals. For example, Amīn Sāmī, "Al-Tarbiyya wa-l-taʿlīm," *Al-Hilāl*, November 1931, pp. 22–24; see also Crabbs, *The Writing of History in Nineteenth-Century Egypt*, p. 120.

56. Amīn Sāmī, *Taqwīm al-Nīl* (Cairo: Dār al-kutub, 1916–1936), vol. 1, preface, pp. 1–3. In 2003, Amīn's work was once more reissued. *Al-Hayāt*, September 29, 2002, p. 16.

57. Sāmī, *Taqwīm al-Nīl*, vol. 1, preface, pp. 1–3.

58. Crabbs, *The Writing of History in Nineteenth-Century Egypt*, p. 120.

59. See, for instance, Sāmī, *Taqwīm al-Nīl*, vol. 1, pp. 96–97, appendix; and Crabbs, *The Writing of History in Nineteenth-Century Egypt*, p. 122.

60. Sāmī, *Taqwīm al-Nīl*, vol. 3, part 1, pp. 434–439, and part 3, pp. 1569–1575.

beasts."[61] After all, it was not appropriate for the "founder" to say such unkind words, particularly at a time when the people were distinguished as the linchpin of Egypt's modern national experience. As we shall see in chapter 3, though Amīn Sāmī was the first to manipulate source material on behalf of the monarchy, by no means would he be the last, nor would he be the most systematic in doing so.

Cognizant of linguistic and conceptual language, Sāmī provided *Taqwīm al-Nīl* with an impressive manifesto, which was obligated to "science and history." In it, he promised to narrate history as a causal chain of events free of sentimental stories. He even criticized other historians for their unorganized style.[62] The promise was easier said than done, however, just as Zaydān had discovered a quarter of a century earlier; like him, Amīn was unable to write the history that he himself had called for.

Aḥmad Shafīq's natural environment was the court of Tawfīq and ʿAbbās Ḥilmī II. Shafīq's father held several administrative positions under Ismāʿīl and Tawfīq and was married to a woman of Circassian origins. Under Tawfīq's royal patronage, Shafīq attended several schools where he achieved a full command of English, French, German, Arabic, and, of course, Turkish. In 1887, before he moved to Paris to pursue his higher education, he had already concluded two years of service in the khedival court. On his return from France, Shafīq was nominated as head of the court's Translation Department. His ties with ʿAbbās were significantly strengthened, and he remained ʿAbbās's closest adviser as late as 1921.[63] All the while, Shafīq was writing history books and compiling documents for his magnum opus, *Ḥawliyāt Miṣr al-siyāsiyya* (Political Annals of Egypt).[64] Beginning in 1926 and continuing over the next ten years, he published this work in ten monumental volumes, a total of ten thousand pages. The project was so ambitious and wide in scope that Shafīq opened his own publishing house.

Similar to Amīn Sāmī, *Ḥawliyāt Miṣr al-siyāsiyya* tried to be nationalist, monarchist, and also continue the canonized tradition of al-Jabartī.[65] Though

61. Khaled Fahmy, *All the Pasha's Men: Mehmed Ali, His Army and the Making of Modern Egypt* (Cambridge: Cambridge University Press, 1997), p. 282.

62. Sāmī, *Taqwīm al-Nīl,* vol. 1, pp. 117–118. Crabbs, too, considered Sāmī's statement of purpose to be highly sophisticated. Crabbs, *The Writing of History in Nineteenth-Century Egypt,* p. 121.

63. ʿAbd al-ʿAzīz Rifāʿī, *Aḥmad Shafīq muʾarrikh: Hayatuhu wa athruhu* (Cairo: al-Dār al-Miṣriyya li-l-taʾlīf wa-l-tarjama, 1965), pp. 1–59; Goldschmidt, *Biographical Dictionary of Modern Egypt,* p. 186.

64. In addition to an autobiography, he also published books on slavery in Islam, the Suez Canal, and the foreign influence in modern Egypt (in French), as well as numerous journalistic articles. See a review in *Al-Hilāl,* February 1932, pp. 619–620. For his journalistic writing, see Aḥmad Shafīq, "Qaṣir al-muntazah," *Al-Hilāl,* November 1931, pp. 70–72; and Aḥmad Shafīq, "Lammā kuntu talmidhan," *Al-Hilāl,* April 1937, pp. 682–685.

65. Aḥmad Shafīq, *Aʿmālī baʿd mudhakkirātī* (Cairo: Maṭbaʿa miṣriyya, 1941), pp. 225–227.

the work was influenced by the founder paradigm and provided some definitive statements on behalf of the modernizing role of Muḥammad ʿAlī, Shafīq accepted the negative prevailing views on ʿAbbās and Saʿīd and decided not to write about them because "nothing of importance happened in their day."[66] Like the writings of his predecessors, this work could not carry the burden of Shafīq's presumption.

These chronicles were written and even canonized because, just like the great classic chronicles of Ibn Iyās and even those of al-Jabartī, they provided an intimate sense of the landscape—human and physical—of Egypt. They presented themselves as an updated, modern continuation of these men's classics and thus responded to a much-needed sense of cultural continuity. For all its political worth, modern history that purported to start anew (1798 or 1805) was to some degree culturally alienating. These chronicles were more truthful to the cultural landscape of Egypt. For instance, Amīn Sāmī's celebration of the Nile Valley could accord cultural authority to the Pharaonic perception of the Nile as the place that shaped a distinct "Egyptian personality."

In addition, these chronicles provided crucial historical source material, which continues to be crucial. This is especially true with regard to Amīn's work. Again, for the most part, the documentation of these two writers was not available anywhere else. It was compiled in a certain order under the combination of Egyptian-Ottoman-monarchic and nationalist rationale. Though an impossible concoction, it was true to the experience of this specific generation. Indeed, these were intimate memoirs, written by individuals who witnessed, participated in, and to some degree shaped fin de siècle Egypt. Their perspective was historically valuable. Even in today's Egypt, almost eighty years after its publication, *Taqwīm al-Nīl* is regarded as an important source.

However, despite their status as cultural monuments, the main problem of these chronicles was their fundamental incompatibility with the demands of historicism.[67] Taken in their entirety, these works did not offer any coherent narrative of the Egyptian past. With no narrative, the capacity for moral judgment was compromised. Not unrelated to this lack, significant parts of these chronicles convey the sense that historical events are incomprehensible: like natural events, they simply happen. Hence, there is no sense of progression, no end to the monotonous flow of events, and thus no end point. If an important intellectual development of late nineteenth-century Egypt was the discovery of the future, these works were entirely indifferent to it.

66. Aḥmad Shafīq, *Ḥawliyāt Miṣr al-siyāsiyya* (Cairo: Maṭbaʿat shafīq bāshā, 1926), vol. 1, p. 6.

67. The following discussion draws on Hayden White, "The Value of Narrativity in the Representation of Reality," in White, ed., *The Content of the Form: Narrative Discourse and Historical Representation* (Baltimore: Johns Hopkins University Press, 1987), pp. 1–25.

Instead, Sāmī and Shafīq could issue only vague statements (a desire to "serve the beloved fatherland") that were not supported by the actual literary structure of the work.[68] These compositions were structurally unable to offer any interpretation of or assign modern meaning to the events they recorded. Clearly, they functioned outside the developing linguistic and political field and were in dissonance with the new spirit of national times and its historicized habits. Therefore, they carried little political value. In a rapidly moving national age of short economical statements, it was impossible to read a work of ten thousand pages and extract political capital from it.

The predicament of both authors was that as active politicians they were cognizant of the spirit of times but, naïvely, still thought that by paying historiographical tribute to the monarchy, they could actually change the cultural power balance in its favor.[69] In fact, already during the time of the books' preparation, well before 1919, the rules of public survival were clear: historicize or perish. Erecting literary monuments of this kind was no longer a guarantee for political survival. Indeed, in some respect, "it was a thankless job."[70] By the late 1930s, this form of being, along with an entire generation of works, was gone forever. The two remaining chronicles, but especially that of Amīn Sāmī, were the last ones to be crated, temporarily sealing this classic historiographical canon.

WRITING ARABIC IN FRENCH: MUḤAMMAD ṢABRĪ AND HIS/STORY

If by Zaydān's death a new generation opted for a different kind of history, Muḥammad Ṣabrī gave it to them. He gave it on time, and he gave it with passion. Born in 1894, Ṣabrī was the first historian to write full-fledged national history. By all means, Ṣabrī was a product of the rapid social and cultural dynamics of de-Ottomanization. Almost from childhood, he was drawn to Arab literature. At sixteen, he published his first book on contemporary Arabic poetry.[71] Not even a trace of Ottomanism was in his work. Ṣabrī himself knew no Turkish.[72] In 1915 he was already doing graduate work at a Ph.D. level in the Sorbonne. He soon came

68. For the quoted phrase, see Sāmī, *Taqwīm al-Nīl*, vol. 1, preface. See also Crabbs, *The Writing of History in Nineteenth-Century Egypt*, p. 120.

69. The last such attempt was Amīn Sāmī's *Miṣr wa-l-Nīl* (Cairo: Maṭbaʿat dār al-kutub al-miṣriyya, 1938).

70. Crabbs, *The Writing of History in Nineteenth-Century Egypt*, p. 125.

71. Aḥmad Ḥusayn al-Ṭamāwī, *Ṣabrī al-Surbūnī: Sīra tārīkhiyya wa ṣūrat ḥayā* (Cairo: Aʿlām al-ʿarab, 1986), pp. 21–44.

72. In the 1930s while working in the royal ʿĀbdīn archive he used the archive's translators. Ibid., pp. 84–85.

to be known as "al-Surbūnī."[73] In 1919, when the Egyptian Wafd arrived in Paris to present its postwar claims, Ṣabrī was employed as its secretary. He befriended Sa'd Zaghlūl, who almost immediately recognized Ṣabrī's literary potential and, later on, asked him to write a book on the 1919 Revolution and its historical background.[74] By all accounts, it seemed Ṣabrī was the right person for the job.

A very short while afterward, the first volume was out, properly prefaced "mon cher Sabry" by his adviser Alphonse Aulard.[75] To understand Ṣabrī's *La révolution égyptienne,* we need to get a taste of the republican intellectual environment that his adviser and his colleagues created. Aulard was famously known as the official republican historian of the French Revolution. As one contemporary historian observed, "It seems clear to Aulard that the natural and logical consequence of the principle of egalitarianism is democracy and that the idea of national sovereignty should find its implication in the form of a republic."[76] His entire corpus—several seminal studies of the political history of the French Revolution—was wrapped around this sort of understanding. To be sure, Aulard was a loyal disciple of the French academic tradition, in which historians were largely regarded as "molders of opinion who had been entrusted with the task of employing the lessons of history to restore a sense of national pride among the citizens of a recently humiliated fatherland in search of regeneration and revenge."[77] This is what the young Ṣabrī was exposed to while in Paris.

Ṣabrī's 1919 *La révolution égyptienne* was designed to celebrate the impending birth of the Egyptian republic after a long revolutionary process. In Ṣabrī's words: "One would not exaggerate if he said that the Egyptian revolution is the son of the French Revolution."[78] And in another place: "The Egyptian national hymn could certainly be called the 'Marseillaise' of an oppressed people."[79] Every place Ṣabrī turned his eyes, he saw only the dynamics of European revolutionism at play. Thus, he was the first Egyptian historian to consider popular struggle as a domain in which both sexes operate on an equal basis. He was especially impressed with the national role of the so-called liberated Egyptian women. Quite ironically, at one point he even cast the wife of the Wafd's vice-president,

73. Contrary to common knowledge, which credits Ṭaha Ḥusayn for being the first Egyptian to graduate from the Sorbonne with a literature degree, Ṣabrī pursued a higher degree in literature and was actually the first Egyptian to graduate from this program. Ibid., pp. 79, 83.

74. Ibid., pp. 55–60.

75. Mohamed Sabry, *La révolution égyptienne* (Paris: Librairie Vrin, 1919), vol. 1, p. 7.

76. James Godfrey, "Alphonse Aulard 1849–1928," in William Halperin, ed., *Essays in Modern European Historiography* (Chicago: University of Chicago Press, 1970), p. 33.

77. See William Keylor, *Academy and Community: The Foundation of the French Historical Profession* (Cambridge, MA: Harvard University Press, 1975), p. 3; see also pp. 36–54.

78. Sabry, *La révolution égyptienne,* vol. 1, p. 135.

79. Ibid., pp. 61–62.

ʿAlī Sharʿawī, as Delacroix's "Liberty Guiding the People."[80] In his other books, Ṣabrī brought into focus the history of the popular Egyptian struggle from 1798 to 1919.[81] Later developed by al-Rāfiʿī, Ṣabrī's perception enjoyed an especially enduring presence in Egyptian historiography.

Even though Ṣabrī began writing in French, the political implications of his work resonated in Arabic. Thus, he defined which sort of historical thinking was to be associated with the nation and, by implication, which type of politics was legitimized by it. In doing so he exposed and highlighted the contradiction between the idea of dynasty and that of nation. This led him to believe that the Egyptian monarchy had no place in the post-1919 order, as it did not initiate, nor did it participate in, the revolution. Finally, he argued, Fu'ād was not popular. When writing about the Egyptian monarchy, Ṣabrī had Louis XVI in mind. Almost a king, Prince Fu'ād knew a thing or two about history, and he was certainly unhappy with what he read. Almost instantly, Ṣabrī's books were boycotted in Egypt.[82]

Money for Nothing

In 1922, Ilyās al-Ayyūbī (1874–1927), a Palestinian-born historian, won a prize of three hundred Egyptian pounds. It was, all things considered, a decent sum of money, as an annual subscription for *Al-Hilāl* cost only 120 piasters, and the average price of a book was 10 piasters.[83] Al-Ayyūbi, then, could have purchased an entirely new library or perhaps relaxed a bit and taken a luxurious trip to his hometown, Acre. And relaxation he probably needed, for during the preceding five years, ever since Fu'ād had declared a public competition for the best book on the Ismāʿīl era, al-Ayyūbī had worked hard. In fact, he was seemingly so exhausted that when the king offered him an additional sum of money to translate his book into French (probably as a countermove to Ṣabrī), al-Ayyūbī politely declined, and the book was never translated.[84]

It was in 1917, then, that Fu'ād began coming to terms with the historiographical challenge with which the monarchy was confronted. Thus, dynastic history, which had functioned merely as a facet of royal dignity, was now seen as an essential element of political survival.[85] As we have seen, more than being a

80. Ibid., pp. 42–43, 65–66.

81. Mohamed Sabry, *La question d'Égypte depuis Bonaparte jusqu'à la révolution de 1919* (Paris: Association égyptienne de Paris, 1920); see also al-Ṭamāwī, *Ṣabrī al-Surbūnī sīra*, pp. 62–68.

82. al-Ṭamāwī, *Ṣabrī al-Surbūnī sīra*, pp. 58–59, 156.

83. I took these figures from the back cover of a later composition by Ilyās al-Ayyūbī. *Muḥammad ʿAlī* (Cairo: Dār al-hilāl, 1923).

84. Al-Ayūbbī was fluent in French. Ziriklī, *Al-Aʿlām*, vol. 2, p. 9.

85. For a classic example of this function, see ʿAzīz Zand, *Al-Qawl al-ḥaqīq fī rathā' wa tārīkh Muḥammad Tawfīq* (Cairo: Maṭbaʿat al-maḥrūsa, 1892).

matter of direct challenge in the form of history books, the nationalist struggle involved a new language that excluded and threatened the monarchy. In order to deal with it, al-Ayyūbī and other writers tried to appropriate the struggle by presenting the royal house as its ultimate historical agent. By embracing official nationalism, they strove to play down the differences between the dynastic and the national realms.

Prince ʿUmar Ṭūsūn, an amateur historian, was the most classic practitioner of this strategy. Well into the 1920s, he continued to claim the credit for the initial idea of the national delegation (the Wafd) to Versailles and the mobilization of the 1919 Revolution soon afterward.[86] Hardly anyone took his claims seriously. Thus, despite the keen efforts of al-Ayyūbī and others, it became increasingly apparent that while subscribing to the founder paradigm was a basic historiographical requirement, it did not automatically deliver political capital to the side of the monarchy.[87] Especially in the wake of the events of 1919, Fuʾād understood that a different kind of reaction was needed. The next two chapters are dedicated to this response.

Toward a Genre of History

Ṣabrī's distinction as a Sorbonne student who footnoted some of his work encouraged Crabbs to think that "his *La révolution égyptienne* marked the beginning of professional Egyptian historiography."[88] Thus, the Darwinist rationale of al-Shayyāl and Crabbs defined "professionalism" as the ultimate point of the new genre's maturity. Naturally, Ṣabrī's work is taken to embody the entire trajectory of modern historiography, from traditionalism to professionalism. Two major points challenge this view.

First, as mentioned before, the appearance of a literary genre demands a series of finely synchronized developments that take into consideration an extremely wide range of intellectual, social, cultural, and political variables. Hence, identifying a genre with one, or a few, pioneering works is entirely meaningless. For this modern genre to prevail, Egyptian culture needed to develop a critical mass of libraries, publishing houses, journals, archives, teaching institutions, conferences, professional communities, and funding opportunities. Only the successful synchronization of all of these elements, conducted mainly in Arabic, can serve

86. See a publication of monarchic declarations and statements on behalf of the national struggle starting a year before the 1919 Revolution: ʿUmar Ṭūsūn, *Kalimāt fī sabīl Miṣr* (Cairo: al-Maṭbaʿa al-salafiyya, 1928), especially part 1. For the alleged nationalist activity of Ṭūsūn, see Shafīq, *Aʿamālī baʿd mudhakkirātī*, p. 251; and Qalinī Fahmī, *Al-Amīr ʿUmar Ṭūsūn* (Cairo: Maṭbaʿat kusta tsumashī, 1944).

87. For a work besides al-Ayyūbī's, see ʿAbd al-Ḥalīm Ḥilmī, *Muḥammad ʿAlī al-kabīr munshiʾ Miṣr al-ḥadīth* (Cairo: Maṭbaʿat maṭar, 1919).

88. Crabbs, *The Writing of History in Nineteenth-Century Egypt*, p. 209.

as an indication of the maturity of modern history as a genre. Such an environment came into existence only toward the end of the 1920s.

Second, even if we accept Crabbs's point of departure and terms of discussion, Ṣabrī still cannot be seen as the originator of professional historiography. Though he certainly contributed to so-called professional writing, he did so only at a later stage, when there were already enough influential writers in a rather developed historiographical scene. Even then, however, he was never able to gain any influential position and was continually censored and repressed. These circumstances would eventually drive him to quit history writing altogether. As we shall see in chapter 5, the honor of initiating professional scholarship, and indeed of substantiating it in thought as well as in practice, goes to his long-time friend and colleague Muḥammad Shafīq Ghurbāl.[89]

CONCLUSION

Egypt's first mass experience of history was the 1919 Revolution. Like the historicized protagonists in Zaydān's novels, the thousands who participated in these revolutionary events must have had some historical understanding of what they were there for. Thus, the 1919 Revolution was a series of events that, at least in the urban centers, were grasped in nationalist historical terms as they unfolded. For the first time, historically driven ideologies were tailored to mass-scale action. Thus, the historicization of the Ottoman-Egyptian worldview was largely completed; the irrevocable link among the nation, modernity, and history was firmly secured; and, eventually, the historicist divide was put in place. Furthermore, history, as analyzed here, became a privileged mode for experiencing all forms of culture, starting with literature, mythology, art, and rituals and ending with poetry.

However, historicism brought with it the uneasy question of continuity. Although the great classic historiographer Arnaldo Momigliano could attempt to trace the origins of modern Western historiography back to classical times and argue for organic continuity, modern Arab historiography, that of Egypt included, could not have done the same with regard to the Islamic, Pharaonic, or any other dimension of its past.[90] Consequently and quite paradoxically, a central

89. Youssef Choueiri also argues against Crabbs's judgment. Choueiri, *Arab History and the Nation-State*, p. 65.

90. Since Western historians such as Oswald Spengler and Arnold Toynbee subscribed to the cyclical understanding of human dynamics, Ibn Khaldūn is perhaps the only example of an Islamic historian whose methodology had any practical relevancy. For Momigliano's enterprise, see David Konstan, "The Classical Foundations of Modern Historiography," *History and Theory* 31, no. 2 (1992): pp. 224–230.

function of modern historiography was to sever this link philosophically and start anew rather than strengthening its ties with the past. From a cultural point of view, denying the philosophical relevancy of Islamic thought during a period of profound transformation in all spheres of life was especially disorienting. Indeed, Egyptian intellectuals invested much energy over the years in elaborating on the idea of continuity *(istimrāriyya)* in an attempt to illustrate a meaningful organic relation to the past (though this pursuit falls outside the scope of this work).[91]

So far we have focused on the people and dynamics through which modern historiography rose to epistemological prominence. For the remainder of the book, the discussion and analysis will focus on modern history books. As we proceed, however, we need to lower the level of abstraction and explore in far greater detail the precise operating mechanisms in history writing and the forms of historical reasoning they employed.

91. For the project of Jamāl Ḥamdān, see Samah Selim, "The New Pharaonism: Nationalist Thought and the Egyptian Village Novel, 1967–1977," *Arab Studies Journal* 8, no. 2 (Fall 2000): pp. 10–24.

3

The ʿĀbdīn House of Records

The 1920s

An anecdote expresses the founding myth of ʿĀbdīn, the powerful archive that shaped Egypt's historiographical horizons for generations to come:

> There is a story told in Egypt concerning a visit by king Fuad to the citadel, where the early records of his dynasty had been thrown underfoot. Upon seeing these papers scattered about and covered with dust, one of the men in the King's party exclaimed: "Your highness, is it not unfitting that we should be treading on the records that deal with reigns of your illustrious ancestors?" According to the story, the King then ordered that all records bearing on the history of the ruling dynasty should at once be moved to ʿĀbdīn Palace and safeguarded there.[1]

Despite such anecdotes, the actual circumstances behind the establishment of the ʿĀbdīn archive and the true nature and scope of the project were more complex. For in reality, the ʿĀbdīn archive played two complementary and, for its time, unusual roles: First, its creation represented a pioneering attempt to establish a modern research archive in Egypt; and second, it simultaneously functioned as a state-governed royal workshop for politicized writing. Initially established in order to cope with the post-1919 national tide, ʿĀbdīn became the headquarters of royal historiography for the next thirty years. This chapter will pay close attention to the archive as the linchpin of the royal historiographical effort.

In recent years, there has been a growing interest in the process through which history is produced, disseminated, and "consumed." French scholars have led this

1. Helen Rivlin, *The Dār al-wathāʾiq in ʿĀbdīn Palace at Cairo as a Source for the Study of the Modernization of Egypt in the Nineteenth Century* (Leiden, the Netherlands: E. J. Brill, 1970), p. 1.

movement. Their underlying assumption is that "all historiographical research is articulated over a socioeconomic, political, and cultural place of production."[2] The story of the archive at ʿĀbdīn represents one such place, which is highly relevant to the broader concerns of Egyptian historiography.

As a well-coordinated and informed initiative, ʿĀbdīn was nourished by the pre-1952 concoction of political interests, colonial knowledge, and the middle-class aspiration to modernize. Concurrently, the heart of the royal historiographical effort was to explain the modern Egyptian experience as part of a story of modernization and transition whose center was the dynasty itself. Each file in ʿĀbdīn was consciously constructed to support this particular founder thesis. In that sense, ʿĀbdīn was a classic *nahḍawī* project built around a certain interpretation of the modern nation.

Since ʿĀbdīn functioned as both an archive and a workshop, its history brings important questions to the fore: What was the scope and long-term influence of this project? In what ways were its aims achieved? Precisely what kind of history could be imagined there? And, finally, what role did foreigners play in all of this? In answering these questions, I will clarify the main argument of this research: ʿĀbdīn was carefully designed to forge a rather limited sense of historical meaning. In doing so, it dictated what would be historically thinkable. This effort was intentional, and it utilized a wide range of techniques, methods, tactics, and strategies, beginning with the selection of what source material would be classified and displayed and ending with the claim of the archive's scientific value and objectivity. By the late 1920s the royal project was already developed enough to impose a veil of silence over several competing versions of the past and their historical actors, who were incompatible with the project's specific, though as yet undeclared, mission.

FORGING THE ARCHIVE

Anarchy in the Records?

In late 1919, just when King Fu'ād began to evince interest in the historiographical potential of archives, historical records could be found almost everywhere around center-city Cairo. The Sharīʿa Courts held a huge collection of registries *(sijillāt)* belonging to at least fifteen different courthouses from all over Egypt and covering a period stretching from the sixteenth to the nineteenth century.[3] The

2. Michel de Certeau, *The Writing of History* (New York: Columbia University Press, 1988), p. 48. See also Paul Ricoeur, *La mémoire, l'histoire, l'oubli* (Paris: Éditions du Seuil, 2000), especially pp. 209–230; and Michael Rolph Trouillot, *Silencing the Past: Power and the Production of History* (Boston: Beacon Press, 1995).

3. Muḥammad Aḥmad Ḥusayn, *Al-Wathā'iq al-tārīkhiyya* (Cairo: Jāmiʿat al-Qāhira, 1954), pp. 88–89.

various archives of the Ministry of Awqāf possessed *waqfiyyas* from the past six centuries, which contained exhaustive and precious information ranging from family and personal status to household economy, finance, and land ownership.[4] The Mixed Courts held their own collection; both the Royal Geographical Society (hereafter RGS) and Qaṣr al-ʿAynī hospital had libraries with rare documents. Valuable sources could also be retrieved from the records and library of al-Azhar University. In addition, several other vast private libraries and collections, such as that of the bibliophile Aḥmad Taymūr, possessed rare state documents.[5] Another important archive was the original ʿĀbdīn Palace collection, which stored various documents pertaining to the rulers of the house, stretching back to the 1870s. To be sure, however, the Daftarkhāne (established in 1829) was Egypt's largest and most centralized reservoir of state documents. Situated at the back of Cairo's citadel, the Daftarkhāne contained the bulk of nineteenth-century Ottoman documents and much more.

Despite the Daftarkhāne's size and significance, its popular reputation was of a constantly chaotic and disorganized place.[6] Its gloomy image was brilliantly captured by Muḥammad al-Muwayliḥī in his comic and acerbic *maqama*-structured tale *Ḥadīth ʿĪsā ibn Hishām*. In a chapter titled "The Record Office" and situated in the Daftarkhāne itself, the author recounts the adventures of his protagonist, ʿĪsā, in search of an endowment document he needed to present in court. Accompanied by his lawyer's assistant, ʿĪsā is searching for the record clerk to assist them:

> After a while we got hold of him [the record clerk], but realized that the wretch was dragging his feet so that we would try to ingratiate ourselves by offering him money. "I'll tell you the truth," he said, "and nothing but the truth. Knowing only the date and name of its owner, we cannot possibly expect to find the text of the endowment in this case. We also need to know the name of the scribe and secretary who wrote it out. One just cannot envisage the Record Clerk coming across it amongst all these piles of paper. He would need to be inspired."[7]

4. These documents were placed in three sites: a special branch of the Daftarkhāne located in the basement of the ministry, another one situated in al-Rifāʿī mosque, and several smaller collections found in the *maḥkama al-sharʿiyya*. Daniel Crecelius, "The Organization of *Waqf* Documents in Cairo," *IJMES* 2, no. 3 (1971): pp. 266–277.

5. The Taymūr family was famous for its library, which included original documents belonging to Muḥammad ʿAlī. Jean Deny, *Sommaire des archives turques du Caire* (Cairo: Société royale de géographie d'Égypte, publications spéciales, 1930), pp. 221–222; *Dhikra Aḥmad Taymūr bāsha*, edited anonymously (Cairo: Maṭbaʿat al-Nīl, 1945), pp. 8–9, 21–27, 40–41, 54–56.

6. Deny, *Sommaire des archives turques du Caire*, p. 170.

7. Roger Allen, *A Period of Time: A Study and Translation of Ḥadith ʿĪsā ibn Hishām by Muḥammad al-Muwayliḥī* (Oxford: Middle East Centre, St. Anthony's College, Oxford, by Ithaca Press, 1992), p. 182.

Then the record clerk invites ʿĪsā to tour the archive as a way of illustrating to him the impossibility of such an undertaking:

> When we passed through the doorway where all the clerks were sitting, we found piles of timber propped up against other blocks of strong wood. . . . It was so dark in this gloomy place that you could not distinguish one man from another. . . . We made our way through this cellar until I imagined that I was either in the midst of the graves of ancient Egyptians, in the sacramental temples at some Roman devotions, or else in the course of examination among freemasons. My heart leaped. I was panic-stricken and was scared that a trap had been set or some sort of trick arranged. . . . "What is it that you want from me by bringing me into this gloom? I have no silver or gold, nor anything that you can grab from me?" . . . [The guard] then proceeded to swear by God and repeat the divorce formula twice, all in order to assure me that we were perfectly safe while walking among the sacks of ledgers and bundles of scrolls. . . . The wretch had barely finished explaining things to me when I tripped over a package and fell over onto pile of scrolls. All of a sudden, someone started shouting from underneath them. "What's the matter with you, you blind idiot?" . . . "Who's this man?" I asked. "Just one of the Records Clerks," the assistant replied, "unearthing his scrolls in the records of the title deeds." "But how can he find such things in this darkness?" I asked. "These are people," he replied, "who are used to working without any light, like bats they can see in complete darkness." (182–184)

They continue to wander in darkness until ʿĪsā finally gives up:

> "Come on, you fraud, take us back to the door so we can return to light of day. I've despaired achieving anything here. How can this clerk conduct a search in such a huge abyss in pitch darkness?"
>
> *Lawyer's assistant:* "Don't assume that people like him cannot find things in total darkness! Don't be put off by the scattered ledgers and piles of scrolls. They're all arranged and stamped in his memory as an inheritance from his father and grandfather. . . ."
>
> *Clerk:* "God bless you . . . God knows that this Record Office has been imprinted on my mind from earliest childhood according to the very best methods of arrangement and description." (184–185)

The clerk embarks on an endless recitation of records and documents to be found in the archive, ranging from royal Ottoman decrees to military and land confiscation records, until ʿĪsā and the assistant decide to leave the building and let the clerk complete the task all by himself. "Days and months went by. . . . At last one day the Assistant brought us the news that the text of the endowment had been found" (188).

Amusing as this passage may be, the Daftarkhāne, as we shall now see, was not as chaotic a place as al-Muwayliḥī and especially King Fuʾād would have had us believe. The latter, in particular, as the opening anecdote to this chapter suggests, had an obvious interest in exaggerating the poor state of the Daftarkhāne and thus creating the founding myth of his "organized" ʿĀbdīn archive. But in order to understand properly what the vantage point was for the royal archival project, a few words are in order about the history of the Daftarkhāne, an institution that was established in 1828 and whose name was Arabized to Dār al-maḥfūẓāt al-Miṣriyya in 1905 but was commonly referred to as the "documents in the citadel."[8]

Quite surprisingly, very little is known about the Daftarkhāne's history and close to nothing about the exact methods in which records were deposited, distributed, classified, and cataloged. The fact of the matter is that until now no serious attempt has been made to tackle this missing information. Some students of modern Egyptian archival science, whose well-developed insights have languished at the academic level, unable to gain substantial foothold in actual practice, have gone as far as arguing that from the time of the Daftarkhāne's establishment until the death of the royal librarian in 1925, no major changes occurred in its method of organization.[9]

Originally, the Daftarkhāne was established and operated by clerks of the treasury. The organization of the large body of documents was a specialty of treasury officials, whose proficiency was an important asset to the state. The more skillful these clerks were, the more revenues the state could farm. Indeed, the Daftarkhāne was mostly needed in order to enhance Muḥammad ʿAlī's control over the country's resources.[10] It was not merely a depot for documents, as one might think, but an institution that operated according to an articulated protocol that stipulated its functions and defined its authority. Unfortunately, the original protocol was lost, and its contents are largely unknown. From its description in *Al-waqāʾiʿ al-miṣriyya* (the official journal, still in circulation since 1828), scholars salvaged some of the original material and were thus able to reconstruct the guidelines and working regulations of the Daftarkhāne: First, official state documents were defined as state property, and officials were required to return them on leaving office. Second, all provinces were required to submit their records to Cairo. In case provincial officials failed to notice the significance of this odd policy, one hundred whips were prescribed to the person in charge.

8. The common view is that the Daftarkhāne was established eight years after the 1820 fire that consumed all existing records. Deny, *Sommaire des archives turques du Caire*, pp. 15–16. However, in 1938, Muḥammad Tawfīq, an enthusiastic student of history and an archivist, located many of the presumably lost documents. Thus, we do not know for sure what precisely was lost in the 1820 fire. Muḥammad Muḥammad Tawfīq, "Al-Ḥalqa al-mafqūda," *Al-Hilāl*, May–June 1941, pp. 588–590.

9. Maḥmūd ʿAbbās Ḥamūda, *Al-madkhal ila dirāsat al-wathāʾīq al-ʿarabiyya* (Cairo: Maktabat nahḍat al-sharq, 1995), pp. 48–49.

10. Jean Deny argues that Muḥammad ʿAlī's excessive centralization is also reflected in the organization of the records. Deny, *Sommaire des archives turques du Caire*, pp. 33–34.

Third, the various government branches could keep their records for a period that would not exceed two years.[11] Despite gaps in our knowledge, it is clear that the Daftarkhāne's prime goal was to function as a modern administrative tool that facilitated swift and easy access to records. [12]

By the 1840s all provincial officials had complied with the new regulations, so that piles of records overwhelmed Daftarkhāne employees. This reality prompted them to rethink their guiding rationale and methods of work. Soon enough, a certain Monsieur Rousse was summoned to consult Egyptian officials on how to manage their inventory. Whoever this consultant was, he drew heavily on the newly developed French methods of archival organization. In postrevolutionary France, archival science rapidly developed, and some of today's bedrock archival principles were established in this very period. The French consultant introduced the practice of selectivity by keeping only valuable records.[13] What were the standards by which clerks could determine the value of a document? Unfortunately, we do not know.

In any event, at Rousse's advice, a new protocol was written in 1846 in accordance with the need to improve record selectivity. The new protocol specified which documents should be kept in the provinces and for how long. It also stipulated regulations according to which documents should be handled and submitted before being deposited in Cairo.[14] All administrative branches submitted an annual report, specifying which records had been submitted for storage. In addition, new standards stipulated which documents had no value and, hence, should be destroyed. On their inspection, useless documents in reasonable physical condition were sent to the paper mill *(kāghid-khāne)* for recycling.[15]

Several organizational developments took place in subsequent years. In 1848 the Daftarkhāne was divided into several sections, each dealing with a separate *diwān*. This change in organization gave administrative meaning to the new European tendency to classify documents according to their origin/source. In 1863 the Daftarkhāne's structure was further developed in order to reflect the changes in the country's administration.[16]

11. Nāhid Ḥamadī Aḥmad, *Al-Muqtanayāt al-arshīfiyya, takwīnihā wa tanmiyatuhā* (Cairo: Dār al-kutub al-miṣriyya, 1996), pp. 67–69.

12. Ibid.; Mūṣṭafa Abū Shuʿaysha', *Dirāsāt fī-l-wathā'iq wa marākiz al-maʿlūmāt al-wathā'iqiyya* (Cairo: al-ʿArabī, 1994), pp. 49–50.

13. Ibid., pp. 52–53; Aḥmad, *Al-Muqtanayāt al-arshīfiyya*, pp. 67–71.

14. Agencies depositing documents in the Daftarkhāne had to mark each deposit clearly with the name of the record group (corresponding to the *daftar*) and the number of documents in each record group. Abū Shuʿaysha', *Dirāsāt fī-l-wathā'iq*, pp. 52–54.

15. The paper factories were established by Ismāʿīl. Cole, *Colonialism and Revolution*, p. 29; Aḥmad, *Al-Muqtanayāt al-arshīfiyya*, pp. 69–71.

16. Ḥusayn, *Al-Wathā'iq al-tārīkhiyya*, p. 75.

In 1865 Khedive Ismāʿīl decommissioned the provincial archives after an act of forgery and embezzlement had occurred. This event reinforced the need to tightly control state records because they contained sensitive information. Ismāʿīl's new policy resulted in greater centralization of all records in Cairo.[17] When the khedive moved from the citadel to live in the more luxurious and newly established ʿĀbdīn Palace, an additional depository was established there. The new ʿĀbdīn archive and the old Daftarkhāne coexisted. Since the original ʿĀbdīn archive contained the records of the palace's daily activity, it would later become the basis for the establishment of Fu'ād's modern research archive. In addition, ʿĀbdīn annexed several other collections, such as the correspondence between Muḥammad ʿAlī and Ibrāhīm during and after the latter's campaign in Syria (1831–48), several dozen Ottoman decrees, and some documents from the formative era of Muḥammad ʿAlī's rule (1807–13).[18]

The next significant administrative act of archive organization occurred during the 1890s. Following the British occupation, the new state bureaucracy produced records that were not under the control of the as yet unestablished monarchy. These were deposited in the Daftarkhāne along with other royal documents. In 1895, as part of the British attempt to improve government access to documents, a new protocol regularized the classification of these records according to four different categories: the archive level *(maḥfūẓāt),* chapters *(faṣl),* subchapters *(qism),* and a special group for correspondence *(taḥrīrāt).*[19] Although this classification method shows growing sophistication in inventory management, we can assume that this British intervention had its own biases. Unfortunately, almost no sources remain concerning this chapter in the history of the archive. In any event, we can clearly determine that the new protocol redefined the archive's organization according to which criteria records were to be kept or dispersed. Once again, unimportant records were not kept. This time, however, they were sold to paper merchants as scrap paper.[20]

Though their parameters are as yet unclear, several changes occurred also at the beginning of the twentieth century. One of these changes, of which close to nothing is known, specified which documents would be open to the public.[21] With the establishment of the parliamentary system, the monarchy was no longer legally and administratively responsible for Dār al-maḥfūẓāt. In 1920, the institution was directed by a certain Muḥsayn Fawzī, who supervised a team of 104

17. The work of the provincial archives was resumed only in 1895. Aḥmad, *Al-Muqtanayāt al-arshīfiyya,* pp. 69–71; Abū Shuʿaysha', *Dirāsāt fī-l-wathā'iq,* p. 55.

18. Deny, *Sommaire des archives turques du Caire,* pp. 10–11, 14–15.

19. According to Deny the reorganization took place in 1890; ibid., pp. 30–31.

20. Abū Shuʿayshaʿ, *Dirāsāt fī-l-wathā'iq,* pp. 55–56.

21. Aḥmad, *Al-Muqtanayāt al-arshīfiyya,* p. 71.

employees.[22] At least theoretically and with the exception of the Ministry of Foreign Affairs, all government ministries were commanded to hand in their documents to Dār al-maḥfūẓāt.[23] Whether this procedure was enforced at all, though, is uncertain.

Who used Dār al-maḥfūẓāt and why? By and large, this institution was used for what it literally means: a place in which documents/registers are stored. It was not a place where scholars came to work. It was simply a warehouse that needed to be reasonably organized so that important documents could be retrieved on demand for official use (mainly in legal and fiscal cases). More than anything else it was a tool of administration, an executive branch, helping to enhance government control. Scholars, inasmuch as they needed a place to work, went to a library; quite often the royal one.

During the 1890s several attempts to retrieve information from Dār al-maḥfūẓāt were recorded. Some of these efforts were administrative in nature, while others were more scholarly.[24] Thus, in 1893, Edward Cecil, a financial adviser, browsed the Daftarkhāne in search of financial information from Saʿīd's reign, regarding the Suez Canal. In 1897 the first scholarly usage of this institution occurred when Agop Faraḥyān, a clerk in the treasury, collected and translated, but never published, some of Muḥammad ʿAlī's correspondence. On the basis of his work, in 1913 Talamas Bey finally prepared a compilation titled *Recueil de la correspondance de Mohamed Aly, Khédive d'Égypte, 1807–1848*. But again, for some unknown reason, its publication was not permitted at the last minute, and only a few copies have survived.[25] All in all, up until 1920 no institution offered scholars the possibility of access to a cataloged collection of historical records. To the best of my knowledge, with the exception of the works of Muḥammad Shafīq, Amīn Sāmī, and, to a lesser extent, Aḥmad Fatḥī Zaghlūl, no history book was written using such records. As we have already seen, these court officials were able to write historical accounts simply because they enjoyed unrestricted access to state records.

22. Muḥsayn Fawzī supervised six officials, each responsible for a different section: Three were geographically divided (into Upper, Middle, and Lower Egypt); a fourth was a state-administrative section; the fifth was dedicated to accountancy; and the last was a processing section for the reception, distribution, and classification of documents. Deny, *Sommaire des archives turques du Caire*, pp. 29–30.

23. Ibid., p. 30.

24. In 1825, Muḥammad ʿAlī's secretary made the earliest attempt to publish official state documents. Hayret Darendevî, *Insa-yi Hayret Efendi* (Cairo: Maṭbaʿat būlāq, 1826). The book is also known as *Insha-i Hayret Efendi: Riyaz-i Küteba ve hiyaz-i üdeba*.

25. Stanford Shaw, "Turkish Source Material for Egyptian History," in Holt, ed., *Political and Social Change in Modern Egypt*, pp. 41–42; Ḥussayn, *Al-Wathāʾiq al-tārīkhiyya*, p. 91; Deny, *Sommaire des archives turques du Caire*, pp. 6–8.

This brief account raises two interesting points. First, despite its popular image, the Daftarkhāne/Dār al-maḥfūẓāt was not an anarchic institution. It did follow a certain line of reasoning, even if this reasoning was essentially different from that which informed the European-modeled archive that Fu'ād aspired to build. For all its worth, the Daftarkhāne, at least until the end of Ismāʿīl's reign, served its creators quite efficiently in their attempts to build a centralized household regime with a modern bureaucracy. Thus, it should have been properly organized for the retrieval of financial information as well as for the discovery of when and who issued new laws and regulations. Other functions were to enable the location of title deeds and criminal records. Therefore, the habit of document shredding and selling, which is usually mentioned as the ultimate proof of institutional chaos, was quite the opposite of anarchic conduct and instead represented a carefully chosen and administered procedure.[26] Even if historical value (as defined by modern historians) was patently not a main criterion for the preservation of documents, it nevertheless is far from being an indication of anarchy. This, of course, is not meant to imply that by the 1920s one could find only well-preserved and organized records in Dār al-Maḥfūẓāt. However, the few sources and studies that we do have cast serious doubts on the popular image of a chaotic archive. This perception, then, should be treated with much suspicion.

Second, and no less important, is the original order in which documents were stored and arranged at their creation. The various protocols suggest that all documents were ordered in relation to both their source (i.e., the government branch that created them) and associated documents. That is to say, regardless of the physical conditions under which documents were stored (for example, how much light or mold there might have been in the Daftarkhāne), when they were first deposited they were arranged in a certain organic order.[27] Though it is plausible that during the course of time some records were separated from others originating from the same source, in most cases original series of documents remained intact.[28] I emphasize this point, since preserving the original context has tremendous historiographical implications, as we shall shortly see. It is precisely this particular order, burned into the mind of al-Muwayliḥī's record clerk, that finally enabled him to hand ʿĪsā his endowment record. This was the archival reality that royal employees found in 1920, at the beginning of their project. In

26. For a mention of institutional chaos, see Deny, *Sommaire des archives turques du Caire,* pp. 31–32.

27. This information was also confirmed by Deny. Ibid., pp. 12, 187.

28. According to Deny, the original order of the *rūzname* (the executive department of the [old] Ottoman treasury) series was disrupted, and parts of it were lost in a fire. The condition of the *rūzname* series was used in order to make the point of chaos. However, in 1941 lost registers of the *rūzname* series were found. Ibid., p. 190; Tawfīq, "Al-Ḥalqa al-mafqūda," pp. 585–594.

order to complete this picture, however, a brief discussion of several common archival practices and their historiographical implications is needed.

A Note on Archival Principles of Arrangement

"Archives are already arranged—supposedly. That is to say, an arrangement was given them by the agency of origin while it built them up day after day, year after year, as a systematic record of its activities and as part of its operations."[29] The discussion in the previous section substantiates the premise that Egyptian records followed a certain organic order. Naturally, all classification or arrangement of records involves a breakdown of a whole into its parts. Thus, whatever action royal employees took while building the ʿĀbdīn archive, it undoubtedly involved a breakdown of the original body of records in order to bring it into harmony with a certain interpretation or philosophy of arrangement. The questions then become, What was the royal philosophy of arrangement? And what were the historiographical consequences of the chosen method?

Since the mid-ninetieth century, Western archives have unanimously accepted two bedrock principles for the arrangement of historical records: *respect des fonds* (the principle of provenance) and *respect pour l'ordre primitif* (the maintenance of original order). The French names of these principles explain their origins. In the wake of the French Revolution, France spearheaded several developments in archival administration, including a conceptualization of the public status of documents and the state's responsibilities both to guard the nation's heritage and, most important, to make that heritage widely accessible.[30] In addition, with the rise of history as an independent profession in its own right, "[European] archives became preponderantly scientific institutions and lost some of their character as a government office."[31] As more archives and records were now open to public scrutiny, with more historians than ever before making use of them, archives were forced to develop, and a core of archival technique and theory was established. Soon enough, *respect des fonds* and *respect pour l'ordre primitif* were overwhelmingly accepted as the foundational principles of the emerging archival profession (as distinguished from librarianship).

29. Oliver Holmes, "Archival Arrangement—Five Different Operations as Five Different Levels," in Maygene Daniels and Timothy Walach, eds., *A Modern Archives Reader: Basic Readings on Archival Theory and Practice* (Washington DC: National Archives and Records Services, 1984), p. 162.

30. For a comprehensive study of developments in France, see Lara Moore, "Restoring Order: The *École des Chartes* and the Organization of Archives and Libraries in France 1820–1870," unpublished Ph.D. dissertation, Stanford University, 2001; Ernest Posner, "Some Aspects of Archival Development since the French Revolution," in Daniels and Walach, eds., *A Modern Archives Reader*, pp. 5–6.

31. Posner, "Some Aspects of Archival Development since the French Revolution," p. 9.

What are these principles, and why are they so important? "Reliance on provenance *(respect des fonds)* assumes that records result from organized purposeful activity and that they were created organically and have a relationship to one another. It assumes that important information can be derived from examining the records in the context of their creation and their relationship. It keeps related groups of records intact, enabling a review of them in their totality."[32] Hence, the *quality* of historical evidence is dependent on these principles of organization. Evidently, the only way to ensure this unique quality is to order documents in relation to their source, that is, the institution/body that created them.[33]

The second principle, *respect pour l'ordre primitif,* is basically an elaboration of the first one. In addition to considering their origin, it touches on the general order of records and holds that records should be kept in the order in which they were first created or that which was imposed on them by the person, organization, or institution that created them. It posits that all individual records are part of a larger series.

> Since series generally reflect action they should be preserved intact as a record of action. They should not be torn apart to create new series. While the arrangement of the particular record item within a series may not significantly reflect action, the series as a whole does. Each record item in it is thus a part of an organic whole. To separate it from the series in which it is embodied will impair its meaning, for the series as a whole has a meaning greater than its part, that is, than the individual record item.[34]

Presumably, the original order illustrates a certain administrative process. "Individual documents achieve *status* only through linkage to the entity which created them as records. . . . If the link is broken the value and reliability of the record are diminished."[35] Undoubtedly, this is the only order that might allow historians to retrieve the original context of an action. If documents were to be reorganized according to author, date of creation, or subject headings, the original context would be lost.

Thus, to return to our discussion, archives that correspond with these two principles will facilitate the appreciation of a document in the most inclusive way, enabling a researcher to "know exactly where it was created, in the framework of what process, to what end, for whom, when and how it came to [the archivists']

32. Bruce Dearstyne, *The Archival Enterprise: Modern Archival Principles, Practices, and Management Techniques* (Chicago: American Library Association, 1993), p. 130.

33. Theodore Schellenberg, "Archival Principles of Arrangement," in Daniels and Walach, eds., *A Modern Archives Reader,* p. 150.

34. Ibid., p. 154.

35. Dearstyne, *The Archival Enterprise,* p. 130.

hands."[36] Close scrutiny of the degree to which these principles were applied in ʿĀbdīn will reveal acts of intentional and manipulative intervention and will assist us in uncovering the royal historiographical agenda and the way in which it was imprinted into the archive's structure. Thus, *respect pour l'ordre primitif* and *respect des fonds* will serve here as an analytical framework for historiographical investigation. What allows us to employ this framework is the very fact that these principles were already well known to those who were in charge of the ʿĀbdīn project.[37]

Eugenio Griffini and the Beginning of the Royal Project

It is difficult to know exactly what kind of library Fu'ād envisioned in ʿĀbdīn Palace when, in 1920, he appointed the autodidact Italian philologist and manuscript hunter Eugenio Griffini (1878–1925) to the position of royal librarian. Griffini was not a newcomer to Egypt. Already in 1910, Fu'ād, then a prince, had invited him to teach in the embryonic Egyptian University.[38] At the time, Griffini could not accept the offer, but the prospects for future cooperation remained open. Unlike other Orientalists, Griffini had much experience in surveying Ottoman archives. His work in the colonial administration of Libya and other scholarly experience in Yemen, Algeria, and Tunisia had trained him to work with Ottoman documents.[39] However, despite his prodigious linguistic capabilities, he lacked any apparent training as a librarian, let alone as an archivist. Though he had experience in preparing catalogs and registering all "unknown/lost" manuscripts, these were essentiality a librarian's work.[40] It is one thing to list and translate a document but a totally different thing to catalog and index entire collections properly. Hardly anyone in Griffini's Orientalist milieu was trained as an archivist. However, given the magnitude of the documents that were stored in ʿĀbdīn and especially in Dār al-maḥfūẓāt, Griffini was certainly viewed as the right person to deal with the task. According to his cousin and to Italian official correspondence, he accepted the position not only because of its prestige but also because he hoped that Italians could reclaim their cultural influence, overwhelmed by that of the Greeks, French, and British. Tacitly, this aspect of colonial competition would have a significant impact on the entire project and is precisely what prompted the Italian Ministry of Foreign Affairs to become intimately

36. Michel Duchein, "Theoretical Principles and Practical Problems of *Respect de Fonds* in Archival Science," *Archivaria* 16 (Summer 1983): p. 64.

37. Deny directly referred to these principles in his published manual. Deny, *Sommaire des archives turques du Caire*, pp. 14–33, 190.

38. Luca Beltrami, *Eugenio Griffini Bey 1878–1925* (Milan: Allegretti, 1926), pp. lxi–lxii.

39. Ibid., pp. li–lii.

40. Ibid., pp. xxviii–xxvix.

involved in Griffini's mission.[41] Apparently, Griffini was also fully aware that he was taking part in a well-orchestrated project, bordering on propaganda.[42]

Shortly after his arrival in Cairo, a new era of extensive archival intervention is said to have begun. Griffini is mostly identified with the first phase of the project, when the vision of a library was gradually transformed into that of an archive. Most probably in the early months of 1923, Fu'ād made an important decision to launch the historiographical project on a scale that was far beyond that of a simple library. It is important to note, however, that the distinction between these two types of institution became clear only as the project unfolded.[43] The modern concept of an archive and the function of an archivist were still foreign in Egypt. In contrast, that of the librarian seems to have been quite familiar, yet it was equally vague. Hence, a shift from a library to an archive was in fact a process in which the modern institution of an archive was borrowed and put to work.

Unfortunately, aside from several journalistic articles about historical subjects, Griffini did not write anything while in Cairo. He left no records describing his work, let alone a comprehensive manual articulating his professional agenda.[44] Hence, the precise mechanisms through which the royal library turned into an archive will remain unknown to us. The little we do know about Griffini's work in ʿĀbdīn comes from his cousin's commemorative account, from the Italian Central State Archives, and especially from his successor, Jean Deny.

According to Deny the only work carried out by Griffini on original source material was limited to records that were already part of the collection in ʿĀbdīn. Thus, Griffini most likely visited Dār al-maḥfūẓāt but never translated or cataloged its records. Likewise, he almost certainly did not transfer any records to ʿĀbdīn. He started working on Muḥammad ʿAlī's documents from the years 1807–13. His job was translation. Since the documents were in Ottoman, a language that had been brushed aside as the residue of a decadent world, hardly any scholar, local or foreign, could read it. Arabic and French, in contrast, were languages that enabled a greater number of writers to engage with this kind of material. Hence, the records were translated into those two languages. In that

41. ASMAE/ISAP 1919–30, Pacco 1001, May 23, 1923.

42. Beltrami, *Eugenio Griffini Bey,* pp. lxiv, lxvil.

43. A letter to the Italian minister of foreign affairs, dated May 23, 1923, stated that Fu'ād desired to prolong Griffini's mission for future extensive projects such as the collection and publication of European documents pertaining to the history of the monarchy. ASMAE/ISAP 1919–30, Pacco 1001.

44. Several of Eugenio Griffini's journalistic articles were: "Man huwa al-ṭabīb Abū Qasīs?" *Al-Ahrām,* December 12, 1923; and "Fī Sabīl al-ḥaqq wa-l-tārīkh: Al-ḥaqīqa fī ḥarīq maktabat al-Iskanderiyya," *Al-Ahrām,* January 21, 1924; as quoted in the bibliography of Beltrami, *Eugenio Griffini Bey.*

way, scholars who were admitted to the archive did not have to bother with the original source material, which in any case was difficult to decipher. This is how the era of archival mediation started. By 1925 this collection was already fully translated, and parts of it were easily published.[45]

Deny found the system of linguistic mediation acceptable, and, indeed, in the following years it was widely adopted. However, when he scrutinized Griffini's translations, he noted that they were inaccurate. Under Griffini's directorship, translations had been made first into Arabic and then into French. As a result the French translations were grossly dissimilar to the Ottoman originals. Apparently, royal officials were cognizant of the problem but could not find anyone who could adequately translate from Ottoman directly into French.[46] In 1924 Griffini himself admitted having difficulties in making the translations.[47] This problem was not solved, and in the future, translation from Ottoman into French was made only on special request.

Another archival activity that seems to have started under Griffini was the building of a collection of foreign documents relating to the dynasty's history. If done properly, such an undertaking involves a tremendous amount of work. In fact, it is difficult to imagine how Griffini could possibly have supervised both the work on the Ottoman records and the creation of a foreign collection. Already in late 1920, Griffini was sent on the first knowledge-gathering expedition to Europe's most important archives. His task was to locate, request official copies, and translate all relevant documents dealing with nineteenth-century Egypt, and especially those associated with the reigns of Muḥammad ʿAlī and Ismāʿīl. Reading descriptions of the work he carried out in the archives of Turin, Naples, Venice, Livorno, Trieste, and Vienna, one gets the impression that more than anything else Griffini was interested in his own hobby—searching for "lost" manuscripts that had little to do with the job for which he was hired.[48] It was while working in Europe that Griffini was undoubtedly faced with the overwhelming nature of his task. Thus, his mission ended up being mainly one of reconnaissance and evaluation. As we shall shortly see, following Griffini's preliminary findings, a score of European scholars were sent to conclude the project and publish their findings.

In accordance with the needs of royal historiography dictated by Fu'ād, Griffini defined the periodization of the project as stretching from 1798/1805

45. Deny, *Sommaire des archives turques du Caire*, p. 10.

46. Ibid., p. 11.

47. Rivlin, *The Dār al-wathā'iq in ʿĀbdīn Palace at Cairo*, p. 115.

48. Indeed, Griffini's major scholarly discoveries were in the field of philology. Beltrami, *Eugenio Griffini Bey*, pp. lxx–lxxi; Georgio Levi Della Vida, "Eugenio Griffini," *Rivista degli Studi Orientali* 10 (1925): pp. 726–730.

into the nineteenth century, though no later than 1882. This periodization was adopted by Griffini's successors and was imprinted onto royal historiography. It was, no doubt, a significant step in the de-Ottomanization process of Egypt's recent history and in the creation of a historiographical substitute for it. In addition, through his work in European archives, Griffini facilitated the formulation of criteria for what was thenceforth considered historically important. These criteria framed the building of the archive around well-defined themes and subjects that were first and foremost related to Muḥammad ʿAlī and, in fact, to the founder paradigm. Grffinni's work in Egypt and Europe illustrates the undecided nature of the royal institution, which was neither an archive nor a library. The exact nature of this institution was yet to be determined.

Griffini was greatly appreciated by his collogues as well as by the king, who, as a token of his appreciation, nominated him to the Order of Ismāʿīl.[49] However, despite Griffini's great erudition, he proved to be too delicate and fragile a person for the job. During his five years in office and in spite of his young age, he continually suffered from all sorts of difficulties and malaises, ranging from the summer heat of Cairo to multiple medical indispositions that hampered his work. For every eight months of work in Cairo, he took four months of vacation to rest in the area of northern Italy's Lombardian lakes.[50] His friends and family often dramatized his working environment: "He [Griffini] is holding his position with much skill and dignity in such a difficult environment, in an Oriental court among an equally difficult, heterogeneous, and international population, often agitated by material moral, political, religious, social, and economic contrasts in a city such as Cairo."[51]

It was during the preparations for the International Geographical Congress in Cairo (April 1925) that Griffini succumbed to yet another random malaise and finally passed away. By the time of his death, the work on Ottoman documents was progressing all too slowly, and, in fact, little seems to have been accomplished relative to the overwhelming nature of the project. Griffini was indeed a gifted philologist but not much of a project manager and certainly not an archivist.[52] However, the practices of translation, periodization, and selection of materials that he established were continued with greater skills and efficiency by a team of archive employees well into the 1940s.

49. Beltrami, *Eugenio Griffini Bey*, p. lxxx.

50. Carlo Alfonso Nallino, "Eugenio Griffini," *Rivista della Tripolitana* 2 (1925): p. 130.

51. Beltrami, *Eugenio Griffini Bey*, p. lxvi. See also Giuseppe Ricchieri, "Il dott. Eugenio Griffini," *Rendiconti*, ser. 2, vol. 58 (May 1925): pp. 467–468.

52. Egyptian historians who worked with Griffini, such as Muḥammad Rifʿat, greatly appreciated his skills in understanding the Ottoman source material and seem to have learned much from him. Beltrami, *Eugenio Griffini Bey*, p. lxxiv.

From Library to Archive

Griffini's untimely death brought with it a change in organization, as by that time the limitations of the royal project had become all too apparent. Clearly, if the royal library was to support a historiographic movement of any weight, it needed to be reorganized along different lines. Put differently, its character as either a library or an archive needed to be decided. Fu'ād was ready for the challenge. This time, with the recognition that one man was simply not enough for the job, a special committee was formed in order to cope with the magnitude of the project. The new steering committee was composed of four erudite members: Ḥasan Nash'āt (head of the royal cabinet), Adolphe Cattaui Bey (secretary-general of the RGS), Marine Lieutenant Georges Douin (attaché of the Suez Canal Company and an independent historian), and Aḥmad Taymūr Pasha (a bibliophile, writer, diplomat, and member of Parliament). All four members had some experience in librarianship, historical scholarship, or coordination of such projects. None of them, however, specialized in reading and understanding Ottoman records. Nor did they have any archival experience.[53]

For these skills they needed Jean Deny. Born in 1879, Deny had a long career behind him as an expert on Turkish language and history. He was educated in the École nationale des langues orientales in Paris, where he had earned his bachelor's in law and linguistics. He had published several general works on history, religion, and folklore and a host of more specialized studies on Turkish etymology and grammar. Like Griffini, he had also worked in the Algerian archives, which he had surveyed extensively. On several occasions he served as French consul and translator in Beirut, Jerusalem, and Tripoli.[54] He arrived in Cairo in 1926 and immediately embarked on an extensive survey of Ottoman (and other) historical records. A month later he submitted to Fu'ād a detailed report of his findings. My opening discussion of Egypt's Ottoman and other depositories is partly based on this report. Following his survey, he was asked to remain in Cairo and was officially nominated as Griffini's replacement. His four years in office saw a profound change in Egypt's archival history. In 1930 he published *Sommaire des archives turques du Caire,* a valuable work that allows a rare view into the vicissitudes of Egypt's history of records. On the completion of this

53. Aḥmad Ḥussayn, *Al-Wathā'iq al-tārīkhiyya,* pp. 91–92; Asad Rustum, *Al-Maḥfūẓāt al-malakiyya al-Miṣriyya: Bayān bi wathā'iq al-shām 1810–1832* (Beirut: American Press, 1940), vol. 1, pp. i–iii; Deny, *Sommaire des archives turques du Caire,* p. 10.

54. Jean-Paul Roux, "Jean Deny," in János Eckmann, Agáh Sirri Levand, and Mecdut Mansuroğlu, eds., *Jean Deny Armağani: Mélanges Jean Deny* (Ankara: Türk Tarih Kurumu Basimevi, 1958), pp. 1–4; Jean-Paul Roux, "Portraits: Hommage à Jean Deny," *Orbis* (Belgium) 7, no. 2 (1959): pp. 558–569.

publication, he returned to Paris and was later nominated director of L'École nationale des langues orientales.[55]

As far as Deny was concerned, the work carried out under his predecessors was far from satisfactory and in several instances had even damaged the records' original order.[56] Nevertheless, Deny did not change the historiographical priorities, for he, too, defined the era of Muḥammad ʿAlī as pivotal. Thus, the work on Ibrāhīm's correspondence from Syria was continued, and most of it was translated into French and Arabic.[57] However, in contrast to Griffini, Deny aspired to study and organize all existing nineteenth-century records in spite of their location and possibly to unite them under one roof.

It did not take long before Deny ascertained that there was no rupture between records situated in ʿĀbdīn and those placed at Dār al-maḥfūẓāt. In other words, documents emanating from the same point of origin could be found in either place. This, for itself, is the ultimate refutation of the anarchy thesis described above. Once this fact was established, Deny embarked on a four-year, single-handed project to study all existing documents and create a united inventory for them.[58] The published inventory suggested a system of classification for all records according to their origins.

Deny's inventory focused entirely on the history of the dynasty. Though he must have come across Ottoman documents that preceded Muḥammad ʿAlī, Deny did not survey them. With this approach, he continued a long tradition of periodization that, in fact, became more dominant as an archival practice than any of the above-mentioned principles of organization.[59] The inventory's structure mirrored nineteenth-century royal administration. Thus, each chapter was dedicated to a different executive branch, such as Dīvān-i-khedīvi (Department of Civil Affairs), Dīvān al-dākhiliyya (Department of Interior), Majlis al-khuṣūṣī (Privy Council), et cetera. A brief history of each *diwān* was attached.[60] Deny surveyed each *diwān* and provided a detailed account of the contents of each box. All boxes were numbered. Outgoing and incoming correspondence was properly marked. This system ensured that regardless of the

55. Ibid.

56. Nonetheless, he did praise some specific aspects of it, as well as Griffini's good intentions. Deny, *Sommaire des archives turques du Caire,* pp. vii, 11.

57. Ibid., pp. 10, 13.

58. Ibid., p. 12.

59. In many archives chronology/periodization was prioritized as an organizing principle over *respect des fonds.* This means that a record group was cut in the middle in accordance with a certain decisive event, quite usually a political one. Françoise Hildesheimer, "Périodisation et archives," *Sources: Travaux Historiques* 23–24 (1990): pp. 39–46.

60. Deny, *Sommaire des archives turques du Caire,* pp. 104–131.

documents' location, researchers could easily trace them from one archive to another.[61]

What Deny did not include in his inventory, which he admitted frankly, were documents that had no immediate relevance to the process of state building under royal guidance (again, the founder paradigm).[62] Thus, when Fu'ād requested a survey of *awqāf* (religious endowment) documents, Deny responded that they were irrelevant for the project. Indeed, *awqāf* documents were extraneous to the royal collection, which only supported the myth of their historical redundancy.[63] Similar treatment also became the norm for the numerous court *sijillāt* collections, which were also defined as stretching beyond the historiographical horizons of the monarchy.[64]

Deny concluded the survey and published the inventory but probably did not prepare the accompanying catalog that eventually guided researchers. During his tenure as head of the royal project, the records of ʿĀbdīn and Dār al-maḥfūẓāt were not yet united. Documents were not moved to ʿĀbdīn before 1932, when the secretary of the court approached the Egyptian government, which legally had to approve an act such as relocation. Only as late as 1934 were 16,589 registries *(sijillāt),* 3,176 record groups *(milafāt),* and 623,917 individual documents *(wathā'iq)* united with those in ʿĀbdīn.[65]

But what exactly was moved to ʿĀbdīn, according to which criteria, and who articulated those criteria? These important questions, which could further expose the royal agenda, cannot be answered. The only thing we know is that records of the Maʿiyya saniyya (Viceregal Cabinet) were moved to ʿĀbdīn.[66] This suggests that the criteria of relocation were based on records that were relevant only to high offices of power. Scrutiny of the many histories that were eventually written in ʿĀbdīn substantiates this assumption.[67] Thus, it might be that quite plainly an official seal of the khedive was the only criterion for records unification and, by implication, availability.

61. Ibid., pp. 228–229.

62. These omitted documents were defined as "Turkish." Under this definition, several collections were excluded from the project.

63. This was the second time in which Fu'ād asked to survey *awqāf* documents. Ibid., pp. 219–220.

64. Ibid., pp. 214–217.

65. This particular professional terminology *(sijillāt, milafāt, wathā'iq)* was used by the general director of *dār al-maḥfūẓāt* in his report on how many documents were moved to ʿĀbdīn. It might be that since then the terminology was changed. Aḥmad Ḥussayn, *Al-Wathā'iq al-tārīkhiyya,* pp. 91–93; Aḥmad Badr, *Dalīl dawr al-maḥfūẓāt wa-l-maktabāt wa marākiz al-tawthīq wa-l-maʿāhid al-bīblyūjrāfiya fī-l-duwal al-ʿarabiyya* (Cairo: UNESCO, 1965), p. 49.

66. Ibid.

67. Chapter 4 is dedicated to these histories.

Furthermore, once the Ottoman documents arrived in ʿĀbdīn, the classification system applied to them is not clear. What should be indexed but not translated? What should be translated? Should all files be made available to researchers? Deny's work clearly portrays the contours of the royal archival effort but is entirely silent on these questions because he was no longer in office. It seems that the process of selectivity was not transparent. Obviously, the only way to make it so would be by a detailed inventory that would indicate what was moved, from which origin, and how it was classified in its new place. To the best of my knowledge, such a document was never written. In addition, successive directors of ʿĀbdīn applied new numbering systems that rendered the older catalogs of little use.[68] Hence, it is not likely that we will ever get an answer regarding the criteria for indexing and translating records. Once more, we are left to wonder and free to make our own educated guesses on the basis of the substance of royal histories.

The sources that were finally made available in ʿĀbdīn were cataloged under two systems: *biṭāqāt al-dār* and *maḥāfiẓ abḥāth*. The first comprised Arabic summaries of documents. The second included only translations. These directing tools led researchers to well-indexed collections that were arranged according to subject heading. For instance, one collection comprised "155 boxes of dossiers containing copies of reports, decrees, statutes, organic laws and information on members of the viceregal family and other prominent personalities."[69] This collection was fully indexed and contained materials copied from the Turkish and Arabic registers of the Maʿiya saniyya, the Dāʾira saniyya (Central Office for Management of Royal Estates and Properties), the Majlis khuṣūṣī, and other central holdings.[70]

Despite what one may think, these documents, once placed in ʿĀbdīn, were not simply untouched originals waiting to be dusted and discovered after years of negligence. There are several indications that a deliberate intervention violated the *fond* principle by classifying documents according to subject heading, author, and date. For example, one index shows the following thematic concerns: administration, railroads, education, commerce, biographies, Syria, a study of Muḥammad ʿAlī's origins, a collection of speeches by Ismāʿīl, and a bibliography in French of Ismāʿīl's reign.[71] These subjects seem suspiciously attractive to cater to the thematic concerns of royal historiography.

68. Shaw, "Turkish Source Material for Egyptian History," p. 43; Robert Hunter, "The Cairo Archives for the Study of Élites in Modern Egypt," *IJMES* 4, no. 4 (1973): p. 481.

69. Hunter also mentions *maṣādir wa tārīkh Miṣr,* which apparently was another collection that was cataloged in the same system. Robert Hunter, *Egypt under the Khedives 1805–1879: From Household Government to Modern Bureaucracy* (Pittsburgh: University of Pittsburgh Press, 1984), p. 267.

70. Ibid. Rivlin provides the subject classification index of original documents and registers in Arabic and Turkish. Rivlin, *The Dār al-wathāʾiq in ʿĀbdīn Palace at Cairo,* pp. 38–40.

71. Hunter, "The Cairo Archives for the Study of Élites in Modern Egypt," p. 478.

It is important to note that the index was not merely a general roadmap for material that could be retrieved in the archive but, in fact, mirrored the exact contents of the boxes. Hence, the index entry "a study of Muḥammad ʿAlī's origins" will lead to a specific box with various documents on the subject. Most probably some of these boxes were created in ʿĀbdīn, since their titles and language do not seem to reflect nineteenth-century thought. This assumption is supported by the fact that in his original survey Deny did not list such entries. The historian Robert Hunter found a specific carton (no. 137) that focused on "the development of the state under Muḥammad ʿAlī."[72] It clearly joined documents with a wide and varied array of origins (laws, decrees, statements, appointment letters, etc.), making it highly unlikely it was originally arranged that way.

Another indication of the habit of placing specific records outside their original context is the instance of the official gazette *Al-waqāʾiʿ al-miṣriyya*. Though several collections of this journal existed, none of them was complete. The journal was first published in Turkish and only later appeared also in Arabic. The usage of this important source was facilitated through the translation of segments of it from Turkish into Arabic and through its arrangement according to subject heading (education, officials, administration, etc.). Similarly, according to Hunter, "some of the cartons help document Muḥammad ʿAlī's efforts to bring the state under greater regulation."[73] Stanford Shaw noticed a similar disruption in the financial registers which "have been arranged together by date, regardless of their origin."[74] Thus, all in all, the index did lead scholars to documents that had been separated from their original *fond*.

What conclusions can be drawn from the way the ʿĀbdīn collection was put together? The liberty that royal employees took in deciding what constituted a proper subject heading determined, by implication, which pasts would become accessible and which would remain unknown. Thus, it goes (almost) without saying that the archive was not intended to support historical work on Egyptian history across time. Rather, it was thematically and chronologically organized in order to lend support to the saga of state formation under Muḥammad ʿAlī and his successors. It was carefully designed to help circumvent the apparently unpatterned nature of the records and provide easily accessed, essentially edited data about the monarchy and its material contribution to Egypt's progress. Thus, the formation of biased criteria for moving, translating, and indexing records

72. Ibid., p. 479.

73. Ibid., p. 481. See also Cuno, "Muhammad ʿAli and the Decline and Revival Thesis," p. 118, fn. 39.

74. Shaw, "Turkish Source Material," p. 43. Juxtaposing Deny and Shaw clarifies that financial registers were joined together from different origins. Deny, *Sommaire des archives turques du Caire*, p. 187.

violated the two basic archival principles: the principle of provenance and the maintenance of original order. All records that fell outside meaningful historical categories as defined by ʿĀbdīn (*awqāf,* court *sijillāt*) remained entombed in historiographical graveyards (basements, sealed rooms, temporary housing, forgotten chambers, etc.).

Since historical value was a highly subjective concept, documents relevant for understanding the lives of, for example, peasants, merchants, soldiers, corvée workers, slaves, lower-class women, and other disenfranchised populations were simply ignored. Consequently, much of their history was never written or, as we shall see in later chapters, was written from a very particular angle so that it was imprinted with the state's superstructure. The assumption behind this reality was that history acted on these people without ever being influenced by them. The Ottomans, as a polity and as a culture, represented another silenced entity, any positive portrayal of which was, rather more systematically, wiped from historical memory. In the words of a royal historian: "The constant refrain of Ottoman venality could be kept up almost indefinitely. There is enough material in the Royal Egyptian Archives to continue this same note for chapter after chapter."[75]

As shown elsewhere, "certain textual models and modes of representation impart a particular sense of purpose to the archive."[76] ʿĀbdīn was no exception to this habit, and the practices of Griffini, Deny, and their successors imprinted the royal model of history on the archive. Now we move to consider other practices that will further substantiate the argument according to which ʿĀbdīn was an institution that manipulated and silenced various pasts.

Building a Foreign Collection

Translated Ottoman records covered only one desired aspect of royal historical aspirations. Though these translated documents forcefully illustrated the emergence of modern Egypt under the guidance of Muḥammad ʿAlī, they fell short of making sense of Egypt's complex and, at times, troublesome relationship with Europe. In order to account for these aspects of Egypt as well, the work started by Griffini in the Italian archives was now expanded, with even greater enthusiasm, to encompass all of Europe's central archives.

The scope of the project was exceptional. Fu'ād, his father's son, knew how to orchestrate cultural projects of such magnitude. In order to manage the venture, he revived the Royal Geographical Society, which was originally established by his father, Ismāʿīl, in 1876. Under Fu'ād, the RGS was harnessed to the royal

75. Pierre Crabitès, *Ismail the Maligned Khedive* (London: Routledge and Sons, 1933), p. 207.

76. Sam Kaplan, "Documenting History, Historicizing Documentation: French Military Officials' Ethnological Report on Cilicia," *Comparative Studies in Society and History* 44, no. 2 (2002): p. 344.

historiographical project, as well as to other efforts. Unlike Fu'ād University and the Ministry of Education, places in which the monarchy had to share power with other political elements, the RGS was under the exclusive directorship of Fu'ād. Furthermore, it was a respectable and rather accomplished institution that was professionally acknowledged by other European geographical societies.[77] Its worldly prestige contributed a much-needed element of respectability.

Between the years 1921 and 1936, the RGS turned into a highly effective vehicle for ensuring that as many foreign documents as possible would be located, shipped to Egypt, and even published eventually.[78] The building of a foreign collection of records and the subsequent publication of segments of it required the participation of many scholars. The profile of these individuals is nearly homogeneous, since, with the exception of one, they were all European males. Employing European scholars in the service of the dynasty was not a novelty. Since the first quarter of the nineteenth century they were regarded and, in fact, functioned as harbingers and disseminators of modern institutions, techniques, and modes of thinking. Although from the beginning of the twentieth century the decision to employ foreigners gradually came to be seen as an odd and unpatriotic one, in the 1920s foreigners were still viewed as an integral part of Egypt's cultural landscape. Furthermore, Egyptian and Western systems of knowledge were still tightly linked, and extensive borrowing and exchange were fairly common.

While the reasons the king would summon foreign historians to Egypt are clear, Europeans' reasons for wanting to come to Egypt are not at all obvious, nor are the exact perceived benefits of such a choice clear. But to understand Europeans' decision to come work in Egypt is to understand the broad dynamics of intellectual activity in the colonial world. Though some of these individuals were indeed first-class scholars, back in Paris and Rome they were not regarded as leading, unequaled intellectuals. Today, we might recognize the seminal contribution of many of them, but for the European audience of that time these scholars were quite obscure. Many had much greater opportunity overseas. Quite simply, they enjoyed more prestige and appreciation in Cairo or Shanghai than back home. These *intellectuals sans frontières* were warmly accepted by the already-existing foreign communities, as well as by the various Westernized elites. This cosmopolitan environment was extremely dynamic. New people arrived all the time, while others departed. It was common to travel and spend some years overseas in a teaching position, in a job in the colonial administration, or in one

77. Donald Reid, "The Egyptian Geographical Society: From Foreign Laymen's Society to Indigenous Professional Association," *Poetics Today* 13, no. 3 (1993): pp. 539–572.

78. The series of *publications spéciales* started in 1921 and was supervised by the RGS general secretary. Adolphe Cattaui, "La célébration du cinquantenaire de la Société royale de géographie d'Égypte," *Bulletin de la Société Royale de Géographie d'Égypte* 8 (July 1925): p. 117.

of the many European businesses and companies that flourished abroad. Besides the factor of prestige, it might also have been financially profitable. What these mobile intellectuals brought with them from Europe, it seemed, was a taste of the future, a view from the hub of what was about to come. Or, in more precise terms, they brought with them the illusion that the secular and modern experience of Europe was universal. They came to serve as an example and to teach the ways in which this experience could be replicated. They were cultural missionaries of nineteenth-century European beliefs: in the power of science, human reason, and the ability of both to shape human experience in the present.

Though today we are sensitive to the negative consequences of the colonial experiment (many scholars regard the entire colonial project as fundamentally flawed), the intentions of these individuals were good. In fact, as far as they were concerned they were contributing to the creation of a new, more modern world. Indeed, in Egypt and elsewhere, their presence was regarded as a positive portent for the imminence of this new world.

Although the bulk of the colonial intellectual system was manned by minor intellectuals, many others of greater stature were also involved. Ronen Raz, for example, has studied the intensive interaction between some of the great European Orientalists of the time and Egyptian scholars, or *ʿulamʾā*. He described these Europeans as "intimate outsiders and welcomed intruders."[79] For such great minds, Egypt offered unmediated access to a sort of knowledge that, along with its living representatives, was simply unavailable in Europe. The comfortable cosmopolitan environment of Cairo and Alexandria was hospitable and allowed these visitors to create a community of scholars that molded existing knowledge into new fields of study, such as Islamic art history. This intellectual reality was by no means unique to Egypt.[80]

By the 1920s, Europeans were active in several cultural bodies with a significant degree of executive power in hand, such as the Société d'économie politique, de statistique, et de législation (established 1909), the Institut d'Égypte, the Comité de conservation des monuments de l'art arabe (1881–1953), and even the Arab Language Academy. Until the mid-1930s, they also enjoyed much influence in Fuʾād University. Scholars such as Gaston Wiet, Carlo Nallino, Gaston Maspero, Enno Littmann, Louis Massignon, August Bernard, and even the much-maligned K. A. C. Creswell had tremendous influence on the formation of modern Egyptian disciplines of knowledge in the fields of sociology, archaeology,

79. Ronen Raz, "The Transparent Mirror: Arab Intellectuals and Orientalism, 1789–1950," unpublished Ph.D. dissertation, Princeton University, 1997, p. 78.

80. As they did in Egypt, British historians also had a critical influence on the emergence of modern Indian historiography. Michael Gottlob, "Writing the History of Modern Indian Historiography: A Review Article," *Storia della Storiografia* 27 (1995): pp. 125–146, especially p. 131.

religion, economy, and law.[81] The archive project brought similar involvement in creating the field of modern Egyptian history and provided royal historiography with the opportunity to become influential both at home and in Europe.[82]

Nevertheless, the nostalgic image of cultural intimacy in a polyglot and cosmopolitan environment is slightly misleading, for Egypt's semicolonial setting did not afford an equal cultural exchange. The construct of cosmopolitanism is difficult to challenge, because it romantically assumes a fixed condition of equality and happiness for all. Nevertheless, as will become increasingly clear in this volume, many elements, chiefly nationalist, strove against and attempted to redefine this polyglot and cosmopolitan environment with its alleged equality. They did so because over the course of time the power to represent reality also became widely acknowledged as the power to order, administer, and colonize it.[83] Colonial power was involved in the creation process of modern Egyptian culture, and history writing, as one possible field of representation, was not beyond its reach. History writing was intimately tied to a very specific colonial agenda with very tangible consequences for the fate of the national struggle for independence. Hence, the premise of an unbiased and equal cultural exchange is problematic, if not simply wrong.

In any event, despite its structural inequality, Egypt's urban cosmopolitan-polyglot environment did make it easier for the monarchy to recruit scholars and quickly mobilize its project. Thus, in a relatively short span of time, many foreign documents relevant to monarchic history were located, copied, and shipped to ʿĀbdīn. Besides Jean Deny and Douin, Fu'ād invited around ten other amateur scholars and sent them on knowledge-gathering expeditions in Europe and America. Angelo Sammarco was the most prominent of these scholars. Sammarco was a self-made historian or, rather, a combination of his own intellectual curiosity and the king's money. With his eventual publication of several

81. Donald Reid, "Cairo University and the Orientalists," *IJMES* 19, no. 1 (1987): pp. 51–76; Reid, *Whose Pharaohs?* part 2; Raz, "The Transparent Mirror"; ElShakry, "The Great Social Laboratory."

82. Writing about the royal project, Donald Reid has argued, "That most of these [royal] works were in French and by Western authors suggests that Fu'ād saw the security of his throne as more dependent on the West and the francophone Egyptian elite than on the majority of his countrymen, who read only Arabic or nothing at all." As we shall see, this conclusion is not warranted, because, beyond what Reid only hinted at, *most* of Egypt's inhabitants did not read at all. The members of the urban strata that did read translated the royal project into Arabic and replicated its assumptions in their own writing. The works discussed by Reid were conceived in ʿĀbdīn, an institution whose influence stretched far beyond the Francophone Egyptian elite. Donald Reid, "The Egyptian Geographical Society: From Foreign Laymen's Society to Indigenous Professional Association," *Poetics Today* 13, no. 3 (1993): p. 555.

83. Mitchell, *Colonizing Egypt;* and Mitchell, *The Rule of Experts.* For a specific study of the emergence of social sciences in Egypt with relation to European knowledge, see ElShakry, "The Great Social Laboratory."

influential history books, his cooperation with the royal project was the longest and, by far, the most extensive one. Born in Naples in 1848, Sammarco arrived in Egypt only in 1922 as a history teacher in the Italian school of Cairo. On Griffini's death he joined the royal project and was asked to continue the work in the Italian and Austrian archives.[84] In 1933, already deeply involved with the monarchy, Sammarco edited the court's official organ, *Liberté*.[85]

Historians Georges Douin and Édouard Driault, editor of the *Revue des Études Napoléoniennes,* took care of the French archives.[86] A certain Miss Fawtier-Jones, the only woman to participate in the project, browsed the British Public Record Office (hereafter PRO) and closely cooperated with Douin.[87] Athanasios Polites, an official in the Greek Ministry of Foreign Affairs, dwelled on Greek state documents. Ḥayyim Naḥūm, the grand rabbi of the Jewish community, translated Ottoman *firmans.* René Cattaui deciphered Russian records. ʿAlī Ismāʿīl, a diplomat in the Egyptian legation in Washington, culled documents relevant to the Ismāʿīl era in the American state archive. The consuls general of Poland in Cairo, Georges Benis and Ludwig Widerszal, worked on Polish state documents.

The copied documents, on their arrival in Cairo, were arranged chronologically and, thus, immediately and irretrievably lost their original context.[88] Gradually, a significant number of these documents was published by the RGS in a series of *publications spéciales.* Over all, the RGS published fifty-two works in eighty-seven volumes, each of which were printed in eighteen thousand copies.[89] The years 1927–33, however, were the most intensive ones in terms of publication. Here, I treat the compilations of published source material as representative of the thematic and temporal concerns of the ʿĀbdīn archive foreign section.[90]

84. Georgio Levi Della Vida, "Angelo Sammarco," *Bulletin de l'Institut d'Égypte* 31 (1948–49): pp. 205–207; Ettore Rossi, "In Memoriam: Angelo Sammarco 1883–1948," *Oriente Moderno* 28 (December 1948): pp. 198–200.

85. ASMAE/ISAP 1931–45, Egitto/Busta no. 6 (1933).

86. Born in 1844, Douin published several books on Chinese history. I was unable to find any biographical information on Driault. René Cattaui Bey, "Georges Douin," *Bulletin de l'Institut d'Égypte* 27 (1944–45): pp. 89–95.

87. Miss E. C. Fawtier-Jones was the daughter of medieval historian Robert Fawtier, who taught in Fuʾād University until 1928. Most likely he introduced her to his French colleagues in the service of the king. FO 371/13130 and personal communiqué from her granddaughter Elizabeth Stone, May 2003.

88. Rivlin, *The Dār al-wathāʾiq in ʿĀbdīn Palace at Cairo,* pp. 5–6.

89. Information extracted from *Bulletin de la Société Royale de Géographie d'Égypte* 19 (1937): p. 483.

90. The foreign collection was assembled during the 1920s and was completed in the late 1930s. It should not be confused with the original foreign section in ʿĀbdīn, known as *arshīf ifranjī.* This collection contained correspondence in European languages. Rivlin, *The Dār al-wathāʾiq in ʿĀbdīn Palace at Cairo,* pp. 5–6, 72ff.; Hunter, *Egypt under the Khedives,* p. 267.

The temporal organization for the entire foreign collection was the standard modern one. Thus, as a royal employee Sammarco coordinated the arrival of documents from at least three locations (Rome, Vienna, and Naples) and conducted gathering missions of his own on several occasions, such as in 1930. During 1928–29, Sammarco continually specified to Italian archivists that ʿĀbdīn was not interested in pre-1798 material. Concomitantly, he requested that they send only the materials that were relevant to Muḥammad ʿAlī and Ismāʿīl.[91] Indeed, as shown in Table 1, the documentation effort focused on royal and modern Egyptian history, stretching from 1798/1805 to 1879 (when Ismāʿīl was deposed) and only rarely beyond it.[92] Concurrently, this framing chronology was fully compatible with the general structure of the ʿĀbdīn archive, which, through its chosen temporal order, excluded the Ottomans and ignored sensitive events such as peasants' revolts, financial blunders, the ʿUrābī affair, and the subsequent British occupation.

From a thematic point of view, the overarching concern of the collection was the bedlam diplomacy of Europe's backyard, which came to be known as the "Eastern Question." The royal project covered Egypt's "Eastern Answer" to this question and especially its growing political autonomy. Quite predictably, most of the documents focused on majestic events of diplomacy and war making. The diplomatic and military moves behind each campaign and crisis, such as the Ḥijāz expedition, the war in Sudan, the battle of Navarin, and especially the military campaigns of Ibrāhīm in Syria, were extensively researched. In covering the British side, sources originated primarily in the Admiralty, the Foreign Office, and the Office of War.[93] Similar documents provided by the Italian, French, and Russian conveyed their official perspectives. It goes without saying that the project focused on the individuals who were believed to have engendered these grand acts of diplomacy and war. The following published titles of correspondence were typical: "Le Grand Vizir à Lord Hawkesbury," "Le Major Général Stuart au Grand Vizir," "Le Général Hutchinson à Lord Hobart," "Lord Elgin à Lord Hawkesbury,"[94] "General Fox to Vice-Admiral Sir John T. Duckworth," "Major Vogelsang to Major-General Frazer," "Captain Hallowell to Lord Collingwood,"

91. See correspondence from December 1928, February, and April 1929, ASMAE/ISAP 1919–30, Pacco 1001. See also ASMAE/ISAP 1931–45, Egitto/Busta no. 3 (1932).

92. The only exception to this was Hayyim Nahumm, *Recueil de firmans impériaux ottomans, 1597–1904,* which was criticized for its inaccuracy: Yaʿqūb Sarkīs, "Tarjamat farāmīn Miṣr," *Al-Muqtaṭaf* (March 1936): pp. 407–410.

93. Georges Douin and E. C. Fawtier-Jones, *L'Angleterre et l'Égypte: La campagne de 1807* (Cairo: Société royale de géographie d'Égypte, publications spéciales, 1928), p. lxxi.

94. Georges Douin and E.C. Fawtier-Jones, *L'Angleterre et l'Égypte: La politique mameluke 1801–1803* (Cairo: Société royale de géographie d'Égypte, publications spéciales, 1929–30), vol. 1, pp. 63, 167, 303, 339.

et cetera.[95] Indeed, ambassadors, councils, attachés, ambitious generals, and other policy makers were the ultimate subjects of the ʿĀbdīn foreign collection and its published records. Browsing these compilations, the reader may come across many references to Muḥammad ʿAlī, Ibrāhīm, and Ismāʿīl. The historical account was carefully woven around them. The documents say close to nothing about low-profile actors.

Despite these clear preferences, the compiled documents also offered readers varied information on a host of less fantastic subjects and events, such as the Ottoman politics of religious minorities, Ottoman administration, slavery, Egyptian administration and public health, education, transportation, commerce, customs treaties, taxes, and the legal status of foreigners.[96] As opposed to the abundance of systematic data on military campaigns and diplomacy, this "other" information was not presented in any orderly way but can be painstakingly fished out of the wider account. It was simply not particularly useful from the perspective of the aims of the royal project, as it did not neatly knit itself together into an exalted epic of national grandeur. Nevertheless, unless one took a trip to Europe, these "less important" data were simply unavailable anywhere else.

We have seen how both thematically and temporally the foreign collection was tailored to royal historiographical needs. However, before we move on there is one more point to consider: the substance of historic evidence. What was written, or written out, in the documents that arrived from Europe? Thus far, one might have gotten the impression of a spirit of harmonious collegiality among the various participants in the project. Reality was quite different, however. Thus, beneath the mutual warm greetings of "Mon cher M. Sammarco" and "Mon cher

95. Douin and Fawtier-Jones, *L'Angleterre et l'Égypte: La campagne de 1807*, pp. 7, 74, 157.

96. On the Ottoman politics of religious minorities, see Georges Douin, *La première guerre de Syrie* (Cairo: Société royale de géographie d'Égypte, publications spéciales, 1931), vol. 1, pp. 65–67; Athanasios Polites, *Les rapports de la Grèce et de l'Égypte pendant le règne de Mohamed Ali 1833–1849* (Rome: Société royale de géographie d'Égypte, publications spéciales, 1937), p. 30; and Athanasios Polites, *Le conflit turco-égyptien de 1838–1841* (Cairo: Société royale de géographie d'Égypte, publications spéciales, 1931), pp. 1, 12–14. On the Ottoman administration, see Douin, *La première guerre de Syrie*, p. 5. On slavery, see Polites, *Les rapports de la Grèce et de l'Égypte*, pp. 257–259, 262–264, 272–276, 288, 339–340; Ḥayyim Naḥūm, *Recueil de firmans impériaux ottomans, 1597–1904* (Cairo: Société royale de géographie d'Égypte, publications spéciales, 1934), p. 854; and Georges Douin, *L'Égypte de 1828 à 1830* (Cairo: Société royale de géographie d'Égypte, publications spéciales, 1935), pp. 29, 38–41. On Egyptian administration and public health, see Douin, *La première guerre de Syrie*, pp. 547–553, 568–578; and Polites, *Le conflit turco-égyptien de 1838–1841*, pp. 170–171. On education and transportation, see Douin, *L'Égypte de 1828 à 1830*, pp. 10–13, 24, 29. On commerce, see Polites, *Les rapports de la Grèce et de l'Égypte*, pp. 99–101, 239–240; and Douin, *La première guerre de Syrie*, p. 569. On customs treaties, taxes, and the legal status of foreigners, see Naḥūm, *Recueil de firmans*, p. 887; and Polites, *Les rapports de la Grèce et de l'Égypte*, pp. 6–8, 78.

TABLE 1. Published Source Material from the ʿĀbdīn Project

Year	Author	Abridged Title	Notes
1923	Georges Douin	*Une mission militaire française auprès de Mohamed Aly*	Military correspondence
1924	Georges Douin	*L'Égypte indépendante, projet de 1801*	Documents from the British Foreign Office
1925	Georges Douin	*L'Égypte de 1802 à 1804*	Consuls correspondence; emphasis on French sources
1925	Édouard Driault	*Mohamed Aly et Napoléon*	Consuls correspondence; emphasis on French sources
1926	Georges Douin	*Mohamed Aly, pacha du Caire (1805–1807)*	Consuls correspondence
1927	Georges Douin	*La mission du baron de Boislecomte (Égypte et la Syria en 1833)*	Consuls correspondence
1927	Édouard Driault	*La formation de l'empire de Mohamed Aly de l'Arabie au Soudan*	Documents from the French Foreign Ministry Archives
1928	Georges Douin and E. C. Fawtier-Jones	*L'Angleterre et l'Égypte: La campagne de 1807*	Emphasis on British documents
1929	Angelo Sammarco	*Il viaggio di Mohammed Ali al Sudan*	Documents from various Italian archives
1929–30	Georges Douin and E. C. Fawtier-Jones	*L'Angleterre et l'Égypte: La politique mameluke 1801–1803*	2 vols.; emphasis on British documents
1930	Édouard Driault	*L'expédition de Crète et de Morée (1823–1828)*	Consuls correspondence
1930	Georges Douin	*Mohamed Aly et l'expédition d'Alger*	Emphasis on French sources
1930	Jean Deany	*Sommaire des archives turques du Caire*	Ottoman documents from Cairo
1930	Angelo Sammarco	*Il regno di Mohammed Ali nei documenti diplomatici italiani inediti*	10 vols. Italian Archives
1930–34	Édouard Driault	*L'Égypte et l'Europe: La crise oriental de 1839–1841*	5 vols.

1931	Athanasios Polites	*Le conflit turco-égyptien de 1838–1841*	Official Greek documents
1931	Athanasios Polites	*Un projet d'alliance entre l'Égypte et la Grèce en 1867*	Official Greek documents
1931	Angelo Sammarco	*La marina egiziana sotto Mohammed Ali*	Italian and other documents, translated and annotated
1931	Georges Douin	*La première guerre de Syrie*	2 vols. French documents
1931–36	René Cattaui	*Le règne de Mohamed Aly d'après les archives russes en Égypte*	4 vols. Russian Archives
1934	Ḥayyim Naḥūm	*Recueil de firmans impériaux ottomans (1597–1904)*	Ottoman firmans
1930–34	Édouard Driault	*L'Égypte et l'Europe: La crise de 1839–1841*	5 vols. consuls correspondence; emphasis on French sources
1930	Édouard Driault	*L'expédition de Crète et de Morée (1823–1828)*	Consuls correspondence
1935	Georges Douin	*L'Égypte de 1828 à 1830*	Consuls correspondence; emphasis on French sources
1935	Athanasios Polites	*Les rapports de la Grèce et de l'Égypte pendant le règne de Mohamed Aly, 1833–1849*	Consuls correspondence and other Greek state documents
1936	Asad Rustum	*The Royal Archives of Egypt and the Origins of the Egyptian Expedition to Syria 1831–1841*	Original source material plus historical commentary
1938	Georges Adam Benis	*Une mission militaire polonaise en Égypte*	2 vols.; emphasis on Polish documents
1940	Giovanni Marro	*Il corpo epistolare di Benardino Drovetti*	Private archive and correspondence of French council Drovetti
1940	Asad Rustum	*A Calendar of State Papers from the Royal Archives of Egypt relating to the Affairs of Syria*	4 vols.; based on Ottoman sources from ʿĀbdīn archive
1947	Jūrj Jundī and Jacques Tagher	*Ismāʿīl kama tuṣawwiruhu al-wathāʾiq al-rasmiyya*	Published by the archivists in ʿĀbdīn

NOTE: This table contains data regarding most of the published works. I was not able, however, to locate a certain number of tomes that were part of the same project.

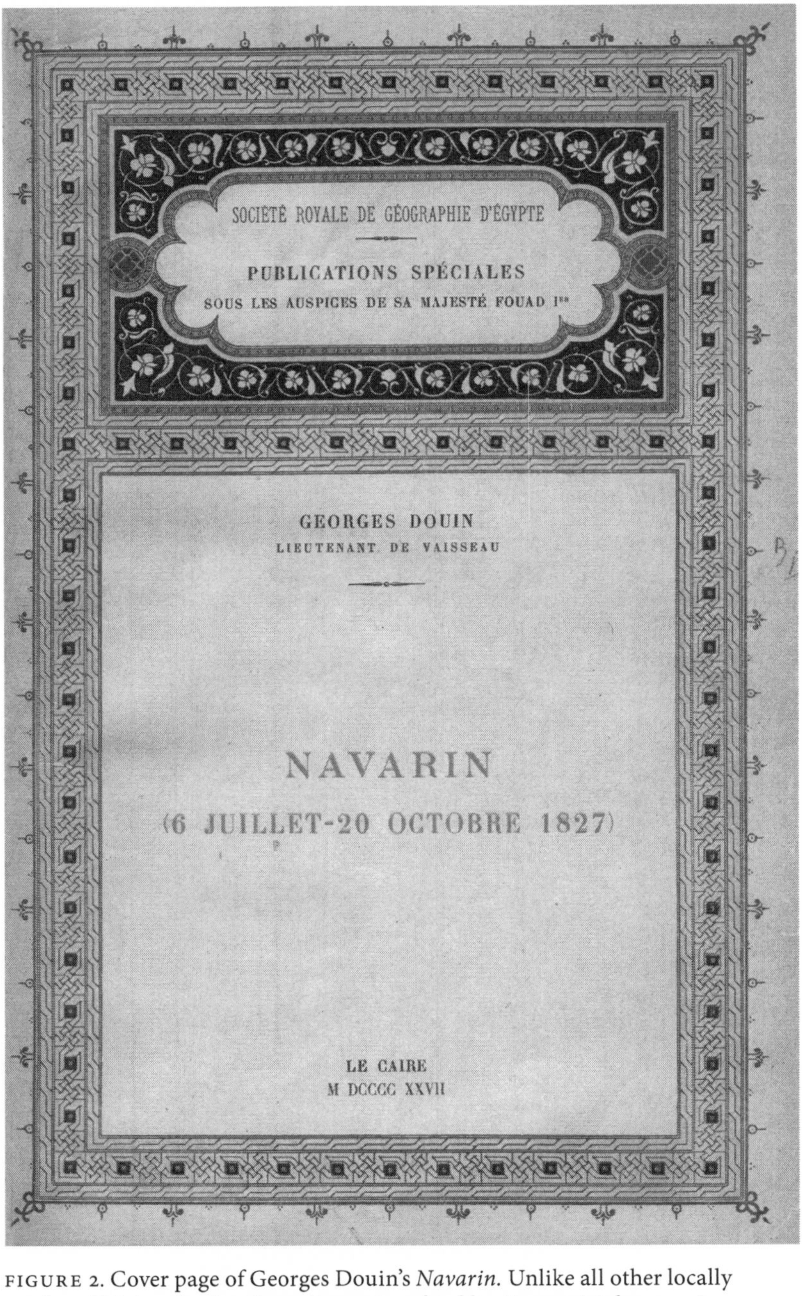
SOCIÉTÉ ROYALE DE GÉOGRAPHIE D'ÉGYPTE

PUBLICATIONS SPÉCIALES

SOUS LES AUSPICES DE SA MAJESTÉ FOUAD Ier

GEORGES DOUIN

LIEUTENANT DE VAISSEAU

NAVARIN

(6 JUILLET-20 OCTOBRE 1827)

LE CAIRE

M DCCCC XXVII

FIGURE 2. Cover page of Georges Douin's *Navarin.* Unlike all other locally produced history books, the entire series of *publications spéciales* was given special attention regarding its design and aesthetic appearance.

Bey," there was fundamental distrust, because Italians and French were in harsh competition.[97] Especially the Italians were eager to illustrate their own contribution to Egyptian history (as, for example, in the case of their alleged contribution to the construction of the Suez Canal).[98] In fact, national prestige in a semicolony was the only reason that the Italian government readily committed its national resources for this project. It is against this background of colonial competition that the Italians manipulated original sources.

The scene was Rome. The protagonist was, once more, Angelo Sammarco, and the crime was changing the original contents of historical documents. Sammarco, playing by the rules of colonial competition, shamelessly asked Italian archivists to erase the "sensitive" references that might present Italy in a negative light or strengthen the French case. Simultaneously, he held the original uncensored documents and promised not to share them with the French.[99] Even the intimate involvement of Fu'ād's cordial relationship with Sammarco and his genuine appreciation of Sammarco's professionalism did not spare him from these wicked tactics. Fu'ād, too, received censored documents.[100]

Over the years and until our times, these publications have been extensively used, because they offered accessibility to a properly indexed and neatly summarized material. Back in the 1930s, aside from the actual scholarly contribution of this material, it brought to the consciousness of local historians the need to base one's work on primary source material and to document it properly. For a certain group of young academic historians, this was indeed a welcome novelty. Even though the royal publications did not sell well, they were extremely popular among academic historians and especially among those who did not have the opportunity to visit foreign archives.[101] Besides, if we take them as an indication of the inventory of the foreign section in ʿĀbdīn, they gave scholars perfectly good reason to go there. Little did these scholars know, however, that the project of the *publications spéciales* was built, at least in part, on shabby foundations of deliberately censored records. Thus, while reading a work such as Douin's *Navarin* (Mutton Stew, in French), one indeed knows only very little of what one is digesting. Even today, scholars still regard these publications, such as *The Cambridge History of Egypt,* as "classics" and use them in canonical texts.[102]

97. For these greetings, see August 12, 1932, ASMAE/ISAP 1931–45, Egitto/Busta no. 3 (1932).

98. See a letter dated June 22, 1933, in which Sammarco explains how he emphasized "our contribution." ASMAE/ISAP 1931–45, Egitto/Busta no. 6 (1933). Later, Sammarco established an entire collection dedicated to Italy's role in the construction of the Suez Canal.

99. Ibid., letters dated August 13, 1933, and May 5, 1936.

100. In particular, the documents that Fu'ād requested concerning his father were censored. Ibid.

101. For statistics on the marketability of royal publications, see a discussion in chapters 3 and 4.

102. See references in Daly, ed., *The Cambridge History of Egypt,* vol. 2, pp. 116, 133, 145, 148.

All in all, these published sources functioned as building material for the writing of Egypt's superstructure history, that is, in writing the contours of Egypt's transition into an Oriental power decreasingly dependent on the Sublime Porte and increasingly entangled with Europe. This story develops along the following lines: from subjection (in the Ottoman era), through evolution and reconstruction (during the reigns of Muḥammad ʿAlī and his successors), to independence.[103] The chosen temporal and thematic order of the foreign collection, as well as the substance of evidence, supported and strengthened this line of historiographical reasoning.

THE ARCHIVE IN ACTION

Paying for History

One can see in retrospect that, because the project initially focused on publishing source material, its immediate impact was similar to that of the pro-monarchic encyclopedic works of Aḥmad Shafīq and Amīn Sāmī. That is to say, it did not provide an inclusive, continuous, coherent, and meaningful historical interpretation that would support the monarchic cause. Since the royal orchestrators of the project were fully aware of this difficulty, they attached long historical introductions to some of the compilations, especially those published in the late 1920s. These learned additions were designed to create the impression that the compiled documents are indeed part of a greater historiographical understanding. In reality, however, they were written from myriad angles (Russian, Polish, French, British, Ottoman, and Greek), were not properly edited, and, therefore, only increased the confusion.

Equally problematic was the internal temporal order of the project. A brief glance at the titles of the published records presents a very confusing picture: Douin collected documents from the years 1801–3, 1802–4, 1805–7, and 1828–30. Driault focused on 1823–28, October 1838 to March 1839, and 1839–41. Polites covered 1838–41 and 1838–49. What temporal order, then, governed nineteenth-century monarchic history? Did royal scholars share a coherent notion of what constituted a "historic period"? Toward the late 1920s, the specificity, fragmentation, and vagueness of the royal historical story became apparent, and a change was needed.[104]

103. The theme of independence, however, was not supported by source material because of the proximity of the event (which took place in 1923) to the present. Nonetheless, as shown in chapter 4, royal historiography did perceive independence as the result of its own actions.

104. In the project's next phase, in which comprehensive history books were published, more emphasis was put on making the internal periodization of the modern era compatible with the reigns of dynasty members (1805–48, 1848–54, 1854–63, and so on).

Cognizant of the shortfalls of the documentation project, Fu'ād soon took the next step. In March 1928, Gabriel Hanotaux, a former French politician, diplomat, historian, and distinguished member of l'Académie française, visited Egypt by invitation from King Fu'ād. Their friendly meeting in Cairo was characterized by mutual appreciation. Hanotaux was impressed with Egypt's intellectual renaissance under Fu'ād. The king presented the great obstacles hampering his project. He mentioned the still existing gaps in Egyptian scholarship. Despite his efforts, the project did not yet suggest an inclusive, comprehensive, and authoritative statement regarding modern Egyptian history. From Fu'ād's perspective, Egypt was still in need of a general work that would encompass the whole course of Egyptian history, emphasize the modern era, and be currently relevant at the same time. Hanotaux knew fairly well what Fu'ād was aiming at, since he had just finished nine years of work that essentially orchestrated a similar project: *Histoire de la nation française,* fifteen volumes of a dense, unapologetically republican, and patriotic history of France. Ironically, although Hanotaux always claimed that it was the "enigma of history" that attracted him to write, he unfortunately contributed little to its resolution throughout his career as a historian, a career accented by a distinctly political undertone.[105] Nonetheless, Fu'ād was extremely impressed.

Hanotaux was no stranger to the vibrant and stimulating Egyptian intellectual scene. In fact, in the 1930s, Egyptian intellectuals still remembered, with much disdain I may add, the great turn-of-the-century debate between Hanotaux and the reformer Muḥammad ʿAbduh. This exchange, including Hanotaux's original articles, was published in Egypt only a few years before the cooperation with Fu'ād had started. Understanding the exact course of this debate and the various arguments put forward by the two parties regarding the value of Islam versus Christianity is not important for our discussion here. It is enough to say that Egyptians remembered Hanotaux's *bête noire* attitude, particularly his comments on Islam, as being racist and degrading.[106]

Fu'ād, nevertheless, was entirely taken by Hanotaux's historical agenda and especially by his conviction that "a historian has to lead his people on the road from past to future."[107] Hence, he inquired if the maestro, a well-known

105. Vesta Sweitzer Vetter, "Gabriel Hanotaux 1853–1944," in William Halperin, ed., *Essays in Modern European Historiography* (Chicago: University of Chicago Press, 1970), pp. 91–118.

106. For Muḥammad ʿAbduh's refutation of Hanotaux, see his *Al-Islām wa-l-radd ʿala muntaqidīhi* (Cairo: Maṭbaʿat al-tawfīq, 1924), pp. 3–61; and Muḥammad Farīd Wajdī, "Mā qālahu Hanotaux," in Muḥammad Rashīd al-Khaṭīb, *Khulāṣat al-radd* (Damascus: Maṭbaʿat al-fayḥāʾ, 1925), pp. 1–77. See also Zaki Badawi, *The Reformers of Egypt* (London: Croom Helm, 1978), pp. 52–54; and Raz, "The Transparent Mirror," pp. 132–133.

107. Quoted in H. L. Wesseling, "Gabriel Hanotaux: A Historian in Politics," *Itinerario* 25, no. 1 (2001): p. 78.

FIGURE 3. Gabriel Hanotaux (1853–1944), a politician, diplomat, statesman, and historian who began his career as an archivist in the French Ministry of Foreign Affairs.

Anglophobe like the king himself, would be willing to supervise a similar project on Egyptian history. "I want my people to know their history and I want others to know the history of my people," explained Fu'ād.[108] It is important, he continued, to write this project in French, the language of universal culture (53). "Until now, Egypt has been the African connection of European civilization. . . . Our history written under your supervision can greatly help us to carry out this providential role" (56). After all, explained the king, it was Napoleon who "exposed Egypt to modern civilization," and this project needed to be continued (53). When the meeting with Fu'ād ended, Hanotaux promised to consider the deal and embarked on a journey to Palestine.

On his return, Hanotaux gave Fu'ād a positive response, and the two sat down to discuss the project's details. Apparently, though a republican, Hanotaux did

108. Gabriel Hanotaux, *Regards sur L'Égypte et la Palestine* (Paris: Librairie Plon, 1929), p. 53.

not mind working for a monarchy. In fact, he too was supposed to help the king to downplay such political differences. Hanotaux presented the possibilities and scope of this venture and also the logistical difficulties of supervising such a work from Paris. Fu'ād responded by delegating Fakhrī Pasha, the Egyptian ambassador to Paris, to coordinate all the necessary administrative aspects of the work. Other considerations, such as the identity of the writers, the publication process, and distribution of the work, were discussed as well. Fu'ād gave Hanotaux free rein.[109] Then, just before the end of the meeting Fu'ād urged Hanotaux:

> Compose the work as soon as you possibly can, and do not lose even a minute. There is indeed much to say about ancient Egypt under the pharaohs, and you know how attached I am to these studies. However, as for now, start with the modern period! . . . The history of my grandfather Muḥammad 'Alī is hardly known; tell it, speak of the ingenious soldier Ibrāhīm, of the great transformations accomplished under Sa'īd, and of my father Ismā'īl. Tie us again to the living world . . . render us justice by telling the truth.[110]

Hanotaux and his comrades did just that, and in 1930 the first volume was ready for publication. At the same time, Pierre Crabitès, Douin, Sammarco, and a host of other writers, all on the king's payroll, began to work on central aspects of Egypt's modern history. A new recruit, British historian Henry Dodwell, joined the team. In 1936, when Fu'ād was already on his deathbed, royal historiography finally appeared as a full-fledged interpretation of modern Egyptian history. These histories were written in 'Ābdīn. Before I move to a discussion of these books in the next chapter, I will investigate at some length the precise process of their production in the rest of this chapter.

'Ābdīn as a Workshop for History Writing

Historians usually take pride in saying that they "live in the archives." But for a group of royal historians this was not merely a trite metaphor born out of professional pride; it was a daily factual experience. Like so many other European scholars, the newly drafted royal historians lived and worked in Cairo. Their workplace was the 'Ābdīn archive, and their job was refuting nationalist historiography and glorifying that of the monarchy. The following section focuses on their daily working environment. In it, I postulate that rational technical decisions, though usually routinized and enacted on the microlevel, are essentially ideological and political and, as such, may have a profound influence at the macrolevel. In our case, the archivists of 'Ābdīn both forged and marketed historical meaning.

109. Ibid., pp. 53–54, 195.
110. Ibid., pp. 196–197. Note that Fu'ād did not mention 'Abbās.

The historian Helen Rivlin was lucky enough to be allowed access to the original collection of ʿĀbdīn. Not many people have had the opportunity to explore it ever since. In 1970, after an extensive investigation, she published a detailed and most revealing inventory. Rivlin, who actually did live in the archive, made a curious discovery. In a subchapter titled "Miscellaneous Collection of Materials in European Languages," she lists a significant body of evidence pertaining to the work of royal historians in ʿĀbdīn. In fact, what Rivlin discovered was the "archive of the ʿĀbdīn archive," which enables us to reconstruct some of the working procedures and practices prevailing there. Most of this collection consists of the personal papers of Douin, Sammarco, Asad Rustum (a Lebanese historian), Crabitès, and others.

The establishment of the Comité des archives in 1925 was, without doubt, a turning point in the royal historiographical effort. Headed by Deny and Douin, with the very active and growing participation of Sammarco, the *comité* was eager to work. The ʿĀbdīn archive was its headquarters. From here, the *comité*'s members directed the translation of Ottoman records as well as the ongoing collection of original documents in Europe and their subsequent translation, editing, and publication.[111] In 1929, the regular office of translation in the palace could no longer cope with the intensity of the task, and a new translator's section was established. In 1934, after five years of tedious work, a second section was established for the preparation of summaries and synopses of translated documents. All records from Muḥammad ʿAlī's era to the end of Ismāʿīl's reign were treated and cataloged accordingly.[112] Bit by bit, particular segments of Deny's inventory were transformed into a translated and well-indexed collection.

The next stage of the royal project was the use of the translated and abridged Ottoman and foreign sources as part of a larger royal research scheme in which entire history books were written. Undoubtedly, such a project necessitated complicated logistics and would have required careful coordination. The royal research agenda, however, could not have materialized without the work carried out by archivists and translators.

The names Maḥmūd Nafʿī, Samʿān Yūsuf, Muḥammad Khalīl, ʿAbd al-Hādī ʿAbd al-ʿĀl, Sāmī Saraj, Fuʾād Ḥilmī, ʿAzīz Mīrzā, and Muḥammad ʿAlī ʿUwaynī, to mention only a few, would probably mean nothing to most students of Egyptian intellectual history. Indeed, they should have little resonance. After all, they were

111. Joseph Galat Pasha, head of the court's European Section, conducted much of the administrative work. Rivlin, *The Dār al-wathāʾiq in ʿĀbdīn Palace at Cairo*, pp. 101, 106–107, 114, 118–120, 124, 126–127; Crabitès, *Ismail the Maligned Khedive*, p. ix.

112. Jūrj Jundī and Jacques Tagher, *Ismāʿīl kama tuṣawwiruhu al-wathāʾiq al-rasmiyya*, published in memory of Ismāʿīl (Cairo: Maṭbaʿat dār al-kutub al-miṣriyya, 1947), pp. 1–2.

not renowned historians, prolific journalists, or engaged public intellectuals who were associated with an influential body of thought. They were merely archivists and translators.[113] However, the success of the royal project rested almost entirely on their shoulders.

Since neither the standard translations from Ottoman and Arabic nor the European records were sufficient for the writing of inclusive royal histories, personal translators and assistants were assigned to key historians such as Douin, Crabitès, and Dodwell.[114] Probably Dodwell especially, in his capacity as a former curator in the Madras Record Office, was accustomed to such archival practices. It is important to stress that the tasks translators were asked to perform were not part of the daily routine of translating important *fonds.* Rather, they translated specifically selected documents on special demand. During the course of work, archivists and translators were expected not merely to translate but also to guide their clients through the records in question, helping them to locate the most needed and relevant material.

Interestingly enough, after browsing a certain *fond,* Rivlin found that only a few selected documents had been translated while other records from the same *fond* were not touched.[115] In many cases, the chosen documents were then separated from their original *fond,* and their context was lost forever.[116] No doubt, the preservation of records within their original context was not a prime concern of the work process. Misplacement of original documents was probably common. As a matter of fact, Ḥasan Aḥmad Ibrāhīm, an independent historian who worked in ʿĀbdīn, recorded a case in which original documents had disappeared and only a translated copy survived. Thus, even if one happened to read Ottoman, there was no way to verify the translation.[117]

Clearly, these procedures entrusted archivists with a significant amount of power in terms of shaping historical interpretation. Conveying his gratitude for the help rendered to him in ʿĀbdīn, Pierre Crabitès wrote, "Though my name appears on the title page of this book, it is not I who have written it. It is a compila-

113. I recorded these names while reading through introductions, acknowledgments, and other by-the-way texts that made a passing reference to one or a few of them. I estimate the number of archivists to be a couple of dozen at the peak of the project. See, for instance, Georges Douin, *Navarin, 6 juillet–20 octobre 1827* (Cairo: Société royale de géographie d'Égypte, publications spéciales, 1927), p. xxxi.

114. Ibid., pp. xxxi, 119, 249, 252; and Georges Douin, *Histoire du Soudan égyptien* (Cairo: Société royale de géographie d'Égypte, publications spéciales, 1944), pp. vi–vii.

115. Rivlin, *The Dār al-wathā'iq in ʿĀbdīn Palace at Cairo,* pp. 100, 106, 114–115, 119.

116. However, for some documents, archivists cited their original *fond* affiliation.

117. Ḥasan Aḥmad Ibrāhīm, "Wathā'iq tārīkh al-Sūdān fī-l-qarn al-tāsiʿ ʿashar," in *Nadwat wathā'iq tārīkh al-ʿarab al-ḥadīth 7–12 May 1977* (Cairo: Maṭbaʿat jāmiʿat ʿayn shamas, 1977), unpaginated.

tion. I have collected source material and allowed it to deliver its own message."[118] Crabitès had no idea how right he was. Many documents were indeed collected and translated for him by the ʿĀbdīn staff, which he wholeheartedly thanked. However, the message he is referring to was not merely that of the "sources" but also, and perhaps even primarily, that of the archivists and translators who handled them. In contrast with librarians, who have no influence whatsoever on the contents of the books they shelve and on the way in which their readers might understand them, archivists and translators in ʿĀbdīn seem to have had a considerable influence in forging historical meaning.

When one considers the quality of the translations in ʿĀbdīn, the question of accuracy becomes relevant. By this I do not mean that random mistakes are to be found. As shown above, both Deny and Griffini were aware of these objective difficulties and did their best to avoid them. More significantly, some evidence suggests that a conscious process of manipulation in translation took place. In other words, through the very process of translation the collection was de facto nationalized and appropriated. The existing evidence is by no means conclusive and would become so only if a comprehensive study of translations were to take place. However, neither is the existing evidence something we can afford to ignore. Khaled Fahmy recorded such a case of manipulative translation when he noticed that Muḥammad ʿAlī's words *devlet-i aliyye* (the Sublime Porte) were translated as "my country."[119] As we have already seen in the career of Amīn Sāmī, manipulation, or shall I say creativity in translation, was common. Some more examples of tendentious translations are suggested below.

A most striking example of the ability of some archivists to go beyond their daily routine and actually direct their knowledge toward the public arena is found in an edited collection of documents on Ismāʿīl. This collection was published by the royal archivist and independent historian Jacques Tagher and coedited with archivist Jūrj Jundī. The preface to their book reads: "In the following pages there is enough evidence to reevaluate the image of this great epoch [of Ismāʿīl].

118. Crabitès, *Ismail the Maligned Khedive,* p. vii. In another book, Crabitès thanked Fu'ād, whose "initiative dominates this work." Pierre Crabitès, *Ibrahim of Egypt* (London: Routledge, 1935), pp. vii–viii.

119. The manipulated translation was adopted by Afaf Lutfi al-Sayyid-Marsot in her *Egypt in the Reign of Muhammad Ali* (Cambridge: Cambridge University Press, 1984). Douin also used "my nation" as his preferred translation: Douin, *Navarin,* p. 243. Fahmy believes that the source of Lutfi al-Sayyid-Marsot's mistake was a manipulative translation from ʿĀbdīn. Over the past years Fahmy has made several references to the intentional manipulation of translation: Fahmy, *All the Pasha's Men,* pp. 24–25; Cuno, "Muhammad ʿAli and the Decline and Revival Thesis," p. 118, fn. 39. See also the special issue of the literary supplement of *Akhbār al-adab: Al-Bustān* 463 (May 26, 2002): pp. 16–22.

Evidently, reading this era in light of official documents will restore justice and reveal to us a true and proper picture of the great Ismāʿīl. This picture is that of a strong personality with a proper place among the famous persons of the time."[120] In a long historical introduction they focused on key episodes in Ismāʿīl's career: the public debts, material development, the spread of "civilization" to Africa (i.e., its colonization), the Mixed Courts, intellectual and cultural progress, and constitutional reform.[121] Throughout the work, they backed each of these topics with documents or parts of documents. These were designed to refute "common myths" about the khedive and unveil *(kashf al-niqāb)* important aspects of Egyptian history.[122] However, more than anything else, the titles and subtitles for the book's sections unveil the agenda of the editors: "The Modernity of Ismāʿīl," "Ismāʿīl the Father," "Ismāʿīl and Islam," "Patronage of Other Religions," et cetera.[123] Specific sections were dedicated to Ismāʿīl's efforts in the fields of education, literacy, agriculture, industry, public works, public health, and so forth.[124] All of these were manifestations of state building and progress to which the khedive is said to have been wholeheartedly dedicated.[125]

The terminology used in the translations and section titles is overtly nationalistic: *"istiqlāl," "shaʿbī," "bilādī and shaʿbī,"* and *"maṣlaḥat bilādī."*[126] Whether these were the actual words of Ismāʿīl or the manipulated translations of royal employees is not at all clear. The editors, however, provided the nationalistic section titles. General statements and opinions of Ismāʿīl were taken out of the records, and the original documents themselves were neither referred to nor published or translated. Hence, Ismāʿīl's quotes, while heroic and moralistic, were devoid of any meaningful context: "It is about time that everyone understands that differences in color should not turn human beings into merchandise. Life and freedom are sacred" (245). And in another place: "By introducing judicial reform in Egypt I am setting an example and providing a great service to all those who are interested in the well-being of the people" (84).

120. The title of their book, which translates as "Ismāʿīl as Described by the Official Documents," illustrates their profound belief in presenting a "true" unbiased picture. Jundī and Tagher, *Ismāʿīl kama tuṣawwiruhu al-wathāʾiq*, p. 26.

121. Ibid., pp. 7–26.

122. Ibid., p. 3.

123. Ibid., pp. 5–8, 9–13, 20–26, 27–32.

124. Ibid., pp. 122–130, 131–146, 150–172, 173–180, 180–190.

125. Several years earlier Tagher had published a history book on Muḥammad ʿAlī that followed the same thematic lines of nation making. There, too, he believed that his impartial account merely let the "facts speak for themselves." Jacques Tagher, *Mohamed Ali: Jugé par les Européens de son temps* (Cairo: Editions Horus, 1942), pp. 9–10.

126. Jundī and Tagher, *Ismāʿīl kama tuṣawwiruhu al-wathāʾiq*, pp. 38–39, 60, 65, 227–228.

In what way did these heroic words become historically useful when separated from the original document from which they were quoted? Without context these quotes could be used merely as ornaments or source material for a manipulated story. Nothing in Tagher and Jundī's collection will assist the historian in reconstructing the circumstances in which Ismāʿīl's actions occurred. Instead, the reader is left with an impressionistic view of a nationalist modernizer and caring father named Ismāʿīl. Sure enough, this collection used the credibility of the archive, as the place where historical truth resides, in order to market this distorted historical meaning.[127]

But translators and archivists in ʿĀbdīn had many tasks to perform in addition to the specific translations and publication of source material, efforts that apparently were not sufficient to make royal historiography influential at home. For this influence, a reaction to local historiography was needed as well. Especially troubling to the monarchy was the critical work of ʿAbd al-Raḥmān al-Rāfiʿī. Hence, royal employees were asked to translate several relevant chapters of his work into French, notably those that dealt with the Ismāʿīl era and the national movement.[128] It is also plausible that Fu'ād, with his partial command of Arabic, also read these translations of al-Rāfiʿī's work into French. As demonstrated in the next chapter, such translations enabled royal historians to refute hostile indigenous scholarship and participate in Egyptian public debates.

At the completion of a specific research project, a stage of writing and proofreading started. Preliminary manuscripts were sent to the RGS, which supervised the printing process, and the press galleys were returned to the archive. Entire drafts of books in press galley form are found in the ʿĀbdīn collection with handwritten remarks on them. Sammarco's and Douin's major works on nineteenth-century Egypt, which formed the backbone of the royal historiography, were reviewed and commented on by their peers before being considered ready for final publication.[129] The archive, then, was home to an intimate, yet competing,

127. The Lebanese historian Asad Rustum was intimately associated with the ʿĀbdīn project as well as the Egyptian academia. He dedicated years of painstaking work in order to publish four thick tomes of Ottoman documents in translation titled: *Al-Maḥfūẓāt al-malakiyya al-miṣriyya: Bayān bi wathāʾiq al-shām*. The published documents related to Egypt's policies in Syria. According to Stanford Shaw, Rustum's documents, which were "published under the subsidy by the late dynasty, ignore entirely the Turkish documents available on the subject of the Cairo archives, and are highly selective even among the Arabic ones, so they should be used with caution." Shaw, "Turkish Source Material for Egyptian History," p. 42. See also "Jalālat al-malik Fārūq al-awwal wa riʿāyat al-baḥth al-ʿilmī al-tārīkhī," *Al-Hilāl*, April 1940, p. 461.

128. Rivlin, *The Dār al-wathāʾiq in ʿĀbdīn Palace at Cairo*, p. 120.

129. The following press galleys and drafts were found in ʿĀbdīn: Douin's *Histoire du Soudan égyptienne;* Sammarco's *Histoire de l'Égypte moderne depuis Mohammed Ali jusqu'à l'occupation britannique, 1801–1882* (3 vols.) (Cairo: Société royale de géographie d'Égypte, 1937); Sammarco's *Les*

community of Western scholars who closely interacted with one another—so intimate that even their personal correspondence with their wives and their photographs remained in the boxes of the collection.[130]

Finally, when manuscripts were ready, Fu'ād had to find a foreign publishing house, since no press in Egypt was big enough to print the project. France (Douin) and Italy (Sammarco) volunteered to assist. Again, competition followed. The French won, but the Italians did not give up easily. In 1931, Roberto Cantalupo, the Italian ambassador to Cairo, finally managed to persuade the court, most probably by reducing print prices, to deliver the publication process to Rome. From then on, all manuscripts were sent directly to the Italian Embassy and several weeks later were returned in the form of beautifully decorated and bound books.[131] Sill, the production process was expensive. Judging from the bills that were sent back to Fu'ād, each book edition cost around twenty thousand Italian liras, which equals almost one hundred thousand dollars in today's value.[132] Thus, the entire printing project alone cost several millions. Paying these sums of money, Fu'ād reprimanded the Italians and threatened to return the project to the French on finding many spelling mistakes and other errors.[133]

But the historiographical process of ʿĀbdīn did not end here, either. Archive employees were also responsible for the press release at the completion of each work. Consequently, royal historiography was extensively reviewed in the Egyptian press and was even said to have mobilized Western scholarship on the subject.[134] Thus, ʿĀbdīn was not simply an archive but also an actual workshop for history writing and a powerful memory maker. This workshop united the court's unlimited resources of translation, editing, proofreading, publishing, publicity, and ultimately distribution (through the RGS). Thus, while independent scholars, such as university students, conducted research in ʿĀbdīn but wrote and published their work independently, royal historians were part of the lubricated

règnes de ʿAbbas, de Sa'id et d'Isma'il (1848–1879), vol. 4 of *Précis de l'histoire d'Égypte,* par divers historiens et archéologues, ed. Zaky el-Ibrachy Pacha and Angelo Sammarco (Cairo: l'Imprimerie de l'Institut français d'archéologie orientale du Caire, 1935); and Sammarco's *Il regno di Mohammed Ali nei documenti diplomatici italiani inediti* (8 vols.) (Cairo: Société royale de géographie d'Égypte, publications spéciales, 1930); and other books on the Italian community of Egypt. These works are discussed at length in chapter 4. Rivlin, *The Dār al-wathā'iq in ʿĀbdīn Palace at Cairo,* pp. 116–119, 122–123.

130. Ibid., pp. 117, 121, 123.

131. ASMAE/ISAP 1931–45, Egitto/Busta no. 2 (1931).

132. For comparison, a bus ride in Rome at the same time cost a quarter of a lira. ASMAE/ISAP 1931–45, Egitto/Busta no. 6 (1933). For bills sent to Cairo, see correspondence from March 11, 1933.

133. Ibid., correspondence of June 1933.

134. Rivlin, *The Dār al-wathā'iq in ʿĀbdīn Palace at Cairo,* p. 117; Carlo Alfonso Nallino, "Una recente storia dell'Egitto dale origini al 1879," *Oriente Moderno* 15, no. 8 (August 1935): pp. 421–425.

machine of court administration. The very personal and daily involvement of King Fu'ād in every detail of the work, trivial as well as crucial, was another aspect of this rather unusual archive.[135]

Maḥmūd Nafʿī, Samʿān Yūsuf, Muḥammad Khalīl, and other archivists were ordinary people who reported at the royal archive in the morning, sat at their desks, translated, indexed, or cataloged, had lunch, worked several hours more, took a coffee break, chatted with a friend, and, by the end of the day, went home only to begin this cycle again the next morning. They were, seemingly, no more than clerks performing chores of archival routine. Yet, however mundane and repetitive was the microprocess of the work in which they were involved, it had a crucial impact on deciding what would become historically thinkable.

By the mid-1930s, ʿĀbdīn was no longer a library, but it was also not much of what we might think of as an archive. It was a site where a grand plan of historical manipulation took place. It functioned as a workshop, as a place where documents were turned into history books. Through the adaptation of a set of archival decisions and practices, ʿĀbdīn did its best to ensure that once Egypt's modern history was written, only particular aspects of it would be visible. However, in order to complete the historiographical process of production, ʿĀbdīn had to influence the reception of its output. It did so by attempting to establish the credibility of the archive as the home of scientific accuracy and historical truth.

The Objectivity of ʿĀbdīn

The front-cover inscription on Sammarco's book *Histoire de l'Égypte moderne* declared "D'après les documents originaux, Égyptiens et étrangers."[136] In 1925 Douin prefaced his book with the following statement: "L'histoire, au sens scientifique du mot, c'est en premier lieu, la connaissance exacte des faits, basée sur une étude approfondit des documents."[137] In the historiographical era that preceded World War II, these declarations could mean only one thing: unmediated and direct access to a thing called "historical truth." On the basis of their experience in ʿĀbdīn, what royal historians believed they were presenting to their readership was an impartial and objective judgment of modern Egyptian history—quite simply, the truth.

135. "Juhūd al-malik Fu'ād fī-l-iṣlāḥ al-ijtimāʿī," *Al-Hilāl,* May 1940, p. 731 (written by an anonymous senior court official); Tawfīq, "Al-Ḥalqa al-mafqūda," pp. 585–594; Karīm Thābit, *Al-Malik Fu'ād, malik al-nahḍa* (Cairo: Maṭbaʿat al-maʿārif, 1944), pp. 49–55.

136. Sammarco, *Historie de l'Égypte moderne,* vol. 3, front cover.

137. Later in the passage, Douin referred directly to the Egyptian archive as the basis for practicing scientific history. Georges Douin, *L'Égypte de 1802 à 1804* (Cairo: Société royale de géographie d'Égypte, publications spéciales, 1925), p. iv.

Both Douin and Sammarco adopted the language and assumptions of the archive's scientific value. Thus, Douin contended that the true history of modern Egypt could be retrieved only through archival work. Documents, he asserted, are the key to historical truth.[138] A similar understanding presided over the monumental project of Angelo Sammarco (ten volumes in total), who wished that his work would put an end to superficial and arbitrary historical narratives and, instead, assist in revealing the truth.[139]

As Douin saw it, his work was doing no less than the "scientific construction of the Egyptian Risorgimento."[140] Furthermore, the term *impartial* or *impartiality* recurs in a number of his writings with no attached explanation as to what it actually means. Unquestionably, however, the royal claim to historical truth or impartiality made use of a new language of science.[141] More than anything else, science was presented as universal, that is, detached of any cultural, social, and political context. Thus, instead of presenting testimonies regarding a forgotten past, the archive suggested solid proofs that were invested with a higher epistemological status and thus appeared to be truthful and credible.[142] It is precisely this language of scientific universality that enabled royalists to claim that the archive could easily bridge differences of culture and nationality.[143] Hence, regardless of their nationality, ethnic origins, cultural orientation, or religious affiliation, researchers could find in the royal archive only a single universal truth waiting to be revealed.

Though it was as early as the mid-1930s that Muḥammad Shafīq Ghurbāl, his disciples, and colleagues presented an articulated agenda of scientific history and used it as their professional ideology, royalists were the first to propose these ideas and put them to work. As we shall see in later chapters, the adoption of a scientific language allowed the monarchy and academia to exclude nationalist writers, who viewed the royal historical interpretation as being biased and unscientific and did not accept it. Meanwhile, belief in the scientific quality of the archive shaped its policy of accessibility.

138. George Douin, *Histoire du règne du Khédive Ismaïl* (Cairo: Institut français d'archéologie orientale pour la Société royale de géographie d'Égypte, publications spéciales, 1933), vol. 1, p. viii.

139. Angelo Sammarco, *Il regno di Mohammed Ali*, vol. 1, pp. i–viii.

140. Letter to Foreign Office, dated February 14, 1933, ASMAE/ISAP 1931–45, Egitto/Busta no. 6 (1933).

141. Douin, *Histoire du règne du Khédive Ismaïl*, pp. vii–viii. However, at least one member of the royal school argued that "History is only a partial consciousness." Édouard Driault, "Mohamed-Aly et Ibrahim," in Mohamed Zaky el-Ibrachy Pacha and Angelo Sammarco, eds., *Précis de l'histoire d'Égypte* (Cairo: l'Institut français d'archéologie orientale du Caire, 1933), vol. 3, part 3, p. 263.

142. I borrowed the distinction between *proofs* and *testimonies* from Ricoeur, *La mémoire, l'histoire, l'oubli*, pp. 224–230.

143. Douin, *Navarin, 6 juillet–20 octobre 1827*, pp. vii–viii.

An Archive Open to All?

Accessibility to archival material has been a delicate matter. Quite often, accessibility polices are motivated by rather curious considerations. Thus, the story goes that the keeper of the Berlin archives explained the liberal politics of accessibility by joking that "Prussia had nothing to fear from publicity because the worst was already known."[144] The reality that the Egyptian monarchy faced was not dissimilar. A liberal accessibility policy to the ʿĀbdīn was considered a possible cure for the monarchy's historiographical woes. This policy rested on the conviction that the archive was the conduit for pristine historical truth. The royal assumption seems to have been that, regardless of the historians' political, social, or cultural dispositions, they would inevitably adopt a very particular, and unquestionably favorable (to the monarchy), understanding of modern history following their experience in ʿĀbdīn.[145] Consequently, the court allowed access even to staunch nationalists who were not affiliated with the royal project.

However, royal officials soon acknowledged the limitations of this policy when, following their work in the archive, nationalist-popular historians reached undesirable and surprising conclusions. The most famous case was that of ʿAbd al-Raḥmān al-Rāfiʿī, who after extensive research in the archive, for which he profusely thanked the king, concluded that Muḥammad ʿAlī was not at all the founder of modern Egypt. Instead, al-Rāfiʿī accorded this role to the "people." To royal officials such conclusions must have come as a great shock, since every inch of the archive was designed to prove otherwise. Al-Rāfiʿī never gained admittance to this building again.[146] The opinionated historian Muḥammad Ṣabrī was among the first victims of the new screening policy, and he, too, was denied access. Nonetheless, the myth of an archive accessible to all remained intact. Undoubtedly, the royal experience shaped the politics of archive accessibility and records availability in twentieth-century Egypt. In fact, one could discern certain continuity in accessibility policies well into the 1960s and beyond, although that time frame is outside the scope of our discussion.

CONCLUSION

What history, then, could be envisioned from the stacks of the ʿĀbdīn archive? Even before we turn to a systematic analysis of royal historiography, guessing some of its contours is possible. Thus, the periodization of the archive will most

144. Quoted in Geoffrey Giles, "Archives and Historians," in Geoffrey Giles, ed., *Archivists and Historians* (Washington DC: German Historical Institute, 1996), p. 8.

145. Douin, *Histoire du règne du Khédive Ismaïl*, vol. 2, p. xi.

146. See discussion in the next chapter.

probably frame the story as stretching between 1798/1805 and the end of Ismāʿīl era. The protagonists of this history will be the members of the dynasty, especially Muḥammad ʿAlī, Ibrāhīm, and Ismaʿīl. The main theme will be Egypt's transition to a modern nation-state. Royal history will tend to focus on reforms and developments in the administration, army, public works, and education. Europe will appear as a benevolent entity, the home of reason and order, which strove to tie Egypt to modern civilization. Egypt, in turn, having its own domestic *mission civilisatrice,* will export these goods to black Africa. The Ottoman Empire will have the role of the villain. Ordinary Egyptians will not have an active role in this story. Modern Egyptian history will be shaped from "outside" and from "above."

Whether it was the archive that was built around the story or the story that was wrapped around the archive is not so important.[147] Most probably it was a dialectical process, that is, a bit of both. What is quite obvious, though, is that, ultimately, documentary practices, such as the one that took place in ʿĀbdīn, were organized around certain concepts, perceptions, and historical notions. "Only by drawing out the historicity of [these] modes of representation can we fully appreciate how a text can encode, define, evaluate, and produce facts on paper, and how these facts, in turn, acquire credibility and legitimacy."[148] Coping with this challenge will be my task in chapter 4.

The impact of the archive, however, was not solely the result of its structure and contents but also a result of the rhetoric and language of which it was part and the way it was talked and thought about. ʿĀbdīn's founding myth, quoted in this chapter's opening, underscored its emergence from a state of total anarchy and disarray to one of meticulous order and organization. Consider, for example, Édouard Driault's contribution to this myth: "The historian could see in the seventeenth and eighteenth centuries only pitiful distress; for it was the ransom of this troubled *époque* to be able to leave neither monuments nor documents nor any other clear testimony, and thus to be as if they had never been."[149]

In yet another outpouring of gratitude, Pierre Crabitès wrote, "His majesty's privy purse bore the heavy expense of collecting and publishing *all this hitherto widely scattered and in some cases almost inaccessible source material.* It is thus obvious that King Fuad's initiative dominates this work. My debt to him is indeed very great."[150]

147. Nonetheless, the story of ʿĀbdīn was quite ubiquitous. Thus, for instance, by excavating the citadel in Cairo, amateur Egyptian archaeologists who believed in the founder paradigm tried to prove it by means of scientific archaeological research. Muḥammad ʿAbd al-Jawwād al-Aṣmaʿī, *Qalʿat Muḥammad ʿAli lā qalʿat Nābuliyūn* (Cairo: Maṭbaʿat Dār al-kutub, 1924).

148. Kaplan, "Documenting History, Historicizing Documentation," p. 347.

149. Driault, "Mohamed-Aly et Ibrahim," p. 188.

150. Crabitès, *Ibrahim of Egypt,* p. vii (emphasis added).

The royal working assumption, then, was rather simple: There are no alternative sources for the study of Egyptian history, nor have there ever been. The previous era left no records. Quite remarkably, this royal myth of a medieval era that evaporated into thin air had an enduring persistence in Egyptian as well as in Western historiography.[151] It is precisely this nihilistic quality, a complete disregard for the premodern past, that makes ʿĀbdīn a truly modern institution: nothing preceded it.

But the rhetoric of ʿĀbdīn aimed at something more substantial than simply bashing the previous so-called medieval era and presenting itself as novel:

> Toute nation a des racines qui plongent dans le passé. Celui-ci conditionne le présent qui lui-même engendre l'avenir. Il est impossible de comprendre les grands problèmes politiques qui agitent la vie des peoples, si on ne les suit pas dans leur développement historique. *C'est ce qu'avait compris le Roi Fouad. Il savait que l'histoire d'Égypte réside dans ses archives, et qu'acucunne oeuvre historique sérieuse ne pourrait jamais être construite, tant que celles-ci demeureraient dans l'état lamentable de désordre où ils avaient trouvées lors de son avènement au trône.*[152]
>
> (Each nation has deep roots in the past. These roots condition the present, which, itself, engenders the future. It is impossible to comprehend the great political problems that agitate people's lives without single-handedly understanding their historical developments. *King Fu'ād understood it. He knows that Egyptian history resides in the archives and that no serious historical work could never be written as long as the archives remain in this lamentable and chaotic state in which he found them on becoming a king.*)

ʿĀbdīn, we are made to believe, incarnates the historical trajectory of the Egyptian nation itself and serves as a metaphor for its emergence from a state of anarchy to one of order and organization.[153] By extension, in building an archive ex nihilo, King Fu'ād replicated and reaffirmed the success of his ancestors, who allegedly founded modern Egypt from scratch.[154] But this was not all. In addition, ʿĀbdīn promised its clients that inside it, in well-organized index boxes, the history of the Egyptian nation was waiting to be discovered and redeemed. This process was, of course, scientific, precise, definitive, and final. But above all—it was real.[155] Indeed, after a long period in which Dodwell "lived" in ʿĀbdīn, he

151. The profound belief in this myth, even among academic historians, was challenged only in the 1960s. For a replication of this myth, see Ḥusayn, *Al-Wathā'īq al-tārīkhiyya,* p. 67. In the West, Crabbs reiterated the belief that "archives . . . were either nonexistent or else in a state of almost complete chaos." Crabbs, *The Writing of History in Nineteenth-Century Egypt,* p. 200.

152. Douin, *Histoire du règne du Khédive Ismaïl,* vol. 3, pp. ix–x (emphasis added).

153. Ibid. Douin continues to describe how ʿĀbdīn substituted order for anarchy in the records.

154. Sammarco described Fu'ād's achievement in almost the same wording: Sammarco, *Il regno di Mohammed Ali,* vol. 1, p. vii.

155. Sammarco, *Historie de l'Égypte moderne,* vol. 3, p. v.

hoped that for the first time he would be able to "ascertain by a study of original materials what Muhammad Ali really did."[156] Thus, at one and the same time, ʿĀbdīn was both the ultimate gate for gaining total and scientific comprehension of modern Egypt and a metaphor for its very emergence. ʿĀbdīn was purposely promoted as both the conduit for understanding and the incarnation of the thing to be understood. This self-referential and self-sufficient nature of the archive is another aspect of its modernity.

Undeniably, the royal project introduced three complementary elements to the field of modern history writing. First, it set the criteria for what would count as "proper historical knowledge" with regard to modern Egypt and what evidence constituted that knowledge. Since, by definition, only one story of modern Egypt is true, what was considered as valid historical knowledge should obviously be consistent with that story. Second, the project disseminated the assumption that both physically and epistemologically no valid historical evidence exists outside ʿĀbdīn and that the true story is to be found only there. That is to say, a particular kind of evidence was gathered in the archive, and certain styles of reasoning were associated with it (hence epistemology). Third, ʿĀbdīn also generated ethical credibility, since the archive became a sign of status, authority, and a certain right to speak. The royal project created a powerful reaffirming circle of individuals who could judge what "proper knowledge" is. These experts were counted as both the source of authority and its ultimate embodiment. In that way, expert authority was introduced into the field of history writing.[157]

The ethical and epistemological credibility of ʿĀbdīn afforded royal historians "the right to make statements about the past, about history, about change, about fate and, by extension, if in any deliberately delimited way, about the future."[158] Historians could remain relatively immune to the seductions and influence of ʿĀbdīn only if they came there consciously searching for evidence to sustain a kind of story different from the royal story. Historians like Muḥammad Ṣabrī and al-Rāfiʿī had both the experience and the maturity to do so. More gullible researchers, such as graduate students, ended up working within the royal paradigm.

Was ʿĀbdīn a national public archive in the twentieth century? Royal historians certainly referred to it as such, and there seems to be a general understand-

156. Henry Dodwell, *The Founder of Modern Egypt: A Study of Muhammad Ali* (Cambridge: Cambridge University Press, 1931), p. vii.

157. These three elements come into focus in Angelo Sammarco, "I documenti diplomatici concernenti il regno di Mohammed Ali e gli archivi di stato italiani," *Oriente Moderno* 9, no. 6 (June 1929): pp. 287–296.

158. Thomas Osborne, "The Ordinariness of the Archive," *History of the Human Sciences* 12, no. 2 (May 1999): p. 54.

ing that ʿĀbdīn was the Egyptian equivalent of the British PRO and the French Archives Nationales.[159] Furthermore, it was allegedly accessible to all citizens. In that sense alone, ʿĀbdīn certainly had the appearance of a civic public archive. However, a close analysis proves otherwise. Consider, for instance, the architecture of the building itself as indicative of its function and status.

Sure enough, in its architectural and civic presence, the ʿĀbdīn archive was not reminiscent of Egypt's other archives, past, present, or future. The wide old decorated building of the Daftarkhāne, situated in the back of the citadel, certainly has much character attached to it. It has a central monumental entrance, carefully carved in brown stone. Its artistic style quotes Byzantine military architecture and impresses visitors even today. Yet, as we know, despite its presence it was not a public archive. Dār al-wathāʾiq, the Nasserist archive of the 1960s that replaced ʿĀbdīn, occupies a typical eastern European modernist building. Even though its aesthetic value is questionable, the combined complex of the National Library and the National Archive, situated on Cairo's Nile *corniche*, is, indeed, a clear statement on behalf of state authority. In contrast with these two institutions, however, the ʿĀbdīn archive was not even situated in a building but rather in a hidden wing in the royal palace. Looking at the palace from the outside, one will not see the archive, nor will she or he be able to guess its location. It is as if the archive never really had its own existence. In fact, it had no public or civic presence whatsoever.

Nonetheless, in reality, more state authority was attached to the indiscernible archive in ʿĀbdīn than to any of Egypt's other visible archives. ʿĀbdīn enjoyed both absolute authority and total invisibility. It was a place that struck Egypt's historical imagination and fused it into the history of the monarchy. The two became inextricably linked. Obviously, ʿĀbdin was a national archive only in the sense that it proposed to its clients a very specific understanding of the nation. The public, as a historical and legal entity, was not part of ʿĀbdīn's historical perception. This situation raises interesting questions: Is the monarchy merely a custodian of documents or their legitimate and lawful owner? Who owns the nation's documents, and what is the desirable relationship between the state and the public in the context of historical investigation?

The public status of records is located in the intersection where state authority and civil rights meet. The precedent set by the ʿĀbdīn archive is important in this regard. Apparently, no ethical code or ideal of service established the relationship among the monarchy, the records, and the public. Needless to say, from a legal point of view, ʿĀbdin was not a public, national archive but a private, royal one.

159. Sammarco, *Histoire de l'Égypte moderne*, vol. 3, p. v. For the public position of the NA-UK, see Patrick Joyce, "The Politics of the Liberal Archive," *History of the Human Sciences* 12, no. 2 (May 1999): pp. 35–49.

A law administrating the establishment of a national archive was issued only in 1954. Historians required a significant amount of practical experience before they sought to reformulate answers to the questions stated above. For the time being, ʿĀbdīn was celebrated as the only existing modern archive and the best institution to start working with.

What role did foreign scholars such as Griffini, Deny, Douin, and Sammarco play in setting the stage for modern Egyptian historiography? Simply put, European historians and archivists contributed their conception of what is modern about Egyptian history and how this modernity should be found, organized, judged, and promoted. Needless to say, they themselves cherished this modernity. As we know, however, ideas about modernity, nationalism, and history (for example, ideas about Egypt's Pharaonic phase) came from a huge number of individuals and cultural agencies over a long period of time and manifested themselves in various ways. These foreign employees were by no means alone in this intellectual effort. Nonetheless, they built the archive around their historiographical notion, perpetuating and objectifying that notion. In this way, they gained a critical influence over modern Egyptian historiography. This, unquestionably, was a unique contribution.

A telling anecdote, involving people from the same milieu and from about the same time, captures the tangible side of this kind of intellectual intervention. In the late nineteenth century, European art historians, architects, and archaeologists formed the Comité de conservation des monuments de l'art arabe. In operation in Egypt between 1881 and 1953, the *comité*, a civil branch of government, was responsible for the renovation and preservation of everything from fountains to mosques and madrassas. Its hands were full. Over the years, *comité* members proposed several philosophies of conservation and preservation that aimed at defining accurate aesthetic principles for deciding what is an authentic Islamic monument. They operated in accordance with these strict principles, which resulted in the modification of hundreds of monuments. In one instance, the *comité* regarded an Ottoman minaret on top of a Fatimid mosque as a distortion of Fatimid authenticity; the minaret was destroyed. Some other buildings were moved from their original locations.[160] Modern colonial knowledge did

160. Similar the royal historians and their work, the Comité de conservation also influenced the periodization of Islamic art. Alaa El-Din Elwi El-Habashi, "*Athar* to Monuments: The Intervention of the *Comité de conservation des monuments de l'art Arabe*," unpublished Ph.D. dissertation, University of Pennsylvania, 2001. For the exemplary career of one prominent *comité* member, see István Ormos, "Preservation and Restoration: The Methods of Max Herz Pasha, Chief Architect of the Comité de Conservation des Monuments de l'Art Arabe," in Jill Edwards, ed., *Historians in Cairo: Essays in Honor of George Scanlon* (Cairo: American University in Cairo Press, 2002), pp. 123–153.

have a tangible impact. With this in mind, we would probably not be surprised to find that Georges Douin resided in the house of Zaynab Khaṭūn, a central Cairo palace renovated by the *comité*.[161] Khaṭūn was a powerful woman who was affiliated with the Turkish elite, which Douin and his colleagues invested much scholarly energy in forgetting.[162]

I mention the work of the Comité de conservation because I deem Fu'ād's Comité des archives to be a similar agency of intervention. Though the royal project was physically invisible and, hence, not as tangible, it was preponderantly influential. I do not argue here that the archive, as the ultimate expression of a certain historical mindset, was imposed on Egypt. This is simply not true. As shown here, it developed through a process of dialectical engagement. However, once it was put to work, the archive introduced to Egyptian historiography, with more force than ever before, a certain view of modern Egypt with very tangible political implications. I dare to say, therefore, that the Egyptian struggle for independence cannot be fully understood without a basic comprehension of the various historiographical views that framed and nourished this struggle. This argument will be substantiated in the next chapter with its close examination of the actual texts that were produced in ʿĀbdīn and their relation to opposing nationalist historiography. Meanwhile, it is important to bear in mind that the archival practices of ʿĀbdīn were politically and ideologically influential. Since the ʿĀbdīn archive systematically silenced periods (the Ottoman, the Mamluk, the era of Khedive ʿAbbās), sources (private papers, *maḥākim sharʿiyya, awqāf*), and people (subalterns), it was not merely a guardian of memory but its actual manufacturer and disseminator.

161. "Georges Douin," *Bulletin de l'Institute d'Égypte* 27 (1944–45): pp. 89–95.
162. Egyptian Archaeological Authority, *Manzil Zaynab Khātūn* (Cairo, n.d.).

4

Competing for History

1930–1952

This chapter is about historiographical competition. What began with the modern conceptual innovation of the founder paradigm, continued with the development of compatible linguistic and conceptual resources and, supported by powerful scholarly institutions such as the ʿĀbdīn archive, culminated with the advent of modern historical narration. Driven by the post-1919 sociocultural and political changes, the most important of which was the rise of a new middle class, a qualitative and quantitative change in the arena of history writing occurred in the next two decades. An unprecedented outpouring of historical knowledge reflected the demand for modern historical meaning. Circulated in popular magazines, newspapers, and books, this knowledge became a desired intellectual commodity. Since in a rapidly transforming environment, history was believed to offer a profound understanding of almost everything that surrounded Egyptians, engagement in it was no longer an arcane intellectual activity reserved for an elevated elite. Instead, it became a ubiquitous intellectual habit of the urban middle class. During these same decades, modern historical arguments were also advanced enough to win political capital. Then, an irreversible process of historiographical competition and rivalry ensued. Consider, for example, the following quotes:

> Henry Dodwell: And yet it is clear that he [Muḥammad ʿAlī] created modern Egypt, bringing it into new and fruitful touch with the West. The part of his work was not, and could not be, undone. He succeeded, for he impressed his purpose deeply on the people over whom he ruled, and even now, almost a century after his death his tradition still lives.[1]

1. Dodwell, *The Founder of Modern Egypt*, p. 268.

> ʿAbd al-Raḥmān al-Rāfiʿī: The right history is that of people, not of kings. The people are an entity that lives, develops, and renews itself through a sequence of successive generations. The people persist, whereas the kings desist. The Egyptian people fabricated the positive aspects of their history. The people's vitality, struggle, sacrifice, traits, progress, willingness, and commitment to freedom fabricated Egyptian history.[2]

Arguably, Dodwell and al-Rāfiʿī were worlds apart from each other. The first was an accomplished and expert historian of India from London University;[3] the second, a maverick Cairene lawyer and political activist who began to write history in the late 1920s and would leave his historiographical mark for generations to come. They came from different environments and different intellectual and political communities, and they especially had different professional orientations, yet they both intentionally competed for the attention of the Egyptian public. What were the circumstances that afforded such an unusual meeting? What sort of public debate were they attempting to manipulate? Who participated in it, and what views were exchanged?

In this chapter I set out to answer these and other questions by discussing the emergence of a full-fledged historiographical field, the circumstances that created it, the forces that shaped it, and the scholarship it produced. Special emphasis is put on the significance of history writing in a semicolonial environment. The chapter ends with a preliminary comment about the actual experience of history writing in an atmosphere of political rivalry and struggle for independence. In discussing these issues, I examine a body of literature written during the twenty-five years that preceded the 1952 Revolution and analyze its various perceptions of early modern Egyptian history from 1798/1805 to 1882.

THE FORMATION OF THE HISTORIOGRAPHICAL FIELD

Any serious attempt to understand intellectual competition should take into account the sociocultural context that framed and conditioned the life cycle of ideas involved. We have already seen how, beginning in late nineteenth century, several sociocultural trends ushered in new modes of historical thinking and writing and created a new, yet very immature, historiographical field. In the late 1920s, however, historical writing began to emerge as a vibrant arena in which a myriad of independent intellectuals and schools of thought closely interacted.

2. Quoted from al-Rāfiʿī's personal papers by Ḥamāda Maḥmūd Aḥmad Ismāʿīl, *Ṣināʿat tārīkh Miṣr al-ḥadīth: Dirāsa fī fikr ʿAbd al-Raḥmān al-Rāfiʿī* (Cairo: al-Hay'a al-miṣriyya al-ʿāmma li-l-kitab, 1987), p. 207.

3. Dodwell was also the editor of *The Cambridge History of India.*

The circumstances that brought about the crystallization of this historiographical field deserve special attention.

The standard explanation for the knowledge boom of the late 1920s revolves around the consolidation of a new middle class, which is commonly referred to as the new *effendiyya*.[4] Initially, during the 1890s, *effendi* was an honorific title bestowed on educated bureaucrats and graduates of the khedival schools who had gone on to pursue advanced education in Europe, but in the late 1920s the title reflected a particular social and economic class composed of well-to-do families that had shifted their urban alliances from al-Azhar, the family business, and the neighborhood to modern avenues of participation in education and professional specialization. Several processes, all of which culminated in precisely that period, facilitated this shift: large-scale urbanization, rapid population growth, the creation of a national economy, and the expansion of the education and communications systems. The post-1919 expectation for a swift revolutionary change on the economic, social, cultural, and, especially, political fronts framed these culminating processes.

Beyond class, as a broad cultural category, *effendis* "lie at the intersection of the merchant and the bureaucrat, of the rural second stratum and the professional, or even the national elite, yet they were distinct as *effendis*."[5] Coming into wealth was not requisite for becoming an *effendi*, and evidently many of them were worse off financially than their parents. First and foremost, what *effendis* did and dreamed of doing qualified them as members of this stratum. Since both functionally and conceptually they were linked to modernity, *effendis* served as teachers, students, bureaucrats, technicians, clerks, engineers, physicians, managers, journalists, and public intellectuals. A process of professionalization was quintessential for this class, and indeed, during the 1930s, they established new professional associations that strove to standardize, codify, certify, and ultimately monopolize specific occupations. As we shall see in chapter 5, history writing and writing in general were part and parcel of this process.

Undoubtedly, as a career pursuers, *effendis* were most significant in terms of their contribution to various types of intellectual engagement, such as the diverse forms of Egyptian nationalism and even socialism.[6] Political activism followed

4. For a history of this emerging class in a broad social context, see Mu'min Kamāl al-Shāfi'ī, *Al-Dawla wa-l-ṭabaqa al-wūsṭa fī Miṣr* (Cairo: Dār qibā', 2000), especially pp. 173–229.

5. Lucie Ryzova, "Egyptianizing Modernity: The 'New Effendiyya' Social and Cultural Constructions of the Middle Class in Egypt under the Monarchy," in Arthur Goldschmidt, Amy Johnson, and Barak Salmoni, eds., *Re-envisioning the Egyptian Monarchy* (Cairo: AUC Press, 2005), p. 125.

6. For a discussion of the new *effendiyya* in relation to nationalist thought, see Israel Gershoni and James Jankowski, *Redefining the Egyptian Nation, 1930–1945* (New York: Cambridge University Press, 1995), pp. 7–22; Israel Gershoni, "The Evolution of National Culture in Modern Egypt:

naturally, and for these reasons, an *effendi* of the 1930s symbolized "the ideal citizen of the state who also fulfilled the role of a modern public."[7]

Since most of the processes that contributed to the consolidation of this class are measurable, scholars have been able to portray the contours of a quantitative change. In almost any given factor (for example, academic institutions, professional associations, and written and broadcast media), one can discern a dramatic quantitative shift toward a full-fledged intellectual arena.[8] Within this dynamic, a distinctive realm that was dedicated to history writing, especially writing about the modern era, came into existence.

Clearly, this lively arena owes its existence to the increase in the number of writers, journalists (from twelve hundred to eighty-two hundred between 1937 and 1947), publishing houses, and academic institutions and to the expanding public education system.[9] Particularly important was the impressive gallery of journals, magazines, and newspapers, in which much of the historiographical competition took place. It seems that in this very period a long process that started in the first half of the nineteenth century was successfully completed, namely, from *maṭbaʿa* (press) to *maktaba* (bookstore) to *dār* (publishing house). Nevertheless, books, in spite of the steady increase in their production, were far outdistanced by the periodic press.[10] These developments generated the vital circulation of ideas without which historical writing could not have subsisted.[11]

Additionally, history writing profited from the establishment of public and

---

Intellectual Formation and Social Diffusion, 1892–1945," *Poetics Today* 13, no. 2 (Summer 1992): pp. 325–350; Marius Deeb, *Party Politics in Egypt: The Wafd and Its Rivals 1919–1939*, St. Antony's Middle East Monographs 9 (London: Ithaca Press, 1979), pp. 11–12; and Kamāl al-Shāfiʿī, *Al-Dawla wa-l-ṭabaqa*, pp. 204–207.

7. Ryzova, "Egyptianizing Modernity," p. 131.

8. Nevertheless, some writers lamented that most citizens did not really read and believed that those who did never processed the information or appreciated the writers. Ibrāhīm Maṣrī, "Li man yaktub al-kātib fī Miṣr?" *Al-Hilāl*, July 1938, pp. 987–991.

9. For the increasing number of journalists, see Jean-Jacques Wardenburg, *Les universités dans le monde arabe actuel* (Paris: Mouton, 1966), vol. 2, p. 81; quoted in Gershoni and Jankowski, *Redefining the Egyptian Nation*, p. 13. For the expansion of public education in the context of history teaching, see Barak Ahraon Salmoni, "Pedagogies of Patriotism: Teaching Socio-political Community in Twentieth-Century Turkish and Egyptian Education," unpublished Ph.D. dissertation, Harvard University, 2002, pp. 514–550, 672–712, 820–926, 990–1065.

10. Some writers called this reality "the book crisis." Muḥammad ʿAbdallāh ʿAnān, "Azmat al-kitāb wa maṣīr al-kutub," *Al-Risāla*, July 30, 1934, pp. 1286–1288.

11. See references to book circulation in "Jawla fī maʿraḍ al-kitāb al-ʿarabī," *Al-Kitāb*, July 1947, pp. 364–367; and Muḥammad Kurd ʿAlī "Kitābunā wa taʾlīfunā," *Al-Hilāl*, July 1939, pp. 841–852. See also Israel Gershoni, "Secondary Intellectuals, Readers, and Readership as Agents of National-Cultural Reproduction in Modern Egypt," in Yaakov Elman and Israel Gershoni, eds., *Transmitting Jewish Traditions: Orality, Textuality, and Cultural Diffusion* (New Haven, CT: Yale University Press, 2000), pp. 324–347.

TABLE 2. Number of History Books Published in Arabic on Modern Egypt

	1900–1915	1916–1925	1926–1940	1941–1950
Books published	2	47	62	94

SOURCES: ʿĀyida Ibrāhīm Nuṣayr, *Al-Kutub al-ʿarabiyya allatī nushirat fī Miṣr bayna ʿāmay 1926–1940* (Cairo: Cairo University, 1966); ʿĀyida Ibrāhīm Nuṣayr, *Al-Kutub al-ʿarabiyya allatī nushirat fī Miṣr bayna ʿāmay 1900–1925* (Cairo: AUC Press, 1983); and Aḥmad Muḥammad Manṣūr, *Al-Kutub al-ʿarabiyya allatī nushirat fī Miṣr 1940–1956* (Cairo: AUC Press, 1975).

NOTE: The books I took into account belong to several different genres, such as biographies, memoirs, school textbooks, and works in translation.

academic libraries in various locations, even outside the two big urban centers. New libraries were regarded as signposts on the highway of Egyptian renaissance, and their activities were closely monitored.[12] Thus, between 1921 and 1950, at least fifty-nine public libraries were established.[13] An increase in the quantity of readership is discernable as well. In 1927 alone, there were 74,420 visitors to Dār al-Kutub, which reorganized itself in order to improve students' accessibility and to enhance cooperation with local libraries in the provinces.[14] As illustrated in Table 2, in accordance with all of these developments, the 1930s and 1940s saw a dramatic increase in the number of published history books on the modern era. In 1945 the Cairo Library Association was established and with it a plan for the creation of the Institute of Librarianship. The British Council in Egypt seems to have been particularly involved in the development of library resources.[15]

By the mid-1930s, a host of history teaching institutions, archives, museums, libraries, orchestrated historical projects, teaching grants, fellowships, students' delegations, conferences, and specialized journals, all interacting and working toward similar ends, constituted the historiographical field. These opinion-forming enterprises, many of them voluntary, toiled to counter, refashion, or support every historical idea that was circulated. Chiefly, but not entirely, funded by public money, these enterprises participated in historical writing and research and were the linchpin in the formation and reformulation of the public's opinion and his-

12. See a report on a new library in Damanhūr with statistics on numbers of books and readership in *Al-Ahrām*, May 6, 1932, p. 9.

13. Egyptian Government, *Dalīl al-maktabāt al-miṣriyya: Al-ʿāmma wa al-mutakhaṣiṣa wa al-aqādīmiyya* (Cairo: al-Maktaba al-aqādimīyya, 1998), p. 13.

14. Shaʿbān ʿAbd al-ʿAziz Khalīfa, *Dār al-kutub al-qawmiyya fī riḥlat al-nushū' wa-l-irtiqā' wa-l-tadahwūr* (Cairo: al-ʿArabī, 1991), pp. 140–145.

15. According to an official British survey of Cairo libraries, by 1950 there were 15 municipal libraries, 2 university libraries, 150 in secondary schools, 10 in government ministries, and 10 libraries in various institutions such as the Arab League headquarters. BW 29/52.

torical consciousness.[16] Although many of these enterprises were in existence prior to the 1930s, the increased number of published works strongly suggests that a successful synchronization of these developments occurred only in this period.

Cognizant of the impact of this sphere on the formation of public opinion, Italy, France, and England tried to influence which history books Egypt would import and which would be displayed in public libraries.[17] On other occasions, historical mindedness was harnessed for the cause of straightforward propaganda. For instance, at one point in 1940, the Italian government, in attempt to win Egyptians to the side of the fascists, appealed to their sense of history. In a covert operation, the Italians distributed in Cairo six hundred thousand pamphlets urging Egyptians to remember their "glorious history," the 1882 British occupation, and the dead Egyptian patriots who fought in Alexandria.[18]

Despite overwhelming illiteracy, even among the urban population, the visualization of the past through popular magazines, stamps, banknotes, statues, and street names, as well as oral forms of reproduction (notably radio and cinema), shaped the population's historical consciousness. Especially prone to such influences was the rising young nationalist generation, which almost immediately translated historical understanding into political action.[19] Consequently, whether they were political associations, parties, cultural institutions, or interested individuals, almost all of the participants in Egypt's public life competed in finding, propagating, and controlling the spread of historical meaning. This chapter tells their story.

Introducing the Protagonists

Just when Fu'ād's historiographical efforts were on the verge of completion, other historical interpretations, which, to say the least, were not necessarily flattering to the monarchy, flooded the Egyptian public arena. Unlike the highly orchestrated royal project, independent scholars, usually outside academia, wrote this litera-

16. On awareness of public opinion, see Niqūlā Ḥaddād, *Al-Hilāl,* June 1936, p. 890.

17. For example, in July 1945, the French government complained that the British government had assisted the Egyptians in creating a black list of prohibited French books. Specifically, they disapproved the ban of the La librairie delà renaissance series. Though the British strongly denied such allegations, they did play a dominant role in the politics of book distribution. FO 924/169, FO 924/170. For an Italian plan to influence Egyptian public opinion through books and films, see ACS/MCP/Propaganda/Egitto/61. In 1937 the Italians planned to open a library with special literature on the history of the Orient: ACS/MCP/Propaganda/Egitto/62.

18. ACS/MCP/Propaganda/Egitto/63.

19. Haggai Erlich, *Students and University in Twentieth Century Egyptian Politics* (London: Frank Cass, 1989), pp. 95–132. Following the demonstrations of 1936, the political potential of educated youth was publicly acknowledged. The April 1936 issue of *Al-Hilāl* was dedicated to youth. See also Maḥmūd Kāmil, *Miṣr al-ghad taḥta ḥukum al-shabāb* (Cairo: Dār al-jāmiʿa, 1945).

ture. Since encompassing the vast literature of this era is virtually impossible, I will confine myself to presenting the work of several key historians and one school of thought. Other, less central writers will be referred to in the notes.

Four independent historians of the same generation, with a similar middle-class social background, operated in the same historiographical scene as the royalists. This quartet, ʿAbd al-Raḥmān al-Rāfiʿī, Muḥammad Shafīq Ghurbāl, Muḥammad Ṣabrī, and Muḥammad Rifʿat, had a critical influence on the thought and practice of modern historiography. Ṣabrī and Rifʿat, both trained in Europe, contributed greatly to the formation and dissemination of historical meaning, but in terms of both quality and quantity their work falls somewhere between al-Rāfiʿī's and the royalists'. Hence, the discussion will focus mainly on the independent writer al-Rāfiʿī and the group of royal historians. Ghurbāl has a special place in the formation of professional academic writing, and it was there that he invested most of his energies. The next chapter is dedicated to his influential professional ethos. Nevertheless, Ghurbāl, who was trained in London under the supervision of Arnold Toynbee, participated also in more accessible forms of writing. In addition to these writers were dozens of journalists, teachers, state officials, and a host of intellectuals, such as the semiofficial historian prince ʿUmar Ṭūsūn, who expressed their historical views, often reiterating or expanding on points already raised by the historians mentioned above.

Despite his confrontation with the monarchy and the falling out with the Wafd, Muḥammad Ṣabrī was still an active historian in the 1930s. Yet he no longer took part in the writing of populist and politically inclined history of the kind that had shocked the monarchy only a decade earlier. Less agitated and obviously more mature than he used to be, Ṣabrī reconciled with the monarchy and was readmitted to the ʿĀbdīn archive, paying the price, like most others, of having his work closely monitored. In the early 1930s he published his findings only after, as he revealed in an interview, he was asked by Fuʿād to "delete some of the more unflattering references to Khedive Ismāʿīl."[20] Despite some criticism for it, he insisted on writing mainly in French, a language he considered most suitable for professional and scientific writing.[21] His works were well received by European historians and especially by those working for Fu'ād.[22] Perhaps because he deserted his confrontational role, leaving it to others, but also because he tended to ignore local Egyptian scholarship, he was relegated to a marginal position from which he never reemerged.

20. Jack Crabbs, "Politics, History and Culture in Nasser's Egypt," *IJMES* 6, no. 4 (1975): p. 390.

21. al-Ṭamāwī, *Ṣabrī al-Surbūnī*, pp. 90–91.

22. Dodwell, Sammarco, and Charles-Roux praised Ṣabrī's achievements. Ibid., pp. 74–75. For their praises, see also the cover jacket of Ṣabrī's book: Mohamed Sabry, *L'empire égyptien sous Ismaïl et l'ingérence anglo-française* (Paris: Paul Geuthner, 1933).

Sadly enough, despite this new successful attempt at writing unconfrontational, politically balanced scholarship, Ṣabrī was still not allowed to became a permanent faculty member in the university. Lacking a position in any of Egypt's academic strongholds, he held several bureaucratic positions, which were always subjected to the whims of the monarchy and the political party in power. Thus, though for many years Ṣabrī was employed as deputy director of Dār al-Kutub and was expected to be appointed as its director, the position was not given to him, and he was forced to resign.[23] Unlike Ghurbāl and Rif'at, who had already captured prominent and influential positions, Ṣabrī was never able to secure professional stability for himself. Frustrated and vulnerable, he gradually gave up historical writing in favor of literary subjects. From a monarchic point of view, his practical suppression was a worthwhile effort. Perhaps because of his temperament (as one writer suggested), Ṣabrī was the only historian who was suppressed both before and after the 1952 Revolution.[24] Neglected and forgotten, he died in Cairo in 1978.[25]

In contrast to Ṣabrī, Muḥammad Rif'at was not renowned for being a prolific and daring writer. Quite the contrary, he wrote only a few books, all of which were closely attuned to where the political wind was blowing. Nevertheless, beginning in the early 1920s, he composed the standard history school textbook and was responsible for its constant updating until 1952. Likewise, he held several key positions in the Ministry of Education, including that of a minister. Cooperating on several occasions with Ghurbāl, Rif'at had a pivotal role in the propagation of historical meaning in the school system.[26] A review of three editions of his school textbook indicates the erosion of royal interpretation and the acceptance of more nationalist themes. In 1947 he published *The Awakening of Egypt*, which was modeled on George Antonius's classic *The Arab Awakening*.

Born in 1889, al-Rāfi'ī had the most versatile career of all. Given al-Rāfi'ī's strong socialization into the nationalist movement of the turn of the twentieth century, one may recognize in his work the particular ideological and political influence of the National Party. Indeed, al-Rāfi'ī's thought was formed in a volatile and lively environment in which national change was promoted on all possible fronts. Lawyers, publishers, journalists, writers, and political activists participated in journalistic and editorial writing.[27] After several years of these writers'

23. al-Ṭamāwī, *Ṣabrī al-Surbūnī*, pp. 161–162.

24. 'Abd al-Mun'im al-Jumay'ī, *Itijāhāt al-kitāba*, pp. 171–178.

25. Shukrī al-Qāḍī, *Mi'at shakhṣīyya miṣrīyya wa shakhṣīyya* (Cairo: al-Hay'a al-'āma li-l-kitāb, 1987), p 235; Yūsuf al-Qa'īd, "Ẓalamnāhu ḥayyan fahal nanṣifuhu mayyitan?" *Al-Muṣawwar*, March 24, 1978, pp. 57–58.

26. For more on his role in the Ministry of Education, see Salmoni, "Pedagogies of Patriotism," pp. 1010–1025.

27. Crabbs, *The Writing of History in Nineteenth-Century Egypt*, pp. 146–184; al-Shayyāl, *Al-Tārīkh wa al-mu'ārikhūn*, pp. 157–181.

intense public activity, their language, rhetoric, and assumptions began to sink in. Al-Rāfiʿī was strongly affiliated with this milieu and acted on its behalf.

Al-Rāfiʿī came from a middle-class Muslim background, the very background that was the dynamic social element that was to usher in the national age.[28] Those of this background spoke and thought in Arabic but were familiar also with Turkish. A strong European influence left its mark on their education. They were polyglots whose culture and political orientation were geared toward imperial Istanbul.[29] The Ottoman framework was so solid in their minds that even during the heyday of World War I, when the Ottomans were already disintegrating, a nationalist al-Rāfiʿī refused to consider any alternative to the Ottoman order.

Like many young ardent nationalists at the turn of the twentieth century, al-Rāfiʿī strongly believed law was a vocation necessary for changing the national reality in Egypt.[30] Indeed, his only formal education was in the field of law. He never studied history but began to write it independently. A man of almost limitless energies, he did not narrow his activity to any particular field; he was a part-time journalist, a lawyer engaging in political activity, and a member of Parliament and cabinet minister on behalf of the National Party.[31]

In 1926, al-Rāfiʿī began working on a modest biography of Muṣṭafa Kāmil, the legendary leader of the National Party, whom he considered the founding father of the anti-British struggle. However, as he began writing, he quickly understood that he must undertake a broader task: to search for the roots of the nationalist struggle.[32] This agenda compelled him to explore the whole history of modern Egypt, from the French expedition to the present.

An industrious scholar, every two to three years al-Rāfiʿī published a new history book, which often set the historical agenda for other historians as well. Thus, popular-nationalist historians adopted his perception, royal historians strove to refute it, and academic historians were bothered first and foremost with his

28. Al-Rāfiʿī's father was a distinguished shaykh in al-Azhar University, and he opposed his son's inclination toward secular education. Muḥammad Bahāʾ al-Dīn ʿUlwān, *ʿAbd al-Raḥmān al-Rāfiʿī: Muʾarīkh Miṣr al-ḥadīth* (Cairo: al-Hayʾa al-miṣriyya al-ʿāmma li-l-kitāb, 1987); Ḥamāda Maḥmūd Aḥmad Ismāʿīl, *Ṣināʿat tārīkh Miṣr.*

29. Toledano, "Social and Economic Change in the 'Long Nineteenth Century,'" pp. 264–267.

30. For law and nationalism, see Donald Reid, *Lawyers and Politics in the Arab World, 1800–1960* (Chicago: Bibliotheca Islamica, 1981), pp. 52–53, 59–60.

31. In addition to being secretary of the party, during the years 1924–25 al-Rāfiʿī was a member of Majlis al-nuwwāb and, between 1939 and 1951, a member of Majlis al-shuyūkh and a minister of provisions (the latter in late 1949). ʿAbd al-Raḥmān al-Rāfiʿī, *Arbaʿat ʿashar ʿām fī-l-barlamān* (Cairo: Maṭbaʿat al-saʿāda bi Miṣr, 1955), pp. 1–5.

32. ʿAbd al-Raḥmān al-Rāfiʿī, *Tārīkh al-ḥaraka al-qawmiyya wa taṭawwur niẓām al-ḥukum fī Miṣr* (Cairo: Dār al-maʿārif, 1987), vol. 1, pp. 23–24.

scholarly methods. By the eve of the 1952 Revolution, al-Rāfiʿī was able to offer the Egyptian public a dozen detailed tomes and probably more than a hundred articles encompassing Egyptian history from 1798 to the present.[33] This project, which came to be known as the National Corpus *(al-mawsūʿa al-waṭaniyya),* was a true work of scholarship.[34] Until today, no other historian or work has suggested to the Egyptian readership such a powerful and accessible account of their entire modern past.

For both Western and local scholars, the work of al-Rāfiʿī is well known yet little studied.[35] Although I do not purport that this account is a full-fledged biography of al-Rāfiʿī, I attempt to shed light on his career as the foremost representative of nationalist popular historiography. In doing so, I focus on two major themes: first, al-Rāfiʿī's efforts to refute the royal historiography of the period 1805–82, through the writing of a systematic and coherent national epic; and second, his central role in the de-Ottomanization of Egyptian history. The rest of al-Rāfiʿī's corpus (1882–1959) will be analyzed in chapter 6.

THE MYRIAD FACETS OF EGYPT'S MODERN PAST

The aim of this section is to offer a close reading of the main corpus of historical literature on modern Egyptian history between 1798/1805 and 1882. At the basis of this very detailed account lies the understanding that a work on historiography must also engage with the actual contents of history books and not merely with the surrounding circumstances of their creation. For an overview of the historiographical scene during the 1920s, the 1930s, and the 1940s, see Table 3, near the end of this chapter.

33. Al-Rāfiʿī's writing career can be divided into four different stages: The first (1912–22) included the publication of four books on various issues, such as the union trades that were dominated by legal thinking. In the second and the longest period (late 1920s to early 1950s), he wrote the "national corpus." In the third phase (late 1950s), he composed two books on the history of the 1952 Revolution up to 1959. In the fourth period, he composed several less important publications on poetry and premodern nationalism.

34. The term *corpus* became prevalent in the 1960s. *Al-Ahrām,* September 2, 1964, p. 30; *Al-Majalla,* January 1962, pp. 22–27.

35. So far, three scholars have evaluated al-Rāfiʿī's life and work. Jack Crabbs focused mainly on the political aspects of al-Rāfiʿī's career in the wake of the 1952 Revolution, in "Egyptian Intellectuals and the Revolution: The Case of ʿAbd al-Raḥmān al-Rāfiʿī," in Shimon Shamir, ed., *Egypt from Monarchy to Republic: A Reassessment of Revolution and Change* (Boulder, CO: Westview Press, 1995), pp. 251–266. Other works provide valuable information but lack analysis. ʿUlwān, *ʿAbd al-Raḥmān al-Rāfiʿī;* Aḥmad Ismāʿīl, *Ṣināʿat tārīkh Miṣr.* Anthony Gorman located al-Rāfiʿī in a wide intellectual and institutional context but overlooked the unified structure and the uniqueness of his historical outlook: Gorman, *Historians, State and Politics,* pp. 84–88, 117–119.

Action, Passivity, and the Egyptian People

No matter what their professional background, religion, ethnicity, political orientation, or national affiliation, virtually all the historians we are about to encounter were in consensus with regard to Egypt's Ottoman experience. Al-Rāfiʿī was no exception. Thus, his tour de force of modern Egyptian history unoriginally starts in 1798, the day Napoleon first stepped onto Egyptian soil. To the Ottomans he dedicated only one short and insignificant chapter, in which he downplayed their historical role.[36] Periods and events that preceded Ottoman rule, such as the Mamluk and Pharaonic era, were not even mentioned.[37] In the words of al-Rāfiʿī, all events prior to 1798 belong to an era of "nationalist *jāhiliya*."[38] Although likely not the first to adopt this view, al-Rāfiʿī was certainly the first to systematize and propagate it in a popular-nationalist vein.

Henry Dodwell was another great popularizer of early modern Egyptian history, but unlike the independent al-Rāfiʿī, he was a full-time history professor operating from that bastion of Oriental studies, London University. Dodwell's field of specialization was Indian history. He did not read, nor did he speak, Arabic. Nevertheless, thanks to the archivists and translators of the ʿĀbdīn archive, he wrote what became one of the most influential accounts of Muḥammad ʿAlī's career. Though originally written in English, it was available in an Arabic translation six years after its publication.[39] In this book Dodwell failed to acknowledge that he, too, was on Fu'ād's payroll. It was important for Dodwell to maintain the illusion of academic integrity, which was naturally incompatible with such an allegiance. Years later, however, while already back in London, he complained to Muḥammad Anīs, a young Egyptian Ph.D. candidate in London University, that Fu'ād did not pay him enough for his efforts.[40] Nevertheless, despite his very

36. al-Rāfiʿī, *Tārīkh al-ḥaraka al-qawmiyya wa taṭawwur,* vol. 1, pp. 27–70.

37. However, in 1963, al-Rāfiʿī updated his corpus by publishing one last volume, which traced the origins of the modern nationalist spirit back through the Pharaonic, Greco-Roman, and Byzantine eras. Al-Rāfiʿī, *Tārīkh al-ḥaraka al-qawmiyya fī Miṣr al-qadīma min fajr al-tārīkh ila al-fatḥ al-ʿarabī* (Cairo: Maktabat al-nahḍa al-miṣriyya, 1963). Posthumously, drafts of another book, covering the period from the Arab to the Ottoman conquest, were edited and published as well. ʿAbd al-Raḥmān al-Rāfiʿī and Saʿīd ʿAbd al-Fattāḥ ʿĀshūr, *Miṣr fī-l-ʿuṣūr al-wūsṭa min al-fatḥ al-ʿarabī ḥatta al-ghazw al-ʿuthmānī* (Cairo: Dār al-nahḍa al-ʿarabiyya, 1970).

38. Like Ṣabrī, al-Rāfiʿī acknowledged the importance of ʿAlī Bey's rule but did not see its relevance to the modern era.

39. Henry Dodwell, *Muḥammad ʿAlī mu'assis Miṣr al-ḥadītha,* trans. ʿAlī Aḥmad Shukrī and Aḥmad ʿAbd al-Khāliq (Cairo: Maktabat al-adāb 1937). See also a review by Maḥmūd Yūsif Zāyid in *Al-Thaqāfa,* January 9, 1950, pp. 25–26.

40. Muḥammad Anīs, "Shafīq Ghurbāl wa madrasat al-tārīkh al-miṣrī al-ḥadīth," *Al-Majalla,* November 1961, p. 13. The translator's preface for the Arabic edition of Dodwell's book reveals the scope of cooperation with the royal project: Dodwell, *Muḥammad ʿAlī mu'assis,* preface.

different background from that of al-Rāfiʿī or Ṣabrī, Dodwell, like Charles-Roux, Driault, and others, held similar views to the two Egyptians when considering Egypt's Ottoman heritage.[41] Thus, Dodwell contended that the period that preceded the French occupation was exceptionally chaotic and repressive.[42] Édouard Driault, for example, was convinced that during the seventeenth and eighteenth centuries Egypt practically disappeared from history.[43]

Regarding the cultural impact of the 1798 French expedition, disagreements continue to this very day. Muḥammad Ṣabrī's perspective on this issue was simple: "En un mot, l'expédition française a posé en Égypte le principe d'un mouvement civilisateur" (In a single word, the French expedition had proposed the principle of a civilizing movement in Egypt).[44] According to al-Rāfiʿī, however, the French invasion was the continuation of Western-Crusader aggression against Egypt.[45] Al-Rāfiʿī was not willing to consider any positive aspects of the French expedition. Thus, he opined, as in previous failed attempts to subdue Egypt by force, the French had to face the fierce resistance of the Egyptian people. The revolutionary character of the people, and hence their utter resistance to any foreign rule whatsoever, was regarded by al-Rāfiʿī as a self-evident metaphysical force, a force that governed al-Rāfiʿī's entire project. Interestingly enough, already in the first volume, al-Rāfiʿī drew an analogy between the Egyptians' struggle against the French and their 1919 Revolution against the British.[46]

In al-Rāfiʿī's version of the story, this popular struggle against France started as the French troops approached Alexandria. Al-Rāfiʿī regarded the confrontation between the inhabitants of Alexandria, headed by Muḥammad Kurayyim (Alexandria's *naqīb al-ashrāf*), and the French forces as an indication of Egypt's nationalist and revolutionary nature.[47] He argued that it was the people and their leaders, rather than the Mamluks, who organized the opposition to the invaders.[48] The military opposition to the French continued after the arrest of

41. Mohamed Sabry, *La genèse de l'esprit national égyptien, 1863–1882,* published dissertation (Paris: Libraire Picart, 1924), p. 8. See also Muḥammad Ṣabrī, *Tārīkh Miṣr min Muḥammad ʿAlī ila al-ʿaṣr al-ḥadīth* (Cairo: Madbūlī, 1991), pp. 19–24.

42. Dodwell, *The Founder of Modern Egypt,* pp. 1–3. See also François Charles-Roux, "L'Égypte de 1801 à 1882," in Gabriel Hanotaux, ed., *Histoire de la nation égyptienne* (Paris: Ouvrage publié sous les auspices et le haut patronage de sa majesté Fouad Ier, Roi d'Égypte, 1937), vol. 6, pp. 2–4; and Driault, "Mohamed-Aly et Ibrahim," pp. 192–204.

43. Driault, "Mohamed-Aly et Ibrahim," p. 187. See also Étienne Combe, "L'Égypte ottomane 1517–1798," in Mohamed Zaky el-Ibrachy Pacha and Angelo Sammarco, eds., *Précis de l'histoire d'Égypte* (Cairo: L'institut français d'archéologie orientale du Caire, 1933), vol. 3, part 1, pp. 41–50.

44. Sabry, *La genèse de l'esprit national égyptien,* p. 8.

45. al-Rāfiʿī, *Tārīkh al-ḥaraka al-qawmiyya wa taṭawwur,* vol. 1, pp. 75–80.

46. Ibid., pp. 155–156.

47. In secondary literature, Kurayyim is usually referred to as Muḥammad Karīm.

48. Ibid., pp. 169–172.

Kurayyim. Although praised by Napoleon himself for his bravery, Kurayyim refused to cooperate with the French and was therefore executed.[49] In this nationalist interpretation, Kurayyim is considered to be the first revolutionary martyr who chose death in the face of a humiliating surrender.

Al-Rāfiʿī's account of the French presence in Egypt was that of an uncompromising popular struggle. The various skirmishes and other incidents were treated as the outcome of an inherently nationalist consciousness. According to al-Rāfiʿī, the French, following two popular Cairo revolutions (the first against Napoleon in 1798 and the second against General Kléber in 1800),[50] were driven out of the country *(al-jalā')*, the Ottoman *wālī* was deposed, and the people appointed Muḥammad ʿAlī. Since Muḥammad ʿAlī understood that he could "not seize power by the force of his soldiers but only by that of the people," he collaborated with them for the purpose of driving the newly appointed Ottoman *wālī*, Khūrshīd Pasha, out of Egypt.[51] Acknowledging the importance of the nationalist factor, Muḥammad ʿAlī joined hands with the authentic popular leadership, headed by ʿUmar Makram, Cairo's *naqīb al-ashrāf*, and other religious leaders. The ultimate result of these moves was the appointment of Muḥammad ʿAlī "by the will of the people."[52] The events of these years further consolidated the nationalist factor *(al-ʿunṣur al-qawmī)*, which had engulfed the entire population of Cairo.[53]

Al-Rāfiʿī's interpretation of Muḥammad ʿAlī's seizure of power was a historiographic novelty. Before his publication, no Egyptian historian would have dared to claim that the forefather of the monarchy was a mere tool in the hands of indigenous nationalist forces. By emphasizing the role of ʿUmar Makram, the catalyst for the election of Muḥammad ʿAlī, al-Rāfiʿī contradicted the pro-monarchic interpretation. Furthermore, for al-Rāfiʿī, Makram embodied the revolutionary nature of the Egyptian people as a whole, a view that was further popularized by historical novelists à la Jurjī Zaydān.[54]

Despite al-Rāfiʿī's four hundred detailed pages, the nationalist factor and its agents were the central, and quite simplistic, thread that runs through the fabric of Egypt's modern history. Al-Rāfiʿī's historical anachronism continued to govern his entire work. By 1930 his project brought into focus a series of historical key concepts that he masterfully presented: the people, hero, enemy, and the nation-

49. Ibid., pp. 178–180.

50. Ibid., p. 268. Although the headquarters of the second Cairo revolution was at the Islamic al-Azhar University, al-Rāfiʿī does not ascribe any religious character to that revolution.

51. Ibid., vol. 2, pp. 327, 289–290, 322–326.

52. Ibid., p. 337.

53. Ibid., p. 257.

54. Muḥammad Farīd Abū Ḥadīd, *Sīrat al-sayyid ʿUmar Makram* (Cairo: Lajnat al-ta'līf wa-l-tarjama wa-l-nashr, 1937), see especially pp. 20, 37, 40, 50, 69–70.

alist factor". Pro-monarchic concepts, such as dynasty and monarchy, did not play any significant role in al-Rāfiʿī's framework.

It goes without saying that royal historiography had a different story to tell, one in which Muḥammad Kurayyim, ʿUmar Makram, and other popular elements were not even mentioned. Furthermore, for royal historiography the French expedition was not a story of Egyptian resistance led by popular heroes but, in the words of a different kind of hero, the beginning of a wonderful friendship. The dynamics of this friendship were rather simple: Europe gave and Egypt took. In the words of Hanotaux, who by now was already quite familiar to the Egyptian readership: "Le plus grand service rendu à l'Égypte par l'expédition de Bonaparte, c'est d'avoir fait resurgir en elle le sens national" (The most important service that the Napoleonic expedition rendered to Egypt was to reawaken its nationalist feeling).[55] Another historian stated: "Ce que l'expédition de 1798 a encore laissé en Égypte, c'est la diffusion de la pensée, de la langue, des lois françaises. . . . La réussite, dans le domaine spirituel, a été longue et brillante" (The diffusion of French thought, language, and laws was another important legacy of the 1798 expedition. . . . The success [of the expedition], in the spiritual realm, has been longstanding and brilliant).[56] Holding a similar view, King Fu'ād declared that Egypt would never forget the contribution of the French expedition.[57]

As for Muḥammad ʿAlī, royal historians, in sharp opposition to al-Rāfiʿī, depicted him as an active and vibrant leader who provoked and incited the various factions against one another until he emerged triumphant. According to Dodwell, for instance, it was Muḥammad ʿAlī who "headed the Cairenes against Kūrshīd" until "at last securing for himself the sanction of the Sultan's authority."[58] On Muḥammad ʿAlī's early career, the general standpoint of Ṣabrī, a die-hard Francophone shifting back and forth between popular and royal perspectives, was essentially royalist and, in fact, nourished some of the foreigners' writings.[59] As we shall see, disagreements among popular-nationalists, royalists,

55. Hanotaux, ed., *Histoire de la nation égyptienne,* vol. 1, p. lxxvii. The press frequently referred to Hanotaux. In 1939 Ṭaha Ḥusayn was asked to supervise the translation work of *Histoire de la nation égyptienne.* For some unknown reason, the project was not completed: *Al-Risāla,* December 12, 1939, p. 2322. See also *Al-Risāla,* July 13, 1936, p. 1160; and Gabriel Hanotaux, "Miṣr mabʿath ḥaḍārat al-ʿālam," *Al-Hilāl,* January 1932, pp. 425–427. For a review of Hanotaux's project, see Nallino, "Una recente storia dell'Egitto dalle origini al 1879."

56. Jacques Bainville, "L'expédition française en Égypte, 1798–1801," in Mohamed Zaky el-Ibrachy Pacha and Angelo Sammarco, eds., *Précis de l'histoire d'Égypte,* vol. 3, part 2, 1933, pp. 177–178.

57. Declaration of the king reported in Hanotaux, ed., *Histoire de la nation égyptienne,* vol. 7, pp. iii–iv.

58. Dodwell, *The Founder of Modern Egypt,* p. 21. Driault, however, inclined more toward the popular explanation: Driault, "Mohamed-Aly et Ibrahim," pp. 204–214.

59. Ṣabrī had an important role in developing and propagating the notion of a ninetieth-century Egyptian empire. Mohamed Sabry, *L'empire égyptien sous Mohamed Ali et la question d'Orient 1811–*

and those situated in between with regard to Muḥammad ʿAlī's career did not end here.

Who Founded Modern Egypt?

In 1930, when the "founder" Muḥammad ʿAlī was at the heart of the historiographical consensus, al-Rāfiʿī published the first inclusive and critical account of his reign. As we might expect, he presented the success of Muḥammad ʿAlī's role as the work of popular forces, especially given the assistance that ʿUmar Makram rendered to him.[60] Similarly, he argued that without the active support of the people against the British fleet at Rashid and other places, Muḥammad ʿAlī would certainly have lost his position.[61] Muḥammad ʿAlī's decision to exile ʿUmar Makram and to massacre the Mamluk forces at the citadel (1811) were regarded by al-Rāfiʿī as betrayal.[62] Despite al-Rāfiʿī's harsh judgment, historian Prince ʿUmar Ṭūsūn and others played down the significance of the citadel massacre and argued that Muḥammad ʿAlī had had no other choice.[63] European royal historians were divided over the moral implications of this act, with their opinions dependent on their national affiliation.[64]

Al-Rāfiʿī was quite ambivalent about Muḥammad ʿAlī's career. While he presented Muḥammad ʿAlī as a mere instrument in the hands of popular forces, he also dedicated hundreds of pages to discussing the achievements of his reforms.[65] Specifically, Al-Rāfiʿī was impressed with Egypt's political, economic, and territorial autonomy. Likewise, he hailed Muḥammad ʿAlī's refusal to grant the Suez Canal concession to the European powers and his stubborn resistance to offers

---

1849 (Paris: Paul Geuthner, 1930), pp. 23–27. See reviews of the book in *Al-Muqtaṭaf,* June 1930, pp. 105–106; and *Al-Hilāl,* June 1930, pp. 1009–1010.

60. Reviewers were impressed with al-Rāfiʿī's ability to forcefully present a new historic interpretation that was not guided by flattery *(mujāmala). Al-Muqtaṭaf,* February 1931, pp. 244–246; *Al-Hilāl,* February 1931, pp. 616–617.

61. ʿAbd al-Raḥmān al-Rāfiʿī, *ʿAṣr Muḥammad ʿAlī* (Cairo: Matbaʿat al-fikra, 1930), pp. 19–29, 45–46, 55–56, 75–73.

62. Ibid., pp. 80–121. In *Al-Hilāl,* al-Rāfiʿī dismissed apologetic attempts to justify the massacre, which he regarded as a well-organized conspiracy that terrorized the entire population and hurt national morale. ʿAbd al-Raḥmān al-Rāfiʿī, "Madhbaḥat al-mamālīk bi-l-qalʿa," *Al-Hilāl,* November 1930, pp. 89–96.

63. ʿUmar Ṭūsūn, "Kayfa intaha al-mamālīk baʿda majzarat al-qalʿa," *Al-Hilāl,* May 1933, pp. 874–877; Anwar Zaqlama, "ʾĀkhar ʿahd Miṣr bi-l-mamālīk," *Al-Hilāl,* February 1929, pp. 474–478.

64. According to Dodwell, the British were the first to consider the moral dimension of the massacre, because it brought about the demise of their allies. Dodwell, *The Founder of Modern Egypt,* p. 36. Charles-Roux considered the massacre a barbaric act that, nevertheless, was "still within the traditions of the Orient." Charles-Roux, "*L'Égypte de 1801 à 1881,*" pp. 44–45.

65. See especially an article lauding Muḥammad Ali's reforms: ʿAbd al-Raḥmān al-Rāfiʿī, "Muḥammad ʿAlī Bāshā wa-l-khadīvī Ismāʿīl," *Al-Hilāl,* November 1933, pp. 33–35.

of Western financial assistance. The lack of constitutional life in that era stood as an exception in al-Rāfiʿī's assessment. However, his accentuation of the achievements of Muḥammad ʿAlī served to allude to the failures of his successors, who had subjected the country to the rule of foreign authority.[66]

For royal historians, Muḥammad ʿAlī's domestic policies were the very heart of the matter. These reforms were total, touching on every possible aspect of life, from personal hygiene to land reclamation.[67] In royal historians' minds, reforms were crucial, because they transformed Egypt into a more modern, progressive, and European-like entity. As such, European observers used reforms as the ultimate measuring tool for Egypt's progress. According to Dodwell, for example, the pasha's reforms were successful because "he had opened his country so widely and so wisely" to Europe.[68] Likewise, Charles-Roux, concluding his account, cited a nineteenth-century British observer who leaves us no doubt as to whom we should thank: "Acune nation n'a autant contribué à la civilization et au progrès de l'Égypte que les Français" (No other nation has contributed as much to Egypt's progress and civilization as the French).[69] And so, obsession with reforms became a hallmark of royal historiography and remained a central theme in local as well as Western historiography for many years to come.[70] Writing in the same period of time, Ṣabrī completely subscribed to this outlook. Already in 1920, Ṣabrī had identified Muḥammad ʿAlī as the "organizer of modern Egypt."[71] However, in his *L'empire égyptien sous Mohamed Ali,* Ṣabrī also referred to British polices that, according to him, hampered these very reforms and foiled the emergence of an independent and sovereign Egyptian state.[72]

By the early 1930s, al-Rāfiʿī's views positioned him not only in opposition to the royalists but also in a sharp opposition to Muḥammad Shafīq Ghurbāl, of Fu'ād University, who himself had much to say about this era. Ghurbāl was thirty-four years old when he finally published his influential book *The Beginnings of*

66. al-Rāfiʿī, *ʿAṣr Muḥammad ʿAlī,* pp. 662–665.

67. Charles-Roux , *"L'Égypte de 1801 à 1881,"* pp. 47–91; Driault, "Mohamed-Aly et Ibrahim," pp. 192–204, 296–308.

68. Dodwell, *The Founder of Modern Egypt,* p. 241.

69. Charles-Roux, *"L'Égypte de 1801 à 1881,"* p. 91.

70. See ʿUmar Ṭūsūn, *Al-Ṣanāʾiʿ wa-l-madāris al-ḥarbiyya fī ʿahd Muḥammad ʿAlī* (Alexandria: Maṭbaʿat ṣalāḥ al-dīn al-kubra, 1932). Academics subscribed to the reforms paradigm as well: Muḥammad Fu'ād Shukrī et al., eds., *Bināʾ dawla: Miṣr Muḥammad ʿAlī* (Cairo: Maṭbaʿat lajnat al-ta'līf al-tarjama wa-l-nashr, 1948). See also Lutfi Sayyid-Marsot, *Egypt in the Reign of Muhammad Ali;* and Rivlin Helen, *The Agricultural Policy of Muhammad ʿAlī in Egypt* (Cambridge, MA: Harvard University Press, 1961).

71. Sabry, *La question d'Égypte depuis Bonaparte,* pp. 16–17. Muḥammad Rifʿat held an identical view: Muḥammad Rifʿat, "Muḥammad ʿAlī, bāʿith nahḍat al-taʿlīm wa-l-thaqāfa," *Al-Hilāl,* April 1937, pp. 617–621.

72. Sabry, *L'empire égyptien sous Mohamed Ali,* pp. 579–592.

the Egyptian Question and the Rise of Mehmet Ali. He was young, extremely energetic, and just about to embark on his lifetime academic mission to "professionalize" historical writing. Al-Rāfiʿī was already an influential historian in his own right. Their bitter differences began at this very point.

In brief, whereas al-Rāfiʿī maintained that "Egypt created Muḥammad ʿAlī," Ghurbāl, in step with the European and royal historiographical view, insisted that it was "Muḥammad ʿAlī [who] created modern Egypt."[73] These differences were not symbolic. Ghurbāl started his account of modern Egypt's defining moment overseas, as part of what seemed a strictly internal European affair. The European power politics of the Orient was the womb in which modern Egypt was conceived. The matchmaker was Napoleon; and the father, Muḥammad ʿAlī ("the founder," in Ghurbāl's terms). Foreigners with well-calculated interests dominated Ghurbāl's story: Consuls, ambassadors, statesmen, generals, admirals, and opportunistic politicians pushed Egypt into the modern era, awakening it from a long medieval slumber. All indigenous players were reduced to nothing: "The Mamelukes and their fellow plunderers—the Bedouins—perpetrated, on their part, similar horrors. They moved in Upper Egypt under four chiefs: Ibrahim, the 'doyen' of the corps but now so enfeebled in body and mind . . . Bardissy . . . whose character was formed by vanity and arrogant ignorance, Elfi, the 'bête noire,' an energetic barbarian, and Osman Hassan, the keeper of the best of the traditions of the race. . . . The Egyptians were the helpless and abject victims of these tyrants."[74] And in another place: "The force with which he [Khorsev, the first Ottoman viceroy after the French withdrawal] had to vanquish the Mamelukes was comprised partly of Turks and partly of Albanians; and the Egyptians never saw a more filthy and immoral and drunken rabble. The Turks were only slightly better than the Albanians."[75]

Thus, in opposition to al-Rāfiʿī, Ghurbāl claimed that local heroes played no significant role in this drama. He deemed ʿUmar Makram a marginal figure and did not even mention Muḥammad Kurayyim.[76] As was nicely put by Youssef Choueiri, "Ghurbāl has a story to tell. It is dominated by a single hero, Muḥammad ʿAlī. All the others are either villains, ignorant, or simply unlucky."[77]

73. After the revolution, al-Rāfiʿī felt more comfortable in attacking Ghurbāl: ʿAbd al-Raḥmān al-Rāfiʿī, "Miṣr khalaqat Muḥammad ʿAlī," *Al-Hilāl,* August 1953, pp. 40–43. See also later articles by Ghurbāl: Shafik Ghorbal, "Dr. Bowring and Muhammad Ali," *Bulletin de l'Institut d'Égypte* 24 (1941–42): pp. 107–112; and Shafik Ghorbal, "The Building-Up of a Single Egyptian Sudanese Fatherland in the 19th Century: The Achievement of the Viceroys Muhammad Ali and Ismail," in ʿAbbās Muṣṭafa ʿAmmar et al., eds., *The Unity of the Nile Valley* (Cairo: Government Press, 1947), pp. 61–63.

74. Shafik Ghorbal, *The Beginnings of the Egyptian Question and the Rise of Mehmet Ali* (1928; repr., New York: AMS Press, 1977), p. 208.

75. Ibid., p. 207.

76. On ʿUmar Makram, see ibid., pp. 227–228.

77. Choueiri, *Arab History and the Nation-State,* p. 71.

Al-Rāfiʿī had a story to tell as well. A single collective hero, the Egyptian people, dominated it. All the others were mere decoration, insignificant ornaments to the true historical forces.

Ghurbāl quoted at length from primary French sources. Numerous footnotes meticulously documented every archival finding. Al-Rāfiʿī's account was essentially free of footnotes. In order to understand Ghurbāl, one should have full command of English and French.[78] Elementary Arabic is enough for one to be completely immersed in al-Rāfiʿī's account. Nothing in Ghurbāl's story makes it distinctively Egyptian. Indeed, as his supervisor Arnold Toynbee suggested, "The writer, while conscious of the blemishes of the work of a beginner writing in a foreign language, submits this essay to the British public."[79] Al-Rāfiʿī's account is an intimate nationalist tale written by a credited nationalist politician who was exceptionally closely attuned to the dynamics of public sentiment.

Some years later, toward the beginning of the 1940s, several publications on the role of Muḥammad ʿAlī were available in Arabic. Karīm Thābit's biography, unimaginatively titled *Muḥammad ʿAlī,* was the most comprehensive attempt to fuse royal historiography, academic research, and popular writing in favor of the monarchy. Thābit, the first royal media consultant in modern Egypt and editor-in-chief of the pro-British organ *Al-Muqaṭṭam,* knew his job fairly well.[80] In the preface to his book Thābit wrote, "All I have done is to read what the Geographical Society has published [i.e., the royal project] and used what I felt is indispensable for us to know about Muḥammad ʿAlī."[81] Thābit's stylistic choice was to narrate Muḥammad ʿAlī from "childhood to adulthood," metaphorically alluding to the very same trajectory supposedly experienced by the Egyptian nation as a whole under the pasha's stern command. Thābit ornamented each chapter with a quote that he either found, or paraphrased, or invented. For example, he quoted Muḥammad ʿAlī as saying, "I took Egypt by the sword, and I am not going to give it [away] in any way but the sword."[82]

Despite a growing number of opposing interpretations, many of them from

78. Even the words of the Egyptian peasants, "Je suis occupé à mes affaires . . . nous sommes devenus les paysans du Pasha" (I am busy with my business . . . we became the pasha's peasants), were cited in French. Ghorbal, *The Beginnings of the Egyptian Question,* p. 281.

79. Ibid., p. xiv.

80. Karīm Thābit was appointed in the wake of the February 1942 incident, during which the British imposed a government and forced the king to accept it in order to handle the flood of negative and undermining publications against the monarchy. See a preface by Muḥammad Ḥasanīn Haykal in Karīm Thābit, *Farūq kama ʿaraftuhu* (Cairo: Dār al-shurūq, 2000), vol. 1, pp. 12–13.

81. Karīm Thābit, *Muḥammad ʿAlī* (Cairo: Maktabat al-maʿārif, 1942), p. 7.

82. Ibid., p. 65.

young academic circles, al-Rāfiʿī's view of Muḥammad ʿAlī hardly changed throughout his career. In contrast, in *Muḥammad ʿAlī al-Kabīr,* Ghurbāl significantly reappraised his previous views: "Muḥammad ʿAlī began, lived, and ended his life as an Ottoman. His mission, as he defined it, was to revive Ottoman power and dress it in a new costume."[83]

The rift between Ghurbāl and al-Rāfiʿī, however, went far deeper than the issue of Muḥammad ʿAlī's role in history; it brought to the fore theoretical questions of objectivity, concerns about the methodological use of source materials, and historical notions of change and agency. Thus, while Ghurbāl's work reflected countless painstaking hours in numerous archives, al-Rāfiʿī drew on secondary sources to discuss remote periods and on newspaper clippings, journals, and personal connections for his discussions of contemporary events.[84] His success triggered Ghurbāl to take action. In *Muḥammad ʿAlī al-Kabīr,* Ghurbāl tried to popularize the insights of his students who worked in the archive. He was eager to prove that serious academic scholarship could also be relevant and popular. As is often the case among scholars, these disagreements soon developed into overt rivalry, and accordingly Ghurbāl and his disciples banned al-Rāfiʿī from the newly established Egyptian Historical Society.

Ibrāhīm's Career as a Historical Accident

Ibrāhīm, a courageous military general and governor of Syria, was Muḥammad ʿAlī's eldest son. He came to Egypt from Macedonia when he was sixteen years of age. Before his untimely death in November 1848, he governed Egypt for a brief period of several months. Naturally, his promising career and its speculative future were the subject of several historical compositions and debates.

Struggling to prove its organic Egyptian roots in a nationalist age, royal historiography was highly invested in Ibrāhīm. As the son of the pasha, Ibrāhīm has been mainly known for his military achievements. Under him, as the story goes, the army emerged victorious to the extent that Egypt became a regional empire, winning nominal independence from Istanbul. These achievements were partly ascribed to Ibrāhīm's intimate relationship with his soldiers: "Ibrāhīm became

83. Muḥammad Shafīq Ghurbāl, *Muḥammad ʿAlī al-kabīr* (Cairo: Dā'irat al-maʿārif al-islāmiyya, 1944), p. 62. On the political circumstances that conceived this book see discussion in the next chapter.

84. After al-Rāfiʿī's death, his family contributed his library to Dār al-Kutub. Its inventory illustrates al-Rāfiʿī's research orientation: 2,024 books in Arabic, 544 books in foreign languages, and 420 periodicals. With the possible exception of Maḥmūd ʿAbbās al-ʿAqqād, no other library in Dār al-Kutub has such a large number of periodicals. Amīn Fu'ād Sayyid, *Dār al-kutub al-miṣriyya, tārīkhuhā wa taṭawwurihā* (Cairo: Awrāq sharkiyya, 1996), p. 57.

so familiar with his men, always living among them, even playing with them and continuously praising the nation from which they sprang, that they came to look on him as a bulwark against their officers and carried matters so far that they were known to refuse to execute orders and to say that they would appeal to Ibrāhīm."[85]

This spirit of comradeship was supposed to have nationalized the army and fostered the growth of a renewed Egyptian patriotism.[86] Two great popularizers of these assumptions were 'Umar Ṭūsūn and 'Abd al-Raḥmān Zakī, a retired military officer, director of the military museum, and amateur historian.[87] Some writers even went so far as to consider Ibrāhīm's occupation of Palestine and Syria as an important stage in Pan-Arab unity.[88]

Beyond that, royal historians contended that Ibrāhīm was not merely a soldier but also, and perhaps even principally, an independent statesman. Crabitès, who dedicated an entire book to Ibrāhīm alone, emphasized his independence from his father: "We insist on this point . . . Ibrāhīm held to his views. They must have been known to the Pasha."[89] For instance, in opposition to his centralist father, Ibrāhīm is said to have been inclined toward modern liberal thought.[90] Yet, by far the biggest difference between father and son was that of identity. As opposed to Muḥammad 'Alī, who was undeniably Turk, Ibrāhīm was considered to be a true Egyptian: "Je ne suis pas Turc, reprit vivement Ibrahim; je suis venu enfant en Egypte et, depuis ce temps, le soleil de l'Égypte a change mon sang et l'a fait tout Arabe" (I am not a Turk, Ibrāhīm retorted with feeling; I came to Egypt as a child and since

85. Crabitès, *Ibrahim of Egypt*, p. 183, based on Georges Douin, *La mission du Baron Boislecomte* (Cairo: Société royale de géographie d'Égypte, publications spéciales sous les auspices de sa majesté Fouad Ier, 1927), p. 239.

86. Charles-Roux, "*L'Égypte de 1801 à 1881,*" pp. 154–156.

87. See 'Umar Ṭūsūn, *Al-Jaysh al-miṣrī al-barrī wa-l-baḥrī fī 'ahd Muḥammad 'Alī Bāshā* (Alexandria: Maṭba'at ṣalāḥ al-dīn al-kubra, 1931). Parts of Ṭūsūn's book on the Egyptian army in Crimea were serialized on *Al-Ahrām*'s first page. 'Umar Ṭūsūn, "Al-jaysh al-miṣrī," *Al-Ahrām*, May 8–11, 1932. 'Abd al-Raḥmān Zakī, *Ibrāhīm Bāshā* (Cairo: Dār al-kutub al-miṣriyya, 1948); 'Abd al-Raḥmān Zakī, *Al-Tārīkh al-ḥarbī li-'aṣr Muḥammad 'Alī* (Cairo: al-Jam'iyya al-mālikiyya li-l-dirāsāt al-tārīkhiyya, dār al-ma'ārif, 1950).

88. Amīn Sa'īd, "Muḥammad 'Alī wa al-imbaraṭūriyya al-'arabiyya," *Muqtaṭaf*, June 1936, pp. 90–96. Dodwell, however, speaks of the "humiliating memory of Egyptian occupation." Dodwell, *The Founder of Modern Egypt*, pp. 128, 257–258.

89. Crabitès, *Ibrahim of Egypt*, p. 125. This work was translated to Arabic by Muḥammad Badrān, a school principal. King Fu'ād granted Badrān a prize of fifty Egyptian pounds for the translation. *Al-Risāla*, September 20, 1937, p. 1552. Parts of the work were serialized in *Al-Risāla*, July 26 and August 2, 1937, pp. 1221–1223 and 1263–1265, respectively.

90. Crabitès, *Ibrahim of Egypt*, p. 125. Nineteenth-century observers were the first to draw a distinction between son and father. Douin, *La mission du Baron Boislecomte*, p. 239. Cultural magazines criticized Crabitès for ignoring important works in Arabic, such as those of al-Rāfi'ī: *Al-Muqtaṭaf*, March 1936, pp. 394–396; *Al-Risāla*, February 24, 1936, pp. 316–317.

then the sun of Egypt has changed my blood and rendered it entirely Arab).[91] The historic accident of Ibrāhīm's early death came as a great shock that derailed Egypt from the right path of modernization. Quite simply: "Aucun autre membre de la famille de Mohamed ʿAli n'était par consequent mieux indiqué qu'Ibrahim Pacha pour continuer et developer la grande oeuvre du fondateur de l'Égypte moderne" (No other member of Muḥammad ʿAlī's family was more suited to continue and develop the important work of the founder of modern Egypt than Ibrāhīm Pasha).[92] Consequently, less qualified personalities, notably ʿAbbās and to a lesser extent Saʿīd, ruled Egypt. Monarchists contended that Egyptian nationalism, taken in its entirety, emerged because of the policies of Muḥammad ʿAlī and, especially, to the nationalized militarism of Ibrāhīm.[93] As we shall see below, this was not their last attempt to appropriate nationalism.

Al-Rāfiʿī's treatment of Ibrāhīm was somewhat reserved. Although he acknowledged Ibrāhīm's extraordinary military capabilities on almost every page of the book, he denied Ibrāhīm's special status as a ruler in his own right. Later, perhaps in response to the royal top-down approach to the rise of national sentiment, al-Rāfiʿī published several articles in which he played down Ibrāhīm's importance by generally referring to his military campaigns as the "the wars of Muḥammad ʿAlī" and by ignoring Ibrāhīm's alleged Egyptian origins.[94]

Another scholar who influenced Egyptian historiography of the 1930s was the Lebanese professor Asad Rustum, an accomplished scholar who had been trained at the University of Chicago and taught at the American University of Beirut. Doing extensive archival work in ʿĀbdīn, Rustum believed that his insights into the era were so revisionist that he considered Dodwell, Ṣabrī, and al-Rāfiʿī to have left "the truth half told."[95] In reality, however, his overall understanding was not all that original: "Through his contact with Europe and the European officers Ibrahim Pasha seems to have been personally convinced of the soundness of the nationalistic philosophy of the day, and to have been determined to try it. In

91. Douin, *La mission du Baron Boislecomte,* p. 249. The same text was reproduced in *Al-Hilāl,* December 1938, p. 120.

92. Angelo Sammarco, *Les règnes de ʿAbbas, de Saʾid et d'Ismaʾil (1848–1879),* vol. 4 of *Précis de l'histoire d'Égypte,* par divers historiens et archéologues, ed. Zaky el-Ibrachy Pacha and Angelo Sammarco (Cairo: l'Imprimerie de l'Institut français d'archéologie orientale du Caire, 1935), p. 2.

93. For a refutation of these arguments, see Fahmy, *All the Pasha's Men,* pp. 239–277.

94. al-Rāfiʿī, *ʿAṣr Muḥammad ʿAlī* (1947), pp. 166–186, 191–220, 230–300; ʿAbd al-Raḥmān al-Rāfiʿī, "Ṣafḥa min tārīkh Miṣr al-qawmī," *Al-Hilāl,* December 1930, pp. 226–232; ʿAbd al-Raḥmān al-Rāfiʿī, "Al-Umarāʾ al-qawād fī-l-usra al-muḥamadiyya al-ʿalawiyya," *Al-Hilāl,* February 1938, pp. 411–413; ʿAbd al-Raḥmān al-Rāfiʿī, "Muḥammad ʿAlī: Hal qaṣada min ḥurūbuhi mulkan wa istiqlālan?" *Al-Hilāl,* August 1937, pp. 1105–1109.

95. Asad Rustum, *The Royal Archives of Egypt and the Origins of the Egyptian Expedition to Syria 1831–1841* (Beirut: American Press, 1936), pp. 30–31.

this sense Ibrahim Pasha certainly deserves the place of honor in the history of nationalism in the Arab Middle East. *He is the first Moslem of rank in the Arab world who conceived of an Arab Nationalist Movement and who was determined to make it effectual.*"[96]

Though by the time Rustum conducted his research all of these nationalist assumptions were already in place, he gave them scientific validity by supporting them with original Ottoman documents. Rustum firmly believed that ʿĀbdīn enabled him to tell a truth-revealing story. As we shall see, some years later, Ghurbāl's young disciples reiterated Rustum's arguments.

ʿAbbās as a Scapegoat

It is difficult to ascertain exactly when, and in what process, the public image of ʿAbbās was fixed as that of a reactionary tyrant. To be sure, this demonization had already started in his lifetime as a form of political opposition that was later transformed into an historiographical trope.[97] British colonial officials certainly played a key role in its propagation. In any event, by the late 1920s, there was already a consensus that the reign of ʿAbbās was a deviation from the right monarchic path, which had been taken and, indeed paved by Muḥammad ʿAlī. ʿAbbās's negative image is very telling, not because it is contested, as the memories of Muḥammad ʿAlī and Ismāʿīl are, but precisely because a consensus view emerged around his heritage. What was the essence of this pejorative image, and why, in fact, is there a consensus around it?

Habitually taking an extreme position, al-Rāfiʿī titled the ʿAbbās era the "age of reaction," because it was during this period that the nationalist momentum came to a full halt. Academic institutions were shut down, reforms in the army were suspended, vocational-training delegations were asked to return home, and industry collapsed. The historical reason for this failure was, according to al-Rāfiʿī, ʿAbbās's weak, conservative, and incapable personality.[98] Regardless of his real worth, ʿAbbās's image as a royal wimp was further popularized, thanks to al-Rāfiʿī. The views of royal historians on that matter hardly differed. Influenced by Muḥammad Ṣabrī, Charles-Roux argued that ʿAbbās's era was characterized by his reaction against Europe and opposition to the political heritage of Muḥammad ʿAlī.[99]

96. Ibid., p. 96 (emphasis added).

97. Toledano uncovered the process of ʿAbbās's demonization during his lifetime. Ehud Toledano, *State and Society in Mid-nineteenth Century Egypt* (Cambridge: Cambridge University Press, 1990), pp. 108–148.

98. ʿAbd al-Raḥmān al-Rāfiʿī, *ʿAṣr Ismāʿīl* (1932; Cairo: Dār al-maʿārif, 1987), vol. 1, pp. 15–27.

99. Sabry, *L'émpire égyptien sous Ismaïl*, pp. 13–28; Charles-Roux, *"L'Égypte de 1801 à 1881,"* pp. 242–247.

According to Crabitès, 'Abbās was recorded as saying, "For the consuls of Europe he [Muḥammad 'Alī] was just a shoe. If I must submit to someone, let me be then the servant of the Khalif, and not of the Christians whom I hate."[100] And, on a more personal level, "The new ruler ['Abbās] was a combination of intellectual nonentity, coward, and fanatic. He was capricious and reactionary. He despised European procedure and progress. He dreaded Christian influence upon Egypt."[101]

Delivering the final blow Sammarco wrote,

> Le caractère le plus marqué de son gouvernement: son hostilité farouche pour la civilisation européenne, son aversion profonde pour tous les ouvrages qui avaient été la *gloire* de son aïeul et à la destruction desquels il travailla peu à peu. *On aurait dit que 'Abbas, en montant sur le trône, s'était chargé de détruire tout ce que Mohammed 'Ali avait fait de bon et d'utile.*[102]
>
> (The most distinctive feature of his government: his ferocious hostility to European civilization, his profound aversion to all the works that had been the glory of his forefather and which he sought, little by little, to destroy. *One would have said that from the time he took power, Abbas took it upon himself to destroy all that Muhammad Ali did that was good and useful.*)

Evidently, 'Abbās's xenophobic rejection of Europe was incompatible with the royalist vision of a modern Egyptian entity inspired and directed by Europe. Likewise it was in opposition to Fu'ād's present politics of intimate affiliation with continental Europe. Hence, for these heavily biased reasons the monarchy itself struggled to distance itself from 'Abbās's heritage.[103] However, despite this general consensus, there were disagreements about why 'Abbās rejected Europe. Al-Rāfi'ī, who wanted modernization with no European intervention (he never specified how this was supposed to happen), reminded his readers, "'Abbās had a peculiarity that history ought to remember; he did not open Egypt's doors to foreign intervention. . . . thus, he kept its treasury free from the burdens of foreign debts, which his successors accepted."[104] In response, Sammarco insinuated that al-Rāfi'ī's views were biased and unscientific, since they were not based on work

100. Crabitès, *Ismail the Maligned Khedive,* p. 1.

101. Ibid.

102. Sammarco, *Précis de l'histoire d'Égypte,* vol. 4, pp. 4–5 (emphasis in original).

103. During the 1930s, Prince 'Umar Ṭūsūn and others made several attempts to revise 'Abbās's image, but they ultimately failed. 'Umar Ṭūsūn, *Al-Ba'thāt al-'ilmiyya fī 'ahd Muḥammad 'Alī, 'Abbās al-awwal wa Sa'īd* (Alexandria: Maṭba'at ṣalāḥ al-dīn, 1934); and *Al-Hilāl,* January 1935, pp. 374–375. Following these publications, Ṭāhir al-Ṭanāḥī, a prolific pro-royalist writer, argued that 'Abbās appreciated education and fought for reforms. "Ba'that 'Abbās Bāshā al-awwal ila almānyā," *Al-Hilāl,* December 1939, pp. 174–181.

104. al-Rāfi'ī, *'Aṣr Ismā'īl,* vol. 1, pp. 26–27.

in ʿĀbdīn. Original documents, contended Sammarco, prove that ʿAbbās's rejection of Europe could have been inspired neither by patriotism nor by his concern for the well-being of Egypt.[105]

Ismāʿīl: A Daring Modernizer or a Reckless Squanderer?

By the early 1930s, writing the history of the early modern era had become a highly sensitive matter. It was during this period that al-Rāfiʿī published *ʿAṣr Ismāʿīl,* a critical account of the reigns of ʿAbbās, Saʿīd, and Ismāʿīl, tying them together as the "Ismāʿīl era." To be sure, this book marked a turning point in al-Rāfiʿī's relationship with the monarchy. As opposed to other voices in Egyptian historiography, his was vehement, simple, and slightly relentless: ʿAbbās, Saʿīd, and Ismāʿīl were responsible for the monetary collapse of Egypt and its growing subjugation to Europe.[106] Once again, al-Rāfiʿī was the only Egyptian historian who presented a very coherent and essentially negative picture of this era. His book set the historiographical agenda and forced royal historians to refute his arguments by personally addressing him. However, since al-Rāfiʿī wrote and published only in Arabic, employees of the ʿĀbdīn archive had to translate segments of his *ʿAṣr Ismāʿīl* into French so that royal historians could rebut it.[107] This is yet another example of the political intervention of archive employees. Far more political, however, was Fu'ād's response; then in the midst of his corrective historiographical effort, he requested that the Ministry of Education prohibit public libraries and schools from using the book.[108] His request was granted. Eight years later the court tried to win al-Rāfiʿī's sympathy by granting him access to the ʿĀbdīn archive, from which he had been expelled in the early 1930s. In return, al-Rāfiʿī was supposed to amend and soften his misguided views; he turned the offer down.[109]

For al-Rāfiʿī, there was no real difference between Saʿīd and Ismāʿīl, because the deterioration of Egypt's financial and political system began under Saʿīd and continued under Ismāʿīl.[110] Thus, by way of generalization, al-Rāfiʿī referred to all of these (negative) trends as the "Ismāʿīl era," about which he wrote, "In terms

105. Sammarco, *Précis de l'histoire d'Égypte,* vol. 4, pp. 4–7.

106. As usual, on the completion of each project, al-Rāfiʿī popularized his views through the press: ʿAbd al-Raḥmān al-Rāfiʿī, "Muḥammad ʿAlī Bāshā wa-l-khidīwī Ismāʿīl," *Al-Hilāl,* November 1933, pp. 33–35. See also a concise review that favorably underscored al-Rāfiʿī's arguments: *Al-Muqtaṭaf,* February 1932, pp. 234–235.

107. Rivlin, *The Dār al-wathā'iq in ʿĀbdīn Palace at Cairo,* p. 120.

108. ʿAbd al-Raḥmān al-Rāfiʿī, *Mudhakkarātī 1889–1951* (Cairo: Dār al-hilāl, 1952), pp. 66–67, 75–76.

109. ʿUlwān, *ʿAbd al-Raḥmān al-Rāfiʿī,* pp. 264–265.

110. In particular, al-Rāfiʿī was critical of Saʿīd's Suez Canal concessions and his use of foreign loans. al-Rāfiʿī, *ʿAṣr Ismāʿīl,* vol. 1, pp. 31–40, 60–63, 69–71.

of its relation to the present, this era is the most significant. This is because the system and most of its negative factors appeared then, and are prevalent also today: the Mixed Courts, the influence of Egypt's foreign inhabitants, debts, and, finally, Western interference in Egypt's political and financial matters. These negative aspects originated in the Ismāʿīl era."[111]

Again, royalists presented an opposing view. Cognizant of the somehow awkward position of a foreign historian rebutting nationalist Egyptian writers, Sammarco's publisher assured the readership that, though an Italian citizen, the author was the first one to present a balanced, objective, and patriotic account, as if he himself were an Egyptian.[112] Whether Sammarco was or was not a true patriot, one thing is sure: he was deeply and personally involved in that historiographical debate. Thus, in his riposte to al-Rāfiʿī, Sammarco also presented Ismāʿīl's heritage as highly relevant for present-day Egypt, but for entirely different reasons: "L'Égypte contemporaine est toute pénétrée de l'infatigable activité civilisatrice d'Isma'il et s'en alimente encore. De quelque côté que l'on tourne les yeux on rencontre les marques de ses bienfaits et de ses oeuvres qui sont toujours debout, vivants, évidentes, indestructibles" (Contemporary Egypt is entirely penetrated and still being nourished by the tireless civilizing activity of Ismāʿīl. No matter where one turns one's gaze, one encounters the marks of his kindness and of his works, which are still standing, alive, and indestructible).[113] Crabitès, who dedicated an entire book to correcting the maligned image of Ismāʿīl, opined, "Ismail was systematically slandered and his heritage distorted. The *leit-motif*... can be compressed into three epithets, 'spendthrift,' 'profligate,' 'squanderer,' into three adjectives, 'reckless,' 'luxurious,' and 'voluptuous,' and into one verb, 'throw away.'"[114]

However, the debate was not merely an exchange of general statements but also touched on the fine details of economic history. Though a central theme in al-Rāfiʿī's work was the collapse of Egypt's fiscal system, his analysis of Egypt's

111. Ibid., p. 73.

112. The Egyptian publisher of Sammarco's "La verità sulla questione del canale di Suez" also argued that Ismāʿīl's history was hitherto written by tendentious politicians who distorted the facts and blackened his name. Angelo Sammarco, "La verità sulla questione del canale di Suez," *Oriente Moderno* 19 (1939): pp. 5–30; Angelo Sammarco, *Al-Ḥaqīqa fī mas'alat qanāt al-suwīs*, trans. into Arabic by Ṭaha Fawzī (Cairo: n.p., 1940), pp. 2–9.

113. Sammarco, *Précis de l'histoire d'Égypte*, vol. 4, p. 240.

114. Crabitès, *Ismail the Maligned Khedive*, p. 33. Crabitès's work was translated into Arabic by Fu'ad Saffūf, editor-in-chief of *Al-Muqtaṭaf*, as *Ismāʿīl al-muftara ʿalayhi* (Cairo: Dār al-nashr al-ḥadīth, 1937). A highly critical analysis of Saffūf's translation and guidelines for future translators were serialized in *Al-Risāla*. "Ismāʿīl al-muftara ʿalayhi," *Al-Risāla*, April 10—May 31, 1937. For more reviews, see *Al-Muqtaṭaf*, December 1933, pp. 605–609; and *Al-Muqtaṭaf*, April 1937, pp. 494–495, 644–645.

financial difficulties was simplistic and demagogic. According to his reasoning, the cause of Egypt's bankruptcy was solely Ismā'īl's prodigality: lavish journeys to Europe, glamorous receptions, extravagant festivals, and the building of numerous immodest mansions and palaces. Other economic, political, and social factors were conspicuously ignored. Al-Rāfi'ī's financial calculations seem to be problematic, if not totally groundless, but they were substantiated by Ṣabrī, who subscribed to the thesis of Ismā'īl's prodigality.[115] In a sharp and personal response to al-Rāfi'ī, Sammarco wrote:

> Si 'Abd ar-Rahman ar-Rafi'i avait étudié à l'aide de documents originaux sûrs les circonstances qui poussèrent effectivement Isma'il à son premier emprunt, il n'aurait pas affirmé que les veritable raison de l'emprunt de 1864 était la vie de luxe, de passion et de gaspillage qu'Isma'il aurait menée . . . , nous n'en trouvons la moindre trace dans aucun des documents des années 1863–1874. Bien au contraire.[116]

> (Had 'Abd al-Raḥmān al-Rāfi'ī made use of original documents in studying the circumstances that effectively drove Ismā'īl to take the first loan, he would never have asserted that the loan of 1864 was taken out to satisfy the allegedly luxurious and wasteful habits of Ismā'īl. . . . We cannot find even the slightest evidence of such behavior in the documents of 1863–1874. Quite the contrary.)

Furthermore, Sammarco condemned al-Rāfi'ī's ill judgment in accusing him of ignoring the complexity of the matter by not distinguishing among the various loans.[117] Al-Rāfi'ī's sources were deemed by Sammarco to be hostile, unscientific, and, above all, quoted in a very selective and manipulative manner.[118] Crabitès, for instance, substantiated Sammarco's view, refuting the reliability of the Cave report on which al-Rāfi'ī grounded his argument.[119] However, as groundless and ultimately out of character as they were, al-Rāfi'ī's bogus calculations supported his thesis in a very persuasive way. Al-Rāfi'ī, in addition to criticizing Ismā'īl's

115. Although factual mistakes are uncharacteristic of al-Rāfi'ī, the eclectic financial evidence provided by him was based on a partial reading of secondary sources, among them Lord Cromer's *Modern Egypt*. al-Rāfi'ī, *'Aṣr Ismā'īl*, vol. 2, pp. 55–58. Ṣabrī scored other minor reasons for Egypt's bankruptcy, among them British exploitation. Sabry, *L'empire égyptien sous Ismaïl*, pp. 108–111.

116. Sammarco, *Précis de l'histoire d'Égypte*, vol. 4, p. 173.

117. Royalists published historical accounts with meticulously documented calculations that refuted the arguments of financial misadministration. Joseph Cattaui, *Le khédive Isma'il et la dette de l'Égypte* (Cairo: Impr. Misr, 1935).

118. Ibid., pp. 174, 189. See also a refutation of al-Rāfi'ī's argument concerning Ismā'īl's prodigality: Sammarco, *Histoire de l'Égypte moderne*, vol. 3, pp. 20–21.

119. He convincingly argued that the ledgers that were submitted to the committee were written in the coded professional jargon of the Coptic accountants, who did their best to keep them intelligible only to themselves so that they could continue to monopolize that profession. Crabitès, *Ismail the Maligned Khedive*, pp. 224–242.

habit of spending money, also depicted him as an incapable and naive manager who sold the Suez Canal shares at a bargain price and thus provided the British with the ultimate excuse to conquer Egypt.[120]

But aside from refuting al-Rāfiʿī, in what ways did royal historians explain Egypt's financial collapse? The most common strategy was not to deny the fiasco but to demonstrate that the money was spent in a careful and calculated manner and channeled into projects such as administrative reforms, an attempt to alleviate the unbearable burden on the Egyptian masses, "bringing civilization" to black Africa, fighting slavery, and supporting scientific reconnaissance, such as exploring the unknown headwaters of the Nile.[121] With this in mind, Douin dedicated a thick tome to Ismāʿīl's African empire and Egypt's civilizing mission in it.[122] According to Crabitès, Lord Cromer and Milner did their best to blacken Ismāʿīl's image and deliberately ignored all of these achievements.[123]

An original argument made by Crabitès considered the khedive's career in terms of what he called Ismāʿīl's "moral balance sheet." Thus, Ismāʿīl is said to have fought not only the slave trade but also the horrors of the corvée system, which enslaved dozens of thousands of Egyptian peasants and was as "stupid as it was immoral."[124] Since "corvée labourers were cruelly treated and died like flies," Ismāʿīl decided to limit it at any cost. Indeed, he was forced to pay a financial fine to Napoleon III for breaching a contract (signed by Saʿīd) and defending the *fallāḥ*.[125] Along with royal historians' demonstration of Ismāʿīl's good use of funds, they also acknowledged the magnitude and consequences of Egypt's financial fiasco and blamed ʿAbbās and Saʿīd for leaving him with a disastrous financial situation.[126] Much of the blame, however, was cast on the eternally corrupt Ottoman Empire. Here, once again, all historians (royalists and popular-nationalists) shared common ground. They all considered the Ottoman entity to be so corrupt and greedy that it forced Egypt to pay fantastic sums of money in order to maintain reasonable relations with it.[127]

For example, Ismāʿīl's 1866 request to change the hereditary order, making it from father to son, was used as an example of Ottoman covetousness. According

120. al-Rāfiʿī, *ʿAṣr Ismāʿīl,* vol. 2, pp. 58–65, 83–87.

121. On administrative reforms, see Sammarco, *Histoire de l'Égypte moderne,* vol. 3, p. 123. On the burden on the Egyptian masses, see ibid., pp. 108–109. On exploring the Nile, see Crabitès, *Ismail the Maligned Khedive,* pp. 70–87, 101–118.

122. Douin, *Histoire du règne du Khédive Ismaïl,* p. iii.

123. Crabitès, *Ismail the Maligned Khedive,* p. 127.

124. Ibid., p. 47.

125. Ibid., pp. 47–69; Sammarco, *Précis de l'histoire d'Égypte,* vol. 4, p. 150. See also Sammarco, *Al-Ḥaqīqa,* pp. 79–86.

126. Sammarco, *Histoire de l'Égypte moderne,* vol. 3, p. 96.

127. al-Rāfiʿī, *ʿAṣr Ismāʿīl,* vol. 1, pp. 85–6; Crabitès, *Ismail the Maligned Khedive,* pp. 171–233.

to royal historiography, by changing the hereditary law, Ismāʿīl hoped to correct the "mistake" that had brought ʿAbbās, rather than a son of Muḥammad ʿAlī, to power. The Ottomans agreed to amend the *firman,* provided that Ismāʿīl would pay an outrageous sum of money, which, according to Sammarco, he did pay for the benefit of Egypt as a whole.[128] While royal historians celebrated the costly act as a realization of Egypt's dream of complete sovereignty, al-Rāfiʿī treated it as nothing but a waste of public funds.[129] Annoyed with al-Rāfiʿī, once more Sammarco was moved to respond personally and condemn the "Egyptian historian who is mainly busy with the national movement."[130]

As was to be expected, none of the royalist scholars identified colonial Europe, with its outrageous interest rates and aggressive politics, as bearing any responsibility for Egypt's financial collapse. An exception was Crabitès, an American, who condemned Europeans for launching psychological warfare against Ismāʿīl, using unacceptable tactics such as threats and intimidation.[131]

Besides Egypt's public debt, a second major bone of historiographical contention revolved around the development of "constitutional life." Here, once again, al-Rāfiʿī acted fast. The political context was interesting, too. Constitutional life in the post-1919 era was never characterized by a broad political consensus regarding the content of the constitution. The 1923 constitution accorded much power to the king and, by extension, to the British in order to counterbalance, but in fact simply to limit, the immense political impact of the Wafd. As the supreme head of state, the king had a very broad mandate that included the right to adjourn Parliament sessions temporarily and to dismiss cabinet ministers. In one form or another, since the first 1923 elections the king often used his powers in order to override the Wafd and later to impose anti-Wafd minority governments. As the culmination of this trend, in 1930 Prime Minister Ismāʿīl Ṣidqī inaugurated a new constitution, which gave Fu'ād even more executive powers and ushered in a period of undemocratic executive unilateralism. The suspension of the 1923 constitution and Parliament was engraved on Egypt's collective memory as two acts of sheer despotism. Though a member of the National Party, which after 1919 was reduced by the Wafd to a symbolic political force, al-Rāfiʿī remained a staunch constitutionalist. Thus, in the midst of this political upheaval, he dedicated his time to the writing of constitutional history under Ismāʿīl. This work was among the most daring political statements of the time. For, while ostensibly

128. Sammarco, *Histoire de l'Égypte moderne,* vol. 3, p. 131–132.

129. Sammarco, *Précis de l'histoire d'Égypte,* vol. 4, p. 221; Douin, *Histoire du règne du Khédive Ismaïl,* vol. 1, pp. 205–232; al-Rāfiʿī, *ʿAṣr Ismāʿīl,* vol. 1, pp. 85–86.

130. Sammarco, *Histoire de l'Égypte moderne,* vol. 3, p. 135.

131. Crabitès, *Ismail the Maligned Khedive,* pp. 259–297.

a mere historical composition, in reality it openly subverted and severely criticized authority.

Al-Rāfiʿī's interpretation presented constitutional reform as the outcome of an intimate relationship between the nationalist movement and constitutional principles. According to him, Ismāʿīl's original Parliament was passive, incompetent, and lacked any judicial power. Hence, it failed to prevent the financial fiasco and succumbed to Ismāʿīl's tyranny *(istibdād)* and absolute rule *(ḥukum muṭlaq)*. Then, continued al-Rāfiʿī, in 1876 the popular forces transformed the Parliament into an active, assertive legislative body and introduced a type of protoconstitution.[132] When Ismāʿīl finally capitulated and agreed to implement constitutional ideals in the form of the Sharīf Pasha government, al-Rāfiʿī contended that Sharīf Pasha was the forefather of constitutional life in Egypt.[133] Yet again, al-Rāfiʿī brought a relatively unknown figure to the fore and presented him as a popular hero who embodied the national spirit and its historical ambitions. Conversely, he presented Ismāʿīl as a marginal figure guided by Sharīf Pasha.

Answering back, royal historians dedicated much space to discussing Ismāʿīl's judicial reforms, which they identified as constituting an important milestone in Egypt's journey into the autonomous modern world.[134] "Popular forces" played no role in these reforms, and Sharīf Pasha was not a popular hero but a mere employee of Ismāʿīl.[135] Interestingly enough, royalists deemed the establishment of the Mixed Courts the most important aspect of the judicial reforms and an answer to the exploitative capitulations system. Established in 1876 in order to solve legal conflicts between Europeans and Egyptians, these courts, in the royalists' view, were the pinnacle of justice and moral order as well as institutions that further emphasized Egyptian sovereignty.[136] A staunch defender of the system was Crabitès, himself a judge in the Mixed Courts. He argued that though the British exploited the system, it terminated a situation in which foreigners were practically untouchable.[137]

Al-Rāfiʿī, in contrast, was not at all interested in the original 1870s context in which the Mixed Courts were established and favored, instead echoing the Egyptian public opinion of the 1930s, which regarded the Mixed Courts as institutions that perpetuated colonial injustice. Thus, he held Ismāʿīl responsible for

132. al-Rāfiʿī, *ʿAṣr Ismāʿīl,* vol. 2, pp. 89ff., 137–138, 200–203, 206–207.

133. Ibid., p. 223.

134. Sammarco, *Histoire de l'Égypte moderne,* vol. 3, pp. 229–247ff.

135. Douin, *Histoire du règne du Khédive Ismaïl,* vol. 1, pp. 294–313.

136. Sammarco, *Précis de l'histoire d'Égypte,* vol. 4, pp. 288–289; Sammarco, *Histoire de l'Égypte moderne,* vol. 3, pp. 252–255, 271–273.

137. Crabitès, *Ismail the Maligned Khedive,* p. 250. Ṣabrī had a similar opinion: Sabry, *L'empire égyptien sous Ismaïl,* pp. 207–255.

their establishment, because "Egyptians were put under the jurisdiction of foreigners who became the masters of the land" and because "the Mixed Courts contradicted Egypt's sovereignty and its judicial independence."[138]

Thus far, with the exception of Ibrāhīm's career, royal historians were rather mute on issues related to the rise of nationalism. However, when studying the era of Ismāʿīl, they identified an intellectual revival, which, in their mind, was intimately associated with the spread of nationalism among the urban middle class. This new interpretation challenged that of al-Rāfiʿī and other popular writers. Unlike al-Rāfiʿī, who simply interpreted all popular acts as true manifestations of the national spirit, royal historians suggested a sophisticated explanation that linked the rise and spread of education to the emergence of public opinion in Egypt.

However, royal historians owed this theory to someone else. Here the credit goes to Ṣabrī, whose concept of public opinion was his last original contribution to the historiography of the era. Unlike all other local and foreign historians, Ṣabrī choose to appraise the Ismāʿīl era under an umbrella concept that encompassed a host of developments in the social, cultural, technological, and intellectual realms. He called this rather vague, and very French, concept "public opinion." Despite Ṣabrī's rather murky notion of what public opinion consisted of and how exactly it was formed, it was clear to him that public opinion ushered in a new era of nationalist activism that culminated in the ʿUrābī revolt.[139] Thus, Ṣabrī was the first Egyptian historian who provided an inclusive explanation for the rise of national activism, bringing into account the transformation of Egyptian public life under Ismāʿīl. As we shall see below, this notion was highly effective in explaining the ʿUrābī revolt, in regard to which he, once more, shifted to the nationalist side.

Using Ṣabrī's ideas, royal historians persuasively tied intellectual and constitutional developments under Ismāʿīl to the social context, thus showing how these trends facilitated the emergence of a full-fledged nationalist middle class. In Sammarco's words: "C'est dans cette bourgeoisie que naquit un sentiment véritablement national auquel l'introduction des institutions parlementaries donna une forte impulsion" (It was in this bourgeoisie that a truly national sentiment was born, one that received a strong boost from the introduction of parliamentary institutions).[140] New terms such as *waṭan, ḥukūma,* and *ḥuriya* were considered the natural expression of these trends.[141]

138. al-Rāfiʿī, *ʿAṣr Ismāʿīl,* vol. 2, pp. 270–276.

139. Sabry, *La genèse de l'esprit national égyptien,* pp. 96–164. See especially Sabry's *L'empire égyptien sous Ismaïl,* pp. 315–371.

140. Sammarco, *Histoire de l'Égypte moderne,* vol. 3, p. 328.

141. Sammarco, *Précis de l'histoire d'Égypte,* vol. 4, pp. 291–318 and especially pp. 316–318.

This explanation directly challenged al-Rāfiʿī's hegemonic interpretation of nationalism. His monolithic notion of a united nationalist Egyptian people was broken down into various classes with different motivations, aspirations, and capabilities. (The only exception to that was a shy acknowledgment that the Ismāʿīl era saw the "revival of women" regarding participation in public affairs.)[142] Now royal historiography could appropriate nationalism as a relatively late development that emerged out of Ismāʿīl's creation of an intellectually curious middle class. Such views formed the essence of the monarchy's official nationalism.

In sum, the historiography of the Ismāʿīl era uncovers two opposing agendas for the future of modern Egypt. According to the royal historical reading, Ismāʿīl's agenda consisted of four elements: engaging Egypt in the life of European civilization, securing its autonomy, developing its infrastructure, and turning Egypt into a leading African power with its own mission to civilize. With a direct monarchic line stretching all the away from Muḥammad ʿAlī, through Ibrāhīm, to Ismāʿīl, Fu'ād was the proud heir of this heritage.[143] By contrast, al-Rāfiʿī was mute on the issue of modernization, its sources, and its inspiration. He relentlessly emphasized the role of the people and identified Europe as an essentially hostile entity. *ʿAṣr Ismāʿīl* makes this point clearly. It was a carefully constructed political statement. The timing of publication, the sensitive issues it dealt with, and especially its controversial and categorical conclusions made the book indigestible to those in power. To cite just one final example, al-Rāfiʿī writes, "Turkish was the spoken language in the houses of the princes of Muḥammad ʿAlī's dynasty. More attention was directed to the study of foreign languages, such as French, than to Arabic. This is the reason for the loosening of ties between them and the people and for their lack of activity on the national level. This alienation between the princes and the people increased because some of them lived in Europe and Istanbul."[144]

142. The inclusion of women in nationalist historiography had begun after the 1919 Revolution. al-Rāfiʿī, *ʿAṣr Ismāʿīl,* vol. 2, pp. 9–32, 299–300; ʿAbd al-ʿAẓīm al-Rāfiʿī, "Muḥammad ʿAlī Bāshā wa-l-Khidīwī Ismāʿīl," *Al-Hilāl,* November 1933, pp. 33–35.

143. Pro-monarchic writers systematically selected this line of four monarchic rulers, which excluded ʿAbbās. Ṭāhir al-Ṭanāḥī, "Al-Dīmuqrāṭiyya ṭabīʿat muḥammad ʿalī wa khulafā'ihi," *Al-Hilāl,* November 1936, pp. 45–48; Sammarco, *Les règnes de ʿAbbas, de Sa'id et d'Isma'il,* pp. 129–130; Crabitès, *Ismail the Maligned Khedive,* pp. 101–118; Muḥammad ʿAbd al-Ghanī Ḥasan, "Al-Khidīwī Ismāʿīl bāʿith al-jamāl fī Miṣr, 1830–1895," *Al-Kitāb,* January 1948, pp. 137–145; Sammarco, *Histoire de l'Égypte moderne,* vol. 3, pp. 105–106, 107–108, 295–310; Charles-Roux, "L'Égypte de 1801 à 1882," pp. 284–332; Driault, "Mohamed-Aly et Ibrahim," pp. 371–372; Douin, *Histoire du règne du Khédive Ismaïl,* vol. 3, pp. iv–v.

144. al-Rāfiʿī, *ʿAṣr Ismāʿīl,* vol. 2, pp. 301–302. See also a review of his book: *Al-Hilāl,* February 1933, p. 51.

Why was this statement political? Like his predecessors, Fu'ād was part of this categorization. His Turkish was far better than his Arabic. Turkish, French, and some Italian were the languages used in his court, and, in fact, as mentioned previously, he would even have preferred to have been king of Albania.

The Coming of the British

The historiography of the 1882 British occupation and its immediate aftermath had to grapple with the 'Urābī movement, the first organized revolt against the monarchic order. The historical responsibility for the British occupation was a sensitive and extremely relevant political issue that served as a focal point for already existing disagreements between royalists and nationalists. The subverting political meaning of a nationalist interpretation brought the monarchy to treat the topic of the 'Urābī affair as taboo and to employ measures of censorship in order to silence interpretations other than its own. However, regardless of this intolerant historiographical environment, the 'Urābī revolt was continually subjected to new, controversial interpretations that symbolized an erosion in the political status of royal historiography.

In accordance with their tendency to limit the historiographical debate on this era, royal works on this period are rather scarce. The pro-royal accounts that do exist began somehow apologetically: "Le nouveau Khédive [Tawfīq] est très diffrérent de son père. . . . Moins brillant, moins intelligent, moins actif, moins volontaire, il est aussi moins ambitieux et moins entreprenant" (The new khedive is very different from his father. . . . He is less brilliant, less intelligent, less active, less stubborn, and also less ambitious and enterprising).[145]

The Ottomans, we are told, were the first to take advantage of the new *moins* khedive, and aggressive European involvement was gently alluded to as well (however, never as a form of imperialist exploitation).[146] Then, the discussion shifted to 'Urābī, "un agitateur sans connaissances militaries" (an agitator without any military knowledge),[147] who decided to rebel because the army discriminated against him and his colleagues. Ironically, the diplomatic and military showdown with the rebels was treated as a domestic European affair.

Since the central historiographical point was to excuse Tawfīq for his role in bringing about the long-lasting British occupation, Tawfīq was presented as a kind of a mediator between the Europeans and the rebels.[148] The bombardment of Alexandria and the occupation that followed it were a direct response to the "Alexandria massacre," in which the xenophobic and anti-European masses,

145. Charles-Roux, "L'Égypte de 1801 à 1882," p. 360.
146. Ibid., pp. 361–365.
147. Ibid., p. 365.
148. Ibid., pp. 369–382.

agitated by nationalists, encroached on the foreign population.[149] The physical destruction of Alexandria and the death toll of the local population were played down.[150] If, thus far, it had been possible for some nationalist Egyptians to identify with several aspects of royal historiography, this account would undoubtedly now estrange them. Ṣabrī, as stated below, is a good case in point.

For al-Rāfiʿī, the landing of the British in Egypt was a tragedy of epic proportions.[151] In 1937 he published his first account of the unfolding British occupation and the ʿUrābī revolt. In relation to the rest of his series, this book stands as an exception, since it is the only one that he was forced to rewrite. Thomas Mayer, who studied the place of the ʿUrābī revolt in Egyptian historiography, has convincingly demonstrated that, until 1922, the revolt was perceived as a mutiny *(ʿiṣyān)*, which led to dangerous chaos *(fitna)*.[152] Not only did the monarchy identify the revolt as a dangerous precedent for a military coup d'état, but certain nationalist circles as well were critical of it, having witnessed the defeat at al-Tall al-Kabīr. A fierce critic of the revolt was Muṣṭafa Kāmil, who argued that it divided the people and ultimately led to the British occupation.[153] As early as 1909, the young al-Rāfiʿī identified with this view and attacked ʿUrābī.[154]

However, in his 1937 book, al-Rāfiʿī claimed that the ʿUrābī revolt was yet another popular revolution.[155] In conformity with al-Rāfiʿī 's central argument, a direct and invisible cause—the revolutionary spirit of the people—linked previous revolts to ʿUrābī's. According to al-Rāfiʿī, the goals of the revolt were just: saving the people from autocratic rule, the establishment of the constitutional system, and the prevention of foreign intervention.

However just the revolt may have been, it utterly failed. Al-Rāfiʿī cast the blame for this fiasco on both the army and Tawfīq: the former because they abused the power granted to them by the people, and the latter because he collaborated with the British. ʿUrābī was presented as a weak and impulsive military leader who deserted the nationalist movement at a decisive moment. Hence, as much

149. Ibid., pp. 385–395.

150. Ibid., pp. 395–411

151. Al-Rāfiʿī was the only historian who tried to evaluate the total numbers of casualties and identify them by name. In his later books, al-Rāfiʿī lists all the Shuhadāʾ by name. ʿAbd al-Raḥmān al-Rāfiʿī, *Al-Thawra al-ʿurābiyya wa-l-iḥtilāl al-inglīzī* (Cairo: Maktabat al-nahḍa al-miṣriyya, 1949), pp. 293–294.

152. Mayer, *The Changing Past*, p. 7.

153. Ibid., pp. 7–8; Crabbs, *The Writing of History in Nineteenth-Century Egypt*, pp. 161–162.

154. The young al-Rāfiʿī published his views in Muṣṭafa Kāmil's ultranationalist organ *Al-Liwāʾ*. Aḥmad Ismāʿīl, *Ṣināʿat tārīkh Miṣr*, p. 233.

155. ʿAbd al-Raḥmān al-Rāfiʿī, *Al-Thawra al-ʿurābiyya wa-l-iḥtilāl al-inglīzī*, 2nd ed. (Cairo: Dār al-Qawmiya li-l-ṭibāʿa wa-l-nashr, 1966), pp. 5–16.

as the defeat in battle was military, it was also moral. Therefore, it paralyzed the national movement and facilitated Egypt's capitulation to the British.[156]

In contrast, Ṣabrī understood the history of the 'Urābī revolution in French revolutionary terms. Along these lines, by 1881 Egyptian public opinion was ripe enough to protest the political submissiveness of Tawfīq, whom Ṣabrī considered a weak autocrat. Further ethnic and social tensions destabilized the country. The British suppressed the revolutionary movement, supported Tawfīq, and remained in Egypt.

According to Ṣabrī, "Ce n'était donc pas une révolte, mais une révolution faite par les Égyptiens, qui aspiraient au self-gouvernement et voulaient secouer le joug de l'étranger" (This was not a revolt but a revolution made by Egyptians who aspired to self-government and wanted to shake off the yoke of the foreigner).[157] Considering the 'Urābī revolt to be the first sizable national movement, Ṣabrī argued that the Egyptian national spirit was not inherently xenophobic and chauvinist, since the revolt was directed only toward those who exploited Egypt; and these, by mere chance alone, happened to be foreigners.[158]

Such views gained currency. Toward the end of the 1940s, other nationalist writers mythologized 'Urābī and attacked al-Rāfi'ī for his biased views.[159] Al-Rāfi'ī, hitherto at the forefront of nationalist historiographical changes, was forced to reappraise 'Urābī's legacy.[160] Thus, with no apparent explanation, in January 1952, he published his new account of the events in the form of *Al-za'īm Aḥmad 'Urābī*. Although many of the themes of the 1937 edition repeated themselves, in this book 'Urābī was portrayed as a war hero who was undermined by "external forces."[161] Thereafter, 'Urābī joined the pantheon of popular heroes and martyrs whose original curator was al-Rāfi'ī. The monarchy, for its part, decided to ban the book. A few months later, the 1952 Revolution occurred, and al-Rāfi'ī's account was immediately released and sold out.[162]

A Requiem to Royal Historiography

Despite the untiring royal efforts recorded here, the monarchists lost the competition for historiographical hegemony. For all its worth, by the mid-1930s, after

156. al-Rāfi'ī, *Al-Thawra al-'urābiyya* (1949), pp. 595–605; Mayer, *The Changing Past*, pp. 18–19.

157. Sabry, *La question d'Égypte depuis Bonaparte*, p. 53.

158. Ibid.; and Sabry, *La genèse de l'esprit national égyptien*, pp. 188–225, especially p. 224.

159. Especially groundbreaking was Maḥmūd al-Khafīf's *Ahmad 'Urābī, al-za'īm al-muftara 'alayhi* (Cairo: Maṭba'at al-risāla, 1947). See also Mayer, *The Changing Past*, pp. 20–21.

160. This reappraisal is also an indication that despite al-Rāfi'ī's prominence, he shared the field with many other, far less systematic writers.

161. 'Abd al-Raḥmān al-Rāfi'ī, *Al-za'īm Aḥmad 'Urābī* (Cairo: Dār al-hilāl, 1952), pp. 36–156.

162. The postrevolution title was changed to *Al-za'īm al-thā'ir Aḥmad 'Urābī* (Cairo: Dār wa maṭābi' al-sha'ab, 1968).

fifteen years of extensive exertion, the organized royal project disintegrated. The published source material and history books were far from being a commercial success, and between 1925 and 1936 Fu'ād financed the RGS far beyond the costs of the publications themselves. In fact, the king's allowances constituted the lion's share of the RGS's annual budget (around 63 percent of the 1928–29 budget).[163] Especially intensive were the years 1927 to 1931, when the publication process was in full swing. A significant part of the expenses went for financing the copying of documents in overseas archives (8.5 percent of the RGS's expense during 1932 and 16 percent during 1933).[164] Disappointingly enough, however, despite the RGS's efforts to market these publications, the revenues from book sales were marginal (12 percent of the entire expenses).[165]

Though some aspects of the royal project had a surprising and long-lasting influence, by and large, popular nationalist interpretations à la Rāfiʿī gained momentum. Nowhere was this reality more apparent than in the official textbooks of Muḥammad Rifʿat, first published in 1925 and constantly updated until the 1952 Revolution. Rifʿat was a cautious official who knew fairly well how to find his way around opposing political parties. His long service in the Ministry of Education under changing political circumstances testifies to this. His language and arguments were extremely careful, as he was fully aware of what was at stake. His textbooks had the same quality. Fusing royal and nationalist accounts, Rifʿat always kept a fine balance, which represented the historiographical consensus of the day.

Reading through three editions of Rifʿat's canonical text and other textbooks of the era, one finds a growing acceptance of the nationalist interpretation. Thus, the ʿUrābī revolt was no longer mentioned as a minor military mutiny *(ʿiṣyān* or *tamarrud)* of embittered officers, but rather as a revolt *(thawra)* that had some noteworthy nationalist aspects. Brief discussions of mistakes and shortcomings on the part of the dynasty became more common. The monetary fiasco in the days of Khedive Ismāʿīl and the general incapability of his successor, Tawfīq, figured strongly among these.[166]

163. *Bulletin de la Société Royale de Géographie d'Égypte* 17 (1931): p. 356.

164. Ibid., 18 (1934): pp. 369, 383.

165. See the budget report of 1928–29. Ibid., p. 357. On Fu'ād's death, the publication ceased, and the annual budget shrank substantially.

166. Muḥammad Rifʿat, *Tārīkh Miṣr al-siyāsī fī-l-azmina al-ḥadītha* (Cairo: al-Maṭbaʿa al-amīriyya, 1938), pp. 158–164, 214–232, 244–263; (1941 edition), pp. 185–223, 238–239; (1949 edition), pp. 121–140, 183–196, 200–224. See also conspicuous historiographical changes in Tawfīq Ḥāmid al-Marʿashlī, *Al-tarbiya al-waṭaniyya* (Cairo: Maṭbaʿat dār al-kitāb, 1926), pp. 77–81; Ḥasan Salīm Afendī et al., eds., *Ṣafwat tārīkh Miṣr wa-l-duwal al-ʿarabiyya* (Cairo: Wizārat al-maʿārif, 1930), vol. 2, pp. 128–133; and ʿAbd al-ʿAzīz Bashrī, *Al-Tarbiya al-waṭaniyya* (Cairo: Wizārat al-maʿārif, 1930), pp. 159–160.

Generally, in an ultra-anti-colonial age of young and fervent nationalist agitation, it was no longer possible to hide the fundamental discrepancy between the idea of the sovereign nation and that of the ruling monarchy. The presence of the royal team of European historians, who were deemed foreign to the nation, only emphasized this discrepancy. Indeed, Egyptian intellectuals were puzzled by Fu'ād's choice to employ them, and they grew to resent it.[167]

Fu'ād's death brought about an end to organized royal historiography, and the monarchy was back at the starting point, except that this time, a young, inexperienced, and disinterested king was in charge. Under Fārūq, if a hostile history book appeared, the monarchy did not seek to combat it with a counterpublication; rather, it simply banned the book and persecuted its author. A good case in point was the works of Maḥmūd al-Khafīf, a senior official in the Ministry of Education, who published the most anti-monarchic interpretation of the ʿUrābī revolt. Though several chapters of the books were already serialized in *Al-Risāla,* al-Khafīf was fired and his book was banned.[168] Thus, by the end of this era, historiographical competition took the form of open rivalry as pro-monarchic writers ceased to produce original interpretations.

BEHIND THE DIVIDE

The analysis of the above historiographical debates could be insightful in at least two different ways:

In understanding the basic positions that generated the historiographical controversies between popular-nationalists and royalists. The vantage point for such comprehension is embodied in their different notions of nation and modernity.

In accounting for the actual day-by-day experience of history writing in the period. With what forces did history writers have to reckon?

Nation, Modernity, Historiography

As demonstrated above, the historiographical range of interpretation consisted of royal historiography at one extreme edge and al-Rāfiʿī's project at the other. Many other writers operated along this spectrum. The interaction between these opposing outlooks was intense. Despite what would seem an insurmountable language

167. See, for instance, a comment in Tawfīq Wahba, "Tārīkh Miṣr al-siyāsī al-ḥadīth," *Al-Muqtaṭāf,* March 1933, pp. 372–373.

168. Mayer, *The Changing Past,* pp. 20–27. See the book jacket of Maḥmūd al-Khafīf, *Aḥmad ʿUrābī, al-zaʿīm al-muftara ʿalayhi* (Cairo: al-Hilāl, 1971). Al-Khafīf's title paraphrased that of Crabitès's book on Khedive Ismāʿīl: *Ismāʿīl al-muftara ʿalayhi.*

barrier, works in French, English, Italian, and Arabic were published on a regular basis in the form of summary articles, reviews, and complete chapters, thanks to a dedicated group of translators, editors, and publishers. Essentially, this passionate cultural exchange was not different from the one conducted between local scholars and foreign Orientalists, "intimate intruders" in Raz's words, at about the same time.[169]

Interestingly, royal and nationalist historiographies shared the main working assumptions of the founder paradigm: (a) the acceptance of the modern European-type nation-state as the "culmination of history" and (b) the view of Egypt as a unified, singular, self-conscious player. Thus, both schools selected Egypt as the ultimate subject of modern histories and a suitable unit of analysis. With so much in common, what divisive element sparkled such a debate?

Hanotaux's question epitomizes disagreement: "Où serait l'Égypte sans l'Europe?" (Where would Egypt be without Europe?)[170] Al-Rāfiʿī and his like would have probably answered, "in a far better place," but royalists would argue otherwise. Surely enough, a striking feature of royal historiography was its overwhelming acceptance of Europe's dominance as the basic assumption of history and of that continent's experience as universal and, hence, replicable. Correspondingly, the overriding feature of this historiography was the attempt to replicate European history through an emphasis on Egypt's transition from medievalism to modernism, from despotism to the rule of law, from feudalism to industrialism, and, in short, from barbarity to civilization. As long as the modernization of Egypt was still underway, royal historians, as well as Europeans, regarded Egyptian history as incomplete, as a sort of project that should be brought to a successful close. In this regard, a comparison with India is called into mind. In fact, the Indian example was apparent to royal historians already during the 1930s. Thus, Dodwell's opening quote was Muḥammad ʿAlī's words: "Je n'ai fait en Égypte que ce les Anglais ont fait aux Indes" (I have done in Egypt only what the English did in India).[171]

Concurrently, the monarchy perceived itself, especially the axis of Muḥammad ʿAlī, Ibrāhīm, Ismāʿīl, and Fuʾād, as the sole historical local force that was capable of modernizing Egypt. Hence, it denied the "inadequate" Egyptian people any active role in Egypt's modern history.[172] For monarchists, modern Egyptian history appeared to be the outcome of the monarch's personal capabilities and the extent of his successful collaboration with Europe. Thus, until its very last

169. Raz, "The Transparent Mirror," p. 78.

170. Hanotaux, ed., *Histoire de la nation égyptienne*, vol. 1, p. lxxxvil.

171. Dodwell, *The Founder of Modern Egypt*, front cover.

172. For a classic example of this monarchic view, see Thābit, *Al-Malik Fuʾād, malik al-nahḍa*, pp. 49–55.

days, the monarchy considered the Egyptian people to be passive recipients of sublime royal polices inspired by Europe and executed by a lineage of skillful monarchs. Unsurprisingly, this royal perception of the Egyptian people was borrowed directly from the British, who, wherever they ruled, considered the local population to be inadequate and, thus, in constant need of tutelage until at some, always unspecified, point in the future, it would be considered ready for self-government and citizenship. In the meantime, they offered subjecthood. In this frame of things, the monarchy simply strove to take over the job of "civilizing" from the British.[173]

In contrast, for nationalists the story of modern Egypt is that of its active people. Al-Rāfiʿī appointed himself to speak on behalf of the nation's unquestionable authority and, like his counterparts in India, argued that Egypt "possessed a unitary self and a singular will that arose from its essence and was capable of autonomy and sovereignty."[174] With this in mind, al-Rāfiʿī strove to transform the nation from being "passive to active, inert to sovereign, capable of relating to history and reason."[175] As all nationalists, he resented the royal/colonial assumption of the inadequacy of the people and their need for constant tutelage. What al-Rāfiʿī wanted was not merely to free the nation from the yoke of Europe's political occupation but to free the Egyptian individual in a profound, existential way. By acknowledging the people's ability to think and act, he defied the monarchy and the British on the most significant level: the place of the Egyptian individual within the universal European order.[176]

Politically then, the prime concern of nationalists was independence and an end to the illicit, implicit, and explicit forms of foreign domination. From this point of view, the main task was to unleash the nation's subjectivity from colonial

173. For interesting similarities with India, see Dipesh Chakrabarty, "Postcoloniality and the Artifice of History: Who Speaks for 'Indian' Pasts?" *Representations* 37, special issue (Winter 1992): pp. 1–26; and Gyan Prakash, "Writing Post-Orientalist Histories in the Third World: Perspectives from Indian Historiography," *Comparative Studies in Society and History* 32, no. 2 (April 1990): pp. 383–408. For a critic of Chakrabarty, see Jacques Pouchepadass, "Pluralizing Reason," *History and Theory* 41, no. 3 (October 2002): pp. 381–391.

174. Al-Rāfiʿī's position is similar to that of Indian nationalist historians. Prakash, "Writing Post-Orientalist Histories in the Third World," p. 389.

175. Ibid., p. 388.

176. Ironically, however, al-Rāfiʿī's notion of the nation was instrumental in writing the Egyptian people out of history. For al-Rāfiʿī, political and other changes always come from the top down and from city to countryside. To the extent that he wrote about places other than Cairo, such as revolts in the countryside, it was only in order to demonstrate an action on behalf of Cairo as the hometown of Egyptian nationalism. For al-Rāfiʿī, as for royal historiography, Egypt was Cairo and occasionally Alexandria, whose repeated resistance to foreigners secured its position as a central player in the birth of modern Egyptian nationalism. As we shall see in chapter 8, Marxist historians criticized al-Rāfiʿī's notion of the people.

and royal control. Thus, as all nationalist histories, al-Rāfiʿī's story of the nation would not end until Egypt achieved no less than complete independence *(istiqlāl tāmm)*. Indeed, his theme of recurrent popular revolutions can be endlessly replicated until independence arrived. Indeed, as we shall see in later chapters, al-Rāfiʿī continued to employ this theme effectively in relation to 1919 and 1952, until Egypt won its de facto independence in 1956. Thus, for al-Rāfiʿī, present time was something to move through into the future.

Beyond liberation lay the problem of modernity. While nationalists had a recipe for independence but had no idea how to modernize (al-Rāfiʿī never suggested dismantling the fruits of colonial materialism, such as railways, communications, and hospitals), the royalists knew how to modernize but compromised the independence and authenticity of Egyptian culture. The two groups together had no idea how to modernize, become independent, and yet remain culturally authentic. This dilemma has been the intellectual impasse of many colonized societies that have fought a colonial entity whose logic they have strived to adopt. This anti-colonial nationalism, "even as it challenged the colonial claim to political domination, . . . also accepted the very intellectual premises of 'modernity' on which colonial domination was based."[177] With minor adjustments, this paradox remains a central cultural challenge to this very day.

Quite tragically, this paradox governed the work and lives of Egyptian historians. Al-Rāfiʿī, Ghurbāl, Ṣabrī, Rifʿat, and their followers did not properly understand it, and foreign historians simplistically suggested that if Egypt could only imagine itself as part of the European universal experience, things would naturally fall into place. Only Egypt's luminaries, such as Muḥammad Ḥusayn Haykal, Ṭaha Ḥusayn, and their like, embarked on a thoughtful and systematic journey in search of answers. Their solutions ranged from full assimilation of European culture to periodical emphasis on the cultural authenticity of Egypt. However, since these intellectuals only wrote about history but never studied history per se, the historiographical front was void of answers. It was only in the 1950s and more so in the early 1960s that Marxist historians attempted to engage the question of modernity and nationalism in a new and original way.

Shaping the Experience of History Writing

The monarchic attempt at monopolizing the past by rather passive means, such as limiting accessibility to documents, mass producing literature, and establishing an atmosphere of taboo around sensitive events was a partial success at best. Hence, the royal establishment resorted to more active means in order to enhance its grip on the formation and dissemination of historical mean-

177. Partha Chatterjee, *Nationalist Thought and the Colonial World: A Derivative Discourse?* (Minneapolis: University of Minnesota Press, 1993), p. 30.

ing. Censorship was not a novelty in post-1882 Egypt. However, it was usually restricted to the political press alone and was applied only in rather extreme cases. In the post-1919 era, active monarchic measures of censorship supported by legislation poisoned the intellectual climate, which hitherto had been more or less a free market of ideas.[178] Especially during the first half of the 1930s, when the monarchy collaborated with the autocratic policies of Prime Minister Ismāʿīl Ṣidqī, historians were offered a fixed menu of options: collaborate, apply self-censorship, or risk persecution. Thus, in many ways, like cinematographers, historians worked under an unwritten code of production in which politically inflammatory issues topped the list: "Communism or any anti-establishment ideologies; expressions of popular mass dissent, such as mass gatherings, demonstrations, strikes or even discussions—and certainly speeches—related to incendiary issues like labor rights. Political violence and the depiction of historical personages and any historical depiction of resistance to foreign occupation, even in Pharaonic dress."[179]

In September 1934, the influential literary weekly *Al-Risāla* published a rare anonymous editorial written by a frustrated historian who aired the grievances of his colleagues regarding the restrictive intellectual atmosphere.[180] In it, he conveyed the sense that when criticizing past events and personalities, historians were acutely conscious of the unwritten rules of what, and what not, to write. Those who crossed the fine line of permissible interpretation were sometimes punished, though in many other instances not. Retaliatory measures had always been restricted and usually targeted specific "undisciplined" individuals. The intellectual community of historians as a whole had never been subjected to any inclusive policies, let alone legislation, that curbed its freedom.

The historian who wrote this editorial was particularly alarmed by the liberty that some higher authority had taken in determining what was, and especially what was not, a permissible historical interpretation and, even worse, by his readiness to enforce it through the use of state power. This literary role, he argued, should be left to the public. This historian understood the new active approach to

178. The new press law was a subject of intense public debate and was considered too autocratic. The law was applied only to the indigenous Egyptian press. Newspapers such as the *Egyptian Gazette* were rarely subjected to censorship, ban, or closure. See a stern critique of it accompanied by an acerbic caricature in the popular journal *Al-Ithnayn wa-l-Dunyā*, August 30, 1936, p. 3. In his memoirs, Ḥasan Yūsuf, a high-ranking palace official, provided a fascinating insider perspective on the palace censorship of the press: Ḥasan Yūsuf, *Al-Qaṣr wa dawruhu fī-l-siyāsa al-miṣriyya 1922–1952* (Cairo: al-Ahrām, 1982), pp. 41–53.

179. Joel Gordon, *Revolutionary Melodrama: Popular Film and Civic Identity in Nasser's Egypt* (Chicago: Middle East Documentation Center, 2002), p. 60.

180. "Ḥaqāʾiq al-tārīkh la yumkin an yaṭmusuhā al-tashrīʿ," *Al-Risāla,* September 9, 1934, pp. 1481–1482.

monitoring and censoring historical writing as a kind of official response to the criticism, slander, and defamation that had been directed toward previous rulers (notably members of the house of Muḥammad ʿAlī). After offering an analysis of past and present policies, the historian, in despair, argued:

> Our message is that historical truth is not divisible. Records and documents alone bind the historian's analysis. The historian is subjected only to his conscience in accordance with [standards of] truth and impartiality. The lives of past rulers and leaders belong to history. Neither a man nor a sulṭān has any right over these past lives. This right is reserved for the sulṭān of science alone. The use of legislative means to obliterate historical truth is an unjustified intervention in the freedom of science and research. Concealing the truth does not suit our era, one of science, truth, and enlightenment.[181]

Quite telling, the prime concern of this editorial was not to save the skin of any particular historian but rather to ensure the future freedom of all historians. In particular, the writer was concerned about sanctions that would ruin scholarship, complicate free scientific research, and ultimately undermine its credibility. In a final belligerent statement, the anonymous historian vowed not to abide by the new measures: "Legislation cannot turn defamation into virtues. The science of today knows no borders or homeland. If the legislator succeeds in fettering our pens in Egypt, he will not be successful in doing so in a foreign country, as the land of God is indeed vast. History is being written in all the living languages, and all of these languages are being read in Egypt."[182]

Put simply, the message was that current Egyptian rulers perceived history writing to be subversive because it claimed to be true. But despite such a sincere critique and regardless of the liberalist and democratic image of pre-1952 Egypt, censorship became so much a part of the writers' daily diet that some of them began considering it a natural aspect of intellectual life. Hence, it is perhaps not that surprising to find that, among other intellectuals, Muḥammad Farīd Abū Ḥadīd, a prominent literary critic and historical novelist who was very much an integral part of the liberalist stratum, headed the censorship office *(maṣlaḥat al-riqāba)* and at the end of his tenure could naturally return to normal intellectual activity.[183] Thus, an integral aspect of this full-fledged historiographical field and of the very experience of writing was the making of careful political calculations.

181. Ibid., p. 1482.

182. Ibid.

183. Abū Ḥadīd was by no means the only intellectual employed as a censor. More obscure professors from Fu'ād University, such as Muḥammad ʿAwaḍ and a British professor of literature, performed similar duties. Yūsuf, *Al-Qaṣr wa dawruhu*, pp. 45–53.

TABLE 3. Selected Nationalist and Royalist Publications

Year*	Author	Title	Notes
1925–52	Muḥammad Rifʿat	*Tārīkh Miṣr al-siyāsī fi-l-azmina al-ḥadītha*	School textbook. Successive modified editions were published until the revolution.
1928	Shafik Ghorbal	*The Beginnings of the Egyptian Question and the Rise of Mehmet Ali*	Probably because of the way Muḥammad ʿAlī is portrayed as dismissive toward the people, the author avoided translating this work into Arabic
1929	ʿAbd al-Raḥmān al-Rāfiʿī	*Tārīkh al-ḥaraka al-qawmiyya wa taṭawwur niẓām al-ḥukum fī Miṣr*	2 vols. Following the publication, the author was denied access to the ʿĀbdīn archive.
1930	ʿAbd al-Raḥmān al-Rāfiʿī	*ʿAṣr Muḥammad ʿAlī*	
1930	Mohamed Sabry	*L'empire égyptien sous Mohamed Ali et la question d'Orient 1811–1849*	
1930–37	Gabriel Hanotaux, ed.	*Histoire de la nation égyptienne*	7 vols. Translation stopped in 1939 for unknown reasons.
1931	Henry Dodwell	*The Founder of Modern Egypt: A Study of Muhammad Ali*	Translated into Arabic in 1937
1931	ʿUmar Ṭūsūn	*Al-Jaysh al-miṣrī al-barrī wa-l-baḥrī fī ʿahd Muḥammad ʿAlī Bāshā*	
1932	ʿAbd al-Raḥmān al-Rāfiʿī	*ʿAṣr Ismāʿīl*	2 vols. Distribution in schools and libraries was banned. Royalists translated parts of the book into French.
1932	ʿUmar Ṭūsūn	*Al-Ṣanāʾiʿ wa-l-madāris al-ḥarbiyya fī ʿahd Muḥammad ʿAlī*	
1932–35	Mohamed Zaky el-Ibrachy Pacha and Angelo Sammarco, eds.	*Précis de l'histoire d'Égypte*	4 vols.

1933–36	Georges Douin	*Histoire du règne du Khédive Ismaïl*	3 vols.
1933	Pierre Crabitès	*Ismail the Maligned Khedive*	Translated into Arabic
1933	Mohamed Sabry	*L'empire égyptien sous Ismaïl et l'ingérence anglo-française*	
1935	Pierre Crabitès	*Ibrahim of Egypt*	Translated into Arabic
1935	Joseph Cattaui	*Le khédive Isma'il et la dette de l'Égypte*	Former president of the Egyptian Geographical Society
1937	'Abd al-Raḥmān al-Rāfi'ī	*Al-Thawra al-'urābiyya wa-l-iḥtilāl al-inglīzī*	The account of the 'Urābī revolt was modified in 1952.
1937	Angelo Sammarco	*Histoire de l'Égypte moderne depuis Mohammed Ali jusqu'à l'occupation britannique, 1801–1882*	3 vols.
1938	Aḥmad 'Izzat 'Abd al-Karīm	*Tārīkh al-ta'līm fī 'aṣr Muḥammad 'Alī*†	An academic publication by one of Ghurbāl's advisees
1939	Angelo Sammarco	*La verita sulla questione del canale di Suez*	Translated into Arabic
1942	Karīm Thābit	*Muḥammad 'Alī*	
1942	'Abd al-Raḥmān al-Rāfi'ī	*Miṣr wa-l-Sūdān fī awwal 'ahd al-iḥtilāl . . . 1882–1892*	
1944	Shafīq Ghurbāl	*Muḥammad 'Alī al-Kabīr*	Awarded the title bey for this publication
1944	Georges Douin	*Histoire du Soudan égyptien*	
1947	Maḥmūd al-Khafīf	*Aḥmad 'Urābī, al-za'īm al-muftara 'alayhi*	Book was banned.
1948	Muḥammad Fu'ād Shukrī et al., eds.	*Binā' dawla: Miṣr Muḥammad 'Alī*	A nonacademic collection by academic historians
1949	The Royal Historical Society	*Al-Dhikra al-mi'awiyya li-wafāt al-maghfūr lahu Muḥammad 'Alī al-kabīr 1849–1949*†	A collection of academic studies by Ghurbāl and his students

*The year indicates the original date of publication, but I did not necessarily refer to the first edition.

†An academic publication.

CONCLUSION

Several arguments have framed our discussion up to this point. We have seen how the historiographical field achieved an unprecedented maturity, evident in terms of its institutional infrastructure, number of writers and readers, circulation of historical output, and, above all, the sophistication, profoundness, and intensity of historiographical debates. The voluminous body of literature this era created, especially the ʿĀbdīn project and the work of al-Rāfiʿī, shaped the historical understanding of Westerners and Egyptians alike for generations to come. Used as both primary source material and complete authoritative and final analysis, this literature produced an image of nineteenth-century Egypt that was galvanized during this era.

Thus, during the 1930s, some thirty years after its institution, the founder paradigm achieved a stunning hegemony on the thought and practice of modern Egyptian history. All writers—nationalists, royalists, and those in between—accepted its premises. All that was left to discuss was who played what role and why within this framework. The historiographical competition discussed here occurred in this context and has been framed here through a discussion of opposing notions of nation and modernity. Finally, the politicization of history writing and the harsh measures of censorship that accompanied it stifled the work of historians. All things considered, historical writings of that period represent a remarkable scholarly achievement that illustrates the interconnectedness between Western and local modes of historical knowledge.

For the picture of historiographical development in this era to be completed, it is necessary to account for a set of general attitudes and methodological and theoretical concerns with regard to the process of history writing: What is historical truth? How is it found? Who has the authority to tell true from false? Is there a hierarchy according to which works of history could be classified and judged? Is history writing a profession or a hobby? And, most important, what is the ultimate purpose of history writing?

Examining the answers Egyptian historians gave to these questions would reveal yet another great historiographical divide between academic and independent historians. Perhaps, as a prelude to this discussion, the following quotes of Egypt's most prominent twentieth-century historians illustrate some of the existing gaps:

> al-Rāfiʿī: I have loved history since I was young, and perceived it as means for the moral upbringing of the people and for national and political revival. . . . in light of my experience, *I see [history] as an instrument for education and for enhancing the national consciousness in the hearts of the people.*[184]

184. al-Rāfiʿī, *Mudhakkarātī,* p. 61 (emphasis added).

Ghurbāl: Science *('ilm)* in and of itself has a responsibility that cannot be borne by our nationalist forces in their current stage. Hence, for the society at large, science should be the slogan of the current cultural revolution . . . both for the realization of the goals of the nation *and for the sake of science itself.*[185]

185. Quoted in Aḥmad 'Abd al-Raḥīm Muṣṭafa, "Shafīq Ghurbāl mu'ārikh," *MTM* 13 (1963): p. 278 (emphasis added).

5

Ghurbāl's School

1930–1952

The story goes that when Muḥammad Shafīq Ghurbāl was asked to identify his most important publications he pointed at his students and said, "These are my most important books."[1] True or not, this anecdote captures the very essence of Ghurbāl's career: Although his publications were fragmentary and on multiple subjects, he nevertheless had an unprecedented influence as a teacher and intellectual leader.[2] From the perspective of intellectual history, then, his career did not provide the historian with a significant body of literature to work with. The historian's task becomes even more frustrating once the basic tension of Ghurbāl's career is considered, for despite a genuine longing to shape the historical consciousness of the public, he was notorious for shying away from public activity. Thus, Ghurbāl gave almost no interviews and never wrote his memoirs; nor did he leave an organized archive, as other intellectuals of his magnitude often did. Ghurbāl left few traces in general, further complicating the work of his future biographers.

Consequently, both Western and local scholars have tended not to focus their research on Ghurbāl. The few who have ventured to study his life and work have had to explain or take for granted his already established canonical position as

1. Muḥammad Anīs, "Shafīq Ghurbāl wa madrasat al-tārīkh al-miṣrī al-ḥadīth," *Al-Majalla*, November 1961, p. 13. For a different version of the same story, see Muḥammad 'Izzat 'Abd al-Karīm, "Muḥammad Shafīq Ghurbāl: Ustādh jīl wa ṣāḥib madrasa," *MTM* 19 (1972): p. 25.

2. Ghurbāl was aware of this state of affairs and nevertheless made a conscious decision to focus on graduate teaching. 'Abd al-Tawwāb 'Abd al-Ḥayy, *'Aṣīr ḥayātī* (Cairo: al-Dār al-qawmiyya li-l-ṭibā'a wa-l-nashr, 1966), p. 156.

the "founder of modern historical writing." Typically, they have chosen to do so by studying his incoherent body of literature and especially his 1928 pioneering work, *The Beginnings of the Egyptian Question and the Rise of Mehmet Ali*. Thus, according to Youssef Choueiri, with *Beginnings*, "Egyptian historiography can be said to have entered a new stage in its development."[3] Particularly, Choueiri conveyed the sense that Ghurbāl was important because of his narrative of the nation-state. Another scholar, Gabriel Piterberg, rightly perceived Ghurbāl as "the doyen of twentieth century Egyptian historiography." However, studying the impact of the "Orientalist discourse" on Egyptian historiography, he wrongly saw Ghurbāl as an important agent of Orientalist thought in academia. Piterberg assumed that Ghurbāl absorbed this mode of thinking from his mentor Arnold Toynbee.[4] Intimately acquainted with the local historiographical scene, Anthony Gorman saw Ghurbāl as the founder of a certain "liberal school" that transferred the historiographical balance "from the palace to [the] people."[5] His view echoes the similar position of Ibrāhīm ʿAbd al-Munʿim al-Jumayʿī.[6]

With all due respect to these fine studies, in reality, Ghurbāl did not have any original, or particularly popular, "national narrative." This credit should be reserved for al-Rāfiʿī.[7] Likewise, the Orientalist mode of thinking that Ghurbāl allegedly brought back home from London has been active in Egypt since the turn of the twentieth century. Ghurbāl was never a major agent of such thought. Inasmuch as Ghurbāl, like everybody else at that time, subscribed to Orientalist ideas, his main source of influence was the ʿĀbdīn project. Though extremely vague and undersubstantiated, Gorman's notion of Ghurbāl's relationship with a liberal school comes closer to his true role. However, rather than studying what made Ghurbāl the father of this school, Gorman repeated the methodological mistake of trying to understand Ghurbāl from the narrow angle of his book *The Beginnings of the Egyptian Question*. In sum, a consistent flaw in these three studies was the inability to explain Ghurbāl's monumental status within the Egyptian historiographical scene in general and the historiographical field in particular. Thus, in this chapter, I return to the starting point: What makes Ghurbāl the doyen of Egyptian historiography?

3. Choueiri, *Arab History and the Nation-State*, p. 65.

4. Gabriel Piterberg, "The Tropes of Stagnation and Awakening in Nationalist Historical Consciousness," in James Jankowski and Israel Gershoni, eds., *Rethinking Nationalism in the Arab Middle East* (New York: Columbia University Press, 1998), pp. 49–50.

5. Gorman, *Historians, State and Politics*, pp. 113–115.

6. al-Jumayʿī, *Itijāhāt al-kitāba*, pp. 159–170.

7. Choueiri studied only "Arab historians and intellectuals who had direct or indirect access to Western education, knew a foreign language, and attempted to use academic techniques in their history writing." Hence, he ignored the impact of al-Rāfiʿī and ascribed to Ghurbāl a role he never had. Choueiri, *Arab History and the Nation-State*, p. 65.

The way to answer this question is to break away from existing accounts of Ghurbāl's career and treat the person himself as a metaphor for or a symbol of academic writing in general. I intend to take literally Ghurbāl's answer, "These are my most important books," and study these "publications": as students, as historians, and, above all, as a homogeneous intellectual community, much as one might ordinarily study the important books of another, perhaps more typical, scholar. Thus, a focus on Ghurbāl's disciples, rather than a study of his fragmented writings alone, will help to clarify his significance and the centrality of his school.

Two major arguments constitute this chapter: First, the academic school of writing continued royal historiography in terms of its focus, assumptions, methods of work, style of writing, institutions, and, most important, its general historiographical and political orientation. Second, gradually, albeit continually, Ghurbāl and his disciples consciously replicated the academic standards of the ʿĀbdīn project and formed a school that regarded itself as professional. Over time, they developed an ideology of professionalism that distinguished them from populist/amateur historians. A major component of this new ideology was their insistence on vigorous archival research as the only way to discover "truth in history." Operating against the background of a concurrent dramatic increase in the writing of popular historiography, they developed a specific notion of historical objectivity that strengthened their claim to expert authority. By the 1940s, the academic school appeared as the only group of history writers with a strong ethical commitment.

THE MAKING OF A SCHOOL

Beginnings in Cairo

Born in 1894 to a middle-class Muslim family of merchants in Alexandria, Ghurbāl could have easily ended up being anything from a lawyer to an engineer. Apparently, his parents had the means to afford to send their son to a prestigious professional school, in the company of the sons of many other members of the emerging *effendiyya* class. But Ghurbāl preferred history to law or engineering.

In 1915 he graduated from the Higher Teacher College (Dār al-muʿalimīn al-ʿulyā), which, being the only institution that offered a degree in the humanities, attracted many literary-minded students such as the literary critic and novelist Muḥammad Farīd Abū Ḥadīd.[8] Although far less prestigious than a professional college, this school was still a central avenue to the social world of the tarboosh-wearing *effendis*.

8. Muḥammad Farīd Abū Ḥadīd, "Kalimat ta'bīn," *MTM* 11 (1963): pp. 36–45.

Unlike other young students who had access to nationalist ideas, Ghurbāl evinced little interest in actual political activity or in political writing. This tendency away from politics became the hallmark of his career. His diligence at school bore fruit, and in 1915 at the age of twenty-one, he was sent to the University of Liverpool to complete a B.A. degree in history. The Ministry of Education paid for the trip. On his arrival at Liverpool, Ghurbāl met Muḥammad Rifʿat, who was just about to graduate. Rifʿat, a friend, colleague, and future influential historian in his own right, would later cooperate with Ghurbāl in a mutual effort to Egyptianize *(tamṣīr)* history writing.[9] While Ghurbāl was in Liverpool, World War I reshaped the Middle East, and he was quick to discern the incompatibility between a distinctive Egyptian nationalism and an Ottoman unity.[10] In 1919, he graduated with honors, returned home, and discovered an essentially different Egypt, far less Turkish and much more nationalist than before.

Ghurbāl's B.A. thesis dealt with the French expedition and the rise of Muḥammad ʿAlī. It was based on extensive archival work with primary sources and served as the basis of his future graduate work in London.[11] Working in archives was not yet a professional habit of Egyptian historians, and, thus, in the eyes of Egyptian intellectuals, Ghurbāl was regarded as a pioneer whose work carried much methodological potential.

The 1919 Revolution found Ghurbāl focused on his studies rather than on political activity, unlike al-Rāfiʿī.[12] After three years of teaching, he was accepted into the prestigious London University to pursue his MA degree under the supervision of Arnold Toynbee. As an ambitious universal historian, Toynbee became Ghurbāl's mentor, and his thought significantly influenced Ghurbāl's writing and general attitude. Toynbee's perception of "elites," "mimetic masses," and the need of the elite to control and administer those much-feared masses was essentially whigish in its advocacy of cultural patronage and intellectual aloofness. Many of these traits would also manifest themselves in Ghurbāl's personal and intellectual attitudes as well as in his political preferences.

As Toynbee himself testified, he was quite ignorant of the political history of the early nineteenth-century Ottoman Empire and seems to have learned from Ghurbāl more than he could have taught Ghurbāl on that subject.[13] In London, Ghurbāl returned to work on his B.A. thesis, added several chapters, reshaped some of his arguments, visited as many as nine different European archives, and, two years later, submitted an innovative and authoritative thesis, which was later

9. Muḥammad Rifʿat, "Kalimat ta'bīn," *MTM* 11 (1963): pp. 7–9.
10. Abū Ḥadīd, "Kalimat ta'bīn," p. 43.
11. Ghorbal, *The Beginnings of the Egyptian Question*, p. xiii.
12. Aḥmad ʿIzzat ʿAbd al-Karīm, "Kalimat ta'bīn," *MTM* 11 (1963): p. 11.
13. Ibid.

published as *The Beginnings of the Egyptian Question and the Rise of Mehmet Ali*. In response, London University accorded him an M.A. degree with distinction. Curiously, the father of academic scholarship in Egypt, who throughout his career would examine many Ph.D. candidates, never continued his official education beyond that point. In 1924 he returned to Egypt with four things: his M.A. thesis, a letter of recommendation from Toynbee, Toynbee's rather snobbish attitude toward history and other human affairs, and one Miss Gertrude Humberstone, a British colleague and his future wife.[14] These were enough to open the doors of the history department in Fu'ād University, where he started teaching in 1928.

In the same year, after almost thirteen years of research and writing, Ghurbāl finally published his *Beginnings*. Printed in London, the book was designed to satisfy the curiosity of the British public. It was never translated into Arabic. In a preface to the first edition Toynbee noted that "it would be difficult to guess from internal evidence whether the author were an Englishman, a Frenchman, an Egyptian or none of these."[15] In retrospect, as some of Ghurbāl's critics noted, this was also an aspect of Ghurbāl's problematic role as an agent of Western thought. Nevertheless, *Beginnings* was assigned to all of Ghurbāl's history students and acquired canonical status.

Egyptianizing an Elite of History Students

In a preface to the first academic publication of one of his students, Ghurbāl lamented the state of historical writing and put forward a new and comprehensive research agenda. According to Ghurbāl, the fascination with the history of great military campaigns and expeditions was indeed justified and important. But equally crucial, and rarely studied, were the reforms carried out under Muḥammad 'Alī. "For this reason," he wrote, "I direct young historians toward the study of these reforms."[16] Indeed, a glance at the works of Ghurbāl's students reveals a certain pattern: Aḥmad 'Izzat 'Abd al-Karīm wrote on education, Aḥmad Aḥmad al-Ḥitta studied agricultural reforms, 'Alī al-Jiritlī focused on industrialization, and, similarly, other students focused on various aspects of Egypt's dynastically sponsored modernization process, such as the advent of the printing press.

Table 4 illustrates the historical horizons of the first generation of Ghurbāl's

14. In his published M.A. thesis, Ghurbāl acknowledged his fellow student and friend Miss Humberstone. Ghorbal, *The Beginnings of the Egyptian Question*, xiv. See also Yaḥḥya al-Khashab, "Kalimat ta'bīn," *MTM* 11 (1963): p. 20.

15. Ghorbal, *The Beginnings of the Egyptian Question*, pp. ix–x.

16. Aḥmad 'Izzat 'Abd al-Karīm, *Tārīkh al-ta'līm fī 'aṣr Muḥammad 'Alī* (Cairo: Maktabat al-nahḍa al-miṣriyya, 1938), pp. i–iv.

history students. All of his advisees focused on nineteenth-century Egypt up to the 1882 British occupation. They all examined various aspects of Muḥammad ʿAlī's contribution to the creation of the modern Egyptian nation-state. The founder paradigm framed and conceptualized the scope of their historical investigation. Many of these works were eventually published as either books or articles. Equally important is the composition of the first generation of graduate students: Egyptian males of middle-class origin, members of the new *effendiyya*.

A glance at some of the published works immediately reveals the scope of cooperation with the ʿĀbdīn project.[17] Students sweepingly accepted the royal chronology, especially with regard to Muḥammad ʿAlī. A "before and after" approach, marked by Muḥammad ʿAlī's accession to power, served as a clear point of departure for any historical discussion. Accordingly, they identified a significant transformation in the status of education, commerce, industry, and agriculture. The achievements of the dynasty—strengthening Egyptian leadership in the East, reviving the national spirit, and facilitating the restoration of the Arabic language and sciences—directed Egypt toward a modern, European-oriented nation-state.[18] The suppression of Egypt's Ottomanness during this period was a common denominator in royal and popular-nationalist historiographies. However, fully aware of the debates between al-Rāfiʿī and pro-monarchic historians, these young students, and especially their mentor Ghurbāl, tried to establish their own unique and independent point of observation. The efforts to distinguish themselves from the ʿĀbdīn project in general, and from foreign historians in particular, are usually referred to as the *tamṣīr* (Egyptianization) project.

Eulogizing Ghurbāl in a period during which his legacy was already under fire, socialist historian Muḥammad Anīs echoed his pioneering role in this regard: "Ghurbāl [was entrusted] with the mission of taking historical studies away from the monarchy and the foreigners. In more precise terms, he [was entrusted] with the mission of Egyptianizing *(tamṣīr)* history a quarter of a century before the idea of *tamṣīr* gained currency."[19]

Forming an elite of indigenous Egyptian students was certainly an integral part of the *tamṣīr* efforts. Deeply committed to this task, Ghurbāl often reminded his students that "foreign historians are interested in imperial aspects, and our

17. The works I discuss here were selected according to considerations of availability.

18. See, for example, ʿAbd al-Karīm, *Tārīkh al-taʿlīm fī ʿaṣr Muḥammad ʿAlī*, pp. 1–3, 27, 82–92, 555–593, 653–664; ʿAlī Jiritlī, *Tārīkh al-ṣināʿa fī Miṣr f ī-l-niṣf al-awwal min al-qarn al-tāsiʿ ʿashar* (Cairo: Dār al-maʿārif bi Miṣr, al-Jamʿiyya al-malakiyya li-l-dirāsāt al-tārīkhiyya, 1952), pp. 9–25, 35–81, 169–183; and Aḥmad Aḥmad al-Ḥitta, *Tārīkh al-ziraʿa al-Miṣriyya fī ʿaṣr Muḥammad ʿAlī al-kabīr* (Cairo: Dār al-maʿārif bi Miṣr, al-Jamʿiyya al-malikiyya li-l-dirāsāt al-tārīkhiyya, 1950), pp. 1–4, 27–49, 105–106, 145–168.

19. Anīs, "Shafīq Ghurbāl wa madrasat al-tārīkh," p. 13.

TABLE 4. The First Generation of Academic History Students, 1934–1952

Student	Year	Thesis Title	Degree	Notes
Aḥmad Aḥmad al-Ḥitta	1934	Al-Fallāḥ al-miṣrī fī ʿahd Muḥammad ʿAlī	M.A.	
Raḍwān Abū al-Futūḥ*	1936	Tārīkh maṭbaʿat būlāq	M.A.	Published as a book
Aḥmad ʿIzzat				
ʿAbd al-Karīm*	1938	Tārīkh al-taʿlīm fī ʿaṣr Muḥammad ʿAlī	M.A.	Published as a book
Iyād Hasanīn Dūs*	1939	Al-Fatḥ al-miṣrī li-l-Sudān fī ʿahd Muḥammad ʿAlī	M.A.	
Ibrāhīm ʿAbduh*	1940	Tārīkh al-ṣaḥāfa al-miṣriyya 1798–1882	M.A.	
Aḥmad ʿIzzat ʿAbd al-Karīm*	1941	Tārīkh al-taʿlīm mundhu awākhīr ʿaṣr Muḥammad ʿAlī ila awāʾil ḥukum Tawfīq	Ph.D.	Published in 1945 as two separate books
ʿAbd al-Ḥamīd Muḥammad al-Baṭrīq*	1943	Al-ḥukum al-miṣrī fī bilād al-ʿarab	M.A.	Completed his graduate work under Dodwell's supervision at London U.
Muḥammad Muḥammad Tawfīq*	1943	Muṣṭalaḥ wathāʾiq tārīkh al-ḥukūm al-ʿuthmānī fī Miṣr	M.A.	Hired by the ʿĀbdīn archive on his graduation
Ibrāhīm ʿAbduh*	1943	Taṭawwur al-ṣaḥāfa al-miṣriyya wa athrihā fī al-nahḍatayn al-fikriyya wa-l-ijtimāʿiyya	Ph.D.	

Muḥammad Rifʿat Ramaḍān*	1945	Thawrat ʿAlī bīk al-kabīr 1768–1772	M.A.	
Jamāl al-Dīn al-Shayyāl†	1945	Tārīkh al-tarjama wa-l-ḥaraka al-thaqāfiyya fī ʿaṣr Muḥammad ʿAlī	M.A./ Alexandria University	Published as a book.
ʿAlī al-Jiritlī*	1947 (?)	Tārīkh al-ṣināʿa fī Miṣr fī-l-niṣf al-awwal min al-qarn al-tāsiʿ ʿashar	M.A.	Jiritlī completed his graduate studies at London U. Published by EHS.
Aḥmad Aḥmad al-Ḥitta*	1946	Taṭawwur al-zirāʿa al-miṣriyya fī al-niṣf al-awwal min al-qarn al-al-tāsiʿ ʿashar	Ph.D.	Published by EHS in 1950 under a different title.
ʿAbd al-ʿAzīz Muḥammad al-Shanāwī*	1948	Al-Sukhra fī ḥafr qanāt al-Suwīs	M.A.	Worked as an archivist in ʿĀbdīn. His M.A. thesis and Ph.D. dissertation were published as books.
Aḥmad ʿAbd al-Raḥīm Muṣṭafa††	1951	Al-Khidīwī Ismāʿīl wa ʿalāqatihi bi-l-bāb al-ʿālī	M.A.	Published as a book.

SOURCES: Qāsim Hishmat, *Dalīl al-rasāʾil al-jāmiʿiyya* (Cairo: Kulliyat al-ādāb, 1996); *MTM* 13 (1967); and *MTM* 16 (1969).

*An advisee of Ghurbāl.

†An unofficial advisee of Ghurbāl.

††A joint advisee of ʿIzzat ʿAbd al-Karīm and Ghurbāl.

mission is to focus on society."[20] For Aḥmad 'Izzat 'Abd al-Karīm, *tamṣīr* was not merely studying Egyptian history in Arabic rather than in French or English. Much more than that, it was "directing attention to the study of modern national history."[21] Thus, especially following his appointment as chair of the history department (1936), replacing the British historian Arthur J. Grant, and later as dean of the Faculty of Arts, replacing Ṭaha Ḥusayn (1938–40), Ghurbāl was credited for successfully Egyptianizing both faculty and students.[22] But what did it really mean to ensure that Egyptians rather than foreigners would teach and write Egyptian history? How did it affect the contents of their writing? And did it, in reality, mark a fundamental shift in interpretation and focus?

By and large, the working assumption was that Egyptians would and should write different history. First, their middle-class social profile differentiated them from all other history writers past and present. Evidently, this fact also influenced their historical perspective. Moreover, although they had intimate familiarity with the 'Ābdīn project, drew heavily on its institutions, and were well versed in its publications, they envisioned a certain division of labor between themselves and the foreign historians.[23] Thus, in terms of their self-image and historical task, Ghurbāl's disciples certainly did not perceive themselves as royal employees, symbolically on the university payroll.

Indeed, these historians had a decidedly different approach and emphasis from that of their foreign colleagues, primarily in that they displayed a more critical view of monarchic history. Here, young historians followed the standard nationalist criticism of the day.[24] Emphasizing their differences with royal historiography, which concentrated almost entirely on power politics and the higher political pyramid, Ghurbāl and his students purported to take the next step and

20. "Ta'bīn Shafīq Ghurbāl," *Al-Majalla*, December 1961, p. 135.

21. 'Abd al-Karīm, "Kalimat ta'bīn," p. 12.

22. Arthur J. Grant (1862–1948) was the author of *Europe in the Nineteenth and Twentieth Centuries*. For *tamṣīr* in Fu'ād University, see Reid, *Cairo University and the Making of Modern Egypt*, pp. 99–102, 126, 162–164.

23. Toward the late 1940s, the *MTM* published detailed lists of sources relevant for the study of the reforms under Muḥammad 'Alī. The students listed the published sources of the 'Ābdīn project as the first body of knowledge they turned to. See, for example, Aḥmad Aḥmad al-Ḥitta, "Marāji' tārīkh al-zirā'a al-Miṣriyya: 'Ahd Muḥammad 'Alī 1805–1848," *MTM* 1, no. 1 (May 1948): pp. 239–254. See also Aḥmad 'Izzat 'Abd al-Karīm, "Tārīkh al-ta'līm fī 'aṣr Muḥammad 'Alī: Maṣādiruhu wa wathā'iquhu," *MTM* 1, no. 1 (May 1948): pp. 255–276; and Amīn Muṣṭafa 'Abd Ilāh, "Tārīkh al-tijāra fī 'aṣr Muḥammad 'Alī: Maṣādiruhu wa wathā'iquhu," *MTM* 2, no. 2 (October 1949): pp. 97–112.

24. Common topics were decline, 'Abbās's reactionary tenure, and Muḥammad 'Alī's policies toward soldiers and peasants. Jiritlī, *Tārīkh al-ṣinā'a*, pp. 179–183; Asmā' Ḥasan Fahmī, "*Tārīkh al-ta'līm fī Miṣr tahta ḥukum 'Abbās wa Sa'īd wa Ismā'īl*," *MTM* 1, no. 1 (May 1948): pp. 330–335; al-Ḥitta, *Tārīkh al-zirā'a*, pp. 107–112; 'Abd al-Karīm, *Tārīkh al-ta'līm fī 'aṣr Muḥammad 'Alī*, pp. 633–637; 'Abd al-'Azīz Muḥammad al-Shinnāwī's published M.A. thesis focused on the corvée system:

study the "people." Elucidating this vision, Ghurbāl declared, "The subjective historian deems redundant what is not related to the elite politics of the sultans and their representatives. The records in the archives, however, provide us with crucial information about the daily livelihood of the soldiers, their food, and their clothes. Hence, it is possible to write the history of the Egyptian army only with these kinds of documents."[25]

Thus, in contrast with the royal historians, academic historians, through exhaustive archival effort, aspired to focus on the lives and deeds of ordinary men and women. Furthermore, unlike popular historians, who employed the notion of the "people," , academic historians aspired, at least ideally, to have a less faceless view of the crowd. Years later Aḥmad ʿIzzat ʿAbd al-Karīm recalled, "If the official school of British and French historians wrote the history of Muḥammad ʿAlī and Ismāʿīl, Ghurbāl directed the students of his school to study the history of the Egyptian nation and society. He directed them to study the history of education, industry, the printing press, commerce, the Egyptian peasant, et cetera."[26] In hindsight, however, ʿAbd al-Karīm's observation was inaccurate, for nothing of real methodological substance marks an elementary break from the essence of monarchic historiography. Rather, what one sees is a fusion of the concerns of popular-nationalist historiography with the theoretical and methodological framework prescribed by ʿĀbdīn.

This reality means that Egyptianization was a problematic enterprise. Indeed, the main challenge of *tamṣīr* was to navigate between the advantages and disadvantages of European historiography and ideally to profit from both worlds. Thus, while resisting the presence of foreign professors and pushing them out of the university, Egyptians venerated their methods and objects of work. For this reason, the *tamṣīr* project may be seen to represent an impasse for the Egyptian intelligentsia, whose modernist anti-colonial project was somehow contradictory. Though historians were not alone in this impasse, their task was far more complicated than that of anthropologists, sociologists, and scientists. This is because they had to grapple with a massive and coherent body of long-established historical knowledge already written on Egypt and because that history was the ultimate medium through which the general question of modernity was addressed.[27]

Consequently, despite their rhetoric, they mostly offered a division of labor and a great degree of philosophical continuity with the monarchic project, rather

---

Al-Sukhrah fī ḥafr Qanāt al-Suways (Alexandria: Munsha'at al-Maʿārif al-ḥadītha, 1958). For his imprisonment, see chapter 7.

25. EHS, *Dhikra al-baṭal al-fātiḥ Ibrāhīm Bāshā 1848–1948*, 2nd ed. (Cairo: Maktabat Madbūlī, al-Jamʿiyya al-malakiyya li-l-dirāsāt al-tārikhiyya, 1990), preface, ii.

26. ʿAbd al-Karīm, "Kalimat ta'bīn," p. 13.

27. For the case of Egyptian sociologists, see ElShakry, "The Great Social Laboratory."

than a fundamental change in focus and interpretation. Historians of future generations, notably during the 1950s and 1960s, noticed this gap between reality and ideal and, as we shall see, decided to come to terms with it by shifting to radical historiographical solutions. Nevertheless, at least as late as 1953, Ghurbāl still held that the most important foundation of his school was its focus on new historical aspects other than power politics.[28] As we shall see now, their professional identity, claim to expert authority, and ethics commitment were the crucial features that defined Ghurbāl's school. These traits were the gift of the royal school and the diligent foreigners who populated it.

Forging a Professional Identity

The prominent essayist, literary critic, and novelist Luwīs 'Awaḍ recalled that in the beginning of the 1930s, while he was a first-year history student at Cairo University, Ghurbāl asked his class to write a paper titled "History: Is It Science or Art?"[29] In the following discussion it will become clear that history professors did everything in their capacity to persuade their students that this question had only one possible answer: History is science, historians are scientists, and their investigations produce objective truth.

The consolidated group of young academic students at Fu'ād University was headed by an equally homogeneous group of faculty members, all of whom shared the following working assumption: Only through painstaking archival work could one find truth in history. These professors, chief among them Ḥasan 'Uthmān, Muṣṭafa Ziyāda, and, of course Ghurbāl, regarded archival work as the single most important practice that distinguished academic professional writing from what they termed "amateur writing."

The advance of the royal project, coupled with the return of the first generation of history professors from their training in Europe, resulted in the adoption and celebration of "scientific history."[30] Writing on the possibility of revealing the true Ibrāhīm through archival research, Ghurbāl maintained that archival material is free of any possible form of bias, because people who had no personal interests or overt public cause to promote wrote the documents years ago, away from the public eye. Hence, Ghurbāl believed that the archive

28. Raḍwān Abū al-Futūḥ, *Tārīkh maṭbā'at būlāq* (Cairo: al-Maṭabā'a al-amīriyya bi-l-Qāhira, 1953), preface, i–iii.

29. Luwīs 'Awaḍ, "Al-Tārīkh bayna al-dhāt wa-l-mawḍū'," *Al-Muṣawwar,* May 11, 1984, p. 24.

30. All previous attempts to discuss questions of theory and method were incoherent, because they drew on an immature historiographical field. Ḥusayn Labīb, "Al-Tārīkh wa al-ṭarīqa al-tārīkhiyya," *Al-Muqtaṭaf,* February 1923, pp. 176–177; Ismā'īl Maẓhar, "Māhiyat al-tārīkh," *Al-Muqtaṭaf,* June and July 1924, pp. 17–21, 172–175, respectively.

is the complete guide to the truth and to the detailed construction of historical reality.[31]

Ghurbāl contended that for the successful exercise of "scientific history," several conditions should be met: First, there should be public acknowledgment of the right of historians to study the documents. Second, documents should be stored in a proper and safe place. (Ghurbāl was especially concerned about the traditional enemies of Egyptian state documents: shredding, selling, fires, and mice.)[32] Third, they should be carefully classified, cataloged, and indexed.[33] Fourth, historical scholarship demanded a capable, reliable, and trustworthy historian who was trained to recover the "truth" from the archive *(yastakhrij al-ḥaqā'iq).*[34] Since the first two conditions were generally met after the 1952 Revolution, Ghurbāl focused on cultivating new historians who would be trained in the archives: "Ghurbāl oriented his students to take interest in collecting original source material, and his students were the first group of Egyptian research students to explore and 'dig out' the contents of the Egyptian archives. In doing so, they assisted in the organization, systematic arrangement, and facilitation of the archives for other scholars. Through these activities Ghurbāl and his students laid the foundations for the modern national history of Egypt."[35] A quote, written in the third person by another student, is indicative of both the task and the self-importance of Ghurbāl's disciples: "The documents of Egyptian history remained buried in the warehouses until Ghurbāl and his outstanding students used them, putting the history of Egypt on a scientific and sound base."[36]

Reiterating the myth of 'Ābdīn was a crucial aspect of university training. Emphasis on archival work brought the first generation of historians to recount their pleasurable experiences in the archive, as though it were the ultimate academic rite of passage. The metaphors of the "unveiling" *(kashf al-niqāb)* and "uncovering" *(kashf al-sitār)* of truth became prevalent in describing the historian's task in the archive.[37] The celebration of source material resulted in a unique academic genre in which students published articles focusing exclusively on "their sources" while, ironically, ignoring the main theses of their works

31. EHS, *Dhikra al-baṭal al-fātiḥ Ibrāhīm Bāshā*, preface, pp. ii–iii. See also a rare interview with Ghurbāl in which he speaks about his work with archival documents: 'Abd al-Ḥayy, *'Aṣīr ḥayātī*, p. 157.

32. 'Abd al-Karīm, *Tārīkh al-ta'līm fī 'aṣr Muḥammad Alī*, preface by Ghurbāl, pp. i–v.

33. In the early 1940s, Ghurbāl and other historians had lamented that their right to investigate sources was limited and that state records were in disarray.

34. Ibid.

35. 'Abd al-Karīm, "Kalimat ta'bīn," p. 13.

36. Abū al-Futūḥ, *Tārīkh maṭbā'at būlāq*, p. ix.

37. 'Abd al-Karīm, *Tārīkh al-ta'līm fī 'asr Muḥammad 'Alī*, preface, pp. i–ii.

altogether.[38] Years later, M.A. student ʿAbd al-ʿAzīz al-Shinnāwī complained that Ghurbāl's pedantic insistence on the quality of archival work was extreme to the degree that it took him ten years to graduate.[39]

While students worked in the archive, cooperation with the archivists seems to have been of great significance. The archivists guided the students through the labyrinth of documents to the much-desired historical truth (sometimes already waiting for them in the form of a translated document in nicely legible Arabic calligraphy). Some of the students who worked in the archives expressed their gratitude not only to the institution itself but also to a particular archivist who accompanied them during their work.[40] This intimate tutorial attention only strengthened the already firm bond between academic historians and royal historiography. Cooperation was so close that after graduation some of Ghurbāl's students took official positions as archivists in ʿĀbdīn.[41]

Academic historians, however, were not the only ones who were using the services of the archives, of course. What, then, distinguished Ghurbāl's disciples from other history writers? The answer to this question is rather complicated and will become clearer below. For the time being, however, it is enough to say that academic historians operated within certain professional conventions, which required a particular style and form of writing. To borrow from Anthony Grafton: "Historians perform two complementary tasks. They must examine all the sources relevant to the solution of a problem and construct a new narrative or argument from them. The footnote proves that both tasks have been carried out. . . . By doing so, moreover, it identifies the work of history in question as the creation of a professional."[42]

All of Ghurbāl's students had plenty of footnotes in their books and articles. The adoption of extensive footnoting, as a form of official prose, embodied the ideology of the emerging profession. This, in and of itself, apparently seemed

38. See *MTM* 1 (1948); and al-Ḥitta, "Marājiʿ tārīkh al-zirāʿa al-Miṣriyya," pp. 239–254. See also ʿAbd al-Karīm, "Tārīkh al-taʿlīm fī ʿaṣr Muḥammad ʿAlī," pp. 255–276; and Amīn Muṣṭafa ʿAbd Ilāh, "Tārīkh al-tijāra fī ʿaṣr Muḥammad ʿAlī," pp. 97–112.

39. Indeed, for his Ph.D., al-Shināwwī left Cairo University and went to the University of Alexandria, where he graduated in one year. Muḥammad Bahāʾ al-Dīn ʿUlwān, *ʿAbd al-ʿAzīz al-Shinnāwī muʾarīkhan* (al-Manṣūra: Dār sanābil, 1999), pp. 9–10.

40. ʿAlī Jiritlī thanked Maḥmūd Nafʿī in *Tārīkh al-ṣināʿa*, p. i. Aḥmad Aḥmad al-Ḥitta expressed general gratitude in *Tārīkh al-zirāʿa*, preface; ʿAbd al-Karīm, *Tārīkh al-taʿlīm fī ʿasr Muḥammad ʿAlī*, introduction, p. ii.

41. On the close cooperation among students, archivists, and translators, see Muḥammad Muḥammad Tawfīq, "Al-Ḥalqa al-mafqūda," *Al-Hilāl*, May–June 1941, pp. 585–594; and Bahāʾ al-Dīn ʿUlwān, *ʿAbd al-ʿAzīz al-Shinnāwī*, p. 12.

42. Anthony Grafton, *The Footnote: A Curious History* (Cambridge, MA: Harvard University Press, 1999), pp. 4–5.

enough to set them apart from other history writers, such as Prince ʿUmar Ṭusūn, whose sources remained obscure. Thus, the first signs of professionalization involved the adoption of methods and practices and the exclusion of competitors who used other methods of investigation.

With truth in history as the historian's ultimate, ideal goal and archival research as the only means of getting there, it was along these lines that the professional identity of historians began to take shape. This was their ideal of service. Perhaps the most authentic expression of historians' professional identity was a series of manuals on "how to write history."[43] As we shall see, these publications were not mere guidelines in dry academic language but vivid manifestos of the emerging academic school in history. The first to be concerned with modern historical methodology in the Arab world was the Lebanese historian Asad Rustum, who, in 1939, published his *Muṣṭalaḥ al- tārīkh* (loosely translated as "The Practice of History"). Trained at the University of Chicago, he became familiar with the subject of methodology and sought to apply and customize it to Arab historiography.[44] As we have already seen, Rustum closely collaborated with the royal project and, hence, was intimately familiar with the Egyptian historiographical scene. During his frequent visits to Cairo, he met not only with court officials and archivists but also with professors and students with whom he shared similar views on how to think, talk, and write about history.

For these reasons and because of the clarity of Rustum's writing, *Muṣṭalaḥ al-tārīkh* enjoyed great popularity among Egyptian scholars, who drew heavily on it and at points entirely plagiarized it in their new publications on methodology.[45] On a practical level, Rustum, who also believed in the accessibility and validity of historical truth, wrote a guidebook for "how to find it." Almost each of the book's chapters ended with a "lesson." Chapter 1 called for basing the work on original source material, since, as he wrote, this was the only way to find historical truth.[46] The second chapter encouraged historians to master foreign languages and auxiliary sciences, such as sociology, so that they could

43. Starting in the mid-1930s, there seems to have been a growing concern with questions relating to the process of history writing in academic circles, as well as in the popular journals. For the reflections of an Arab visiting professor from Budapest, see ʿAbd al-Karīm Jarmanush, "Kayfa yajibu an yuktab al-tārīkh wa man huwa al-mu'arīkh al-kāmil?" *Al-Hilāl,* March 1935, pp. 201–204. Some writers sought to compare the European mode of history writing with the Islamic one: "T'alīf al-tārīkh: Muqābalat al-ṭuruq al-ḥadītha bi al-qadīma," *Al-Hilāl,* April 1927, pp. 729–730.

44. Ilyās al-Qattār et al., eds., *Asad Rustum al-insān wa-l-mu'arīkh 1897–1965* (Beirut: al-Maktaba al-būlisiyya, 1984), pp. 19–26.

45. See a series of articles by Muḥammad Muṣṭafa Ziyāda, "Sinaʿat al-tārīkh fī Miṣr," *Al-Thaqāfa,* nos. 97, 100, 105, 111 (November 1940—February 1941).

46. Asad Rustum, *Muṣṭalaḥ al- tārīkh* (1939; Sidon, Lebanon: al-Maṭbaʿa al-ʿaṣriyya, 1955), pp. 1–3.

study the sources properly.[47] In opposition to Ghurbāl, Rustum argued in his third chapter that source material was often manipulated and sometimes even entirely forged. Hence, a close analysis of the documents and their context was necessary for revealing historical truth.[48] Other chapters suggested that it was not enough to "gather facts"; historians should also pay attention to questions of organization and writing style, having in mind their future readership.[49] Most of Rustum's examples were based on his working experience in 'Ābdīn, which further enhanced the book's popularity among Egyptian historians.

Writing a series of articles in *Al-Risāla* from August to December 1941, Ḥasan 'Uthmān, a former student of Ghurbāl and an influential history professor in his own right at the University of Alexandria, articulated the "ten commandments" for the historian.[50] Drawing heavily on Rustum and others, 'Uthmān repeated the conventional wisdom regarding the historian's task of uncovering historical truth.[51] Somehow contradictory, however, was a statement on the possibility of reaching absolute philosophical objectivity, wherein 'Uthmān admitted that, philosophically speaking, it is impossible to grasp historical truth in any categorical and objective fashion. Because of this difficulty, he continued, historians ought to present the results of their investigations as relatively truthful and reasonable *(natīja ma'qūla)*.[52] Although this statement was in opposition to the common understanding of historical truth, no debates on that issue appear to have taken place. In fact, even 'Uthmān himself ignored his statement and returned to the professional notion of historical truth, using it as a tool for the demarcation of the professional boundaries of academics and for the exclusion of popular historians and historical novelists, whose goal was not considered to be historical truth and thus, allegedly, could not tell reality from fiction. 'Uthmān writes,

> Not everyone who writes history is a historian. A historian must have the necessary qualities of those who are working in science. He needs to love and be devoted to his work regardless of all the possible difficulties of research. The rarity of sources should not discourage him. The obscurity and confusion of facts should not distract him. He should spend months and years and travel from country to country in pursuit of the truth. A historian should have a critical mind. He should not sub-

47. Ibid., pp. 5–9.

48. Ibid., pp. 10–28.

49. Ibid., pp. 124–126, 141.

50. Ḥasan 'Uthmān (1908–73) completed his master's degree in Middle Eastern history and continued his doctoral studies in Italy, where he specialized in Italian history. He was a prolific writer, who, among other things, translated Dante into Arabic. A member of the first generation of middle-class professional historians, he was committed to the development of historical methodology. Muḥammad Maḥmūd al-Sarūjī, "Khiṭāb ta'bīn," *MTM* 21 (1974): pp. 1–12.

51. Ḥasan 'Uthmān, "Kayfa yuktab al-tārīkh?" *Al-Risāla*, August 11 (1941): pp. 1000–1002.

52. Ibid.

scribe to any views or sources without first investigating them carefully. He should adopt only the just and the truthful and suggest nothing but that. He should be truthful, loyal, and courageous. He should not lie. Nor should he be a hypocrite. He should not hide facts that others do not know. . . . He should not be an exhibitionist in his desire for fame. He should have a strong personality . . . should be sensitive, empathic, tolerant, and have much imagination.[53]

ʿUthmān's text is designed to answer a crucial question: How do "we," as professional historians, write history? ʿUthmān conveys the sense that "our" way, that of the real historians, is the only way to find objective truth in history. Like other academic historians, ʿUthmān reconfirms the premise that methodologically controlled research makes objective knowledge possible.

Studying the way in which communities of scholars create a shared notion of objectivity, Allan Megill, a scholar of European historiography, has defined this process as the creation of "disciplinary objectivity." Megill writes, "Defined institutionally, disciplinary objectivity refers to the claim by practitioners of a particular discipline to have authoritative jurisdiction over its area of competence."[54] In other words, disciplinary objectivity serves as an important form of academic authority and a tool in asserting the academic monopoly over historical knowledge. Once this particular notion of objectivity was accepted by academic historians, they were confident that they were the only ones capable of writing worthy history. Consequently, academic historians were eager to persuade other writers of the validity of their professional authority and ready to impose it on them.

In 1943, four years after the publication of Rustum's *Muṣṭalaḥ al-tārīkh*, Ḥasan ʿUthmān published the first book on historical methodology in Egypt, titled *Manhaj al-baḥth al-tārīkhī*. *Manhaj* was the central keyword that governed ʿUthmān's work. Narrowly defined, *manhaj* simply means "methodology" and is still used in that sense today. However, it acquired an additional meaning that was incorporated into the jargon of professional historians, making it pivotal for the understanding of their scholarly community. Beginning in the late 1930s, the concept of *manhaj* came to represent academic historians' claim to professional authority. Or, put differently, *manhaj* was the vehicle through which professional historians presented their theoretical apparatus as scientific *(ʿilmī)*, that is, as empirical, objective, politically impartial, and disinterested knowledge.

The time in which history was regarded as mere description of events, for the purpose of remembering and for the glorification of key events in the life of individuals and nations, has passed. History is no longer regarded as part of culture in

53. Ibid., p. 1001.
54. Allan Megill, "Four Senses of Objectivity," *Annals of Scholarship* 8, nos. 3–4 (1991): p. 305.

> general, necessary for the training of individuals for political or military life. Nor is history regarded any longer as a branch of literature studied for the purpose of pleasure alone. Educated amateurs, on the one hand, and scholarly researchers, on the other, have up to now dealt with history, until scientists began to turn their attention toward the subject, at which point scientifically based historical research was established. . . . scientific circles collected and published historical sources, wrote in all fields of history, and studied historical methodology *(manhaj al-baḥth al-tārīkhī)*. This methodology is one of the most important bases for the progression of historical studies.[55]

At the same time in which *manhaj* incorporated the methodological assumptions of the community, it also adopted the ethical code and, especially, the superior self-image of the modern professional historian. Thus, the above quotes characterize the professional personality of the new historian as devoted, honest, careful, courageous, impartial, sensitive, empathic, and tolerant and as having a critical mind and much imagination.[56] Years later, when the first generation of professional historians began to pass away, the eulogies of their colleagues repeated and, thus, perpetuated the claim to these traits.[57]

By creating a professional ideology and forming a professional self-image, academic historians clearly distinguished themselves from "other" historians. Consider, for example, the words of Ḥasan 'Uthmān: "Many who write history do not understand history. They are not critical, and their writings are nothing but unorganized information. These books are not worthy of their titles or even of the paper on which they are printed."[58]

This patronizing and dismissive attitude justified the problematic tendency among academic historians not to read or even seriously take into consideration any work that did not originate in their circles. Ironically, this approach was in opposition to the *manhaj*'s declared aim of bringing into account all possible sources. Although constituting the lion's share of published historical literature, popular works were not reviewed in the academic's professional journal.

Interestingly enough, although academics left behind copious materials concerning their personnel, institutions, and ideology and, in fact, provided us with a rather coherent sense of their intellectual community, they did not tell us much

55. 'Uthmān hoped that Fu'ād University and the University of Alexandria would assign the book to history students. Ḥasan 'Uthmān, *Manhaj al-baḥth al-tārīkhī*, 2nd ed. (1943; Cairo: Dār al-ma'ārif bi Miṣr, 1965), preface (unrevised from 1st ed.), pp. 9–10.

56. 'Uthmān, "Kayfa yuktab al-tārīkh?" pp. 1000–1002.

57. Sa'īd 'Abd al-Fattāḥ 'Āshūr, "Uatādh al-tārīkh fī dhimat al-tārīkh: al-Duktur Muḥammad Muṣṭafa Ziyāda," *Al-Majalla* (January 1969): pp. 31–37. Muḥammad Muṣṭafa Ziyāda, "Wafā' wa rathā'," *MTM* 9–10 (1960–62): pp. i–ii. See also a special issue in memory of Ghurbāl: Muḥammad Rif'at, "Kalimat ta'bīn," *MTM* 11 (1963): pp. 7–9. Abū Ḥadīd, "Kalimat ta'bīn," pp. 36–45.

58. Ḥasan 'Uthmān, "Kayfa yuktab al- tārīkh?" *Al-Risāla*, September 1, 1941, p. 1002.

about the excluded "amateurs." Even from academics' own perspective, questions such as who the amateur historians were, what they wrote, and how, if at all, they were organized, remain unanswered. The silence of the academic circles and their deliberate politics of exclusion are manifestations of this group quest for monopoly in the field of history writing. Academic historians perceived themselves as superior to popular writers and sought to standardize historical investigation and supervise the process of training and certifying young historians, thus controlling the final quality of the work. Put in that context, the ideal of historical objectivity was instrumental in strengthening and enforcing the norm of scholarly rectitude. Once Ghurbāl's disciples were reasonably organized, anarchic criteria for writing were no longer acceptable.

'Ā'isha 'Abd al-Raḥmān (known also by her pen name "Bint al-shāṭī'"), a student and a future influential scholar in her own right, remembered that her history professors, Ghurbāl and Muṣṭafa Ziyāda, insisted that history writing requires specialization. Specialization, she recalled, clearly leads to a monopoly in history writing *(iḥtikār)*, and this monopoly is a necessary practice to ensure the quality of historical writing. Writing in 1961, she echoed the views of her professors, arguing, "The gate of writing in the sciences is locked and will open only to those who specialize."[59] By the early 1940s, Ghurbāl and his disciples had vouchsafed for themselves the task of gatekeepers, ensuring that no despised amateur historian would ever inadvertently slip in.

GHURBĀL'S SCHOOL IN CONTEXT

Thus far, the discussion has focused exclusively on a rather small group of students and professors whom I deem pivotal for the development of historical writing in general and for that of modern Egypt in particular. We have seen how this group developed its distinctive professional identity and practiced it through painstaking archival work, centered almost entirely on nineteenth-century Egypt. However, important as the study of this elite may be, when put in a quantitative context, it is far from representative of the overall trends in Egyptian academia. The following discussion is dedicated to some of the other features of academic historiography.

A survey of Ph.D. dissertations and M.A. theses written during the years 1925–54 reveals three important characteristics of academic historiography in this period:[60] (a) a distinctly Egypto-centric, inward-looking self-absorption, (b) an emphasis on the study of the Islamic and medieval periods, and (c) an abstention from writing on contemporary issues. Table 5 presents the few dissertations and

59. 'Ā'isha 'Abd al-Raḥmān, "Al-Takhaṣṣuṣ wa-l-iḥtikār," *Al-Ahrām*, October 27, 1961, p. 12.

60. The survey begins in 1925, when Fu'ād University was inaugurated, and ends in 1954, when revolutionary institutions eventually managed to gain control over much of the academy.

TABLE 5. Geographical Focus of Ph.D. Dissertations and M.A. Theses on Modern History, 1925–1954

Degree	Institution	Works on Egypt	Other
M.A.	Fu'ād/Cairo	14	1
M.A.	Alexandria	0	1
Ph.D.	Fu'ād/Cairo	5	0
Ph.D.	Alexandria	1	0

SOURCES: Qāsim Hishmat, *Dalīl al-rasā'il al-jāmi'iyya; MTM* 13 (1967); and *MTM* 16 (1969).

NOTE: 'Ayn Shams University was not yet productive in the period under discussion.

theses written on the modern period and shows that most of the works on the modern era focused exclusively on Egypt alone. Out of twenty-two M.A. theses and Ph.D. dissertations combined, only two studied areas outside Egypt.

Although following the rise of Pan-Arabism more attention was paid to other countries, the overall emphasis nonetheless remained on Egypt. In hindsight, we can plausibly speculate that this focus on Egypt was the endowment of a distinctive Egyptian nationalism. Thus, even at times in which supra-Egyptian orientations gained currency, scholarship's focus on the history of the modern era remained on Egypt.[61] Once more, the historiographical output illustrates the scale of the de-Ottomanization and the close affinity between the modern notion of history and the nation.

Table 6 demonstrates that most of the academic output was directed toward Islamic and medieval history. During the period under discussion, forty-three M.A. theses in Islamic-medieval history versus fifteen in modern history were submitted to Fu'ād University. Accordingly, Ph.D. students submitted seventeen dissertations in Islamic-medieval history versus five alone in the modern field (all of which were supervised by Ghurbāl). In the University of Alexandria, the ratio was four Ph.D. dissertations in the Islamic-medieval field to one in the modern. Only one work focused on contemporary history.[62]

61. Emmanuel Sivan found a connection between the increase in works on other regions and supra-Egyptian orientations. Notwithstanding these changes, the focus of history writers remained Egypt. Emmanuel Sivan, "Megamot Bahistoriographia Hamitsrit-Indikatorim Kamutiyim" (Trends in Egyptian Historiography—Quantities Indicators), *Ha-Mizraḥ Ha-ḥadash* 91, no. 3 (1973): pp. 296–298.

62. I believe it was only during the 1950s that a separate category was employed in order to distinguish "modern history" *(tārīkh ḥadīth)* from "contemporary history" *(tārīkh mu'āṣir)*. Until then, 1882 remained a watershed year, beyond which historians knew they were entering a zone dominated by politics.

TABLE 6. Temporal Focus of Ph.D. Dissertations and M.A. Theses, 1925–1954

Degree	Institution	Islamic and Medieval History (sixth–eighteenth century)	Modern History (nineteenth century)	Contemporary History (post-1882)
M.A.	Fu'ād/Cairo	43	15	0
M.A.	Alexandria	2	0	1
Ph.D.	Fu'ād/Cairo	17	5	0
Ph.D.	Alexandria	4	1	0

SOURCES: Qāsim Hishmat, *Dalīl al-rasā'il al-jāmi'iyya; MTM* 13 (1967); and *MTM* 16 (1969).
NOTE: 'Ayn Shams University was not yet productive in the period under discussion.

By and large, professional academic historians and their students refrained from engaging in research and teaching on modern Egypt. Studying contemporary Egypt, then, was hardly an option. Given the absence of any official restricting guidelines for history writing in monarchic Egypt or even in the early 1950s, the voluntary inaction of historians regarding contemporary Egypt is indeed very curious. In part it may be explained by the measures of censorship that were applied to the press. However, it seems that professors themselves imposed and enforced limitations on writing that focused on this period. Ḥaṣan 'Uthmān, for example, refused to supervise any graduate work dealing with contemporary history and strongly objected to his students' attempts to study the period.[63] The only professors who focused on contemporary issues were Muḥammad Muṣṭafa Ṣafwat and Muḥammad Fu'ād Shukrī, but even Ṣafwat preferred to tie his research to benign questions of foreign relations rather than to the risky terrain of domestic politics.[64] Shukrī, on the other hand, was more daring and thus ended up having bitter disagreements with Ghurbāl over questions of objectivity. Consequently he was academically isolated.[65] Whatever Egyptian historians were writing, they always had to reckon, gradually, albeit steadily, with these self-imposed limitations on contemporary history.

63. 'Abd al-'Aẓīm Ramaḍān, "Madāris kitābat tārīkh Miṣr al-mu'āṣir," in Aḥmad 'Abdallāh, ed., *Tārīkh Miṣr bayna al-manhaj al-'ilmī wa-l-ṣirā' al-ḥizbī* (Cairo: Dār shuhdī li-l-nashr, 1988), p. 61.

64. Muḥammad Muṣṭafa Ṣafwat, "Mawqif Almānyā izā' al-mas'ala al-Miṣriyya, 1876–1914," *MTM* 1, nos. 1–2 (May–October 1948): pp. 87–153; Muḥammad Muṣṭafa Ṣafwat, "Baḥth fī-l-jalā' al-Inglīzī 'an Miṣr wa ba'that Sir Henry D. Wolf," *MTM* 2, no. 1 (May 1949): pp. 77–114.

65. Muḥammad Fu'ād Shukrī was born in Ḥilwān in 1904. In 1931 he was sent to Liverpool on behalf of the government. He studied the history of modern and contemporary Sudan. In 1936 Ghurbāl hired him as part of the *tamṣīr* project. He died in 1963. al-Jumay'ī, *Itijāhāt al-kitāba*, pp. 179–187.

Only Ghurbāl was able to act in exception to this rule. In his 1952 *Tārīkh al-mufāwaḍāt,* he tried to depoliticize the most sensitive national issue of the time: Anglo-Egyptian negotiations. The book was in print when the 1952 Revolution broke out, and some people suggested he modify some of his statements. Ghurbāl daringly refused.[66] His task, as he himself understood it, was to provide the public with an account that would not play into the hands of any of the parties and would serve as a tool for self-improvement: "I wish to inform the reader that I originally wrote this book for myself as an attempt to organize my reflections [on current affairs] and establish my judgment [of it] on sound understanding. I did not write it for the sake of what is commonly referred to as politics. I do not take part in that kind of writing. My writing is that of an Egyptian citizen who aspires to be a better one, capable of evaluation and discrimination."[67]

Originally, however, the book was designed in part as a response to al-Rāfiʿī and was supposed to show the way to a new type of politically impartial writing. The events of the 1952 Revolution sealed Ghurbāl's attempts in that direction, for the second volume of this project was never published. Instead, popular writing emerged triumphant.

Curiously, Ghurbāl sometimes violated his own objection to the writing of politically biased accounts aiming to support a narrow party line. In June 1948, in the wake of Egypt's participation in the war in Palestine, Ghurbāl's patriotism harnessed his historical perspective to the cause. The result, as noted by Choueiri, was a text that tracked the long historical commitment of Egypt to the land of Palestine from the dawn of history to the time of King Fārūq. Ghurbāl put special emphasis on military leadership, beginning with Ṣalāḥ al-Dīn and spanning the centuries to Muḥammad ʿAlī, Ibrāhīm, and Fārūq. In contrast with his own agenda, he offered an analogy between Fārūq's struggle and the heroism of the second caliph ʿUmar b. al-Khaṭāb, whose honorific title was al-Fārūq (he who distinguished truth from falsehood).[68] Ghurbāl, whose entire academic project aimed at undermining populist writing built around simplistic historical analogies, should, perhaps, have known better how to distinguish "truth from falsehood."

With the intensification of the struggle against the British in the early 1950s, political impartiality became difficult to sustain. Nevertheless, academic historians sweepingly abstained from writing on contemporary history, beginning to

66. "Ta'bīn Shafīq Ghurbāl," *Al-Majalla,* December 1961, p. 135.

67. Ghurbāl, *Tārīkh al-mufāwadāt al-miṣriyya al-briṭāniyya* (Cairo: Maktabat al-nahḍa al-miṣriyya, 1952), pp. i–ii.

68. Ghurbāl, "Ḥurūb Miṣr fī Filasṭīn," *Al-Kitāb,* June 1948, pp. 189–194; Choueiri, *Arab History and the Nation-State,* pp. 69–70.

challenge this dogma only toward the late 1950s and, in a more organized fashion, in the wake of the 1961–62 socialist turn.[69]

Explanations for this state of affairs vary. Muḥammad Anīs, a member of the second generation of university historians and the one responsible for introducing socialist historiography to academia, argued that the constant oppressive measures taken by the monarchy and its attempt to monopolize writing hampered historians from focusing on modern history.[70] His student ʿAbd al-ʿAẓīm Ramaḍān contended that before the 1952 Revolution the common assumption was that "historical perspective" takes fifty years to achieve; only then could a sound and objective study be executed. ʿĀṣim Disūqī spoke of "pressures," censorship, and the difficulties of obtaining sources.[71]

It seems, then, that a combination of all of the above "encouraged" historians to study a past as remote and politically irrelevant as possible. The unwritten professional code that stressed political impartiality was certainly an important factor in validating this prohibition. More important, however, were the archival policies restricting access to official documents that might shed light on recent events. The lack of an organized and well-administered state archive discouraged contemporary scholarship as well. Consequently, nonacademic writers filled this empty space. Cognizant of this situation, academic historians moved to establish a professional association.

The Foundation of the Royal Historical Society

Loyal to the ideal of the university as separate from politics and committed to the segregation of politics from "science," scholars such as Ghurbāl found their ideals unrealizable at Fu'ād University. As skillfully demonstrated by Donald Reid, the university was dominated by a mélange of domestic and colonial politics. French and British functionaries struggled over influence in the curriculum and management. Furthermore, the royal palace played favorites with a core of politically affiliated professors. By the mid-1940s, academia had become another possible route to a cabinet seat. Parliamentary politics and academic life were almost synonymous. Agitated, politicized students who supported politically committed professors completed this picture.[72] Against this background, historians decided to reorganize their scholarly community.

The call for the establishment of a professional association went hand in hand

69. Another shift occurred after the 1967 war, when the institution of new independent research centers, modeled on the American "think tank," necessitated an independent perspective.

70. Anīs, "Shafīq Ghurbāl wa madrasat al-tārīkh," p. 13.

71. ʿĀṣim Disūqī, *Miṣr al-muʿāṣira fī dirāsāt al-muʾārikhīn al-miṣriyyīn* (Cairo: Dār al-ḥuriyya, 1977), pp. 18–19.

72. Reid, *Cairo University and the Making of Modern Egypt*, pp. 71–156.

with the development of the *manhaj*. In 1940, Muṣṭafa Ziyāda first called for its establishment, and Ḥasan ʻUthmān joined the call a year later. In 1945, it was officially founded by Ghurbāl. Ziyāda deemed the association crucial, because, as a medievalist, he felt a certain shortage of historical source material, especially for the Ottoman period. He maintained that only an association such as the RGS could carry out an extensive survey of relevant sources throughout the world and bring them to Egypt.[73] ʻUthmān's vision was apparently more comprehensive and, in essence, similar to that of Ghurbāl, who held that a professional association was crucial in order to organize and develop the work and ensure its high quality and the integrity of the historical profession.[74]

Though, sociologically speaking, conditions were favorable for the association's establishment, it was not an easy matter, as it had to reckon with a host of political variables. The politics behind the scenes form an interesting, though not unusual, corollary to the scandalous politics of the 1940s. I was able to reconstruct only segments of it.

The February 1942 incident in which the British imposed a Wafd government headed by Muṣṭafa al-Naḥḥās, with the king's consent and in opposition to public opinion, was a watershed in the public status of the monarchy. With the public image of the royal house at its lowest level in years, the long-neglected efforts of Fu'ād to strengthen the image of the monarchy through cultural enterprises had become clear even to the inexperienced king Fārūq. The agenda of the monarchy had changed little over the years, and the same was true of its unwavering support for the creation of a glorifying nationalist historiography. Since academics wanted a professional association, they desperately needed political and financial patronage. Hence, the ground was ready for tighter cooperation with the monarchy, a cooperation that would go beyond the realm of the archive.

In 1940, after two years as dean of the Faculty of Arts and much university politics, Ghurbāl was nominated as undersecretary of state in the Ministry of Education, working with his close friend Muḥammad Rifʻat. Though not a party member, Ghurbāl was associated with the pro-monarchic Saʻdist and the Liberal Constitutionalist parties, and his strong convictions regarding education were in line with the elitist orientation of these parties.[75] Under the sway of his cultural experience in London as well as the intellectual influence of Toynbee, who viewed

73. Muḥammad Muṣṭafa Ziyāda, "Ṣināʻat al-tārīkh fī Miṣr," *Al-Thaqāfa* 5 (November 1940): pp. 16–17.

74. ʻUthmān, "Kayfa yuktab al- tārīkh?" pp. 1088–1089.

75. The Saʻdists were headed by Aḥmad Māhir, Maḥmūd Fahmī al-Nuqrāshī, and others. They had a close relationship with King Fārūq and abhorred Mūṣṭafa al-Naḥḥās (the Wafd). Choueiri, *Arab History and the Nation-State*, p. 67.

the entire historical trajectory of "civilization" as the outcome of the skills of the elite, Ghurbāl became a staunch supporter of elitism as a cultural and political mission. Thus, as a top official in the Ministry of Education, he favored a policy that aimed at cultivating a small and capable elite, just as he had done while in the history department at Fu'ād University. This policy was in opposition to the Wafd's position, which advocated the universal availability of education, even at the expense of quality. Ghurbāl's firm resistance to universal education resulted in his automatic removal from the Ministry of Education each time the Wafd came to power (during 1942–45 and 1950–52).[76] Exacerbating Ghurbāl's rocky experience in government service were his thorny personal relationships with some prominent politicians from the Wafd. For instance, in 1942, when Prime Minister Muṣṭafa al-Naḥḥās was searching for a new residence in Cairo, his extensive search yielded a schoolhouse, which he asked to be evacuated for his convenience. Ghurbāl objected. Al-Naḥḥās insisted, won, and sent Ghurbāl back to academia.[77]

This particular episode might have been what pushed Ghurbāl to seek a tighter cooperation with the court. In any event, Ghurbāl sensed that the time was ripe for him to write a popular history book on a subject that was the focal point of royal historiography: the history of Muḥammad 'Alī. In 1944, Ghurbāl published *Muḥammad 'Alī al-Kabīr,* in which, inter alia, he intentionally popularized the insights of his students, proving that academic knowledge could also be popular.[78] The book was published in the abridged popular series A'lām al-Islām. Influenced by the Islamic reorientation of Egyptian culture since the 1930s, the publisher popularized Muslim figures of great importance, such as Muḥammad 'Abduh, the philosopher al-Farābī, and the poet Abū Nuwwās.

Ghurbāl had consistently refused to translate *Beginnings of the Egyptian Question* into Arabic, primarily because Muḥammad 'Alī was presented there as a mere Albanian foreigner who had laid violent hands on property.[79] Thus, publishing a popular book rendering Muḥammad 'Alī a more central position in the historical foundation of modern Egypt seemed not such a bad idea. Fārūq was delighted, and on the publication of the first edition, he held an official reception in honor of Ghurbāl.[80] The title "bey" was part of this parcel. Commenting on

76. Each time following his removal, Ghurbāl returned to his previous position, until his retirement in January 1954. Yūsuf Niqūlā, *A'lām min al-Iskandariyya* (Alexandria: Mu'asasat al-ma'ārif, 1969), pp. 296–297.

77. Aḥmad 'Abd al-Raḥīm Muṣṭafa in a preface to Ghurbāl's *Muḥammad 'Alī al-kabīr,* 2nd ed. (Cairo: al-hilāl, 1987), pp. 10–11.

78. Some of Ghurbāl's former students did the same. Muḥammad Muḥammad Tawfīq, "Dīwān al-muḥāsaba fī 'ahd Muḥammad 'Alī Bāshā al-kabīr," *Al-Hilāl,* March–April 1943, pp. 261–264.

79. Ghorbal, *The Beginnings of the Egyptian Question,* p. 281.

80. Ibid., p. 12.

this episode, Choueiri writes, "His [Ghurbāl's] passionate and highly subjective defense of his hero [Muḥammad ʿAlī] leaves us no doubt about his political and ideological loyalties."[81]

Consequently, Ghurbāl's personal rapprochement with the palace resulted in the establishment of the Royal Historical Society (al-Jamʿiyya al-malakiyya li-l-dirāsāt al-tārīkhiyya), the first historical association in the Arab world, which renamed the Egyptian Historical Society in 1952. Although far less skilled than his father in supervising cultural maneuvers and with a dubious level of commitment to such projects, Fārūq, nevertheless, was clearly motivated to establish a pro-monarchic cultural branch. As a measure of vigilance, Fārūq nominated Muḥammad Ṭāhir as president, a close friend who had more experience in nightclubbing than in professional writing. The board of directors was in the king's hands as well. As for the professional side, in his capacity as the de facto director and the editor-in-chief of its journal, Ghurbāl had enough room to promote his agenda.

Notwithstanding the patronage of the palace, the formative years were quite difficult. Those who expected lavish financial support, similar to that granted by Fu'ād to the RGS, were extremely disappointed.[82] The resources of the EHS were always very limited. In fact, it did not even have a permanent office, to say nothing of a monumental building in the heart of Cairo, as the Royal Geographical Society had had.[83] For years, the acting members met in Ghurbāl's temporary office in the Ministry of Education. Wherever Ghurbāl was working, the offices of the EHS moved with him.

However, as modest as the royal support was, its patronage paid off. In 1946, Ghurbāl and his disciples learned of the establishment of the Association for Arab Historical Studies under the presidency of the eminent Muḥammad Ḥusayn Haykal. Not much is known about this episode, but it is obvious that the young EHS felt threatened and tried to avoid competition. With royal support, the EHS was eventually able to incorporate the new association in 1948. Muḥammad Ḥusayn Haykal and Gaston Wiet joined the EHS board of directors, but if they

81. Choueiri argues that the Islamic orientation of Ghurbāl's account was influenced by Fārūq's idea of declaring himself as a caliph of all Muslims. Choueiri, *Arab History and the Nation-State*, pp. 102–103.

82. Ghurbāl himself was a member of the RGS board of directors and was well aware of the large sums of money channeled to historical writing during the 1930s.

83. Such a building was established in 2001 when the *EHS* resurrected itself after years of forced marginalization on the part of the authorities. Ibrāhīm ʿAbd al-Munʿim al-Jumayʿī, *Al-Jamʿiyya al-miṣriyya li-l-dirāsāt al-tārīkhiyya wa dirāsa tārīkhiyya li-l-muʾassasa ʿilmiyya 1945–1985* (Cairo: al-Jamʿiyya al-tārīkhiyya al-miṣriyya, 1995), pp. 22–24.

had any influence in the EHS, it appears to have been invisible.[84] Ghurbāl and his circles were successful in defending their professional agenda.[85]

The price the EHS had to pay for this sort of protection was clear. The monarchy used the EHS to reintroduce into the nation's festive calendar the celebration of its founding fathers, who were gradually being marginalized by nationalist commemorative events. Thus, both the centennial commemoration of the deaths of Ibrāhīm (1848–1948) and Muḥammad Alī (1849–1949) were celebrated by the EHS in grand style. Many of Egypt's political, intellectual, and cultural elites, as well as some foreign delegates, attended the ceremonial commemoration of Muḥammad ʿAlī. An attempt was made to contact Americans who had served in the Egyptian army during 1870–82 in order to interview them.[86] In special publications of the EHS dedicated to these events, Egypt's best historians reconfirmed the relevancy and primacy of the monarchic history to current times. Their celebratory writing, comparing, for instance, Muḥammad ʿAlī to George Washington, was politically transparent.[87]

No doubt, under the leadership of Ghurbāl, the EHS was successful in propagating its creed, but it still never managed to popularize it. Ghurbāl was famous for seeing that the academic output of his students was published either as books or as articles. He harnessed the resources of the EHS for that purpose. His level of commitment was unrivaled. No other Egyptian historian before or after him invested so much energy in cultivating a young generation.[88] Despite the limited autonomy of the EHS, under Ghurbāl's leadership it had enough power to consolidate and promote its professional hegemony in the academic world. A close analysis of the EHS's organ, *Al-Majalla al-tārīkhiyya al-miṣriyya* (cited hereafter as *MTM*), illustrates the scope of the society's efforts.

Initially appearing in May 1948, the journal was the first academic publication to focus entirely on history. Until then, perhaps once in a while, academic

84. Ibid., pp. 25–30.

85. Another historiographical initiative was the establishment of an independent historical journal titled *Cahiers d'Histoire Égyptienne* in 1948. The founder was Jacques Tagher, an archivist and chief curator at the royal library. His journal focused on the same issues as the *MTM* but was published in French and did not seem to have posed a professional threat. Tagher did not seek any political patronage. Gaston Wiet, "Jacques Tagher," *Cahiers d'Histoire Égyptienne* 4, no. 3–4 (October 1952): pp. 163–165. See also *Cahiers d'Histoire Égyptienne* 3, no. 3 (March 1951): pp. 221–281.

86. al-Jumayʿī, *Al-Jamʿiyya al-miṣriyya*, p. 175.

87. Ghurbāl tackled the question of Muḥammad ʿAlī, Ibrāhīm, and Arab unity. EHS, *Dhikra al-baṭal al-fātiḥ Ibrāhīm Bāshā 1848–1948*, introduction; EHS, *Al-Dhikra al-miʾawiyya li-wafāt al-maghfūr lahu Muḥammad ʿAlī al-kabīr 1849–1949* (Cairo: Dār al-maʿārif bi Miṣr, 1949), pp. 1–37; Zakī, *Al-Tārīkh al-ḥarbī li-ʿaṣr Muḥammad ʿAlī.*

88. Disūqī, *Miṣr al-muʿāṣira*, p. 2.

historians had been able to "insert" an article into the journal of the Faculty of Humanities.[89] As chief editor, Ghurbāl insisted on a politics-free journal to a degree of absurdity. The 1948 war, the great 1952 fire in Cairo, and even the 1952 Revolution were never referred to by the journal. The avoidance of current political events was coupled with the continual neglect of contemporary history.

A major academic concern, at least for those who were educated abroad, was to promote Western intellectual infrastructure in order to nourish the work of young historians and colleagues. The archival work as the major source of academic inspiration resulted in the production of inductive, and even empiricist, scholarship, which became one of the dominant and continuing features of Egyptian historiography. "Common sense" seems to have been the favored tool for analysis. Cognizant of this reality while paradoxically functioning as its major perpetuator, Ghurbāl facilitated the translation of several texts in the philosophy of history, hoping it would trigger a deeper philosophical understanding of history. Thus, classic texts by Kant and Descartes, and also more contemporary works by Toynbee and Robin George Collingwood, were made available.[90] However, Collingwood's text *The Idea of History* argued that historical analysis depends solely on the historian's own imagination and his or her capacity to reenact the past in his or her mind.[91] Typically British, such an attitude only strengthened the already prevailing deductive mood of Egyptian historians.

It is therefore fair to say that the academic atmosphere was hostile to any form of historical abstractions. For instance, when a former student, ʿAlī Jiritlī, returned from London University with a Ph.D. thesis that, among other things, offered a leftist critique of the Egyptian "ruling classes," Ghurbāl reacted emotionally: "Every Egyptian belongs to the ruling classes. All Egyptians rule and are being ruled. Those who argue otherwise deny reality and evade responsibility."[92] Ghurbāl's instinctive reaction betrays his analytic limitations, which excluded class analysis as a worthy tool of historical interpretation. Perhaps, after all, it is

89. See, for instance, Muḥammad Shafīq Ghurbāl, "Amīr Sūrī fī Italiya fī-l-qarn al-sābiʿ ʿasahr," *Majallat Kulliyat al-Ādāb* 2, no. 1 (May 1934): pp. 75–110; Muḥammad Shafīq Ghurbāl, "Miṣr ʿinda muftaraq al-ṭuruq 1798–1801," *Majallat Kulliyat al-Ādāb* 4, no. 1 (May 1936): pp. 1–70; and Muḥammad Fu'ād Shukrī, "Baʿtha ʿaskariya būlūniya fī Miṣr fī ʿahd Muḥammad ʿAlī," *Majallat Kulliyat al-Ādāb* 7, no. 1 (May 1946): pp. 27–48.

90. *MTM* 1, no. 1–2 (May–October 1948): pp. 155–179; *MTM* 2, no. 2 (October 1949): pp. 135–153, 171–172; *MTM* 5 (May–October 1956): pp. 157–166. The *MTM* was always committed to the publications of new sources. *MTM* 1 (May 1949): p. 139; *MTM* 3, no. 2 (October 1950): pp. 75–157.

91. This understanding of the historian's task characterized British historiography in general. Doris Goldstein, "The Professionalization of History in Britain in Late Nineteenth and Early Twentieth Centuries," *Storia della Storiografia* 3 (1983): pp. 3–27.

92. See Ghurbāl's review of Jiritlī's *The Structure of Modern Industry in Egypt: MTM* 2, no. 1 (May 1949): p. 231.

not so surprising that after 1945, the most challenging analysis of Egyptian history was offered by Egyptian Marxists independent of academia.

Standardizing historical investigation was one of the *MTM*'s main concerns. Particularly revealing in that sense is the "book review" section, which apart from its informative nature provided criteria for answering the question: What is a good academic work? Emphasis on source material, the demand for objectivity, and political neutrality seem to draw much of the reviewers' attention.[93] Another function of the journal was to serve as "meeting place" for the community. Announcements on coming conferences and new publications as well as eulogies were fairly common.[94] It was a vital, intimate, and homogeneous community of several dozen scholars. Some Syrian and Iraqi scholars joined it as well.[95]

Since the establishment of the *MTM* heralded the building of a professional community with an urgent mission to accomplish, that mission required a broad professional consensus. Thus, if any major debates or differences of opinion occurred over questions of methodology and subject matter, they were pushed aside. The association's journal was the place where the *manhaj* was fully exercised and celebrated, and the exclusion of those who did not follow it, even if they were already dead, characterized the community and its journal. Hence, al-Rāfiʿī was ignored even at his death.[96]

Like any other form of organization, the establishment of the EHS increased the bargaining power of historians vis-à-vis the state, or at least historians felt that this was the case. Although fairly happy with the free hand granted them in the ʿĀbdīn archive, the society's historians were far from content with the patronage of the state in regard to source material.[97] Concerned with the authority of the state over the nation's documents, historians sought to remodel this relationship. Thus, in 1947 Ghurbāl proposed that the state amend its rules with regard to certain documents so that they would be guarded rather than simply destroyed. Ghurbāl's central argument was that documents are not the property of the state alone but also the property of "history" and historians.[98] The issues of availability and regulation of accessibility were also raised. No apparent change occurred until after the 1952 Revolution, when in 1954 a new archival law was issued. But,

93. *MTM* 3, no. 2 (October 1950): pp. 193–202; *MTM* 1, no. 1–2 (May–October 1948): pp. 323–329. See also the above-mentioned review of Jiritlī's work.

94. *MTM* 1, no. 1–2 (May–October, 1948): pp. 357–425.

95. al-Jumayʿī, *Al-Jamʿiyya al-miṣriyya*, pp. 135–136.

96. al-Jumayʿī, however, reports that in the formative years of the EHS, one failed attempt for cooperation with al-Rāfiʿī took place. Ibid., p. 100.

97. The scholarly limitations of the royal archive were quite apparent by this time. Muḥammad Muṣṭafa Ziyāda, "Ṣināʿat al-tārīkh fī Miṣr," *Al-Thaqāfa* 31 (December 1940): p. 91; ʿUthmān, "Kayfa yuktab al- tārīkh?" pp. 1088–1089.

98. al-Jumayʿī, *Al-Jamʿiyya al-miṣriyya*, pp. 14–15.

as we shall see in the last two chapters, even progressive legislation fell short of satisfying the historians.

PROFESSIONALISM AND PREMODERN HISTORICAL THOUGHT

During the 1930s, professionalism was forged as a secularist ideology that celebrated and institutionalized objectivism as an organic part of modern historical narration. Helped by that narration's status as a product of a due scientific process, historians argued that their histories were not only "true" but also "real." Borrowed straight from the logic of the 'Ābdīn project, this powerful claim was a crucial element in the fortification of professional historians' authority vis-à-vis that of other historians and other modes of historical comprehension. Viewed in a wider context, the institution of this professional mode usually entailed a certain antipathy toward irrationality and superstition. This fundamental position characterized all modern professions. The Egyptian doctor would not prescribe a coffee bean solution for an infected eye any more than the irrigation engineer would develop an elaborate system of mules and buckets rather than pumps and channels. By and large, modern medicine, engineering, and a host of other professions treated premodern forms of organization with contempt. Egyptian historians could not escape the manifestations of their scientific professionalism. Once, they even asked their students to name another modern profession that resembles history writing. (One innovative student chose tin smithing.)[99] In this scheme of things, the unavoidable question is, What was the position of academic historians in regard to the premodern Islamic historiographical tradition?

With one famous exception, modern historical thinking rendered the premodern historiographical heritage obsolete in terms of its capacity to serve as a useful cognitive tool. The exception was the work of Ibn Khaldūn, whose cyclical notion of history was motivated by group spirit *('aṣabīya).* Taking into account an enormous number of variables, such as geography, climate, religion, politics, culture, and economics, he suggested a theory of historical change that identified a cyclical process of the rise, stagnation, and fall of ruling groups and the power structures they create.[100] Engaging with the elementary structures of historiography, Ibn Khaldūn contributed a groundbreaking conceptual framework that was equal in its importance to the Islamic contribution in the fields of algebra and astronomy. In the time that had passed since the fourteenth century, Ibn Khaldūn's philosophy of history was not lost. Yet, given the challenges of modern

99. "Sina'at al-tārīkh fī Miṣr," *Al-Thaqāfa* 97 (November 1940): p. 1867.

100. Mehradad Kia, "Ibn Kahldūn," in D.R. Woolf, ed., *A Global Encyclopedia of Historical Writing* (New York: Garland Publishing, 1998), vol. 1, pp. 440–441.

Arab historiography, the modern era was the right time to "rediscover" it.[101] Born in Tunis in A.D. 1331 but living and operating also in Cairo, his contribution to universal knowledge could be seen as an essentially Egyptian effort.

Compared with cyclical perceptions of history, a linear understanding of the past was more compatible with the idea of progress and thus more popular in the modern era. Nonetheless, a cyclical explanation of historical change was still a valid and rather influential intellectual choice. Thus, in the first half of the twentieth century, the conceptual contribution of Ibn Khaldūn was visible in the works of two central European thinkers of history: Oswald Spengler (1880–1936) and Arnold Toynbee. Spengler's apocalyptic study *The Decline of the West* (1918–22) argued that civilizations go through a life cycle. Influenced by the horrific experience of World War I, he reached the conclusion that the West had begun its decline. In no time, Spengler's end-of-progress perspective haunted European thought. Toynbee's monumental work *A Study of History* (1948–61) was a much broader and scholarly study based on similar philosophical grounds. Toynbee's basic unit of analysis was "civilization," a mélange of religious, political, and geographical traits. According to Toynbee, the emergence of a certain civilization occurred through a mechanism of "challenge and response," in which a creative minority provided adequate solutions to emerging challenges. In a robust civilization, the interaction between the innovative minority and the mimetic masses would result in progress. Thus, challenge-response-mimesis was the basic process that defined the success or failure of every civilization.[102] Given the cultural status of this historiographical mode, Ibn Khaldūn's ideas acquired an unexpected relevancy. As such, they were seen as an assuring sign that modern Egyptian historiography was based on solid and especially organic theoretical tradition.[103] Ghurbāl's radio lecture on Ibn Khaldūn was envisioned in this context, and so was his public lecture on Arab historians.[104]

Besides this claim for organic historiographical continuity, Egyptian and Arab scholars made an interesting argument regarding the scientific methodological value inherent in the Islamic tradition of source analysis. Thus, with relation to the study of *ḥadīth,* they contended that, just as in the modern historiographi-

101. Rustum, *Muṣṭalaḥ al-tārīkh,* introduction.

102. John Galtung, "Arnold Toynbee: Challenge and Response," in John Galtung and Sohail Inayatullah, eds., *Macrohistory and Macrohistorians: Perspective on Individual, Social and Civilizational Change* (London: Praeger, 1989), pp. 120–128. This perception of history was elitist, since it placed responsibility for historical success solely in the hands of a capable elite.

103. For a similar cultural formulation in India, see Gyan Prakash, *Another Reason: Science and the Imagination of Modern India* (Princeton, NJ: Princeton University Press, 1999), pp. 86, 89, 90, 94, 228.

104. *MTM* 11 (1963): p. 25; Muḥammad Shafīq Ghurbāl, "Asālīb kitābat al-tārīkh 'inda al-'Arab," *Majallat Mujma' al-lugha al-'arabiyya* 14 (1962): pp. 25–34.

cal process, *ḥadīth* criticism involved the identification of all existing sources for a given event, the systematic comparison of these sources, and, finally, the hierarchization of sources and even the elimination of the unfounded ones. The popular methodological guide of Asad Rustum strongly emphasized this point.[105] Ghurbāl followed suit by emphasizing the modernity of al-Jabartī's historical methodology, which followed these practices.[106]

However, even in cases in which academic scholars could not claim theoretical and methodological universality, they never dismissed the entire corpus of Islamic historiographical heritage. Unlike doctors and irrigation engineers in their contemptuous attitude toward anything premodern, historians had a tremendous amount of respect at all times for the cultural and aesthetic value of Islamic historiography. Aḥmad ʿIzzat ʿAbd al-Karīm, for instance, used to begin his classes with readings from the classic account of Ibn Iyās.[107]

On another level, Toynbee's inevitable reliance on Ibn Khaldūn and his great respect for both the Egyptian and the Islamic civilizations proved the point Egyptians were making. Thus, Toynbee's cyclical theory of civilization was particularly welcomed among Arab academic circles. Given Toynbee's mentorship and support of Ghurbāl ever since his graduation, his becoming a sort of father figure for Egypt's fledging academic school of history is not surprising.[108] And thus, even in times in which Toynbee's monumental work of analyzing civilization was severely criticized in the West for being presumptuous, Middle Eastern historians fiercely defended it.[109] In fact, Toynbee's idea of history had a long-lasting influence on Ghurbāl and on the Egyptian intellectual trend that sought continuity in history.

Indeed, already before the 1950s, Ghurbāl popularized Toynbee's unique perception of civilization and change in history. Though Ghurbāl's *Beginnings of the Egyptian Question* was free of Toynbee's theory, in *Takwīn Miṣr* and also in *Muḥammad ʿAlī al-Kabīr,* Toynbee's challenge-response-mimesis theory guided Ghurbāl's interpretation of Muḥammad ʿAlī's experience with the Ottomans.[110]

105. Rustum, *Muṣṭalaḥ al- tārīkh,* pp. 29–37, 88–118.

106. Ghurbāl, "Asālib kitābat al-tārīkh," p. 34.

107. Yunān Labīb Rizq, "Aḥmad ʿIzzat ʿAbd al-Karīm: Al-muʿālim," *Miṣr al-Ḥadītha* 2 (2003): p. 457.

108. Toynbee was also a staunch anti-imperialist, a stance that positioned him as a true philosophical alternative to other European historians.

109. For concise summaries of the controversy around Toynbee's theories, see H.R. Trevor-Roper, "The Prophet," *New York Review of Books* (October 12, 1989): pp. 28–32; and Zaki Saleh, *Trevor-Roper's Critique of Arnold Toynbee: A Symptom of Intellectual Chaos* (Baghdad: al-Ma'aref Press, 1958).

110. According to Ghurbāl, the Ottomans had failed to respond to European progress and thus declined. Ottoman narrow-mindedness *(ḍayq al-'ufuq)* had dragged Egypt to the "bottom of history." Muḥammad ʿAlī understood these historical dynamics and was the only regional leader

As we shall see in chapter 7, toward the end of his career Ghurbāl would take this analysis one step further, fusing it with the idea of historical continuity *(istimrāriyya)* from Pharaonic to modern times.[111] In short, resorting to the legacy of Ibn Khaldūn and to the selection methods of *ḥadīth* scholars was the only solution to the inorganic connection of professionalism and Islamic historical thought. As we shall see in chapter 9, this cultural problem of authenticity in historical thought was a burning issue for the Islamists of the 1970s.

CONCLUSION

Organizing and coordinating the process of professionalization, Ghurbāl became an extremely busy man. He matched researchers to subjects, made books happen, and found jobs for his students. In short, he became an academic fixer and the person who led the elaborate process through which historical writing became methodologized. Under his leadership, four elementary conditions for the creation of a professional discipline were met: (a) the development of a body of esoteric historical knowledge that the practitioners were required to master, (b) autonomy of the profession in controlling the work, its practitioners, and the relation between the two, (c) a bid for monopoly on historical knowledge, and (d) the creation of an ideal of service that was both a commitment and an ethical imperative that lay above the interests of the practitioners.[112] All of these conditions were what made Ghurbāl the father of the academic school and the chief architect of the institutionalization of history writing.

Undoubtedly, the ability of the historical profession in Egypt to impose its conviction was, inter alia, the outcome of this institutionalization.[113] However, what distinguished academic historians from other professions, say, Egyptian blue-collar workers, and accorded them the authority with which they spoke

---

capable of responding to them. Ghurbāl argued that Muḥammad ʿAlī cultivated a creative Turkish-Egyptian elite whose role was to respond to European challenges. The pasha's popular peasant army (cast as Toynbee's mimetic masses) was the central tool with which he sought to reform the Ottoman Empire and to "civilize" Sudan as well. Ghurbāl, *Muḥammad ʿAlī al-kabīr* (1944), pp. 5–7, 13–14, 34–35, 62–73, 78–79, 84–85, 114–119, 130–131, 148.

111. In 1949 in his capacity as top official in the Ministry of Education, Ghurbāl established the museum of civilization, which was built around Toynbee's historical notions. Anīs, "Shafīq Ghurbāl wa madrasat al-tārīkh," p. 16.

112. Thomas Broman, "Rethinking Professionalization: Theory, Practice and Professional Ideology in Eighteenth-Century German Medicine," *Journal of Modern History* 67, no. 4 (December 1995): p. 835; Jan Goldstein, "Foucault among the Sociologists: The Disciplines and the History of Professions," *History and Theory* 23, no. 2 (1984): p. 175; Andrew Abbot, *The System of Professions: An Essay on the Division of Expert Labor* (Chicago: University of Chicago Press, 1988), pp. 1–15.

113. For institutionalization of the historical profession, see Pim den Boer, *History as a Profession* (Princeton, NJ: Princeton University Press, 1998), pp. 309–365.

was the approach to academic history as a theory-driven practice. As such, it purports to make reference to unobservable phenomena and thus chart the path of future experiences. In order to substantiate their claim to such power, academic historians developed the concept of objectivity, which positioned them as disinterested viewers who, in virtue of their special location, could account for "historical truth." As Peter Novick illustrated, historians could not conceive their practice without relating it to objectivity. Whether as an aim within reach or as an abstract ideal that is only worth aspiring to, objectivity justified the historians' claim to expert authority.[114]

From this new position, they held that historical truth requires authorization and that only Ghurbāl and his colleagues could and should master and regulate this process. Only they could provide the scientific validation and the ability to safeguard this truth. As expert historians, they purported to monopolize the ability to speak truth and to decide whether a statement is true or false. In the process of regulating historical truth, they hoped to produce even more authority in a cyclical process. Speaking with the authority of what was believed to be objective, empirical, and disinterested knowledge, they quite naturally followed this with the exclusion of others.

On the ground, however, the success of Ghurbāl's school in acquiring the status from which their expert authority would be widely acknowledged, especially by independent writers, was limited. The capacity to create hierarchic relationships rests not on abstract concepts of truth and objectivity, which in any event are very difficult to establish, but on the practice of history as an independent, vibrant, daring, and intellectually involved interpretative community. For all their efforts, Ghurbāl's community of academic historians was not yet there. Nonetheless, despite their limited success in persuading others to respect their expert authority, their ethical commitment to a due historiographical process of investigation clearly distinguished them from all other history writers. In an increasingly ideological age, when a growing number of politicized writers passed judgment on the past without ever studying it, the methodological checks and balances of academia safeguarded historical scholarship from the dangers of metahistorical reasoning and its detachment from historical reality.

114. Peter Novick, *That Noble Dream: The "Objectivity Question" and the American Historical Profession* (Cambridge: Cambridge University Press, 1988).

6

Partisan Historiography

The 1940s and Beyond

After the outbreak of World War II and increasingly throughout the 1940s, Egyptian public life was radicalized. Parliamentary politics was viewed as detached from the country's real problems, and politicians appeared as self-serving and corrupt. Successive governments rose and fell, and the existing political order began to lose both credibility and respect. Thus, the largest opposition group, the Muslim Brotherhood, openly challenged the state by murdering Prime Minister Maḥmūd Fahmī al-Nuqrāshī. The government responded in the same fashion and eliminated the brotherhood's leader, Ḥasan al-Bannā. On a number of occasions the state brutally suppressed the communists. The popular anti-British struggle in the Suez Canal area propagated ideological violence, and, all in all, there was a greater willingness to solve problems by force alone.

Writing history in such violent and uncertain political times further politicized the historiographical scene. Given the inherent biases to which all histories are subject, the main question these events evoke is, At what point does the calculated selection of facts exceed the limits of randomness and turn into a systematic mechanism of distortion and bigotry? This chapter examines a new type of history writing that systematized the selection of facts and the organization of historical reality in an essentially political manner. Here dubbed "partisan," this historiography was structurally political. In partisan historiography, the impact of the political world no longer comes from the outside, for example, in the form of censorship or monopoly. Rather, it is an organic part of the work's logic. Even by the standards of royal history and its manipulated apparatus, partisan historiography created an extreme degree of interplay between politics and historical thought, in which political parties, most notably the Wafd and the National Party, strove to prescribe and enforce the meaning of history.

Thus far in this book, I have examined only the history of the pre-1882 era. I have briefly mentioned that secondary scholars have designated the post-1882 era as "contemporary history" *(tārīkh muʿāṣir),* which was commonly acknowledged as political, and hence, off limits. In this chapter I show how and why contemporary history became the exclusive realm of party politics. In doing so I discuss two forms that partisan historiography embraced: the national allegory and Marxist historiography. The first was extremely powerful and popular. The second was an innovative fringe movement. Both, however, were politically conditioned and thus permitted a rather narrow range of historical interpretation.

The first form, partisan historiographies as allegories for the nation, proliferated in this period. By focusing on two classic cases, in which al-Rāfiʿī's National Party equated to Muṣṭafa Kāmil and the Wafd equated to Saʿd Zaghlūl, the first two sections of the discussion illustrate how post-1882 history was harnessed to serve a narrow party line. Both parties and their leaders were elevated to the status of allegorical figures, a move that was enormously politically profitable. The third section strives to explain why national allegories acquired such significance.

The fourth, and last, section deals with partisanship in Marxist historiography. Until the 1950s, this historiography was a nonallegorical fringe phenomenon. By being indifferent to the high politics of kings and wars as the generators of the historical transition from tradition to modernity, Marxists located themselves outside the mainstream of Egyptian historiography. Their ideas on history were derived from a standard Marxist dogma of historical materialism. Though Marxists were certainly nationalists, their main preoccupation was not with the nation but with "real" people and their "real" problems. Thus, in light of existing historical thought in Egypt, they proposed an innovative framework of interpretation that engaged with new subjects, such as how social roles enabled economic and political control. This literature would influence mainstream history only during the late 1950s. Though its historical approach was original, it too exacerbated a damaging cultural tendency to think about history as part of a political apparatus.

AL-RĀFIʿĪ'S HISTORY OF 1882–1952

Surviving the repression of the 1930s and the ban on his books, ʿAbd al-Raḥmān al-Rāfiʿī emerged from this era stronger than ever before. His perseverance paid off. By the 1940s he had become a one-man school of history, a class of his own. While his work was seen as controversial, writing a book on modern history without quoting him at some point or another was impossible. Though this remains the case even today, his achievement was not merely an academic one. Young nationalist radicals in search of new order also found their collective biographies in his histories. His formula resonated well across the political spectrum. According to al-Rāfiʿī, the series of popular revolutions that started in 1798 and led to the ʿUrābī revolt in 1882 continued well into the twentieth century, including the 1919 Revolution, the multiple skirmishes with the British, and the student demonstrations of the mid-1930s and 1940s. Thus, as long as al-Rāfiʿī could identify the impact of these purportedly revolutionary forces on current politics, he continued to toil on his "National Corpus" *(al-mawsūʿa al-waṭaniyya).* Revolt after revolt until national redemption was his simple motto. For cadets in the military academy and especially for one particular core group *(shilla)* of them, al-Rāfiʿī's work was the definitive history of their generation.[1] Less than twenty years later, this *shilla* would put his history to work in real life. This section looks at al-Rāfiʿī's writing after his triumph over Fu'ād's foreigners was secured. It illustrates how al-Rāfiʿī wove Egypt's contemporary history around the political agenda of the National Party, thus becoming the foremost historian of partisanship. Al-Rāfiʿī's unique capability for matching tales from the past with the rhythm of historical progression, his masterful developing and blending of the two, is best sensed by reviewing his project book-by-book.

Miṣr wa-l-Sūdān fī awwal ʿahd al-iḥtilāl (Egypt and Sudan at the Beginning of the Occupation, 1882–1892) (1942)

The ten years discussed in this work, from the British occupation to the beginning of Muṣṭafa Kāmil's public activity, were characterized as an era of national decadence.[2] The most significant marker of Egypt's helplessness was the 1899 separation of Sudan. During that period, Egypt lost critical elements of its national sovereignty: an independent army, political autonomy, and even the constitutional order (parties, elections, and Parliament). Written during the growing anti-British atmosphere of World War II, this book was one of the strongest anti-colonial texts of that era, for it contradicted the typical colonialist claim for material progress and modernization, an argument that had accompanied Egyptian historiography for a very long time.[3] Although this work was published only three years after his biography on the life and times of Muṣṭafa Kāmil appeared, through it al-Rāfiʿī laid the groundwork for the "big bang" of Egyptian nationalism—the appearance of Muṣṭafa Kāmil in national politics.

1. Anouar Abdel-Malek, *Egypt: Military Society* (New York: Random House, 1968), pp. 208–209.

2. ʿAbd al-Raḥmān al-Rāfiʿī, *Miṣr wa-l-Sūdān fī awwal ʿahd al-iḥtilāl: Tārīkh Miṣr al-qawmī fī sanat 1882 ila sanat 1892* (Cairo: Maktabat al-nahḍa al-miṣriyya, 1948), pp. 174–179.

3. Ibid., pp. 179–190. Compare François Charles-Roux, "*L'Égypte de l'occupation anglaise à l'indépendance égyptienne,*" in Hanotaux, ed., *Histoire de la nation égyptienne,* vol. 7, pp. 3–151.

Muṣṭafa Kāmil: Bāʿith al-ḥaraka al-qawmiyya (Mustafa Kamil: Instigator of the National Movement) (1939)

The central topic of the book was Kāmil's political legacy as it was understood, elaborated, dogmatized, and propagated for over thirty years by al-Rāfiʿī and other party members, such as Fatḥī Raḍwān. In al-Rāfiʿī's own words, Muṣṭafa Kāmil revived the national dynamic that would culminate in the 1919 Revolution, making him nothing less than the Christopher Columbus of Egyptian nationalism.[4] The following is a list of the six most important principles laid down by Kāmil and the National Party: (a) the immediate and unconditional withdrawal of all foreign forces from Egyptian soil (known as *al-jalā'*); (b) continuous and total struggle (jihad) against all forms of occupation, whether military, economic, or cultural;[5] (c) the necessity of positioning constitutional life *(al-dustūr)* at the center of Egyptian public life;[6] (d) the general affinity between the Ottoman Empire and the Islamic world (As we have seen, Kāmil could not resolve the contradiction between a distinctive Egyptian nationalism and Pan-Islamic affiliations. In this book, al-Rāfiʿī tried to conceal this contradiction by arguing that Kāmil's priority was first fighting the British and, only then, separation from the Ottomans.);[7] (e) the unification of Egypt and the Sudan *(waḥdat wādī al-nīl);*[8] and (f) national unity. (Despite Kāmil's Islamic rhetoric and political thought, the stress was on Egyptians belonging to one nation, whether they were Copts or Muslims.)[9]

These principles guided not only the National Party but also, as has been made clear, al-Rāfiʿī's entire project. Seen in this light, the Kāmil era brought to a close a period of unorganized nationalism and loosely coordinated resistance. Out of the despair of previous years, a new, self-confident movement emerged under Kāmil's assuring leadership, one that was ready to challenge the British.

Muḥammad Farīd ramz al-ikhlāṣ wa-l-taḍḥiya (Muhammad Farid, the Symbol of Loyalty and Sacrifice) (1941)

This biography of National Party leader Muḥammad Farīd covered the years 1908–19 as seen through the narrow prism of the National Party. The distinction between the historical national movement and the National Party became so vague that the principles introduced by Kāmil were depicted here as those of

4. ʿAbd al-Raḥmān al-Rāfiʿī, *Muṣṭafa Kāmil: Bāʿith al-ḥaraka al-qawmiyya: Tārīkh Miṣr al-qawmī min sanat 1892–1908* (Cairo: Maktabat al-nahḍa al-miṣriyya, 1950), pp. 12, 13.

5. Ibid., pp. 106–108ff.

6. Ibid., p. 41. See also Kāmil, *Al-Shams al-mushriqa.*

7. al-Rāfiʿī, *Muṣṭafa Kāmil,* pp. 346–369.

8. Ibid., pp. 401–402.

9. Ibid., pp. 432–433.

the Egyptian people as a whole.[10] The focus on the people represents the ongoing struggle within the nationalist camp for historiographical hegemony. The main issue of debate was: Who deserved the most credit for the 1919 Revolution and the independence that followed it? Al-Rāfiʿī's answer was that, while the Jarīda-Umma group, especially Saʿd Zaghlūl, had collaborated with the British, the National Party led the people to the 1919 Revolution. Moreover, al-Rāfiʿī blamed the Jarīda-Umma group and the palace for helping the British to encroach on the National Party and its leaders.[11]

Thawrat sanat 1919 (The 1919 Revolution) (2 vols., 1946)

After Kāmil and Farīd had prepared the ground, the last modern revolution in Egyptian history was launched. Al-Rāfiʿī tried to evaluate whether the 1919 Revolution was a success or a failure.[12] According to him, the long-term causes for the outbreak of the revolution had originated in World War I: the atmosphere of military suppression, encroachment on constitutionalism and political freedom, and the deposition of the first nationalist khedive, ʿAbbās II.[13] More direct and immediate causes were the formation of the Wafd and the arrest of Zaghlūl, who headed it. Once begun, the revolution followed the pattern of earlier revolutions: it spread to the countryside and encompassed all social classes, including women.[14] Al-Rāfiʿī's emphasis on women's participation was part of a growing acknowledgment of their role in the nationalist struggle, an emphasis initiated by Ṣabrī.[15]

Al-Rāfiʿī also highlighted the violent nature of this revolution, a violence from which he falsely claimed to exempt himself.[16] He concluded this book by arguing that the success of the revolution was partial. Though it succeeded in its moral, social, and, to some degree, political aspects (notably the creation of the constitution), it completely failed to secure Egypt's full independence. Hence, al-Rāfiʿī perceived the revolution as an "unfinished revolution." This epithet for the 1919 Revolution was to be appropriated by the revolutionary rhetoric of the 1950s, when the Free Officers presented themselves as those who would "finish it."

10. ʿAbd al-Raḥmān al-Rāfiʿī, *Muḥammad Farīd ramz al-ikhlāṣ wa-l-taḍḥiya: Tārīkh Miṣr al-qawmī min sanat 1908 ila sanat 1919* (Cairo: Dār al-maʿārif, 1984), pp. 485–491.

11. Ibid., pp. 71–78, 137, 179, 485–486. See a review in *Al-Hilāl,* February 1949, pp. 166–167.

12. On why al-Rāfiʿī wrote the book, see *Al-Hilāl,* February 1952, pp. 12–14.

13. ʿAbd al-Raḥmān al-Rāfiʿī, *Thawrat sanat 1919: Tārīkh Miṣr al-qawmī min sanat 1919 ila sanat 1921* (Cairo: Maktabat al-Nahḍa al-miṣriyya, 1955), pp. 12, 18–19, 52.

14. Ibid., pp. 170, 185, 190–191, 202–203, 209.

15. For instance, see Sabry, *La révolution égyptienne,* vol. 1, pp. 42–43, 65–66.

16. Though al-Rāfiʿī expressed his reservations about violence, evidence suggests that he was a member of the "black hand" organization, which targeted individuals during the revolution. Ibid., pp. 170, 185, 190–191, 202–203, 209; ʿUlwān, ʿAbd al-Raḥmān al-Rāfiʿī, pp. 136–143; Crabbs, "Egyptian Intellectuals and the Revolution," p. 251.

Fī aʿqāb al-thawra al-miṣriyya (In the Aftermath of the Egyptian Revolution) (3 vols., 1947, 1949, 1951)

In 1947, 1949, and 1951, al-Rāfiʿī published the last three volumes of his project; they narrated the history of Egypt from 1919 to 1951, the eve of the 1952 Revolution. Al-Rāfiʿī's main concerns were to establish the historical credentials of his political party and to systematically discredit his political rivals. In these works he resorted to moralism: "The intellectuals and educated people should function as messengers of nationalism," he intoned. And in another place, "The educated youth, especially university graduates, should serve in their communities as a model for national principles."[17]

As an active lawyer, a part-time publicist, and a political leader, al-Rāfiʿī also invested a great deal of his time in party politics.[18] Much of his attention was now directed to what he perceived as a public violation of the *al-jalāʾ* principle: "We are in need of citizens who are truly committed to the national idea. These citizens are the nation's soldiers. . . . they should propagate the ideology of *al-jalāʾ*. The evacuation of the Nile Valley is not merely a national demand but an ideology that should be deeply rooted in the hearts."[19]

A classic example of al-Rāfiʿī's concerns is expressed in his account of the 1936 Anglo-Egyptian agreement, which, he argued, was signed by the Wafd in order to ensure the persistence of its political hegemony. In direct opposition to everything that the National Party stood for, this agreement was a shameful act of surrender: "The Wafd alone bears responsibility for the decline of the national spirit and the individualization of national life by propagating an atmosphere of selfishness and opportunism."[20] But his disappointment was not restricted to the Wafd alone: "Egypt is responsible for the futility of this submission. It was incumbent upon it to continue the resistance and to refuse to accept an agreement that would foil independence and reaffirm occupation."[21] Frustrated by the decline of his party since 1919 and by the marginality of its creed, al-Rāfiʿī warned the nation: "Establishing political life on the basis of hollow declarations, shiny words, personal connections, and the pursuit of personal interests will lead to regression in the quality of public life and hinder the progress of the nation."[22]

17. ʿAbd al-Raḥmān al-Rāfiʿī, *Fī aʿqāb al-thawra al-miṣriyya thawrat 1919* (Cairo: Dār al-maʿārif, 1989), vol. 3, pp. 338, 339, respectively.

18. Crabbs, "Egyptian Intellectuals and the Revolution," pp. 250–255.

19. al-Rāfiʿī, *Fī aʿqāb al-thawra*, vol. 3, p. 340.

20. Ibid., 163–164.

21. Ibid., p. 41.

22. al-Rāfiʿī, *Fī aʿqāb al-thawra*, vol. 3, p. 342. As a prominent figure in the post-1919 National Party leadership, al-Rāfiʿī personally experienced the breakdown of his party and the rise of the Wafd. For comprehensive analyses of the rivalry between those groups, see Walid Kazziha, "The

Once more, such an account triggered Ghurbāl to answer back. For him it was not about the Wafd, with which, as already mentioned, he had his own troubles. Rather, Ghurbāl could not bring himself to ignore such a ruthless attack on his professional ideology. As we have seen, less than a year after the publication of al-Rāfiʿī's third volume, Ghurbāl published a comprehensive history of the Anglo-Egyptian conflict from 1882 to 1936. The precise contents of this book are of little interest. It is enough to say that Ghurbāl resolved to illustrate the merits of balanced academic scholarship that would not tendentiously support a narrow party line and would not see itself as a representation of the nation in history. The idea was to write the history of the Anglo-Egyptian relationship, perhaps the most sensitive national issue, and a history that would go beyond the exiting myths. Once more, Ghurbāl situated himself in a position of intellectual leadership. And once more, the effort would prove half-successful at best.

Naturally, Ghurbāl focused his attention on the refutation of al-Rāfiʿī's judgment. He was seriously interested in conveying the sense of political complexity, which al-Rāfiʿī systematically chose to ignore. Under the circumstances that prevailed at the time, Ghurbāl argued, negotiations were a reasonable and acceptable way to end the conflict: "Only a naive historian expects nations to live constantly in a stage of revolution, and only a naive historian would regard a return to normal life as a setback and [political] corruption.[23] The return of students to study, clerks to their office, and peasants, workers, and traders to their work . . . is the natural thing. . . . [On the contrary,] the trading-in of the principles and the norms of [these] politics is the true corruption."[24]

Thus, the 1936 agreement was not an act of political corruption but a natural outcome of complex circumstances from which Egypt had also much to gain.[25] Summarizing his view, Ghurbāl stated that although al-Rāfiʿī based his account on an impressive array of sources, his interpretation was simplistic and flawed. At one point, just to make sure things were indeed personal, Ghurbāl insinuated that al-Rāfiʿī was, after all, a mere "lawyer."[26]

By the eve of the revolution, al-Rāfiʿī's entire series covering the history of the popular-revolutionary spirit from 1798 to 1951 was ready, lacking only one more revolution and an accompanying Wagnerian soundtrack to complete it. Not a musi-

---

Jarida-Umma Group and Egyptian Politics," *Middle Eastern Studies* 13, no. 3 (1977): pp. 373–385; ʿAbd al-ʿAẓīm Ramaḍān, *Taṭawwur al-ḥaraka al-waṭaniyya fī Miṣr min sanat 1918 ila sanat 1936* (Cairo: Dār al-kitāb al-ʿarabī li-l-ṭibāʿa wa-l-nashr, 1968), pp. 23–46; and Arthur Goldschmidt, "The National Party from Spotlight to Shadow," *Asian and African Studies* 16, no. 1 (1982): pp. 13–30.

23. For al-Rāfiʿī's complaints, see al-Rāfiʿī, *Fī aʿqāb al-thawra,* vol. 3, pp. 337–340.

24. Ghurbāl, *Tārīkh al-mufāwaḍāt,* p. 6.

25. Ibid., pp. 1–8, 270–271.

26. Ghurbāl claimed that al-Rāfiʿī's lawyerly methods were simplistic and inappropriate. However, he praised al-Rāfiʿī for his ability to document. Ibid., pp. 14–15.

cian but a reasonable scriptwriter named Fatḥī Raḍwān realized the artistic vision of al-Rāfiʿī's history. In 1951 he was in the final stages of the production of a new film titled *Muṣṭafa Kāmil.* He completed the work, but the film was immediately banned, and Raḍwān was allocated a nice cell in prison.[27] With one more setback for his cause, al-Rāfiʿī was patiently waiting for the next revolution. A few months later, such an event indeed found him—sooner than he had ever expected.

THE WAFD'S HISTORY

They say that in a remote village in Upper Egypt, some people saw sprouts of beans emerging from the ground in readable shapes—"Long live Saʿd." They also say that in another place, while examining a pregnant lady only days before labor, her doctor could clearly hear the fetus shouting, "Long live Saʿd."[28] This Saʿd was, of course, Saʿd Zaghlūl, the celebrated Wafd leader who passed away in 1927. On his death, legends of all sorts proliferated. A stream of panegyric publications, the majority of which were historical biographies, flooded the book market. In 1936, an imposing art deco mausoleum combining Pharaonic motives was inaugurated in the heart of Cairo. Zaghlūl was commemorated on a grand and unprecedented scale. Yet, during the late 1930s, such commemoration was quite ubiquitous. It was, in fact, the age of commemoration, and the monarchy did not lag far behind the Wafd. The names and figures of the monarchy's ancestors were engraved on the urban landscape of Alexandria, Cairo, and other cities. More neglected heroes were Muṣṭafa Kāmil and Muḥammad Farīd. Despite al-Rāfiʿī's relentless efforts, the Wafd activists and their allies systematically foiled his attempts to establish a statue or a mausoleum similar to Zaghlūl's granite edifice.[29]

As was recently shown by Gershoni and Jankowski, the scandalous politics of commemoration was not restricted to the field of public architecture but was particularly evident in historiography, where it left a very strong mark.[30] Simply by their sheer quantity, Zaghlūl's biographies formed the core of the Wafd's historiography, even surpassing the number of school textbooks on the Wafd. (See Table 7.) Unlike the colossal and ordered story of the National Party, the Wafd version of the post-1882 era was conveniently wrapped around Zaghlūl's biography. For everything that preceded this year, al-Rāfiʿī's version was com-

27. Yoav Di-Capua, "Embodiments of the Revolutionary Spirit: The Commemoration of Mustafa Kamil and Muhammad Farid," *History and Memory* 13, no. 1 (Spring–Summer 2001): pp. 101–102.

28. These anecdotes were told by Dr. Muḥammad Ḥusayn Haykal. Aḥmad ʿAbd al-Raḥīm Muṣṭafa, "Ḥawla taqwīm zaʿamāt Miṣr fi mā bayna thawratay 1919–1952," in ʿAbdallāh, ed., *Tārīkh Mīsr,* p. 263.

29. Di-Capua, "Embodiments of the Revolutionary Spirit," pp. 85–113.

30. Gershoni and Jankowski, *Commemorating the Nation.*

TABLE 7. Selective Publications on Sa'd Zaghlūl to 1952

Year	Author	Title	Orientation
1927	Aḥmad Ḥusayn al-Qurāni	*Dhikra Sa'd*	Obituaries
1927	Muḥammad Ismā'īl al-Buḥayrī	*'Ibarāt al-sharq*	Biography
1927	Aḥmad Fahmī Ḥāfiẓ	*Sa'd Zaghūl Pasha*	Political biography
1927	Foulad Yéghen	*Sa'd Zaghloul*	Biography (in French)
1927	Muḥammad Ibrāhīm al-Jazīrī	*Āthār al-za'īm Sa'd Zaghlūl*	Biography
1928	'Uways 'Uthmān, ed.	*Dumū' al-shu'arā'*	Elegies
1929	Karīm Khalīl Thābit	*Sa'd*	Biography
1930	'Ubayid Makram	*'Azamat Sa'd*	Biography
1936	'Abbās Maḥmūd al-'Aqqād	*Sa'd Zaghlūl*	Biography
1942	'Abduh Ḥasan al-Zayyāt	*Sa'd Zaghlūl*	Biography
1952	Joseph Naḥḥās	*Dhikrayāt: Sa'd*	"Sa'd and I"

NOTE: The titles listed exclude school textbooks.

monly accepted. In fact, only the Marxist historians differed from al-Rāfi'ī in their view of the pre-1882 era.

The first thing that strikes the reader of Zaghlūl's biographies is their familiar evolutionary pattern from childhood to adulthood. The various signposts along the way are of particular interest: received an Islamic education in al-Azhar, was a disciple of the 'Abduh-Afghānī circle, received a modern professional education, learned a foreign language, experienced a happy marriage within an aristocratic family, held ministerial positions, was a popular political leader, was a leader of the independence struggle, was tried, punished, and ultimately experienced victory as the head of a de jure independent nation-state. Thus, Zaghlūl was portrayed as a true son of the people *(ibn al-sha'b)* who rose to prominence in order to save the nation.[31]

However, Zaghlūl's life is not a mere metaphor for the nation but rather an idealistic correction of the nation's actual experience. As we have seen in chapter 4, Egypt's transition, or transformation, into a modern capitalist nation-state with a developed sense of citizenship was always deemed grievously incomplete.

31. Muḥammad Ismā'īl al-Buḥayrī, *'Ibarāt al-sharq* (Cairo: Maktabat al-sa'āda, 1927), pp. 7–47.

Zaghlūl's biographies corrected this trajectory. In them, he appears as the embodiment of an absolute and successful transition to modernity.[32] Furthermore, by emphasizing his commitment to Islamic heritage as well as his capacity for modern science and reason, the biographies depict Zaghlūl as the solution for the challenges of modernity. Thus, since Zaghlūl was portrayed as both modern and authentic, the aspirations of an entire generation could find in him a perfect example of the feasibility of its collective project.

Biography, autobiography, diary, and memoir are literary genres that celebrate individuality and thus express the longing of the urban literates for bourgeois individualism and citizenship. In the case of Zaghlūl, however, this literature was entirely devoid of a celebration of individuality. Instead of focusing on the individual Zaghlūl, these biographies allegorically accounted for "Egypt."

The Western split between the private and the public, the poetic and the political, does not exist in allegorical writing. There, the private and the public are presented as one.[33] Even Zaghlūl's wife, Ṣafiyya, is mentioned only in her capacity as an allegory for feminine resistance and as "the mother of the nation" *(umm al-miṣriyyīn)*.[34] Everything personal, let alone private, such as Zaghlūl's social calculations of prestige in marrying the daughter of Prime Minister Muṣṭafa Fahmī or his alleged love affair with Princess Nazlī, is overlooked.[35] Even writings on Zaghlūl's psychology, the ultimate domain of individuality, "discovered" in his character collective ideals such as progress *(rajul taqaddum)*.[36] Thus, the myriad compositions dedicated to Zaghlūl and Kāmil were nothing but disguised collective accounts with a strong hagiographic character.[37] Sa'd was elevated to an allegorical level of existence.

Through corrective prediction and reference, allegory brought the nation to life, but it also appropriated the right to speak on behalf of the people at all times and in all situations. When Sa'd died, his holy leadership *(al-za'āma al-muqaddasa)* passed to the party's leadership and especially to Muṣṭafa al-Naḥḥās.[38] After

32. Ibid., pp. 11–12; Karīm Thābit, *Sa'd fī ḥayātihi al-khāṣṣa* (Cairo: n.p., 1929), pp. 21–22.

33. Fredric Jameson, "Third-World Literature in the Era of Multinational Capitalism," *Social Text* 15 (Autumn 1986): p. 69.

34. Muḥammad Ibrāhīm al-Jazīrī, *Āthār al-za'īm Sa'd Zaghlūl* (Cairo: Māṭba'at dār al-kutub, 1927), preface.

35. On alleged love affair, see Mostyn, *Egypt's Belle Époque*, p. 130; and Beth Baron, *Egypt as a Woman: Nationalism, Gender, and Politics* (Berkeley: University of California Press, 2005), pp. 136–138.

36. al-Buḥayrī, *'Ibarāt al-sharq*, pp. 175ff.; 'Abbās Maḥmūd al-'Aqqād, *Sa'd Zaghlūl* (Cairo: Maṭba'at jamāzī, 1936), pp. 543–572.

37. With a few rare exceptions (for example, Ṭaha Ḥusayn's *Al-Ayām*) this hagiographic tendency was quite prevalent.

38. Gorman, *Historians, State and Politics*, p. 120.

the 1919 Revolution, Sir Alfred Milner arrived in Egypt to tour the country to investigate the causes of the revolution. As the story goes, he came across a local *fallāḥ* in some remote field and had the following short exchange with him:

Sir Milner: What is your name?
fallāḥ: (silence).
Sir Milner: Are you married?
fallāḥ: (silence).
Sir Milner: Do you have children?
fallāḥ: Ask Saʿd Pasha.
Sir Milner: What time is it?
fallāḥ: Ask Saʿd Pasha.[39]

The allegorical Saʿd took on a life of his own and now spoke on behalf of whomever and whatever. In light of this reality, in July 1925, the frustrated Mr. Nevile Henderson, acting British high commissioner in Egypt, exclaimed, "Before the country could enter upon a period of calm Saad must be killed—morally."[40] However, allegorical historiography persisted, and by the 1950s it constituted the core of partisan historiography. Thus, morally speaking, Saʿd Zaghlūl was more alive than ever before. In the following section, I attempt to explain why and how allegorical historiography persisted and what its possible long-term cultural consequences were.

NATIONAL ALLEGORY AS A HISTORIOGRAPHICAL PROBLEM

More than fifteen years ago, the literary phenomenon of national allegory was the subject of a fierce debate. Frederic Jameson's controversial statement that *all third-world texts are necessarily to be read as national allegories* ignited the theoretical reservoir of the postcolonial school in literary criticism. Though this school of thought was only in the formative stages of theoretical elaboration, the postcolonial critics blamed Jameson for the deadly sins of "essentialism" and reduction of the "other."[41] In one quick move, Jameson, a distinguished Marxist theoretician, was theoretically bayoneted, and national allegories were

39. Rifʿat al-Saʿīd, *Saʿd Zaghlūl bayna al-yamīn wa-l-yasār* (Beirut: Dār al-qaḍāyā, 1976), pp. 5–6.

40. FO 371/10888.

41. Jameson, "Third-World Literature in the Era of Multinational Capitalism," p. 69; and response by Aïjaz Ahmad, "Jameson's Rhetoric of Otherness and the 'National Allegory,'" *Social Text* 17 (Autumn 1987): pp. 3–25.

marked as no less than essentially racist.[42] Cognizant of the positions of all sides in this debate, I maintain that while only a minority of Egyptian histories were national allegories, their disproportionate cultural and political impact needs to be explained.

Though in the short term, histories based on national allegories were useful in mobilizing the people against colonialism, in the long run they stifled historical interpretation and limited its horizons. The process that created this state of affairs was rather simple. As illustrated throughout this book, Egypt was forged as the ultimate subject of modern history. There were hardly any alternative subjects or historical themes. Gradually, however, the irrevocable link between history and the nation was extended to those who purported to represent the nation. Hence, quite logically, if the nation is the subject of history, and the political parties and their leaders embody the nation, by extension, they become the subjects of history as well and an allegory for the nation.

Partisan historiography owes its existence to this realization. Both al-Rāfiʿī and the Wafd wrote histories that competed for the same goal of freeing the nation's subjectivity from colonial and royal control. Henceforth, the past became each party's bank of credit; and the future, its next realm of operation. After the formative stages of historiographic solidification, there were two irreconcilable subjects of history: the nation according to the National Party, and the nation according to the Wafd. But which to believe?

The paradoxical nature of anti-colonial modernity further polarized this binary historiography. As already mentioned, Egyptians opposed the colonizer and at the same time tried to replicate its culture. Those who admired Western and British culture and sought to put it to work in Egypt were deemed collaborators, even if they also honestly advocated freedom from occupation. Members of the Wafd and the Liberal Constitutionalists clearly fall within this category. Their acquisition of some of the external characteristics of British colonialists, such as aloofness, elitism, and the exclusion of the lower classes, only validated the accusation of their betrayal. In contrast, those who were more ambivalent toward Western culture, espousing a more belligerent plan for struggle, regarded themselves as more authentic and patriotic, even if they offered no solutions to the challenge of modernity. The National Party, Young Egypt, and even the Muslim Brotherhood fall within this category. Thus, depending on the multiple ways parties and individuals reacted to this paradox, they were perceived as either heroes or traitors.

A binary tendency was endemic to anti-colonial nationalism, and national allegory was the medium that captured and amplified this tendency. By defini-

42. Imre Szeman, "Who's Afraid of National Allegory? Jameson, Literary Criticism, Globalization," *South Atlantic Quarterly* 100, no. 3 (Summer 2001): pp. 803–827.

tion, allegory is a symbolic story that serves as a disguised representation of meanings deeper than those indicated on the surface. As we have just seen, the characters in an allegory often have no individual personality. Instead, they embody moral qualities and other abstractions. Allegory is a total system of meaning, all the more total when backed by political power. The totality of national allegories makes them rigid and unrevisable intellectual systems. Thus, Saʿd Zaghlūl and Muṣṭafa Kāmil either fully embody the struggle of the new modern Egyptian for independence or not. A partial allegory is a meaningless concept. Since both leaders stood for different national solutions, as allegories, they could not coexist.

This definitive mode of historical understanding became common, and an increasing number of histories were to be found on one or the other side of the villain/hero equation. A scene from the film *Miramar* (1969), based on a novel by Naguib Mahfouz bearing the same title, illustrated the persistence of this divide. In it, ʿAmr Wajdī, a retired journalist and Wafdist supporter, and Ṭulba Marzūq, a former palace official whose property was confiscated during the 1952 Revolution, exchange the following impressions:

Ṭullba: Do you know who is the cause of the misfortunes we face today?

ʿAmr: Which misfortunes?

Ṭullba: Cut the nonsense! The misfortunes in our country.

ʿAmr: Who?

Ṭullba: Saʿd Pasha. He kept heaping attack on the king and cursing the English; all the talk of revolution and democracy, just so the people would applaud him. The people are still clapping—they will applaud almost everything.

ʿAmr: God rest his soul. He was a patriot and a revolutionary—and he was trustworthy.[43]

Whether academic or not, studies that were indifferent to the paradox of anti-colonial modernity ended up perpetuating this exchange. The following section goes beyond our time framework, into the 1970s, to briefly examine a particular tradition in which serious and accomplished historians wrote themselves into a corner.

The Chronic Debates of Partisan Historiography

Shortly after the accession to power of Premier Ismāʿīl Ṣidqī, opposition leader Muṣṭafa al-Naḥḥās hurried to the safe of Bank Miṣr. With him he carried a rather large package, which he asked to deposit. It was not money or even jewelry.

43. Gordon, *Revolutionary Melodrama,* pp. 221–222.

Instead, concerned for the fate of Zaghlūl's memoirs under the new government of Ismā'īl Ṣidqī, al-Naḥḥās entombed behind the doors of the bank's sturdy steel vaults the fifty-three precious notebooks. Untouched, they stayed there until 1948, when Ṣidqī began publishing his own memoirs. Ṣidqī's memoirs, however, raised rather unpleasant questions regarding the issue of the Wafd's integrity. Knowing that properly punctuated responses to the uncomfortable questions raised by Ṣidqī's notes could be found only in Zaghlūl's memoirs, al-Naḥḥās hurried to the safe again. Unfortunately, only a select fraction of the material was used, as Zaghlūl's handwriting was, apparently, virtually unreadable. A short while afterward, the Wafd's response was published, and the memoirs were once again returned to the silence of their steel abode. Al-Naḥḥās gained custody of these memoirs, because Zaghlūl stipulated that the Wafd's leader and his nephew should get them after his death. His will was respected.[44]

Then, the 1952 Revolution occurred. When all political parties were officially dissolved, al-Naḥḥās, no longer the head of an existing party, lost legal ground for custodianship of Zaghlūl's memoirs. Unsatisfied with al-Naḥḥās's opportunistic attitude, Ṣidqī's family requested the memoirs, and the case was taken to court.[45] Aware of the sensitivity of this issue, the court put the case to rest and, only in 1963, ruled in favor of al-Naḥḥās. Approaching his end, the elderly leader al-Naḥḥās deposited the memoirs with Dr. Barakāt Bahā' al-Dīn, the son of Zaghlūl's nephew and a legal co-custodian. A short while after the documents were delivered from the bank to Bahā' al-Dīn's house, the phone rang in Bayt al-umma, Zaghlūl's former residence and a national museum. Frida, Zaghlūl's seventy-seven-year-old German translator, answered the phone. Bahā' al-Dīn was on the other end of the line. Apparently, he too could make little headway with the pasha's cryptic handwriting, and he pleaded for her help. The old lady came to his aid, but while unpacking the notebooks she had carefully put in order thirty-six years earlier, three days after Zaghlūl's death, she found something truly disturbing. Flipping through the notebooks she exclaimed: "One hundred pages are missing!" An unfortunate human error? Or a deliberate act, perpetrated by unknown entities? Also, the nagging question, What secrets had been contained within those missing pages? Speculation proliferated. The pages were never found.[46]

44. *Al-Ahrām,* June 22, 1963, p. 7; 'Abd al-'Aẓīm Ramaḍān, *Mudhakkirāt Sa'd Zaghlūl* (Cairo: al-Hay'a al-Miṣriyya al-'āmma li-l-kitāb, 1987), pp. 26–29.

45. According to another version, after July 1963 the government sought to get hold of the memoirs. See more in chapter 8. See also Ḍiyā' al-Dīn Baybars, *Asrār ḥukūmat yūliū* (Cairo: Maktabat madbūlī, 1976), pp. 36–38; and Jalāl al-Sayyid, "Maṭlūb ḥimāyat jamī' al-mudhakkarāt al-siyāsiyya," *Al-Jumhūriyya,* June 22, 1963, p. 5.

46. *Al-Ahrām,* June 22, 1963, p. 7.

Nevertheless, despite the court's ruling, powerful forces operated to achieve full state custodianship of all historical material of national value. Zaghlūl's memoirs were a top priority for all concerned. Socialist historian Muḥammad Anīs lobbied strongly. He had envisioned a new historiographical era, a complete rewriting of modern Egyptian history. Documents were the cornerstone of this ambitious plan.[47] After meeting with the minister of culture, Anīs got what he wanted. The state was harnessed to the project, al-Naḥḥās joined his ancestors, and Zaghlūl's memoirs were deposited in the newly established Markaz wathā'iq wa tārīkh Miṣr al-mu'āṣir, where they were officially, though perhaps not always efficiently, opened to public scrutiny.[48]

By that time, however, after fifteen years of intense revolutionary experience, Zaghlūl, al-Naḥḥās, and the Wafd were buried under an avalanche of nihilistic historical rhetoric. No one ventured to study Egypt's national figures academically. Anīs, in spite of his own biases, opted to change this state of affairs. With the gradual change of atmosphere after the 1967 war, a historiographical window of opportunity was opened.

In 1968, M.A. student 'Abd al-Khāliq Lāshīn became the first scholar to use Zaghlūl's memoirs in order to critically study his legacy. By 1975, he completed his study at the doctoral level. The result was a controversial composition that sparked an endless debate. Prefacing his advisee's study, Aḥmad 'Abd al-Raḥīm Muṣṭafa accentuated the academic and objective character of Lāshīn's work. Lāshīn himself stated that this was a scholarly study about truth. The premise was that Zaghlūl was not a mythical hero but an ordinary human being who should be studied as such.[49] Sensing Zaghlūl's fascination with colonial institutions, styles of reasoning, and Western culture in general, Lāshīn presented Zaghlūl as an elitist leader who, while arguing for independence, closely collaborated with the British.[50] Though Lāshīn was cautious enough not to question Zaghlūl's commitment to independence, he cast doubt on his patriotism and mounted an effective attack against the allegorical figure of Zaghlūl and his role in national history.[51]

'Abd al-'Aẓīm Ramaḍān, a student of Muḥammad Anīs and a contemporary of Lāshīn, disapproved of his colleague's book. In a study on the national movement that was published at the same time, he once again presented the Wafd as the representative of the people and the history of the national movement after World

47. See discussion in chapter 8.

48. *Al-Ahrām*, June 22, 1963, p. 7; al-Sayyid, "Maṭlūb ḥimāyat," p. 5.

49. Aḥmad 'Abd al-Raḥīm Muṣṭafa, "Taqdīm," in 'Abd al-Khāliq Lāshīn, *Sa'd Zaghlūl wa dawruhu fī-l-siyāsa al-Miṣriyya* (Beirut: Dār al-'awda, 1975), pp. 8, 11–15.

50. See, for instance, Lāshīn, *Sa'd Zaghlūl wa dawruhu*, pp. 50–59.

51. Ibid., pp. 503–504.

War I as a reflection of this party. In this historical scheme, the place of Zaghlūl as a national allegory was secured.[52] Quite expectedly, Ramaḍān also highlighted the objective nature of his academic work, which had allowed *him* to discover the truth.[53] Following the publication of these books, Gamal Abd al-Nasser died, the revolution ended, and Sadat's regime eventually forced Lāshīn to flee the country,[54] but the debate around Zaghlūl's legacy persisted.

In 1980, Ramaḍān was officially nominated to edit Zaghlūl's memoirs and prepare them for publication. He concluded his work seven years later, and the old debate immediately resurfaced. In a long introduction to the official edition, Ramaḍān celebrated his success, glorifying seven years of tedious work. Zaghlūl's handwriting had given him no end of trouble, yet, not as much, he argued, as it had given Lāshīn's thesis, which he once more took the trouble to refute. He did so by means of a personal attack, alluding to what he saw as Lāshīn's poor academic analysis. For him Lāshīn's work was no more than a condemnation of Zaghlūl.[55] Lāshīn and other historians, who had meanwhile joined the fray, fired back. In the March 1987 issue of *Al-Hilāl*, the legacy of Zaghlūl was described as a "romantic dream in need of a realist interpretation."[56] Lāshīn attacked Ramaḍān for regarding himself as an authority on Zaghlūl's memoirs and, by extension, on Egypt's national history. His counterattack also highlighted his opponent's mistakes in the reading of Zaghlūl's handwriting. Just to drive his point home, he generously insulted Ramaḍān's entire academic career as cheap "boutique scholarship" and his work as written and published at great speed and, thus, of inferior quality.[57]

Tensions remained high as the 1987 conference on the state of modern Egyptian historiography neared. As already mentioned in the introduction to this work, it was an exciting and unprecedented event, the first to discuss historiography in such an open manner after an entire decade of self-examination. As was to be expected, the legacy of national leaders figured strongly in the various discussions. Many attendees called for revision.[58] In his opening address, the elderly ultranationalist Fatḥī Raḍwān, loyal promulgator of an exaggerated version of al-Rāfiʿī's histories, described Zaghlūl as a traitor and a collaborator. Raḍwān's demagogic style and especially the fact that he was not an academic historian

52. ʿAbd al-ʿAẓīm Ramaḍān, *Taṭawwur al-ḥaraka al-waṭaniyya fī Miṣr 1918–1936* (Cairo: al-Hay'a al-miṣriyya al-ʿāmma li-l-kitāb, 1998), vol. 1, pp. 5–7.

53. Ibid., p. 5.

54. Gorman, *Historians, State and Politics*, p. 70.

55. Ramaḍān, *Mudhakkirāt Saʿd Zaghlūl*, pp. 44–46.

56. Editorial, *Al-Hilāl*, March 1, 1987, p. 7.

57. ʿAbd al-Khāliq Lāshīn, "Al-Ḥaqā'iq al-ghā'iba fī nashr mudhakarāt Saʿd Zaghlūl," *Al-Hilāl*, March 1, 1987, pp. 15–20.

58. ʿAbd al-Raḥīm Muṣṭafa, "Ḥawla taqwīm zaʿamāt," pp. 261–276.

infuriated Ramaḍān. In a series of belligerent articles, Ramaḍān set out to discredit Raḍwān's authority to talk about history in public.[59] He did not need to put much effort into this project, since a year later Raḍwān was dead. He was buried alongside al-Rāfi'ī, Muṣṭafa Kāmil, and Muḥammad Farīd.[60]

On the second day of the conference, Ramaḍān and Lāshīn were scheduled to participate on a special panel dedicated to the debate on Zaghlūl. Ramaḍān delivered an eleven-point speech, in which he once more refuted Lāshīn's critical view of Zaghlūl. The cryptic handwriting issue was once again brought to the fore. Lāshīn simply did not fully understand Sa'd Pasha's words. Ramaḍān's lecture was rich with details but otherwise provided very little insight into the heart of the matter. It ended with a personal note, with Ramaḍān alluding to the offensiveness of Lāshīn's accusations against him. Lāshīn, however, appeared to have been even more offended by Ramaḍān's belligerent style and, in retaliation, decided to boycott the panel altogether. Ad hominem attacks flew around the room, and the heated debate reached a deadlock.[61]

This controversy was by no means an isolated episode in Egyptian historiography. It was partisan historiography's inheritance to future generations. Though Egyptian academia was potentially capable of renewal, this sort of debate remained something of a blind spot. In fact, with minimal effort, similar stories could be retrieved regarding Muṣṭafa Kāmil, Muḥammad Farīd, Muṣṭafa al-Naḥḥās, and others.[62] In hindsight, it is quite puzzling to see how generation after generation of historians accepted these terms of discussion and continued to wrangle over one episode or another in which either Zaghlūl or Kāmil appeared insufficiently nationalist or one appeared more or less nationalist than the other. One of the prime tasks of revisionist historiography is to arrive at a profound change in the methods of investigation and the conceptual framework for inquiry, and scholarship that was grounded in national allegories was structurally incapable of making those changes. For Lāshīn and Ramaḍān, revisionism simply meant contradicting each other as well as attempting to achieve a more truthful reading of Zaghlūl's indecipherable handwriting, which was essentially impossible because by this time Frida, Zaghlūl's German translator, was dead.

In sum, as long as the partisan system of thought and its nationalist assumptions were accepted, writing about national leaders could be politically daring, but it was not likely to be revisionist. During the 1980s, academics certainly felt

59. 'Abd al-'Aẓīm Ramaḍān, *Tārīkh miṣr wa-l-muzawirūn* (Cairo: al-Zahrā' li-l-I'lām al-'arabī, 1993), pp. 136–155.

60. Di-Capua, "Embodiments of the Revolutionary Spirit," pp. 103–104.

61. Aḥmad 'Abdallāh, "Taqdīm al-ḥiwār al-maftūḥ bayna Dr. 'Abd al-'Aẓīm Ramaḍān and Dr. 'Abd al-Khāliq Lāshīn," in Aḥmad 'Abdallāh, ed., *Tārīkh Miṣr,* pp. 277–280.

62. See the discussion in the next two chapters.

FIGURE 4. Allegory as political power. SHAYKH ʿULAYSH: Every hour you make up a reason to visit Saʿd's tomb to the degree that you would prompt him to escape his grave. At the same time, you never visit the grave of Muṣṭafa Kāmil, even though he is a veteran of nationalism who sacrificed much more. What is the reason? AL-NAḤḤĀṢ PASHA: You are so stupid. We are going to Saʿd's grave for [political] business *(tijāra)* not for visitation *(ziyāra)*. Muṣṭafa Kāmil's tomb is not even useful for a clearance sale. *Al-Kashkūl*, no. 562, February 1, 1932.

the impasse, but rather than critically engaging with the nexus among history, modernity, and the paradox of anti-colonial modernity, they left the nationalist assumptions that define Egyptian historiography untouched. Instead, other explanations abounded. One popular way to explain national allegories was to argue that they are the outcome of historical work that took Thomas Carlyle's idea of the "hero" in history all too seriously.[63] Another way was to understand allegory merely as a political problem between Right and Left. Rifʿat al-Saʿīd's short composition *Saʿd Zaghlūl bayna al-yamīn wa-l-yasār* (Saʿd Zaghlūl between Right and Left) is a good case in point.[64] According to this view, historians got used to judging leaders in the "court of history," either acquitting them as heroes or condemning them as villains, all in accordance with the historian's own political creed.[65] As we shall see in chapter 9, this practice was usually referred to as the problem of politicization and factionalism *(ṣirāʿ ḥizbī).*

THE FIRST WAVE OF MARXIST HISTORIOGRAPHY

King Fārūq used to joke, "If a future historian would one day like to write a book on the formation and development of the communist movement in Egypt, he could find all the necessary sources in my closet."[66] A committed archenemy of communism, he obsessively collected any piece of information. Whether it came from open, published sources, like newspapers, from the publications of the communists themselves, or from the confidential reports of the secret service, Fārūq had it. Communists, he used to say while waving his pistol, should be kept at bay.[67] His closet was the proper place to keep their works. Though the king was by no means the only person to be alarmed by the so-called Marxist/communist peril, against all odds, the Marxist option persisted.[68]

Three factors make Egyptian Marxism an extremely important school within the modern historiographical tradition: the cultural and social background of its leadership, its highly fragmented political structure, and the wide selection of other left-wing political thought that influenced it. Combined, these factors accorded the Egyptian Marxist movement an organizational flexibility and modularity, a natural propensity toward intellectual engagement, and a ready-made leftist public that could relate to its ideas.

As a rule, key Marxist activists came from the urban middle and upper classes. Many were members of ethnic and religious minorities with a cosmopolitan and polyglot background. While some were veterans of previous socialist and communist organizations, others were young activists who were heavily influenced

63. ʿAlī Barakāt, "Al-Tārīkh wa-l-qaḍāyā al-manhaj fī Miṣr al-muʿāṣira," *Qaḍāyā Fikriyya* 11–12 (July 1992): p. 78.

64. al-Saʿīd, *Saʿd Zaghlūl bayna al-yamīn wa-l-yasār,* pp. 5–7.

65. ʿAbd al-ʿAẓīm Ramaḍān, *Muṣṭafa Kāmil fī maḥkamat al-tārīkh* (Cairo: al-Hay'a al-miṣriyya al-ʿāmma li-l-kitāb, 1987), pp. 3–10.

66. Thābit, *Fārūq kamā ʿaraftūhu,* vol. 1, p. 78.

67. Ibid., pp. 77–78, 144.

68. Distinctions between Marxists and communists were not yet very clear.

by the radical political environment of the 1930s. Save for a growing, though not yet dominant, number of working-class members, the rank and file of the Marxist movement originated from similar, largely humble, social origins.

After a decade of repression and the demise of the first Communist Party beginning in the late 1930s, the Marxist movement made a gradual comeback.[69] Less than a decade later, a host of political and cultural groups were already active. Thus, leading the Egyptian Movement for National Liberation (EMNL) was a major activist from comfortable Jewish origins, Henri Curiel (1914–78).[70] Hillel Schwartz formed ISKRA (the Spark). Israel Marcel headed a small group known as the People's Liberation (Taḥrīr al-sha'b). Another, slightly bigger, organization was the New Dawn group (al-Fajr al-jadīd). In addition, the core of the Marxist movement was composed of multiple committees, youth groups, cultural centers, clubs, artistic associations, and loosely affiliated individuals.[71] This milieu accorded the movement a strong intellectualizing tendency. Structurally, the Marxist scene was extremely vibrant, and too often organizations tended to unite and then split. For instance, in April 1947, ISKRA and the EMNL united and formed the strong Democratic Movement for National Liberation (DMNL, al-Ḥaraka al-Dimuaqrātīya li-l-tuḥarrur al-Waṭanī).[72] Though in hindsight, the ideological differences between some of the factions may seem symbolic, this modular structure increased the survival capability of the Marxist option.[73]

Marxists were isolated because they were always external to the legitimate political system, which pushed the movement to engage with its environment ideologically. A constantly reinforced intellectual dynamism became one of its main features. With few real political options at hand, Marxists turned to publishing as a central form of political activity. Correspondingly, the impressive number of newspapers and independent publishing houses was disproportionate to the size and resources of the movement. In most cases, its publishing houses were nothing but crowded apartments.[74] Such was the case for the New Dawn

69. The history of the first communist movement has little relevancy to the subject of Egyptian historiography. Tareq Ismael and Rifa'at El-Sa'id, *The Communist Movement in Egypt, 1920–1988* (Syracuse, NY: Syracuse University Press, 1990), pp. 12–31.

70. Also known by its Arabic acronym HAMITU (al-Ḥaraka al-Miṣriyya li-l-Taḥarrur al-Waṭanī).

71. One such cultural association was Georges Henein's Art et Liberté. Selma Botman, *The Rise of Egyptian Communism 1939–1970* (Syracuse, NY: Syracuse University Press, 1988), pp. 12–16.

72. Ibid., pp. 69ff.

73. For a detailed map of the structure and organization of the Marxist milieu, see ibid., p. 13. For a firsthand description of some major disagreements, see Aḥmad Ṣādiq Sa'd, *Ṣafaḥāt min al-yasār al-miṣrī fī a'qāb al-ḥarb al-'ālamiyya al-thāniyya, 1945–1946* (Cairo: Maktabat madbūlī, 1976), pp. 25–60.

74. Sa'd, *Ṣafaḥāt min al-yasār al-miṣrī*, pp. 46–47.

group's publishing apparatus, House of the Twentieth Century (Dār al-qarn al-ʿashrīn). Their newspaper was *Al-Fajr al-jadīd*. Their declared goal was to study Egyptian society.[75] The young activist and writer Shuhdī ʿAṭiyya al-Shāfiʿī generated ISKRA's House of Scientific Studies (Dār al-abḥāth al-ʿilmiyya, established 1944).[76] *Al-Jamāhīr* was their newspaper.[77] They covered a wide array of subjects ranging from poverty and unemployment in Egypt to various economic developments around the world. They promoted regional awareness, especially among third-world countries sharing similar stages of development. The House of the Dawn (Dār al-fajr) was affiliated with Israel Marcel's People's Liberation.[78] The EMNL was especially prolific and innovative. Under the leadership of Henri Curiel, it initiated the Green Book series, which offered local as well as European Marxist literature, much of it available in translation. Fawzī Girgis, who was later to become a historian in his own right, was the head of the EMNL translation bureau. Cooperating with an impressive cadre of specialists, including members of the distinguished Arab Language Academy, they produced translations of high quality. The writings of Marx, Engels, Lenin, and Stalin formed the bulk of the translated library. All of this semilegal material was sold in Henri Curiel's bookshop, al-Midān.[79]

Thus, in a relatively short span of time, a broad selection of periodicals, daily newspapers, leaflets, pamphlets, and works of more established scholarship such as books on Marxist theory, science, agrarian reforms, culture, politics, and economy was available to the public.[80] Cheaply printed pamphlets such as *Mashākil al-ʿummāl fī Miṣr* (The Problem of the Workers in Egypt) (1941), *Lā ṭabaqāt* (No Class . . . !) (1945), and *Afyūn al-shaʿb* (Opium for the People) (1948) elaborated new concepts and ideas (such as class structure), even if some of them were not necessarily committed to communism or were actually critical of it.[81] Many of them were circulated free of charge. History figured strongly in Marxist publications. The House of the Twentieth Century, for instance, specialized in applying Marxist historical thought to Egypt. All in all, the message of these Marxist publications was in sharp dissonance with that of the government, as well as with the existing scholarship on Egyptian history.

75. Botman, *The Rise of Egyptian Communism*, p. 54.

76. Ibid., pp. 48–49.

77. Ibid., pp. 161–162.

78. Roel Meijer, *The Quest for Modernity: Secular Liberal and Left-Wing Political Thought in Egypt 1945–1958* (London: Routledge-Curzon, 2002), p. 106.

79. Anwar Moghith, "Marxisme égyptien et Marxisme occidental: Traduction et idéologie," *Égypte/Monde Arabe* 30–31, nos. 2–3 (1997): pp. 86–87; Meijer, *The Quest for Modernity*, p. 106; Botman, *The Rise of Egyptian Communism*, p. 38.

80. Botman, *The Rise of Egyptian Communism*, pp. 38, 48.

81. Meijer, *The Quest for Modernity*, pp. 124–125.

In July 1946, Premier Ismāʿīl Ṣidqī moved against all opposition groups. Marxists were a prime target of this wide campaign. Hundreds of people from the urban intelligentsia (students, journalists, professionals, and political activists) were arrested. ISKRA's House of Scientific Studies, the New Dawn's House of the Twentieth Century, and a host of other establishments, such as the Committee to Spread Modern Culture, were shut down.[82] Several bookstores, including that of Henri Curiel, were also closed.[83] Even after 1946, the secret police kept a watchful eye on the movement. In 1950, Curiel was deported from Egypt. However, despite government encroachment on anything that was remotely communist,[84] this lively intellectual scene, much of it underground, continued to flourish, and young activists continued to compose, translate, and publish. Thus, the twenty spin-off groups that made up the Marxist movement lent it a certain organizational durability.[85]

In his novel *The Man Who Lost His Shadow,* Fatḥī Ghānim captured the secretive lifestyle of young Marxist activists in this period. The protagonist, Comrade Shawqī, is portrayed as serial pamphlet producer. Shawqī owns a cheap printing press, which is hidden in his tiny flat. This is also the nightly meeting place of Shawqī's cell. Their main occupation is circulating ideas.[86] Indeed, "the communist movement was by far the most important promoter of modernist political ideas in Egypt."[87] However, since their entire ideological apparatus was dependent on history, they directed much of their creative zeal to this area.

Early Historical Materialism

In terms of theory of history, Marx and Engels left only scattered reflections and a few methodological examples. Though their historical heritage was dogmatic, it was highly ambiguous and unsystematic.[88] Thus, the next generation of Marxist intellectuals was left with the task of developing a more coherent sense of a Marxist theory of history. Largely known as historical materialism, this theory

82. Saʿd, *Ṣafaḥāt min al-yasār al-miṣrī,* pp. 46–47.

83. The closing of Curiel's bookshop interrupted the translation movement, which was organized around it. Moghith, "Marxisme égyptien et Marxisme occidental," p. 87; Botman, *The Rise of Egyptian Communism,* pp. 64–66.

84. The government was rather blind to the differences among Marxists, socialists, and communists.

85. Ismael and El-Sa'id, *The Communist Movement in Egypt,* p. 37.

86. Fathy Ghanem, *The Man Who Lost His Shadow* (London: Chapman and Hall, 1966), pp. 61–71.

87. Meijer, *The Quest for Modernity,* p. 126.

88. Georg Iggers, *Historiography in the Twentieth Century* (Hanover, NH: University Press of New England, 1997), p. 79.

postulates that a system of social roles conditions the economic structure of any given society. This structure is composed of three elements: productive forces, relation of production, and the political and ideological superstructure. The task of the theory is to provide a functional explanation for the relationship among these elements. In this regard, it holds (a) that the condition of productive forces explains the nature of the society's relation of production and (b) that this relation of production shapes the superstructure. Thus, it was commonly accepted that class divergence expresses the distinction between those who own the means of production and those who labor using the means of production.[89] Another important component of Marxist thought is its dialectic conception of historical development, in which the contradictions inherent to each historical phase are revealed and superseded by a higher phase of development. "The dialectic method thus becomes the basis for critical theory that looks at the irrationalities, in this case the violation of human dignity, contained in every social formation."[90] With this in mind, Marxists expected the inevitable overthrow of capitalism and the rise of socialism. By studying history, they thought they could predict and plan the triumph of socialism.

Believing in the scientific value of Marxist theory, socialist thinker and reformer economist Rāshid al-Barrāwī (1907–87), during the 1940s, began translating into Arabic canonical writings such as Marx's *Capital* and Lenin's *Imperialism, the Higher Stage of Capitalism*. Al-Barrāwī was a key figure in socialist and reformist thought in the prerevolutionary era. Continuing the Fabian socialist-modernist tradition of Salāma Mūsa,[91] al-Barrāwī also relied on another source of inspiration—the two traditions of British socialism: the authoritarian option that sought to eliminate inefficacy (represented by Sidney Webb [1859–1947] and Beatrice Webb [1858–1943]), and the democratic option that espoused liberty, individualism, moral regeneration, and social fulfillment (advocated by Harold Laski [1893–1950].[92] Though he accepted the Marxist view of base and superstructure as pivotal elements in the shaping of societies, al-Barrāwī rejected the Marxist-Leninist notion of violent revolution and favored instead state-initiated authoritarian solutions. As a professor of economics in Fu'ād University, al-Barrāwī coauthored a study of the economic history of modern Egypt (1798–present), his most significant historiographical contribution. Following an analysis of the various successful (Muḥammad 'Alī's)

89. Stephan Rigby, *Marxism and History* (New York: St. Martin's Press, 1987), p. 4; Stephan Rigby, "Marxist Historiography," in Michael Bentley, ed., *Companion to Historiography* (London: Routledge, 1997), pp. 893–894.

90. Iggers, *Historiography in the Twentieth Century*, p. 80.

91. On Musa, see Meijer, *The Quest for Modernity*, p. 89.

92. Ibid., pp. 70–72.

and failed (Britain's) economic policies,[93] its message was that "only an etatist program of planning, collectivization, and mass industrialization, imposed from above, could guarantee development."[94] For Marxists and specifically for Stalinists, this conclusion was very appealing.

However, despite such studies, the wide array of left-wing reformist ideas about history and economics was by no means fused into a comprehensive theory of history. Only scattered ideas and several non-Marxist case studies of Egypt informed the writing of the first generation of Marxist historians.[95] By and large, until the 1940s, even the most loyal communist veterans, survivors of the first Communist Party, knew only little about Marxism and even less about its ideas on history.[96] A systematic application of historical materialism began in earnest only during the late 1940s.

One of the first writers to consider Egypt's modern experience in Marxist terms was Aḥmad Ṣāliḥ Rushdī. A prominent member of the New Dawn group and chief editor of its organ, *Al-Fajr al-jadīd,* in 1945 he published *Krūmir fī Miṣr.* The aim of this book was to explain why the British came to Egypt, why they stayed, and what the impact of their policies was. Its subject was the social and economic condition of Egypt. According to Rushdī, under Ismāʿīl, Egypt suffered from heavy foreign financial involvement that left it at the mercy of the capitalist market and its predatory politics. By the 1880s, when Egypt's market was already wide open, the British conquered the country and established their own monopoly system.[97] Free trade was no longer advocated. According to Rushdī, British economic policy in Egypt enabled it to find markets for its products, maintain its capacity for manufacturing, and thus keep the lid on its own interclass tensions, which would otherwise have resulted in civil war.[98] Indeed, "the essential purpose of Cromerian reforms was to open the Egyptian market to foreign capital in general and to British goods in particular."[99] Illustrating the long-term domestic damage of reforms, Rushdī argued that these policies benefited the foreigners, who, in any case, lived in Egypt only because it was

93. Al-Barrāwī believed in technological determinism as a central shaping force in history. Rāshid al-Barrāwī and Muḥammad Ḥamza ʿUlaysh, *Al-Taṭawwūr al-iqtiṣādī fī Miṣr fī-l-ʿaṣr al-ḥadīth,* 5th ed. (Cairo: Maktabat al-nahḍa al-miṣriyya, 1954), pp. 53–88, 136–184.

94. Meijer, *The Quest for Modernity,* p. 82.

95. These writings were *British Imperialism in Egypt,* by Elinor Burns, and *Egypt's Ruin: A Financial and Administrative Record,* by Fedor Aronovich Rothstein. The latter was translated into Arabic by Muḥammad Badrān as *Tārīkh al-mas'ala al-miṣriya, 1875–1910* (Cairo: Lajnat al-ta'līf wa-l-tarjama wa-l-nashr, 1936).

96. Botman, *The Rise of Egyptian Communism,* p. 39.

97. Aḥmad Ṣāliḥ Rushdī, *Krūmir fī Miṣr* (Cairo: Dār al-qarn al-ʿishrīn, 1945), pp. 14–15, 18, 28, 38.

98. Ibid., pp. 33–34.

99. Ibid., p. 62.

extremely profitable.[100] Thus, while the upper classes accumulated wealth, the peasants were impoverished, and a new stratum of landowners emerged at their expense.[101] Though clearly not a full-fledged implementation of historical materialism (such studies would appear only a decade later), Rushdī's analysis was still an alternative to royal and academic schools of history.

Meanwhile, at about the same time, Aḥmad Ṣādiq Sa'd published *Mushkilat al-fallāḥ* (1945). A cofounder of the New Dawn group, he set out in this work to explain the miserable condition of peasants in twentieth-century Egypt and why they were denied the benefits of modernity. The book echoed the social agenda of the New Dawn group, which supported radical agrarian policies. Drawing on a broad framework of analysis, Sa'd showed how social and economic problems were the outcome of capitalist and imperialist intervention in Egypt. Thus, he provided a functional explanation for the misery of the *fallāḥ* in relation to the large landowners, whom he viewed as parasites.[102]

The next and most impressive stage in Marxist historical thought was established by Fu'ād Mursī (1925–90). The son of railway worker and a future leader of the communist movement, he published *Taṭawwur al-ra'smāliyya wa kifāḥ al-ṭabaqāt fī Miṣr* (The Development of Capitalism and Class Struggle in Egypt) in May 1949. Mursī's book ushered in a new systematic understanding of historical materialism. Only twenty-five years old, Mursī made it his modest mission to implement in Egypt what he had seen and learned from French communists. A history book was the proper place to begin.[103] According to him, the history of Egypt since 1798 was a "precise implementation of the laws of dialectic materialism *(al-mādiya al-jadaliya).*"[104] Based on such laws, his understanding of modern Egyptian history from 1798 to 1949 was the following: Napoleon brought the ideas of the French bourgeoisie to Egypt, and Muḥammad 'Alī's policies of centralization, national unity, elimination of backward political elements, industrialization, agrarian reform, and close commercial ties with Europe established the Egyptian bourgeoisie on firm ground. Drawing on these trends, Ismā'īl deepened ties with Europe and introduced capitalism to Egypt with greater force than ever before. The bourgeoisie flourished (17–19).In 1881 the exploited peasants revolted against this feudalist-capitalist order, and the increasingly nationalized bourgeoisie joined in with a call for constitutionalism (20–22). However, despite initial success, the revolt failed because of the coalition of colonialism and feudalism,

100. Ibid., p. 46.

101. Ibid., pp. 77–81, 84–85, 88–89.

102. Meijer, *The Quest for Modernity,* pp. 110–111

103. Botman, *The Rise of Egyptian Communism,* pp. 104ff.

104. Fu'ād Mursī, *Taṭawwur al-ra'smāliyya wa kifāḥ al-ṭabaqāt fī Miṣr* (1949; Cairo: Kitābāt al-miṣrī al-jadīd, al-maktaba al-ishtirākiyya, 1990), p. 17.

the weakness of the peasants' leadership (including that of the army), and the lack of decisive action on the part of the bourgeoisie (24). Next, the landowners collaborated with the British. Thus, the forces of reaction *(rajʿiyya)* grew stronger, and the revolutionary movement was halted (24–25).

By the turn of the century, the nationalized bourgeoisie formed political parties, fought against imperialism, and perennially collaborated with the toiling classes. However, the diverse economic interests of the bourgeoisie and its fear of a Bolshevik-style revolution postponed the socialist revolution (24–25), hence, the partial success of the 1919 Revolution. During the 1930s the bourgeoisie began to collaborate with the landowners, forming new parties with them. The fear of fascism drove the bourgeois Wafd Party to collaborate closely with colonialism and sign the 1936 agreement (31–32). During World War II, Egypt was put in the service of imperialism, and the class struggle intensified (33–34). Since by that stage, the bourgeoisie had lost its national thrust and supported only policies that coincided with its own economic interests, it moved against the workers, betrayed the revolutionary cause of democracy, and eliminated the revolution from within (38). With Ismāʿīl Ṣidqī in mind (38–39), Mursī ended his analysis with the inevitable conclusion that only the working class could fight against imperialism and feudalism (53–55). With this conclusion, it is hardly surprising that the rest of his history book was a blueprint for the formation of the Egyptian Communist Party. He established it in 1950.[105] Some Marxists, especially those who espoused Leninism, had now joined the already established tradition of partisan historiography.

Partisan Yet Innovative

Shaped by Marxist ideology, these historians tended to focus on a number of issues that were organic to the doctrine: tracing the growth of the productive forces, characterizing the various relations of production, explaining transitions among various modes of production, studying class formation, and analyzing revolutionary changes in the superstructure. Even though the motivation for studying these subjects was political, Marxist historiography raised crucial questions that were extremely productive for social history. For instance, before Marxist historiography, there was little interest in studying the history of landownership or the wretched poverty of the *fallāḥ*. Class was not a category for historical investigation. None of Ghurbāl's students studied such things. The same is true also for nationalist and royal historians. Though Marxist historiography was just in its formative stages of development, already during the 1940s it had carved out for itself a theoretical space that was innovative and ambitious.

105. The new Communist Party was not the biggest Marxist organization in Egypt.

Under the critical eye of Marxists, terms that had gained meaning directly from colonial historiography were now viewed differently. For instance, according to Mursī and to a lesser extent Rushdī, historical change is caused by the interplay of productive forces and relations of production that necessitate a change on the political and ideological level (i.e., the superstructure). Such changes were usually conceived in revolutionary terms, since they provide evidence for the truthfulness and the inevitability of the Marxist doctrine. Indeed, in place of "reforms," Marxists were always fascinated by the concept of revolution as the ultimate marker of changes in the superstructure level.[106]

Yet, the different notions of reform and revolution were just the tip of a linguistic and conceptual iceberg. By the 1950s, the Marxists had firmly established an elaborate linguistic apparatus. Investing cultural energy in developing appropriate linguistic resources was a conscious effort; new modes of thought and action necessitated new language.[107] Thus, the following terms became increasingly ubiquitous: progressive thought *(tafkīr taqaddumī),* revolutionary movement *(ḥaraka thawriyya),* revolutionary theory *(naẓariya thawriyya),*class struggle *(kifāḥ al-ṭabaqāt),* feudalism *(iqṭāʿ),* dialectic materialism *(al-mādiya al-jadaliya),* reaction *(rajʿiyya),* police state *(dawla bulīsiyya),* class consciousness *(waʿy ṭabaqī),* and class formation *(tabalwur al-ṭabaqāt).*[108]

In hindsight, however, we can see that much of this terminology was not yet persuasively tied into comprehensive historical explanations. Hence, rather than being an organic part of the text, it usually appeared in introductions and conclusions. Nonetheless, what distinguished Marxist historians from royal, academic, and nationalist historians was their language, concepts, and shared body of interests, questions, hypotheses, and historical emphases. Novelist Fatḥī Ghānim comically captured the appeal of this language when Shawqī's girlfriend, Mabrūka, describes the answers she often heard to her queries: "long phrases whose meaning I did not understand (but even still, I could not resist his eyes.)"[109]

Like all other local schools of historical thought that were rooted in the nineteenth century, Marxism believed that objective scientific knowledge was possible and that the progress of mankind was exclusively centered in Europe.[110] However,

106. Rigby, "Marxist Historiography," p. 902.

107. Aḥmad Saʿīd, "Qāmūs al-iqtiṣād al-siyāsī," originally published in *Al-Fajr al-jadīd* (January 11, 1949), reprinted in Saʿd, *Ṣafaḥāt min al-yasār,* pp. 358–363; Moghith, "Marxisme égyptien et Marxisme occidental," pp. 78–81.

108. Mursī, *Taṭawwur al-ra'smāliyya,* pp. 15, 17, 24, 40; and Rushdī, *Krūmir fī Miṣr,* p. 5.

109. Later in the novel Mabrūka becomes a committed revolutionary. Ghanem, *The Man Who Lost His Shadow,* p. 64.

110. Mursī also thought that Egypt was backward. Mursī, *Taṭawwur al-ra'smāliyya,* p. 17.

notwithstanding this common ground, the conceptual world of Marxists differed markedly from that of the other schools. Specifically, Marxists believed that "scientific knowledge expresses itself in general statements about the lawful behavior of phenomena."[111] History was thus conceived as a law-bound process with permanent categorical structures. The task of the historian, therefore, was to uncover these hidden laws of historical development.[112]

From a political perspective, conventional, European-inspired Marxism assumed that the overall direction of historical progress is a given and that the role of politics is merely that of shaping specific forms within a given process. Leninism, in turn, "modified this notion by voluntarism that stressed the centrality of the party."[113] Thus, in Lenin's conception, the party was a suprahistorical force that could influence the pace and direction of historical progress and engender revolution. In the Soviet Union, this understanding led to "the subordination of historical research and writing to day-by-day strategies of the party."[114] In Egypt, it encouraged pioneers such as Mursī to think seriously about how to "help history" by establishing an efficient political mechanism. Evidently, Leninism shaped Mursī's interpretation of history to such a degree that the natural extension of it was the establishment of the Egyptian Communist Party.[115]

CONCLUSION

In 1945 socialist thinker Salāma Mūsa published a short manifesto titled "Ḥurriyat al-ʿaql fī Miṣr." It was issued by Israel Marcel's Dār al-fajr. A year later both the author and the publisher ran into trouble. The author was arrested on charges of sabotage, and the Marxist publishing house was closed down. "Ḥurriyat al-ʿaql" protested "press censorship, licensing of the press, and anti-socialist laws."[116] Though this article was undoubtedly a courageous statement on behalf of freedom of speech, limits on thought were also posed from within, at least where history writing was concerned. In this chapter, I have argued that, as much as partisan historiography was an essential tool for the success of national struggle, it made a dubious long-term contribution to independent nonpolitical thinking.

Of the two forms of partisanship discussed here, the allegorical one appears to have been especially detrimental to the free flow of ideas. Allegory was an

111. Iggers, *Historiography in the Twentieth Century,* p. 79.

112. Mursī, *Taṭawwur al-ra'smāliyya,* pp. 12–13.

113. Iggers, *Historiography in the Twentieth Century,* p. 81.

114. Ibid.

115. Mursī, *Taṭawwur al-ra'smāliyya,* pp. 111–113.

116. Vernon Egger, *A Fabian in Egypt: Salamah Musa and the Rise of the Professional Classes in Egypt, 1900–1939* (Lanham, MD: University Press of America, 1986), p. 239. See also Meijer, *The Quest for Modernity,* p. 106.

extremely succinct and visually expressive mode. An image of Zaghlūl, let alone a huge edifice in his memory, was enough to tell the entire story of modern Egypt. In a country in which high levels of illiteracy still existed, allegory increased the fictional component of history at the expense of the part that is true to historical reality. By this means, allegorical writing created histories that were contingent on fictions and thus could easily capture one's imagination. In addition, this type of historiography evolved over a long period of time and seems to have become a natural part of the cultural landscape.[117] This degree of cultural prominence made it difficult for a free historiographical marketplace of meaning to evolve. In other words, allegorical historiography threatened the process of cultural rejuvenation, as it enabled "old" and unuseful meanings to stay around simply because they were backed by political power. When finally substituted, a new, yet structurally similar, political dogma prevailed.

Marxism, the second type of partisanship, was more complex and innovative yet, in the end, equally problematic. Intellectually, Marxists assumed that lawful historical development is the outcome of social conflict rooted in economic inequality. Politically, they thought they possessed the key to a comprehensive solution to Egypt's problems. Hence, there was no separation of theoretical knowledge and (political) practice, and, naturally, each could be compromised in order to satisfy the demands of the other. Their ability to provide a critical view of the present in light of past experience was dependent on the prevailing political circumstances.

In contrast with partisanship, only the activity of academic historians was framed by a strong ethical commitment by the 1950s. Though academics had their own biases, they intentionally avoided contemporary historiography, since its practice contradicted their scholarly values of rectitude and impartiality. While admittedly nationalist, academic historiography did not see itself as an allegory for the nation. This was its main source of authority. Undoubtedly, this situation created a tremendous pressure on young historians to use their authority in support of partisanship. The question is, for how long could subsequent generations of young academic historians resist the lures and temptations of partisan engagement and political power? As long as the power-balance impasse among popular political organizations, party politics, the monarchy, and the British remained stable, there was enough room for historiographical pluralism and independent thought. But what would happen if political power were to be concentrated in the hands of the few?

117. For criticism of this phenomenon, see Yunān Labīb Rizq, "Bayna al-mawḍū'iyya wa-l-taḥazzub fī kitābat tārīkh al-aḥzāb al-siyāsiyya fī Miṣr," in 'Abdallāh, ed., *Tārīkh Miṣr,* pp. 363–374.

7

Demonstrating History

The 1950s

The decade that followed the events of July 1952 critically altered the conventional assumptions of post–World War I Egyptian historiography. This impact was obvious. A variety of state-owned media invoked the memory of past events on a daily basis. Indeed, over the years, scholars had been drawn to the extensive usage of the past during the 1950s. Subscribing to the idea that the task of historiography is mainly that of studying shifts in historical representation, they emphasized the changing image of several rulers and popular leaders.[1] Though the issue of changing historical images was the most visible historiographical trait of post-1952 Egypt, more significant developments in the conceptualization of the past took place during this era.

Attentive to the weight of these conceptual changes, I argue in this chapter that the hermeneutic process of analyzing historical evidence was replaced with the tendency to demonstrate the historic value of present political acts. Rather than extracting new meaning out of history, the historians' only task was to draw analogies and identify metaphors and symbolism that justified and celebrated the political present. While this usage of the past was extremely efficient in forging Egypt's new revolutionary identity, it came at the price of sacrificing a more realist process of historical representation that insisted on analyzing historical testimonies. When history writers no longer had to prove the validity of their

1. Thomas Mayer's study on the changing image of Aḥmad 'Urābī was the most original and exhaustive survey of this kind. Mayer, *The Changing Past*, pp. 28–57. According to Gorman, early revolutionary historiography was characterized by "a negative view of the monarchy." Gorman, *Historians, State and Politics*, p. 53.

statements by submitting them to an elaborate process of scrutiny, the very value of truthfulness in historical writings was undermined as well.

The first section of the chapter's five covers the appropriation and transformation of al-Rāfiʿī's national epic and of Amīn Saʿīd's Pan-Arab histories into a new brand of revolutionary historiography. This epic and these histories treated the past as a mere series of analogies and metaphors whose object was to demonstrate the glorious achievement of the postcolonial moment of triumph. The second section shows that this evasion of a critical engagement with the past was turned into a practical philosophy of history that favored a historic act in the present over the understanding of the historical past. Together, these two sections form the core of my argument.

The rest of the chapter provides additional background on other historiographical and intellectual developments. The third and fourth sections supplement the central argument by dealing with changes in the structure of the intellectual elite and the viable networks that secured its existence. An analysis of Ghurbāl's post-1952 intellectual role illustrates the degree of academic incompatibility with the prevalent revolutionary culture.

The last section examines in great detail the writings of a second generation of Marxist historians. The fact that many of these historians were active in various communist organizations complicated their relationship with the state and subjected them to the regional and international politics of communism as such. It thus made them vulnerable to accusations of collaboration with foreign political forces. Communist writers began developing an Egyptian brand of scientific socialism in contrast to the self-congratulatory revolutionary historiography and the marginalized position of academic writings. Far more analytical and engaging with concrete political dilemmas, they channeled their energies into developing methods and mechanisms of central planning. Thus, rather than "demonstrating history," Marxists sought to control it. Indeed, as we shall see in chapter 8, in 1962 the state embraced a similar form of scientific socialism as its guiding theoretical framework.

HISTORY AS A CURSORY REVIEW OF THE PAST

Postmonarchic Egypt was hungry for a new view of itself. Referring to the past seventy years since the end of the British occupation, writer and journalist Anwar al-Jindī maintained that though "there were many books on Farūq, Fu'ād, Ismāʿīl, Saʿd Zaghlūl, al-Naḥḥās, politics, nationalism, and society, most of them were false."[2] According to him, save for al-Rāfiʿī, Fatḥī Raḍwān, and a few members of

2. Al-Jindī was associated with the Muslim Brotherhood. Anwar al-Jindī, "Hal yuktabu al-tārīkh min jadīd?" *Al-Risāla,* September 1, 1952, p. 985.

the Muslim Brotherhood, everyone else compromised the truth.[3] Thus, according to al-Jindī, a culture of systematic falsification governed Egypt's public life. Following a brief analysis of what he thought truth in history was, al-Jindī ordered scholars to "rewrite history!"[4] In calling for rewriting, he in fact referred to a comprehensive process of cultural reshuffling, since, as he said, "our entire history is in disarray."[5] His words resonated well, yet history was not rewritten.

As far as al-Rāfiʿī was concerned, there was not much rewriting to do. All that was needed was a public acknowledgment that he was right and all the others (royal historians, academics, and Wafdists) were wrong. Thus, rather than involving a profound process of rethinking historiographical procedures and methods of work, rewriting was limited to changes in the representation of historical figures and events. For a prolific writer such as al-Rāfiʿī, this was an easy task. In fact, he regarded the entire rewriting process as no more than a limited surgical intervention: "In many nations, true history requires only the correction of mistakes and not its rewriting in each generation and each regime change. Only distortions should be corrected in order for truth to prevail."[6] Thus, although opposing rewriting, al-Rāfiʿī set out to do precisely that in a series of articles titled "mistakes and distortions in the modern history of Egypt."[7] Over the course of four months he corrected all of these "mistakes" with no fear of retaliation.[8] Once the job was completed, the true revolutionary story of Egypt, as al-Rāfiʿī had toiled to narrate it since 1928, was ready for mass consumption.[9]

From the point of view of the Free Officers, who instigated the 1952 Revolution, gaining control of the radio building, broadcasting their manifesto, and even

3. Though politically outspoken, Raḍwān and the Muslim Brotherhood did not write history. Ibid.

4. Ibid.

5. Anwar al-Jindī, "Taṭhīr al-tārīkh," *Al-Risāla,* September 15, 1952, p. 1043.

6. ʿAbd al-Raḥmān al-Rāfiʿī, "Akhṭāʾ wa akādhīb fī tārīkh Miṣr al-hadīth," *Al-Hilāl,* March 1952, p. 31.

7. Various calls for rewriting had been heard since 1952, but al-Rāfiʿī objected to all of them (see more below). Aḥmad Ismāʿīl, *Ṣināʿat tārīkh Miṣr,* p. 252.

8. Among the corrected "mistakes" were a few rather major issues: the leadership of the people, the authoritarian style of Muḥammad ʿAlī, the compulsive financial habits of Khedive Ismāʿīl, the history of the Mixed Courts, the myth of constitutional life under Ismāʿīl, the incompetence of Khedive Tawfīq, and his role in bringing about the British occupation. ʿAbd al-Raḥmān al-Rāfiʿī, *Al-Hilāl,* February 1952, pp. 20–24, March, pp. 26–31, May, pp. 33–37.

9. See a condensed form of this revolutionary history from 1798 to 1952: ʿAbd al-Raḥmān al-Rāfiʿī, "10 ḥawādith ʿuzma fī-l-sittīn sana al-akhīra," *Al-Hilāl,* January 1953, pp. 29–35.

exiling King Fārūq three days later were the easiest parts of the revolution. A much more complicated issue was explaining their place in the overall scheme of history. Who were they and what did they want? The first few days of the revolution were indeed marked by uncertainty as the Officers reiterated the slogans and general statements of their generation: national liberation and socioeconomic justice. But there was nothing unusual or revolutionary about any of this. They needed, at least in the short run, something more concrete to hold on to. Conveniently, then, just at that point, the heritage, prestige, and historical perception of the National Party were made available to them.

Thus, exactly two days after the army took power, at around two in the afternoon the phone rang in the office of the chief warden in a formerly British prison facility, seven miles north of Cairo. On the line was a staff member of the prime minister's office. He asked to make sure that in four hours, Fatḥī Raḍwān, a prisoner since the burning of Cairo eighteen months earlier, would arrive at the airport, where a special airplane would be waiting to take him to Alexandria. That evening, Raḍwān was already making suggestions to Egypt's new and perplexed leadership.[10] Some months later he assumed a ministerial office that revolutionized the public style of Egyptian politics. For the next six years, he headed Egypt's Ministry of National Guidance (Wizārat al-irshād al-qawmī). With many resources at his disposal, he put the historical perception of the National Party to work for Egypt's new government.

Almost immediately, al-Rāfiʿī's history was officially embraced. Marking the six-month anniversary of the revolution in a colorful "liberation festival," General Muḥammad Naguib, the figurehead of the revolution, delivered the following speech:

> What our forefathers said on May 13, 1803 [ʿUmar Makram's revolt], the grandsons say on July 23, 1952. We should internalize these lessons and teach our children that this is the only way to end tyranny in Egypt. It is the heritage of ʿUmar Makram that we carry on. Throughout history the Egyptian people were continuously chained until they raised their heads again in September 1881, when ʿUrābī repeated Makram's words. And this is precisely what we say again in July 1952. Then Muṣṭafa Kāmil along with Muḥammad Farīd gathered the people around them and brought about the 1919 Revolution.[11]

These words stemmed from Naguib's acknowledgment that al-Rāfiʿī's books "serve as the basis for the military movement and national ammunition for the

10. Baybars, *Asrār ḥukūmat yūlyū,* pp. 94–102.

11. During the festival the name of Ismāʿīliyya Square was changed to Liberation Square (Maydan al-taḥrīr). *Al-Ahrām,* January 24, 1953, pp. 1, 9.

nation as a whole."[12] Al-Rāfiʿī reciprocated with an article about the fifty-one-year-old general and Aḥmad ʿUrābī.[13] The analogy was not lost on anyone.

Simultaneously, Raḍwān's previously banned film on Muṣṭafa Kāmil was released. The film was a true cinematographic event that visually supported the Free Officers' claim to power. According to Joel Gordon, "Punctuated by excerpts from Kamil's spellbinding oratory, delivered with conviction by acting novice and striking look-alike Anwar Aḥmad, the film is the first to depict the British occupation, as well as nationalist resistance to it."[14] Next, a new torso statue of Muṣṭafa Kāmil was inaugurated.[15] Then, in February 1953, on the annual memorial day of Muṣṭafa Kāmil and, in November 1953, on Muḥammad Farīd's memorial day, the two legendary leaders were reburied in an official state ceremony. The burial location was a recently completed pseudo-Mamluk domed mausoleum. It was, in fact, the same mausoleum that al-Rāfiʿī had envisioned in response to the inauguration of Saʿd Zaghlūl's mausoleum some twenty years earlier. The funeral procession was joined by thousands of civilians. The new revolutionary leadership attended it. Various speeches reminded the crowds of the dedication and sacrifice of past generations. Those who spoke vowed to continue the struggle in the path of Muḥammad Kurayyim, ʿUmar Makram, Aḥmad ʿUrābī, and, of course, Muṣṭafa Kāmil and Muḥammad Farīd. Both memorial services inspired writers, publicists, and journalists to retell the new revolutionary history of modern Egypt. All that was written and said in the months following the 1952 Revolution was a reiteration, and at times an elaboration, of al-Rāfiʿī's histories.[16] As time went by, more commemorative projects were initiated, such as the building of the ʿUmar Makram mosque in center city Cairo and the changing of street and square names.[17]

Nonetheless, the political life of dead bodies was not enough to ground the revolution in the hearts and minds of young Egyptians. Only profound events, such as the 1956 nationalization of the Suez Canal, transformed the public image of the revolution. Nasser's defiance of the old colonial instinct of gunboat diplomacy brought the colonial era in the Middle East to a close and ushered in a more

12. The interview is cited by Aḥmad Ismāʿīl, *Ṣināʿat tārīkh Miṣr al-ḥadīth,* p. 264. See also Crabbs, "Egyptian Intellectuals and the Revolution," pp. 259–262.

13. ʿAbd al-Raḥmān al-Rāfiʿī, "ʿUrābī wa Muḥammad Najīb," *Al-Hilāl,* September 1952, pp. 9–12.

14. Gordon, *Revolutionary Melodrama,* p. 62.

15. Di-Capua, "Embodiments of the Revolutionary Spirit," pp. 101–103.

16. Ibid. See also Muhammad Naguib, *Egypt's Destiny* (London: Victor Gollancz, 1955), pp. 48, 148; and ʿAbd al-Bāsiṭ Muḥammad Ḥasan, "Al-Sayyid Muḥammad Kurayyim," *Al-Risāla,* September 22, 1952, pp. 1063–1064.

17. Di-Capua, "Embodiments of the Revolutionary Spirit," p. 106.

overt phase in regional cold war politics. The aim of the Suez nationalization act and the deeper meaning embedded in it were to free Egypt from all forms of colonial domination—military, political, economic, cultural, and intellectual. Along with modernization, this was the historic task of the anti-colonial project.[18] Hence, unleashing part of the nation's subjectivity from colonial control was a staggering triumph that concluded the unfinished 1919 Revolution. This moment fell squarely into the logic of revolutionary historiography.

Following the war, the minister of education Kamāl al-Dīn Ḥusayn asked al-Rāfiʿī to prepare an abridged version of his project, suitable for the usage of pupils. Titled *Miṣr al-mujāhida fī-l-ʿaṣr al-ḥadīth* (Militant Egypt in the Modern Age), it hit the market in 1957.[19] This abridgement of the series located quotes from President Nasser's speeches with each relevant historical event, a form of authoritative commentary that bonded past and (political) present.[20] Simultaneously, a growing number of writers began entertaining the metahistorical idea of popular struggle. The result was a stream of publications, in fact a trend in its own right, that continued well into the 1960s.[21] One of the most comprehensive accounts was written by a certain Muḥammad Amīn Ḥasūna. Hostile to the royal project, right after the revolution he returned to ʿĀbdīn archive. Salvaging materials that had been systematically ignored, he published a corrected account of Egypt's modern history in two volumes: *Kifāḥ al-shaʿb* (The People's Struggle). This book began with ʿUmar Makram and ended with Nasser and, as expected, followed the evolution of nationalist revolutionary consciousness.[22]

Thus, though it was by no means a rethinking of history writing, the historiography of popular struggle seeped deep into culture. Especially influenced was the education system. The questions on the final history exam of secondary schools asked pupils to compare the revolutionary events of 1881–82 with those of 1952, the French defeat in Acre (1799) with resistance to the British in Port Saʿīd

18. Indeed, one of the popular slogans of the 1919 Revolution, "al-qanā li-Miṣr la Miṣr li-l-qanā" the canal for Egypt, not Egypt for the canal), invoked the problem of the Suez Canal. Ibrāhīm ʿĀmir, *Taʾmīm al-qanā* (Cairo: Dār al-nadīm, October 1956), p. 20.

19. ʿAbd al-Raḥmān al-Rāfiʿī, *Miṣr al-mujāhida fī-l-ʿaṣr al-ḥadīth* (1957; repr., Cairo: Dār al-hilāl, 1989), vol. 1, p. 7.

20. Ibid., vol. 2, p. 110. See another example on p. 164.

21. Wafīq ʿAbd al-ʿAzīz Fahmī, *Qaḍiyyat al-jalāʾ: Thawrat 23 Yūlyū 1952* (Cairo: Kutub qawmiyya, al-dār al-qawmiyya li-l-ṭibāʿa wa-l-nashr, n.d.); Masʿūd ʿAbd al-Hādī, *Al-Thawrāt fī Miṣr* (Cairo: Maṭbaʿat mukhaymar, 1954); *Kifāḥ al-shaʿb wa-l-jalāʾ*, Ikhtarnā laka 26 [series] (Cairo: Dār al-Maʿārif, n.d.).

22. Muḥammad Amīn Ḥasūna, *Kifāḥ al-shaʿb min ʿUmar Makram ila Jamāl ʿAbd al-Nāṣir* (Cairo: Maṭābiʿ al-ṣabāḥ, 1955), vol. 1, pp. 8–10.

(1956), and also the failed British attack in 1807 with their defeat of 1956.[23] At the same time, in some parts of Egypt, pupils were asked to get rid of their old history books. In a relatively short span of time, Egypt's history was reduced to a transcendental continuum of several evolutionary dates (1798, 1882, 1919, 1956) in which each event miraculously led to another. It would take al-Rāfiʿī some years to realize that he had authorized the abuse of Egypt's historiography. Meanwhile, he celebrated. In the pages of *Al-Hilāl,* al-Rāfiʿī urged young Egyptians to internalize the lessons of this history.[24]

With surprising speed, the theme of popular struggle was adapted to the screen. As early as 1957, the film *Port Said (Būr saʿīd)* was released. According to Joel Gordon, it was a "heroic tale of underground resistance to foreign aggression."[25] Another film of comradeship and anti-British struggle was *The Prisoner of Abu Zaʿbal (Sajīn abū zaʿbal).* Both films added a visual aspect to the histories that were already sold in bookshops and broadcast over the radio. Thus, a historiographical tradition that began with Muḥammad Ṣabrī and continued with al-Rāfiʿī reached its zenith only after 1956, when it appeared as a full-fledged multimedia presentation of epic proportions.

But, especially after 1956, Nasserism, too, had a strong Pan-Arab emphasis, which also was in need of a history to support it. Though we tend to think of Eastern Arab nationalism as one coordinated project, it was divided between two different nationalist efforts until Nasser's time. The first, with which we are already familiar, was the politics of Egyptian nationalism. The second was Syrian nationalism, which, according to most writers, originated with the great Arab Revolt of World War I and was later fragmented into Syrian, Iraqi, Jordanian, and Saudi streams. Despite the will for a meaningful Pan-Arab project, present since the 1930s, the Egyptian and the Syrian movements continued to run parallel to each other, both politically and intellectually.[26] By squeezing a broad cultural vision into a sensational program for political unity, Nasserism made the most serious attempt to bring these two movements together. For the first time in its history, the 1956 constitution declared Egypt an Arab state. Concrete regional political steps followed. The February 1958 establishment of the United Arab Republic (hereafter UAR) with Syria marked the success of this agenda. This act shook the Arab world and its allies in the postcolonial world.

23. Riyāḍ Baqariūs et al., eds., *Mūjaz al-tārīkh al-muṣawwar, al-tarbiyya al-waṭaniyya* (Cairo: Wizārat al-tarbiyya wa-l-taʿlīm, 1958), pp. 161–163.

24. ʿAbd al-Raḥmān al-Rāfiʿī, "Fī tārīkh durūs li-l-shabāb," *Al-Hilāl,* April 1953, pp. 20–23.

25. Gordon, *Revolutionary Melodrama,* pp. 74–75.

26. Neither the institution of the Arab League nor the 1948 war united these two nationalist streams.

Never before had a state that had so recently won its independence after a long struggle willfully succumbed to rule by a polity with which it did not even share a border. But whatever reservations Syrians might have had with relation to this project—and these were many—they had little influence on how the unification was viewed and legitimized historically. Here, the focus of discussion shifts to Amīn Saʿīd.

Amīn Saʿīd, born in 1890 in Ladhakiyya, Syria, was one of the most prolific of all Pan-Arab history writers. His father introduced him to the family business of publishing in an early age. After leaving the family's small publishing house, Saʿīd traveled extensively in Syria, Lebanon, and Egypt, often working as a journalist. Later, he initiated his own Damascus-based journal, *Al-Kifāḥ* (The Struggle).[27] For Amīn Saʿīd, the Arab cause was a way of life. He met several of the leading figures of Syrian nationalism and began writing the history of the Arab/Syrian nationalism when Nasser was still in high school. And so, by the time Nasser's Pan-Arab agenda was launched, a host of Amīn's publications on Arab struggle and unity were already circulating.

In his writings, Amīn Saʿīd traced the revolutionary element in the histories of various Arab countries. A series of revolts—the 1916 revolt on the Arabian Peninsula, the 1919 in Egypt, the 1920 in Iraq, the 1921 in Tunisia, and the 1945 in Algeria—were regarded as true manifestations of this spirit.[28] Tying it to a greater historical sequence, he invoked the memory of the so-called unified Arab resistance to the Crusaders, the Mongols, the Ottomans (1831–39), and, of course, the 1956 Suez campaign. Like al-Rāfiʿī, yet independently of him, Saʿīd put forward a logic of history that perceived Arabism as a unified metahistorical force that permanently resisted foreign intrusion. Saʿīd's motto, "History repeats itself,"[29] assured the readers that the success of Pan-Arabism was guaranteed. Thus, in terms of scope, style of reasoning, and organization, Amīn Saʿīd's histories resembled those of al-Rāfiʿī. The histories of both were consumed as a transcendental series of unbelievable triumphal events. Both writers promoted a well-defined political cause and witnessed the triumph of their vision.[30] New

27. Ziriklī, *Al-Aʿlām,* vol. 2, pp. 20–21.

28. See Amīn Saʿīd, *Al-Thawra* (Cairo: Dār iḥyāʾ al-kutub al-ʿarabiyya, 1959), pp. 9–10; and especially Amīn Saʿīd, *Thawrāt al-ʿarab fī-l-qarn al-ʿishrīn* (Cairo: Dār al-hilāl, 1960), pp. 5–10.

29. Amīn Saʿīd, *Al-Jumhūrīya al-ʿarabiyya al-muttaḥida* (Cairo: Dār iḥyāʾ al-kutub al-ʿarabiyya, 1959), vol. 1, pp. 7–11.

30. Nonetheless, the two men had some scholarly differences. Saʿīd's account of ʿUrābī's motivations and achievements was far more critical and skeptical than the revised version of al-Rāfiʿi. Amīn Saʿīd, *Tārīkh Miṣr al-siyāsī min al-ḥamla al-fransiyya sanat 1798 ila inhiyār al-malakiyya 1952* (Cairo: Dār iḥyāʾ al-kutub al-ʿarabiyya, 1959), pp. 87–118.

histories were tailored to this model, and popular radio anchor Aḥmad Saʿīd broadcast this message.[31]

In hindsight, however, though Pan-Arabism achieved an overwhelming political presence and was able to mobilize various political, economic, and cultural resources on its behalf, it left hardly any historiographical mark. Regardless of the plethora of publications and radio broadcasts on the subject, no one clearly understood how to approach writing Pan-Arab history.[32] What sort of historiography suited Pan-Arabism? There was also a basic problem of the entrenchment of historiographical habits, for both theoretically and methodologically Egyptian historiography was firmly centered on the nation-state. In the perception of the Egyptian historiographical tradition, Pan-Arabism was first and foremost an Egyptian project, woven around the idea that Egypt should play a historically pivotal role in the region.[33] In 1959 the government prescribed to the universities several classes on national Arab history. Regardless of which ideas professors subscribed to, they were required to teach these classes.[34] However, neither they nor their students were obliged to write such histories themselves. It seems that students had difficulties imagining histories that transcended national boundaries.[35] As late as 1965, only a handful of students ventured to translate the Pan-Arab cause into history.[36]

Hence, neither academic historians nor amateur writers were able to create thought-provoking Pan-Arab histories. Though rhetorically Pan-Arab historiography protested the colonial division of the Arab lands, it also perpetuated the fragmentation of the Arab subject in practice and theory.[37] For instance, the

31. Anwār al-Jindī, *Maʿrakat al-muqāwama al-ʿarabiya* (Cairo: Maṭbaʿat al-taḥrīr, 1961), pp. 3–5.

32. Meijer found Pan-Arabism an intellectual trend of secondary importance. Meijer, *The Quest for Modernity,* p. 6. Anthony Gorman thinks there was never a clear sense of what Pan-Arab historiography was. Gorman, *Historians, State and Politics,* p. 63.

33. The ideas of rightful Egyptian hegemony and Egypt's self-perception of grandeur are unexplored territory. Early on, but especially since the nineteenth century, Egyptians perceived themselves as natural leaders in the region and made concerted efforts to play an important role in Africa as well as Greater Syria. The books of Muḥammad Ṣabrī on the "Egyptian Empire" echoed this idea.

34. Fauzi Najjar, "State and University in Egypt during the Period of Socialist Transformation, 1961–1967," *Review of Politics* 38, no. 1 (1976): p. 61.

35. Even graduate students who did not study Egypt were narrowly focused on one state alone.

36. The same was also true in relation to Nasser's third-world agenda. For a survey of graduate theses and dissertations, see Qāsim Hishmat, *Dalīl al-rasāʾil al-jāmiʿiya* (Cairo: Kulliyat al-ādāb, 1996), vol. 1, pp. 181–204; and *MTM* 13 (1967): pp. 411–415.

37. In the 1970s, when Egyptian historians actually went to live and teach in Arab countries, some longtime beliefs were shaken.

persistent vilification of the Ottomans and the denial of the synchronic value of the Ottoman past blinded Arab historians to their common experience. More than anything else, however, Pan-Arab histories à la Amīn Saʿīd, because of their utopian sense of history as a projection of future success, were philosophically incapable of coping with the political failures of Pan-Arabism. If we are to comprehend events such as the 1961 disintegration of the UAR and the war in Yemen by Amīn's logic, they can have been only historical accidents or conspiracies. Such incomprehensible failures paralyzed this most eloquent and prolific advocate of Pan-Arabism. He died in 1967.

LIFT UP YOUR HEAD, MY BROTHER! (WE ARE GOING TO MAKE HISTORY)

The Nasser regime's sense of history, however, did not involve merely an appropriation and modification of already existing histories. Though the Free Officers had much respect for present nationalist writers, by their own actions they introduced a practical distinction between "writing history" and "making history."[38] Obviously, they sought to make it. The drive to make history originated from the populist nature of Nasserism. Like other political systems of this kind (such as Castro's Cuba), Nasserism had a constant need for public demonstration of its achievements. It was exhibitionist.[39] Thus, public display became a central feature of Nasserite politics. Indeed, through popular festivals and ceremonies the revolution demonstrated how it actually made history happen.

Orchestrated by the Ministry of National Guidance, an endless stream of festivals, holidays, congresses, memorials, inaugurations, commemorations, and other political rituals demonstrated that the revolution was making history by actually producing events.[40] Some of those events, such as the Festival of Science

38. The following discussion is based on recent observations about the philosophy of history and fascist Italy. While I do not claim that Nasserism was fascist, its populist style of operation and thought had a strong resemblance to some populist traits that exited in Mussolini's Italy. Claudio Fogu, "Actualism and the Fascist Historic Imaginary," *History and Theory* 42, no. 2 (May 2003): pp. 196–221.

39. Other traits of populism are: being urban in nature and origin, having a multiclass orientation, having charismatic authority, and having a militaristic appearance. Michael Conniff, "Introduction: Towards a Comparative Definition of Populism," in Conniff, ed., *Latin-American Populism in Comparative Perspectives* (Albuquerque: University of New Mexico Press, 1982), pp. 13–27. See also Elie Podeh and Onn Winckler, eds., *Rethinking Nasserism* (Gainesville: University Press of Florida, 2004), pp. 1–69.

40. See a list of "historic" revolutionary achievements that the regime published for its six-month anniversary: *Al-Ahrām*, January 23, 1953, pp. 1, 7. See also Aḥmad ʿAṭiyya

(ʿĪd al-ʿilm) and Chickens' Week (aimed at encouraging agricultural production), were quite meaningless in and of themselves, yet, when seen as part of a stream of happenings, they persuasively conveyed the sense that Egypt was making progress.[41] The agrarian reform was a good example of this style of politics. Such reform was debated for years during the monarchic era, but hardly anything of substance happened. Certainly, peasants with no land had no expectation of a change in their condition.

Under Nasser, the agrarian reform was launched immediately. Once completed, a popular festival took place for several days, during which Nasser and his comrades traveled to remote villages, met peasants, and personally distributed the land to them. It was a revolutionary extravaganza of justice making that was called the "procession of benevolence" *(mawkib al-khayr)*.[42] The redundancy of endless monarchic talk on reform was substituted at once with swift and visible action. Historic events unfolded in front the citizens' eyes.

Speech making was the center of these revolutionary congregations. A striking example was Nasser's astounding Suez nationalization speech on the evening of July 26, 1956 (the commemoration of Farūq's exile). The speech was coded. When Nasser mentioned the code word *De Lesseps*, the French engineer who envisioned the Canal, special teams on alert stormed into the offices of the Suez Canal Company and nationalized it.[43] That night, Egyptians learned that Nasser's words had activated history. The war broke out, Nasser became Nasserism, and Egypt won its long awaited bid for independence. With more fantastic historic events unfolding each week, Nasserism appeared as "an historic agent whose acts were not merely significant in the eyes of history (and historians) but rather actively *signified* history in the present."[44] Thus, history was a present act that was called *historic*. History as a past act became marginal. This notion of historic acts collapsed past, present, and future into a continuum of sublime spectacle. It

---

Allāh, *Qāmus al-thawra al-miṣriyya* (Cairo: al-Maktaba al-anglū-miṣriyya, 1954), pp. 119, 134, 138–139.

41. On the two celebratory events, see ibid., p. 16.

42. See *Al-Muṣawwar,* July 2, 1954, p. 15; and *Al-Akhbār,* July 17, 1954, p. 3.

43. This codification was the reason that Nasser mumbled the name of the French engineer several times during this speech. This event was beautifully pictured in the film *Nasser 56* (1996).

44. Fogu, "Actualism and the Fascist Historic Imaginary," p. 200. Several such historic events transpired within a mere six years: the day of the revolution itself, the deposition of the king, the agrarian reform, the declaration of a republic, the Bandung conference (April 1955), the nationalization of the Suez Canal, the decision to build the High Dam, the 1956 defeat of imperialism, and the 1958 unification with Syria.

conveyed a simple, coherent, and logical sense of time that was generally referred to as the revolutionary era *('ahd)*. In a sense, it was as if the revolution nationalized time.

Developed out of action and without much philosophical fuss, this actualist philosophy of history lacked any theoretical text to support it. Instead, it was based on a fundamental distinction between *historic* and *historical*. While *historic* meant to engender history in the present, *historical* referred to a pluralist hermeneutic process whose object is the past. Slowly but surely, the revolution's *historic* sense of the present substituted the more realist politics of historical representation that had been the pillar of historical thought and practice since the late nineteenth century. Commenting on a similar reality in post-1968 Czechoslovakia, the dissident playwright Václav Havel complained about the substitution of history with what he called pseudohistory (i.e., *historic* events):

> Instead of events, we are offered nonevents; we live from anniversary to anniversary, from celebration to celebration, from parade to parade, from a unanimous congress to unanimous elections and back again; from a Press Day to an Artillery Day, and vice versa. *It is no coincidence that, thanks to the substitution for history, we are able to review everything that is happening in society past and future, by simply glancing at the calendar. . . .* whereas for our ancestors the repeated rituals always had a deep existential meaning, for us they are merely a routine performed for its own sake. *The government keeps them going to maintain the impression that history is moving.*[45]

With the horizons of Egyptian expectation opened wide as never before, this highly speculative vision of history became the principal codifier of Egyptian revolutionary identity. For some prominent members of the former cultural order, the elimination of the historical ideal was too much.

Thus far, the intellectual giant of the Egyptian Nahḍa, Ṭaha Ḥusayn, has not made an appearance in the pages of this work. As dean of Fu'ād University, he was familiar with Ghurbāl's project and had even sympathized with it. Yet, Ṭaha Ḥusayn never ventured into history writing proper and hardly commented on modern writing. He left this task to historians. This long silence on matters of historical thought and practice was broken in 1957, for he saw the celebration of the *historic* moment as a form of cultural threat. Hence, with the help of some friends, he decided to edit a school textbook that was designed, in both form and content, to challenge the actualist philosophy of history and its simplistic succession of historic triumphs in the present.

45. Václav Havel, *Open Letters: Selected Prose 1965–1990* (London: Faber and Faber, 1991), p. 74 (emphases added).

Structurally, Ḥusayn and his colleagues decided not to write a regular historical narrative. Instead, they fragmented Egypt's history by compiling original texts from the medieval era (Ibn Baṭṭūṭa, Ibn Khaldūn) to the present (Aḥmad Shafīq, Muḥammad Ḥusayn Haykal, al-Rāfiʿī, and even Nasser). Thus, rather than presenting one familiar story (modernistic transition under European tutelage or revolutionary struggle), they presented history as a confusing, yet beautifully rich and colorful, experience. In the preface to the book, Ṭaha Ḥusayn invited the young readership to make sense of this kaleidoscopic presentation and to form their own opinions and views about the past. In doing so, he substantiated his argument according to which history is a dynamic process of discovery and interpretation. In an era of exclamation marks, he encouraged pupils to be at ease with doubt: "[On reading these different versions of the same past,] your perplexity increases to the degree that you might question the entire value of history. You might even ask yourself, What is the best way to know the truth with regard to a past that is so distant from you in terms of time and place?"[46]

In order to convince the young readers that different points of view with regard to the past are not a dangerous anomaly but a welcome, and even a natural, cultural phenomenon, Ṭaha Ḥusayn then went on to explain some basic concepts of the philosophy of history. In plain language he clarified basic concepts of historical objectivity, perception of time, and possible causes for distortion of facts. Finally, he placed the responsibility for making sense out of the past on the reader himself: "Choose for yourself what you deem proper and reject what you think is erroneous."[47] Instead of being a mere spectator of historical events, the reader of this book was asked to bear responsibility.

Subverting the ruling vision of history, this modest compilation was a strong statement on behalf of historical interpretation and a sophisticated criticism of revolutionary certainties. In sharp contrast to cursory thought about the past, it conveyed the sense that history is a complicated, dynamic, and ever-changing process of search for meaning. History is a multilayered phenomenon in a permanent process of formation and reformation. Though the book included all the canonical revolutionary texts, it cast profound doubt on the uniform logic they called for. In that sense it was subversive. Nonetheless, this book was one drop in a sea of histories that provided only a cursory review of the past and thus undermined historical reasoning. Within this state of affairs, academia's task of defending this view comes into focus.

46. Ṭaha Ḥusayn et al., ed., *Fuṣūl mukhtāra min kutub al-tārīkh, min awāsiṭ al-qarn al-sābiʿ ila al-ʿaṣr al-ḥadīth* (Cairo: al-Maṭbaʿa al-amīriyya bi-l-Qāhira, wizārat al-tarbiyya wa-l-taʿlīm, 1957), p. i.

47. Ibid., p. v.

ON THE NETWORKS OF HISTORICAL THOUGHT

After reviewing the contours of early revolutionary historiography, we should examine more carefully what happened to the intellectuals of the old regime. Since the two years that followed the 1952 Revolution were marked by political uncertainty, there was room for cultural continuation. Later, in the wake of the 1954 power struggle between Nasser and Naguib, a more definitive direction in politics was taken. This shift critically influenced the human networks and the infrastructure on which history writing depended.

In February 1954, Egyptians went to the streets in support of Naguib's leadership over that of Nasser. A month later Naguib was ousted. Less than an hour after Naguib's deposition, Nasser, the new president of the republic, hurried to the old radio building in Cairo. With him was comrade Ṣāliḥ Sālim. It was the second time in less than two years that the Free Officers rushed to the radio station. Unlike in July 1952, this time they did not come in order to register another revolutionary message on empty tapes. This time there was no shocking message to air. Instead, the two arrived to erase Naguib's tapes. Every speech made by him since July 1952 and every mention of him, insignificant and remotely related to the politics of the day, were erased from the tapes.[48] This event was not an anomaly. In the months and years following the revolution, an enormous project of orchestrated amnesia took place. Everything from films and books to statues was treated in accordance to this harsh code of erasure and elimination. Even a beautiful laudatory poem by Ibrāhīm Ḥāfiẓ, written in the context of the centennial celebration of Muḥammad ʿAlī some fifty years earlier, was not spared.[49]

This new atmosphere marked the permanent suspension of liberalism as the primary source of inspiration for political and cultural organization.[50] At that point, it became clear that the political pluralism of parliamentary life was a thing of the past. Instead, Nasser had offered a benevolent dictatorship whose primary aim was liberation and modernization.[51] Gradually, major cultural establish-

48. The radio station workers were ready for the task, since they had just finished erasing tapes from the monarchic era. Baybars, *Asrār ḥukūmat yūlyū*, pp. 49–50.

49. In 1904, poet Muḥammd Shawqī had composed a poem in praise of the royal family. This poem presented Muḥammad ʿAlī as the founder of modern Egypt. Ibrāhīm Ḥāfiẓ responded with a laudatory poem of his own, but the lines that mentioned the royal family were expurgated from the seventh edition (of 1955). Sasson Somekh, "The Neo-classical Arabic Poets," in Muhammad Mustafa Badawi, ed., *Modern Arabic Literature* (Cambridge: Cambridge University Press, 1992), pp. 67–69.

50. Joel Gordon, *Nasser's Blessed Movement: Egypt's Free Officers and the July Revolution* (Oxford: Oxford University Press, 1992), pp. 125–156.

51. Meijer, *The Quest for Modernity*, pp. 162–167.

ments such as publishing, radio, and cinema were put under the direct control of Raḍwān's Ministry of National Guidance. A growing number of educated professionals worked in this sector. Their rise to prominence was coupled with the militarization of civilian life, in which junior military officers, with basic education, were assigned key positions only because they were trustworthy.[52] Hence, it was not unusual to find a military officer working as a cultural technocrat of sorts in a senior position, such as newspaper editor. As one historian ironically put it, "[The officers] became experts in all fields of life, including foreign policy, social affairs, atomic and nuclear energy, soccer, general sports, agrarian and educational reform, economics, transportation, urban planning, journalism, cinematography, and even ballet. . . . [They were experts] in everything and for everything."[53]

These officers were joined by various groups of low-level intellectuals who, under the monarchy, had been obscure figures of little importance. Some, such as Mas'ūd 'Abd al-Hādī, had come from humble origins. They were the first generation of urban literates with basic higher education or less, intellectual curiosity, and much drive for success. The intellectual icons of their generation were Ṭaha Ḥusayn, Maḥmūd 'Abbās al-'Aqqād, and Muḥammad Ḥusayn Haykal. This group had opted for social mobility and cultural status under the monarchy. However, they settled for less. Positions such as university professor, editor, and journalist were respected enough, but much to their disappointment, the rigid cultural hierarchy of the monarchic era hampered their upward mobility. In particular, they lacked the institutional and financial support of a university or a publishing house. As members of a generation that had experienced the second wave of modernization and its discontents (post-1930s), they readily selected radical solutions (Young Egypt). Eager to shape their own future with the modernistic tools they had acquired, they overlooked the dangers of authoritarianism.

Though ostensibly defenders of the previous order, after the 1952 Revolution they crossed the lines. A score of minor intellectuals joined Nasser's apparatus. The national goal of radical modernization through guided authoritarianism appealed to them.[54] The revolution gave them a stage, an agenda, protection, and a sense of freedom and self-importance. Their cultural activity in newspapers, haphazard cheap-print editions, new series of books, and radio lectures

52. In that period the tension between civilian experts and loyal ex-military men was known as the crisis of "ahl al-thiqa wa ahl al-khibra" (the people we trust and those who have knowledge and expertise). 'Ādil Ḥamūda, *Azmat al-muthaqafīn wa thawrat yūlyū* (Cairo: Maktabat madbūlī, 1985), pp. 239–242.

53. Ibid., p. 239.

54. On this issue, see part 2 of Meijer, *The Quest for Modernity.*

brought about a significant increase in the field of public information. Originally a Wafdist, Muṣṭafa al-Hifnāwi was one such low-level intellectual who contributed his expertise to the new regime. As a graduate student of history in Paris, he wrote a thesis on the history of the Suez Canal. On the basis of the confidential records of the Suez Canal Company, he illustrated the connection between the canal administration and "Egypt's impoverished and colonial status."[55] Nasser then appointed al-Hifnawī, as a self-proclaimed expert on the canal, its history, and why it should be nationalized, to the executive board of the Egyptian Canal Authority.[56]

Not all of those who went on to serve the new order, however, were marginal figures of mediocre intellectual achievements. Many, such as Rāshid al-Barrāwī, were capable individuals with full-fledged programs for reform. Believing in both modernity and authoritarianism, prominent intellectuals who had initially responded negatively to Nasserism eventually joined the system. As Meijer clarifies: "This change of attitude was . . . part of the authoritarian modernism most intellectuals upheld in their writing even before the July [1952] Revolution."[57] Hence, at least initially, the structure of the revolutionary bureaucracy consisted of professionals who had been in the previous order.

As time went by and competent professionals achieved prominence in economics and other fields, ex-military personnel and the least successful intellectuals of the previous era dominated the state-guided cultural scene. Their activities alienated the establishment—consisting of the old-guard intelligentsia—which, in turn, refused to cooperate with the revolution or did so half-heartedly. Nonalignment at home was the old guard's undeclared cultural policy, but they also openly criticized the compromise of democratic principles. Eventually, in the annals of Nasserism, this reality came to be known as the 1961 "crisis of the intellectuals." For a while, the government handled it with care, but it soon took a more aggressive turn.

Whatever the real intentions of those in power were, one thing was obvious: supporters of political pluralism, such as journalists Aḥmad Bahā' al-Dīn and Iḥsan ʿAbd al-Quddūs, were regarded first with suspicion and later as a threat. Yet, they carried on. In fact, many other educated people also were willing to defend the pluralist order. And thus, hundreds of intellectuals from all across the ideological spectrum who vocally protested in the months that followed Naguib's expulsion from office were arrested, censured, intimidated,

55. Robert Tignor, *Capitalism and Nationalism at the End of Empire: State and Business in Decolonizing Egypt, Nigeria and Kenya, 1945–1963* (Princeton, NJ: Princeton University Press, 1998), p. 100.

56. Ibid., pp. 100, 116–117.

57. Meijer, *The Quest for Modernity*, p. 202.

and removed from their positions in universities, publishing houses, and government service.

The impact of this policy on historical thought and practice was nothing short of profound. As we have seen in chapter 4, an entire web of institutions and functionaries sustained the monarchic historiographical order. The regime's campaign undermined the normal circulation of information and ideas, which was vital to history writing. Thus, though the majority of those imprisoned were not historians, the removal from public life of hundreds of participating journalists, writers, editors, students, university professors, and low-level cultural functionaries, such as archivists and librarians, damaged the operational basis of pluralistic historiography. For instance, the ʿĀbdīn project was terminated, and its staff was sent to support Egypt's diplomatic efforts abroad.[58] For a while, there was no archive to work in, not even a distortedly selective one like ʿĀbdīn. Since the universities officially campaigned for the return to parliamentary life, they particularly suffered from this heavy-handed policy.[59] Because of the centrality of history in the new order, Ghurbāl's academic network was especially vulnerable. Some of its members went directly to jail.[60]

Among those harassed were Ibrāhīm ʿAbduh and ʿAbd al-ʿAzīz al-Shinnāwī. Both were former students of Ghurbāl. ʿAbduh was a historian of journalism and an assistant professor at Cairo University. Under the monarchy he had also been employed as a government censor, a position that put him at odds with the new regime. In 1954 he was dismissed from the university and subsequently left Egypt.[61] Dr. al-Shinnāwī was a professor of history and an archivist in ʿĀbdīn. Studying the Suez Canal for a period of fifteen years, he was almost unrivaled in his intimate familiarity with the relevant historical sources.[62] In 1955, as the Egyptian government secretly prepared the case for the nationalization of the Suez Canal, some crucial historical documents that justified Egypt's right to nationalization disappeared. Investigated by very high levels of the intelligence community, al-Shinnāwī was suspected of smuggling the records to France and

58. ʿĀdil al-Ḥusaynī, "Al-Tārīkh kadhāb," *Rūz al-Yūsuf,* July 2, 1962, pp. 30–31.

59. Ḥamūda, *Azmat al-muthaqafīn,* p. 206.

60. However, as early as January 1953, at least one former student, ʿAlī Jiritlī, joined the revolution and became a leading economist. Meijer, *The Quest for Modernity,* pp. 76–77, 179; Tignor, *Capitalism and Nationalism at the End of Empire,* pp. 73, 86, 158, 398.

61. ʿAbduh returned in the 1970s after a successful career as founder and chief editor of the cultural journal *Al-ʿArabī.* He published extensively but never returned to teach in the university. J. J. G. Jansen, "Ibrahim Abduh, His Autobiographies and His Political Polemical Writings," *Bibliotheca Orientalis* 37 nos. 3–4 (1980): p. 130; Ḥamūda, *Azmat al-muthaqafīn,* p. 181.

62. See al-Shinnāwī 's article in *MTM* 6 (1957): pp. 135–155.

was immediately arrested on charges of spying. After two years in prison, during which he was brutally tortured, al-Shinnāwī was released and later politically rehabilitated.[63] On his release he taught history at al-Azhar.

Not all those arrested were supporters of the monarchic order; the state instinctively reacted against all opposition forces, including communists and moderate socialists. Thus, although a tenured professor in Cairo University such as Fu'ād Mursī or the eminent literary critic and part-time historian Luwīs 'Awaḍ were not followers of Ghurbāl's school, they were an integral part of the same academic fabric that sustained the opposition and was deemed liberal.[64] In short, as communist historian Anouar Abdel-Malek put it, 1954 brought a "massive purge that destroyed the careers of almost seventy professors, lectures and instructors in Egypt's universities. All those who were affected—and some of them were outstanding—belonged to the liberal wing, whether they were Wafdists, Marxists or merely freethinkers, even advocates of constitutionalism, and not one was later restored to his post."[65]

The attack on these networks was so sweeping and abrupt that even al-Rāfi'ī was put in an awkward position. Despite his militant political agenda, al-Rāfi'ī supported political pluralism. After all, he acknowledged the advantages of a political system that, in spite of occasional harassment, had allowed him to act as a voice of opposition for nearly three decades. He and the National Party were an organic part of this political order. For a short period of time, between July and November 1949, he had even held a ministerial position. Thus, quite naturally and contrary to the position of his National Party comrades, he defended the idea of political pluralism. As a lawyer and politician, he joined the official committee for the drafting of a new constitution. Naively, he hoped to change things from within.[66] As editor-in-chief of the daily newspaper *Al-Qāhira,* he fiercely objected to what he described as the dictatorship of the one-party system.[67] He even called the Free Officers to run for elections.[68] As a historian, he must have been discouraged to see that, though he had paid such careful attention to his-

63. 'Ulwān, *'Abd al-'Azīz al-Shinnāwī,* pp. 14–16; 'Abd al-Mun'im al-Jumay'ī, *Itijāhāt al-kitāba,* pp. 204–208.

64. Samah Suhayl Idriss, "Intellectuals and the Nasserite Authority in the Egyptian Novel," unpublished Ph.D. dissertation, Columbia University, 1991), pp. 44–45.

65. Abdel-Malek, *Egypt: Military Society,* p. 213.

66. *Al-Ahrām,* March 18, 1954, pp. 7, 11; Aḥmad Ismā'īl, *Ṣinā'at tārīkh Miṣr,* pp. 84–85.

67. Yet, like many others who witnessed the monarchic party system, he feared anarchy. See 'Abd al-Raḥmān al-Rāfi'ī, "Ḥizb wāḥad am aḥzāb?" *Al-Qāhira,* November 20, 1953, p. 3; and 'Abd al-Raḥmān al-Rāfi'ī, "Mithāq al-ḥizbiyya wa kayfa yataḥaqaq," *Al-Qāhira,* November 28, 1953, pp. 3, 6.

68. *Al-Ahrām,* March 18, 1954, pp. 7, 11.

torical details, his books were reduced to catalysts for a series of revolutionary events. The value of painstaking research was simply meaningless. Far worse, much to his astonishment, he soon found out that government operators did not appreciate his fondness for historical details. Visiting his publishing house, they censored his books.[69] Thus, we see that hardly anyone was spared this official backlash. Certainly not the Muslim Brotherhood.

Despite their relative strength, being the largest and most cohesive popular organization, the Muslim Brotherhood operated on the margins of the public sphere. It had been in the best interest of the previous political system to perpetuate this situation. Following a sensational assassination attempt on Nasser's life in October 1954 and the ensuing falling out with Nasser's movement, the Muslim Brotherhood was pushed even further away from mainstream politics. As part of this process, the organization was not allowed to publish its history. Yet, outside Egypt the Muslim Brotherhood attracted scholarly attention. In 1952, the renowned Palestinian scholar of Arabic literature Isḥāq Mūsa Ḥusaynī completed the first academic study on the Muslim Brotherhood. In a preface to the 1956 English edition he wrote, "Any person reading this book with a view to finding in it propaganda with or against the Brethren is heading for disappointment. Such books are now plentiful in the market, written by friends and foes of the Brethren. . . . It is to be lamented that the reading public has got used to books that distort history. And these constitute the majority of our history books, old and new, to the extent that rarely can we find one that does justice to an issue by stating the facts objectively."[70]

Whether the author was true to his call for objectivity is open to debate. In any event, Ḥusaynī presented an original and well-documented study that put the Muslim Brotherhood at center stage in contemporary politics. By providing the organization with such a serious study, he accorded the Brotherhood a much needed recognition. As we have seen, studies on contemporary affairs were a rarity. Unable to respond by other means, the Egyptian government banned the circulation of this book.[71] And thus, until the 1970s, neither the Muslim Brotherhood nor any other Islamic organization was allowed to historicize its modern experience publicly. With this background, we now turn to a discussion of the decline of Ghurbāl's school.

69. A worker at the printing press testified that the original copy of al-Rāfiʿī's account of the 1952 Revolution was censored by the deletion of the history of ex-president Naguib. ʿAbd al-Munʿim al-Jumayʿī, *Itijāhāt al-kitāba*, p. 58.

70. Ishak Musa Husaini, *The Moslem Brethren: The Greatest of Modern Islamic Movements* (Beirut: Khayat, 1956), p. v.

71. ʿAbdallāh, ed., *Tārīkh Miṣr*, p. 414.

ACADEMIA CHALLENGED

Early on, Nasser had evinced an interest in history writing in the context of the university. "[Though] I do not claim the Chair of History for myself," he wrote, ". . . I would immediately say that the July Revolution represented the realization of a long-cherished hope—a hope entertained by the Egyptian people . . . —to determine their own destiny."[72] With this in mind, Nasser expected history professors to probe "in search of roots that penetrate into the depths of the history" of their nation.[73] Thus, he hoped for, if not a direct call for the rewriting of history, then at least a reorientation or, as we shall see in chapter 8, more awareness of the present needs of society at large. Though at the beginning of the new era, academic historians entertained the idea of participating in the building of it, they were soon disenchanted. Hence, the government, rather than relying on university professors to forge its historical perceptive, sought the assistance of others. This was the practical meaning of the "crisis of intellectuals." When we consider this crisis, we should also have Ghurbāl and his disciples in mind. The following section views the 1952–61 era from the point of view of this group.

Immediately following the revolution, Ghurbāl made several attempts to participate in public historical discussion. First, in July 1953, he apologetically tried to explain the place of the 1952 Revolution in Egypt's modern history. Unavoidably, he ended up accepting much of al-Rāfiʿī's observations. For a moment it seemed as if even Ghurbāl had succumbed to the political pressures of the day. But then, just when al-Rāfiʿī took the liberty of claiming his triumph publicly, Ghurbāl decided to make the effort to stand for the convictions of his school. He faithfully did so until his death.[74]

Undoubtedly, the revolutionary era marks the end of Ghurbāl's career as an intellectual leader in the field of historiography.[75] However, despite his basic incompatibility with the prevalent self-congratulatory historiography, he was not a minor figure who could simply be purged. Instead, he was repeatedly eased aside, or rather upward. Always revered, in 1954 at the death of his wife, he

72. Gamal Abdel Nasser, *The Philosophy of the Revolution* (Cairo: National Publication House, 1954), p. 10.

73. Ibid., p. 9.

74. Muḥammad Shafīq Ghurbāl, "Makān al-thawra al-miṣriyya," *Al-Hilāl,* July 1953, pp. 32–35. Al-Rāfiʿī revived his old debate with Ghurbāl on who created modern Egypt. See again al-Rāfiʿī, "Miṣr khalaqat Muḥammad ʿAlī," *Al-Hilāl,* August 1953, pp. 40–43.

75. Though he was a member of the 1953 committee for investigating the state of higher education, this distinguished forum was assembled before the revolution. See the discussion in chapter 8.

took early retirement from his position as undersecretary of the Ministry of Education. A short while afterward, he was nominated as head of the newly established Institute of Arabic Studies (Maʿhad al-dirāsāt al-ʿarabiyya).[76] Ghurbāl readily accepted this appointment, even though he was not a staunch supporter of the Nasserite brand of Pan-Arabism and did not covet the power and prestige bestowed on the revolution's supporters. He had had plenty of these earthly powers and honorific prestige before the revolution and was always very modest about how he used them. To be sure, while he did not mind Pan-Arabism, after such a long and successful career Ghurbāl did not wish to become another Amīn Saʿīd. Surely, the Institute of Arabic Studies was a proper place from which to sustain and defend his professional agenda. It should be remembered that for his entire professional life, Ghurbāl always preferred to support his cause from within an institution. He was, by any measure, a "man of the system."

Once, in a rather personal note, Ghurbāl wrote, "I have taught myself to learn from life."[77] If he was to be true to this declaration, now, some years after the revolution, was the proper time to put it to work. Indeed, right after assuming office, he swiftly reevaluated the historiographical scene. Since, for all intents and purposes, revolutionary historiography practically monopolized the writing on the modern era, he shifted his interest to the less politicized territory of premodern Egypt and Arab-Ottoman history.[78] This new position was highly compatible with the official aims of an Arab League institution and also made it easier for Ghurbāl to defend his creed with regard to questions of methodology and ethics. Thus, with a prestigious institution behind him, he relocated Egypt's modern experience to a wider premodern and unpoliticized context. By doing so, Ghurbāl hoped to rescue it from the claws of popular writers. Cognizant of the surrounding reality, he maintained that as long as historians were "bounded by methodology *(quyūd al-fann wa uṣūl al-ṣināʿa),*" they could belong to any political party without risk of compromising their mission.[79] If judged by the sort of history that was published, this last call for moderation and perspective went unanswered. Yet, always nonconfrontational, he carried on.

Ghurbāl's renewed academic activity was now mainly directed toward a pan-

76. This institution was established and financed by the Arab League, not by the Egyptian government. While in this position, Ghurbāl began supervising the preparation of a new Arab encyclopedia, *Al-Mawsūʿa al-ʿarabīya al-maisura.*

77. Muḥammad Shafīq Ghurbāl, *"Al-Ḥayā jadīra bi-an naḥyāhā,"* in Aḥmad Amīn, ed., *ʿAllamatnī al-ḥayā* (Cairo: Dār al-hilāl, 1953), p. 52.

78. Muḥammad Shafīq Ghurbāl, "Maṣādir al-ilhām ʿinda baʿḍ al-muʾarikhīn," *Al-Hilāl,* November 1954, pp. 43–49.

79. Muḥammad Shafīq Ghurbāl, "Aḥkām al- muʾarikhīn ʿala al-rijāl," *Al-Hilāl,* April 1955, p. 42.

oramic study of Egyptian history and civilization from Pharaonic times to the present. Modern Egyptian intellectuals were always fascinated by long-term historical change in the Nile Valley. From whatever angle they approached the subject, they all dealt with what is still commonly known in Egyptian intellectual circles as the question of continuity *(istimrāriyya)* in Egyptian history.[80] Two sources of intellectual inspiration guided Ghurbāl: previous writings on how the environment shaped a distinctive "Egyptian character" and the intellectual agenda of his mentor Arnold Toynbee. As we have already seen, Toynbee's monumental project *A Study of History* was a strong statement on behalf of the inner force of civilization as the generator of history. Under present conditions, it made much sense for Ghurbāl to revisit Toynbee's theories, apply, and tailor them to the history of Egypt, the Arabs, and Islam. Already in 1954, in a series of radio lectures and a book titled *Takwīn Miṣr* (The Formation of Egypt), Ghurbāl began to implement this agenda.[81]

A full analysis of Ghurbāl's postmonarchic historical agenda, however, would take us away from the scope of this study. In brief, he tried to navigate the history of Egyptian civilization among the West, the Ottomans, the Muslims, and the Arabs. However, despite this effort, his work was eclectic, unfocused, and lacked the revolutionary enthusiasm of the day.[82] Ghurbāl's last publication, *Manhaj mufaṣṣal li-l-durūs* (An Elaborate Agenda for Research), was an attempt to come up with a compatible research agenda similar to the one he had in the 1930s and with which he once revolutionized history writing. Hardly anyone found this program appealing. On the verge of ending his career, Ghurbāl made perhaps the single most important statement of his entire second career: "The Arabs developed a habit of ascribing all of their troubles to the Ottomans."[83] Though Ghurbāl did not offer any groundbreaking interpretation of the relationship between Ottoman and Arab histories, he put his finger on a field that was in serious need of revision.[84]

80. On the idea of *istimrāriyya,* see Selim, "The New Pharaonism."

81. In spite of the nationalist motto "Egypt is the gift of the Egyptians," the work hid a broad historiographical agenda. Muḥammad Shafīq Ghurbāl, *Takwīn Miṣr ʿibra al-ʿuṣūr* (Cairo: al-Hayʾā al-miṣriyya al-ʿāmma li-l-kitāb, 1990), p. 77.

82. Even though Ghurbāl deemed Egyptian history to be essentially different from—indeed, superior to—that of the Arabs generally, he insisted on trying to bring them together. See another series of radio lectures that have been published posthumously. Muḥammad Shafīq Ghurbāl, *Min zāwiyat al-qāhira* (Cairo: Dār al-idhāʿa wa-l-tilifizyūn, n.d.), pp. 7–38.

83. Muḥammad Shafīq Ghurbāl, *Manhaj mufaṣṣal li-l-durūs: Al-ʿawāmil al-tārīkhiyya fī bināʾ al-umma al-ʿarabiyya ʿala ma hiya ʿalayhi al-yawm* (Cairo: Maʿhad al-dirāsāt al-ʿarabiyya, 1961), p. 130.

84. Already in his previous work, Ghurbāl argued that under the Ottomans Egypt had a distinctive experience and thus, unlike the rest of the Ottoman provinces, it did

While Ghurbāl continued to supervise the work of graduate students from the Institute of Arabic Studies and Cairo University, none of his post-1952 advisees rose to academic or intellectual prominence.[85] By this time the point of academic gravity had shifted to ʿAyn Shams University, where the most promising students went to work with Aḥmad ʿIzzat ʿAbd al-Karīm.[86] In 1955, ʿAbd al-Karīm began the meetings of the Advanced Seminar in Modern History. Over fifty years later, it still convenes every Thursday at 6 P.M. Probably the most advanced and innovative forum in which to discuss history, it trained the next generation of social historians. There, they combined the ethical and methodological creed of Ghurbāl with the social sensitivity of the Left. As a new generation of scholars took over, Ghurbāl's role became symbolic. The prospective visit of Toynbee to Cairo in October 1961 was planned also as a symbolic event, in which the lifetime achievements of Ghurbāl would be celebrated, a sort of a collective acknowledgment of three decades of a shy, yet highly influential, presence.

Among Egyptian historians, Toynbee and Ghurbāl were often mentioned in one breath. Toynbee was a reminder of the possibility of a lively cooperation with European academia. As a result of his long-term support of the Arab cause and his criticism of Zionism, Toynbee was also very popular in the Arab world. Indeed, days before his arrival, the British ambassador to Cairo assured Toynbee, "The people here regard you at present as kind of St. George to the Zionist dragon."[87] Ghurbāl was looking forward to this visit. In his last letter to Toynbee he wrote,

---

not undergo decline. Thus, quite originally, Ghurbāl singled the Ottoman era as Egypt's reservoir of successful historical experience. Nonetheless, he could not explain why, during the nineteenth century, Egypt failed to respond to the challenges posed by the West. Ghurbāl, *Takwīn Miṣr,* pp. 25–26, 96, 98, 110, 104, 106–107.

85. These students studied Sudan, East Africa, the Red Sea, nineteenth-century legal and tax history in Egypt, the Egyptian-Ottoman relationship, and Ottoman Yemen. Hishmat, *Dalīl al-rasāʾil al-jāmiʿiya,* vol. 1, pp. 184, 186, 195, 197, 201, 203–204.

86. Nominated as assistant professor in ʿAyn Shams University in 1951, ʿAbd al-Karīm gradually made his way up. Beginning in June 1958, he initiated a new series of studies on history titled al-Maktaba al-Tārīkhiyya. From 1961 to 1964 he served as dean of the humanities in ʿAyn Shams, and in 1965 he was elected president of the EHS. Yunān Labīb Rizq, "Aḥmād ʿIzzat ʿAbd al-Karīm: Al-muʿalim," *Miṣr al-ḥadītha* 2 (2003): pp. 457–460; Giuseppe Contu, "Aḥmad ʿIzzat ʿAbd al-Karīm (1909–1980): Storico arabo contemporaneo," in Clelia Sarnelli Cequa, ed., *Studi arabo-islamici in onore di Roberto Rubianacci nel suo settantesimo compleanno* (Naples: Istituto Universitario Orientale, 1985), vol. 1, pp. 219–238; "Al-Maktaba al-tārīkhiyya," *MTM* 8 (1959): pp. 295–303; ʿAbd al-Munʿim al-Jumayʿī, *Itijāhāt al-kitāba,* pp. 195–203.

87. William McNeill, *Arnold J Toynbee: A Life* (New York: Oxford University Press, 1989), p. 250; Saleh, *Trevor-Roper's Critique of Arnold Toynbee.*

"When you come to Cairo you are going to stay with me."[88] As Toynbee mused sadly later, God disposed it otherwise. Unfortunately, the two could not meet, for Ghurbāl suddenly died. Arriving in Cairo a short while after, Toynbee attended the commemorative session of the EHS. Introduced by Ṭaha Ḥusayn, he eulogized his disciple and friend: "I could tell what kind of career Shafeek Ghorbal was going to have. Some people are born with the gift of scholarship, he was one of those. Above all, he had the gift of character and objectivity both of which have been referred to already. It was very marked in Shafeek Ghorbal that he had independence of mind, and the dedication and determination to see his own researches to the end. It is so rare that people are distinguished in both the field of learning and the field of administration."[89]

Sometime before Ghurbāl's death the press depicted him as a withdrawn elderly man who spent much of the day in his rose garden. He was seen as a defeated giant whose approval, however, was still needed. And approval for the cultural policies of the day was precisely what Ghurbāl declined to provide. Hence, he minimized his public appearances and stubbornly shied away from television interviews.[90] At his death, newspapers mentioned his various public positions as member, affiliate, teacher, director, and president of various institutions.[91] But the loss of Ghurbāl meant much more than a formal newspaper eulogy could possibly capture. His death was a reminder of the days in which academia was at the forefront of cultural innovation. Ghurbāl, said one colleague, was a distinguished member of the passing generation of intellectual giants.[92] Practically his heir 'Izzat 'Abd al-Karīm said he was a one-man school of history.[93] Others mentioned that he brought to Egypt the professional notion of objectivity in historical research and revolutionized historical methodology in the entire Arab East.[94] His close friend, historian Muḥammad Rif'at, hoped that worthy students would carry on Ghurbāl's message.[95] Such words strengthened the commitment to the common denominator around which this professional community was originally formed.

Meanwhile, at the same university in which Ghurbāl had established his

88. Arnold Toynbee, "A Word of Appreciation," *MTM* 11 (1963): appendix.

89. Ibid.

90. Crabbs, "Politics, History and Culture in Nasser's Egypt," p. 403. Particularly see *Al-Ahrām*, October 7, 1958.

91. *Al-Ahrām*, October 20, 1961, p. 7.

92. Aḥmad 'Abd al-Raḥīm Muṣṭafa, "Shafīq Ghurbāl mu'arikhan," *MTM* 11 (1963): p. 255.

93. *MTM* 11 (1963): pp. 19–20.

94. Ibid., pp. 21–45.

95. Ibid., pp. 7–9.

school, a young history professor named Muḥammad Anīs advised a student who had changed his opinion following the reading of new source material, "You have to be systematic. . . . objectivity is a relative thing."[96] And so, within academic circles, outside pressures began showing their mark, and an era of partisan historiographical "commitment," or engagement, was about to begin.

THINKING SOCIALISM SCIENTIFICALLY

Compared with state-manufactured historical meaning, Marxist historiography continued to be a fringe movement. Despite that, its intellectual significance cannot be exaggerated. With the gradual dismantling of the networks of the liberalist intelligentsia, Marxists remained the largest and, by far, the most organized and systematic school of thought. Still tightly connected to the communist movement, their critical engagement with the past differentiated them from revolutionary-inspired historiography. This section investigates a lacuna of Marxist historical knowledge that would shape the historical imagination of the 1960s generation.

Though Marxists continued to experience oppression, between 1956 and 1959 they coexisted with those in power. In the aftermath of the Bandung conference, which turned Nasser into a recognized third-world leader, the rapprochement with the Eastern Bloc and the 1956 victory over imperialism in Suez, it seemed as though, against communist doctrinal logic, the nationalized bourgeoisie had been successful in confronting imperialism on a world scale. Thus, the multiple communist organizations began to rethink their relationship with the state. Pressured to act in unison by Nasser's series of regional successes, four different communist groups formed the Egyptian Communist Party in January 1958. For its part, the momentum of Nasserism allowed the regime to enter the dialogue from a position of power. Consequently, the communists, and the critical Left in general, were accorded relative freedom of action.[97]

Almost immediately, new publishing houses were established, of which two, Dār al-nadīm and al-Dār al-Miṣriyya li-l-ṭibāʿa wa-l-nashr wa-l-tawzīʿ, were especially active in publishing history.[98] In addition, Nasser ordered the foundation of a new evening newspaper, *Al-Masāʾ*. Edited by leftist officer Khālid Muḥyyīʾ al-Dīn, *Al-Masāʾ* was the most vibrant and innovative ideological workshop in Egypt and attracted a very broad audience for its theses.[99] Unlike any other

96. Quoted in ʿAbd al-Raḥīm Muṣṭafa, "Ḥawla taqwīm zaʿamāt Miṣr fī mā bayna thawratay, 1919–1952," p. 268.

97. Ismael and El-Sa'id, *The Communist Movement in Egypt*, pp. 89–105.

98. Abdel-Malek, *Egypt: Military Society*, p. 121.

99. Ibid., pp. 120, 86.

daily, "it devoted numerous sections (almost four of its eight pages every day) to heavily documented studies in which communists and leftists alike analyzed Egyptian society in transition and offered their solutions."[100] The political intellect of Egypt, with its half-paralyzed universities, was exclusively situated within these leftist circles.

As we have seen, the first wave of Marxist scholarship was incapable of translating its political lexicon and interest in history into a mainstream political agenda. A decade later, during the mid-1950s, Marxist historians came closer to achieving this mission, and during the 1960s they witnessed, according to their own account, a sort of ideological triumph. With more resources and experience at their disposal, they produced a series of historical writings whose aim was to influence the regime's political direction. Three writers, Shuhdī 'Aṭiyya al-Shāfi'ī (1912–60), Fawzī Jirjis (1914–86), and Ibrāhīm 'Āmir (1922–76), mark the renaissance of Marxist historiography in this period.[101] Together, they composed fine studies in scientific socialism and elaborated on the meaning of this worldview. Yet, though their works are usually lumped together as though they were one work written by a single writer, great differences in quality and sophistication exist among them, as well as some disagreements and differences in emphasis.[102]

Though he was the youngest of the three, Ibrāhīm 'Āmir was the most sophisticated in his theoretical understanding of the nexus among scientific socialism, Egyptian history, and the philosophy of history. "I maintain," he wrote, "that there is a national and international need for the writing of a study on the Egyptian national movement in the context of both social and world forces."[103] Since the magnitude of such a project was apparent to him, he began by publishing an articulated political guide and research agenda. In brief, on the basis of updated contributions to the theory of historical materialism, 'Āmir set out to elucidate the various stages of development from feudalism through imperialism (commercial, industrial, and financial) to the highest stage of socialism. He argued that by bribing elements of the bourgeoisie, capitalism subverted struggles for national liberation. "[All] nationalist revolutions begin, develop, and aim at securing the interests of local capitalists and the middle class. If they remain in

100. Ibid., p. 120.

101. Anouar Abdel-Malek (b. 1924) was another active Marxist who, following government repression, left Egypt in 1959. His most influential works were published in French, yet his *Egypt: Military Society* was highly influential in Egypt as well.

102. For previous analyses of this group, see Meijer, *The Quest for Modernity*, pp. 222–227; 'Alī Barakāt, "Fī-l-ṭarīq ila madrasa ijtimā'iyya fī kitābat tārīkh Miṣr al-ḥadith 1798–1952," *Al-Fikr* 5 (1985): p. 58; and Gorman, *Historians, State and Politics*, pp. 91–93.

103. Ibrāhīm 'Āmir, *Thawrat Miṣr al-qawmiyya* (Cairo: Dār al-nadīm, 1957), pp. 5–7.

the hands of these, they will never accomplish any of the people's demands."[104] The task of socialism, therefore, was to forge a front with the toiling classes and defeat the bond among capital, colonialism, and domestic collaborators.[105] To achieve this end, one first needed to understand history.

Doing precisely that, ʿĀmir offered a historical perspective on Egypt's social structure. He dated the formation of large landowners back to the policies of Muḥammad ʿAli and associated the emergence of the financiers and the agrarian wing of the upper bourgeoisie with the profound structural changes of the Ismāʿīl era.[106] He then reviewed the revolutionary nature of the people: a conglomerate of peasants, workers, merchants, shop owners, and clerks, who repeatedly failed to overcome the coalition of reactionary forces.[107] ʿĀmir's historical analysis brought to the fore a series of critical concerns: when and how the class of large landowners was formed; what the roots of capitalism in Egypt were; who profited from the occupation and how; what the relation was between party politics and social structure; and what the living conditions of the Egyptian peasant were. In short, ʿĀmir proposed to study, from scratch, Egypt's entire socioeconomic structure and its relation to power politics. It was an appealing plan.

Fawzī Jirjis, ʿĀmir's senior comrade, took this research agenda and tailored from it an elaborate study on political change. His scope ranged throughout the Ottoman occupation, from 1517 to 1952. For political reasons, Jirjis, as ʿĀmir before him, refrained from writing on Egyptian society under Nasser. Yet, he had plenty to say about earlier periods. According to Jirjis, the Ottomans had suppressed the middle class and thus perpetuated the feudal system of rule.[108] By the time of the French occupation, Egypt was already struggling for independence.[109] After the French eliminated the feudal order of the Mamluks, the middle class was strengthened and was thus able to nominate Muḥammad ʿAlī.[110] The pasha, however, reciprocated with feudal-style state centralism, which frustrated the growth of the middle class.[111] Consequently, Egypt did not experience a transition to a capitalist stage of development. Jirjis then showed how frail and superficial industry was under Muḥammad ʿAlī. According to him, the only goal of the pasha was state power. Thus, despite an increase in economic production, uneven

104. Ibid., p. 60.

105. Ibid., pp. 10–39.

106. Ibid., pp. 41–45.

107. Ibid., pp. 10–39.

108. Fawzī Jirjis, *Dirāsāt fī tārīkh Miṣr al-siyāsī mundhu al-ʿaṣr al-mamlūkī* (1958; Cairo: al-ʿArabī, 1989), pp. 11–21.

109. Ibid., pp. 22, 24–25.

110. Ibid., p. 30.

111. Ibid., pp. 34–37, 41.

income distribution assured that Egypt would remain a semifeudal system.[112] Meanwhile, during the second half of the nineteenth century, the financial form of capitalism became dominant, and the new class of large landowners readily collaborated with the British occupation of 1882. Their shared goal was to keep Egypt in the underdeveloped stage of feudalism.[113] In various forms their collaboration continued all the way to 1952. Elaborating on the diverse revolutionary actions mentioned by ʿĀmir, Jirjis discussed at great length how the upper bourgeoisie, large landowners, and capitalists foiled each of them.[114] All in all, Jirjis dealt with an enormous number of issues such as standard of living, income distribution, class formation, social justice, and sociopolitical structure. Rather than being a conclusive study, this was an illustration of the enticing possibilities offered by this historical approach.

Upon charting the contours of future historical research, ʿĀmir published a second and much more focused study on the "problem of the *fallāḥ*." Published in 1958 and drawing on an impressive, and previously unconsulted, body of sources, ʿĀmir's *Al-Arḍ wa-l-fallāḥ* was the historical companion to al-Sharqāwī's definitive novel of this generation, which carried a similar title: *Al-Arḍ* (The Earth, 1954). Like the novel, ʿĀmir's study aimed to show that "the question of the *fallāḥ* is that of the entire Egyptian people."[115] Since in the past this question had been analyzed only according to "misleading standards that were borrowed from Europe and other places," the problem of the *fallāḥ* was not solved.[116] Rethinking the state of the *fallāḥ*, he redefined "the heart of the agriculture problem in Egypt" as "landownership, its usage, the economy of product distribution, and the balance of social power in the countryside."[117] ʿĀmir's actual analysis of this problem was revisionist on two counts. First, he argued that feudalism, in the European sense of the term, did not exist in Egypt and that the large landowners of the 1870s were not feudalist but capitalists. Challenging the common wisdom with regard to a mechanistic development of history from feudalism to capitalism, he now stated that each country followed a distinctive historical process that should be acknowledged and studied.[118] Second, by identifying four forms

112. Ibid., pp. 41–42.

113. Ibid., pp. 71–79, 91, 106, 111–112, 115.

114. "Nation liberation struggles in other countries demonstrated that bourgeois leadership could not carry the revolution toward fulfilling its aims." Jirjis, *Dirāsāt fī tārīkh Miṣr*, p. 138. For his analysis of the traitorous 1936 Anglo-Egyptian treaty, see p. 178.

115. Ibrāhīn ʿĀmir, *Al-Arḍ wa-l-fallāḥ: Al-masʾala al-zirāʿiyya fī Miṣr* (Cairo: al-Dār al-Miṣriyya li-l-ṭibāʿa wa-l-nashr wa-l-tawzīʿ, 1958), p. 12.

116. Ibid., pp. 13–14, 15.

117. Ibid., p. 18.

118. Ibid., pp. 19–20, 80–81, 86–89.

of peasantry and five forms of landownership, he provided the most detailed analysis of the socioeconomic structure in the countryside.[119] On the basis of this understanding, ʿĀmir identified the "enemies" of history and called for more profound agrarian reforms.[120] Believing in the scientific and objective value of historical knowledge, he assured his readers that "it is impossible to distort all history all of the time."[121]

A study of lesser historiographical importance was that of Shuhdī ʿAṭiyya al-Shāfiʿī, on the development of the national movement between 1882 and 1956. A prominent member of this group and an active communist, he stated their cause: "[This book] was written with an eye toward the future. Its aim is to outline the contours of this future. By using past experience, it outlines the ways in which the people should struggle against imperialism, feudalism, and monopoly [and should strive for] the amelioration of cultural and material conditions, freedom, and democracy."[122]

Focusing on how the peasants and workers collaborated for the success of the 1952 Revolution, al-Shāfiʿī fused the standard nationalist narrative of al-Rāfiʿī with ʿĀmir's reading of Egyptian history.[123] Undoubtedly, this book embodied the short-lived rapprochement between the communists and the national agenda of the regime.[124] Al-Shāfiʿī's most original contribution was in making important notional connections among workers' organizations, legislation, representation, poverty, taxation, and the fundamental agenda of workers' rights.[125] On the basis of these abstract links, he called on the regime to eliminate monopolies by expanding the public sector and implementing central planning.[126] However, although al-Shāfiʿī was the most educated of the three historians, he should be remembered more for his uncompromising political activity than for his historical or theoretical contribution. Indeed, it was due to his political bravery that he was imprisoned and tortured to death.[127]

119. Ibid., pp. 115–124.

120. Ibid., pp. 139–160.

121. Ibid., p. 23.

122. Shuhdī ʿAṭiyya al-Shāfiʿī, *Taṭawwur al-ḥaraka al-waṭaniyya al-miṣriyya 1882–1956* (Cairo: al-Dār al-Miṣriyya li-l-ṭibāʿa wa-l-nashr wa-l-tawzīʿ, 1957), p. 4.

123. Ibid., pp. 49, 60.

124. Following the nationalization of the Suez Canal, communists hurried to "write themselves" into the hegemonic nationalist story. See, for instance, ʿĀmir, *Ta'mīm al-qanā.*

125. al-Shāfiʿī, *Taṭawwur al-ḥaraka al-waṭaniyya*, pp. 38–39, 42–45, 84–86.

126. Ibid., pp. 218–219, 225–228, 228–231.

127. Joel Beinin, "The Communist Movement and Nationalist Political Discourse in Nasirist Egypt," *Middle East Journal* 42, no. 2 (Autumn 1987): pp. 568–584.

This second wave of Marxist writing was interrupted by the 1959 crackdown.[128] The ideological and acute political differences between the communist groups that formed the Egyptian Communist Party and the government were too wide to bridge, despite three years of their coexistence. On the theoretical level, even the Democratic Movement for National Liberation, the largest communist organization that supported the revolution in 1952, did not subscribe to Nasser's notion of Arab nationalism and Arab political unity. Rather than seeing nationalism and unity as the ultimate goal, the communists perceived it as a mere stage along the way to the higher developmental plain of socialism. In place of unity, communists emphasized the necessity of class struggle and a proletarian revolution, to which Nasserism strongly objected. Furthermore, while Nasser publicly endorsed the importance of religion, the communists considered religion a hindrance to progress. Some of these differences left the communists quite perplexed and unsure about the "true nature of Nasserism" and the desired level of coordination with it. Thus, the communists remained divided from the government on a host of doctrinal and tactical concerns.[129]

Ultimately, these differences were expressed in the communists' skepticism and direct criticism regarding the unification with Syria and the right approach toward General Qāsim's regime in Iraq. After the fall of the Iraqi monarchy in July 1958, the emerging coalition of Iraqi communists and nationalist forces was seen by Egyptian communists as a desired model to be replicated at home. For Nasser, however, the communist endorsement of Qāsim was a treacherous act aimed at undermining his leadership in the Arab world. This view in addition to his permanent suspicion of the communists led to the January 1959 crackdown, which influenced the entire spectrum of leftist and Marxist thought. Until April 1964, when Soviet leader Nikita Khrushchev visited Egypt, most communist and Marxist thinkers would remain in prison.

Notwithstanding this act of suppression, from an intellectual perspective Marxists ushered in a new historiographical era by proposing theoretically neat explanations for historical problems that had thus far been engaged mainly through the prism of colonial historiography. Though they did not conduct archival research, for the first time since the beginning of the royal project, an entire research agenda that focused on socioeconomic factors and elements previously considered nonsensical, such as class, was made available to the public. Even though these studies pointed toward a specific communist solution that was viewed with much suspicion, young academics could easily see how promising the underlying agenda was.

128. The crackdown was caused by differences over policy toward the 1958 coup in Iraq and the success of the communists there.

129. Ismael and El-Sa'id, *The Communist Movement in Egypt*, pp. 106–109.

Furthermore, the accumulated body of pre-1959 writings had already established a sound sense of historical progression into a scientifically planned future. While during the 1940s, Marxists regarded their cause only as a just one, in the 1950s they also described it as scientific and thus inevitable. Viewing historical prediction as a collective project, Marxists were confident that discovering the exact historical laws that hampered or pushed modernization forward made such prediction possible. This belief fed into a broader intellectual trend that was represented by the noncommunist Rāshid Barrāwī, whose "concept of history was largely future-oriented, deterministic, instrumentalist, and emancipatory, leading ruthlessly to national progress, which was objectified and reified by being expressed mainly in quantifiable units of production and material development."[130] Together, yet not in any coordinated fashion, the various leftist circles would ultimately push Egypt into the ideological era of scientific socialism. In this era, which began in earnest only after the elaboration of Arab socialism in the early 1960s, an analytical perception of the past and a critical view of the present were fused into an extremely optimistic, if not a utopian, vision of a modern future. Once operative, it was applied to all fields of action, foreign policy and culture included.

Though we cannot speak of scientific socialism in some true Soviet sense, the gradual acceptance of central planning as a major tool of governance was driven by a communist ideology. It also brought to the fore a new class of functionaries. Thus, the self-reflective liberal intellectual was replaced by the high priests of modernity and science, who were given the prestigious social status of "experts," "engineers," and, by extension, "ideologues." Their source of authority, like that of the regime itself, was based on the application of science for the benefit of progress. They developed a centrist ideology of planning, which launched extreme projects of social engineering. Though officially denied, the structural historical analysis of Marxists conditioned many of the programs of collectivization and industrialization. As argued by Meijer, in the late 1950s this logic became consensual, and central planning in various formulations *(takhṭīṭ, tarshīd,* and *tawjīh)* was applied to culture, political education, and the idea of democracy itself.[131] Furthermore, once extreme rationalization became standard, it was believed that, much like economic planning, "cultural production" *(intāj al-thaqāfa)* could be guided by the state—hence, the unprecedented increase in state patronage of books of guidance *(kutub tawjīhiyya).*[132]

130. Meijer, *The Quest for Modernity,* p. 90.

131. Ibid., p. 209.

132. The history of books during the Nasserite era is outside the scope of this work. For some first impressions on this topic, see Meijer, *The Quest for Modernity,* pp. 209–210, 222; Menachem Klein, "Egypt's Revolutionary Publishing Culture, 1952–1962," *Middle*

the autumn of 1963, the government officially appointed Anīs director of the project of historiographical revision. The aim of this initiative was to "rewrite modern Egyptian history from the French expedition, or from the late eighteenth century, to the present . . . in a scientific and socialist fashion."[10] Left open were questions such as, What was to be the scope of this project? How should it be rewritten? And who should do so?

Though the government spoke of rewriting, or revision *(iʿādat kitāba),* Anīs and his friends spoke of "the project" *(al-mashrūʿ).* They envisioned a quest for a new historiographical regime that sought to reverse the influences of the ʿĀbdīn project, tone down the influence of celebratory nationalist historiography, bring agency back to the people, and thus create independent indigenous knowledge about Egypt.[11] In the following years, Anīs strenuously labored to realize this state-supported vision and led the project into unexplored territory. Debates and scandals of all sorts proliferated. Facing the passive opposition of the second generation of academic historians and hampered by the tragic collapse of Nasserism, the project was eventually quietly brought to an end.

The story of this historiographical project is the subject of this chapter. Its centrality within the Nasserite experience did not escape the attention of Western scholars. Nissim Rejwan, Jack Crabbs, and Anthony Gorman have covered much of this historiographical terrain. They identified and did their best to explain some of the most important developments in this field. All three scholars illustrate how, during the heyday of the Nasserite era, culture became less open to experiments of trial and error and more inclined toward planned "production." Nissim Rejwan discussed how the modern past was used to sustain the "ideology of Nasserism." In a seminal article on politics and culture, Jack Crabbs set out to illustrate how Nasserism shaped culture. He was the first to record in some detail the historiographical debates in the daily press. Both Rejwan and Crabbs, however, represent a typical top-down unidirectional approach to the study of Nasserism. This approach reduces an extremely nuanced and complex intellectual scene to a flat, monotonic power relationship.[12] This perspective particularly damaged the study of historiography by limiting the discussion to who has the power to dictate historical representation.[13]

10. Muḥammad Anīs, "Al-Tārīkh fī khidmat al-taṭawwur al-ishtirākī," *Al-Ahrām,* July 7, 1963, p. 11.

11. Anīs denied that the government controlled the project and insisted that its only role was to facilitate research and provide support that the universities could not give. Ibid.

12. A classic example of such a "top-down" approach is Harir Dekmejian, *Egypt under Nasir* (Albany, NY: State University of New York Press, 1971), pp. 70–81.

13. Nissim Rejwan, *Nasserist Ideology: Its Exponents and Critics* (New York: John Wiley and Sons, 1974), pp. 11–26.

Recently, Anthony Gorman elucidated the connection between historiography and institutional change. His work is much more sensitive to the existence of a plethora of intellectual streams and cultural interest groups. However, subscribing to the notion of "official history," he, too, neglected the motivations for and the intellectual roots of ideas.[14] In the context of history writing, Gorman focused mainly on the political process and its impact on individuals and organizations (universities, think-tanks). For Crabbs, Rejwan, and Gorman, of secondary importance, and sometimes even of none at all, were changes in the methods of historical investigation and in the philosophical assumptions on which they were based. Put differently, these three scholars overlooked the role of historical thought. Consequently, regardless of their important contribution, crucial questions remain unanswered: On what philosophical grounds did the proposed socialist history legitimize itself? To what notions of truth in history did it subscribe? How did this philosophy plan to shape the actual experience of history writing?

In light of these questions, this chapter will reappraise the historiographical process during the 1960s. Again, the general argument is that a Marxist theory of history provided Arab socialism with a notion of historical change and with suggestions for how it could be planned and controlled. In almost every significant respect—its perception of time, of the agents of historical change, and of the problem of objectivity—this theory of history was at odds with idealistic histories of progressive human betterment, for example, the writings of Ghurbāl's students. Hence, the success of the socialist cultural revolution depended on the complete elimination of the ʿĀbdīn project's mode of historical thinking. The first section of the discussion focuses on the Marxist idea of lawful and ordered behavior of history in the context of the Charter. As mentioned in previous chapters, the belief in the existence of these laws led to central planning, short-term forecasts, and even long-term prophecies. It thus formed the basis for thinking about any form of change. The second and third sections deal with the political attempts to reorganize historiographical resources and to pressure individuals and institutions to subscribe to this Marxist theory of history. Together all three sections substantiate the meaning of the rewriting project to make the point that much more than rewriting was at stake. As the title of this chapter suggests, this was an expression of a cultural revolution whose ambitious aim was to be in control of history.

SOCIALIST HISTORIOGRAPHY IN THEORY

Achieving control over history, that is, forging an authentic, independent selfhood out of the past, necessitated a comprehensive theoretical statement tailored

14. Gorman, *Historians, State and Politics*, p. 59.

to such an enormous project. A prime task was to distinguish the current project from previous efforts in this field. In doing so, the proposed theoretical framework needed to facilitate a radical transformation in the methods of thinking and arriving at historical truth. Though flirting with the borders of utopianism, the Charter was written and accepted as the authentic theoretical skeleton for achieving modernity and liberation. Scholars have long acknowledged the Charter's significance and origins. Particularly, they have elaborated on the economic and political agenda of this document and located its origins in socialist thought that was not communist. Haykal's editorials in *Al-Ahrām* appeared a year or more before the actual writing of the Charter and charted its contours in advance.[15] Essentially Marxist thinkers who were systemically imprisoned for their political activities, such as Luṭfī al-Khūlī, could easily identify the influence of their thought in this document.[16] As in the final analysis, the scientific exposition of Arab socialism was historical materialism, the heart of Egyptian Marxist thought.

Though much of the scholarly discussion centered on how economy and politics were forged into an ideology, scholars were conscious of how much the Charter had to say about modern Egyptian history. For instance, it reiterated the conventional logic of the founder paradigm, which views the flow of modern Egyptian history from the "darkness of the Ottoman invasion" through the nationalist awakening of the nineteenth century to the struggle for liberation.[17] It pointed out common mistakes of interpretation made by previous historians and condemned them for their inability to deduce simple truths from history.[18] Aside from condemnations, the Charter also made recommendations: "The 1919 revolution of the Egyptian people is worthy of deep study."[19] Though the Charter indicates a change of attitude toward both the heritage of the 1919 Revolution and the national role of Saʿd Zaghlūl, its comments about Egyptian history contributed nothing new. The only significance of the Charter to modern historiography lies in its representation of the moment at which the historical understanding of scientific socialism emerged triumphant. Changes in representation of historical figures and events are of minor importance. Hence, rather than a watchful reading of what the Charter has to say about such issues, what is important is to account for how the historical philosophy of scientific socialism shaped the

15. Tignor, *Capitalism and Nationalism at the End of Empire*, p. 171.

16. Kirk Beattie, *Egypt during the Nasser Years: Ideology, Politics and Civil Society* (Boulder, CO: Westview Press, 1994), pp. 162–166, 168–170; Rami Ginat, *Egypt's Incomplete Revolution: Lutfi al-Khuli and Nasser's Socialism in the 1960s* (London: Frank Cass, 1997), pp. 69–77, 134–139.

17. UAR, *The Charter* (Cairo: Information Department, 1962), pp. 19–26.

18. Ibid., p. 24.

19. Ibid., p. 23.

Charter and, with it, the politics it prescribed. Therefore, notwithstanding the many political differences and the many doctrinal differences between Arab socialism and the scientific socialism of communists, the two were structurally similar as far as historical thought was concerned.

As the discussion in the third section will illustrate, the Charter was widely accepted as a constitutive text to the degree that Egyptian historians and historical ideologues such as Jalāl al-Sayyid, ʿAbd al-Ḥamīd al-Baṭrīq, Muṣṭafa Sāmī, and Muḥammad Anīs insisted on the importance of interpreting history through the Charter's prism. On this ground, scholars published several commentaries in the style of "the Charter for historians." The motto signified that applying the Charter's rationale to the field of history writing would guarantee the much-desired result of firm historical knowledge on which Egypt could plan and build its future. By implication, it would also erase the traces of colonial scholarship, most particularly the ʿĀbdīn project. In order to grasp the full theoretical and methodological significance of the Charter, we need to combine our previous knowledge on Marxist thought (as discussed in the two preceding chapters) with these new methodological manuals for historians.

Philosophically, the Charter was based on familiar Marxist principles that had been part of the intellectual scene since the late 1940s. As we saw in chapter 6, early Egyptian Marxists came to view history as a law-bounded process. I have emphasized that this understanding rested on the premise that objective scientific knowledge is possible and that this knowledge expresses itself in general statements about the lawful behavior of any given phenomenon. Thus, in order to be elevated to the epistemological status of science, Marxist history had to discover (and also formulate) laws of historical development. Unbounded by the specific chains of time and place, these scientific laws point in the direction of future change and, thus, understanding them enables large-scale forecasts. This notion of science and historical progression afforded unconditional historical prophecy.

Moral vision guided this formulation of science and history. The motive behind it was not to have knowledge for its own sake (i.e., to satisfy one's curiosity and need for spiritual adventure) but to solve practical problems in the future. Put differently, this philosophy of history guided ideology. Thus, rather than interpreting social change, Marxists were busy planning it. The historians' task was to write the history of these future solutions. Since the entire frame was scientific, the solutions and the historical analysis that justified them were believed to be objective, truthful, and, above all, inevitable. Egyptian ideologues and historians especially emphasized this last point, the inevitability of the socialist solution.[20]

20. Muḥammad Anīs, "Tārīkhunā al-qawmī fī-l-mithāq," *Al-Kātib,* June 1966, pp. 69–70.

The Charter took this position as its philosophical vantage point for the planning of economy, social change, and foreign policy. Hence, it had a special section dedicated to inevitability: "The socialist solution to the problem of economic and social underdevelopment in Egypt . . . was never a question of free choice. The socialist solution was an historical inevitability imposed by reality."[21] Affirming this prognosis, Muḥammad Anīs added, "The Charter's concept of Egyptian social development emerges from fundamental and objective truths."[22]

Backed by the power of science, truth, and a just cause and armed with a theory of history as their weapon, socialist historians had an urgent mission to accomplish.[23] Slightly euphoric, they now came to believe that simply by writing history they could begin to remedy "Egyptian backwardness."[24] But first, even before they began writing, they needed to subdue the existing historiographical infrastructure and bring it under their direct control. The status of historical records was their first realm of operation. The state, as we shall now see, was, of course, sympathetic to their effort. But it was not always helpful.

RECORDS TO THE PEOPLE!

April 1, 1963. The writer: Muḥammad Anīs. The addressee: ʿAbd al-Qādir Ḥātim, minister of culture. The subject: "Our National Heritage." The medium: *Al-Ahrām*.

> I do not know any other issue to which, time and again, the Egyptian press has dedicated so much attention as to that of national records and documents. And I do not know any other issue which the Ministry of Culture has ignored so persistently. . . . If political independence necessitates that power be transferred from foreign to Egyptian hands, and if economic independence requires the handing over of capital to our hands, so, surely, intellectual independence demands the concentration of our intellectual capital in national hands, first and foremost, with regard to official records, which constitute our national heritage.[25]

With these words Anīs began a wide public campaign to alter the management and availability of historical records fundamentally. These efforts were crowned with only partial success. As we saw in chapter 3, an insurmountable barrier of archival intervention stood between Egyptian historians and historical

21. UAR, *The Charter,* p. 49.

22. Anīs, "Tārīkhunā al-qawmī fī-l-mithāq," p. 71.

23. Jalāl al-Sayyid, "Tārīkhunā al-qawmī fī ḍaw' al-ishtirākiyya," *Al-Kātib,* August 1963, p. 91.

24. Ḥusayn Fawzī al-Najjār, "Al-Ishtirākiyya al-ʿarabiyya wa tafsīr al-tārīkh," *Al-Fikr al-Muʿāṣir* 6 (June 1966): pp. 15–16; Anīs, "Tārīkhunā al-qawmī fī-l-mithāq," p. 71.

25. Muḥammad Anīs, "Turāthunā al-qawmī . . . Ya wazīr al-thaqāfa! Hal yasbiqunā al-ajānib li-dirāsat whathā'iqunā?" *Al-Ahrām,* April 1, 1963, p. 9.

records. Entire periods, events, and groups had been silenced. The situation at ʿĀbdīn had never escaped the critical eyes of historians—in particular, those who did not profit from the power relations of which the archive was part. Besides, among all modern historians was a common consensus that no records existed from which they could write contemporary Egyptian history.[26] Now, as part of a comprehensive cultural revolution, it was the right time to correct this reality. Two related goals were defined: The first was to obtain various political memoirs and ascertain their unknown condition. In this regard, the names of Muḥammad Farīd, Saʿd Zaghlūl, and ʿAbd al-Raḥmān Fahmī came to mind, along with many others. The second goal concerned the shameful malfunctioning of the national archive. It needed to be reformed.

Anīs and a close circle of supporters began by pursuing the cause of political memoirs, a patriotic issue of the first degree. They called on the government to defend Egypt's national heritage.[27] They were young, bold, resolute, and willing to put as much energy as needed behind this cause. Their group consisted of literary critics, journalists, historians, and various ideologues from the group of public intellectuals of the 1960s. Anīs headed them.[28]

Anīs grew up in the Darb al-aḥmar neighborhood in Cairo. It was a popular area largely inhabited by the working class. His father was a construction worker who specialized in mosque restoration. The family lived on little money. Two years after the 1919 Revolution, when Anīs was born, the neighborhood was one of the strongest bastions of Wafdist support. The family later moved to al-ʿAbbāsiyya, another politicized neighborhood. The great nationalist demonstrations of the 1930s attracted Anīs, who became fully immersed in the political street scene.[29] In his own testimony, he was a sworn nationalist, like his father. For both father and son, nationalism meant the Wafd.[30] That would change. If not for the intimate tutelage of Shaykh ʿAlī al-Shahdāwī, a family relative, Anīs might have dropped out of school altogether and probably become a blue-collar worker himself. The shaykh's dedication to Anīs's educational upbringing ensured that he would graduate from high school and continue well beyond it.[31] At Fu'ād University he chose to study history. He graduated with a bachelor's degree in 1943, just when the influence of Ghurbāl's school had reached its zenith. Had he

26. Muṣṭafa Sāmī, "Al-Ḍurūra allatī tafruḍ iʿādat kitābat tārīkh Miṣr al-ḥadīth," *Al-Ahrām,* March 24, 1963, p. 7.

27. Jalāl al-Sayyid, "Maṭlūb ḥimāyat jamīʿ al-mudhakkarāt al-siyāsiyya," *Al-Jumhūrīya,* June 22, 1963, p. 5.

28. Other affiliated members, to name a few, were Jalāl al-Sayyid, Rajā' al-Naqqāsh, Fawzī al-Najjar, ʿAbd al-ʿAẓīm Anīs, and Rushdī Saʿīd.

29. Barakāt, "Al-Tārīkh wa qaḍāyā al-minhāj fī Miṣr al-muʿāṣira," pp. 83–84.

30. Majdī al-Daqāq, "Baʿd taqdīm istiqālatahu," *Al-Muṣawwar,* May 25, 1985, p. 16.

31. ʿAbd al-Munʿim al-Jumayʿī, *Itijāhāt al-kitāba,* pp. 212–213.

continued to an advanced degree in Fu'ād University, he might have become a staunch supporter of this academic school. He chose otherwise. Using Ghurbāl's connections abroad, he departed to Birmingham University on receiving a government scholarship and then to London. Hamilton A. R. Gibb and Toynbee supervised his work.[32]

Postwar England seethed with leftist political activity. Radical ideas constantly circulated. In academic circles and among historians in particular, Marxism was alive and kicking. It was while in England, away from the intellectual atmosphere of Fu'ād University, that Anīs became acquainted with socialist thought.[33] The social realties of Egypt, with which he was intimately familiar, illustrated the validity, urgency, and power of such ideas. Already in England, Anīs translated some of his insights into political protest.[34] Back in Egypt, he was nominated assistant professor at Fu'ād University.

During the 1950s, in both his scholarship and political activity, he kept a low profile. Though not as publicly engaged as Ibrāhīm 'Āmir, Anīs regularly contributed to the innovative leftist workshop of the newspaper *Al-Masā'* and was an active member of a mixed leftist group called Jam'iyat al-ghadd.[35] Already then, in 1959, his socialism figured strongly, and he expressed skepticism toward the celebratory histories of Arab unity, such as those of Amīn Sa'īd. "These," he wrote, "should be substituted by objective, scientific studies that reveal history's inner laws and logic."[36] This was the most daring intellectual statement he made.

Though politically prudent, he was never indifferent. Always attentive, Anīs emotionally and even assertively engaged with his surroundings. Legend has it that when the 1956 war broke, Anīs canceled his class and called on his students to come to the country's defense. Certainly not for the last time, he preferred action to words. The students obeyed.[37] It was precisely Anīs's ability to bring together a burning sense of patriotism, a socialist approach to human affairs, and an academic prestige that positioned him at a politically and intellectually influential junction.

Cognizant of his position, he began building himself as a political intellectual. Certainly, Anīs was among the very few who could bridge the gaps among the

32. Jalāl al-Sayyid, "Muḥammad Anīs: Al-rajūl wa-l-qaḍiyya," pp. 145–146.

33. Ṣalāḥ al-'Aqqād, "Muḥammad Anīs mu'arrikhan wa mufakiran," *Al-Ahrām*, September 4, 1986, p. 13; Barakāt, "Al-Tārīkh wa qaḍāyā al-minhaj," pp. 83–84.

34. al-Sayyid, "Muḥammad Anīs: Al-rajūl wa-l-qaḍiyya," pp. 145–146.

35. Ibid., p. 146; Aḥmad 'Abd al-Raḥīm Muṣṭafa, "Muḥammad Anīs mu'ārikhan wa munāḍilan," *Al-Hilāl*, November 1986, pp. 60–61; Meijer, *The Quest for Modernity*, p. 157.

36. Meijer, *The Quest for Modernity*, p. 238.

37. 'Ādil Ghunaym, "Muḥammad Anīs: Al-mu'arīkh al-waṭanī alladhī faqadnāhu," *Al-Ahrām*, September 7, 1986, p. 7.

sluggish and reluctant academia, the marginalized but vibrant Marxist forces outside it, and the nationalist will of regime supporters. When the socialist option gradually turned into policies, Anīs secured for himself a leading role as an ideologue in the Secretariat of the Propaganda and Socialist Thought, a body that belonged to the newly established Arab Socialist Union.[38] This is only a speculation, but it might be that from this position Anīs was involved in the drafting of the Charter's historical section. In any event, the government decision of autumn 1963 to nominate him as head of the rewriting committee did not surprise anyone. Organizing his task force, he created a subcommittee for historical records and documents.[39]

At about the same time the American University in Cairo (AUC) conducted a large-scale project to collect—in fact, to salvage from oblivion—modern Egyptian documents of historical significance. Some Egyptian scholars participated in this project. It was a well-intentioned enterprise, but it brought some unanticipated results. Soon, Muḥammad Farīd's son handed a copy of his father's unpublished memoirs to AUC.[40] Few people had ever seen them, and, save for al-Rāfiʿī, no Egyptian historian had studied them. Egyptian universities had previously failed to persuade the family to deposit a copy into their hands.[41] Anīs had worked closely with AUC, which extended to him an open invitation to participate in the project. Instead, he decided to turn this opportunity into a national scandal.[42] He cast AUC in the role of colonizers who encroached on the Egyptian national heritage. This theme resonated well to patriotic ears. The fact that a Harvard graduate student, Arthur Goldschmidt, was allowed to examine Farīd's memoirs well before Egyptian students or scholars could lay their eyes on them sounded outrageous enough to attract government attention.[43] Anīs lobbied hard. A short while afterward, the government declared that it would seek ownership of the political memoirs of Saʿd Zaghlūl, Makram ʿUbayd, ʿAbd al-Raḥmān Fahmī, Ismāʿīl Ṣidqī, and Muḥammad Farīd.[44] The AUC project failed. Meanwhile, Anīs was promoted to chair as professor of modern history in Cairo University.[45]

38. Najjar, "State and University in Egypt during the Period of Socialist Transformation," p. 65.

39. Maḥmūd al-Sharqāwī, "Fī dirāsat tārīkhunā al-ḥadīth," *Al-Risāla*, November 21, 1963, p. 22.

40. Sāmī, "Al-Ḍurūra allatī tafruḍ," p. 7.

41. Ibid.

42. Anīs, "Turāthunā al-qawmī . . . Ya wazīr al-thaqāfa!" pp. 9, 11.

43. al-Sayyid, "Muḥammad Anīs: Al-rajul wa-l-qaḍiyya," p. 150; Baybars Ḍiyāʾ al-Dīn, *Fatḥī Radwān yarwī li Diyāʾ al-Din Baybars asrār ḥukūmat yūlyū* (Cairo: Maktabut Madabūli, 1976), p. 39. According to Goldschmidt (personal communiqué), the memoirs were suggested to him by Muḥammad Farīd's son, who insisted that, save for al-Rāfiʿī, no one ever asked him to study or publish the memoirs.

44. al-Sayyid, "Muḥammad Anīs: Al-rajul wa-l-qaḍiyya," p. 150.

45. Crabbs, "Politics History and Culture in Nasser's Egypt," p. 394.

Anīs was militant in pursuing this cause. When the daily newspaper *Al-Akhbār* also got hold of Muḥammad Farīd's memoirs and began publishing them, Anīs was furious.[46] He attacked the newspaper for publishing inaccurate and fabricated material *(muzayyaf)*. Historical documents, he argued, belong in the national archive, not in a newspaper. Seeing no harm in making such information public, *Al-Akhbār* defended itself by rebuking Anīs as a monopolist—a grave insult for any socialist—who wished to keep the memoirs for himself and his colleagues. In response, Anīs explained that in order not to mislead the public, such material should first be submitted to careful scientific study. Besides, when published in a newspaper, historians could not rely on this material for their work. Journalists, he declared, are entirely incapable of accomplishing such a mission and henceforth should leave the job to historians. Defending its journalistic duties and caring very little if historians could use this material or not, *Al-Akhbār* was not persuaded and portrayed Anīs as a lazy professor who did nothing but cry, "Hand them to me!" (i.e., the documents). Instead of pleading for government help, *Al-Akhbār* advised Anīs to learn from newspaper reporters who conducted research and located source material themselves.[47] The personal tone that accompanied this exchange expresses the volatile and sensitive nature of the political memoirs project. Thus, even among those who were in agreement ideologically and believed that historical records should be protected, there was little consensus on how they should be handled and by whom.

From the perspective of the government, things were hardly simpler. Though Anīs was head of an official state-appointed committee, his power was limited. In fact, from an administrative point of view, Anīs was entirely dependent on the cooperation of government officials, whom he tried to persuade that the government could and should exercise its legal right to own the political memoirs of dead leading figures.[48] According to Anīs, the ignorance of many officials hindered progress. At one point, he and professor Aḥmad ʿAbd al-Raḥmān Muṣṭafa approached the minister of culture and explained the problem of political memoirs, hoping for swift cooperation. In a brief, tense meeting the minister fired back, "How much do you need?" and then immediately declared, "The modern

46. *Al-Akhbār* intentionally sensationalized the memories, presenting them as a thriller of espionage, murder, behind-the-scenes dubious politics, and even sex. See the story of spy ʿAzīza (Madame Rushborn), the Egyptian Mata Hari who was after Farīd's secrets. *Al-Akhbār*, June 19–20, 1964, pp. 4, 5.

47. For the exchange, see Muḥammad Anīs, "Daʿwa li-l-waṭaniyya lā daʿwa li-l-iḥtikār," *Al-Jumhūrīya*, July 30, 1964, p. 3; and Mūsa Ṣabrī, "Hātuhā lī ḥabībī," *Al-Akhbār*, August 5, 1964, p. 14. Apparently, journalists, such as the ones working for *Al-Akhbār*, were regularly sent to the British Public Record Office to prospect for forgotten stories. Personal communiqué from Robert Tignor, February 2004.

48. A 1954 law allowed the government to appropriate such documents. See discussion below.

history of Egypt begins in July 23, 1952. It did not have any modern history prior to that date!"[49] Notwithstanding such obstacles, progress was gradually made, and soon the government flatly prohibited the selling or exporting of any historical documents without direct ministerial permission. In chapter 6, I mentioned the legal battle over Zaghlūl's memoirs. It was in this context that those memoirs were seized, and students began analyzing them.[50] In the same year, the first part of the correspondence between ʿAbd al-Raḥmān Fahmī and Saʿd Zaghlūl was also published. Anīs wrote what he felt was a proper preface for the publication.[51] Later, part of Muṣṭafa Kāmil's unpublished correspondence was made available as well.[52]

After the issue of political memoirs, the second burning issue was that of the reorganization of the national archive (Dār al-wathāʾiq). Quite naively, Anīs was now pushing for a huge reform that had been on the minds of academic historians for quite some time. Before we continue, however, a brief history of archival organization since 1952 is in order. Since the 1930s, historians had advocated for greater availability of twentieth-century source material. We have seen how this issue was an important element in the historians' efforts to gain professional recognition and cultural bargaining power. Over the years, a host of pleas, subcommittees, and reports calling for archival reforms failed to produce results. During the 1950s, Aḥmad ʿAbd al-Raḥmān Muṣṭafa participated on such a committee.[53] In 1954, the Ministry of National Guidance established Dār al-wathāʾiq, the first national archive. Though close to nothing is known about the circumstances behind this decision, most likely it came from the circles of the National Party, which controlled this ministry. The central motivation was to eliminate the archival reality of ʿĀbdīn.[54] A new progressive law backed the national archive and gave it judicial power over individuals and government agencies alike. For instance, Dār al-wathāʾiq could decide which body of documents constitutes historical heritage and force its owners to hand it into government control. It also

49. ʿAbd al-Raḥīm Muṣṭafa, "Muḥammad Anīs muʾarrikhan wa munāḍilan," p. 63. For the reluctance of Minister Tharwat ʿUkasha to help, see al-Sayyid, "Muḥammad Anīs: Al-rajul wa-l-qaḍiyya," p. 150.

50. *Al-Ahrām*, June 22, 1963, p. 7.

51. It seems that getting a hold of this material was relatively easy. Muḥammad Anīs, ed., *Dirāsāt fī wathāʾiq 1919* (Cairo: Maktaba al-anglū al-miṣriyya, 1963).

52. Published as Muṣṭafa Kāmil, *Ṣafaḥāt maṭwīya min tārīkh al-zaʿīm Muṣṭafa Kāmil: Rasāʾil jadīda li-Muṣṭafa Kāmil min 8 yūniyū 1895 ilā 19 Fabrāyir 1896*, edited by Muḥammad Anīs (Cairo: al-Hayʾa al-Miṣriyya al-ʿamma li-l-kitāb, 1987).

53. Aḥmad ʿAbd al-Raḥīm Muṣṭafa, "Ḥawla iʿādat taqyyīm tārīkhunā al-qawmī," *Rūz al-Yūsuf*, July 8, 1963, p. 12.

54. Maḥmūd ʿAbbās Ḥamūda, *Al-Madkhal ila dirāsat al-wathāʾiq al-ʿarabiyya* (Cairo: Maktabat nahḍat al-sharq, 1995), p. 49.

stipulated that on official demand, all government ministries must submit their records to the archive. Until then, each government branch had been obliged to manage its own records in coordination with Dār al-wathā'iq.[55] Compared with the practices of 'Ābdīn, this progressive law grounded in legislation important standards and values, such as accountability, transparency, accessibility of records, and collection development.

Yet, in reality, none of these progressive ideas was tested. The offices of Dār al-wathā'iq continued to reside in 'Ābdīn, and records under its jurisdiction were dispersed all over Cairo (to al-Azhar, Dār al-maḥfūẓāt in the citadel, and other locations). This huge collection was neither inventoried nor cataloged.[56] Simply, there were too many records and collections to deal with and few means by which to do so. The will to do so was also lacking, and so was an understanding of the cultural importance of such a project. In the pages of *Al-Ahrām,* Anīs wondered how a revision of history could take place when Dār al-wathā'iq was paralyzed and its director was busy organizing foreign archives abroad.[57]

It was clear to everyone involved that Dār al-wathā'iq was in a complete state of disarray. To add insult to injury, the archive's administration was biased against Egyptian scholars and seemed to extend better service to foreign students. The ground was ready for another scandal. This time, it involved Harvard graduate student Helen Rivlin, an advisee of Hamilton Gibb. Working on Egyptian history during the reign of Muḥammad 'Alī, Rivlin was fascinated with the overwhelming historiographical intervention of the 'Ābdīn project. Intimately acquainted with its history, she was granted access to the restricted collection that I described in chapter 3 as the "archive of the 'Ābdīn archive." She spent weeks inventorying that collection but in the process got into a conflict with the archive's directors.[58] Apparently, since 1952, Egyptian scholars had been prohibited access to collections that were open to foreigners.[59] Not only was such a reality was in opposition to the spirit of the revolution; it also violated the 1954 law, which, as a lesson from the royal era, emphasized admission on an equal basis. Like Arthur Goldschmidt before her, Rivlin was too successful in her pursuit of knowledge and a bit unaware of the political circumstances of which her pursuit was a part.

55. For a draft of Law 356, see ibid., pp. 119–142.

56. Abū Shu'aysha', *Dirāsāt fī-l-wathā'iq wa marākiz al-ma'lūmāt al-wathā'iqiyya,* p. 66.

57. Despite the condition of Dār al-wathā'iq, its director turned his attention elsewhere, extending his professional services to the governments of Sudan and Tunisia. Muḥammad Anīs, "Turāthunā al-qawmī . . . Ya wazīr al-thaqāfa!" p. 9.

58. Consequently, Rivlin published *The Dār al-wathā'iq in 'Ābdīn Palace at Cairo as a Source for the Study of the Modernization of Egypt in the Nineteenth Century.* As we saw in chapter 3, it is an invaluable resource—indeed, one of a kind—that completes our understanding of the royal project.

59. 'Abd al-Raḥīm Muṣṭafa, "Muḥammad Anīs mu'arrikhan wa munāḍilan," p. 63.

The imbroglio, about which Rivlin declined to comment, allegedly involved the unauthorized removal of documents. Whether or not this actually occurred, her career in the archive came to an abrupt end.

In an atmosphere of repeated scandals in which foreigners persistently "encroached" on Egypt's cultural legacy, Anīs requested the establishment of a center for the administration of historical records.[60] Most probably, the intercepted model of the AUC project inspired him. In June 1964, the center was officially inaugurated. Though originally founded under a different name, since 1967 it has been known as the Center of Documents and Contemporary History of Egypt (Markaz wathā'iq wa tārīkh miṣr al-mu'āṣir). The center's mission statement declared that by collecting source material it would facilitate the study of contemporary Egyptian history.[61] As far as the issue of source material was concerned, this mission precisely overlapped with the official duties of Dār al-wathā'iq. No one seemed to care, certainly not Anīs. Almost immediately, Egyptian graduate students such as 'Abd al-Khāliq Lāshīn began working with the political memoirs the center managed to seize. Another group edited memoirs and prepared them for publication. First in a daily newspaper and then in *Al-Kātib,* the main organ of the socialist cause, the political memoirs of Muḥammad Farīd were made available to the public.[62] The point was clear: historical documents belong to the people and should always be available to them.

Simultaneously, in a series of articles in *Al-Katib,* Anīs proposed a grand synthesis of modern Egyptian history from the late eighteenth century to the 1952 Revolution.[63] Heavily based on the work of Ibrāhīm 'Āmir and his friends, the articles summed up the socialist historical agenda along the lines of Egypt's transformation from feudalism to socialism. Working from within the logic of the founder paradigm, they established the groundwork for much of what was to follow.[64] Nonetheless, the focus of activity remained historiographical reorganization and not actual writing.

In the field of source material, the job of administering historical records was

60. *Al-Ahrām,* April 5, 1963, p. 13.

61. *Miṣr al-Ḥadītha* 1 (2002): p. 445; Sayyid, *Dār al-kutub al-miṣriyya,* p. 95.

62. Beginning in November 1969 and throughout 1970, *Al-Kātib* serialized and commented on the memoirs of Muḥammad Farīd. Ra'ūf 'Abbās, Sayyid Muṣṭafa, and Muḥammad Anīs, "Muḥammad Farīd wa mudhakkarātuhu," *Al-Kātib,* November 1969, pp. 2–80; *Al-Jumhūrīya,* October 16, 1969, pp. 5, 14.

63. Muḥammad Anīs, "Dirāsa fī-l-mujtama' al-miṣrī," *Al-Kātib,* serialized from June–November 1965 to March 1966.

64. Cowritten with another colleague, the articles were processed into a book. It was dedicated to "the masses": Muḥammad Anīs and Rajab Ḥarāz al-Sayyid, *Thawrat 23 Yūlyū 1952 wa uṣūluhā al-tārīkhiyya* (Cairo: Dār al-nahḍa al-'arabiyya, 1969), introduction, pp. 110–146. See also Gran, "Modern Trends in Egyptian Historiography,".

far from finished. Locating its next field of operation, the subcommittee for historical records requested permission from the government to search for archival sources abroad. The argument was that a revision of modern history requires such records.[65] The Ministry of Culture consented. And thus, almost forty years after King Fu'ād had dispatched his emissaries to Europe's central archives, Egyptian officials were once again on the hunt. A high-ranking official was sent to England and the United States. Aside from the documents that were copied and sent to Egypt, not much is known about this initiative.[66] This time, however, professors raised the question of the organic order and origin of records. As a result of their experience in 'Ābdīn, they doubted the possibility of putting such an enormous system in order, especially, when Dār al-wathā'iq was practically half-paralyzed.[67] Indeed, the project never amounted to more than one or two trips abroad.

At that point, a crucial administrative development took place. In 1965 the government decided to merge Dār al-wathā'iq and Dār al-kutub. Both intuitions had been reformed in 1954, when progressive legislation was introduced also to Dār al-kutub. It is yet unclear who pushed for the merge. Since Anīs demanded that the Center of Documents and Contemporary History of Egypt would operate from within Dār al-kutub, his circles must have approved of the merger.[68] Certainly they did not fight it. Though the center and the archive were essentially two different institutions, government officials did not seem to grasp the distinctions. In fact, the officials were mainly preoccupied with their symbolic value.

The national archive and the national library were symbols of national sovereignty. They proved that Egypt was in control of its past and that the cultural revolution was making headway. On the symbolic date of July 23, 1961, the government laid the cornerstone for Dār al-kutub.[69] These were busy times during which Cairo's urban landscape was reshaped in order to represent the city's status as a capital of the Arab and nonallied world. Soon, along the recently inaugurated Nile corniche and in the vicinity of other revolutionary edifices, such as the new Radio and Television Building, the long modernistic edifice of Dār al-kutub was being built.[70] No one seemed to have had the time or the patience to delve into archive and library theory. All over the country, huge industrial mergers were

65. Sāmī, "Al-Ḍurūra allatī tafruḍ i'ādat kitābat tārīkh Miṣr al-ḥadīth," p. 7.

66. Maḥmūd al-Sharqāwī, "Fī dirāsat tārīkhunā al-ḥadīth," *Al-Risāla*, November 21, 1963, p. 22.

67. Specifically Aḥmad 'Abd al-Raḥīm Muṣṭafa referred to the problem of unbound records from Europe. 'Abd al-Raḥīm Muṣṭafa, "Ḥawla i'ādat taqyyīm tārīkhunā al-qawmī," p. 12.

68. Sayyid, *Dār al-kutub al-miṣriyya*, p. 95.

69. Ministry of Culture and Guidance, *Dār al-kutub fī 'ahd al-thawra* (Cairo: Dār al-kutub, 1962), p. 7.

70. The corniche was inaugurated in July 1956. *Al-Muṣawwar*, August 17, 1956, pp. 32–34.

taking place, and the library business was probably seen as nothing more than another merger. Furthermore, tight public (government) control over institutions was derived from the socialist creed of public ownership. Thus, mergers of all sorts were built on firm ideological ground. The universities, as we shall now see, could not expect a different kind of treatment.

FOR WHOSE SAKE?

As part of the post–World War II interest in socioeconomic reform, universities were also considered likely candidates for reorganization. Hence, during the early 1950s, a committee on the status of higher education in Egypt was formed. Among its members were the legal expert and judge ʿAbd al-Razzāq al-Sanhūrī and Muḥammad Shafīq Ghurbāl. Though they began working before the 1952 Revolution, their final report was submitted only in August 1953.[71] The final page of this report reads: "The university . . . should be free to formulate its own educational policy and to adopt the ways and means for its realization. It should be free to manage its budgetary and financial matters, appoint, promote and discipline its academic and administrative staff."[72] The day these recommendations were made public, *Al-Ahrām* cried, "Universities in Egypt are isolated from public life; their mission in the new age must be reconciled to activities of the ministries."[73] After that, and particularly in light of the unresolved "crisis of intellectuals," there was a growing realization that the universities remained the only area of the public sector in which the persistence of the old regime was all too visible. For a political leadership that claimed to lead a cultural revolution, this was an unacceptable situation.

Toward the late 1950s, the following view of the higher education system became common: A Western-oriented bourgeoisie had come to dominate the universities and marginalize progressive revolutionary forces. If the task of universities was to train specialists and produce a socialist vanguard, their sociopolitical and intellectual structure rendered them incapable of realizing their mission.[74] Hence, rather than engendering change, the universities perpetuated backwardness *(takhalluf)*. This reactionism *(rajʿiyya)* manifested itself in a dual sociointellectual rupture with the people. On the intellectual level the universities propagated knowledge that was irrelevant to Egypt's social reality and had little to do with the country's pressing needs. This form of intellectual alienation

71. "Tanẓīm al-taʿlīm al-jāmaʿī wa rabṭihi bi-ḥājāt al-bilād," *Al-Ahrām*, August 17, 1953, pp. 4, 9.
72. Najjar, "State and University in Egypt during the Period of Socialist Transformation, 1961–1967," p. 59.
73. Quoted by Najjar, ibid.
74. Muḥammad Anīs, "Al-Maḍmūn al-thawrī li-l-taṭwīr al-jāmaʿī," *Al-Ahrām*, July 4, 1964, p. 9.

resulted in deliberate exclusion of entire social groups.[75] It is an irony that a person like Muḥammad Anīs, whose social mobility was afforded by the university system, would write such lines. Nonetheless, many respectable figures, for instance, Luwīs ʿAwaḍ, believed that this analysis contained truth.

Beginning in 1961, Egypt's leadership forcefully moved to ideologize the universities in the desired socialist direction. Though the immediate goal was to bring about a general change in university atmosphere, the study of history was singled out as a field in urgent need of revision. While it was unclear how to transform sociology or geography, there was a very neat notion of what socialist historiography should be. The Charter and its commentaries showed the way. Other publications also underscored the problematic contradiction between the reactionary university climate and the creation of a truly modern Egyptian historiography. In the view of many, Egyptian history had been stolen from its people.[76] Colonial officials had provided the first information about the making of modern Egypt. Royal employees, such Aḥmad Shafīq and Ilyās al-Ayyūbī, had reiterated and subscribed to these ideas and had striven to perpetuate dynastic rule. Later, through his control of the RGS, King Fu'ād had financed foreigners to complete the job. They wrote in foreign languages. Important documents were concealed. With a highly efficient administrative machine behind them, royalists and their allies had achieved an overwhelming hegemony in the field of historical interpretation.[77] Strict measures of censorship backed their work and suppressed alternative views. Egyptian academic scholars affiliated themselves with this historiographic milieu and, thus, extended its influence. Consequently, academics perpetuated a situation in which Egyptians had lived throughout their entire modern experience without knowing their true history. While the people were in a state of complete disorientation, academic history focused only on kings and rulers.[78] Universities had betrayed their mission of creating an authentic Egyptian history.

Once the relation between the academia and historiography was established, the campaign to reform the universities and the project to revise history became inextricably linked. Wholeheartedly believing in the necessity and interconnectedness of both missions, Anīs's roles as a socialist ideologue, university professor, and historian embodied this relationship. In 1963 he wrote, "Just as it is impossible to grant the forces of reaction freedom to conduct their political and eco-

75. "Ḥawla risālat al-taʿlīm al-jāmaʿī," *Al-Ahrām*, February 4, 1967, p. 7; "Arbaʿa qaḍāyā ra'īsiyya tashku minhā jāmiʿātinā," *Al-Ahrām*, March 30, 1966, p. 7; Muḥammad Anīs, "Al-Maḍmūn al-thawrī," pp. 9, 11.

76. al-Sayyid, "Tārīkhunā al-qawmī fī ḍaw' al-ishtirākiyya," p. 87.

77. Anīs, "Al-Tārīkh fī khidmat al-taṭawwur al-ishtirākī," p. 11; Sāmī, "Al-Ḍurūra allatī tafruḍ iʿādat kitābat tārīkh Miṣr al-ḥadīth," p. 7; al-Ḥusaynī, "Al-Tārīkh kadhdhāb," pp. 30–31.

78. ʿAbd al-Ḥamīd al-Baṭriq, "Al-Tārīkh fī khidmat al-taṭawwur al-ishtirākī," *Al-Ahrām*, July 17, 1963, p. 11.

nomic activities . . . let us also confine intellectual freedom to the nationalist and socialist frameworks. If it is accepted that reaction cannot be allowed to conduct its feudalist or monopolistic-capitalistic activities unchecked, *it should be equally clear that the reactionary outlook cannot be allowed to evaluate our history.*"[79]

Soon, senior historian and president of the EHS, ʿIzzat ʿAbd al-Karīm, and his fellow "old regime" and "reactionary" historians were pulled into a fight for survival. Leading historians were now openly criticized. Once viewed as a paragon of historiographical integrity, in the 1960s Ghurbāl was described as an elitist who had absorbed Toynbee's aloofness. In his histories, he was blamed for overlooking the revolutionary role of the people. Other academic historians, such as Muḥammad Fuʾād Shukrī, were also attacked.[80] While Anīs's efforts in the field of source material gained the respect of "old-guard" historians, many historians were alienated by the campaign to transform the universities from secluded ivory towers to bastions of revolutionary thought and to force a socialist interpretation of history. Hence, with rare exceptions, hardly any academic historian took the trouble to fight for the reorganization of state records.[81] Now, they were all on the defense.

Before we turn to the actual argument regarding the social value of university historians, it is important to acknowledge that in reality the debate reflected the power balance between two opposing philosophies of how culture should function. Each philosophy with its own logic and experience, their intellectual roots stretched back to the intellectual framework of modern Egyptian culture, in place since the late nineteenth century. In brief, the main issue was that of commitment to or engagement with *(iltizām)* society.

Since the early 1950s, Arab intellectuals had called for *iltizām*, usually using the French terms *engagement* and *engagé*.[82] Though in the 1950s the political culture of the Arab East was loaded with slogans, *iltizām* was not one of them. Rather, it was a substantial concept that was borrowed from Jean-Paul Sartre's philosophy of freedom cum personal responsibility. In a nutshell, it meant "art for life's sake," and Arab literary critics translated this idea into *al-adab fī sabīl al-ḥayāt*.[83] It was

79. *Al-Ahrām*, July 10, 1963, p. 9; translated and quoted by Rejwan, *Nasserist Ideology*, p. 12 (emphasis added).

80. Socialist writers avidly searched Ghurbāl's writings for incriminating evidence. "Incriminating" statements such as "the 1919 Revolution was an outburst of *righteous* anger" proved his guilt. Nonetheless, Anīs maintained his respect and appreciation for Ghurbāl and even dedicated his book on Ottoman historiography to him. al-Sayyid, "Muḥammad Anīs: Al-rajul wa-l-qaḍiyya," p. 144; al-Sayyid, "Tārīkhunā al-qawmī fī ḍawʾ al-ishtirākiyya," pp. 88–89.

81. ʿAbd al-Raḥmān Muṣṭafa, who initially lobbied with Anīs, was a rare exception.

82. For *iltizām*, see Paul Starkey, "Commitment," *Encyclopedia of Arabic Literature* (New York: Routledge, 1998), pp. 175–176.

83. Abdul-Nabi Isstaif, "Forging a New Self, Embracing the Other: Modern Arabic Critical Theory and the West—Luwīs ʿAwaḍ," *Arabic and Middle Eastern Literatures* 5, no. 2 (2002): p. 162.

expected that whatever intellectuals wrote or did would influence society and, in turn, would be influenced by it. Almost instantly the call for intellectual engagement became the new ideal of the secular Arab intellectual of the 1950s. Literary writing idolized the cause and the need to fight and sacrifice on behalf of it. For reasons that do not concern us here, over the years, several meanings of *iltizām* coexisted; each called for different form of engagement. In many occasions, *iltizām* was widely translated into a narrowly defined political commitment to a specific ideology. In Egypt for instance, the socialist vanguard regarded *iltizām* as an unconditional political commitment to the socialist cause.[84]

In contrast to *iltizām* was the idealistic striving for human betterment inherent in the phrase "knowledge for its own sake." Rather than serving the cause of direct political engagement, this view conceived culture as a complex process of interaction among multiple players. According to this view, cultural change was the outcome of free interaction and not a result of an imposed state plan. It was commonly accepted that prerevolutionary culture in Egypt was based on the notion of knowledge for its own sake. Ṭaha Ḥusayn and Maḥmūd ʿAbbās al-ʿAqqād were two of its most ardent supporters. Ghurbāl's school fully subscribed to it.[85] In the mid-1960s, when the pressures on the universities mounted, the elderly Ṭaha Ḥusayn reiterated the creed that had unified his generation: "The function of the university is to create a perfect system of higher education and to pursue knowledge for its own sake and not for the sake of a government position." Others agreed: "For the university the discovery of truth is primordial; the needs of society are important but secondary."[86] For the socialists, this laissez-faire philosophy was a fiction that perpetuated foreign control.[87] "Science for its own sake," they argued, "is a luxury Egypt can no longer afford." At the present stage, "science for society should be the motto of the cultural revolution."[88] The issue was now a question of how far the government would go in substituting "history for the sake of the people" for "historical knowledge for its own sake." It was also a question of how cooperative and receptive the Egyptian intelligentsia would be with regard to such an enterprise. Experience showed that they knew how to resist.

But even before university professors began mobilizing to oppose government plans, al-Rāfiʿī's one-man school of history raised its opposition. Like anything else that had to do with this man, his objection was categorical, uncompromising,

84. However, Lūwīs ʿAwaḍ advocated a less political notion of *iltizām*. Abdul-Nabi Isstaif, "Forging a New Self, Embracing the Other," pp. 161–167.

85. Ibid.; Starkey, "Commitment," pp. 175–176.

86. Najjar, "State and University in Egypt," p. 84.

87. Ibid., p. 77. See also Rushdī Saʿīd, "Ḥawla azmat al-thaqāfa," *Al-Ahrām*, May 10, 1967, p. 7.

88. Najjar, "State and University in Egypt," p. 66.

and final. In fact, already during the 1950s, when Fatḥī Raḍwān had entertained the idea of rewriting modern Egyptian history, al-Rāfiʿī had objected to it. Now in his seventies, al-Rāfiʿī was a marginal, yet revered, figure whose work was elevated to a peculiar canonical status in which it was both respected and contested.[89] Marxists could never make sense of his work. (They used it only as a primary source.) They saw absolutely no connection between the heroic deeds he recorded and the social realities that had generated them. To the Marxist mind, his taken-for-granted sense of historical causality illustrated the unscientific nature of his entire enterprise.[90] In addition, socialists argued that al-Rāfiʿī neglected the countryside and focused almost entirely on large cities.[91] Thus, if they needed one more reason why history should be rewritten, al-Rāfiʿī's project was it. In one of his last interviews, al-Rāfiʿī defended himself, invoking, in turn, an archaic sense of historical knowledge: "There is absolutely no need for the rewriting of history, since I have already done so. I wrote history in an honest and correct fashion; thus, there is no need for rewriting it, *as there is no need for the rewriting of engineering and algebra.*"[92]

Al-Rāfiʿī, however, was no match for resourceful young socialists. Even the political leadership treated him with much kindness and compassion and not as an imminent intellectual threat. In 1964 he was talked about as Egypt's candidate for the Nobel Prize (unclear in which category).[93] He did not receive it. Two years later, in December 1966, he passed away, leaving behind him sixteen books, dozens of articles, a rich library, and a very empty bank account.[94] For all the criticism he attracted over the years, the debates, the skirmishes, the bans, the prison, and the insults, al-Rāfiʿī was a symbol. And when this symbol of Egyptian nationhood died, something of Egypt was lost as well. His funeral cortege left from the ʿUmar Makram mosque, turned onto Muṣṭafa Kāmil Square, and ended in the Muṣṭafa Kāmil mausoleum. He was put to rest alongside the forefathers of the

89. In 1963 he updated his corpus by publishing one last volume that traced the origins of the modern nationalist spirit back through the Pharaonic, Greco-Roman, and Byzantine eras. al-Rāfiʿī, *Tārīkh al-ḥaraka al-qawmiyya fī Miṣr al-qadīma.*

90. al-Sayyid, "Tārīkhuna al-Qawmī fī ḍaw' al-Ishtirākīya," pp. 89–90. See also a comment by Muḥammad Anīs in a meeting of the EHS: *MTM* 13 (1967): p. 353.

91. Muḥammad Anīs, "Al-Naẓra al-Ishtirākīya li-tārīkh mujtamaʿinā," *Al-Ahrām,* July 10, 1963, p. 9.

92. Quoted in ʿAbd al-Salām Ḥalaba, "Jabartī al-qarn al-ʿishrīn yataḥadath," *Al-Qūwwāt al-Muṣāllaḥa,* December 1966, p. 20 (emphasis added). In another interview he said, "The right history is to be found in my books." Sāmī, "Al-Ḍurūra allatī tafruḍ iʿādat kitābat tārīkh Miṣr al-ḥadīth," p. 7.

93. Iḥsān Bakr, "Al-Mu'arikh al-miṣri al-murashaḥ li-jā'īzat nūbil," *Al-Ahrām,* February 9, 1964, p. 30.

94. Right after his death, both Harvard University and the Libyan government offered his family significant sums of money for his library. The family patriotically refused and contributed the collection to Dār al-kutub. Crabbs, "Politics History and Culture in Nasser's Egypt," p. 404.

National Party, the leaders whose history he devotedly wrote and courageously defended. In the following days and weeks, Egypt's most important newspapers and journals passionately eulogized him. They wrote about what Egypt had lost. He was called "the Jabartī of the twentieth century."[95]

But tears and sentimentality did not deter those who pushed for reform, and the daily opposition of their adversaries was also visible. Academic historians could simply not bring themselves to write socialist history. As far as they were concerned, reevaluation and rejuvenation of historical meaning were a natural and welcomed process. Central direction and state intervention, however, were deemed disastrous. In fact, as Aḥmad ʿAbd al-Raḥīm Muṣṭafa argued, such direction and intervention evoked the experience of history writing in the Soviet Union and Nazi Germany.[96] Many scholars could not see the difference between the proposed state-backed socialist initiative and Fu'ād's royal project. If the guided experience under the monarchy resulted in severe falsification of history, why should the socialist experiment be any different? Neither royalism nor socialism, "the study of our modern history," they wrote, "should be based on historical veracity *(ṣidq)* and avoid political bigotry, which would empty it from truth."[97] Thus, they warned the public against the predicted grave consequences of Ḥanbalism *(ḥanbaliyya)* in historical research, meaning zealous and partisan scholarship.[98] Committed to the empiricism of the academic school and to its notion of truth in history, ʿIzzat ʿAbd al-Karīm argued that only new evidence, and not new ideas, perspectives, or political inclinations, should warrant rewriting. Revision, he contended, was an active and ongoing process *(mustamir)* that should not be interrupted. State-guidance *(tawjīh),* he warned, would take Egypt away from the truth.[99]

Thus, the debate over rewriting and university reform drifted into the realm of ethics and moralism. At stake was the foundational ethics of Ghurbāl's school. Driven by a definitive notion of science and truth, devoted socialists argued that the very process of rewriting was based on scientific methodology *(manhaj ʿilmī)* and was therefore inherently truthful.[100] To borrow a term from the philosopher Thomas Nagel, what socialist theory offered Egyptians was "a view from nowhere." That is, it offered historical meaning that was presumably uncondi-

95. *Rūz al-Yūsuf,* December 12, 1966, pp. 18–20; *Ākhar Sāʿa,* December 7, 1966, p. 17; *Al-Akhbār,* December 6, 1966, p. 7; *Al-Jumhūrīya,* December 6, 1966, p. 24; *Al-Muṣawwar,* December 9, 1966, pp. 12–13; ʿAbd al-Salām Ḥalaba, "Jabartī al-qarn al-ʿishrīn yataḥadath," pp. 20–21. See also ʿUlwān, *ʿAbd al-Raḥmān al-Rāfiʿī,* pp. 309–328.

96. ʿAbd al-Raḥīm Muṣṭafa, "Ḥawla iʿādat taqyyīm tārīkhunā al-qawmī," p. 12.

97. al-Sharqāwī, "Fī dirāsat tārikhunā al-ḥadīth," p. 23.

98. Ibid.

99. Sāmī, "Al-Ḍurūra allatī tafruḍ," p. 7.

100. al-Sayyid, "Tārīkhuna al-Qawmī fī ḍaw' al-Ishtirākīya," p. 89.

tioned by its environment and hence was beyond judgment, was objective and real at all times—the ultimate knowledge. Forcefully believing in such a view, socialist historiography entirely presupposed the interpretation of its object of investigation. As philosopher Jean Luc-Nancy observed, "Ideological operativity is the operativity of a will that knows itself *already* to be the reality of its representation."[101] Socialist historiography falls squarely into this definition.

Thus, the due process of source material examination, deliberation, consideration of other views, and reconstruction of the historical object was denied. Rewriting history also meant a revision of ethics and methodology and, thus, had profound moral implications. Socialist historians tended to examine a given historical phenomenon only in light of its conformity (or nonconformity) with the objective scientific historical process. The degree of this conformity enabled them to evaluate whether their historical object was right or wrong, good or bad. Put differently, this historiographical process aimed at moral judgment. As we have seen, academic scholarship was not free from biases, political or otherwise. All historiographies are, to one degree or another, ideological. However, while Ghurbāl's school called for the separation of moral judgment from historical analysis, socialists espoused the exact opposite. This was the crucial difference between the groups. Unaware of its own limitations, the socialist creed did not remain on paper.

Over the years, university professors spoke of an atmosphere of bigotry, moral cowardice, and fanaticism. An acute observer, professor of economics Galal Amin recently wrote on what happened to his fellow colleagues during the 1960s: "The government's insistence that its ideology be dominant in university instruction had a corrupting influence on economic scholarship in a number of ways. The weaker spirits in academia hurried to write whatever the government wanted to read. . . . the more independently minded became discouraged, and some even preferred to leave Egypt altogether."[102] Professors of history who did not embrace socialism experienced the treatment. Those who still had any working relationships with Western academia noticed that on some occasions their environment became increasingly hostile. One prominent example comes to mind.

During 1964, Bernard Lewis and Peter Holt, of the School of Oriental and African Studies at London University (SOAS), began organizing an international conference on the modern historiography of Egypt. This was the second time in which the two had ventured to cover the vast territory of Middle Eastern historiography, a sensitive issue.[103] The conference was scheduled to take place in London

101. Jean-Luc Nancy, "Our History," *Diacritics* 20, no. 3 (Autumn 1990): p. 114.

102. Galal Amin, *Whatever Happened to the Egyptians? Changes in Egyptian Society from 1950 to the Present* (Cairo: American University in Cairo Press, 2000), p. 159.

103. The first conference took place in 1958, and its proceedings were published as Lewis and Holt, eds., *Historians of the Middle East.*

on April 1965. Along with Iraqi and Lebanese scholars, several Egyptian historians, ʿAbd al-Ḥamīd Baṭrīq, Jamāl al-Dīn al-Shayyāl, and Muḥammad Anīs, were invited to participate.[104] News traveled fast. When in June 1964 the daily newspaper *Al-Ahkbār* learned of the planned conference, it headlined its article, "Our Modern History between London and Tel-Aviv: The Hard Task of Our Professors at the London Conference."[105] In the body of the article, the symposium was portrayed as a dangerous conspiracy against Egypt. Specifically two papers, one titled "The National Charter" (by Nadav Safran) and the other titled "The Social Development in Egypt since 1952" (by P.J. Vatikiotis) concerned *Al-Ahkbār*. The presence of Israeli scholars did little to pacify anxiety. Hence, *Al-Ahkbār* called Egyptian professors to meet in advance and coordinate their message.

In *Al-Kātib*, Rajāʾ al-Naqqāsh dismissed the conference as an insincere, selective, and manipulative colonial enterprise. He wished to see the day when such a conference would be held in Egypt. Then, however, the academic perspective would be that of Indians, Russians, and other excluded communities.[106] These reactions to the conference transformed the individual business of a university professor into the national case of the "Egyptian delegation." Both in Cairo and London, pressures mounted.

On April 12, 1965, the conference was opened as planned. For whatever reason, Muḥammad Anīs did not attended. However, surprisingly, and probably at the insistence of the Arab Socialist Union, Ismāʿīl Ṣabry ʿAbdallāh and Ibrāhīm Saʿd al-Dīn, two senior communists fresh out of jail, attended the conference. The organizers were well aware of the existing tensions, and "the Director . . . went out of his way to stress that SOAS was an independent body, which had no government connections, and none with Foreign Office in particular."[107] A British Foreign Office official reported, "At the opening session the Chairman began by announcing that two papers," by Dr. Safran and Dr. Vatikiotis, "would not be discussed on the grounds that 13 years was too short a time in which to reach any definite conclusions, that much vital material was still unavailable." The report continued: "I discovered, however, from Dr. Vatikiotis during a tea break that he had in fact been informed only the night before."

Regardless of the great efforts to create a hospitable atmosphere, Egyptian scholars were anxious and uncomfortable.[108] Political pressures at home trans-

104. Al-Shayyāl participated in the previous conference and, under the name el-Din el-Shayyal Gamal, published his pathbreaking work "Historiography in Egypt in the Nineteenth Century," in Lewis and Holt, eds., *Historians of the Middle East*, pp. 401–421.

105. FO 371/183975, document VG 2231/2.

106. "Dawr al-fikr fī-l-mujtamaʿ al-ishtirākī," *Al-Kātib*, January 1965, p. 20.

107. This and the following quotes are taken from FO 371/183975.

108. Ibid.

formed what should have been a standard academic experience into a daring political test in which foreign ministries were involved behind the scenes. At a time in which Egyptian reaction to the colonial and royal histories was at its peak, the conference came to symbolize the power of historiographical reaction. Within this highly charged atmosphere, it was difficult to expect a different attitude. Socialism, as we have seen, had many latent tendencies, including zealotry and xenophobia. The "knowledge for the sake of society" campaign was accompanied by such a tone.

Just when the tensions within the small community of Egyptian intelligentsia were close to a boiling point, a meeting was convened in order to smooth over some of the differences. Beginning in November 29, 1965, seven months after the SOAS conference, historians met at the offices of the EHS, crowded on the second floor of a large gray building halfway between Taḥrīr and Ṭalʿat Ḥarb squares, in center-city Cairo. They convened for four weekly sessions, dedicated in turn to political, economic, cultural, and social history. In total, around thirty historians, literary critics, and journalists attended the meetings. Some hardly spoke; others could not stop speaking. To judge from the published minutes, unlike the biting exchanges in the press and the pressures of the London affair, this was a very relaxed and polite exchange. Though the original intention was to discuss the very idea of state-sponsored revision, the discussion soon drifted to anything even remotely related to history rewriting. At times thoughtful and at others rather dull and trite, this series of meetings could easily be given the title "What Is History?"

Professor Aḥmad ʿAbd al-Raḥmān Muṣṭafa began by raising a consensual concern: the predicament of modern records. Retreating from his position on what ought to propel revision, he contended that if rewriting was to take place, new source material would be needed. Just as was done in Europe, he said, the Ministry of Foreign Affairs ought to catalog its correspondence and open it to the public.[109] On the same topic, other participants commented on the irony that Egyptian historians were not allowed to benefit from the riches of the Egyptian heritage.[110] Later, the discussion shifted to a question that preoccupied all four sessions: Where should rewriting begin? Some people suggested that though the proposal was to rewrite modern history *(tārīkh ḥadīth),* whenever this period begins, it was meaningless without a serious study of the Mamluk era.[111] Publicist ʿAbd al-Rāziq Ḥasan argued, "Our modern history begins right where the capitalist roots of our society lie."[112] Many thought that the purpose of rewriting was

109. *MTM* 13 (1967): pp. 346–347.

110. Particularly, they referred to *awqāf* records. Ibid., pp. 347–348.

111. Ibid.

112. Ibid., p. 351.

to represent the outlook of the present. When reality changes, new ideas can open the past to new interpretations.[113] Put differently, not only should new historical evidence initiate a process of reevaluation, but also the creation of new meaning can engender rewriting.

A staunch empiricist, Aḥmad ʿIzzat ʿAbd al-Karīm came close to considering a similar position: "It is necessary to study our modern social and national history so that we can better understand the origins of our present ideas and values."[114] Therefore, if the single most important public development was the present socioeconomic change, historians should direct their energy to this arena. This is an extremely important point, because it legitimized and substantiated the school of modern social history within academia. From there, the discussion shifted to the uniqueness of the Egyptian historical experience and the need to clarify professional terminology so that the specificity of Egypt's history would be addressed.[115] Ḥikmat Abū Zayd asked when and how the profession of history writing emerged. He seemed to suggest that historiographical self-awareness would assist in focusing the discussion. It would be twenty years before his proposal would be taken seriously. The meeting ended there, but the debates continued. At the outskirts of mainstream revolutionary culture, under ʿIzzat ʿAbd al-Karīm's reassuring leadership, academia rebounded. Its reluctance to succumb to the state-sponsored historiographical process frustrated the socialist project. But there was also criticism from within the socialist ranks.

One example of this criticism came from the journalist Mūsa Ṣabrī, of *Al-Akhbār,* who sarcastically suggested to Anīs that he might want to stop preaching long erudite lectures on methodology. Egyptians, he said, expect to see some history published. This comment touched the weakest aspect of the entire rewriting project. As we have just seen, it was not really about actual writing and, indeed, not much was rewritten. Apparently, many of those who spoke of the necessity for historical revision were literary critics. In Egypt, they were always at the forefront of intellectual and ideological innovation. However, people like Maḥmūd Amīn al-ʿĀlim, Rajāʾ al-Naqqāsh, and ʿĀbbās Ṣāliḥ never wrote history. Hence, there was a gap between the revisionist rhetoric and the actual historiographical potential of intellectuals.[116] In addition, even when the skill and the will were abundant, it still took years to publish well-researched works. In fact, as we saw in chapter 6, the first scholarly studies using Zaghlūl's memoirs were published only around

113. Ibid., pp. 352–353, 367–369.

114. Ibid., p. 364.

115. ʿIzzat ʿAbd al-Karīm was concerned about economic historians studying Egypt in (Marxist) European terms that blinded them to Egypt's actual past. Ibid., pp. 354–355.

116. See a roundtable discussion about revolutionary thought: "Dawr al-fikr fī-l-mujtamaʿ al-ishtirākī," pp. 4–29.

the mid-1970s, and the memoirs themselves reached the book market only in the 1980s. By that time, however, they were free of scientific socialism.

Intimately acquainted with Egypt's historiographical scene, Peter Gran has argued that "Muḥammad Anīs was a seminal historiographer because he moved from political and institutional history to socioeconomic analysis of political reality."[117] Though true, Anīs immensely profited from the headway made by the Marxist triumvirate of Shuhdī 'Aṭiyya al-Shāfi'ī, Fawzī Jirjis, and Ibrāhīm 'Āmir, though he never properly acknowledged them. It is impossible to imagine any of Anīs's work, including that on the 1952 Revolution, without such studies. Hence, it would be fair to say that, more than anything else, Anīs's importance lies in the field of historiographical action, including that of teaching.[118] His writing per se was of lesser importance.[119]

CONCLUSION

As a system of thought, Arab socialism was no longer able to contain the phenomenal and conceptual world that surrounded it. As a conclusive worldview, it failed, and it did so on a number of fronts. Historical thought and, in particular, the belief in historical laws of destiny were central to the experience of Nasserism. As time passed, when the next generation of historians enjoyed the benefit of perspective and hindsight, they completely distanced themselves from the laws and destiny of history. Clearly, ideology came at a price of liquidating certain kinds of knowledge and even part of the very process of thinking. Being in control of history was acknowledged as an unfeasible project.

To date, one of the best critiques of the scientific historiographical mindset is that of the anti-authoritarian philosopher Karl Popper. His argument develops along the lines that scientific historiography destroyed (liberalist) history by claiming to explain it all. In return, history ruined the scientific mindset by unfolding in an unpredictable way. Published in 1957, *The Poverty of Historicism*

117. Gran, "Modern Trends in Egyptian Historiography," p. 371.

118. Over the years Anīs advised close to seventy graduate students. Hishmat, *Dalīl al-rasā'il al-jāmi'iya,* vol. 1, p. 459.

119. This observation includes Anīs's contribution to the field of Ottoman studies. In line with his general attitude toward historical records, he encouraged young historians to make full use of various Ottoman collections in Cairo. However, Anīs himself did not use these collections. His book on the Ottoman state in the Arab East from 1516 to 1914 acknowledged that Egypt ought to be understood through the Ottoman experience. Though an important and original point, like most scholars Anīs did not read Ottoman, did not use proper archival sources, and therefore did not truly break from the previous anti-Ottoman tradition. Muḥammad Anīs, *Madrasat al-tārīkh al-miṣrī fī-l-'aṣr al-'uthmānī* (Cairo: Dār al-jīl li-l-ṭibā'a, 1962), pp. 7–28; Muḥammad Anīs, ed., *Al-Dawla al-'uthmāniyya wa-l-sharq al-'arabī 1514–1914* (Cairo: al-Maktaba al-anglū al-miṣriyya, 1965), pp. 3–4, 140–164.

was a sensational refutation of scientific socialism and related ideologies. The dedication read: "In memory of the countless men and women of all creeds, nations or races who fell victims to the . . . belief in Inexorable Laws of Historical Destiny."[120] In this work, Popper dissected the idea that "by discovering the 'rhythms,' 'the laws,' or the 'trends' that underlie the evolution of history" *historical prediction* is possible.[121] Appalled by the actual performance of Stalinism and Nazism, Popper warned that "*the belief in historical destiny is sheer superstition, and that there can be no prediction of the course of human history by scientific or any other rational methods.*"[122] Egyptian socialism was, of course, on an entirely different moral scale from that of Nazi Germany and the Soviet Union. The aims of Nasserism, liberation and modernity, were just, and its methods were largely legitimate. Yet, despite that, it, too, subscribed to a deterministic philosophy of history that delivered neither modernity nor liberation. What remained from this experiment was the bittersweet memory of a noble effort and the legacy of proud resistance.

But there was much more to the rewriting project than simply failure. By no means did the disintegration of this project render the effort obsolete.[123] To begin with, it attempted to create a sense of textual hierarchy in which the celebratory histories of the 1950s were put in their right perspective as efforts of identity building alone. Then, the socialist experiment brought to center stage new thematic concerns and a new style of analytical writing. It marked a shift from narrative history to the examination of the historical structure within which individuals had functioned. Specifically, questions related to land tenure, capital, income distribution, and working-class history defined the historiographical agenda of future generations. The geographical focus also shifted from the big cities to the countryside. These were precisely the same topics and areas that socialists urged academia to embrace when they ordered the rewriting project.[124] Another important contribution was related to the ideal that history should emphasize the role of "the people." For scientific socialism, the people were only the "bearers" of the structural forces that shape their destiny. Hence, this historiography was structurally incapable of giving history a human face.[125] Nonetheless, it inherited the ideal and left room for new methods through which it could materialize in the future.

120. Karl Popper, *The Poverty of Historicism* (New York: Basic Books, 1960), front page.

121. Ibid., p. 3.

122. Quoted in John Passmore, "The Poverty of Historicism Revisited," *History and Theory* 14, no. 4 (1975): p. 35 (emphasis added).

123. Gorman, though, had a different impression. Gorman, *Historians, State and Politics,* p. 59.

124. al-Sayyid, "Tārīkhuna al-Qawmī fī ḍaw' al-Ishtirākīya," p. 90; Anīs, "Al-Naẓra al-Ishtirākīya li-tārīkh mujtama'inā," p. 9; Crabbs, *Politics, History and Culture,* p. 395.

125. As a modernistic ideology, scientific socialism was extremely paternalistic toward the "masses" and felt morally obliged to transform their lives by fighting their backward habits. This sense of mission was another aspect of the cultural revolution.

Beginning in the early 1970s, the third generation of academic historians combined these historiographical concerns with the methodological and ethic commitment of first-generation scholars. The result was the emergence of a new school of social and economic history, dominated by the advisees of ʿIzzat ʿAbd al-Karīm and other graduates of his Thursday seminar in ʿAyn Shams University.[126] Raʾūf ʿAbbās, Maḥmūd Mutawallī, ʿĀṣim Disūqī, ʿAlī Barakat, and to some extent Yunān Labīb Rizq proposed a new and enlightening perspective on Egypt's socioeconomic experience. In contrast with earlier writers on the same subjects, they based their work on painstaking archival research, including land registries and other unstudied collections.[127]

In the field of archival management, the tragic mistakes of the 1960s are still visible. Almost forty years after the creation of the Dār al-kutub and Dār al-wathāʾiq conglomerate, archivists, librarians, and historians are in agreement that this act was a dismal failure that betrayed the mission of both the national library and the national archive.[128] In 1971 the national press was added to the merger. As far as original source material was concerned, the progressive 1954 law was never applied, and Anīs's reformist cause was submerged in an ever-expanding and disoriented bureaucracy. Recently, the Center of Documents and Contemporary History of Egypt published a special dossier of documents from the March 1954 crisis: a major turning point in Nasserite politics. None of the published documents was in Arabic.[129] Despite the passage of years, the records of the Nasserite era have still not been subjected to public scrutiny. Many still remain in the hands of individuals who served the regime, such as Muḥammad Ḥasanayn Haykal.[130] Despite high expectations for public accountability, the government persistently refused to submit its own records to the people. The documents to the people project, begun with such enthusiastic declarations, ended silently. Its cause, though, has never been forgotten.[131] As the political establishment of Nasserism began to disintegrate, more room for doubt and new prospects for operation occurred. But so did a great deal of fatigue and concerns about the possible price of a new effort. Given new opportunities, more university professors began taking teaching positions abroad. ʿIzzat ʿAbd al-Karīm and Muḥammad Anīs were among the first to leave. Their students remained.

126. Gran, "Modern Trends in Egyptian Historiography," pp. 367–368.

127. Ibid., pp. 369–371.

128. For how the mission of the national library and the archive was compromised, see Khalīfa, *Dār al-kutub al-qawmiyya*, pp. 5–7ff.; and Sayyid, *Dār al-kutub al-miṣriyya*, pp. 1–2.

129. *Miṣr al-Ḥadītha* 2 (2003): pp. 463–493.

130. Gorman, *Historians, State and Politics*, p. 76.

131. Khālid Fahmī, "Laysa difāʿan ʿan dār al-wathāʾiq: Faṣl dār al-wathāʾiq ʿan dār al-kutub," *Akhbār al-Adab*, March 16, 2003, pp. 31–33.

9

Authoritarian Pluralism

1970–2000

Immediately after Anwar Sadat's accession to power in November 1970, the seemingly united front of Nasserism began to collapse. In less than a decade the authoritarian populism and socialist dogmatism of the previous era were replaced by a political system of authoritarian pluralism. Expanded and bureaucratically perfected by President Husni Mubarak since 1981, this new political system has had a paradoxical quality: For the liberalization of the political and cultural arenas and the diversification and privatization of the media and the economy did not undermine authoritarianism but only strengthened it. The puzzling irony of this counterintuitive sociopolitical system would probably leave even an acute critic like George Orwell speechless.

In this chapter I examine the multiple ways in which authoritarian pluralism shaped the historiographical marketplace. I argue that while authoritarian pluralism allowed previously marginalized groups such as the Muslim Brotherhood to write and publish history, the government monopoly on state records curtailed the ability to ascertain the veracity of historical interpretations. The lack of historical records undermined the value of historical truthfulness and severely damaged the capacity to maintain textual hierarchy. Furthermore, given the state's continuous disregard for other values—such as accessibility, transparency, and public accountability—the professional authority of academic historians, whose agenda of modern research was highly dependent on the maintenance of such values, declined sharply. Consequently, greater sections of the historiographical field became methodologically poor, culturally provincial, and philosophically speculative. Since the 1987 conference on historiography, the various aspects of this process have come to be known as the crisis of historical consciousness.

SETTING THE AUTHORITARIAN ARENA

The *infitāḥ,* the great structural transformations of the 1970s, began already in the wake of the 1967 war. The March 1968 reforms permitted the out-migration of workers to neighboring countries. A decade later, the thin stream of untrained workers was turned into a river of hundreds and thousands of employees, some of whom were the country's best and brightest. Many of the emigrants were members of Egypt's exhausted academic circles. They left because of money, professional opportunities, and the quest for basic civil liberties and personal freedom. Amid the new riches of Arab oil, the freedom to travel, the opportunity to live and work in a less dogmatic cultural climate, and the ability to communicate these new experiences to relatives and friends back home brought with them the collective realization that Nasserism, as a total cultural and economic system, had outlived its expediency.

Though Nasserism had been on the defensive on almost all fronts since 1967, people had, until 1970, largely held their tongues. Even if their acerbic manuscripts were ready for submission, they were never sent to publishers. However, days, if not hours, after Nasser was buried, Egyptians began telling their stories. They did so in any possible medium, whether inside or outside Egypt. A partial list of things that were up for consideration included the following: Why did the revolution restrict basic liberties, such as freedom of expression and association? Why did the state resort to oppression and torture? Why was the state so inefficient and corrupt? What happened in the Yemen and the 1967 wars? And, above all, did the *rais,* Gamal Abd al-Nasser, really know what was going on, or was he manipulated and betrayed by his closest aides?

Many individuals and groups wanted to provide answers to these questions. There were those who under Nasserism were imprisoned, tortured, silenced, purged, fired, and marginalized and others whose property was sequestered. There were patriots, such as Nasser's once-favorite writer Tawfīq al-Ḥakīm, whose book *The Return of Consciousness* was the first pejorative evaluation of the revolutionary era.[1] There was *Zayni Barakat,* the brilliant and unflattering historical allegory by Gamāl al-Ghīṭāni, which criticized the police state. But, alongside these critics, there were also the winners of the previous era and its staunch ideologues, such as Muḥammad Ḥasanayn Haykal and ʿAbd Allāh Imām, author of *Al-Nāṣirīyya* (1971), who were out to defend the deeds and especially the intentions of Nasserism. And so, the past was back, and an unprecedented number of individuals from all walks of life began writing and talking about it.[2]

1. Tawfiq al-Hakim, *The Return of Consciousness,* translated by Bayly Winder (New York: New York University Press, 1985).

2. A comprehensive discussion of the struggle over the heritage of Nasserism is an enormous undertaking, which lies outside the scope of this work. For an overview of this topic, see Meir

Sadat, whose initial political thrust was famously weak, needed to consolidate his power at a time in which a tide of historical writing threatened to undermine his legitimacy. In the aftermath of the May 1971 Corrective Revolution, during which the Nasserist network of political power was swiftly eliminated, and, later, as a result of the successful October 1973 war, Sadat's credentials allowed him to take a series of critical steps. With the shift from socialism to capitalism, a corresponding shifting of state alliances also occurred, from the realm of peasants, workers, and the lower rural classes to the urban middle and upper classes. Because they were the only classes that could relate meaningfully to a capitalist marketplace, Sadat allowed these formerly marginalized urban classes to return to politicoeconomic circles of influence. He thus terminated the isolation of wealthy individuals, returned sequestered property to its previous owners, and protected it by law. Many judges and journalists who were detained and fired under Nasser were reinstated, and clear limitations were set on the use of police powers.[3] Symbolically, the president himself "presided over the public burning of tapes accumulated from over 22,000 telephone taps maintained by the internal security apparatus."[4] Presumably, the police state was dead.

Realizing that economic openness necessitated a corresponding political pluralism, Sadat established a special "hearing committee" *(lajnat al-istimāʿ),* which consulted all the legal and political sectors and registered their complaints. Two years later the Arab Socialist Union was replaced by a left-center-right platform of parliamentary representation, and old political actors such as the Wafd began making their political comeback. In 1979 multiparty elections took place. Since such rehabilitated political forces demanded a legitimate venue for publication in a fashion that would fairly represent the new ideological spectrum, the government relaxed its tight control over the publishing industry, and press censorship was decreased. In a matter of months, new newspapers, journals, and book series were inaugurated. In return for the seemingly democratic environment of the *infitāḥ,* Sadat expected political submission, which he conveniently couched as "responsible behavior." He even proposed a political "code of ethics" to ensure that criticism remained "responsible."[5] As we shall see, both he and Mubarak extended this paternalistic vision to history writing as well.

Seeking to strengthen the social bases of support, educational reform brought

Nuema, "Ha-Natzerism batqufa hapost natzerit" (Nasserism in the Post-Nasserist Era), unpublished Ph.D. dissertation, Bar Ilan University, 2004.

3. Raymond Hinnebusch, *Egyptian Politics under Sadat: The Post Populist Development of an Authoritarian-Modernizing State* (Cambridge: Cambridge University Press, 1985), p. 50.

4. John Waterbury, *Egypt: Burdens of the Past/Options for the Future* (Bloomington: Indiana University Press, 1978), p. 239.

5. Hinnebusch, *Egyptian Politics under Sadat,* p. 75.

more institutions of higher education to small urban centers of the countryside. Thus, between 1974 and 1978, seven new universities were added to the existing four (Cairo, Alexandria, Asyut, and the Suez Canal) in provincial centers such as Tanta, Minya, and Menufiya. In addition, "Sadat increased the proportion of students admitted to universities from roughly 40 percent of those who took the baccalaureate exam in the early 1970s to more than 60 percent in the late 1970s and early 1980s."[6] These policies allowed a record number of high school graduates to enroll in the higher education system.[7] Among many other things, that meant bringing history writing to entirely new places and publics.

Simultaneously, the government released thousands of political prisoners from across the political spectrum. Many were members of the Muslim Brotherhood. Previously banned from any form of participation in public life, the Islamists of the 1970s burst into this new sphere and became intensely involved in all forms of public life, including history writing. In a matter of a few years, the Islamists defeated the Left and achieved effective control of most rural and urban campuses. Worldly capitalism was one pillar of the *infitāḥ*, and a broadly conceived Islamic culture was supposed to become the other. This structure, however, was famously weak, because many Islamists combined capitalism and Islamic culture and became spectacularly rich, yet resentful of capitalism and the state.[8] Thereafter, they turned their wealth to the publishing industry and established from scratch several strictly Islamic publishing houses, which poured dozens of Islamic history books onto the market.

Despite Sadat's paternalistic expectation of popular gratitude, political realities often took a slightly different turn. Amid violent student demonstrations, the wheat subsidy riots, deepening social cleavages, the rise of an aggressive breed of political Islam, and a host of other domestic, regional, and international challenges that emerged around the time of Sadat's 1977 trip to Jerusalem, his authoritarian pluralism was seen as weak, unstable, and even illegitimate. However, Sadat's sensational death did not terminate this authoritarian project. Under the stern and unimaginative bureaucratic regime of Husni Mubarak, the constitutional and administrative mechanisms of authoritarian pluralism have been significantly fortified.

Though political scientists identify a shift from liberalization (in the 1980s) to deliberalization (in the 1990s), the three survival strategies of Mubarak's regime have remained virtually the same: a winning combination of patronage and cooptation, exclusionary laws, and coercive powers. As Maye Kassem noted, "The

6. Carrie Rosefsky Wickham, *Mobilizing Islam: Religion, Activism and Political Change in Egypt* (New York: Columbia University Press, 2002), p. 38.

7. Kirk Beattie, *Egypt during the Sadat Years* (New York: Palgrave, 2000), p. 94.

8. Ibid., p. 153.

combination of these strategies allows for the existence of contained pluralism within an authoritarian regime and permits it to adopt images of liberalization/democratization without actually conceding to such measures."[9] Thus, Mubarak has ruled by resorting to emergency laws, executive decrees, military and other special courts, constant manipulation of legal procedures, and a good measure of downright repression. The regime has had a good excuse for putting such measures to work.

At war with political Islam, that is, with a significant body of its own citizens, the government has successfully monopolized all legitimate political activity, especially that of the many voluntary associations, professional syndicates, and trade unions. In order to ensure the longevity of its monopoly, most, if not all, elective processes are still being fixed. In sharp contrast with previous political orders, authoritarian pluralism has ruled without a guiding ideology, without elaborate means for popular mobilization, and, ultimately, without a vision.[10] Instead, it has ruled unimaginatively by means of carefully managed violence and routine microbureaucratic practices.

These endless bureaucratic procedures have critically shaped the domain of culture and, more relevant to this discussion, the very possibility of writing critical history. Historians of contemporary Egypt are not famous for running into trouble because of the "message" of their books. Though the penal code contains an article that speaks of "harming Egypt's image," it has never actually been applied to historians of the modern era. It is difficult to recall an incident in which a contemporary historian's work has been deemed to challenge the government monopoly on truth in public life, as opposed to judgments regarding the work (and the resulting fate) of several historians under the monarchy and Nasserism. This is because the authoritarian pluralism of Mubarak has been extremely successful in shaping a pluralistic historiographical marketplace of multiple voices but with little, if any, public agency. We will now turn to see how this came about.

THE THREE WAVES OF ISLAMIST HISTORIOGRAPHY

In 1970, a curious visitor to a bookstore who wanted to read about the history of the Muslim Brotherhood would probably have left the shop empty-handed. State policy prohibited the Brethren—and the loosely held coalition of Islamic cultural and political forces of which they were a part—from writing and publishing books on their role in contemporary Egyptian history, and the prohibition was

9. Maye Kassem, *Egyptian Politics: The Dynamics of Authoritarian Rule* (Boulder, CO: Lynne Rienner Publishers, 2004), p. 3.

10. Eberhard Kienle, *A Grand Delusion: Democracy and Economic Reform in Egypt* (London: I. B. Tauris, 2000), pp. 1–48.

strictly observed. So strict was this taboo that even academic scholars and journalistic pundits, who enjoyed a considerable degree of autonomy and protection, chose their topics carefully. For well over three decades, and especially since the elimination of democratic institutions in 1954, the state treated the Islamists as an exterior social body and not as an organic part of Egyptian society. It was expected that modern, secular state culture would assimilate the Islamic option and that the "problem" would be naturally resolved. Unexpectedly however, when the Islamists exemplified extraordinary organizational persistence and unusual cultural vitality, the Nasserist state forcefully drove the movement out of the public eye. Sadat's conscious decision to favor an Islamic cultural orientation in order to curb the Nasserist Left and appeal to broad social circles terminated this underground phase and opened the once-sealed public arena to broad Islamist participation. Islamists seized the moment.

The quest for a significant public role and the need to unite their own rank and file motivated the Islamists to invest heavily in establishing an Islamic publishing industry. Dozens of "cheap-print" editions by newly established, or recently rehabilitated, Islamic publishing houses, such as the extremely prolific Dār al-Anṣār and the politically conscious Dār Wahba, were made widely available to the public. The expansion of Islamic publishing was a political move beyond, and independent of, the economic considerations of demand and supply. The books were often sold expensively in Saudi Arabia, and the profits were used to subsidize cheap editions at home. Unsubsidized secular books had a hard time competing.[11] Beyond books, periodicals on politics and current affairs also figured strongly. *Al-Daʿwa* and *Al-Iʿtiṣām,* the Muslim Brotherhood's flagship journals, resumed their publication, and historical accounts were high on their agenda. Dozens of cheaply printed history books by unknown authors poured onto the market. This three-phased Islamic historiographical onslaught consisted of a plethora of genres such as prison memoirs, popular historic accounts of fateful and often violent events, integrated works on the history of the Muslim Brotherhood, biographies of Ḥasan al-Bannā, and specific academic studies on selected topics. After a decade of intensive work, around the time of Sadat's assassination, the same bookstore visitor with the same interest would have had multiple Islamic bookstores and publishers from which to choose. He or she could also have bought such books on the sidewalks of big cities. In light of this phenomenon, one Islamist writer openly spoke of an intellectual jihad.[12]

The first and most influential wave of writing was composed of a stream of biographies about the exemplary life of the Muslim Brotherhood's founding

11. Yves Gonzales-Quijano, *Les gens du livre: Édition et champ intellectuel dans l'Égypte Républicaine* (Paris: CNRS Éditions, 1998), pp. 160–164, 193–198.

12. Muḥammad Yiḥya, *Fī-l-radd ʿala al-ʿalmāniyīn* (Cairo: al-Zahra' li-l-iʿlām al-ʿarabī, 1985), p. 4.

father, Ḥasan al-Bannā. The main questions for consideration were, Who murdered him? Why? and How? Answers to these questions needed to address the violent atmosphere of the 1940s and the collapse of the liberal order. Initially, the Islamists, who had never written contemporary history before, failed to rise to this challenge and explained the murder of al-Bannā in general terms of ongoing conspiracy against "Islam." Many of these early, first-wave accounts employed a hidden-hand mechanism of explanation and were based on personal testimonies of al-Bannā's tortured "companions."

The style of writing was Islamic in the sense that more than a few stylistic similarities existed between the exemplary life of al-Bannā and the *sira* (biography) of the prophet Muhammad.[13] Consciously stepping onto the historiographical battlefield of national heroes, the authors of these books were responding to the hagiographies of Nasser, Zaghlūl, Muṣṭafa Kāmil, and many others. As part of this move, the Islamic press published anything that al-Bannā ever said or wrote.[14] Beyond al-Bannā and later Sayyid Quṭb, many other authors of first-wave historical works focused on the fate of the Muslim Brotherhood under the Nasser regime. One of the earliest dramatic compositions in this genre was *Al-Madhbaḥa* (The Massacre), which recounted in great detail the brutal killing of twenty-one Muslim Brotherhood prisoners in the Ṭura prison in June 1957. This chronicle of what the author calls "senseless killing" serves as an allegory for the entire Muslim Brotherhood's experience under Nasser.[15]

Another early publication was a posthumously published memoir by escaped Muslim Brotherhood prisoner Ḥasan 'Ashmāwī, titled *Al-Ikhwān wa-l-thawra* (The Brethren and the Revolution). 'Ashmāwī, who personally met Nasser in conjunction with the 1951 resistance in the canal zone and even assisted the Free Officers in hiding weapons in his family estate prior to the January 1952 "burning of Cairo," tried to understand how he had gone from being an anti-British patriotic warrior to public enemy number one.[16] Other writers had the same message.[17]

13. Jābir Rizq, *Al-Asrār al-ḥaqiqiyya li-ightiyāl ḥasan al-bannā* (Cairo: Dār al-anṣār, 1978), pp. 3–15, 26–27, 40–41; Muḥammad 'Abd Allāh al-Sammān, *Ḥasan al-Bannā . . . : Al-rajul wa-l-fikra* (Cairo: Dār al-i'tiṣām, 1978), pp. 39ff.; 'Abd al-Muta'āl al-Jabrī, *Li-mādhā 'ughtīla al-imām al-shahīd Ḥasan al-Bannā?* 2nd ed. (Cairo: Dār al-i'tiṣām, 1978), pp. 9–27, 109–115; 'Umar Tilimsānī, *Al-Mulham al-mawhūb ustādh al-jīl ḥasan Aḥmad 'Abd al-Raḥmān al-Bannā* (Cairo: Dār al-anṣār, 1981).

14. See, for instance, Ḥasan al-Bannā, *Qaḍīyatunā bayna yaday al-ra'y al-'amm al-miṣrī wa-l-'arabī wa-l-islāmī wa-l-ḍamīr al-'ālamī: Ākhar mā katab al-imām al-shahīd qubayla ightiyālihi* (Cairo: n.p., 1978).

15. Muṣṭafā al-Muṣīlḥī, *Al-Madhbaḥa: Fī-l-dhikrā al-'ishrīn li-l-madhbaḥa allatī ta'arraḍa lahā al-ikhwān al-muslimūn bi-līmān ṭarah yawm al-sabt, 1/6/1957* (Cairo: Dār al-anṣār, 1977), pp. 5–10.

16. Ḥasan 'Ashmāwī, *Al-Ikhwān wa-l-thawra* (Cairo: al-Maktab al-miṣri al-ḥadith, 1977), pp. 19–20.

17. Ḥasan Dawḥ, *Ṣafaḥāt min jihād al-shabāb al-muslim* (Cairo: Dār al-i'tiṣām, 1977).

How could it be that an organization that had fought the British and the Zionists with the utmost dedication imaginable was now treated as an anti-nationalist force worthy of brutal suppression? For the Muslim Brotherhood, this deep sense of betrayal never ceased to be a motivating force. Their style of writing was fiery, demagogic, vociferous, and sometimes even hysterical. Their books were not footnoted.

The high public profile of the Muslim Brotherhood triggered reactions from several academics and journalistic pundits. One such historian, always ready to jump into the fray, was the prolific ʿAbd al-ʿAẓīm Ramaḍān, who in some of his books, but especially in the pages of the daily *Al-Jumhūriyya,* refuted the Brotherhood's pseudohistorical logic of constant victimization and persecution.[18] Another influential writer was the Marxist historian Rifʿat al-Saʿīd, whose footnoted biography of al-Bannā took issue with virtually the entire corpus of public argumentation made by the Muslim Brotherhood.[19] Drawing on Western scholarship, particularly Richard Mitchell's previously banned classic, *The Society of the Muslim Brothers,* as well as the works of Albert Hourani, Hamilton Gibb, and Gustave von Grunebaum, al-Saʿīd made the best of Sadat's lifting of censorship of foreign academic publications.[20] The second wave of Islamist historiography was born against this backdrop.

In 1978 Anwar al-Jindī, an exceptionally prolific scholar of Islamic medieval and early modern history with more than fifty titles to his name, published an extremely influential book—the first of its kind—in which he tried to explain the nationalist paradox from al-Bannā's perspective. This was by far the most seriously researched and well-written biography of al-Bannā. It was also the most articulate statement on the history of the Muslim Brotherhood to date.

His main argument was that the Wafd's admiration for Western institutions and norms undermined its ability to resist the colonizers and that, for this and other reasons, it had ultimately failed the nation. Given the weakness of al-Azhar University throughout the monarchic era, the Brethren were left with the task of speaking for "Islam."[21] Quite conveniently, however, al-Jindī ignored, or

18. Ramaḍān argued that between 1938 and 1947 the Muslim Brotherhood closely collaborated with the monarchy in undermining the liberal order. Shaykh ʿAbd Allāh al-Sammān responded in *Al-iʿtiṣām.* This exchange was republished in ʿAbd al-ʿAẓīm Ramaḍān, *Miṣr fī ʿaṣr al-Sadat* (Cairo: Maktabat madbūlī, 1986), vol. 1, pp. 79–114.

19. Rifʿat al-Saʿīd, *Ḥasan al-Bannā: Matā, kayfa, wa li-mādhā?* (Cairo: Maktabat madbūlī, 1977), pp. 12–17, 22–27, 96–98, 122–125.

20. Mitchell's book was translated into Arabic and published by Madbūlī in 1977; Richard P. Mitchell, *The Society of the Muslim Brothers* (London: Oxford University Press, 1969). See also "Ra'y kātib amrīkī fī ḥasan al-bannā," *Al-Hilāl,* April 1977, pp. 122–129, and May 1977, pp. 112–119.

21. Anwar al-Jindī, *Ḥasan al-Bannā: Al-dāʿiya, al-imām, wa-l-mujaddid al-shahīd* (Beirut: Dār al-qalam, 1978), pp. 21–23, 36–48, 57–59.

explained away, the brutal involvement of the paramilitary wing of the Muslim Brotherhood in violently enforcing public Islamic morality by acts of bombing or arson of cinemas, brothels, and liquor stores. He also claimed that the brotherhood was not responsible for the murder al-Nuqrāshī Pasha in December 1949.[22] More than any other author publishing on this subject around this time, al-Jindī presented the Muslim Brotherhood in a positive light, using clear, level-headed language. The high-quality production of al-Jindī's book, which was a far cry from the standard cheap-print format, accorded the book an aura of professional authority.

Alongside this more systematic, second historiographical wave, longtime activists and writers such as Maḥmūd ʻAbd al-Ḥalīm and Muḥammad al-ʻAdawī continued to follow populist arguments that spoke of a worldwide conspiracy against the *daʻwa* (the cause of promoting Islam) and of a Nasserist betrayal.[23] Dār al-Anṣār and Dār al-Daʻwa willingly published such works. However, despite the persistence and quantitative weight of popular works, leading thinkers continued to push for a more comprehensive understanding of recent Islamist history. And thus, by the late 1970s, a third, and much more reflective, historiographical wave emerged among academic scholars.

Zakarīyā Sulaymān Bayyūmī and, more important, the revered judge Ṭariq al-Bishrī were the leading actors in this third wave. Bayyūmī began his research as a graduate student in al-Shams University and was aided and supported by the Department of History in al-Azhar. The purpose of his work was to defend the Islamic movement by using sound academic methodology that could gain the respect of mainstream intellectuals.[24] In two important and complementary books on the Muslim Brotherhood, Bayyūmī appears as a balanced historian who was not deterred from confronting sensitive issues such as the Muslim Brotherhood's notion of jihad.[25] Bayyūmī employed a cultural prism for understanding the capacity in which the Muslim Brotherhood served as an alternative to the ruling secular culture of monarchic Egypt. While praising the social achievements of the Islamic movement, he emphatically rejected violence. Coming out of mainstream academia, Bayyūmī's influential work ensured that it would no longer be possible to discuss Egypt's nationalist struggle without

22. The state's vengeful murder of al-Bannā on King Fārūq's birthday (February 12) was seen as the ultimate proof of a state-palace conspiracy. Al-Jindī, however, does not mention this argument. al-Jindī, *Ḥasan al-Bannā*, pp. 180–185, 191–234.

23. Maḥmūd ʻAbd al-Ḥalīm, *Al-Ikhwān al-muslimun: Ahdath sanat al-tarikh* (Alexandria: Dar al-Da'wa, 1979, 1985); Maḥmūd al-ʻAdawī, *Haqāʻq wa asrār ḥaqla kitāb al-ikhwān al-muslimūn: Aḥdāth sanʻat al-tārīkh* (Cairo: Dār al-anṣār, 1980).

24. Zakarīyā Sulaymān Bayyūmī, *Al-Ikhwān al-muslimūn wa-l-jamaʻāt al-islāmiya fī-l-ḥayāh al-siyāsiya al-miṣriya, 1928–1948* (Cairo: Maktabat wahaba, 1979), p. 3.

25. Ibid., pp. 123–131.

taking into consideration the contribution of the Islamic movement and its alternative agenda.

Notwithstanding Bayyūmī's contribution, the most important historian of the third wave, a true thinker and intellectual, was Judge Ṭarīq al-Bishrī. He was born in 1933 to a respected family whose head, his grandfather, served as shaykh of al-Azhar. His father was a respected jurist. Yet, al-Bishrī did not follow the family tradition and, like many other young members of his generation inside or outside Egypt, turned to the revolutionary secular world of the 1950s, studied European law, and became a state employee.[26] Besides law, al-Bishrī's other abiding commitment was history writing. Though he started his career in leftist intellectual circles, with the progression of the *infitāḥ* he gradually shifted to a mainstream Islamist position. Since then, he has written from a decidedly Islamist stance and has long been acknowledged as a respected public figure and councilor *(mustashār)* of the Egyptian Conseil d'état (Majlis al-shūra).

As noted in Meijer's original analysis, al-Bishrī's work is intellectually accumulative, highly analytical, and, more than anything else, oriented toward finding a solution to Egypt's weak unity, partial independence, and lack of democratization.[27] From the Wafdists and their political associates on the Marxist-communist Left to the Muslim Brotherhood, al-Bishrī scrutinized all of Egypt's political currents and their respective historiographical schools. He evaluated their performance on the basis of the triple criteria of unity, independence, and democracy.

Al-Bishrī's position was that the deeds and ideas of the Islamic movement can make sense only when juxtaposed to the history of all other political movements. Loyal to this perspective in his first 1972 book on Egyptian political life at the close of the monarchic era, al-Bishrī argued that compared with other political currents the Muslim Brotherhood had performed poorly and that its violent actions were unpatriotic and counterproductive. Furthermore, while all other political forces, especially the Marxist Left, had a coherent ideological platform, the Muslim Brotherhood's message was extremely vague. He thus blamed the organization for intentional obscurantism *(ghumūd)*.[28] Though still loyal to his triple criteria of unity, independence, and democracy, al-Bishrī noticed in the sweeping Americanization of the *infitāḥ* years that on some profound cultural level Egypt was losing its predominantly Islamic heritage *(turāth)*. He thus shifted the focus to the fate of Islamic culture under the pressures of modernity. Hereafter, he used the Islamic term *turāth* as an over-

26. ʿAbd al-Munʿim al-Jumayʿī, *Itijāhāt al-kitāba*, pp. 139–140.

27. Roel Meijer, *History, Authenticity and Politics: Tariq al-Bishri's Interpretation of Modern History,* Occasional Paper no. 4 (Amsterdam: Middle East Research Association, 1989).

28. Ṭāriq al-Bishrī, *Al-ḥaraka al-siyāsiya fī miṣr, 1945–1952* (Cairo: al-Ḥayʾa al-miṣriya al-ʿāma li-l-kitāb, 1972), pp. 51–56; Meijer, *History, Authenticity and Politics*, pp. 9–12.

arching concept, without which independence, unity, and democracy would be quite meaningless.

Furthermore, developing a theoretical prism, al-Bishrī introduced two additional concepts that capture the essence of the struggle that has underlined Egypt's modern history. According to him, it was a struggle between *al-wāfid,* that is, between foreign/European elements, which were alien to local culture, and *al-mawrūth,* cultural elements that are inherited. As Meijer showed, the balance between *al-wāfid* and *al-mawrūth* determines the overall condition of the Islamic *turāth* and has a critical effect on the long-term triple goals of the Egyptian community.[29]

Once Egyptian history was understood in terms of cultural authenticity, the contribution of the Muslim Brotherhood as the only political force that defended *turāth* became abundantly clear. At this point in time, al-Bishrī was no longer troubled by the ideological "vagueness" of the Islamic movement. The discovery of authenticity came to al-Bishrī as a revelation and caused him to desert completely the few Marxist terms of analysis that he had used in the early 1970s. He famously did so in a long introductory essay to the second edition of his book *Al-Ḥaraka al-siyāsiya fī miṣr.*[30] There, al-Bishrī elaborated on his conceptual framework and denied the political, cultural, and especially the moral primacy of the European nation-state. With remarkable persistence over the course of the past three decades, al-Bishrī has examined the many ways in which Western models have deformed the cultural authenticity of Egyptians and mutilated their collective sense of self.[31] Over time and as a result of his scholarly agenda of history for the sake of reform rather than partisanship, al-Bishrī has become a respected member of Egypt's so-called New Islamist school *(al-wassaṭiyya).* This reformist modernist collective aims to rethink the sociocultural and legal foundations of the state and infuse them with moderate Islamic content. In Raymond William Baker's pioneering study of this group, he aptly put it this way: al-Bishrī is considered the "master historian" of the New Islamist school.[32]

A somewhat unexpected side effect of these three historiographical waves was

29. Meijer, *History, Authenticity and Politics,* pp. 19–27; Roel Meijer, "Authenticity in History: The Concepts al-Wāfid and al-Mawrūth in Ṭāriq al-Bishrī's Reinterpretation of Modern Egyptian History," in Manfred Woidich, ed., *Amsterdam Middle Eastern Studies* (Wiesbaden: L. Reichert Verlag, 1990), pp. 68–83.

30. Ṭāriq al-Bishrī, *Al-ḥaraka al-siyāsiya fī miṣr, 1945–1952,* 2nd ed. (Cairo: Dār al-shurūq, 1983), pp. 1–68.

31. Ṭāriq al-Bishrī, *Al-Muslimūn wa-l-aqbāṭ fī iṭātr al-jamā'a al-waṭaniya* (Cairo: al-Ḥay'a al-miṣriya al-'āma li-l-kitāb, 1980), pp. 491–516, 702–724; Raymond William Baker, *Islam without Fear: Egypt and the New Islamists* (Cambridge MA: Harvard University Press, 2003), p. 205.

32. Baker, *Islam without Fear,* p. 35.

the greater legitimacy given the study of Islamic societies. The Ottoman past was a sure candidate for reconsideration, and nationalist-inspired statements such as "Ottomanism is not an ethnicity but a profession of theft, robbery and rape" were not taken for granted anymore.[33] One of the first Islamist scholars who ventured into Ottoman studies was 'Abd al-'Azīz al-Shinnāwī, a former liberalist whose traumatic prison experience under Nasser turned him from a peaceful disciple of Ghurbāl into a devoted Islamist. In the early 1980s, as chair of the history department in one of al-Azhar's colleges, al-Shinnāwī published *Al-Dawla al-'uthmāniya: Dawla Islāmīya muftara' 'alayhā* in four volumes. The governing theme of this monumental work was that the Ottomans were faithful Muslims who promoted Islamic civilization but were suppressed by the ideological apparatus of the secular nation-state. Notwithstanding this important development, the Islamists offered neither a theoretical nor a methodological breakthrough in terms of creating the field of Ottoman studies. This last task would fall to Egyptian students who were trained abroad.

In the end, the combined influence of these three historiographical waves ushered in greater academic standards in history writing about the Islamic movement. Subsequently, elements of this once-forbidden history were integrated into the national historical annals. However, though the three waves of Islamist historiography reached a highly sophisticated stage in the writings of al-Bishrī, his writings did not crown the overall trajectory of Islamist historiography, because the three phases did not succeed one another temporally and, in fact, coexisted simultaneously. From a quantitative point of view, even in the 1990s, most of the available historical works bore the vociferous characteristics of the first historiographical wave: poor, if any, documentation, conflicting oral testimonies, explanations of loose causality, and conspiracy-driven accounts. With this type of speculative historiography dominating the marketplace, the average, unspecialized reader would face difficulties in establishing any kind of certitude regarding even the most elementary episodes in the history of the Islamic movement.

FROM DICTATION TO REGULATION

And so it happened that following the decline of the state as the sole planner and organizer of public life, a barrage of interpretations, counterinterpretations, accusations, and counteraccusations proliferated. This historiographical cacophony took the form of journalistic writing, memoirs, history books, films, television shows, and, perhaps more than anything else, gossip and rumors about

33. From a 1981 newspaper quoted in Rif'at al-Sa'īd, *Safaḥāt min tārīkh miṣr: Ru'īyat al-'alāqa bayna al-tārīkh wa-l-siyāsa* (Cairo: Dār al-thaqāfa al-jadīda, 1984), p. 157.

the "true nature" of Nasserism and about "what really happened" during these years. Some intellectuals, such as Niʿmat Aḥmad Fu'ād, called directly for the rewriting of history.[34]

Not only in Islamist circles but also among die-hard Wafdists, dozens of journalists-turned-historians dominated the cultural scene with accounts of "history by instinct" that were based on subjective impressions and the flimsiest of evidence. All had clear agendas that called for the rehabilitation of historical leaders, such as Muṣṭafa al-Naḥḥās, and for a reevaluation of the 1919 Revolution.[35] Some serious works were also written, such as the notable contribution by former officer Aḥmad Ḥamrūsh, whose *Qiṣṣat thawrat 23 yūliū* is still one of the most detailed and reliable accounts of the revolution. By the mid-1980s, the overwhelming majority of Nasserist officers had already published their memoirs. In short, a record number of individuals—some returning from exile—and previously outlawed political forces began to discuss openly the errors, sins, crimes, mistakes, and shortcomings of Nasserism. Somewhat paradoxically, the more works they published, the less clear it became what actually happened.

Though all parties strove to inculcate their own version of events, no one, not even the Muslim Brotherhood, was as eager to do so as President Sadat, who used any possible media, print or broadcast, to disseminate his story.[36] Against this backdrop, the well-connected Muḥammad Ḥasanayn Haykal, editor-in-chief of *Al-Ahrām* and a staunch defender of Nasser's heritage, established a private committee for the writing of the revolutionary era. Being one of Nasser's closest men, Haykal had access to top-secret documents, some of which he had taken home. Other private initiatives by Free Officers and their coterie, who at some point had gotten their hands on original source material, also occurred.[37] Concerned for the fate of his own historical image, Sadat decided to block Haykal's initiative

34. Fikrī Abāẓa, "Al-Ḥaqiqa al-tā'iha wa-l-ḥaqq al-ḍā'iʿ," *Al-Muṣawwar,* June 28, 1974, p. 47; Muḥamamd ʿAṣfūr, "Fatḥ al-milafāt," *Al-Muṣawwar,* January 10, 1975, pp. 12–13; Fūmil Labīb, "Al-Ḥaqīqa hiya al-hadaf," *Al-Muṣawwar,* July 25, 1975, pp. 28–29; Ṣāliḥ Jawdat, "ʿIndama nuʿīd kitābat al-tārīkh," *Al-Muṣawwar,* March 29, 1974, p. 11; Kamāl al-Najamī, "Al-Tārīkh kaʿūd al-kabrīt," *Al-Muṣawwar,* August 9, 1974, p. 44.

35. Ṣabrī Abū al-Majd, "Muṣṭafa al-Naḥḥās zaʿīm waṭanī," *Al-Muṣawwar,* August 29, 1975, pp. 22–26, and September 5, 1975, pp. 24–27; Aḥmad Abū Kaff, "Muḥāḍir al-jalasāt al-sirriya," *Al-Muṣawwar,* October 25, 1974, pp. 26–27.

36. See, for instance, a long historical series on the revolution that rewrites Sadat's role into the national canon. Ṣabrī Abū al-Majd, "Sanawāt ma qabla al-thawra," *Al-Muṣawwar,* July–December, 1977; Ṣabrī Suwaylīm, "Matā yantahi tasjīl asrār al-thawra?" *Al-Ahram,* January 3, 1977, p. 7.

37. Habitually during the month of February, a month before the anniversary of the revolution, Haykal would sensationally publish some secret documents. See, for instance, Aḥmad ʿAbd al-Raḥīm Muṣṭafa, "Wathā'īq haykal tataqalam: Qayfa inzalaqat miṣr ila hazimat 1967," *Al-Hilāl,* February 1989, pp. 60–65. For the story of another private archive, see *Al-Muṣawwar,* December 27, 1974, p. 52.

and establish an official governmental committee for history writing, especially for the history of the 1967 war. He used this occasion to remove Haykal from his *Al-Ahrām* fiefdom and prohibit him from publishing in the Egyptian press.[38]

The committee convened for the first time in October 1975, only a few days after the weeklong celebrations commemorating the second anniversary of the October victory.[39] Husni Mubarak, the newly appointed vice president and a national hero who had successfully commanded the air force during the October war, headed the committee. Mubarak knew nothing about history writing, let alone how civil society was supposed to function. Yet, he carried with him the prestige of a triumphant general who was not embroiled, politically or otherwise, in the corrupt power structure of the Nasserist state. It was, then, a fresh start, and Mubarak was asked to head a group of nineteen journalists, pundits, politicians, high-ranking military officers, and a few historians. The committee was divided into eight civil and military subcommittees. ʿIzzat ʿAbd al-Karīm represented academia and was the only historian of modern Egypt.[40]

In his opening address Mubarak explained the rationale behind the enterprise and specified the committee's objectives and mandate. The press was attentive. According to him, since the public sphere was flooded with multiple contradictory accounts as to what actually happened during the 1952 Revolution, the "true" story remained unknown, and the public was left confused and perplexed. Echoing the president, he argued that previous interpretations were tainted by ideology and that Egypt was in dire need of an "objective" and "scientifically based" interpretation.[41] He assured the public that the aim of the committee was not to defend the 1952 Revolution but to consider all the economic, political, social, and international factors that had shaped it. Then, in what marked a break from previous state attempts in the field of history, Mubarak said that the president had assured him that committee members would be granted access to secret archival source material and even allowed to question individuals who had played public roles in this era.[42]

As the committee convened for its initial five-day session, Sadat publicly argued that the rewriting of history was Egypt's pressing goal. He said that he was disappointed to learn that individuals intent on propagating biased historical accounts exploited the new freedoms he had granted. He called for the search for historical truth and, specifically, for the real story behind the events of June 1967.

38. ʿAbd al-Munʿim al-Jumayʿī, *Itijahāt al-kitāba*, p. 152.

39. For these celebrations, see Gershoni and Jankowski, *Commemorating the Nation*, pp. 283–295.

40. "Lajnat tārīkh al-thawra," *Al-Ahrām*, October 11 and October 12, 1975, p. 1.

41. "Ḥusnī Mubārak yaftatihu," *Al-Ahrām*, October 13, 1975, pp. 1, 5.

42. Ibid.

He too felt that the next generation had the right to know what had happened since 1952.[43]

Though Mubarak had a point, not everyone was persuaded by the simplicity of the call for order and truth. ʿIzzat ʿAbd al-Karīm read through the official rhetoric and, as if he were not at all an active member of the committee, expressed skepticism toward the entire project. Though it was unclear if the committee's job was to collect records or write history, ʿAbd al-Karīm reminded the government that some Egyptian historians were part of a sound professional tradition. In order to write balanced and objective accounts, these historians needed only a functioning national archive of the kind that existed in England or the United States. ʿAbd al-Karīm forcefully argued that the important and justified principle of "state security" exists in other nations as well but is never used as a wholesale ban on historical contemplation or reflection. State security, he argued, has its limitations, and they ought to be specified by law. Open accessibility to state records was crucial in informing and strengthening the formation of public opinion.[44] As the distinguished president of the EHS, ʿAbd al-Karīm invoked Ghurbāl's historiographical tradition, which was in opposition to the committee's logic of operation. Unfortunately, his calls fell on deaf ears, and, as Gorman has noted, before long he stopped showing up to committee meetings.[45] This was a first sign of spontaneous and solid opposition to the committee's work.

A former student of Ghurbāl's, historian Ibrāhīm ʿAbduh, joined the critics. In a book cynically titled *Tārīkh bi-lā wathāʾiq* (History without Sources), ʿAbduh recounted his failed attempts to write the history of Nasserism on the basis of the available documentation, such as Nasser's speeches, the press, the "Socialist Charter" (i.e., the National Charter), the March 1968 Declaration, and interviews. Nothing in these records, he stated, could explain the war in Yemen, the 1967 war, or any other meaningful event during the 1960s.[46] His conclusion was a straightforward call to release the "imprisoned records" of the 1952 Revolution and to reestablish the lost archival tradition of ʿĀbdīn. The government should understand that "it could not write history" and that "history is not written by decree."[47] Another professor reminded *Al-Ahrām*'s readers that history writing is an open-ended process that is incompatible with the government's tendency to formulate the "last word" on any given subject.[48] In the same spirit, ʿAbd al-ʿAẓīm Ramaḍān published a series of articles on the poverty of Egypt's archival culture.

43. "Al-Masʾala al-qawmiyya," *Al-Ahrām*, October 27, 1975, p. 4.

44. ʿIzzat ʿAbd al-Karīm, "Al-ḥukuma wa kitābat al-tārīkh," *Al-Ahrām*, November 14, 1975, p. 7.

45. Gorman, *Historians, State and Politics*, p. 69.

46. Ibrahīm ʿAbduh, *Tārīkh bi-lā wathāʾīq* (Cairo: Muʾasasat sajl al-ʿarab, 1975), p. 11.

47. Ibid., pp. 81–82.

48. Aḥmad al-nāṣiri, "Kitābat tārīkh al-shaʿb am al-thawra?" *Al-Ahrām*, December 6, 1975, p. 7.

In them, he called on the committee and the government to reform state archives and to leave the rest for the historians, allowing the historiographical marketplace to take its natural course.[49]

Less than a year after the committee's establishment, cautious criticism took the shape of opposition, and Mubarak was pushed to explain why the government thought it could write history. Under pressure, he did his best to assure critics that "history writing will not stop" and that the committee's other tasks were the collection, organization, and classification of records so that no one could falsify the past. He promised to establish another special center to hold and manage these records, similarly to the way the rewriting project of the 1960s was handled. Shifting the focus to the collection of records, *Al-Ahrām* inquired about the private journal and other records of Nasser, the materials of the archive of the Arab Socialist Union, and those of its central committee. Somewhat perplexed, Mubarak promised to find them.[50]

These various pressures were quite successful, and by the early months of 1977 the committee's focus had shifted from writing history to collecting the records of the following: the Revolutionary Command Council and the Free Officers meetings, the 1954 Anglo-Egyptian negotiations, the cabinet and Central Intelligence, Parliament, and the Syrian-Egyptian unity negotiations.[51] Soon enough, the committee publicly admitted difficulties in locating many of the materials, and rumors about hidden and lost materials circulated.[52] Three safes, which originated from the office of the powerful Sāmī Sharaf, were found in the central intelligence building, but the keys were missing. It was rumored that Nasser's personal diary was inside one of them. Other sources were in private hands, and some of these individuals, such as the son of intellectual Muḥammad Ḥusayn Haykal, who had died in 1956, handed them to the committee and were immediately praised for their patriotism.[53] Besides collecting Egyptian records, the committee acknowledged the need to collect international materials and ship them home, where they could be cataloged in the proposed special center for the revolution's historical records.[54]

A few years later, in light of more pressing political events, such as the peace process with Israel and Islamic resistance at home, the interest in the committee's work subsided, and Mubarak stepped down as its chairman. After Sadat's

49. The articles were originally published in *Al-Jumhūriya* during 1975. Ramaḍān, *Miṣr fī 'aṣr al-Sadat,* vol. 2, pp. 88–91, 99–107.

50. "Al-ḥukuma wa kitābat al-tārīkh," *Al-Ahrām,* January 10, 1976, p. 7.

51. Suwaylīm, "Matā yantahi tasjīl asrār al-thawra?" p. 7.

52. Aḥmad Abū Kaff, "Watā'īq khaṭira 'an marākiz al-qūwa," *Al-Muṣawwar,* September 9, 1977, p. 57.

53. Suwaylīm, "Matā yantahi tasjīl asrār al-thawra?" p. 7.

54. Ibid.

assassination, additional urgent issues dominated public discussion, and the committee was quietly dissolved. In hindsight, unlike the efforts of the Nasserist "rewriting committee," which dictated a specific reading of the past, Sadat's effort was designed to manipulate the historiographical process and create a seemingly open marketplace of ideas. Mubarak subscribed to a similar order, yet decided to keep state records secret for a period of half a century.[55]

Deprived of basic archival infrastructure for the post-1952 era, history writers could say and write whatever they wanted, but the overall sum of their activity canceled itself out in a futile, magiclike cycle of one underdocumented account competing against another. Unlike in the Nasserist era, historians were not punished for their opinions, but by the 1980s their opinions did not matter very much either. From an authoritarian point of view, it was a smart solution. As historian Yunān Labīb Rizq observed, though the study of post-1952 era was never forbidden by decree, it became a forbidden land *(arḍ muḥarama)* in practice.[56]

THE RISE AND STALL OF A NEW GENERATION

By and large, until the late 1960s, social and economic histories were synonymous with Marxism. However, after three waves of Marxist- and socialist-inspired scholarship, young students such as Ra'ūf 'Abbās, Maḥmūd Mutawallī, 'Āṣim Disūqī, and 'Alī Barakāt decided to cut the Gordian knot that tied social and economic history to Marxist thought. Though Marxist notions such as class struggle still informed their thought, and though they were still intellectually dependent on Ibrāhīm 'Āmir's work, their general interests, methods of inquiry, and style of argumentation differed from those of their Marxist peers and marked the brief revival of pre-1952 academic professionalism. By the early 1980s, this new generation presented a coherent series of archive-based studies that covered crucial topics such as landownership, workers' movements, class formation, and business and financial history. Other historians, such as Yunān Labīb Rizq, contributed studies that closely scrutinized specific political movements that substantiated the socioeconomic analysis of prerevolutionary Egypt. None of them wrote about the 1952 Revolution. Below is a short discussion of the rise of this new school of historians and of the powerful circumstances that eventually contained it.[57]

This new generation began with independently minded young students. Ra'ūf 'Abbās was its most prolific and academically active member. He was born in 1939

55. 'Abd al-Mun'im al-Jumay'ī, *Itijahāt al-kitāba*, p. 152–151.

56. Yunān Labīb Rizq, "Kitābat tārīkh thawrat 23 yūliū bayna al-taḥrīm wa-l-ibāḥa," *Al-Ahrām*, September 27, 1975, p. 7.

57. For an early assessment of this school, see Gran, "Modern Trends in Egyptian Historiography," pp. 367–371.

to a Port Sa'id working-class family with a background even humbler than that of Muḥammad Anīs. It is to the credit of the 1952 Revolution that 'Abbās, a son of a railway worker, was able to rise in the academic ranks and become one of Egypt's most influential historians. This would not have been likely under the monarchy. In the mid-1950s he enrolled in the vibrant history department of 'Ayn Shams University, researching the history of the Egyptian labor movement since 1889. His work charted the institutional development of this movement and covered many of the legal, organizational, and economic aspects of Egyptian trade unionism.[58] Though in hindsight 'Abbās's work was no match for the monumental working-class trilogy of his contemporary, Marxist historian Amīn 'Izz al-Dīn (published between 1967 and 1972), it was still a pioneering enterprise that called for an empirical investigation of themes such as the relationship among capital, landownership, and class formation.[59]

Social historian 'Alī Barakāt focused on the rise of private landownership all the way up to 1952. Drawing extensively on various types of state registries *(sijillāt)* and other previously unconsulted source material, Barakāt empirically illustrated the extent to which property relations were also political, economic, and social relations. Influenced by the pioneering work of Gabriel Baer, he also maintained that the transfer of landownership from state to private hands was the most important socioeconomic process in prerevolutionary Egypt. Though he also studied the making of the urban administrative, financial, and industrial bourgeoisie, his main focus remained the condition of the *fallāḥ* and the problem of landownership. He therefore regarded the struggle to improve the living conditions of peasants and the nationalist struggle against colonialism to be the same.[60]

A similar nationalist perspective informed the work of 'Āṣim Diṣūqī, who tackled the topic of landownership from a slightly different angle. While previous writers had portrayed a picture of contrasting class distinctions, Diṣūqī explored the gray areas that large landowners and industrialists shared. Though these two groups seemingly belonged to two different classes, he suggested that capital facilitated their wide interclass collaboration.[61] It was an argument that his contemporary Maḥamūd Mutawallī substantiated by studying the history of Egyptian capitalism. In Mutawallī's study, the connection among colonialism,

58. Ra'ūf 'Abbās, *Ḥaraka al-'umaliya fī miṣr, 1899–1952* (Cairo: Dār al-kutub al-'arabī li-l-ṭibā'a wa-l-nashr, 1967), pp. 18–65.

59. Ra'ūf 'Abbās, *Al-niẓām al-ijtimā'ī fi Miṣr fī ẓill al-milkiyāt al-zirā'iyya al-kabīra, 1837–1914* (Cairo: Dār al-fikr al-ḥadīth, 1973), pp. 112–247.

60. Barakāt, *Ṭatawwur al-milkīya al-zirā'iyya fī miṣr*; 'Alī Barakāt, *Al-milkīya al-zirā'iyya bayna thawratayn, 1919–1952* (Cairo: Markaz al-dirāsāt al-siyāsiyya wa-l-istarātijiyya bi-l-ahrām, 1978).

61. 'Āṣim Disūqī, *Kibār mullāk al-arāḍī al-zirā'iyya wa dawruhum fī-l-mujama' al-miṣrī, 1914–1952* (Cairo: Dār al-theqāfa al-jadīda, 1975), pp. 143–209.

foreign capital, and the landed and industrial elite became not only theoretically clear but also empirically founded.[62]

In 1981, ʿĀṣim Diṣūqī summarized the academic achievements of this generation in a short, readable, and eye-opening account. He illustrated the many ways in which his generation had moved away from the theoretical generalizations of historical materialism and, instead, used various pre-1952 records from Dār al-wathāʾīq in order to present a realistic account of a globalized social and economic epoch.[63] Unlike Nasserist official historiography, which celebrated Egypt's progress through concrete socialist stages but appeared to be conceptually bankrupt when, against all theoretical expectations, capitalism reappeared, the work of the new generation had much explanatory power vis-à-vis the *infitāḥ*.

Yet despite the civic academic vitality that characterized this new generation, the scholarly environment of the late 1970s and the state refusal to share its records slowly suffocated it. One of the main reasons for this state of affairs was the aggressive and politicized atmosphere on university campuses all over the country. Under Sadat, government polices turned both new and old universities into political battle zones where state-backed Islamists achieved a firm control, in fact an iron grip, over campus life. Even mild leftists such as ʿAlī Barakāt were treated as dangerous "Nasserists" and were thus made natural candidates for political and academic harassment. With increasing political challenges to the regime, such as the 1977 wheat subsidy riots, the presence of the secret police on campuses increased, and this group became involved in managing campus life on a daily basis. It was thus involved in everything from student politics to faculty appointments and promotions. Elections to the student union were regularly fixed, and faculty and students began spying on one another. Nepotistic appointments were also common, and the administrative protocol was frequently bent to meet "special needs." The meteoric academic career of Egypt's first lady Jihan Sadat, from an insignificant master's student of English literature to a full faculty member in Cairo University in a mere few years, notoriously demonstrated much of what went wrong during these years. The president himself paternalistically treated professors as mere servants of his political agenda.[64] Though Nasserism was gone, the politicization of academic life did not come to an end and in several respects was even made worse.

In addition to political pressures, pressures on infrastructure from the dra-

62. Maḥmūd Mutawallī, *Al-uṣūl al-tārīkhiyya li-l-raʾsmālīya al-miṣrīyya wa taṭwwurihā* (Cairo: al-Ḥayʾa al-miṣriyya al-ʿāmma li-l-kitāb, 1974).

63. ʿĀṣim Diṣūqī, *Naḥwa fahm tārīkh miṣr al-iqtiṣādī wa-l-ijtimāʿī* (Cairo: Dār al-kutub al-jamāʿī, 1981), pp. 5–17.

64. In a typical paternalistic episode, Sadat convened Egypt's best and brightest academics and ordered them to prepare a new national curriculum in accordance with stiff ideological guidelines. For a penetrating criticism of academic life from the perspective of historians, see Abbās, *Mashaynāhā khutān*, pp. 133, 146, 205, 221–247, 236, 253, 257–258, 265, 270–272.

matic increase in enrollment brought about a sharp decline in academic standards. Especially in the humanities, classrooms were packed, and ratios of students to professors reached an all-time high.[65] When students began competing for their professors' attention, the door to unprecedented academic corruption was opened wide, and faculty members began selling their students "extra material" that guaranteed a better grade. Books that were not written by their professors rarely made it into the classroom, which undermined the academic publishing sector and the free flow of ideas necessary for vibrant intellectual life.[66]

Naturally, rich students from the Persian Gulf "excelled" in their studies, and Saudi scholars paid cash dollars in order to publish their "scholarship." Since everyone wanted to become a *duktūr,* bold acts of plagiarism proliferated. In one rumored incident, students plagiarized dissertations and copied footnotes without ever laying their eyes on the original sources cited in those works.[67] Footnoting was thus viewed not as a practice that sustained ethical values of transparency and accountability but as an empty formality and a value-free task, something like building a wall. Supervisors willfully collaborated with the undoing of basic academic standards and integrity by approving these dissertations without even reading them. It was therefore no surprise that even scholars who held a doctorate were caught plagiarizing and that university professors stole primary source material from libraries and special collections.[68]

The most noticeable sign of the deterioration of the historians' professional community was the actual collapse of the EHS. From the time in which 'Izzat 'Abd al-Karīm stepped down as its chairman in 1976 until 1999, when his disciple Ra'ūf 'Abbās financially and organizationally revived it, the EHS was mismanaged and produced nothing of real importance. Thus, a society that bravely survived the heavy-handed cultural policies of Nasser later collapsed under Sadat and Mubarak when its most loyal defenders, members of the third and fourth generation of professional historians, followed their mentors and took jobs in the new universities of the Gulf.

These powerful circumstances undermined the success of this new academic generation and, among other things, condemned it to methodological provin-

65. See, for instance, Muḥammad Sa'īd, "Mashākil jām'āt al-aqālīm," *Al-Muṣawwar,* January 31, 1975, pp. 1–4.

66. Shukrī Muḥammad 'Iyād, "Inqadhū al-kitāb al-jāma'ī," *Al-Hilal,* October 1987, pp. 14–19.

67. Barakāt alluded to a certain "footnote" scandal about which he declined to elaborate on the grounds that the facts are well known. 'Alī Barakāt, "Madrasat al-tārīkh al-ijtimā'ī al-miṣrī fī rub' qarn, 1970–1995," in Muḥammad 'Afīfī, ed., *Al-Madrasa al-tārīkhiya al-miṣriyya,* pp. 110–112.

68. For a famous case of plagiarism, see 'Abd al-'āl al-Bāqūrī, "Iḍbaṭ yā wazīr al-thaqāfa faḍiḥa thaqāfiya," *Al-Hilāl,* January 1977, pp. 59–65, and responses in the February 1977 issue as well. For stolen sources, see Abbās, *Mashaynāhā khutān,* pp. 190–191, 209–210, 266–268.

cialism. Indeed, it did not connect to new and highly relevant modes of interpretation, such as the British neo-Marxist school of E. P. Thompson or the new world systems theory of Immanuel Wallerstein. Methodological poverty was a real problem. Ra'ūf Abbās, for instance, explained that during the 1970s he left for Japan in order to overcome his "methodological ignorance."[69] The students of this generation, however, continued to suffer from the very same problem. Poor as they were, many universities could not afford to purchase even basic foreign publications, and a new generation of students grew apart from Western scholarship.[70] A review of dissertations written between 1980 and the mid-1990s illustrates the degree to which a new generation of students continued to employ outdated modes of analysis.[71] Consequently, it was up to a new generation of young American scholars, who used roughly the same source material, to present a more sophisticated understanding of the very same topics. Years later, some of their work would be translated into Arabic.[72]

The only subfield of history that developed a slightly different professional and scholarly dynamic was Ottoman studies, which were influenced by the French and Anglo-Saxon traditions.[73] During the 1970s, the above-mentioned interest in Islamic history and the cumulative weight of foreign revisionist studies pushed local scholars such as 'Abd al-Raḥīm 'Abd al-Raḥmān 'Abd al-Raḥīm, later a professor at al-Azhar, to view Ottoman Egypt in a new light.[74] Cultural magazines as well began writing about how to save Ottoman history.[75] In a matter of years, Ottoman history of the Arab provinces developed also in Tunisia, and young scholars who were trained abroad, such as Nelly Hanna of the American University of Cairo, introduced an altogether new brand of social history. In the mid-1980s, Ottoman historians figured strongly as active participants in the

69. Abbās, *Mashaynāhā khutān*, p. 153.

70. 'Iyād, "Inqadhū al-kitāb al-jāma'ī," pp. 14–19.

71. 'Āṣim Disūqī, "Tārīkh miṣr al-iqtiṣādī al-ḥadīth fī-l-jāmi'a al-miṣriyya, 1970–1995," in Muḥammad 'Afīfī, ed., *Al-Madrasa al-tārīkhīya al-miṣriyya* (Cairo: Dār al-shurūq, 1997), pp. 96–97.

72. Among these scholars were Joel Beinin, Ellis Goldberg, Zachary Lockman, Robert Vitalis, and Kenneth Cuno.

73. Stanford Shaw's landmark studies *Ottoman Egypt in the Eighteenth Century* and *The Financial and Administrative Organization and Development of Ottoman Egypt, 1517–1798* were available already during the 1960s. André Raymond's *Artisans et commerçants au Caire au XVIIIe siècle* was published in 1973 and was translated to Arabic a year later. Peter Gran's *Islamic Roots of Capitalism* came later and was widely discussed as well.

74. 'Abd al-Raḥīm's *Al-Rīf al-miṣrī fī-l-qarn al-thāmin 'ashar* was the first study to focus on Ottoman rural Egypt. See the conference proceedings by Aḥmad 'Izzat 'Abd al-Karīm, ed., *'Abd al-Raḥmān al-Jabartī: Dirāsāt wa-buḥūth* (Cairo: al-Ḥay'a al-Miṣrīya al-'Āmma li-l-kitāb, 1976).

75. Muṣṭafa Nabīl, "Taqwīm al-dawla al-'uthmāniyya," *Al-Hilāl*, December 1985, pp. 34–43; Sa'īd 'Ismā'īl 'Alī, "Mā hakadhā yunqad al-tārīkh al-'uthmānī," *Al-Hilāl*, June 1987, pp. 128–133.

era of historiographical self-reflection.[76] From that point onward and in sharp opposition to the circumstances of previous generations, knowledge of Ottoman Turkish became mandatory.

SELF-REFLECTION AND THE DECLINE OF PROFESSIONAL AUTHORITY

Academic historians were the first to suffer from and react to the historiographical dissonance of the 1970s and the decline in professional standards that followed it. In an attempt to historicize their own predicament, several historians began writing on method, theory, thought, and practice. This self-reflective tide began with some modest individual publications, continued with a collaborative roundtable discussion, culminated with the 1987 conference, and persisted since then with several conferences and edited volumes.

The tide began in 1977, when ʿĀṣim Diṣūqī published a modest booklet that examined the history of historical writing in post-1952 contemporary Egypt. He argued that compared with "amateur" historians, academic historians have not published enough, have faced more political pressures, and ultimately have failed to shape public opinion. Critical of his colleagues' practice, Diṣūqī warned of the decline of professional authority in the eyes of the public. Obviously unimpressed by such arguments, his senior colleagues considered him an undisciplined young scholar who overstepped his boundary.[77] Diṣūqī was right, and since then things have grown quite a bit worse. A 1984 roundtable discussion *(nadwa)* of academic historians explicitly spoke of an "identity crisis" *(azmat intimā')* and a "true crisis of confidence" *(azmat thiqa ḥaqīqiyya)* in historical writing.[78] In the wake of Sadat's peace agreement with Israel, such "crisis talk" was quite prevalent in the Arab world. But above all were the local circumstances. The strident tide in Islamic writings, the chronic nationalist debates that led nowhere, and a more general feeling that history writing since Nasser was not an accumulative enterprise but a disorienting process pushed historians to begin talking to and about one another. All this time, the public was still asking, *What happened to us since 1952?*

76. ʿAbd al-Raḥīm specified particular topics in need of reevaluation, such as guilds, industries, Ottoman elite's social contacts, and even intellectual history. ʿAbd al-Raḥīm ʿAbd al-Raḥmān ʿAbd al-Raḥīm, "Ḥawla minhajiyat dirāsat tārīkh miṣr ibāna al-ʿaṣr al-ʿuthmānī, 1517–1798," *Al-Fikr* 5 (March 1985): pp. 33–41. For an overview of Ottoman studies, see Neli Hanah, "Al-dirāsāt al-tārīkhiya al-khāṣa bi miṣr fī-l ʿaṣr al-ʿuthmānī," in ʿAfīfī, ed., *Al-madrasa al-tārīkhīya al-miṣriyya,* pp. 161–168.

77. Diṣūqī, *Miṣr al-muʿāṣira fī dirāsāt al-mu'ārikhīn al-miṣriyyīn,* pp. 18–19. For the debate, see Muḥammad Anīs, "Ḍajja fi ṣaff al-tārīkh," *Al-Hilāl,* February 1978, pp. 32–34.

78. The *nadwa*'s proceedings were published in special issue of *Al-Fikr.* See "ʿAn al-tārīkh wa-l-waʿy bi-l-dhāt" and "Ḥajatunā ila waʿy naqdī," *Al-Fikr* 5, March 1985, pp. 5–6, 7–9, respectively.

Convened under great cultural urgency, this relatively low-profile 1984 *nadwa* was the first serious attempt to grasp the dimensions of this crisis, define it, and think of possible solutions. The topics discussed were as critical as they were eclectic: What is objectivity and who is an objective historian? What schools of history writing exist and how did they evolve? Why is methodology so poor? Where does modern Egyptian history begin? And even what is history? In short, discussants touched on many of the elementary particles that compose the thought and practice of history as a modern system of knowledge. However, typical of a preliminary discussion that took on a huge topic, the outcome spoke vaguely of the need to form a critical historical consciousness *(waʿy naqdī)*.[79] The decisive contribution of this collective effort was that it helped shift the focus from what happened in history to "how we study it." This critical move was tantamount to a call for a professional psychoanalysis, and it was only a matter of time until a more serious session would convene.

As mentioned in the introduction to this book, this happened in 1987. The conference "Commitment and Objectivity in Contemporary Egyptian Historiography" was not a naive event, for, among other things, it did not expect the government to serve as therapist. The participants in the conference were prominent history writers. Some were academics, but many were not. Though they had been acquainted with one another, they had never really spoken to one another publicly about the condition of history writing. There were many "affairs" and issues from the past three decades to come to terms with. As we saw in chapter 6, some of the encounters were as chronic as they were explosive. Emotions indeed ran high, fueling discussion in the press in the weeks and months that followed. For the first time since Nasser, one of Egypt's most important intellectual communities decided to come to terms with its own history. As organizer Aḥmad ʿAbdallāh put it, the good name of the profession *(sharf al-mihna)* was at stake.[80]

Four common concerns surfaced constantly during the conference: the lack of access to state records, poor methodological skills and poverty of interpretative frameworks, who is and who is not a professional historian, and the connection between (political) commitment and objectivity. These seemingly unrelated issues were, however, tightly connected to one another. With no original source material from which to write authoritative historical accounts and with outdated theoretical and methodological tools, academic historians, journalists, pundits, and partisan writers were doing virtually the same job. Thus, both academics and so-called amateurs wrote of contemporary history using highly subjective sources, such as interviews, newspapers, magazines, and, especially, personal

79. Ibid., pp. 43–55.

80. Aḥmad ʿAbdallāh, "Al-mubārizūn bi suyūf qadīma yaṭʿanūnu al-ajyāl al-jadīda: Ḥawla kitābat al-tārīkh al-miṣri bi ḥajr al-dubb al-masnūn," in Aḥmad ʿAbdallāh, ed., *Tārīkh Miṣr*, p. 17.

memoirs. Any account was as truthful as any other. As Aḥmad ʿAbdallāh reminded his audience, falsification and distortion of history are rarely a matter of straightforward lies but rather are related to the way the system works.[81]

By the late 1980s, the historiographical field was no longer able to maintain a clear hierarchy of professional quality. All books seemed alike, and historical probability (i.e., the potential to agree with some certitude that something had happened in a certain way) was severely undermined as well. As historian ʿAbd al-Raḥīm Muṣṭafa nicely put it in a 1995 sequel to this conference, ever since the 1952 Revolution the people had been confused and could not even tell if Muḥammad ʿAlī was a hero or a villain or how a criminal like ʿUmar Makram suddenly became a national hero.[82]

The poor standards also contributed negatively to the loss of textual hierarchy. Academic historians publicly blamed one another for publishing cheap "boutique scholarship" and plagiarized "cut-and-paste" books *(al-qaṣṣ wa-l-liṣq)*.[83] The grim reality on campuses was undeniable. ʿĀṣim Diṣūqī maintained that, since the 1980s, dissertations had become works of "description rather than analysis." He blamed this state of affairs on the lack of proper philosophical training.[84] When even academic historians were implicated in politically motivated skirmishes, their ethical claim to objectivity lost its credibility, and their scientific authority was seen as a mere slogan.

Against this backdrop, the academic community began to come to terms with the many ways in which it had lost its once prestigious and authoritative public status. It was as if academics needed to repeat Ghurbāl's project of professional and ethical reconstruction once again. With minimum self-awareness, some historians tried to push for a clear consensual definition of who constitutes a historian. Later, low-ranking historians such as Ibrāhīm ʿAbd al-Munʿim al-Jumayʿī began writing extensively on this issue. They naively thought that by delegitimizing the "amateurs" they would automatically regain what they had lost in professional authority and public status.[85] Except that this time, "the amateurs" knew better and were well situated to fight back.

Though certainly not someone whom academics would classify as an amateur,

81. Ibid., pp. 17–18.

82. Aḥmad ʿAbd al-Raḥīm Muṣṭafa, "Taʿqīb," in Muḥammad ʿAfīfī, ed., *Al-Madrasa al-tārīkhiya al-miṣriyya*, p. 62.

83. Abd al-Khāliq Lāshīn, "Al-haqā'iq al-ghā'iba fī nashr mudhakarāat Saʿd Zaghlūl," *Al-Hilāl*, March 1, 1987, p. 20; Ramaḍān, "Madāris kitābat miṣr al-muʿāṣir," p. 59.

84. Diṣūqī, "Tārīkh miṣr al-iqtiṣādī al-ḥadīth fī-l-jamāʿa al-miṣriyya 1970–1995," in ʿAfīfī, *Al-Madrasa al-tārīkhīya al-miṣriyya*, p. 94.

85. See the discussion in ʿAbdallāh, ed., *Tārīkh Miṣr*, pp. 96–97. On his part, ʿAbd al-Munʿim applied the "amateurs" argument for the entire twentieth century. ʿAbd al-Munʿim al-Jumayʿī, *Itijāhāt al-kitāba*, pp. 33–69.

independent historian Ṭāriq al-Bishrī attacked the various definitions of "amateur" as empty, unfounded, and, especially, unnecessary. He argued that institutional academic historians shy away from contemporary history while preaching to amateurs not to do so.[86] Indeed, he went on, as far as contemporary history is concerned, academic historians can be distinguished from the amateurs only by their professorial titles and the location of their offices.

Though the era of retrospection had yet to create the proposed critical historical consciousness, it articulated a list of imperfections in the historiographical process, from university training and archival procedures to editing, publishing, and ethical conduct. Reflecting this achievement, the debates of the past two decades were a crucial step toward the much-anticipated historiographical rehabilitation. From a political perspective, the self-reflective trend made it abundantly clear that while historians do not need the government to organize and manage their community, a positive historiographical chain reaction will be possible only when the state opens its records to public scrutiny. Since the state has no political interest in following this direction, some historians began thinking of expansive projects of oral history.[87] Among those who turned to oral archiving is a feminist group composed of activists and academics who founded the women and memory forum. Directed by experienced historians such as Amira Sonbol, this project retrieves oral testimonies and helps reconstruct the lost history of Egyptian women.[88]

CONCLUSION

In 2003 a diverse group of university professors formed the "March 9" circle, so called after the exemplary March 1932 decision of Aḥmad Luṭfī al-Sayyid to resign his position as university president in reaction to the political removal of Ṭaha Ḥusayn from his position as dean. Inspired by this form of action, which eventually brought Ḥusayn back to campus, the "March 9" circle tries to subvert the cause-and-effect cycle in which aggressive government intervention in university affairs inevitably leads to poor academic standards.[89]

86. Ibrāhīm ʿAbd al-Munʿim al-Jumayʿī, "Al-Muʾarikhūn al-hawāh wa dawruhum fī kitābat tārīkh miṣr al-ḥadīth wa-l-muʿāṣir," in ʿAfifī, ed., *Al-Madrasa al-tārīkhiya al-miṣriyya*, pp. 28–34. For al-Bishrī's responses, see pp. 35–40.

87. The Economic and Business History Research Center (EBHRC) at the American University in Cairo recently started such a project. Mostafa Hefny, "Listening for History: A Report on Oral History, Scope, Fidelity and Methodology," *EBHRC Chronicle* 1, no. 1 (July 2005): pp. 17–20.

88. The impressive output of Egyptian feminist scholars covers a broad spectrum of subjects, including literature. Much of their work, however, does not strictly fall into the historical tradition that this book examines. For the women and memory forum, see www.wmf.org.eg/ (accessed September 2008).

89. Hoda Elsadda, "Resistance as Prerequisite for Reform," *Al-Ahram Weekly* 813, September 21–27, 2006; available at http://weekly.ahram.org.eg/2006/813/sc131.htm (accessed October 2008).

As for historians, the lesson they drew from authoritarian pluralism is that academic claims for representing historical truth and, in turn, the public notion of this truth ultimately depend on the very ways in which academic research is regulated. Under the tenure of authoritarian pluralism, most types of original source material for the post-1952 era became a forbidden commodity. The circulation of thousands of politically driven historical accounts formed the crux of the new historiographical market. Thereafter, professional authority collapsed, and establishing and maintaining a vertical textual hierarchy and elementary criteria of quality became impossible. Authoritarian pluralism was therefore successful in converting the multiplicity of historical voices into a debilitating historiographical mash.

On another level, this cultural order successfully disrupted the process of intellectual renewal and minimized the possibility that public opinion will ever have a meaningful dialogue with the historiographical process and, in turn, with the political sphere. The most obvious sign of the disruption of the historiographical cycle is the lack of fundamental change since the 1940s in books that are at the two ends of the spectrum involved in this cycle, that is, school textbooks for children and professional literature on method and theory for scholars. Even a cursory review of such books will show that a basic nationalist perspective, similar to the one that al-Rāfiʿī put together half a century earlier, is still in place.[90] In a similar vein, recent books on the thought and practice of historiography have not changed in any meaningful way over the past half century.[91]

Not only has the Egyptian scholarly community not entered a dialogue with the Western historical method and striven to influence it from the stance of an Egyptian experience, but also, for the most part, that community has become entirely removed from what seems to be an emerging global historiographical field. On a final note, the fate of historiography under the purview of authoritarian pluralism is only one aspect of a much broader phenomenon: the general struggle of Egyptian culture. Whether they examine the state of the Egyptian book, cinema, or critical thought, Egyptian critics are cognizant of the role of the state in bringing about and maintaining the state of crisis.[92]

90. ʿAbduh Qāsim Qāsim, "Al-Tārīkh wa kayfa yadrusuhu al-talāmīdh al-miṣriyūn," *Wujhāt Naẓar* 25 (February 2001): pp. 48–53.

91. Ibrāhīm ʿAbd al-Munʿim al-Jumayʿī, *Manhaj al-baḥth al-tārīkhī: Dirāsāt wa buḥūth* (Cairo: Maṭbaʿat al-Jablāwī, 1992); and Muḥammad Ziyān ʿUmar, *Madkhal ila ʿilm al-tārīkh* (Cairo: al-Ḥayʾa al-ʿāma li-l-kitāb, 2000).

92. For the crisis of publishing and the book, see "Azmat al-nashr wa-l-qirāʾa," *Al-Hilāl,* May 1980, pp. 6–11; "Ayna al-kitāb al-ʿArabī?" *Al-Hilāl,* March 1981, p. 3; and the editorial, "Azmat al-ḥiwār fīl thaqāfa al-miṣriyya," *Al-Hilāl,* August 1984, pp. 20–21.

Conclusion

The late historian Albert Hourani once remarked that the Arabs are looking at themselves with eyes given to them by Europe. In a way, this is a study of these "eyes" and the things they saw, failed to see, or chose to ignore. By talking about eyes, Hourani aimed at something more substantial than a mere perspective or view. These eyes were nothing but new categories of knowledge, such as geography, anthropology, sociology, and, the subject of this book, the modern European tradition of making sense of the past. When this European historiography presented itself to the Middle East, it prided itself on having some distinctive features. Thus, it claimed to be the only method that encompassed the idea of progress as cumulative and irreversible change; it was committed to causality, was quantitative in essence, developed useful notions of time, such as anachronism and periodization, was narrated in distinct literary styles, had a strong preference toward individualism as well as collective agency, and, above all, had a close affinity to the natural sciences and the idea of scientific objectivity. The totality of this tradition was derived from its service as both a mode of being and an object of a distinctive scholarly project.

Seriously committed to secularism and rationalism, European historiography defined itself in opposition to mythical, literary, poetic, and other forms of ontological writings that are loosely bound to empirical reality. By the early twentieth century, the Egyptian intellectual community accepted this specific mode of intelligibility as the gold standard for the evaluation of all things past. As Japanese philosopher of history Masayuki Sato observed, "As the complex of politics, culture, society, thought and way of life we call the 'Western system' diffused throughout the world in the second half of the nineteenth century, Western historiography spread as a part of this complex. Therefore it became necessary that the various regions of the world, having placed their new point of reference on this new mode of existence, reconstruct their own past."[1] The direct result of this acceptance was the desertion of the existing tradition of making sense of the past. The Islamic chronicle and the *khiṭaṭ* are examples of extinct genres that fell short of accounting for the new experience of modernity. Hence, though history was only one thread in the greater tapestry of Egypt's intellectual experience, it stood, nonetheless, at the center of the Egyptian project of modernity. But even beyond the Arab lands of Islam were many more examples of this process elsewhere in the world.

Interestingly, both European and Egyptian historiographies of modern Egypt began in Cairo in the 1920s. The working assumptions and scholarly output of the royal project were considered universal, and as much as they shaped local scholarship they also had a tremendous influence on Western scholarship of modern Egypt. Both strains of scholarship, as we have seen, were blinded to the human experience of entire groups and classes and were ready to ignore them as they went about the creation of a full-fledged nation-state system. Though debates and disagreements among the various schools and writers proliferated after the termination of the royal project, they shared, nonetheless, a powerful common denominator. In practice, whether they were colonial officials, foreigners on a payroll, graduate students, royalists, Marxists, socialists, capitalists, revolutionists, academics, or even Islamists, their writing was exclusively wrapped around the structures, institutions, and apparatuses of the nation-state. Even the work of Ṭāriq al-Bishrī, the man who made the most of the identity and authenticity crisis of the modern era, engaged with this problem via the nationalist prism. After five long decades of shared constitutive historiographical assumptions, around the 1970s Western scholarship on Egypt began to take a different path altogether, influenced by a succession of "turns" (linguistic, cultural, and in essence postmodern). In contrast, Egyptian historians of modern times remained largely entrenched in a historiographical system that worshiped the nation-state.

And so, when we think of the legacy of historians in the broader context of modern Egyptian experience and even beyond Egypt, it is therefore possible to speak of their profound association with a nineteenth-century historiographical logic. Situated at the intersection of modernity and nationalism, Egyptian historians were entrusted with maintaining this junction and regulating the flow of traffic through it. This was an extremely strategic place in which to be located—one that should, logically, have given them a front-stage cultural role. To evaluate how historians fulfilled their job—that is, how and why they policed

1. Masayuki Sato, "Cognitive Historiography and Normative Historiography," in Rüsen, ed., *Western Historical Thinking*, p. 130.

this junction the way they did—we need to examine the professional processes that guided and conditioned their work.

Four forms of reasoning (explanatory, normative, organizational, and justificatory) explain the relationship between the seemingly unrelated historiographical aspects. These forms of reasoning make sense of the discipline's values (objectivity, accuracy, accountability, transparency, and truthfulness), concepts (change, reform, revolution, and continuity), historical themes (de-Ottomanization, fetishization of Muḥammad 'Alī), organizational forms (training and accessibility to historical records), and philosophical habits (critical engagement with the worldwide intellectual scene). If these aspects are looked at jointly, they form a professional culture that explains why Egyptian historians thought and practiced modern history the way they did.[2]

Since the beginning of the twentieth century, the founder paradigm was accepted as the central frame of reference for the organization of most historical knowledge on modern Egypt. Taking the modern nation-state as both the subject and object of the historical discipline, the founder thesis placed Egypt as the subject of a historical scheme of transition from medieval backwardness, through renaissance and an anti-colonial struggle, to liberation and modernization. Despite the many variations this original perspective underwent in the past century, its core essence remained virtually unchanged.

For instance, by showing historians how to postulate historical topics and relate them to one another in the form of a transitional or revolutionary account, the founder paradigm provided the discipline with the explanatory reasoning of its practice. Other forms of reasoning followed naturally. Thus, by recommending which histories ought to be written, the founder thesis shaped the normative reasoning of the discipline. Complementing that recommendation with telling historians what history is good for and rewarding or punishing them for their writings and views, this paradigm provided the justificatory mechanisms of the discipline. By being highly suggestive to those in power or those who seek power (the monarchy, the political parties, the revolutionaries, and the state in general), the infrastructure of historical practice (universities, archives, libraries, and the publishing industry) was built around the story of the nation. In that way, it formed the organizational principles of the discipline and established the standards for how to arrange, regulate, and systematize the invention, dissemination, and consumption of historical knowledge. In short, Egypt's historiographical culture prescribed the writing of patriotic accounts of liberation and struggle that are extremely useful in forging identity and inducing group cohesion. Since the state and the nation are practically indistinguishable, critical accounts are treated

2. For forms of reasoning in the history of ideas, see Mark Bevir, *The Logic of the History of Ideas* (Cambridge: Cambridge University Press, 1999).

as unpatriotic, dangerous, and ultimately illegitimate. No matter how tentatively it did so, once Egyptian culture committed itself to this mode of operation, it inevitably committed itself also to the severe implications of that mode.

Four examples for such implications come to mind. First, the periodization of modern Egyptian history, particularly the temporal framework that allowed Egyptians to forget the Ottomans, had a devastating impact on the viability of a Pan-Arab project. Indeed, the denial of four hundred years of common Arab life as an integral community within the larger Ottoman order emptied the modern Arab experience of any meaningful historical substance. Coping with the failure of the unification with Syria, Muḥammad Ḥasanayn Haykal proffered an easy historical explanation: "Following centuries of Ottoman tyranny, the Arab people of Egypt became isolated from the rest of the Arabs. Then came the French expedition, which broke the Ottoman iron wall surrounding Egypt.... However, [despite of the renaissance that followed] Egypt could not yet look across the Sinai to discover its position among the Arabs."[3]

Evidently, rather than being informed by histories that transcended the specific political boundaries of each nation, Pan-Arab thought was built solely on the singular and unified historical experiences of each specific nation, whether Egyptian, Iraqi, or Syrian. This historiographical reality frustrated the Pan-Arab mission, for in order to become a viable political option, it was first necessary to undo, or at least temper, the centric histories of the nation and to reconsider the Ottoman era. The same was true for any other supra-Egyptian orientation. In reality, the secular Egyptian experience of nationalism and its modes of operation were too strong simply to be brushed aside. Hence, for the most part, Pan-Arabism was exclusively based on nationalistic historical works that paid only sentimental homage to it. Indeed, the Egyptian historiographical tradition was, and continues to be, extremely Egypto-centric.[4]

The second implication concerns the way in which this secular nationalist system deemed the Islamic cultural legacy obsolete. It is quite remarkable that during the first eighty years of historical thought and practice discussed here, Egyptian historians did not consider the cultural legacy of Islam to have any meaningful—as opposed to rhetoric and ornamental—relevancy for the making of the modern Egypt. The prohibition of the Muslim Brotherhood from publicly

3. *Al-Ahrām*, November 3, 1961, p. 4.

4. This observation is somewhat in opposition to the argument made by Gershoni and Jankowski regarding a shift to Pan-Arabism during the 1930s and 1940s in their *Redefining the Egyptian Nation, 1930–1945*. Though on the political level there were many indications of the emergence of a Pan-Arab politics (the Arab League for instance), on the intellectual level, Pan-Arabism was frail. As Roel Meijer argued, "I do not believe that there was a general trend from Egyptian nationalism in the 1930s and 1940s.... I found that Pan Arabism was of secondary importance." Meijer, *The Quest for Modernity*, p. 11.

examining and promoting an alternative historical vision eventually resulted in the dramatic explosion of the 1970s whose historiographical implications contributed to the crisis of the 1980s.

A third implication, and perhaps the one that is the most critical, is the inability to distinguish clearly between nation (i.e., the political community of citizens) and the state (i.e., the means by which that community conducts its business). In most historical writings until the 1970s, the state was considered to be the highest form of the nation's realization, and in the eyes of many the two were interchangeable. Especially following the Islamic revival of the 1970s, Egyptian reality proved time and again that the state and the national community have different needs and interests. Notwithstanding this reality, historians continue to nourish the policies of the state, even if these very policies significantly undermine the well-being of the community. This is obviously the case with the issue of state accountability and historical source material. The state, therefore, lies well beyond criticism and has a historical buffer zone to protect it stretching all the way back to the rise of Muḥammad ʿAlī. This is why a critical study of the state in the nineteenth century is likely to be viewed as an iconoclastic and unpatriotic account that undermines the cohesion of the nation in the present.

The fourth implication of the existing historiographical structure is related to the long-lasting influence of empiricism in the field of history writing and the poverty of interpretational frameworks. On both the academic and the popular levels, empiricism remains one of the most striking features of Egyptian historiography. Influenced by their British professors, the first two generations of Egyptian academic historians were taught that historical facts are "analogous to the facts of the natural sciences: discrete, atomic and supremely indifferent to the position of the observer."[5] Within this scheme, the task of the historian was to accumulate facts systematically and interpret them. This practice led to some general—always unfulfilled—anticipation that a certain universal history would finally be exposed.[6] This optimistic anticipation is part of the explanation for the persistence of empiricism.

Especially within academia, students of modern Egypt were instructed to painstakingly gather facts. Systematically covering primary sources, they might end up with a remarkable first-rate factual base but little or no framework for interpretation. The cult of common sense and the ideal of encyclopedic knowledge strengthened the empiricist grip on scholarship and made untangling the intricate relation between historical subject matter and method even more difficult. Indeed, the manuals on methodology of the 1990s were essentially similar to the first methodological works that were written during the 1940s. Both

5. Gareth Stedman Jones, "The Pathology of English History," *New Left Review* 46 (1967): p. 30.
6. Ibid.

sets focus almost entirely on matters of empiricist technique. Correspondingly, they reaffirmed that the historian's task was only to uncover new and previously undiscussed facts, but not to venture into a more expansive critical interpretation that might go beyond the well-established boundaries constructed by the existing historiographical order.

In that sense, empiricism limited the possibility for critical and alternative histories whose aim is to question traditions and norms. Instead, it left the job to literary critics and writers who contested norms and traditions through the world of fiction but lacked the philosophical justification of history, which was necessary to facilitate change.[7] All in all, until today, the discipline of modern history remains essentially empiricist, a well-insulated autarchy in which even comparative work is rarely written.

Until the 1970s, Egyptian historiography was successful in nourishing the anti-colonial struggle, creating a sense of community, and, for a certain period of time, facilitating important social and agrarian reforms, but since then it has lost its ability to play an important public role and engender change. Indeed, in the past three decades history writing has failed to fulfill its intended role as a critical tool for self-examination and reform. In this situation not only critical history suffers but also the kind of history that provides orientation and codifies identity—hence, the 1980s crisis of historical consciousness and the two questions posed in the beginning of this study: *What is the history of modern Egyptian historiography? And which kind of history writing would best serve the collective needs of the Egyptian people?*

Since these questions served as the initial motivation for this inquiry, they are also a good place to terminate it. By critically examining the thought and practice of the historiographic intellectual system, I have attempted to respond to the first question in this work. The second question necessitates a normative judgment and thus lies well beyond the mandate of historical scholarship. Nonetheless, since the Egyptian historiographical experience is not dissimilar to that of other postcolonial societies, considering some of the answers that these societies provided might prove to be insightful for this second question.

A brief review of South and Southeast Asian historiography of the past two decades reveals its heavy involvement with postmodernism. Its analytical tools have thus far proved quite successful (a) in achieving a profound understating of how local disciplines of knowledge operate, (b) in retrieving lost historical experiences, and (c) even in causing Western historiography to reevaluate its own working assumptions regarding South and Southeast Asian societies. These histories, however, are not useful at all as builders of a collective identity. At

7. Egyptian literary critics belong to the only intellectual community that critically and meaningfully engages with new intellectual trends and ideas.

any rate, it is rather impressive that instead of continuing to be confined by a nineteenth-century historiographical momentum, South and Southeast Asian intellectuals perfected the European tradition of counter-Enlightenment in order to emancipate themselves from such conceptual shackles.

Successful as it may be, the South and Southeast Asian historiographical agenda has been suited to address the specific needs of these communities and not those of Egyptians or Arabs. The question is therefore, can Arab intellectuals carve a critical space of their own within the global modern experience? As already mentioned, the limited awareness of alternative historiographical frameworks usually comes from the circles of literary critics.[8] It is quite remarkable that even a senior historian like Ra'ūf Abbās, whose 2004 autobiography was the best-articulated critical account to date of Egypt's present historiographical system, would emphatically reject any historiographical perspective that functions outside or in opposition to the standard historiographical order.[9] Such positions make sure that rather than joining the emerging global discipline of history on their own terms, Egyptian historiographers will remain deeply rooted in a nineteenth-century intellectual tradition.

But we also have another way of comprehending the challenge to Egyptian historiography. When philosopher of history Hayden White was recently asked to address the question of the universality of Western historical thinking, his response left no room for second guessing: "There is no possibility," he said, "of 'adapting' Newtonian or Einsteinian physics to 'local' traditions. If one wants to make airplanes that fly or build an atomic bomb that explodes, one has to use Western physics. And so it is with Westernization of culture. If you want to Westernize, you have to adopt Western historical thinking."[10] The task of Egyptian historians, perhaps of all Arab historians, is to prove this statement partly true.

8. See, for instance, Maḥmūd al-Wardānī, "Manāhij al-tārīkh al-gharbī wa huwīyat miṣr: Laḥaẓātihā al-kubra," *Wujhāt Naẓar* 5, no. 54 (July 2003): pp. 58–63. See also the supplemental special issue of *Al-Bustān* discussing the "myth of Muḥammad 'Alī," *Aḥbār al-adab* 463, May 26, 2002.

9. See, for instance, Ra'ūf Abbās, "Al-Mamālīk al-judud," *Miṣr al-ḥaditha* 1 (2002): pp. 515–520.

10. Hayden White, "The Westernization of World History," in Rüsen, ed., *Western Historical Thinking*, p. 118.

BIBLIOGRAPHY

ARCHIVAL SOURCES

United Kingdom

NATIONAL ARCHIVES (NA-UK), KEW

British Council

BW 29/52

Foreign Office (FO)

FO 371/10888
FO 371/13130
FO 371/183975
FO 924/169
FO 924/170

Italy

ARCHIVIO STORICO MINISTERO DEGLI AFFARI ESTERI (ASMAE), ROME, INVENTARIO SERIE AFFARI POLITICI (ISAP)

ASMAE/ISAP 1919–30, Pacco 1001
ASMAE/ISAP 1931–45, Egitto/Busta no. 2 (1931)
ASMAE/ISAP 1931–45, Egitto/Busta no. 3 (1932)
ASMAE/ISAP 1931–45, Egitto/Busta no. 6 (1933)

ARCHIVIO CENTRALE DELLO STATO (ACS), ROME, MINISTERO DELLA CULTURA POPULARE (MCP)

ACS/MCP/Propaganda/Egitto/61
ACS/MCP/Propaganda/Egitto/62
ACS/MCP/Propaganda/Egitto/63

NEWSPAPERS AND PERIODICALS

Al-Ahrām
Ākhar Sā'a
Al-Akhbār
Akhbār al-Adab
Al-Fikr
Al-Fikr al-Mu'āṣir
Al-Ḥayat
Al-Hilāl
Al-Ithnayn wa-l-Dunyā
Al-Jumhūrīya
Al-Kātib
Al-Kitāb
Al-Majalla
Majallat Kulliyat al-Ādāb (Cairo University)
Majallat Mujma' al-lugha al-'arabiyya
Al-Manār
Al-Muqtaṭaf
Al-Muṣawwar
Qaḍāyā Fikriyya
Al-Qāhira
Al-Qūwwāt al-Muṣāllaḥa
Al-Risāla
Rūz al-Yūsuf
Al-Thaqāfa
Wujhāt Naẓar

SOURCES IN ARABIC

'Abbās, Ra'ūf. *Al-Ḥaraka al-'umāliya fī miṣr, 1899–1952*. Cairo: Dār al-kutub al-'arabī li-l-ṭibā'a wa-l-nashr, 1967.
———. "Al-Mamālīk al-judud." *Miṣr al-ḥaditha* 1 (2002): 515–520.
———. *Mashaynāhā khutān: Sīra dhātiya*. Cairo: Dār al-hilāl, 2004.
———. *Al-niẓām al-ijtimā'ī fi Miṣr fī ẓill al-milkiyāt al-zirā'iyya al-kabīra, 1837–1914*. Cairo: Dār al-fikr al-ḥadīth, 1973.
'Abd al-Hādī, Mas'ūd. *Al-Thawrāt fī Miṣr*. Cairo: Maṭba'at mukhaymar, 1954.
'Abd al-Ḥalīm, Maḥmūd. *Al-Ikhwān al-muslimūn: Aḥdath sana'at al-tārīkh: Ru'ya min al-dākhil*. Alexandria: Dār al-Da'wa, 1985.
'Abd al-Ḥayy, 'Abd al-Tawwāb. *'Aṣīr ḥayātī*. Cairo: al-Dār al-qawmiyya li-l-ṭibā'a wa-l-nashr, 1966.
'Abd al-Jawwād al-Aṣma'ī, Muḥammad. *Qal'at Muḥammad 'Ali lā qal'at Nābuliyūn*. Cairo: Maṭba'at Dār al-kutub, 1924.
'Abd al-Karīm, Aḥmad 'Izzat, ed. *'Abd al-Raḥmān al-Jabartī: Dirāsāt wa-buḥūth*. Cairo: al-Hay'a al-Miṣrīya al-'Āmma li-l-kitāb, 1976.

———. *Tārīkh al-taʿlīm fī ʿaṣr Muḥammad ʿAlī*. Cairo: Maktabat al-nahḍa al-miṣriyya, 1938.

ʿAbdallāh, Aḥmad. "Al-mubārizūn bi suyūf qadīma yaṭʿanūnu al-ajyāl al-jadīda: Ḥawla kitābat al-tārīkh al-miṣri bi ḥajr al-dubb al-masnūn." In Aḥmad ʿAbdallāh, ed., *Tārīkh Miṣr bayna al-manhaj al-ʿilmī wa-l-ṣirāʿ al-ḥizbī*, 15–27. Cairo: Dār shuhdī li-l-nashr, 1988.

———. "Taqdīm al-ḥiwār al-maftūḥ bayna Dr. ʿAbd al-ʿAẓīm Ramaḍān and Dr. ʿAbd al-Khāliq Lāshīn." In Aḥmad ʿAbdallāh, ed., *Tārīkh Miṣr bayna al-manhaj al-ʿilmī wa-l-ṣirāʿ al-ḥizbī*, 277–280. Cairo: Dār shuhdī li-l-nashr, 1988.

———, ed. *Tārīkh Miṣr bayna al-manhaj al-ʿilmī wa-l-ṣirāʿ al-ḥizbī*. Cairo: Dār shuhdī li-l-nashr, 1988.

ʿAbd Allāh al-Sammān, Muḥammad. *Ḥasan al-Bannā . . . : Al-rajul wa-l-fikra*. Cairo: Dār al-iʿtiṣām, 1978.

ʿAbd al-Malik, Anwar. *Nahḍat Miṣr*. Cairo: al-Hayʾa al-miṣriyya al-ʿāmma li-l-kitāb, 1983.

ʿAbd al-Raḥīm Muṣṭafa, Aḥmad. "Ḥawla taqwīm zaʿamāt Miṣr fī mā bayna thawratay 1919–1952." In Aḥmad ʿAbd Allāh, ed., *Tārīkh Miṣr bayna al-manhaj al-ʿilmī wa-l-ṣirāʿ al-ḥizbī*, 261–272. Cairo: Dār shuhdī li-l-nashr, 1988.

———. "Taqdīm." In ʿAbd al-Khāliq Lāshīn, *Saʿd Zaghlūl wa dawruhu fī-l-siyāsa al-miṣriyya*, 7–9. Beirut: Dār al-ʿawda, 1975.

———. "Taʿqīb." In Muḥammad ʿAfīfī, ed., *Al-Madrasa al-tārīkhīya al-miṣriyya*, 62–63. Cairo: Dār al-shurūq, 1997.

ʿAbduh, Ibrāhīm. *Tārīkh bi-lā wathāʾīq*. Cairo: Muʾassasat sajl al-ʿarab, 1975.

ʿAbduh, Muḥammad. *Al-aʿmāl al-kāmila li-l-imām Muḥammad ʿAbduh*. Edited by Muḥammad ʿImāra, 6 vols. Beirut: al-Muʾassasa al-ʿarabiyya li-l-dirāsāt wa-l-nashr, 1972.

———. *Al-Islām wa-l-radd ʿala muntaqidīhi*. Cairo: Maṭbaʿat al-tawfīq, 1924.

Abū al-Futūḥ, Raḍwān. *Tārīkh maṭbāʿat Būlāq*. Cairo: al-Maṭabāʿa al-amīriyya bi-l-Qāhira, 1953.

Abū Ḥadīd, Muḥammad Farīd. *Sīrat al-sayyid ʿUmar Makram*. Cairo: Lajnat al-taʾlīf wa-l-tarjama wa-l-nashr, 1937.

Abū Shuʿayshaʿ, Mūṣṭafa. *Dirāsāt fī-l-wathāʾiq wa marākiz al-maʿlūmāt al-wathāʾiqiyya*. Cairo: al-ʿArabī, 1994.

ʿAdawi, Muḥammad. *Ḥaqāʾiq wa asrār ḥawla kitāb al-ikhwān al-muslimūn: Aḥdāth sanʿat al-tārīkh*. Cairo: Dār al-anṣār, 1980.

Aḥmad, Nāhid Ḥamadī. *Al-Muqtanayāt al-arshīfiyya, takwīnihā wa tanmiyatuhā*. Cairo: Dār al-kutub al-miṣriyya, 1996.

Aḥmad Ismāʿīl, Ḥamāda Maḥmūd. *Ṣināʿat tārīkh Miṣr al-ḥadīth: Dirāsa fī fikr ʿAbd al-Raḥmān al-Rāfiʿī*. Cairo: al-Hayʾa al-miṣriyya al-ʿāmma li-l-kitab, 1987.

ʿAlī, Muḥammad Kurd. *Khiṭaṭ al-shām*. 6 vols. Damascus: al-Maṭbaʿa al-ḥadītha, 1925–28.

ʿĀmir, Ibrāhīm. *Al-Arḍ wa-l-fallāḥ: Al-masʾala al-zirāʿiyya fī Miṣr*. Cairo: al-Dār al-Miṣriyya li-l-ṭibāʿa wa-l-nashr wa-l-tawzīʿ, 1958.

———. *Taʾmīm al-qanā*. Cairo: Dār al-nadīm, October 1956.

———. *Thawrat Miṣr al-qawmiyya*. Cairo: Dār al-nadīm, 1957.

Anīs, Muḥammad, ed. *Al-Dawla al-ʿuthmāniyya wa-l-sharq al-ʿarabī 1514–1914*. Cairo: al-Maktaba al-anglū al-miṣriyya, 1965.

———. *Dirāsāt fī wathā'iq 1919*. Cairo: Maktaba al-anglū al-miṣriyya, 1963.

———. *Madrasat al-tārīkh al-miṣrī fī-l-ʿaṣr al-ʿuthmānī*. Cairo: Dār al-jīl li-l-ṭibāʿa, 1962.

Anīs, Muḥammad, and Rajab Ḥarāz al-Sayyid. *Thawrat 23 Jūlyū 1952 wa uṣūluhā al-tārīkhiyya*. Cairo: Dār al-nahḍa al-ʿarabiyya, 1969.

ʿAqqād, Abbās Maḥmūd al-. *Saʿd Zaghlūl*. Cairo: Maṭbaʿat jamāzī, 1936.

ʿAshmāwī, Ḥasan. *Al-Ikhwān wa-l-thawra*. Cairo: al-Maktab al-miṣri al-ḥadith, 1977.

ʿAṭiyya Allāh, Aḥmad. *Qāmus al-thawra al-miṣriyya*. Cairo: al-Maktaba al-anglū-miṣriyya, 1954.

Ayyūbī, Ilyās al-. *Muḥammad ʿAlī*. Cairo: Dār al-hilāl, 1923.

Badr, Aḥmad. *Dalīl dūr al-maḥfūẓāt wa-l-maktabāt wa marākiz al-tawthīq wa-l-maʿāhid al-bībliyūjrāfiya fī-l-duwal al-ʿarabiyya*. Cairo: UNESCO, 1965.

Badr, Ṭaha. *Taṭawwūr al-riwāya al-ʿarabiyya al-ḥadītha*. Cairo: Dār al-maʿārif, 1963.

Bannā, Ḥasan al-. *Qaḍīyatunā bayna yaday al-ra'y al-ʿamm al-miṣrī wa-l-ʿarabī wa-l-islāmī wa-l-ḍamīr al-ʿālamī: Ākhar mā katab al-imām al-shahīd qubayla ightiyālihi*. Cairo: n.p., 1978.

Baqariūs, Riyāḍ, et al., eds. *Mūjaz al-tārīkh al-muṣawwar, al-tarbiyya al-waṭaniyya*. Cairo: Wizārat al-tarbiyya wa-l-taʿlīm, 1958.

Barakāt, ʿAlī. "Madrasat al-tārīkh al-ijtimāʿī al-miṣrī fī rubʿ qarn, 1970–1995." In Muḥammad ʿAfifī, ed., *Al-Madrasa al-tārīkhiya al-miṣriyya*, 101–112. Cairo: Dār al-shurūq, 1997.

———. *Al-milkīya al-zirāʿiyya bayna thawratayn, 1919–1952*. Cairo: Markaz al-dirāsāt al-siyāsiyya wa-l-istarātijiyya bi-l-ahrām, 1978.

———. *Taṭawwur al-milkīyya al-zirāʿiyya fī Miṣr, 1813–1914, wa athruhu ʿala al-ḥaraka al-siyāsiyya*. Cairo: Dār al-thaqāfa al-jadīda, 1977.

Barrāwī, Rāshid al-, and Muḥammad Ḥamza ʿUlaysh. *Al-Taṭawwūr al-iqtiṣādī fī Miṣr fī al-ʿaṣr al-ḥadīth*. 5th ed. Cairo: Maktabat al-nahḍa al-miṣriyya, 1954.

Bashrī, Abd al-ʿAzīz. *Al-Tarbiya al-waṭaniyya*. Cairo: Wizārat al-maʿārif, 1930.

Baybars, Ḍiyā' al-Dīn. *Asrār ḥukumat yulyū*. Cairo: Maktabat madbūlī, 1976.

Bayyūmī, Zakarīyā Sulaymān. *Al-Ikhwān al-muslimūn wa-l-jamaʿāt al-islāmiya fī-l-ḥayāh al-siyāsiya al-miṣriya, 1928–1948*. Cairo: Maktabat wahaba, 1979.

Bishrī, Ṭāriq al-. *Al-ḥaraka al-siyāsiya fī miṣr, 1945–1952*. Cairo: al-Ḥay'a al-miṣriya al-ʿāma li-l-kitāb, 1972.

———. *Al-ḥaraka al-siyāsiya fī miṣr, 1945–1952*. 2nd ed. Cairo: Dār al-shurūq, 1983.

———. *Al-Muslimūn wa-l-aqbāṭ fī iṭār al-jamāʿa al-waṭaniya*. Cairo: al-Ḥay'a al-miṣriya al-ʿāma li-l-kitāb, 1980.

Buḥayrī, Muḥammad Ismāʿīl al-. *ʿIbarāt al-sharq*. Cairo: Maktabat al-saʿāda, 1927.

Crabitès, Pierre. *Ismāʿīl al-muftara ʿalayhi*. Translated into Arabic by Fu'ād Saffūf. Cairo: Dār al-nashr al-ḥadīth, 1937.

Darendevî, Hayret. *Insa-yi Hayret Efendi*. Cairo: Maṭbaʿat būlāq, 1826.

Dawḥ, Ḥasan. *Ṣafaḥāt min jihād al-shabāb al-muslim*. Cairo: Dār al-iʿtiṣām, 1977.

Dhikra Aḥmad Taymūr bāsha. Edited anonymously. Cairo: Maṭbaʿat al-Nīl, 1945.

Disūqī, ʿĀṣim. *Kibār mullāk al-arāḍī al-zirāʿiyya wa dawruhum fī-l-mujamaʿ al-miṣrī, 1914–1952*. Cairo: Dār al-theqāfa al-jadīda, 1975.

———. *Miṣr al-muʿāṣira fī dirāsāt al-muʾārikhīn al-miṣriyyīn*. Cairo: Dār al-ḥuriya, 1977.

———. *Naḥwa fahm tārīkh miṣr al-iqtiṣādī wa-l-ijtimāʿī*. Cairo: Dār al-kutub al-jamāʿī, 1981.

———. "Tārīkh miṣr al-iqtiṣādī al-ḥadīth fī-l-jāmiʿa al-miṣriyya, 1970–1995." In Muḥammad ʿAfīfī, *Al-Madrasa al-tārīkhīya al-miṣriyya*, 85–98. Cairo: Dār al-shurūq, 1997.

Ḍiyāʾ al-Dīn, Baybars. *Fatḥī Radwān yarwī li Diyāʾ al-Din Baybars asrār ḥukūmat yūlyū*. Cairo: Maktabut Madabūli, 1976.

Diyāb, Muḥammad ʿAbd al-Ḥakam. *Khulāṣat tārīkh Miṣr al-qadīm wa-l-ḥadīth*. Cairo: al-Maṭbaʿa al-amīriyya bi bulāq, 1892.

Dodwell, Henry. *Muḥammad ʿAlī muʾassis Miṣr al-ḥadītha*. Translated from the original English by ʿAlī Aḥmad Shukrī and Aḥmad ʿAbd al-Khāliq. Cairo: Maktabat al-adāb, 1937.

Egyptian Archaeological Authority. *Manzil Zaynab Khātūn*. Cairo, n.d.

Egyptian Government. *Dalīl al-maktabāt al-miṣriyya: Al-ʿāmma wa-l-mutakhaṣiṣa wa al-aqādīmiyya*. Cairo: al-Maktaba al-aqādimīyya, 1998.

EHS. *Dhikra al-baṭal al-fātiḥ Ibrāhīm Bāshā 1848–1948*. 2nd ed. Cairo: al-Jamʿiyya al-malakiyya li-l-dirāsāt al-tārikhiyya, maktabat madbūlī, 1990.

———. *Al-Dhikra al-miʾawiyya li-wafāt al-maghfūr lahu Muḥammad ʿAlī al-kabīr 1849–1949*. Cairo: Dār al-maʿārif bi Miṣr, 1949.

Fahmī, Maḥmūd. *Al-Baḥr al-zākhir fī tārīkh al-ʿālam wa akhbār al-awāʾil wa-l-awākhir*. 4 vols. Cairo: al-Maṭbaʿa al-kubra al-amīriyya bi būlāq, 1894–95.

Fahmī, Qalinī. *Al-Amīr ʿUmar Ṭūsūn*. Cairo: Maṭbaʿat kusta tsumashī, 1944.

Fahmī, Wafīq ʿAbd al-ʿAzīz. *Qaḍiyyat al-jalāʾ: Thawrat 23 Yūlyū 1952*. Cairo: Kutub qawmiyya, al-dār al-qawmiyya li-l-ṭibāʿa wa-l-nashr, n.d.

Farīd, Muḥammad. *Kitāb al-bahja al-tawfīqiyya fī tārīkh muʾāssis al-ʿāʾila al-khudaywiyya*. Cairo: al-Maṭbaʿa al-amīriyya, 1890.

Fikrī, Muḥammad Amīn. *Jughrāfīyat Miṣr*. Cairo: Maṭbaʿat wādī al-Nīl, 1878.

Ghurbāl, Muḥammad Shafīq. "Amīr Sūrī fī Italiya fī-l-qarn al-sābiʿ ʿasahr." *Majallat Kulliyat al-Ādāb* 2, no. 1 (May 1934): 75–110.

———. "Asālīb kitābat al-tārīkh ʿinda al-ʿArab." *Majallat Mujmaʿ al-lugha al-ʿarabiyya* 14 (1962): 25–34.

———. "Al-Ḥayā jadīra bi-an naḥyāhā." In Aḥmad Amīn, ed., *ʿAllamatnī al-ḥayā*, 52–54. Cairo: Dār al-hilāl, 1953.

———. *Manhaj mufaṣṣal li-l-durūs: Al-ʿawāmil al-tārīkhiyya fī bināʾ al-umma al-ʿarabiyya ʿala ma hiya ʿalayhi al-yawm*. Cairo: Maʿhad al-dirāsāt al-ʿarabiyya, 1961.

———. *Min zāwiyat al-qāhira*. Cairo: Dār al-idhāʿa wa-l-tilifizyūn, n.d.

———. "Miṣr ʿinda muftaraq al-ṭuruq 1798–1801." *Majallat Kulliyat al-Ādāb* 4, no. 1 (May 1936): 1–70.

———. *Muḥammad ʿAlī al-kabīr*. Cairo: Dāʾirat al-maʿārif al-islāmiyya, 1944.

———. *Muḥammad ʿAlī al-kabīr*. 2nd ed. Cairo: al-Hilāl, 1987.

———. *Takwīn Miṣr ʿibra al-ʿuṣūr*. Cairo: al-Hayʾa al-miṣriyya al-ʿĀma li-l-kitāb, 1990.

———. *Tārīkh al-mufāwaḍāt al-miṣriyya al-briṭāniyya.* Cairo: Maktabat al-nahḍa al-miṣriyya, 1952.

Ḥalawānī, Amīn b. Ḥasan al-. *Nabsh al-hadhayān min tārīkh Jurjī Zaydān.* 1889. Medina, Saudi Arabia: Maktabat ibn al-qiyam, 1989.

Ḥamūda, ʿAbbās Maḥmūd. *Al-madkhal ila dirāsat al-wathāʾīq al-ʿarabiyya.* Cairo: Maktabat nahḍat al-sharq, 1995.

Ḥamūda, ʿĀdil. *Azmat al-muthaqafīn wa thawrat yūliū.* Cairo: Maktabat madbūlī, 1985.

Hanah, Neli. "Al-dirāsāt al-tārīkhiya al-khāṣa bi miṣr fī-l-ʿaṣr al-ʿuthmānī." In Muḥammad ʿAfīfī, ed., *Al-Madrasa al-tārīkhīya al-miṣriyya,* 161–168. Cairo: Dār al-shurūq, 1997.

Ḥasūna, Muḥammad Amīn. *Kifāḥ al-shaʿb min ʿUmar Makram ila Jamāl ʿAbd al-Nāṣir.* 2 vols. Cairo: Maṭābiʿ al-ṣabāḥ, 1955.

Haykal, Muḥammad Ḥasanīn. *Azmat al-muthaqafīn.* Cairo: Dār al-ʾudabāʾ, 1961.

Ḥilmī, ʿAbd al-Ḥalīm. *Muḥammad ʿAlī al-kabīr munshiʾ Miṣr al-ḥadīth.* Cairo: Maṭbaʿat maṭar, 1919.

Hishmat, Qāsim. *Dalīl al-rasāʾil al-jāmiʿiya.* 2 vols. Cairo: Kulliyat al-ādāb, 1996.

Ḥitta, Aḥmad Aḥmad al-. *Tārīkh al-zirāʿa al-miṣriyya fī ʿaṣr Muḥammad ʿAlī al-kabīr.* Cairo: Dār al-maʿārif bi Miṣr, al-jamʿiyya al-malakiyya li-l-dirāsāt al-tārīkhiyya, 1950.

Ḥusayn, Muḥammad Aḥmad. *Al-Wathāʾīq al-tārīkhiyya.* Cairo: Jāmiʿat al-Qāhira, 1954.

Ḥusayn, Ṭaha, et al., eds. *Fuṣūl mukhtāra min kutub al-tārīkh, min awāsiṭ al-qarn al-sābiʿ ila al-ʿaṣr al-ḥadīth.* Cairo: al-Maṭbaʿa al-amīriyya bi-l-Qāhira, wizārat al-tarbiyya wa-l-taʿlīm, 1957.

Ibrāhīm, Ḥasan Aḥmad. "Wathāʾiq tārīkh al-Sūdān fī-l-qarn al-tāsiʿ ʿashar." In *Nadwat wathāʾiq tārīkh al-ʿarab al-ḥadīth 7–12 May 1977.* Cairo: Maṭbaʿat jāmiʿat ʿayn shamas, 1977. Unpaginated.

Jabrī, ʿAbd al-Mutaʿāl al-. *Li-mādhā ʿughtīla al-imām al-shahīd Ḥasan al-Bannā?* 2nd ed. Cairo: Dār al-iʿtiṣām, 1978.

Jazīrī, Muḥammad Ibrāhīm al-. *Āthār al-zaʿīm Saʿd Zaghlūl.* Cairo: Māṭbaʿat dār al-kutub, 1927.

Jindī, Anwar al-. *Ḥasan al-Bannā: Al-dāʿiya, al-imām, wa-l-mujaddid al-shahīd.* Beirut: Dār al-qalam, 1978.

———. *Maʿrakat al-muqāwama al-ʿarabiya.* Cairo: Maṭbaʿat al-taḥrīr, 1961.

Jiritlī, ʿAlī. *Tārīkh al-ṣināʿa fī Miṣr fī-l-niṣf al-awwal min al-qarn al-tāsiʿ ʿashar.* Cairo: Dār al-maʿārif bi Miṣr, al-Jamʿiyya al-malakiyya li-l-dirāsāt al-tārīkhiyya, 1952.

Jirjis, Fawzī. *Dirāsāt fī tārīkh Miṣr al-siyāsī mundhu al-ʿaṣr al-mamlūkī.* 1958; Cairo: al-ʿArabī, 1989.

Jumayʿī, ʿAbd al-Munʿim Ibrāhīm al-. *Itijāhāt al-kitāba al-tārīkhiyya fi tārīkh Miṣr al-ḥadīth wa-l-muʿāṣir.* Cairo: ʿAyn li-l-dirāsāt wa-l-buḥūth al-insāniyya wa-l-ijtimāʿiyya, 1994.

———. *Al-Jamʿiyya al-miṣriyya li-l-dirāsāt al-tārīkhiyya wa dirāsa tārīkhiyya li-l-muʾassasa ʿilmiyya 1945–1985.* Cairo: al-Jamʿiyya al-tārīkhiyya al-miṣriyya, 1995.

———. *Manhaj al-baḥth al-tārīkhī: Dirāsāt wa buḥūth.* Cairo: Maṭbaʿat al-Jablāwī, 1992.

———. "Al-Muʾarrikhūn al-hawāh wa dawruhum fī kitābat tārīkh miṣr al-ḥadīth wa-l-mu'āṣir." In Muḥammad 'Afifī, ed., *Al-Madrasa al-tārīkhiya al-miṣriyya*, 28–34. Cairo: Dār al-shurūq, 1997.

Jundī, Jūrj, and Jacques Tagher. *Ismā'īl kama tuṣawwiruhu al-wathā'iq al-rasmiyya*. Published in memory of Ismā'īl. Cairo: Maṭba'at dār al-kutub al-miṣriyya, 1947.

Kamāl al-Shāfi'ī, Mu'min. *Al-Dawla wa-l-ṭabaqa al-wūsṭa fī Miṣr*. Cairo: Dār qibā', 2000.

Kāmil, Maḥmūd. *Miṣr al-ghad taḥta ḥukum al-shabāb*. Cairo: Dār al-jāmi'a, 1945.

Kāmil, Muṣṭafa. *Ṣafaḥāt maṭwīya min tārīkh al-za'īm Muṣṭafa Kāmil: Rasā'il jadīda li-Muṣṭafa Kāmil min 8 yūniyū 1895 ilā 19 Fabrāyir 1896*. Edited by Muḥammad Anīs. Cairo: al-Hay'a al-Miṣriyya al-'amma li-l-kitāb, 1987.

———. *Al-Shams al-mushriqa*. Vol. 2 of *Al-Mu'alafāt al-kāmila li Muṣṭafa Kāmil Bāshā*. Cairo: al-'Arabī, 2001.

Khafīf, Maḥmūd al-. *Ahmad 'Urābī, al-za'īm al-muftara 'alayhi*. Cairo: Maṭba'at al-risāla, 1947.

———. *Aḥmad 'Urābī, al-za'īm al-muftara 'alayhi*. Cairo: al-Hilāl, 1971.

Khalīfa, Sha'bān 'Abd al-'Aziz. *Dār al-kutub al-qawmiyya fī riḥlat al-nushū' wa-l-irtiqā' wa-l-tadahwūr*. Cairo: al-'Arabī, 1991.

Kifāḥ al-sha'b wa-l-jalā'. Ikhtarnā laka 26 [series]. Cairo: Dār al-Ma'ārif, n.d.

Lāshīn, 'Abd al-Khāliq. *Sa'd Zaghlūl wa dawruhu fīl-siyāsa al-miṣriyya*. Beirut: Dār al-'awda, 1975.

Manṣūr, Aḥmad Muḥammad. *Al-Kutub al-'arabiyya allatī nushirat fī Miṣr 1940–1956*. Cairo: American University in Cairo Press, 1975.

Mar'ashlī, Tawfīq Ḥāmid al-. *Al-Tarbiya al-waṭaniyya*. Cairo: Maṭba'at dār al-kitāb, 1926.

Ministry of Culture and Guidance. *Dār al-kutub fī 'ahd al-thawra*. Cairo: Dār al-kutub, 1962.

Mubārak, 'Alī. *Al-Khiṭaṭ al-tawfīqiyya al-jadīda li-Miṣr al-qāhira*. 11 vols. Cairo: al-Hay'a al-miṣriyya al-'āmma li-l-kitāb, 1994; originally published in 20 volumes in 1886.

Mursī, Fu'ād. *Taṭawwur al-ra'smāliyya wa kifāḥ al-ṭabaqāt fī Miṣr*. 1949; Cairo: Kitābāt al-miṣrī al-jadīd, al-maktaba al-ishtirākiyya, 1990.

Muṣīlḥī, Muṣṭafā al-. *Al-Madhbaḥa: Fī-l-dhikrā al-'ishrīn li-l-madhbaḥa allatī ta'arraḍa lahā al-ikhwān al-muslimūn bi-līmān ṭarah yawm al-sabt, 1/6/1957*. Cairo: Dār al-anṣār, 1977.

Mutawallī, Maḥmūd. *Al-uṣūl al-tārīkhiyya li-l-ra'smālīya al-miṣrīyya wa taṭwwurihā*. Cairo: al-Hay'a al-miṣriyya al-'āmma li-l-kitāb, 1974.

Naqqāsh, Salīm al-. *Miṣr li-l-miṣriyyīn*. Alexandria: Maṭba'at jarīdat al-maḥrūsa, 1884.

Niqūlā, Yūsuf. *A'lām min al-Iskandariyya*. Alexandria: Mu'assasat al-ma'ārif, 1969.

Nuṣayr, 'Āyida Ibrāhīm. *Al-Kutub al-'arabiyya allatī nushirat fī Miṣr bayna 'āmay 1900–1925*. Cairo: American University in Cairo Press, 1983.

———. *Al-Kutub al-'arabiyya allatī nushirat fī Miṣr bayna 'āmay 1926–1940*. Cairo: Cairo University Press, 1966.

Qāḍī, Shukrī al-. *Mi'at shakhṣīyya miṣrīya wa shakhṣīyya*. Cairo: al-Hay'a al-'āma li-l-kitāb, 1987.

Qāsim, 'Abduh Qāsim. "Al-Tārīkh wa kayfa yadrusuhu al-talāmīdh al-miṣriyūn." *Wujhāt Naẓar* 25 (February 2001): 48–53.

Qattār, Ilyās al-, et al., eds. *Asad Rustum al-insān wa-l-mu'arīkh 1897–1965*. Beirut: al-Maktaba al-būlusīyya, 1984.

Rāfi'ī, 'Abd al-Raḥmān al-. *Arba'at 'ashar 'ām fī-l-barlamān*. Cairo: Maṭba'at al-sa'āda bi Miṣr, 1955.

———. *'Aṣr Ismā'īl*. 2 vols. 1932. Cairo: Dār al-ma'ārif, 1987.

———. *'Aṣr Muḥammad 'Alī*. Cairo: Matba'at al-fikra, 1930, 1947 editions.

———. *Fī a'qāb al-thawra al-miṣriyya thawrat 1919*. 3 vols. Cairo: Dār al-ma'ārif, 1989.

———. *Miṣr al-mujāhida fī-l-'aṣr al-ḥadīth*. 6 vols. 1957. Repr., Cairo: Dār al-hilāl, 1989.

———. *Miṣr wa-l-Sūdān fī awwal 'ahd al-iḥtilāl: Tārīkh Miṣr al-qawmī fī sanat 1882 ila sanat 1892*. Cairo: Maktabat al-nahḍa al-miṣriyya, 1948.

———. *Mudhakkarātī 1889–1951*. Cairo: Dār al-hilāl, 1952.

———. *Muḥammad Farīd ramz al-ikhlāṣ wa-l-taḍḥiya: Tārīkh Miṣr al-qawmī min sanat 1908 ila sanat 1919*. Cairo: Dār al-ma'ārif, 1984.

———. *Muṣṭafa Kāmil: Bā'ith al-ḥaraka al-qawmiyya: Tārīkh Miṣr al-qawmī min sanat 1892–1908*. Cairo: Maktabat al-nahḍa al-miṣriyya, 1950.

———. *Muṣṭafa Kāmil: Bā'ith al-ḥaraka al-waṭaniyya*. Cairo: Maktabat al-nahḍa al-miṣriyya, 1939.

———. *Tārīkh al-ḥaraka al-qawmiyya fī Miṣr al-qadīma min fajr al-tārīkh ila al-fatḥ al-'arabī*. Cairo: Maktabat al-nahḍa al-miṣriyya, 1963.

———. *Tārīkh al-ḥaraka al-qawmiyya wa taṭawwur niẓām al-ḥukum fī Miṣr*. 2 vols. Cairo: Dār al-ma'ārif, 1987.

———. *Al-Thawra al-'urābiyya wa-l-iḥtilāl al-inglīzī*. Cairo: Maktabat al-nahḍa al-miṣriyya, 1949.

———. *Al-Thawra al-'urābiyya wa-l-iḥtilāl al-inglīzī*. 2nd ed. Cairo: Dār al-qawmiyya li-l-ṭibā'a wa-l-nashr, 1966.

———. *Thawrat sanat 1919: Tārīkh Miṣr al-qawmī min sanat 1919 ila sanat 1921*. Cairo: Maktabat al-nahḍa al-miṣriyya, 1955.

———. *Al-Za'īm Aḥmad 'Urābī*. Cairo: Dār al-hilāl, 1952.

———. *Al-Za'īm al-thā'ir Aḥmad 'Urābī*. Cairo: Dār wa maṭābi' al-sha'ab, 1968.

Rāfi'ī, 'Abd al-Raḥmān al-, and Sa'īd 'Abd al-Fattāḥ 'Āshūr. *Miṣr fī-l-'uṣūr al-wūsṭa min al-fatḥ al-'arabī ḥatta al-ghazw al-'uthmānī*. Cairo: Dār al-nahḍa al-'arabiyya, 1970.

Rajabī, Khalīl bin Aḥmad al-. *Tārīkh al-wazīr Muḥammad 'Alī Bāshā*. Cairo: al-Āfāq al-'arabiyya, 1997.

Ramaḍān, 'Abd al-'Aẓīm. "Madāris kitābat tārīkh Miṣr al-mu'āṣir." In Aḥmad 'Abdallāh, ed., *Tārīkh Miṣr bayna al-manhaj al-'ilmī wa-l-ṣirā' al-ḥizbī*, 59–79. Cairo: Dār shuhdī li-l-nashr, 1988.

———. *Miṣr fī 'aṣr al-Sadat*. Cairo: Maktabat madbūlī, 1986.

———. *Miṣr fī 'aṣr al-Sadat*. 2 vols. 2nd ed. Cairo: Maktabat madbūlī, 1989.

———. *Mudhakkirāt Sa'd Zaghlūl*. Cairo: al-Hay'a al-miṣriyya al-'āmma li-l-kitāb, 1987.

———. *Muṣṭafa Kāmil fī maḥkamat al-tārīkh*. Cairo: al-Hay'a al-miṣriyya al-'āmma li-l-kitāb, 1987.

———. *Tārīkh Miṣr wa-l-muzawirūn*. Cairo: al-Zahrā' li-l-I'lām al-'arabī, 1993.

———. *Taṭawwur al-ḥaraka al-waṭaniyya fī Miṣr min sanat 1918 ila sanat 1936*. Cairo: Dār al-kitāb al-'arabī li-l-tibā'a wa-l-nashr, 1968.

———. *Taṭawwur al-ḥaraka al-waṭaniyya fī Miṣr 1918–1936*. 4 vols. Cairo: al-Hay'a al-miṣriyya al-'āma li-l-kitāb, 1998.

Rifā'ī, 'Abd al-'Azīz. *Aḥmad Shafīq mu'arrikh: Hayatuhu wa athruhu*. Cairo: al-Dār al-Miṣriyya li-l-ta'līf wa-l-tarjama, 1965.

Rif'at, Muḥammad. *Tārīkh Miṣr al-siyāsī fī-l-azmina al-ḥadītha*. Cairo: al-Maṭba'a al-amīriyya, 1938, 1941, 1949 editions.

Rizq, Jābir. *Al-Asrār al-ḥaqiqiyya li-ightiyāl Ḥasan al-Bannā*. Cairo: Dār al-anṣār, 1978.

Rizq, Yunān Labīb. "Aḥmād 'Izzat 'Abd al-Karīm: Al-mu'ālim." *Miṣr al-ḥadītha* 2 (2003): 457–460.

———. "Bayna al-mawḍū'iyya wa-l-taḥazzub fī kitābat tārīkh al-aḥzāb al-siyāsiyya fī Miṣr." In Aḥmad 'Abdallāh, ed., *Tārīkh Miṣr bayna al-manhaj al-'ilmī wa-l-ṣirā' al-ḥizbī*, 363–374. Cairo: Dār shuhdī li-l-nashr, 1988.

Rothstein, Fedor Aronovich. *Tārīkh al-mas'ala al-miṣriya, 1875–1910*. Translated into Arabic by Muḥammad Badrān. Cairo: Lajnat al-ta'līf wa-l-tarjama wa-l-nashr, 1936.

Rushdī, Aḥmad Ṣāliḥ *Krūmir fī Miṣr*. Cairo: Dār al-qarn al-'ishrīn, 1945.

Rustum, Asad. *Al-Maḥfūẓāt al-malakiyya al-miṣriyya: Bayān bi wathā'iq al-shām 1810–1832*. 4 vols. Beirut: American Press, 1940.

———. *Muṣṭalaḥ al- tārīkh*. 1939. 2nd ed., Sidon, Lebanon: al-Maṭba'a al-'aṣriyya, 1955.

Ṣabrī, Muḥammad. *Tārīkh Miṣr min Muḥammad 'Alī ila al-'aṣr al-ḥadīth*. Cairo: Madbūlī, 1991.

Sa'd, Aḥmad Ṣādiq. *Ṣafaḥāt min al-yasār al-miṣrī fī a'qāb al-ḥarb al-'ālamiyya al-thāniyya, 1945–1946*. Cairo: Maktabat madbūlī, 1976.

Sa'īd, Aḥmad. "Qāmūs al-iqtiṣād al-siyāsī." In Aḥmad Ṣādiq Sa'd, *Ṣafaḥāt min al-yasār al-miṣrī fī a'qāb al-ḥarb al-'ālamiyya al-thāniyya, 1945–1946*, pp. 358–363. Cairo: Maktabat madbūlī, 1976.

Sa'īd, Amīn. *Al-Jumhūriyya al-'arabiyya al-muttaḥida*. 2 vols. Cairo: Dār iḥyā' al-kutub al-'arabiyya, 1959.

———. *Tārīkh Miṣr al-siyāsī min al-ḥamla al-fransiyya sanat 1798 ila inhiyār al-malakiyya 1952*. Cairo: Dār iḥyā' al-kutub al-'arabiyya, 1959.

———. *Al-Thawra*. Cairo: Dār iḥyā' al-kutub al-'arabiyya, 1959.

———. *Thawrāt al-'arab fī-l-qarn al-'ishrīn*. Cairo: Dār al-hilāl, 1960.

Sa'īd, Rif'at al-. *Ḥasan al-Bannā: Matā, kayfa, wa li-mādhā?* Cairo: Maktabat madbūlī, 1977.

———. *Sa'd Zaghlūl bayna al-yamīn wa-l-yasār*. Beirut: Dār al-qaḍāyā, 1976.

———. *Safaḥāt min tārīkh miṣr: Ru'īyat al-'alāqa bayna al-tārīkh wa-l-siyāsa*. Cairo: Dār al-thaqāfa al-jadīda, 1984.

Salīm Afendī, Ḥasan, et al., eds. *Ṣafwat tārīkh Miṣr wa-l-duwal al-'arabiyya*. 2 vols. Cairo: Wizārat al-ma'ārif, 1930.

Sāmī, Amīn. *Miṣr wa-l-nīl*. Cairo: Maṭba'at dār al-kutub al-miṣriyya, 1938.

———. *Taqwīm al-Nīl*. 3 vols. Cairo: Dār al-kutub, 1916–36.

Sammarco, Angelo. *Al-Ḥaqīqa fī mas'alat qanāt al-suwīs*. Translated into Arabic by Ṭaha Fawzī. Cairo: n.p., 1940.

Sarhank, Ismā'īl. *Ḥaqā'iq al-akhbār 'an duwal al-biḥār*. 3 vols. Cairo: al-Maṭba'at al-amīriyya būlāq, 1896.

Sayyid, Aḥmad Luṭfī al-. *Al-Muntakhabāt.* Cairo: Dār al-nashr al-ḥadīth, 1937.

Sayyid, Amīn Fu'ād. *Dār al-kutub al-miṣriyya, tārīkhuhā wa taṭawwuruhā.* Cairo: Awrāq sharqiyya, 1996.

Sayyid, Jalāl al-. "Muḥammad Anīs: Al-rajul wa-l-qaḍiyya." *Al-Manār* 21 (September 1986): 142–152.

Shāfi'ī, Shuhdī 'Aṭiyya al-. *Taṭawwur al-ḥaraka al-waṭaniyya al-miṣriyya 1882–1956.* Cairo: al-Dār al-Miṣriyya li-l-ṭibā'a wa-l-nashr wa-l-tawzī', 1957.

Shafīq, Aḥmad. *A'mālī ba'd mudhakkirātī.* Cairo: Maṭba'a miṣriyya, 1941.

———. *Ḥawliyāt Miṣr al-siyāsiyya.* 10 vols. Cairo: Maṭba'at shafīq bāshā, 1926.

Shayyāl, Jamāl al-Dīn al-. *Al-Tārīkh wa-l-mu'arrikhūn fī Miṣr fī-l-qarn al-tāsi' 'ashar.* Cairo: Maktabat al-nahḍa al-miṣriyya, 1958.

Shinnāwī, 'Abd al-Azīz Muḥammad al-. *Al-Dawla al-'uthmānīya: Dawla Islāmīya muftara' 'alayhā.* 4 vols. Cairo: Maktabat al-anjlū al-miṣrīya, 1980–86.

———. *Al-Sukhrah fī ḥafr Qanāt al-Suways.* Alexandria: Munsha'at al-Ma'ārif al-ḥadītha, 1958.

Shukrī, Muḥammad Fu'ād. "Ba'tha 'askariya būlūniya fī Miṣr fī 'ahd Muḥammad 'Alī." *Majallat Kulliyat al-Ādāb* 7, no. 1 (May 1946): pp. 27–48.

Shukrī, Muḥammad Fu'ād, et al., eds. *Binā' dawla: Miṣr Muḥammad 'Alī.* Cairo: Maṭba'at lajnat al-ta'līf al-tarjama wa-l-nashr, 1948.

Shuqayr, Na'ūm. *Tārīkh al-Sūdān.* Beirut: Dār al-jīl, 1981.

Ṭamāwī, Aḥmad Ḥusayn al-. *Ṣabrī al-Surbūnī: Sīra tārīkhiyya wa ṣūrat ḥayā.* Cairo: A'lām al-'arab, 1986.

Thābit, Karīm. *Fārūq kama 'araftuhu.* 2 vols. Cairo: Dār al-shurūq, 2000.

———. *Al-Malik Fu'ād, malik al-nahḍa.* Cairo: Maṭba'at al-ma'ārif, 1944.

———. *Muḥammad 'Alī.* Cairo: Maktabat al-ma'ārif, 1942.

———. *Sa'd fī ḥayātihi al-khāṣṣa.* Cairo: n.p., 1929.

Tilimsānī, 'Umar. *Al-Mulham al-mawhūb ustādh al-jīl ḥasan Aḥmad 'Abd al-Raḥmān al-Bannā.* Cairo: Dār al-anṣār, 1981.

Ṭūsūn, 'Umar. *Al-Ba'thāt al-'ilmiyya fī 'ahd Muḥammad 'Alī, 'Abbās al-awwal wa Sa'īd.* Alexandria: Maṭba'at ṣalāḥ al-dīn, 1934.

———. *Al-Jaysh al-miṣrī al-barrī wa-l-baḥrī fī 'ahd Muḥammad 'Alī Bāshā.* Alexandria: Maṭba'at ṣalāḥ al-dīn al-kubra, 1931.

———. *Kalimāt fī sabīl Miṣr.* Cairo: al-Maṭba'a al-salafiyya, 1928.

———. *Al-Ṣanā'i' wa-l-madāris al-ḥarbiyya fī 'ahd Muḥammad 'Alī.* Alexandria: Maṭba'at ṣalāḥ al-dīn al-kubra, 1932.

'Ulwān, Muḥammad Bahā' al-Dīn. *'Abd al-'Azīz al-Shinnāwī mu'arrikhan.* al-Manṣūra: Dār sanābil, 1999.

———. *'Abd al-Raḥmān al-Rāfi'ī: Mu'arrikh Miṣr al-ḥadīth.* Cairo: al-Hay'a al-miṣriyya al-'āmma li-l-kitāb, 1987.

'Umar, Muḥammad Ziyān. *Madkhal ila 'ilm al-tārīkh.* Cairo: al-Hay'a al-'āma li-l-kitāb, 2000.

'Uthmān, Ḥasan. *Manhaj al-baḥth al-tārīkhī.* 1943. 2nd ed., Cairo: Dār al-ma'ārif bi Miṣr, 1965.

Wajdī, Muḥammad Farīd. "Mā qālahu Hanotaux." In Muḥammad Rashīd al-Khaṭīb, ed., *Khulāṣat al-radd,* 1–77. Damascus: Maṭba'at al-fayḥā', 1925.

Wardānī, Maḥmūd al-. "Manāhij al-tārīkh al-gharbī wa huwiyat miṣr: Laḥaẓātihā al-kubra." *Wujahāt Naẓar* 5, no. 54 (July 2003): 58–63.

Yiḥya, Muḥammad. *Fī-l-radd 'ala al-'almāniyīn.* Cairo: al-Zahra' li-l-i'lām al-'arabī, 1985.

Yūsuf, Ḥaṣan. *Al-Qaṣr wa dawruhu fī-l-siyāsa al-miṣriyya 1922–1952.* Cairo: al-Ahrām, 1982.

Zakī, 'Abd al-Raḥmān. *Ibrāhīm Bāshā.* Cairo: Dār al-kutub al-miṣriyya, 1948.

———. *Al-Tārīkh al-ḥarbī li-'aṣr Muḥammad 'Alī.* Cairo: al-Jam'iyya al-mālikiyya li-l-dirāsāt al-tārīkhiyya, dār al-ma'ārif, 1950.

Zand, 'Azīz. *Al-Qawl al-ḥaqīq fī rathā' wa tārīkh Muḥammad Tawfīq.* Cairo: Maṭba'at al-maḥrūsa, 1892.

Zaydān, Jurjī. *Ghadat Karbalā'.* Beirut: Dār maktabāt al-ḥayā, 1969.

———. *Istibdād al-mamālīk.* 1892–93. Repr., Cairo: Dār al-hilāl, 1965.

———. *Al-Mamlūk al-shārid.* 1891–92. Repr., Cairo: Dār al-hilāl, 1965.

———. *Radd rannān 'ala nabsh al-hadhayān.* Cairo: Maṭba'at al-ta'līf, 1891.

———. *Tārīkh Miṣr al-ḥadīth.* Cairo: Maṭba'at al-muqtaṭaf, 1889, 1911 editions.

Ziriklī, Khayr al-dīn. *Al-A'lām, qāmūs tarājim li-ashhar al-rijāl wa-l-nisā' min al-'arab wa-l-musta'ribīn wa-l-mustashriqīn.* 8 vols. Beirut: Dār al-'ilm li-l-malāyīn, 1986.

SOURCES IN HEBREW

Nuema, Meir. "Ha-Natzerism batqufa hapost natzerit." Unpublished Ph.D. dissertation, Bar Ilan University, 2004.

Sivan, Emmanuel. "Megamot ba Historiographia Hamitsrit-Indikatorim Kamutiyim." *Ha-Mizraḥ Ha-ḥadash* 91, no. 3 (1973): 296–298.

SOURCES IN WESTERN LANGUAGES

Abbot, Andrew. *The System of Professions: An Essay on the Division of Expert Labor.* Chicago: University of Chicago Press, 1988.

Abdel-Malek, Anouar. *Egypt: Military Society.* New York: Random House, 1968.

Abou-El-Haj, Rifaat Ali. "The Social Uses of the Past: Recent Arab Historiography of Ottoman Rule." *International Journal of Middle East Studies* 14, no. 2 (1982): 185–201.

Ahmed, Cezzâr, Pasha. *Ottoman Egypt in the Eighteenth Century: The Nizâmnâme-i Misir of Cezzâr Ahmed Pasha.* Edited and translated from the original Turkish by Stanford J. Shaw. Cambridge, MA: Harvard University Press, 1962.

Aïjaz, Ahmad. "Jameson's Rhetoric of Otherness and the 'National Allegory.'" *Social Text* 17 (Autumn 1987): 3–25.

Alleaume, Ghisaline "L'Égypte et son histoire: Actualité et controversés première partie: La presse et l'histoire." *Bulletin du Centre d'Études et de Documentation Économiques* 20, no. 2 (1986): 9–34.

Allen, Barry. "Review Essay: Another New Nietzsche." *History and Theory* 42, no. 3 (October 2003): 363–377.

Allen, Roger. *The Arabic Novel.* Syracuse, NY: Syracuse University Press, 1995.

———. *A Period of Time: A Study and Translation of Ḥadith ʿĪsā ibn Hishām by Muḥammad al-Muwayliḥī.* Oxford: Middle East Centre, St. Antony's College, Oxford, by Ithaca Press, 1992.

Amin, Galal. *Whatever Happened to the Egyptians? Changes in Egyptian Society from 1950 to the Present.* Cairo: American University in Cairo, 2000.

Anderson, Benedict. *Imagined Communities.* 1983. 2nd ed., London: Verso, 1991.

Antonius, George. *The Arab Awakening: The Story of the Arab National Movement.* Philadelphia: Lippincott, 1939.

Ayalon, Ami. *Language and Change in the Arab Middle East.* New York: Oxford University Press, 1987.

———. *The Press in the Arab Middle East: A History.* New York: Oxford University Press, 1995.

Ayalon, David. "The Historian al-Jabartī." In Bernard Lewis and P. M. Holt, eds., *Historians of the Middle East,* 391–402. London: Oxford University Press, 1962.

Azm, Jallal Sadik al-. "Western Historical Thinking from Arabian Perspective." In Jören Rüsen, ed., *Western Historical Thinking: An Intercultural Debate,* 119–127. New York: Berghahn, 2002.

Badawi, Zaki. *The Reformers of Egypt.* London: Croom Helm, 1978.

Badrawi, Malak. *Political Violence in Egypt 1910–1924: Secret Societies, Plots and Assassinations.* Richmond, UK: Curzon Press, 2000.

Bainville, Jacques. "L'expédition française en Égypte, 1798–1801." In Mohamed Zaky el-Ibrachy Pacha and Angelo Sammarco, eds., *Précis de l'histoire d'Égypte,* vol. 3 of 4, part 2: 131–184. Cairo: l'Institut Français d'Archéologie Orientale du Caire, 1933.

Baker, Raymond William. *Islam without Fear: Egypt and the New Islamists.* Cambridge, MA: Harvard University Press, 2003.

Baron, Beth. *Egypt as a Woman: Nationalism, Gender, and Politics.* Berkeley: University of California Press, 2005.

———. *The Women's Awakening in Egypt: Culture, Society and the Press.* New Haven, CT: Yale University Press, 1994.

Beattie, Kirk J. *Egypt during the Nasser Years: Ideology, Politics and Civil Society.* Boulder, CO: Westview Press, 1994.

———. *Egypt during the Sadat Years.* New York: Palgrave, 2000.

Beinin, Joel. "The Communist Movement and Nationalist Political Discourse in Nasirist Egypt." *Middle East Journal* 42, no. 2 (Autumn 1987): 568–584.

Beinin, Joel, and Zachary Lockman. *Workers on the Nile: Nationalism, Islam and the Egyptian Working Class, 1882–1954.* Princeton, NJ: Princeton University Press, 1987.

Beltrami, Luca. *Eugenio Griffini Bey 1878–1925.* Milan: Allegretti, 1926.

Berque, Jacques. *Egypt: Imperialism and Revolution.* London: Faber and Faber, 1972.

Bevir, Mark. *The Logic of the History of Ideas.* Cambridge: Cambridge University Press, 1999.

Botman, Selma. *The Rise of Egyptian Communism, 1939–1970.* Syracuse, NY: Syracuse University Press, 1988.

Broman Thomas. "Rethinking Professionalization: Theory, Practice and Professional Ideology in Eighteenth-Century German Medicine." *Journal of Modern History* 67, no. 4 (December 1995): 835–872.

Brown, Daniel. *Rethinking Tradition in Modern Islamic Thought.* Cambridge: Cambridge University Press, 1999.

Burke, Peter. "Western Historical Thinking in a Global Perspective—10 Theses." In *Western Historical Thinking: An Intercultural Debate,* 15–32. New York: Berghahn, 2002.

Burns, Elinor. *British Imperialism in Egypt.* London: Labour Research Department, 1928.

Cahen, Claude. "Khiṭaṭ." In *Encyclopaedia of Islam,* 5: 22b. 2nd ed. Leiden, the Netherlands: E. J. Brill, 1960–.

Cattaui, Adolphe. "La célébration du cinquantenaire de la Société royale de géographie d'Égypte." *Bulletin de la Société Royale de Géographie d'Égypte* 8 (July 1925): 109–129.

Cattaui, Joseph. *Le khédive Isma'il et la dette de l'Égypte.* Cairo: Impr. Misr, 1935.

Cattaui, René, Bey. "Georges Douin." *Bulletin de l'Institut d'Égypte* 27 (1944–45): 89–95.

Chakrabarty, Dipesh. "A Global and Multicultural 'Discipline' of History?" *History and Theory* 45, no. 1 (2006): 101–109.

———. "Postcoloniality and the Artifice of History: Who Speaks for 'Indian' Pasts?" *Representations* 37, special issue (Winter 1992): 1–26.

———. *Provincializing Europe: Postcolonial Thought and Historical Difference.* Princeton, NJ: Princeton University Press, 2000.

Charles-Roux, François. "L'Égypte de 1801 à 1882." In Gabriel Hanotaux, ed., *Histoire de la nation égyptienne,* vol. 6 of 7: 1–413. Paris: Ouvrage publié sous les auspices et le haut patronage de sa majesté Fouad Ier, Roi d'Égypte, 1937.

———. "*L'Égypte de l'occupation anglaise à l'indépendance égyptienne.*" In Gabriel Hanotaux, ed., *Histoire de la nation égyptienne,* vol. 7 of 7, pp. 3–151. Paris: Ouvrage publié sous les auspices et le haut patronage de sa majesté Fouad Ier, Roi d'Égypte, 1937.

Chatterjee, Partha. *Nationalist Thought and the Colonial World: A Derivative Discourse?* Minneapolis: University of Minnesota Press, 1993.

Choueiri, Youssef. *Arab History and the Nation-State: A Study in Modern Arab Historiography 1820–1980.* London: Routledge, 1989.

Cole, Juan. *Colonialism and Revolution in the Middle East.* Princeton, NJ: Princeton University Press, 1993.

Combe, Étienne. "L'Égypte ottomane 1517–1798." In Mohamed Zaky el-Ibrachy Pacha and Angelo Sammarco, eds., *Précis de l'histoire d'Égypte,* vol. 3 of 4, part 1: 1–128. Cairo: l'Institut français d'archéologie orientale du Caire, 1933.

Commins, David. *Islamic Reform: Politics and Social Change in Late Ottoman Syria.* Oxford: Oxford University Press, 1990.

Conniff, Michael. "Introduction: Towards a Comparative Definition of Populism." In Michael Conniff, ed., *Latin-American Populism in Comparative Perspectives,* 13–27. Albuquerque: University of New Mexico Press, 1982.

Contu, Giuseppe. "Aḥmad 'Izzat 'Abd al-Karīm (1909–1980): Storico arabo contemporaneo." In Clelia Sarnelli Cequa, ed., *Studi arabo-islamici in onore di Roberto Rubianacci nel suo settantesimo compleanno,* vol. 1 of 2: 219–238. Naples: Istituto Universitario Orientale, 1985.

Crabbs, Jack A., Jr. "Egyptian Intellectuals and the Revolution: The Case of 'Abd al-Raḥmān

al-Rāfiʿī." In Shimon Shamir, ed., *Egypt from Monarchy to Republic: A Reassessment of Revolution and Change,* 251–266. Boulder, CO: Westview Press, 1995.
———. "Politics, History and Culture in Nasser's Egypt." *International Journal of Middle East Studies* 6, no. 4 (1975): 386–420.
———. *The Writing of History in Nineteenth-Century Egypt: A Study in National Transformation.* Cairo: American University in Cairo Press, 1984.
Crabitès, Pierre. *Ibrahim of Egypt.* London: Routledge, 1935.
———. *Ismail the Maligned Khedive.* London: Routledge and Sons, 1933.
Crecelius, Daniel. "Al-Jabartī's *'Ajā'ib al-Athār fī-l-Tarājim wa-l-Akhbār* and the Arabic Histories of Ottoman Egypt in the Eighteenth Century." In Hugh Kennedy, ed., *The Historiography of Islamic Egypt, c. 950–1800,* 221–235. Leiden, the Netherlands: E. J. Brill, 2001.
———. "The Organization of *Waqf* Documents in Cairo." *International Journal of Middle East Studies* 2, no. 3 (1971): 266–277.
Cromer, Evelyn Baring. *Modern Egypt.* New York: Macmillan Company, 1908.
Cuno, Kenneth. "Muhammad ʿAli and the Decline and Revival Thesis in Modern Egyptian History." In Ra'ūf 'Abbās, ed., *Iṣlāḥ am taḥdīth? Miṣr fī 'aṣr Muḥammad 'Alī,* 93–119. Cairo: al-Majlīs al-aʿla li-l-thaqāfa, al-jamʿiyya al-miṣriyya li-l-dirāsāt al-tārīkhiyya, 2000.
Daly, M. W., ed. *The Cambridge History of Egypt,* 2 vols. Cambridge: Cambridge University Press, 1998.
Dearstyne, Bruce. *The Archival Enterprise: Modern Archival Principles, Practices, and Management Techniques.* Chicago: American Library Association, 1993.
de Certeau, Michel. *The Writing of History.* New York: Columbia University Press, 1988.
Deeb, Marius. *Party Politics in Egypt: The Wafd and Its Rivals 1919–1939.* St. Antony's Middle East Monographs 9. London: Ithaca Press, 1979.
Dekmejian, Harir. *Egypt under Nasir.* Albany, NY.: State University of New York Press, 1971.
Della Vida, Georgio Levi. "Angelo Sammarco." *Bulletin de l'Institut d'Égypte* 31 (1948–49): 205–207.
———. "Eugenio Griffini." *Rivista degli Studi Orientali* 10 (1925): 726–730.
den Boer, Pim. *History as a Profession.* Princeton, NJ: Princeton University press, 1998.
Deny, Jean. *Sommaire des archives turques du Caire.* Cairo: Société royale de géographie d'Égypte, publications spéciales, 1930.
Di-Capua, Yoav. "Embodiments of the Revolutionary Spirit: The Commemoration of Mustafa Kamil and Muhammad Farid." *History and Memory* 13, no. 1 (Spring–Summer 2001): 85–113.
Dirks, Nicholas B. "History as a Sign of the Modern." *Public Culture* 2, no. 2 (Spring 1990): 25–32.
Dodwell, Henry. *The Founder of Modern Egypt: A Study of Muhammad Ali.* Cambridge: Cambridge University Press, 1931.
Douin, Georges. *L'Égypte de 1802 à 1804.* Cairo: Société royale de géographie d'Égypte, publications spéciales, 1925.

———. *L'Égypte de 1828 à 1830.* Cairo: Société royale de géographie d'Égypte, publications spéciales, 1935.
———. *Histoire du règne du Khédive Ismaïl.* 3 vols., 6 parts. Cairo: Institut français d'archéologie orientale pour la Société royale de géographie d'Égypte, publications spéciales, 1933–36.
———. *Histoire du Soudan égyptien.* Cairo: Société royale de géographie d'Égypte, publications spéciales, 1944.
———. *La mission du Baron Boislecomte.* Cairo: Société royale de géographie d'Égypte, publications spéciales sous les auspices de sa majesté Fouad Ier, 1927.
———. *Navarin, 6 juillet–20 octobre 1827.* Cairo: Société royale de géographie d'Égypte, publications spéciales, 1927.
———. *La première guerre de Syrie.* 2 vols., Cairo: Société royale de géographie d'Égypte, publications spéciales, 1931.
Douin, Georges, and E.C. Fawtier-Jones. *L'Angleterre et l'Égypte: La campagne de 1807.* Cairo: Société royale de géographie d'Égypte, publications spéciales, 1928.
———. *L'Angleterre et l'Égypte: La politique mameluke 1801–1803.* 2 vols. Cairo: Société royale de géographie d'Égypte, publications spéciales, 1929–30.
Driault, Édouard. "Mohamed-Aly et Ibrahim." In Mohamed Zaky el-Ibrachy Pacha and Angelo Sammarco, eds., *Précis de l'histoire d'Égypte,* vol. 3 of 4, part 3: 187–390. Cairo: L'Institut français d'archéologie orientale du Caire, 1933.
Duara, Prasenjit. *Rescuing History from the Nation: Questioning Narratives of Modern China.* Chicago: University of Chicago Press, 1995.
Duchein, Michel. "Theoretical Principles and Practical Problems of *Respect de Fonds* in Archival Science." *Archivaria* 16 (Summer 1983): 64–82.
Egger, Vernon. *A Fabian in Egypt: Salamah Musa and the Rise of the Professional Classes in Egypt, 1900–1939.* Lanham, MD: University Press of America, 1986.
Elshakry, Marwa. "Darwin's Legacy in the Arab East: Science, Religion and Politics, 1870–1914." Unpublished Ph.D. dissertation, Princeton University, 2003.
ElShakry, Omnia. "The Great Social Laboratory: Reformers and Utopians in Twentieth Century Egypt." Unpublished Ph.D. dissertation, Princeton University, 2001.
Erlich, Haggai. *Students and University in Twentieth Century Egyptian Politics.* London: Frank Cass, 1989.
Erlich, Haggai, and Israel Gershoni, eds. *The Nile: Histories, Culture, Myths.* Boulder, CO: Lynne Rienner Publishers, 2000.
Evert, Beth. "Paradigm." In Robert Audi, ed., *The Cambridge Dictionary of Philosophy,* 641–642. Cambridge: Cambridge University Press, 1999.
Fahmy, Khaled. *All the Pasha's Men: Mehmed Ali, His Army and the Making of Modern Egypt.* Cambridge: Cambridge University Press, 1997.
———. "The Police and the People in Nineteenth-Century Egypt." *Die Welt des Islam* 39, no. 3 (1999): 340–377.
Farag, Nadia. "Al-Muqtataf 1876–1900: A Study of the Influences of Victorian Thought on Modern Arabic Thought." Unpublished Ph.D. thesis, Oxford University, 1969.
Fogu, Claudio. "Actualism and the Fascist Historic Imaginary." *History and Theory* 42, no. 2 (May 2003): 196–221.

Galtung, John. "Arnold Toynbee: Challenge and Response." In John Galtung and Sohail Inayatullah, eds., *Macrohistory and Macrohistorians: Perspective on Individual, Social and Civilizational Change,* 120–128. London: Praeger, 1989.

Gasper, Michael. "Civilizing Peasants: The Public Sphere, Islamic Reform and the Generation of Political Modernity in Egypt, 1875–1919." Unpublished Ph.D. dissertation, New York University, 2004.

"Georges Douin." *Bulletin de l'Institute d'Égypte* 27 (1944–45): 89–95.

Gershoni, Israel. "The Evolution of National Culture in Modern Egypt: Intellectual Formation and Social Diffusion, 1892–1945." *Poetics Today* 13, no. 2 (Summer 1992): 325–350.

———. "Imagining and Reimagining the Past: The Use of History by Egyptian Nationalist Writers, 1919–1952." *History and Memory* 4, no. 2 (1992): 5–37.

———. "Secondary Intellectuals, Readers, and Readership as Agents of National-Cultural Reproduction in Modern Egypt." In Yaakov Elman and Israel Gershoni, eds., *Transmitting Jewish Traditions: Orality, Textuality, and Cultural Diffusion,* 324–347. New Haven, CT: Yale University Press, 2000.

———. "The Theory of Crisis and the Crisis in a Theory: Intellectual History in Twentieth-Century Middle Eastern Studies." In Israel Gershoni, Amy Singer, and Y. Hakan Erdem, eds., *Middle East Historiographies: Narrating the Twentieth Century,* 131–182. Seattle: Washington University Press, 2006.

Gershoni, Israel, and James Jankowski. *Commemorating the Nation: Collective Memory, Public Commemoration, and National Identity in Twentieth-Century Egypt.* Chicago: Middle East Documentation Center, 2004.

———. *Egypt, Islam and the Arabs: The Search for Egyptian Nationhood, 1900–1930.* New York: Oxford University Press, 1986.

———. *Redefining the Egyptian Nation, 1930–1945.* New York: Cambridge University Press, 1995.

Ghanem, Fathy. *The Man Who Lost His Shadow.* London: Chapman and Hall, 1966.

Ghorbal, Shafik. *The Beginnings of the Egyptian Question and the Rise of Mehmet Ali.* 1928. Repr., New York: AMS Press, 1977.

———. "The Building-Up of a Single Egyptian Sudanese Fatherland in the 19th Century: The Achievement of the Viceroys Muhammad Ali and Ismail." In 'Abbās Muṣṭafa 'Ammar et al., eds., *The Unity of the Nile Valley,* 64–75. Cairo: Government Press, 1947.

———. "Dr. Bowring and Muhammad Ali." *Bulletin de l'Institut d'Égypte* 24 (1941–42): 107–112.

Giles, Geoffrey. "Archives and Historians." In Geoffrey Giles, ed., *Archivists and Historians,* 5–13. Washington DC: German Historical Institute, 1996.

Ginat, Rami. *Egypt's Incomplete Revolution: Lutfi al-Khuli and Nasser's Socialism in the 1960s.* London: Frank Cass, 1997.

Godfrey, James, L. "Alphonse Aulard 1849–1928." In William Halperin, ed., *Essays in Modern European Historiography,* 22–42. Chicago: University of Chicago Press, 1970.

Goldschmidt, Arthur. *Biographical Dictionary of Modern Egypt.* Boulder, CO: Lynne Rienner Publishers, 2000.

———. "The National Party from Spotlight to Shadow." *Asian and African Studies* 16, no. 1 (1982): 13–30.

Goldschmidt, Arthur, and Robert Johnston, eds. *Historical Dictionary of Egypt*. Lanham, MD: Scarecrow Press, 2003.

Goldstein, Doris. "The Professionalization of History in Britain in Late Nineteenth and Early Twentieth Centuries." *Storia della Storiografia* 3 (1983): 3–27.

Goldstein, Jan. "Foucault among the Sociologists: The Disciplines and the History of Professions." *History and Theory* 23, no. 2 (1984): 170–192.

Gonzales-Quijano, Yves. *Les gens du livre: Édition et champ intellectuel dans l'Égypte Républicaine*. Paris: CNRS Éditions, 1998.

Göran, Therborn. "Routes to/through Modernity." In Mike Featherston, Scott Lash, and Roland Robertson, eds., *Global Modernities*, 124–139. London: Sage Publications, 1995.

Gordon, Joel. *Nasser's Blessed Movement: Egypt's Free Officers and the July Revolution*. Oxford: Oxford University Press, 1992.

———. *Revolutionary Melodrama: Popular Film and Civic Identity in Nasser's Egypt*. Chicago: Middle East Documentation Center, 2002.

Gorman, Anthony. *Historians, State and Politics in Twentieth Century Egypt: Contesting the Nation*. London: Routledge-Curzon, 2003.

Gottlob, Michael. "Writing the History of Modern Indian Historiography: A Review Article." *Storia della Storiografia* 27 (1995): 125–146.

Grafton, Anthony. *The Footnote: A Curious History*. Cambridge, MA: Harvard University Press, 1999.

Gran, Peter. "Modern Trends in Egyptian Historiography: A Review Article." *International Journal of Middle East Studies* 9, no. 3 (August 1978): 367–371.

Habashi, Alaa El-Din Elwi El-. "*Athar* to Monuments: The Intervention of the *Comité de conservation des monuments de l'art Arabe*." Unpublished Ph.D. dissertation, University of Pennsylvania, 2001.

Hafez, Sabry. *The Genesis of Arabic Narrative Discourse: A Study in the Sociology of Modern Arabic Literature*. London: Saqi Books, 1993.

Hakim, Tawfiq al-. *The Return of Consciousness*. Translated by Bayly Winder. New York: New York University Press, 1985.

Hallaq, Wael. "Was the Gate of Ijtihād Closed?" *International Journal of Middle East Studies* 16, no. 1 (1984): 3–41.

Hamilton, Paul. *Historicism*. The New Critical Idiom Series. London: Routledge, 1996.

Hanley, Will. "Foreignness and Localness in Alexandria, 1880–1914." Unpublished Ph.D. dissertation, Princeton University, 2007.

Hanna, Nelly. "The Chronicles of Ottoman Egypt: History or Entertainment?" In Hugh Kennedy, ed., *The Historiography of Islamic Egypt, c. 950–1800*, 237–250. Leiden, the Netherlands: E. J. Brill, 2001 .

———. *In Praise of Books: A Cultural History of Cairo's Middle Class, Sixteenth to the Eighteenth Century*. Syracuse, NY: Syracuse University Press, 2003.

Hanotaux, Gabriel, ed. *Histoire de la nation égyptienne*. 7 vols. Paris: Ouvrage publié sous les auspices et le haut patronage de sa majesté Fouad Ier, Roi d'Égypte, 1931–40.

———. *Regards sur L'Égypte et la Palestine.* Paris: Librairie Plon, 1929.

Hartog, François. "Time, History and the Writing of History: The *Order* of Time." In Rolf Torstendahl and Irmline Veit-Brause, eds., *History-Making: The Intellectual and Social Formation of a Discipline,* 95–113. Stockholm: Kungl. Vitterhets Historie och Antikvitets Akademien, 1996.

Havel, Václav. *Open Letters: Selected Prose 1965–1990.* London: Faber and Faber, 1991.

Hefny, Mostafa. "Listening for History: A Report on Oral History, Scope, Fidelity and Methodology." *Economic and Business History Research Center Chronicle* 1, no. 1 (July 2005): 17–20.

Hildesheimer, Françoise. "Périodisation et archives." *Sources: Travaux Historiques* 23–24 (1990): 39–46.

Hilmi II, Abbas. *The Last Khedive of Egypt: Memoirs of Abbas Hilmi II.* Translated by Amira Sonbol. Reading, UK: Ithaca Press, 1998.

Hinnebusch, Raymond. *Egyptian Politics under Sadat: The Post Populist Development of an Authoritarian-Modernizing State.* Cambridge: Cambridge University Press, 1985.

Holmes, Oliver. "Archival Arrangement—Five Different Operations as Five Different Levels." In Maygene Daniels and Timothy Walach, eds., *A Modern Archives Reader: Basic Readings on Archival Theory and Practice,* 162–180. Washington DC: National Archives and Records Services, 1984.

Hourani, Albert. *Arabic Thought in the Liberal Age, 1798–1939.* Cambridge: Cambridge University Press, 1993.

———. "Historians of Lebanon." In P. M. Holt and Bernard Lewis, eds., *Historians of the Middle East,* 226–245. London: Oxford University Press, 1962.

Humphrey, Richard. *The Historical Novel as Philosophy of History.* Leeds: Institute for German Studies, 1986.

Hunter, Robert F. "The Cairo Archives for the Study of Élites in Modern Egypt." *International Journal of Middle East Studies* 4, no. 4 (1973): 476–488.

———. *Egypt under the Khedives 1805–1879: From Household Government to Modern Bureaucracy.* Pittsburgh: University of Pittsburgh Press, 1984.

———. "Self-Image and Historical Truth: Nubar Pasha and the Making of Modern Egypt." *Middle Eastern Studies* 23, no. 3 (July 1987): 363–375.

Husaini, Ishak Musa. *The Moslem Brethren: The Greatest of Modern Islamic Movements.* Beirut: Khayat, 1956.

Iggers, Georg. "Historicism: The History and Meaning of the Term." *Journal of the History of Ideas* 56, no. 1 (1995): 129–152.

———. *Historiography in the Twentieth Century.* Hanover, NH: University Press of New England, 1997.

Ismael, Tareq, and Rifa'at El-Sa'id. *The Communist Movement in Egypt, 1920–1988.* Syracuse, NY: Syracuse University Press, 1990.

Isstaif, Abdul-Nabi. "Forging a New Self, Embracing the Other: Modern Arabic Critical Theory and the West—Luwīs 'Awaḍ." *Arabic and Middle Eastern Literatures* 5, no. 2 (2002): 161–180.

Jacob, Wilson. "Working Out Egypt: Masculinity and Subject Formation between Colonial Modernity and Nationalism, 1870–1940." Unpublished Ph.D. dissertation, New York University, 2005.

Jameson, Fredric. "Third-World Literature in the Era of Multinational Capitalism." *Social Text* 15 (Autumn 1986): 65–88.

Jansen, J.J.G. "Ibrahim Abduh, His Autobiographies and His Political Polemical Writings." *Bibliotheca Orientalis* 37, nos. 3–4 (1980): 128–132.

Jones, Gareth Stedman. "The Pathology of English History." *New Left Review* 46 (1967): 29–43.

Joyce, Patrick. "The Politics of the Liberal Archive." *History of the Human Sciences* 12, no. 2 (May 1999): 35–49.

Kaplan, Sam. "Documenting History, Historicizing Documentation: French Military Officials' Ethnological Report on Cilicia." *Comparative Studies in Society and History* 44, no. 2 (2002): 344–369.

Kassem, Maye. *Egyptian Politics: The Dynamics of Authoritarian Rule.* Boulder, CO: Lynne Rienner Publishers, 2004.

Kazziha, Walid. "The Jarida-Umma Group and Egyptian Politics." *Middle Eastern Studies* 13, no. 3 (1977): 373–385.

Keylor, William. *Academy and Community: The Foundation of the French Historical Profession.* Cambridge, MA: Harvard University Press, 1975.

Kia, Mehradad. "Ibn Kahldūn." In D.R. Woolf, ed., *A Global Encyclopedia of Historical Writing,* vol. 1 of 2, pp. 440–441. New York: Garland Publishing, 1998.

Kienle, Eberhard. *A Grand Delusion: Democracy and Economic Reform in Egypt.* London: I.B. Tauris, 2000.

Klein, Menachem. "Egypt's Revolutionary Publishing Culture, 1952–1962." *Middle Eastern Studies* 39, no. 2 (April 2003): 149–178.

———. "*Ikhtarna Laka* (We Have Selected for You): A Critique of Egypt's Revolutionary Culture." *Orient* 38, no. 4 (1997): 677–691.

Konstan, David. "The Classical Foundations of Modern Historiography." *History and Theory* 31, no. 2 (1992): 224–230.

Koselleck, Reinhart. *Futures Past: On the Semantics of Historical Time.* Translated from the original German by Keith Tribe. Cambridge, MA: MIT Press, 1985.

———. *The Practice of Conceptual History: Timing History, Spacing Concepts.* Translated from the original German by Todd Samuel Presner et al. Stanford, CA: Stanford University Press, 2002.

Kracauer, Sigfried. "Time and History." *History and Theory,* Beiheft 6 (1966): 65–78.

Lewis, Bernard, and P.M. Holt, eds. *Historians of the Middle East.* London: Oxford University Press, 1962.

Lukács, Georg. *The Historical Novel.* Translated by Hannah and Stanley Mitchell from *A történelmi regény.* Lincoln: University of Nebraska Press, 1983.

Lutfi al-Sayyid-Marsot, Afaf. *Egypt and Cromer: A Study in Anglo-Egyptian Relations.* London: John Murray, 1968.

———. *Egypt and Cromer: A Study in Anglo-Egyptian Relations.* New York: Frederick A. Praeger, 1969.

———. *Egypt in the Reign of Muhammad Ali.* Cambridge: Cambridge University Press, 1984.

Mandelbaum, Maurice. *History, Man, and Reason; A Study in Nineteenth-Century Thought.* Baltimore: Johns Hopkins University Press, 1971.

Mardin, Şerif. *The Genesis of Young Ottoman Thought: A Study in the Modernization of Turkish Political Ideas.* Syracuse, NY: Syracuse University Press, 2000.

Martin, Richard, Mark Woodward, and Dwi Atmaja. *Defenders of Reason in Islam: Muʿtazilism from Medieval School to Modern Symbol.* Oxford: One World, 1997.

Mayer, Thomas. *The Changing Past: Egyptian Historiography of the Urabi Revolt, 1882–1983.* Gainesville: University Press of Florida, 1988.

McDougall, James. "Colonial Words: Nationalism, Islam, and Languages of History in Algeria." Unpublished Ph.D. thesis, University of Oxford, 2002.

McNeill, William. *Arnold J Toynbee: A Life.* New York: Oxford University Press, 1989.

Megill, Allan. "Four Senses of Objectivity." *Annals of Scholarship* 8, nos. 3–4 (1991): 301–320.

Meijer, Roel. "Authenticity in History: The Concepts al-Wāfid and al-Mawrūth in Ṭāriq al-Bishrī's Reinterpretation of Modern Egyptian History." In Manfred Woidich, ed., *Amsterdam Middle Eastern Studies*, 68–83. Wiesbaden: L. Reichert Verlag, 1990.

———. *History, Authenticity and Politics: Tariq al-Bishri's Interpretation of Modern History.* Occasional Paper No. 4. Amsterdam: Middle East Research Association, 1989.

———. *The Quest for Modernity: Secular Liberal and Left-Wing Political Thought in Egypt 1945–1958.* London: Routledge-Curzon, 2002.

Milner, Sir Alfred. *England in Egypt.* London: E. Arnold, 1899.

Mitchell, Richard P. *The Society of the Muslim Brothers.* London: Oxford University Press, 1969.

Mitchell, Timothy. *Colonizing Egypt.* Berkeley: University of California Press, 1991.

———. *Rule of Experts: Egypt, Techno-politics, Modernity.* Berkeley: University of California Press, 2002.

Moghith, Anwar. "Marxisme égyptien et Marxisme occidental: Traduction et idéologie." *Égypte/Monde Arabe* 30–31, nos. 2–3 (1997): 71–91.

Moore, Lara. "Restoring Order: The *École des Chartes* and the Organization of Archives and Libraries in France 1820–1870." Unpublished Ph.D. dissertation, Stanford University, 2001.

Moosa, Matti. *The Origins of Modern Arabic Fiction.* Boulder, CO: Lynne Rienner Publishers, 1997.

Mostyn, Trevor. *Egypt's Belle Époque Cairo 1869–1952.* London: Quartet Books, 1989.

Naguib, Muhammad. *Egypt's Destiny.* London: Victor Gollancz, 1955.

Nahumm, Hayyim. *Recueil de firmans impériaux ottomans, 1597–1904.* Cairo: Société royale de géographie d'Égypte, publications spéciales, 1934.

Najjar, Fauzi. "State and University in Egypt during the Period of Socialist Transformation, 1961–1967." *Review of Politics* 38, no. 1 (1976): 57–87.

Nallino, Carlo Alfonso. "Eugenio Griffini." *Rivista della Tripolitana* 2 (1925): 124–132.

———. "Una recente storia dell'Egitto dalle origini al 1879." *Oriente Moderno* 15, no. 8 (August 1935): 421–425.

Nancy, Jean-Luc. "Our History." *Diacritics* 20, no. 3 (Autumn 1990): 96–115.
Nasser, Gamal Abdel. *The Philosophy of the Revolution*. Cairo: National Publication House, 1954.
Novick, Peter. *That Noble Dream: The "Objectivity Question" and the American Historical Profession*. Cambridge: Cambridge University Press, 1988.
Ormos, István. "Preservation and Restoration: The Methods of Max Herz Pasha, Chief Architect of the Comité de Conservation des Monuments de l'Art Arabe." In Jill Edwards, ed., *Historians in Cairo: Essays in Honor of George Scanlon*, 123–153. Cairo: American University in Cairo Press, 2002.
Osborne, Thomas. "The Ordinariness of the Archive." *History of the Human Sciences* 12, no. 2 (May 1999): 51–64.
Owen, Roger. *Lord Cromer: Victorian Imperialist Edwardian Proconsul*. Oxford: Oxford University Press, 2004.
———. *The Middle East in the World Economy, 1800–1914*. London: I. B. Tauris, 1993.
Passmore, John. "The Poverty of Historicism Revisited." *History and Theory* 14, no. 4 (1975): 30–47.
Philipp, Thomas. "Approaches to History in the Work of Jurji Zaydan." *Asian and African Studies* 9, no. 1 (1973): 63–85.
———. *Ǧurǧī Zaidān: His Life and Thought*. Beirut: Franz Steiner Verlag, 1979.
———. "Language, History and Arab National Consciousness in the Thought of Jurjī Zaydān (1861–1914)." *International Journal of Middle East Studies* 4, no. 1 (1973): 3–22.
Pieterse, Jan Nederveen. "Hybridity, So What? The Anti-hybridity Backlash and the Riddles of Recognition." *Theory, Culture and Society* 18, nos. 2–3 (2001): 219–246.
Piterberg, Gabriel. "The Tropes of Stagnation and Awakening in Nationalist Historical Consciousness." In James Jankowski and Israel Gershoni, eds., *Rethinking Nationalism in the Arab Middle East*, 42–61. New York: Columbia University Press, 1998.
Podeh, Elie, and Onn Winckler, eds. *Rethinking Nasserism*. Gainesville: University Press of Florida, 2004.
Polites, Athanasios. *Le conflit turco-égyptien de 1838–1841*. Cairo: Société royale de géographie d'Égypte, publications spéciales, 1931.
———. *Les rapports de la Grèce et de l'Égypte pendant le règne de Mohamed Aly 1833–1849*. Rome: Société royale de géographie d'Égypte, publications spéciales, 1937.
Popper, Karl. *The Poverty of Historicism*. New York: Basic Books, 1960.
Posner, Ernest. "Some Aspects of Archival Development since the French Revolution." In Maygene Daniels and Timothy Walach, eds., *A Modern Archives Reader: Basic Readings on Archival Theory and Practice*, 3–14. Washington DC: National Archives and Records Services, 1984.
Pouchepadass, Jacques. "Pluralizing Reason." *History and Theory* 41, no. 3 (October 2002): 381–391.
Prakash, Gyan. *Another Reason: Science and the Imagination of Modern India*. Princeton, NJ: Princeton University Press, 1999.
———. "Writing Post-Orientalist Histories in the Third World: Perspectives from Indian Historiography." *Comparative Studies in Society and History* 32, no. 2 (April 1990): 383–408.

Prashad, Vijay. *The Darker Nations: A People's History of the Third World.* New York: New Press, 2007.

Rabbat, Nasser. *The Citadel of Cairo.* Leiden, the Netherlands: E. J. Brill, 1995.

Raymond, André. *Artisans et commerçants au Caire au XVIIIe siècle.* Damascus: Institut français de Damas, 1973.

Raz, Ronen. "The Transparent Mirror: Arab Intellectuals and Orientalism, 1789–1950." Unpublished Ph.D. dissertation, Princeton University, 1997.

Reid, Donald M. *Cairo University and the Making of Modern Egypt.* Cambridge: Cambridge University Press, 1990.

———. "Cairo University and the Orientalists." *International Journal of Middle East Studies* 19, no. 1 (1987): 51–76.

———. "The Egyptian Geographical Society: From Foreign Laymen's Society to Indigenous Professional Association." *Poetics Today* 13, no. 3 (1993): 539–572.

———. *Lawyers and Politics in the Arab World, 1800–1960.* Chicago: Bibliotheca Islamica, 1981.

———. *Whose Pharaohs? Archeology, Museums and Egyptian National Identity from Napoleon to World War I.* Berkeley: University of California Press, 2002.

Reimer, Michael J. *Colonial Bridgehead: Government and Society in Alexandria, Egypt 1807–1882.* Cairo: American University in Cairo Press, 1997.

Rejwan, Nissim. *Nasserist Ideology: Its Exponents and Critics.* New York: John Wiley and Sons, 1974.

Ricchieri, Giuseppe. "Il dott. Eugenio Griffini." *Rendiconti,* ser. 2, 58 (May 1925): 466–470.

Ricoeur, Paul. *La mémoire, l'histoire, l'oubli.* Paris: Éditions du Seuil, 2000.

Rifaat Bey, Mohammed. *The Awakening of Modern Egypt.* London: Longmans, Green, 1947.

Rigby, Stephan H. *Marxism and History.* New York: St. Martin's Press, 1987.

———. "Marxist Historiography." In Michael Bentley, ed., *Companion to Historiography,* 889–928. London: Routledge, 1997.

Rigney, Ann. *Imperfect Histories: The Elusive Past and the Legacy of Romantic Historicism.* Ithaca, NY: Cornell University Press, 2001.

———. "Narrativity and Historical Representation." *Poetics Today* 12, no. 3 (Autumn 1991): pp. 591–605.

Rivlin, Helen. *The Agricultural Policy of Muhammad ʿAlī in Egypt.* Cambridge, MA: Harvard University Press, 1961.

———. *The Dār al-wathāʾiq in ʿĀbdīn Palace at Cairo as a Source for the Study of the Modernization of Egypt in the Nineteenth Century.* Leiden, the Netherlands: E. J. Brill, 1970.

Robinson, Chase. *Islamic Historiography.* Cambridge: Cambridge University Press, 2003.

Rosenthal, Franz. *A History of Muslim Historiography.* Leiden, the Netherlands: E. J. Brill, 1952.

Rossi, Ettore. "In Memoriam: Angelo Sammarco 1883–1948." *Oriente Moderno* 28 (December 1948): 198–200.

Rothstein, Fedor Aronovich. *Egypt's Ruin, a Financial and Administrative Record.* London: A. C. Fifield, 1910.

Roux, Jean-Paul. "Jean Deny." In János Eckmann, Agáh Sirri Levand, and Mecdut Mansuroğlu, eds., *Jean Deny Armağani: Mélanges Jean Deny,* 1–4. Ankara: Türk Tarih Kurumu Basimevi, 1958.

———. "Portraits: Hommage à Jean Deny." *Orbis* (Belgium) 7, no. 2 (1959): 558–569.

Rüsen, Jörn. "Historical Narration: Foundation, Types, Reason." *History and Theory* 26, no. 4 (December 1987): 87–97.

Rustum, Asad. *The Royal Archives of Egypt and the Origins of the Egyptian Expedition to Syria 1831–1841.* Beirut: American Press, 1936.

Ryzova, Lucie. "Egyptianizing Modernity: The 'New Effendiyya' Social and Cultural Constructions of the Middle Class in Egypt under the Monarchy." In Arthur Goldschmidt, Amy Johnson, and Barak Salmoni, eds., *Re-envisioning the Egyptian Monarchy,* 124–163. Cairo: American University in Cairo Press, 2005.

Sabry, Mohamed. *L'empire égyptien sous Ismaïl et l'ingérence anglo-française.* Paris: Paul Geuthner, 1933.

———. *L'empire égyptien sous Mohamed Ali et la question d'Orient 1811–1849.* Paris: Paul Geuthner, 1930.

———. *La genèse de l'esprit national égyptien, 1863–1882.* Published dissertation. Paris: Libraire Picart, 1924.

———. *La question d'Égypte depuis Bonaparte jusqu'à la révolution de 1919.* Paris: Association égyptienne de Paris, 1920.

———. *La révolution égyptienne.* 2 vols. Paris: Librairie Vrin, 1919.

Sadgrove, P. C. "Al-Nadīm Sayyid 'Abdāllah." In *Encyclopaedia of Islam,* 7: 852a. Leiden, the Netherlands: E. J. Brill, 1960–.

Saleh, Zaki. *Trevor-Roper's Critique of Arnold Toynbee: A Symptom of Intellectual Chaos.* Baghdad: al-Ma'aref Press, 1958.

Salmoni, Barak Ahraon. "Pedagogies of Patriotism: Teaching Socio-political Community in Twentieth-Century Turkish and Egyptian Education." Unpublished Ph.D. dissertation, Harvard University, 2002.

Sammarco, Angelo. "I documenti diplomatici concernenti il regno di Mohammed Ali e gli archivi di stato italiani." *Oriente Moderno* 9, no. 6 (June 1929): 287–296.

———. *Histoire de l'Égypte moderne depuis Mohammed Ali jusqu'à l'occupation britannique, 1801–1882.* 3 vols. Cairo: Société royale de géographie d'Égypte, 1937.

———. *Les règnes de 'Abbas, de Sa'id et d'Isma'il (1848–1879).* Vol. 4 of *Précis de l'histoire d'Égypte,* par divers historiens et archéologues, ed. Zaky el-Ibrachy Pacha and Angelo Sammarco. Cairo: l'Imprimerie de l'Institut français d'archéologie orientale du Caire, 1935.

———. *Il regno di Mohammed Ali nei documenti diplomatici italiani inediti.* 10 vols. Cairo: Société royale de géographie d'Égypte, publications spéciales, 1930.

———. "La verità sulla questione del canale di Suez," *Oriente Moderno* 19 (1939): 5–30.

Sato, Masayuki. "Cognitive Historiography and Normative Historiography." In Jören Rüsen, ed., *Western Historical Thinking: An Intercultural Debate,* 128–141. New York: Berghahn, 2002.

Saul, Samir. "Ali Moubarak, un historien égyptien et son oeuvre." *Storia della Storiografia* 5 (1984): 77–85.

Sayyid, Ayman Fuad. "L'évolution de la composition du genre de khiṭaṭ en Égypte musulmane." In Hugh Kennedy, ed., *The Historiography of Islamic Egypt, c.950–1800*, 77–92. Leiden, the Netherlands: E. J. Brill, 2001.

Schellenberg, Theodore. "Archival Principles of Arrangement." In Maygene Daniels and Timothy Walach, eds., *A Modern Archives Reader: Basic Readings on Archival Theory and Practice*, 149–161. Washington DC: National Archives and Records Services, 1984.

Schölch, Alexander. *Egypt for the Egyptians! The Socio-political Crisis in Egypt 1878–1882.* London: Ithaca Press, 1981.

Schorske, Carl E. *Thinking with History.* Princeton, NJ.: Princeton University Press, 1998.

Selim, Samah. "The New Pharaonism: Nationalist Thought and the Egyptian Village Novel, 1967–1977." *Arab Studies Journal* 8, no. 2 (Fall 2000): 10–24.

Shaw, Stanford. *The Financial and Administrative Organization and Development of Ottoman Egypt, 1517–1798.* Princeton, NJ: Princeton University Press, 1962.

———. "Turkish Source Material for Egyptian History." In P. M. Holt, ed., *Political and Social Change in Modern Egypt*, 28–48. London: Oxford University Press, 1968.

Shayyal Gamal, el-Din el-. "Historiography in Egypt in the Nineteenth Century." In Bernard Lewis and P. M. Holt, eds., *Historians of the Middle East*, 401–421. London: Oxford University Press, 1962.

———. *A History of Egyptian Historiography in the Nineteenth Century.* Alexandria: University of Alexandria Press, 1962.

———. "Some Aspects of Intellectual and Social Life in Eighteenth-Century Egypt." In P. M. Holt, ed., *Political and Social Change in Modern Egypt*, 117–132. London: Oxford University Press, 1968.

Somekh, Sasson. "The Neo-classical Arabic Poets." In Muhammad Mustafa Badawi, ed., *Modern Arabic Literature*, 36–81. Cambridge: Cambridge University Press, 1992.

———. "The Sad Millenarian: An Examination of Awlad Haritna." In Trevor Le Gassick, ed., *Critical Perspectives on Nagib Mahfouz*, 101–114. Washington DC: Three Continents Press, 1991.

Sonn, Tamara. "Tawḥīd." In *The Oxford Encyclopedia of the Modern Islamic World*, 194. Oxford: Oxford University Press, 1995.

Southgate, Beverley. *Postmodernism in History: Fear or Freedom?* London: Routledge, 2003.

Spengler, Oswald. *The Decline of the West.* Translated by Charles Francis. New York: Knopf, 1950.

Starkey, Paul. "Commitment." *Encyclopedia of Arabic Literature*, 175–176. New York: Routledge, 1998.

———. "Egyptian History in the Modern Egyptian Novel." In Hugh Kennedy, ed., *The Historiography of Islamic Egypt, c. 950–1800*, 251–262. Leiden, the Netherlands: E. J. Brill, 2001.

Suhayl Idriss, Samah. "Intellectuals and the Nasserite Authority in the Egyptian Novel." Unpublished Ph.D. dissertation, Columbia University, 1991.

Szeman, Imre. "Who's Afraid of National Allegory? Jameson, Literary Criticism, Globalization." *South Atlantic Quarterly* 100, no. 3 (Summer 2001): 803–827.

Tagher, Jacques. *Mohamed Ali: Jugé par les Européens de son temps.* Cairo: Editions Horus, 1942.

Tignor, Robert L. *Capitalism and Nationalism at the End of Empire: State and Business in Decolonizing Egypt, Nigeria and Kenya, 1945–1963.* Princeton, NJ: Princeton University Press, 1998.

———. *Modernization and British Colonial Rule in Egypt, 1882–1914.* Princeton, NJ: Princeton University Press, 1966.

Toledano, Ehud. "Forgetting Egypt's Ottoman Past." In Jayne Warner, ed., *Cultural Horizons: A Festschrift in Honor of Talat S. Halman,* 150–167. Syracuse, NY: Syracuse University Press, 2001.

———. "Social and Economic Change in the 'Long Nineteenth Century.'" In M. W. Daly, ed., *The Cambridge History of Egypt,* vol. 2 of 2: 252–284. Cambridge: Cambridge University Press, 1998.

———. *State and Society in Mid-nineteenth Century Egypt.* Cambridge: Cambridge University Press, 1990.

Topolski, Jerzy. "Historical Narrative: Towards a Coherent Structure." *History and Theory* 26, no. 4 (December 1987): 75–86.

Toynbee, Arnold. *A Study of History.* 12 vols. London: Oxford University Press, 1948–61.

Trevor-Roper, Hugh R. "The Prophet." *New York Review of Books,* October 12, 1989, 28–32.

Trouillot, Michael Rolph. *Silencing the Past: Power and the Production of History.* Boston: Beacon Press, 1995.

United Arab Republic (UAR). *The Charter.* Cairo: Information Department, 1962.

Vetter, Vesta Sweitzer. "Gabriel Hanotaux 1853–1944." In William Halperin, ed., *Essays in Modern European Historiography,* 91–118. Chicago: University of Chicago Press, 1970.

Wardenburg, Jean-Jacques. *Les universités dans le monde arabe actuel.* 2 vols. Paris: Mouton, 1966.

Ware, Lewis Beier. "Jurjī Zaydān: The Role of a Popular History in the Formation of a New Arab World-View." Unpublished Ph.D. dissertation, Princeton University, 1973.

Watenpaugh, Keith David. *Being Modern in the Middle East: Revolution, Nationalism, Colonialism, and the Arab Middle Class.* Princeton, NJ: Princeton University Press, 2006.

Waterbury, John. *Egypt: Burdens of the Past/Options for the Future.* Bloomington: Indiana University Press, 1978.

———. *The Egypt of Nasser and Sadat: The Political Economy of Two Regimes.* Princeton, NJ: Princeton University Press, 1983.

Weiss, Bernard. "Taqlid." In *The Oxford Encyclopedia of the Modern Islamic World,* 187–189. Oxford: Oxford University Press, 1995.

Wendell, Charles. *The Evolution of the Egyptian National Image.* Berkeley: University of California Press, 1972.

Wesseling, H. L. "Gabriel Hanotaux: A Historian in Politics." *Itinerario* 25, no. 1 (2001): 65–83.
White, Hayden. "The Rule of Narrativity: Symbolic Discourse and the Experience of Time." *University of Ottawa Quarterly* 55, no. 4 (1985): 287–299.
———. "The Value of Narrativity in the Representation of Reality." n Hayden White, ed., *The Content of the Form: Narrative Discourse and Historical Representation,* 1–25. Baltimore: Johns Hopkins University Press, 1987.
———. "The Westernization of World History." In Jören Rüsen, ed., *Western Historical Thinking: An Intercultural Debate,* 11–118. New York: Berghahn, 2002.
Wickham, Carrie Rosefsky. *Mobilizing Islam: Religion, Activism and Political Change in Egypt.* New York: Columbia University Press, 2002.
Wiet, Gaston. "Jacques Tagher." *Cahiers d'Histoire Égyptienne* 4, nos. 3–4 (October 1952): 163–165.
———. *Mohammed Ali et les beaux-arts.* Cairo: Société royale d'études historiques, 1950.
Winichakul, Thongchai. *Siam Mapped: A History of the Geo-body of a Nation.* Honolulu: University of Hawaii Press, 1994.
Zammito, John. "Koselleck's Philosophy of Historical Time(s) and the Practice of History." *History and Theory* 43, no. 1 (2004): 124–135.
Zaydān, Jurjī. *The Autobiography of Jurji Zaidan.* Translated and edited by Thomas Philipp. Washington DC: Three Continents Press, 1990.
Zerubavel, Eviatar. *Time Maps: Collective Memory and Social Shape of the Past.* Chicago: University of Chicago Press, 2003.
Zubaida, Sami. *Islam, the People and the State: Essays on Political Ideas and Movements in the Middle East.* London: Routledge, 1989.

FILMOGRAPHY

Muṣṭafa Kāmil. 1951. Director: Aḥmad Badr-Khān.
Nasser 1956. 1996. Director: Muḥammad Faḍl.

INDEX

Italicized page numbers refer to illustrations and tables.

'Abbās, Ra'ūf, 1, 310, 327–28, 330–31, 343
'Abbās ('Abbās Ḥilmī I), 140, 161, 194n24; demonization of, 162–64, 162n97, 167–68; and royal vs. nationalist historiographies, 161, 162–64, 163n103, 167–68, 171n143
'Abbās Ḥilmī II, 27, 27nn22,23, 32, 35, 67, 69, 75–76, 83–84, 223
'Abd al-Ḥalīm, Maḥmūd, 319
'Abd al-Karīm, Aḥmad 'Izzat, 14, *183;* and academic historians, 190, *192–93,* 194–95, 216, 270–71, 270n86, 310; and Arab socialist historiography, 300, 303, 307, 307n115, 310; and authoritarian pluralism, 324–25, 330
'Abd al-Nāṣir, Huda, 2n5
'Abd al-Raḥīm, 'Abd al-Raḥim, 'Abd al-Raḥmān, 331, 331n74, 332n76
'Abd al-Raḥīm, Muṣṭafa, 334
'Abd al-Rāziq, Ḥasan, 306
'Abdallāh, Aḥmad, 2, 333–34
'Abdallāh, Ismā'īl Ṣabry, 305
Abdel-Malek, Anouar, 29, 265, 273n101, 283
'Ābdīn archive, 10, 12–14, 13n, 85n72, 91–140, 164, 184; and academic historians, *192–93,* 195, 197–200, 213, 213n97; accessibility to, 134, 213, 295–96; and anarchy thesis, 92–95, 99, 99n28, 107, 135–36; and Arab socialist historiography, 290, 297; and Deny, 12, 95n10, 97n19, 99n28, 102n37, 103–4, 106–11, 107n56, 110n74, 114, *118,* 126, 139; and foreign collections, 104, 111–22, 112n78, 114n82, 115n87, *118–19, 120,* 126, 139, 154; forging of, 92–122; and Griffini, 12, 102–6, 103nn43,44, 104n48, 105n52, 107n56, 111, 115, 139; and objectivity, 13, 13n, 92, 132–33, 133n141; and al-Rāfi'ī, 130, 134, 137, 164; and revolutionary historiography, 253, 264, 280; and translations, 103–4, 105, 109–11, 126–30, 128n119, 132, 164
'Ābdīn Palace collection, 93, 97
'Ābdīn project, 12–14, 325, 338; and 'Ābdīn archive, 92, 106, 108, 114n82, 115, 116–17, 123–32, 135–37, 140; and academic historians, 187–88, 191, 194, 194n23, 196, 199, 214; and Arab socialist historiography, 285–86, 288, 294–95, 295n58, 303; and revolutionary historiography, 253, 264, 277; and royal vs. nationalist historiographies, 146, 151n40, 158, 175; termination of, 264
'Abduh, Ibrāhīm, *192,* 264, 264n61, 325
'Abduh, Muḥammad, 23–25, 24n13, 27, 32–35, 35n56, 41, 50, 56, 61n154, 64, 74n26, 123, 209; followers of, 27, 67, 70, 227
Abdülhamid, 27, 68–69
Abou-El-Haj, Rifaat Ali, 71n17
abstraction, 16, 19, 30, 36, 60, 62, 66, 71, 90, 212, 218, 230
Abū al-Futūḥ, Raḍwān, *192*

Abū Ḥadīd, Muḥammad Farīd al-, 59n, 181, 181n183, 188
Abū Nuwwās, 209
Abū Zayd, Ḥikmat, 307
academic historians, 2, 7, 10, 10n28, 13–15, 186–218, *192–93, 204, 205*, 341; and ʿĀbdīn archive, 121, 136n151; and Arab socialist historiography, 284–85, 284n8, 291–94, 298–308, 308nn118,119, 310; and authoritarian pluralism, 311–12, 316, 318–19, 322, 324–25, 327–32, 329n64, 333–36; and partisan historiography, 14, 233–35, 243, 245, 247; and revolutionary historiography, 14–15, 249–50, 256, 260, 263–65, 267–72, 270n85; and royal vs. nationalist historiographies, 147, 149–51, 156–59, 156n70, 184. *See also names of academic historians*
l'Académie française, 123
accessibility to archives, 134, 213, 295–96, 325, 339
actualist philosophy of history, 257–60
adab fī sabīl al-ḥayāt, al-, 300–301
ʿAdawī, Muḥammad al-, 319
Advanced Seminar in Modern History, 270
Afghānī, Jamāl al-Dīn al-, 23, 25, 227
African empire, 50, 124, 129, 135, 167, 171, 256n33
agency, collective, 159, 285, 315, 337
agrarian reforms, 190, 239, 243, 258, 258n44, 274–76, 282, 342
"ahl al-thiqa wa ahl al-khibra," crisis of, 262n52
Aḥmad, Anwar, 252
Ahrām, Al-, 31, 279, 287, 289, 295, 298, 323–25
Akhbār, Al-, 293, 293nn46,47, 305, 307
Aʿlām al-Islām (series), 209
ʿĀlim, Maḥmūd Amīn al-, 307
Alleaume, Ghisaline, 72
allegorical writing. *See* national allegory
amateur historians, 10, 77, 88, 114, 160, 188, 196, 202–3, 256, 332–35, 334n85. *See also* independent historians; popular-nationalist historiography; *names of amateur historians*
Americanization, 320
American University in Cairo (AUC), 292, 296, 331, 335n87
American University of Beirut, 161
Amin, Galal, 304
Amīn, Qāsim, 25–26
ʿĀmir, Ibrāhīm, 273–76, 291, 296, 308, 327
analogies, 152, 206, 248–49, 252, 254. *See also* metaphors
anarchy thesis, 92–95, 99, 99n28, 107, 135–36
Anglo-Egyptian agreement (1936), 224–25
Anglo-Egyptian conflict (1882–1936), 225
Anglo-Egyptian negotiations (1954), 206, 225, 326
Anīs, ʿAbd al-ʿAẓīm, 290n28
Anīs, Muḥammad, 15, 151, 191, 207, 233, 272, 307, 328; and Arab socialist historiography, 284–85, 285n11, 288–94, 296–97, 296n64, 299–300, 300n80, 305, 308, 308nn118,119, 310
annals, 4, 41, 43, 322
anti-colonial nationalism, 21–22, 69, 73, 75, 149, 176, 179, 195, 216n108, 282, 317–18, 339, 342; and partisan historiography, 219, 221, 230, 236; and revolutionary historiography, 253–54
Antonius, George, 148
ʿAqqād, ʿAbbās Maḥmūd al-, *227*, 262, 301
Arab Awakening, The (Antonius), 148
ʿArabī, Al-, 264n61
Arabic language, 25, 34, 48, 53, 81, 83, 87–88, 310, 331, 331n73; and ʿĀbdīn archive, 103–4, 107, 109–10, 109n70, 114n82, 127–28, 130; and academic historians, 190–91, 194, 200n50; and royal vs. nationalist historiographies, *146*, 149, 151, 158, 160nn89,90, 164, 165n114, 171–72, 177, *183*
Arabic literature, 36, 36n, 54, 56, 59–60, 85. *See also* historical novel
Arab Language Academy, 113, 239
Arab League, 254n26, 268, 268n76, 340n4
Arab Revolt, 254
Arab Socialist Union, 283, 284n6, 292, 305, 313, 326
archives, 1, 9–10, 71, 78, 82; and academic historians, 196–99, 207, 212; accessibility to, 134, 213, 295–96, 325, 339; and Arab socialist historiography, 289–90, 293–94, 297, 310; and authoritarian pluralism, 15, 325–27; principles of arrangement, 100–102; and revolutionary historiography, 264, 277. *See also names of archives*
Arḍ wa-l-fallāh, Al- (ʿĀmir), 275
Arḍ, Al- (The Earth, al-Sharqāwī), 275
arrests/imprisonment, 13; of ʿAbduh, 35; and authoritarian pluralism, 312, 314, 322; of intellectuals, 263, 265; of Kurayyim, 152–53; of Marxist historians, 240, 246, 276–77, 283–84, 287, 305; of Muslim Brotherhood, 317; of Raḍwān, 226; of Rāfiʿī, 302; of Shāfiʿī, 276; of al-Shinnāwī, 265; of Zaghlūl, 223
Art et Liberté, 238n71
Ashʿarite orthodoxy, 24, 24n13

'Ashmāwī, Ḥasan, 317
'Ashmāwī, Sayyid, 31n35
'Aṣr Ismā'īl (Rāfi'ī), 164, 164n106, 171
Association for Arab Historical Studies, 210
Aulard, Alphonse, 86
authenticity, Islamic, 23, 25, 32, 321
authoritarianism, 4, 75, 241, 262–63
authoritarian pluralism, 15, 311–36; and academic historians, 311–12, 316, 318–19, 322, 324–25, 327–32, 329n64, 333–36; and Islamist historiography, 2, 314–22, 329; and regulation, 322–27, 336; and self-reflection, 332–35
authority, professional, 12–13, 15; and academic historians, 201, 214, 217–18, 247
'Awaḍ, Luwīs, 196, 265, 299
'Awaḍ, Muḥammad, 181n183
Awakening of Egypt, The (Rif'at), 148
Awlād Ḥaritna (Children of Gebelawi, Mahfouz), 279
awqāf (religious endowment) documents, 108, 108n62, 111, 306n110
Ayalon, Ami, 72
Ayalon, David, 7
Ayām, Al- (Ḥusayn), 228n37
'Ayn Shams University, 270, 270n86, 310, 319, 328
Ayyūbī, Ilyās al-, 87–88, 87nn83,84, 299
Ayyubid dynasty, 32n46
Azm Sadik Jallal al-, 16
al-Azhar University, 93, 149n28, 227, 265, 295, 318–20, 322, 331

Badr, Ṭaha, 55
Badrān, Muḥammad, 160n89
Baer, Gabriel, 328
Bahā' al-Dīn, Aḥmad, 263
Bahā' al-Din, Barakāt, 232
Baḥr al-zākhir fī tārīkh al-'ālam wa akhbār al-awā'il wa-l-awākhir, al- (The Bottomless Sea on the Events of World History, Fahmī), 44
Baker, Raymond William, 321
Baker, Samuel, 50
Bandung conference (April 1955), 258n44, 272
Bank Miṣr, 231–32
Bannā, Ḥasan al-, 219, 316–18, 319n22
banned books, 35, 146n17, 174, 176, 220, 266. *See also* censorship
Barakāt, 'Alī, 310, 327–29, 330n67
Baring, Evelyn, Sir. *See* Cromer, Lord
Barrāwī, Rāshid al-, 241–42, 242n93, 263, 278
Bārūdī, Maḥmūd Sāmī al-, 21
Baṭrīq, 'Abd al-Ḥamīd Muḥammad al-, *192*, 288, 305
Bayt al-umma, 232
Bayyūmī, Zakarīyā Sulaymān, 319–20
Beginnings of the Egyptian Question and the Rise of Mehmet Ali, The (Ghurbāl), 156–57, 187, 190, 209, 216
Beinin, Joel, 331n72
Benis, Georges, 115, *119*
Bernard, August, 113
Bey, Talamas, 98
bigotry, 219, 303–4
Bint al-shāṭī. *See* Raḥmān, 'Ā'isha 'Abd al-
Birmingham University, 291
Bishrī, Ṭariq al-, 319–22, 335, 338
biṭāqāt al-dār, 109
black hand organization, 223n16
books, 5, 144–46, 144n10, 146n17, *146*, 278, 278n132, 313, 315–16, 319. *See also* textbooks; *titles of books*
border, political *(ḥadd)*, 48, 50–51
British colonialism, 20, 22, 22n7, 26–27, 35, 66–69; and 'Ābdīn archive, 92, 97–98, 97n19, 116; and academic historians, 191, 206–7; and Arab socialist historiography, 282, 288, 292, 299, 305–6; and authoritarian pluralism, 318, 328; and chronicles, 81–82; and Cromer, 21, 25, 27n22, 50, 62, 64, 66–67, 69, 72–73, 78–79, 78n40; defeat of (1956), 179, 253–54, 258n44; and Dinshaway incident (1906), 27, 64–68; and February 1942 incident, 158n80, 208; and Milner, 22n7, 53, 62, 79; and partisan historiography, 221–23, 229–30, 233, 241–45, 247; protectorate of, 70; and revolutionary historiography, 249, 252–53, 279; and royal vs. nationalist historiographies, 146, 146n17, 152, 162, 166n115, 167, 169, 172–74, 178–79
British Council in Egypt, 145
British Foreign Office, 305
British historians, 113n80, 125, 190, 194–95, 212, 212n91, 331, 341. *See also names of British historians*
British Museum, 53
British occupation, 22, 35, 97, 116, 146, 172–73, 191, 221, 250n8, 252, 274–75
British Public Record Office (PRO), 115, 138
Buḥayrī, Muḥammad Ismā'īl, *227*
bureaucrats/bureaucracy, 21, 22, 25, 73–74, 76–77, 97, 99, 148, 310, 314–15. See also *effendis*
Burke, Peter, 17

Bustānī, Salīm al-, 53
Byzantine era, 151n37, 302n89

Cahiers d'Histoire Égyptienne, 211n85
Cairo: fire (1952), 212; as "Paris along the Nile," 20–21; and space, perception of, 49–51
Cairo Library Association, 145
Cairo University, 74, 74n26, 196, 198n39, *204, 205,* 264, 264n61, 265, 270, 283, 292, 312
calligraphy, Arabic, 198
Cambridge History of Egypt, The, 121
Cantalupo, Roberto, 131
Capital (Marx), 241
capitalism, 8n25, 241–43, 273–75, 283, 300, 306, 313–14, 328–29
capitulations system, 169
Carlyle, Thomas, 236–37
Casino al-Jazera, 284
Castro, Fidel, 257
Cattaui, Adolphe, 106, 112n78
Cattaui, Joseph, *183*
Cattaui, René, 115, *119*
causality, 7, 36, 43–44, 61, 83, 302, 322, 337; in historical novels, 58–59
Cave report, 166
Cecil, Edward, 98
celebratory histories, 211, 285, 291, 309
censorship, 1, 13, 35, 68, 68n5, 89, 121, 121nn98,100, 205, 207, 219, 246, 299; and authoritarian pluralism, 313, 318, 324–25; and revolutionary historiography, 261, 261n48, 266, 266n69; and royal vs. nationalist historiographies, 146n17, 147–48, 164, 172, 174, 176, 179–81, 180n178, 181n183, 184
centennial commemorations, 12, 31, 35, 49, 52, 60, 64, 211, 261
Center of Documents and Contemporary History of Egypt, 296–97, 310
central planning, 15, 249, 276, 278, 286
challenge-response-mimesis theory, 215–16
chaos, institutional. *See* anarchy thesis
Charles-Roux, François, 147n22, 152, 155n64, 156, 162
Charter. *See* National Charter
Chickens' Week, 258
Choueiri, Youssef, 9, 157, 187, 187n7, 206, 210, 210n81
Christianity, 19, 123, 163
Christian Syrians, 7, 20–21, 25, 39–40, 79. *See also* Zaydān, Jurjī
chronicles, 4, 5, 6–8, 11–12, 30, 35, 37, 47, 51, 57, 80–85, 338; and time, perception of, 41, 41n80, 43–46
citadel, 91, 93, 95, 97, 135, 138, 295
citadel massacre (1811), 55, 58, 155, 155nn62,64
citizenship, 12, 73, 178, 227–28
civilization, 23, 26, 124, 129, 177–78; and civilizing mission, 135, 167, 171, 178; and Toynbee, 209, 215–16, 216–17nn110,111, 269
class, 28, 143–44, 212–13, 223, 230, 327–28, 338; and Marxist historians, 239, 241, 243–45, 275, 277, 283, 327–28. *See also* middle class; upper class; working class
code words, 258, 258n43
cold war politics, 252–53
Collingwood, Robin George, 212
colonialism, 2, 4, 10, 10n28, 12–14, 16, 25–26, 28, 168, 282, 292; and ʿĀbdīn archive, 12, 112–14, 121, 139–40; and revolutionary historiography, 256, 272–77. *See also* British colonialism
Comité de conservation des monuments de l'art arabe, 113, 139–40, 139n
Comité des archives, 126, 140
commemoration, politics of, 31, 52, 211, 226, 252, 257–59, 282, 285. *See also* centennial commemorations
"Commitment and Objectivity in Contemporary Egyptian Historiography" (1987 conference), 1–3, 2n2, 9, 11, 15, 234–35, 311, 332–33
Committee of Union and Progress (CUP), 68–69
Committee to Spread Modern Culture, 240
common sense, cult of, 212, 341
Communist Party. *See* Egyptian Communist Party
communists/communism, 180, 320; and Arab socialist historiography, 283–84, 287–88, 305; and partisan historiography, 219, 237, 237n68, 238, 238n69, 239–40, 240n84, 242–44, 244n, 246; and revolutionary historiography, 249, 265, 272–73, 276–78, 276n124, 277n128
conscription, 22, 34, 55
constitution (1923), 168
constitution (1956), 254
constitutionalism, 19, 67–69, 168–69, 221–23, 243, 250n8, 265
contemporary history, 220, 274, 333; and academic historians, 204–7, 204n62, 212, 247;

and Arab socialist historiography, 290, 294, 296; and authoritarian pluralism, 315–17, 335
continuity, 46, 54, 61, 84, 89–90, 215–17, 269, 339
Copts, 68, 68n7, 166n119, 222
Corrective Revolution (May 1971), 313
corvée system, 111, 167, 194n24
cosmopolitanism, 112–14, 237
cotton production, 20
Crabbs, Jack, 6–8, 6n18, 8n25, 36, 60, 81–82, 83n62, 88–89, 150n35, 285–86
Crabitès, Pierre, 12, 125–28, 128n118, 135, 166n119; vs. popular-nationalists, 160, 160nn89,90, 163, 165–68, 165n114, 169, *183*
Creswell, K. A. C., 113
crisis of "ahl al-thiqa wa ahl al-khibra,," 262n52
crisis of confidence, 332–33, 336
crisis of historical consciousness, 15, 311, 342
crisis of historicism, 28
"crisis of the intellectuals" (1961), 263, 267, 282–83, 283n2, 298
Cromer, Lord, 21, 25, 27n22, 50, 62, 64, 66–67, 69, 72–73, 78–79, 78n40, 166n115, 167, 242
cultural revolution, 185, 286, 290, 297–98, 300–301, 309n125
Cuno, Kenneth, 8n25, 31n35, 331n72
CUP. *See* Committee of Union and Progress (CUP)
Curiel, Henri, 238–40, 240n83
cyclical perceptions of history, 44, 61n152, 214–16

Daftarkhāne/Dār al-maḥfūẓāt, 93–99, 93n4, 95nn8,10, 96n14, 98n22, 102–3, 107–8, 108n65, 138
Dante, 200n50
al-Dār al-Miṣriyya li-l-ṭibā'a wa-l-nashr wa-l-tawzī', 272
Dār al-anṣār, 316, 319
Dār al-da'wa, 319
Dār al-kutub, 145, 148, 297–98, 310
Dār al-maḥfūẓāt, 295
Dār al-nadīm, 272
Dār al-'ulūm (teacher-training school), 81
Dār al-wathā'iq (Nasserist archive), 138, 294–98, 295n57, 310, 329
Dār Wahba, 316
Darwinism, 19, 53, 88
da'wa (cause of promoting Islam), 319
Da'wa, Al- (journal), 316
Dawla al-'uthmāniya: Dawla Islāmīya muftara' 'alayhā, Al- (al-Shinnāwī), 322
Decline of the West, The (Spengler), 215
De Lesseps (code word), 258, 258n43
Democratic Movement for National Liberation (DMNL), 238, 277
democratic principles, 73, 86, 168, 181, 231, 241, 244, 263, 276, 278, 315–16, 320–21
Demolins, Edmond, 53, 53n121
demonstrations, 68, 69n8, 146n19, 180, 221, 290, 314
Deny, Jean, 12, 95n10, 97n19, 99n28, 102n37, 103–4, 106–11, 107n56, 110n74, 114, *118*, 126, 139
de-Ottomanization, 12, 70–72, 71n14, 75, 77, 79–81, 85, 105, 150, 204, 339
Descartes, 212
determinism, 57, 242n93, 278, 309
dialectic materialism, 241, 243, 245
Dinshaway incident (1906), 27, 64–68
disciplinary objectivity, 201
Disūqī, 'Āṣim, 207, 310, 327–29, 332, 334
diwān, 96, 107
Diyāb, Muḥammad 'Abd al-Hakam, 43, 47
document shredding/selling, 96, 96n15, 97, 99, 197, 213
Dodwell, Henry, 125, 127, 136–37, *192;* vs. popular-nationalists, 141–42, 147n22, 151–52, 151n40, 154, 155n64, 156, 160n88, 161, 177, *182*
Douin, Georges, 167, *183;* and 'Ābdīn archive, 106, 114–15, *118–19, 120,* 121–22, 125–27, 128n119, 130–33, 132n137, 139–40
Driault, Édouard, 115, *118–19,* 135, 152
Dumas *(père* and *fils),* 53
Dūs, Iyād Hasanīn, *192*
dynastic history, 38, 43, 47, 76, 82, 87–88, 191, 211, 299; and 'Ābdīn archive, 91–92, 104, 107, 122, 122n104, 125, 135. *See also* royal historiography

"Eastern Question," 116
École nationale des langues orientales (Paris), 106–7
Economic and Business History Research Center (EBHRC), 335n87
economic history, 2, 4, 17, 19, 28, 62, 67, 73, 79, 327–28; and Arab socialist historiography, 282–83, 309–10; and Marxist historians, 242–43, 327; and royal vs. nationalist historiographies, 143, 155, 165–69, 166nn115,117,119, 175
education, 15, 74; and academic historians, 190, 195, 208–9; and Arab socialist historiography, 298–301; and authoritarian pluralism, 313–14, 329–31; and revolutionary historiography, 253, 256, 256nn35–37, 278; and royal vs.

education *(continued)*
nationalist historiographies, 143–44, 148–49, 149n28, 170
effendis, 23, 25–26, 30, 65, 76, 188, 191; and royal vs. nationalist historiographies, 141, 143–44, 147, 149. *See also* middle class
Egyptian army, 34–35, 173, 211, 216–17n110, 244, 251; in historical novels, 55–56, 58
Egyptian Canal Authority, 263
Egyptian Communist Party, 238, 242, 244, 244n, 246, 272, 277, 284. *See also* communists/communism
Egyptian Conseil d'état (Majlis al-shūra), 320
Egyptian Criminal Code, 64
"Egyptian Empire," 256, 256n33
Egyptian Gazette, 180n178
Egyptian Historical Society (EHS), 159, 210–13, 210nn82,83, 213n96, 270n86, 271, 300, 306, 325, 330. *See also* Royal Historical Society
Egyptianization project, 189, 191, 194–95, 203–4, 204n61, *204,* 205n65
Egyptian Movement for National Liberation (EMNL), 238–39, 238n70
Egyptian/Syrian relations: occupation of Syria (1831–48), 56, 97, 107, 116, 160, 160n88; unification (1958), 258n44, 277, 326, 340
Egypt in the Reign of Muhammad Ali (Lutfi al-Sayyid-Marsot), 128n119
Egypt: Military Society (Abdel-Malek), 273n101
EHS. *See* Egyptian Historical Society (EHS)
elites, 30, 74, 81, 230, 233, 249, 300, 329, 332n76; and 'Ābdīn archive, 112, 114n82, 140; and academic historians, 191, 195, 203, 208–9, 211, 215n102, 216–17n110; Toynbee's views on, 189–90
L'empire égyptien sous Mohamed Ali (Ṣabrī), 156
empiricism, 201, 212, 218, 284, 303, 307, 328–29, 337, 341–42
Engels, 239–40
England in Egypt (Milner), 22n7, 53
English language, 13, 25, 83, 151, 158, 177, 190, 194
entente cordiale (1904), 27
essentialism, 229–30
ethical codes of operation, 13; and 'Ābdīn archive, 137–38; and academic historians, 15, 188, 196, 202, 218, 247, 268, 270; and Arab socialist historiography, 303–4, 310; and authoritarian pluralism, 330, 334–35; and revolutionary historiography, 14, 268, 270
European/Western historiographical model, 7–8, 13, 17, 22–23, 28, 48–49, 275, 337–38, 342–43; and 'Ābdīn archive, 96, 99–100, 112–14, 116, 135–36, 139; and academic historians, 187n7, 190, 195, 201, 212, 212n91, 215–17n110, 269–70; and Arab socialist historiography, 284–85, 298, 304, 306, 307n115; and authoritarian pluralism, 318, 321, 331, 336; and continuity, 89, 89n90; and partisan historiography, 228, 230; and royal vs. nationalist historiographies, 146, 146n17, 155–57, 163, 165, 177–79, 184; and Zaydān, 37, 39–40
Exceptional Laws, 69, 69n8
exile: of al-Nadīm, 23; of Fārūq, 251, 258; and Nasserism, 323; of ultranationalists, 69, 69n8; of 'Umar Makram, 155; of Urabists, 21, 44
expert authority, 13, 137, 188, 196, 218, 278. *See also* authority, professional

Faculty of Humanities, 212
Fahmī, Maḥmūd, 21, 44, 47. *See also* Muhandis, al-
Fahmī, 'Abd al-Raḥmān, 290, 292, 294
Fahmī, Muṣṭafa, 228
Fahmy, Khaled, 128, 128n119
Fajr al-jadīd, Al-, 239, 242
Fakhrī, Ḥusayn, 68, 125
Farābī, al-, 209
Faraḥyān, Agop, 98
Farīd, Muḥammad, 7, 26, 45, 47, 69, 75, 79, 222–23, 226, 235, 251–52; and Arab socialist historiography, 290, 292–93, 292n43, 296, 296n62
Fārūq, King, 176, 237, 249, 251, 258, 258n44; and academic historians, 206, 208–10, 208n75, 210n81
fascism, 146, 244, 257n38
Fatimid authenticity, 139
Fawtier, Robert, 115n87
Fawtier-Jones, E. C., Miss, 115, 115n87, *118*
Fawwāz, Zaynab, 26, 77n39
Fawzī, Muḥsayn, 97–98, 98n22
February 1942 incident, 158n80, 208
feminism, 26, 77n39, 335, 335n88
Festival of Science ('Īd al-'ilm), 257–58
feudalism, 177, 243–45, 273–76, 296, 300
Fī a'qāb al-thawra al-miṣriyya (In the Aftermath of the Egyptian Revolution, al-Rāfi'ī), 224–26
Fikrī, Muḥammad Amīn, 49
fire (1820, Daftarkhāne), 95n8
firmans, 115, 167–68
footnoting, 44, 56, 88, 158, 198–99, 330, 330n67
foreign collections, 104, 111–22, 112n78, 113n80,

115n87, *118–19, 120,* 126, 139, 154, 297, 297n67, 326, 331
foreign historians, 10, 12, 112, 139, 191, 194–96; and Arab socialist historiography, 295–96, 299, 301, 304–6; and royal vs. nationalist historiographies, 154, 165, 170, 176–77, 179. *See also names of foreign historians*
forgery, 97, 200
founder paradigm/thesis, 12–13, 33, 60–64, 61nn151,152,154, 63nn161,164, 84, 88, 191, 287, 296, 339; and 'Ābdīn archive, 92, 105, 108, 108n62, 135n147; and royal vs. nationalist historiographies, 141, 155–59, 161, 177, 184
freedom of speech/association, 15, 69, 180–81, 246, 312
Free Officers, 223, 250–52, 257, 261–62, 265, 317, 323
French archival science, 91–92, 96, 100–102, 115, 131. *See also names of French archivists*
French Archives Nationales, 138
French expedition (1798), 33, 149, 152–53, 156, 189, 253, 284–85, 340
French historians, 91–92, 115n87, 116, 121, 123, 195. *See also names of French historians*
French language, 13, 25, 81, 83, 87n84, 194, 211n85, 273n101; and 'Ābdīn archive, 103–4, 107, 109, 114n82, 124, 128, 130; and royal vs. nationalist historiographies, 147, 154, 158, 158n78, 164, 171–72, 177; and Ṣabrī, 86–87, 147, 154
French occupation, 6, 11n31, 20, 27, 32n46, 55, 152, 274
French Revolution, 86, 100
Frontiers incident (1894), 69
Fu'ād, Aḥmad, King, 70, 76, 81, 82n55, 87–88, 208, 249, 280, 319n22; and 'Ābdīn archive, 91–92, 94–95, 97, 99, 102–6, 103n43, 108, 108n62; and Arab socialist historiography, 297, 299, 303; death of, 125, 175n165, 176; and foreign collections, 111–12, 114, 121, 121n100; royal project of (*see* 'Ābdīn project); and royal vs. nationalist historiographies, 146–47, 151, 154, 160n89, 163–64, 168, 171–72, 175–77, 175n165
Fu'ād, Ni'mat Aḥmad, 323
Fu'ād University, 112, 113, 115n87, 156, 181n183, 190, 196, 202n55, 241, 259, 290–91; and academic historians, 203–4, *204, 205,* 207, 209
Future (temporal notion of), 11, 29, 46, 52–53, 61–62, 84, 113, 123, 179, 257, 276, 278, 288; in historical novels, 57–59
Galat, Joseph, 126n111
geography, Egyptian, 49–51, 49nn106,109, 51n115, 82
Gershoni, Israel, 226, 340n4
Ghālī, Būṭrus, 50, 65, 68–69
Ghānim, Fatḥī, 240, 245, 245n109
Ghīṭāni, Gamāl al-, 312
Ghurbāl, Muḥammad Shafīq, 13–15, 65, 89, 188–91; and academic historians, 15, 162, 186–218, 186n2, 187n7, *192–93, 204, 205;* and Arab socialist historiography, 286, 290–91, 298, 300–301, 300n80, 303–4; and authoritarian pluralism, 322, 325, 334; death of, 271; and Egyptianization project, 189, 191, 194–95, 203–4, 204n61, *204,* 205n65; and historical methodology, 199–202, 199n43, 200n50, 208, 213, 215–18; and partisan historiography, 225, 225n26, 244; and politicization of history writing, 13, 189, 194–96, 204n62, 205–10, 209nn76,78; and professionalism, 13, 188, 196–203, 196n30, 197n33, 199n43, 207–8, 213–17, 216–17nn110,111; and revolutionary historiography, 14, 249, 259, 264–65, 267–72, 267n75, 268n76, 269–70nn82,84; and Royal Historical Society, *183,* 207–14, 209nn76,78, 210nn82,83, 211n87, 213n96; vs. royal historiography, 147–48, 156–59, 157n73, 158n78, 179, *182–83,* 185; and scientific inquiry, 133, 196–97, 200–202
Gibb, Hamilton A. R., 291, 295, 318
Girgis, Fawzī, 239
global historiographical practice, 16–17, 329, 336, 343
Goldberg, Ellis, 331n72
Goldschmidt, Arthur, 292, 292n43, 295
Gordon, Joel, 252, 254
Gorman, Anthony, 9, 150n35, 187, 256n32, 285–86, 325
Gorst, Eldon, 67, 69
Grafton, Anthony, 198
Gran, Peter, 8n25, 308, 331n73
Grant, Arthur J., 194, 194n22
Greco-Roman past, 5, 11n30, 151n37, 302n89
Greek Ministry of Foreign Affairs, 115
Green Book series, 239
Gregorian calendar, 31, 33
Griffini, Eugenio, 12, 102–6, 103nn43,44, 104n48, 105n52, 107n56, 111, 115, 139
Groppi's Café, 284
Grunebaum, Gustave von, 318

Hādī, Mas'ūd 'Abd al-, 262
Ḥadīth, 38, 215–17
Ḥadīth 'Isā ibn Hishām (Muwaylīhī), 93–94, 99
Hafez, Sabry, 59–60
Ḥāfiẓ, Aḥmad Fahmī, *227*
Ḥāfiẓ, Ibrāhīm, 261, 261n49
Ḥakīm, Tawfīq al-, 312
Ḥalawānī, Amīn al-, 38–43, 39n67, 40n75, 41n78, *42*
Hamidian autocracy in greater Syria, 20
HAMITU. *See* Egyptian Movement for National Liberation (EMNL)
Ḥamrūsh, Aḥmad, 323
Ḥanbalism in historical research, 303
Hanna, Nelly, 8n25, 331
Hanotaux, Gabriel, 123–25, *124*, 154, 154n55, 177, *182*
Ḥaqā'iq al-akhbār 'an duwal al-biḥār (True Narrations of Maritime Nations, Sarhank), 43–44, 44n84
Ḥaraka al-siyāsiya fī miṣr, Al- (al-Bishrī), 321
Ḥasūna, Muḥammad Amīn, 253
Ḥātim, 'Abd al-Qādir, 289
Havel, Václav, 259
Ḥawliyāt Miṣr al-siyāsiyya (Political Annals of Egypt, Shafīq), 83–84
Haykal, Muḥammad Ḥusayn, 76n34, 179, 210, 260, 262, 283, 283n2, 287, 310, 312, 323–24, 323n37, 326, 340
"hearing committee" *(lajnat al-istimā')*, 313
Henderson, Nevile, 229
Henein, Georges, 238n71
hereditary law, 167–68
Ḥifnāwī, Muṣṭafa al-, 263
High Dam, 258n44
Higher Teacher College (Dār al-mu'alimīn al-'ulyā), 188
Ḥijāz expedition, 116
Hijri calendar, 31
Hilāl, Al-, 33, 38, 53–54, 80, 87, 146n19, 234, 254
Ḥilbāwī, Ibrāhīm, 65
Ḥilmī, Fu'ād, 126
Histoire de la nation égyptienne (Hanotaux), 154n55
Histoire de la nation française (Hanotaux), 123
Histoire de l'Égypte moderne (Sammarco), 132
historical consciousness, 28–30, 55, 59, 76–77, 145–46, 186, 333–35; crisis of, 15, 311, 342
historical materialism, 220, 240–44, 273, 287, 329
historical methodology, 10, 13, 15, 199–202, 199n43, 200n50, 208, 213, 215–18, 341–42; and Arab socialist historiography, 284, 288, 303–4, 307, 310; and authoritarian pluralism, 311, 319, 322, 330–31, 333, 336; and revolutionary historiography, 256, 268, 270, 280
historical novels/novelists, 30, 52–59, 59n, 200
historicism, 11–12, 28–30, 36, 38, 46, 51–53, 60–61, 63, 66, 89, 135; and chronicles, 78, 84–85; crisis of, 28
historic moment, 258–59, 282
historiographical competition, 141–85; and 'Abbās, 161, 162–64, 163n103, 167–68, 171n143; and British colonialism, 146, 146n17, 152, 162, 166n115, 167, 169, 172–74; formation of historiographic field, 142–50, *145;* and Ibrāhīm, 157, 159–62, 160nn88–90, 170–71, 177; and Ismā'īl, 147, 162, 164–72, 165n112, 175; and Muḥammad 'Alī, 141, 151, 154–63, 168, 171, 177; protagonists of, 146–50; and 'Urābī revolt, 170, 172–76
Ḥitta, Aḥmad Aḥmad al-, 190, *192–93*
Ḥizb al-Dusturī, al- (Constitutional Party), 67
Ḥizb al-Miṣrī, al- (The Egyptian Party), 67
Ḥizb al-Nubalā' (Party of Nobles), 67
Ḥizb al-'Ummāl (Workers Party), 67
Holt, Peter, 304
Hourani, Albert, 45, 54, 318, 337
House of Scientific Studies (Dār al-abḥāth al- 'ilmiyya), 239–40
House of the Dawn (Dār al-fajr), 239, 246
House of the Twentieth Century (Dār al-qarn al- 'ishrīn), 239–40
Humberstone, Gertrude, 190, 190n14
Hunter, Robert, 109n69, 110
"Ḥurriyat al-'aql fī Miṣr" (Mūsa), 246
Ḥusayn, Kamāl al-Dīn, 253
Ḥusayn, Ṭaha, 86n73, 154n55, 179, 194, 228n37, 259–60, 262, 271, 301, 335
Ḥusaynī, Isḥāq Mūsa, 266

Ibn Baṭṭūṭa, 260
Ibn Iyās, 7, 84, 216
Ibn Khaldūn, 44, 89n90, 214–17, 260
Ibrāhīm, 56, 97, 107, 116–17, 125, 135; and academic historians, 196, 206, 211, 211n87; Egyptian identity of, 160–61; and royal vs. nationalist historiographies, 157, 159–62, 160nn88–90, 170–71, 177
Ibrāhīm, Ḥasan Aḥmad, 127
Ibrahim of Egypt (Crabitès), 160, 160n89

Idea of History, The (Collingwood), 212
ijtihād, 23–24
Ikhwān wa-l-thawra (The Brethren and the Revolution, ʿAshmāwī), 317
Iltizām (commitment), 300–301
Imām, ʿAbd Allāh, 312
imperialism, European. *See* colonialism
Imperialism, the Higher State of Capitalism (Lenin), 241
imprisonment. *See* arrests/imprisonment
independence, 4, 10, 14, 67, 70, 258, 282, 320–21; and ʿĀbdīn archive, 114, 122, 122n103, 140; and partisan historiography, 223–24, 227, 230, 233; and royal vs. nationalist historiographies, 142, 178–79
independent historians, 2, 10, 191, 213, 218, 335; vs. royal historiography, 131, 146–56, 184. *See also names of independent historians*
Indian historiography, 23, 113n80, 151, 177–78, 178n174
individualism, 25, 178, 228, 241, 337
industrialization, 190, 195, 243, 278, 282, 328–29
inevitability, 14, 245, 278, 288–89
infitāḥ, 312–14, 320, 329
Institut d'Égypte, 113
Institute of Arabic Studies, 268, 268n76, 270
Institute of Librarianship, 145
International Geographical Congress (Cairo, April 1925), 105
Iraqi coup, 277, 277n128
ISKRA (the Spark), 238–40
Islam, 23, 39, 123, 314–15, 318, 338, 340
Islamic historiography, 5–9, 11, 11n30, 48, 50, 63–64, 70, 85, 89–90, 89n90, 222, 331; and academic historians, 203–4, *205*, 209–10, 210n81, 214–17; and Zaydān, 37–41, 80
Islamist historiography, 2, 217, 314–22, 329, 341. *See also* Muslim Brotherhood
Ismāʿīl, ʿAlī, 115
Ismāʿīl, Khedive, 20, 35, 35n56, 44, 50, 82–83, 87, 195; and ʿĀbdīn archive, 104, 109, 111, 115, 116–17, 125–26, 128–30, 129n120, 135; and Daftarkhāne, 96n15, 97, 99; and Marxist historians, 242–43, 274; and revolutionary historiography, 249, 250n8, 274; and royal vs. nationalist historiographies, 147, 162, 164–72, 165n112, 175
"Ismāʿīl era," 164–65
Israeli historians, 305
Istibdād al-mamālīk (The Tyranny of the Mamluks, 1892–93, Zaydān), 55–56
Italian archives/archivists, 102–3, 111, 115, 116, *118*, 121, 121n98, 131. *See also names of Italian archivists*
Italian Central State Archives, 103
Italian language, 13, 25, 128, 172, 177
Italian Ministry of Foreign Affairs, 102–3, 103n43
Iʿtiṣām, Al-, 316, 318n18
ʿIzz al-Dīn, Amīn, 328

Jabartī, ʿAbd al-Raḥmān al-, 6–7, 8n25, 35, 41, 43, 45, 83–84, 216
al-jalāʾ principle, 222, 226
Jamāhīr, Al-, 239
Jameson, Frederic, 229
Jamʿiyat al-ghadd, 291
Jankowski, James, 226, 340n4
Japanese history, 45–46, 47
Japanese-Russian war, 46
Jarīda, Al-, 67, 69–70, 73, 75
Jarīda-Umma group, 69–70, 73, 75, 223
Jawīsh, ʿAbd al-ʿAzīz, Shaykh, 26, 68–69, 68n7, 75
Jazīrī, Muḥammad Ibrāhīm al-, *227*
Jewish community, 20, 115, 238
jihad, 222, 319
Jindī, Anwar al-, 249–50, 249n, 318–19, 319n22
Jiritlī, ʿAlī al-, 190, *193*, 212, 264n60
Jirjis, Fawzī, 273–75, 275n114, 308
journalism, 36, 38–40, 68, 72, 74, 144. *See also* journals; newspapers; *names of journals or newspapers*
journalists, 2, 20, 22, 25, 38, 73, 77, 127; and Arab socialist historiography, 284, 290, 293, 293n47, 306–7; and authoritarian pluralism, 313, 316, 318, 322–23, 333; and revolutionary historiography, 255, 262–64; and royal vs. nationalist historiographies, 143–44, 147–49
journals, 2n2, 52–53, 72, 88, 144–45, 159, 303, 313. *See also names of journals*
judicial reforms, 12, 129, 169–70
Jumayʿī, ʿAbd al-Munʿim Ibrāhīm al-, 9, 187, 213n96, 334, 334n85
Jumhūriyya, Al-, 318
Jundī, Jūrj, *119*, 128–30, 129n120

Kabīr, ʿAlī Bey al-, 55
Kāfī fī tārīkh Miṣr al-qadīm wa-l-ḥadīth, al- (A Definitive History of Ancient and Modern Egypt, Shārūbīm), 44–45

Kallīnī, Fahmī, 81
Kāmil, Ḥusayn, Prince, 69–70, 76
Kāmil, Muṣṭafa, 7, 26–27, 27n23, 32, 34–35, 45–47, 47n101, 52, 62–64, 74n26, 251–52, 294; biography of, 149, 221, 317; death of, 68; and National Party, 14, 67, 149, 220–22; and partisan historiography, 220–22, 226, 228, 230, 235, *236*; reburial of, 252; on 'Urābī revolt, 173, 173n154
Kant, 212
Kassem, Maye, 314–15
Katib, Al-, 296, 296n62, 305
Khafīf, Maḥmūd al-, 174n159, 176, *183*
Khalīl, Muḥammad, 126, 132
Khaṭūn, Zaynab, 140
Khiṭaṭ al-tawfīqiyya al-jadīda, Al- (Mubārak), 48–50
khiṭaṭ genre, 7, 8, 30, 41, 48, 50, 81–82, 338
Khrushchev, Nikita, 277, 284
Khulāṣat tārīkh Miṣr al-qadīm wa-l-ḥadīth (A Concise History of Ancient and Modern Egypt, Diyāb), 43
Khūlī, Luṭfī al-, 287
Kifāḥ, Al- (The Struggle), 255
Kifāḥ al-sha'b (The People's Struggle, Ḥasūna), 253
Kitāb al-bahja al-tawfīqiyya fī tārīkh mu'āssis al-'ā'ila al-khudaywiyya (The Grandeur Most Divine in the Account of the Founder of the Khedival Line, Farīd), 47
Kitchener, Herbert, 27n22, 69
Koran, 24n12, 38
Krūmir fī Miṣr (Rushdī), 242
Kurayyim, Muḥammad, 152–54, 152n47, 157, 252, 279

labor movement, 73, 180, 328
landownership, 244, 275–76, 327–29
landscape, 48, 50, 84
Lane, Edward, 284
Lāshīn, 'Abd al-Khāliq, 233–35, 296
Laski, Harold, 241
Lebanese historiography, 45, 53, 161, 199
Le Bon, Gustave, 53, 53n121
legal education, 74, 106, 149
leisured historians, 78, 81–85
Lenin/Leninism, 239, 241, 244, 246, 284n6
Lewis, Bernard, 304
Liberal Constitutionalist Party, 208, 230
liberal school, 187–88, 261, 265, 278. *See also* academic historians
Liberté, 115
La librairie delà renaissance series, 146n17
libraries/librarians, 10, 39, 39n67, 53, 88, 93, 93n5, 98, 100, 264, 310, 330; and 'Ābdīn archive, 102–3, 105–6, 128, 132; and royal vs. nationalist historiographies, 144–46, 145n15, 146n17, 159n84, 164, *182*
linearity (temporal notion of), 7, 37, 45, 48, 58, 61n152, 215
linguistic constructs, 12, 66, 72, 76–77, 79, 83, 85, 245; and 'Ābdīn archive, 104, 106, 141. *See also* semantic field
literacy, 19–20, 22, 29, 63, 73–74, 144–46, 144n8, *145*, 228, 247
literary genres, 16, 30, 48, 59–60, 88, 228
Littmann, Enno, 113
Liwā', Al-, 27, 32, 173n154
Lockman, Zachary, 331n72
London University, 151, 189–90, 212, 304–5
"long nineteenth century," 70
Louis XVI, King of France, 87
Luc-Nancy, Jean, 304
Lukács, Georg, 57
Luṭfī al-Sayyid, Aḥmad, 25, 67, 70, 73–74
Lutfi al-Sayyid-Marsot, Afaf, 128n119

Madhbaḥa, Al- (The Massacre), 317
Maghribī, 'Abd al-Qādir al-, 25
maḥāfiẓ abḥāth, 109
Mahfouz, Naguib, 230, 279–80
Māhir, Aḥmad, 208n75
maḥkama al-shar'iyya, 93n4
Ma'iyya saniyya (Viceregal Cabinet), 108–9
Majalla al-tārīkhiyya al-miṣriyya, Al- (MTM), 211–13, 211n85
Majlis al-nuwwāb, 149n31
Majlis al-shuyūkh, 149n31
Makram, 'Ubayid, *227*
Mamlūk al-shārid, Al- (The Fugitive Mamluk, 1891–92, Zaydān), 55–56, 58
Mamluks, 41n80, 75, 140, 151–52, 155, 157, 252, 274, 306; in historical novels, 55–59
Manār, Al-, 33
Manfalūṭī, Muṣṭafa Luṭfī al-, 59n
manhaj. *See* historical methodology
Manhaj al-baḥth al-tārīkhī ('Uthmān), 200n50, 202n55
Manhaj mufaṣṣal li-l-durūs (An Elaborate Agenda for Research, Ghurbāl), 269
manipulation of source material/translation, 82–83, 128–30, 128n119, 132, 232–35

Manners and Customs of the Modern Egyptians (Lane), 284
Man Who Lost His Shadow, The (Ghānim), 240
Maqrīzī, al-, 7, 48
Marcel, Israel, 238–39, 246
March 1968 Declaration, 312, 325
"March 9" circle, 335
Markaz wathā'iq wa tārīkh Miṣr al-mu'āṣir, 233
Marro, Giovanni, *119*
Marṣafī, al-, Shaykh, 72–73
Marx, Karl, 239–41
Marxist historiography, 2, 10n28, 15–16, 178n176, 179, 213; and Arab socialism, 278, 282–84, 284n6, 286–88, 291–92, 302, 307n115, 308; and authoritarian pluralism, 318, 320–21, 327–28; and crackdown (1959), 277, 277n128; and historical materialism, 220, 240–44, 273, 287; as partisan historiography, 14, 220, 227, 229, 237–47, 237n68, 240n84; as revolutionary historiography, 249, 265, 272–78, 273n101, 281. *See also* socialist historiography
Masā', Al-, 272–73, 291
Mas'ala al-sharqiyya, Al- (The Eastern Question, Kāmil), 47, 47n101
Maspero, Gaston, 113
Massignon, Louis, 113
M.A. theses, *193*, 203–4, *204*, *205*
mausoleums, 226, 252, 302
Mayer, Thomas, 173, 248n1
medieval cultural context, 10, 30, 41, 44–45, 50, 61, 63, 136, 157, 318, 339; and academic historians, 203–4, *205*, 208
Megill, Allan, 201
Meijer, Roel, 256n32, 263, 278, 320–21, 340n4
metahistorical reasoning, 14, 218, 253, 255
metaphors, 47, 57, 136–37, 158, 197, 227, 248–49. *See also* analogies
al-Midān bookshop, 239–40, 240n83
middle class, 21, 25, 73, 273–74, 298, 313, 328; and academic historians, 191, 194, 200n50; and Marxist historians, 237, 243–44; and royal vs. nationalist historiographies, 141, 143, 149, 170–71. See also *effendis*
military campaigns, 56, 61, 97, 107, 116–17, 159–60, 160n88, 161, 190, 194n24. *See also entries beginning with* war
Milner, Alfred, Sir, 22n7, 53, 62, 79, 167, 229
mimetic masses, 189, 215–16, 216–17n110. *See also* Toynbee, Arnold
Ministry of Awqāf, 93, 93n4
Ministry of Culture, 289, 297
Ministry of Education, 112, 148, 164, 175, 189, 208–10, 217n111, 253, 268
Ministry of Foreign Affairs, 98, 306
Ministry of National Guidance, 251, 257, 262, 294
Miramar (1969 film), 230
Miramar (Mahfouz), 230
Mīrzā, 'Aziz, 126
Miṣr, 49–50, 50n110
Miṣr al-mujāhida fī-l-'aṣr al-ḥadīth (Militant Egypt in the Modern Age, al-Rāfi'ī), 253
Miṣr li-l-miṣriyyīn (Egypt for the Egyptians, al-Naqqāsh), 37n63, 44
Miṣr wa-l-Nīl (Sāmī), 85n69
Miṣr wa-l-Sūdān fī awwal'ahd al-iḥtilāl (Egypt and Sudan at the Beginning of the Occupation, 1882–1892, al-Rāfi'ī), 221
Mitchell, Richard, 318, 318n20
Mixed Courts, 22, 93, 129, 165, 169–70, 250n8
Modern Egypt (Cromer), 78–79, 78n40
modern history, Egyptian, 3–11, 8n25, 11nn30,31, 337, 339, 342; and 'Ābdīn archive, 12–13, 114, 123–32, 126n111, 134–40; and academic historians, 194, 203–5, 204n62, *204*, *205*, 207, 214–17; and Arab socialist historiography, 284–85, 284n8, 287, 290, 293–94, 303, 305–7; and authoritarian pluralism, 318, 321, 324, 333; and Cromer, 78–79; hybrid nature of in Ottoman Egypt, 11, 30, 36, 43–44, 60, 63; as literary genre, 88–90; and partisan historiography, 230, 233, 243; and revolutionary historiography, 267–69; and royal vs. nationalist historiographies, 13, 141, 144–45, 149, 150–77; and semantic field, 66, 77; and space, perception of, 51–52; and time, perception of, 38, 43–45
modernity and history, 3–5, 4n14, 8–10, 8n25, 11–12, 14, 20, 320, 338; and 'Ābdīn archive, 92, 137, 139; and academic historians, 13, 195, 216; and Arab socialist historiography, 287, 309, 309n125; and Cromer, 78–79; from global perspective, 16–18; and Marxist historians, 220, 243; and partisan historiography, 220, 228, 230, 236, 243; and revolutionary historiography, 263, 278; and royal vs. nationalist historiographies, 13, 143, 157, 176, 179, 184; and semantic field, 65, 73–74, 77, 89; and subjectivity, 47, 62
Momigliano, Arnaldo, 89
monarchic authority, 12–13, 66, 70, 75–76, 75n32, 81–85, 87–88, 88n86; and 'Ābdīn archive, 137–

monarchic authority *(continued)*
38; and academic historians, 208–11; and Arab socialist historiography, 299, 303; and authoritarian pluralism, 315, 318, 318n18, 319n22, 320, 328; and official nationalism, 76–77, 88, 171; and revolutionary historiography, 258, 261nn48,49, 262, 264–65, 265n67; and royal vs. nationalist historiographies, 153–54, 168–69, 172, 176–81; and Ṣabrī, 87, 134, 137, 147–48. *See also* royal historiography; *names of kings*
monarchic history. *See* dynastic history
monopoly in history writing, 203, 217–19, 293, 300
Moosa, Matti, 40n75, 41n78, 54, 56
moral value of history, 52–53, 57–58, 61n154, 76, 84, 167, 303–4; and partisan historiography, 223–24, 230, 241; and royal vs. nationalist historiographies, 155, 155n63, 169, 184
MTM. See *Majalla al-tārīkhiyya al-miṣriyya, Al- (MTM)*
Mu'ayyad, Al-, 27, 27n23
Mubārak, 'Alī, 7, 48–50, 49n106, 81
Mubarak, Husni, 15, 311, 313–15, 324–27, 330
Muḥammad 'Alī, 10, 11n31, 12, 339, 341; and 'Ābdīn archive, 97–98, 98n22, 103–5, 107, 109–11, 116–17, 122, 125–26, 128, 129n125, 134–35, 137; and academic historians, 189–91, 194nn23,24, 195, 206, 209–11, 211n87, 216, 216–17n110; and Arab socialist historiography, 295; and authoritarian pluralism, 334; centennial anniversary of inauguration, 12, 31, 35, 49, 52, 60, 64, 261; and Daftarkhāne, 95, 95n10; as founder of modern Egypt, 30, 31–35, 32nn46,47, 37n63, 47, 49, 51, 57, 61n154, 62–63, 63nn161,164, 79, 82–84; in historical novels, 55–59; and Marxist historians, 241, 243, 274; and revolutionary historiography, 250n8, 261, 261n49, 274; and royal vs. nationalist historiographies, 141, 151, 154–63, 168, 171, 177; and Taymūr family library, 93n5
Muḥammad 'Alī al-Kabīr (Ghurbāl), 159, 209–10, 210n81, 216
Muḥammad 'Alī (play), 31
Muḥammad 'Alī (Thābit), 158
Muḥammad Farīd ramz al-ikhlāṣ wa-l-taḍḥiya (Muhammad Farid, the Symbol of Loyalty and Sacrifice, al-Rāfi'ī), 222
Muḥammad, Prophet, 23–24, 317
Muhandis, al-, 21. *See also* Fahmī, Maḥmūd
Muḥyyī' al-Dīn, Khālid, 272
Muqaṭṭam, Al-, 27, 158
Muqtaṭaf, Al-, 21, 53, 165n114
Mursī, Fu'ād, 243–46, 265
Mūsa, Salāma, 241, 246
Mushkilat al-fallāḥ (Sa'd), 243
Muslim Brotherhood, 15, 219, 230, 249n, 250, 250n3, 266, 311, 314, 316–21, 318n18, 323, 340–41
Muslims, 20, 26, 149, 188, 209, 210n81, 222, 269, 322
Mussolini, 257n38
Muṣṭafa Kāmil (film), 226, 252
Muṣṭafa Kāmil: Bā'ith al-ḥaraka al-qawmiyya (Mustafa Kamil: Instigator of the National Movement, al-Rāfi'ī), 221
Muṣṭafa, Aḥmad 'Abd al-Raḥīm, *193*, 233, 293–94, 297n67, 303, 306
Muṣṭalaḥ al-tārīkh (Rustum), 199–201
Mutawallī, Maḥmūd, 310, 327–28
Mu'tazila, 24–25, 24nn12,13
Mutual Brotherhood Society, 68
Muwayliḥī, Muḥammad, 93–94, 99

Nabsh al-hadhayān min tārīkh Jurjī Zaydān (Excavating for Nonsense in the History of Jurjī Zaydān, al-Ḥalawānī), 39–40, 40n75, *42*
Nadīm, 'Abd Allah al-, 22–23, 25
nadwa (1984), 332–33
Naf'ī, Maḥmūd, 126, 132
Nagel, Thomas, 303
Naguib, Muḥammad, 251–52, 261, 263, 266n69
Nahḍa, 3, 17, 21, 25, 28, 72, 79, 259
nahḍawī, 25, 92
Naḥḥās, Joseph, *227*
Naḥḥās, Muṣṭafa al-, 208–9, 208n75, 228, 231–33, 235, 249, 323
"Naḥnu wa-l-Shuyū'īya" (Communism and Us, Haykal), 283
Naḥūm, Ḥayyim, 115, *119*, 116n92
Najjar, Fawzi al-, 290n28
Nallino, Carlo, 113
Napoleon, 124, 151, 153–54, 243
Napoleon III, 167
Naqqāsh, Rajā' al-, 290n28, 305, 307
Naqqāsh, Salīm al-, 37n63, 44–45
Nash'āt, Ḥasan, 106
Nāṣirīyya, Al- (Imām), 312
Nāṣiriyya school, 81
Nasser, Gamal Abd al-, 2n5, 234, 283; assassination attempt on, 266; and authoritarian plu-

ralism, 312, 317, 322, 326, 330, 332; death of, 312; and revolutionary historiography, 252–53, 255, 256n36, 257–58, 258n43, 260–63, 266–67, 272, 274, 277. *See also* Nasserism
Nasser 56 (1996 film), 258n43
Nasserism, 15, 49n109, 138, 254–55, 257–58, 257n38, 263, 268, 272, 277; and Arab socialist historiography, 282–83, 285, 308–10; and authoritarian pluralism, 311–13, 312–13n2, 315–16, 319, 323–27, 329
national allegory, 14, 220, 228–37, *236*, 246–47; chronic debates of, 231–37
National Archive, 138
National Charter, 283, 286–89, 292, 299, 325
National Congress of Popular Forces, 283
National Corpus *(al-mawsūʿa al-waṭaniyya)*, 150, 150nn33,34, 151n37, 221
national holidays, 31–32, 35
nationalism, 3, 5–7, 9–12, 67–71, 68n5, 70, 70n12, 85, 87, 89, 91, 235, 338–41, 340n4; and ʿĀbdīn archive, 91, 114, 125, 128–30, 129n125, 133–34, 139–40; and academic historians, 14, 189, 194, 204, 208, 211–12, 233–35, 247; and Arab socialist historiography, 284–85, 287, 290, 292, 300, 302n89; and authoritarian pluralism, 319–20, 322, 328, 329n64, 332, 336; and chronicles, 81, 83–85; and de-Ottomanization, 71, 79–80; and Marxist historians, 220, 243–45, 272, 276–78; and national allegory, 14, 220, 228–37, 236; and official nationalism, 76–77, 88, 88n86, 171; in Ottoman Egypt, 19, 22, 27–29, 34, 50, 63–64; and partisan historiography, 13–14, 220–37, 243–45, 247; and revolutionary historiography, 14, 249, 251–59, 254n26, 262, 272, 276–78; and royal vs. nationalist historiographies, 13, 143, 146, 146n19, 148–79, 151n37, 178n176, *182–83*, 184–85; and semantic field, 73–75. *See also* National Party; Wafd
nationalization, 283; of Suez Canal (1956), 14, 252–53, 253n18, 255, 258, 258n44, 263–64, 272, 276n124
National Library, 138
National Party, 12–14, 27, 67–69, 73–75, 77, 251, 265, 294, 303; and night schools, 74; and partisan historiography, 220–26, 224n22, 230; vs. royal historiography, 148–49, 168
Native Courts, 65
Navarin (Douin), *120*, 121
Navarin, battle of, 116
Nawāfil, Hind, 26
Nazi Germany/Nazism, 303, 309
Nazlī, Princess, 228
nepotism, 312
New Dawn group (al-Fajr al-jadīd), 238–40, 242–43
new historicism, 28
New Islamist school *(al-wassaṭiyya)*, 321
newspapers, 19, 32–33, 40, 52, 82n55, 237–38, 313, 333; and Arab socialist historiography, 293, 296, 303; and revolutionary historiography, 262, 271–73; and royal vs. nationalist historiographies, 141, 144, 159; and semantic field, 72, 74, 77
night schools, 74
Nile corniche, 297, 297n70
Nimr, Fāris, 20–21
1987 conference. *See* "Commitment and Objectivity in Contemporary Egyptian Historiography" (1987 conference)
Nobel Prize, 302
Novick, Peter, 218
Nūbār Pasha, 22
Nuqrāshī, Maḥmūd Fahmī al-, 208n75, 219, 319

objectivity, 2, 7, 10, 159, 337, 339; and ʿĀbdīn archive, 13, 13n, 92, 132–33, 133n141; and academic historians, 188, 196, 200–201, 203, 207, 213–14, 218, 271; and Arab socialist historiography, 286, 288–89, 291, 304; and authoritarian pluralism, 324–25, 333–34; and partisan historiography, 233–34, 245; and revolutionary historiography, 260, 266, 271–72
official nationalism, 76–77, 88, 171
oral archiving, 335, 335n88
Order of Ismāʿīl, 105
organic historiographical continuity, 41, 63, 89–90, 99–101, 159, 214–15
Orientalists, 38–39, 78, 102, 113, 151, 177, 187
Orwell, George, 311
Ottoman Egypt, historicizing of, 3, 6–7, 11–12, 11n30, 19–65, 222, 340; and ʿĀbdīn archive, 13, 93, 97, 99n28, 102, 111, 116–17, 122, 135, 139–40; and academic historians, 189, 191, 208, 216, 216–17n110; and Arab socialist historiography, 287, 300n80, 308n119; and authoritarian pluralism, 322, 331–32, 331n74, 332n76; background of, 19–30; debate over founder paradigm/thesis, 31–35, 31n35, 60–64, 61nn151,152,154, 63nn161,164; and de-Ottomanization, 12, 70–72, 71n14, 75, 77, 79–81, 85; and historical novels, 30, 52–59,

Ottoman Egypt *(continued)*
59n; and revolutionary historiography, 255, 257, 268–69, 269–70n84, 274; and royal vs. nationalist historiographies, 149, 151–52, 159, 167–68, 172; and space, perception of, 11, 30, 36, 48–52, 49nn106,109, 62; and subjectivity, 11, 30, 36, 46–48, 61–62; and time, perception of, 3, 11–12, 30, 36, 37–46, 61
Ottoman language, 103–7, 105n52, 109, 111, 115, *118–19*, 126–27, 162, 308n119

Pan-Arabism, 14, 160, 204, 211n87, 249, 254–57, 256nn32–37, 268, 277, 282, 340, 340n4
Pan-Islamism, 19, 26, 222
paper mill *(kāghid-khāne)*, 96, 96n15
Parliament, 75–76, 106, 149, 168–69, 207
partisan historiography, 13–14, 219–47; chronic debates of, 231–37; and Marxist historians, 14, 220, 227, 229, 237–46, 237n68, 247; and national allegory, 14, 220, 228–37, *236*, 246–47; and al-Rāfi'ī, 220–27, 223n16, 224n22, 225n26, 234–35; and Wafd, 220, 223–30, 224n22, *227*, 232–34, 244
paternalism, 26, 312–14, 329n64
patriotism, 14, 22, 34, 160, 165, 206, 230, 233, 290–91, 326
patronage, 189, 208, 210, 211n85, 213, 278, 314
peasantry, 25–26, 111, 116, 158n78, 167, 194n24, 195, 216–17n110; and authoritarian pluralism, 313, 328; and partisan historiography, 243–44; and revolutionary historiography, 258, 274–76
People's Liberation (Taḥrīr al-sha'b), 238–39
periodization, 4, 43, 45–46, 58–59, 61, 82, 337, 340; and 'Ābdīn archive, 104–5, 107, 107n59, 122, 122n104, 134–35
Pharaonic past, 5, 11n30, 51, 63, 84, 89, 139, 151, 151n37, 180, 217, 226, 269, 302n89
Ph.D. dissertations, *193*, 203–4, *204*, *205*, 330–31, 334
Philipp, Thomas, 54–55
Piterberg, Gabriel, 187
plagiarism, 1, 199, 330, 330n68
pluralistic historiography, 15, 247, 259, 261, 263–65
police state, 240, 245, 312–13, 329
Polites, Athanasios, 115, *119*, 122
political lexicon, 29–30, 49–50, 49n109, 66, 71, 77. *See also* semantic field
political memoirs, 1, 84, 180n178, 186, 228, 232–34, 232n45; and Arab socialist historiography, 290, 292–94, 292n43, 296, 307–8; and authoritarian pluralism, 317, 322–23, 333–34
political parties, 2, 9, 12–14, 66–67, 70, 76–77, 148, 175, 268, 274, 313; and partisan historiography, 220, 224, 230, 232, 244, 246–47. *See also names of political parties*
political slogans, 74, 251, 253n18, 300
political violence, 68, 68n7, 76, 180, 219, 223, 223n16, 319–20
Popper, Karl, 308–9
popular-nationalist historiography, 10n28, 13, 341; and academic historians, 188, 191, 195, 200, 202–3, 206, 209, 209n78, 211; vs. royal historiography, 149–51, 154, 167, 176. *See also* nationalism; *names of popular-nationalist historians*
popular struggle, 86, 152–53, 253–54
populism, 16, 147, 188, 206, 257, 257nn38,39, 319
Port Said (Būr sa'īd) (film), 254
postmodernism, 17–18, 28, 338, 342
Poverty of Historicism, The (Popper), 308–9
premodern historical thought, 3, 8, 11–12, 136, 150n35, 214–17, 268. *See also* Islamic historiography
Press Law (1881), 68
Press Law (1909), 68–69, 68n5, 74
printing press, 190, 195
Prisoner of Abu Za'bal, The (Sajīn abū za'bal) (film), 254
PRO. *See* British Public Record Office (PRO)
production, means of, 241, 244–45, 274, 283, 285
professionalism, 7, 9, 14, 73, 88–89, 327, 332–36; and academic historians, 13, 188, 196–203, 196n30, 197n33, 199n43, 207–8, 213–17, 216–17nn110,111; and royal vs. nationalist historiographies, 143–44, 147–48
progress, 8, 10, 22, 26, 29, 79, 84, 156, 215–17n110, 221, 228, 246, 258, 278, 286, 288, 329, 337; and debate over founder paradigm/thesis, 33, 61n154, 62, 64; in historical novels, 53, 58; and time, perception of, 3–4, 45–46
"proper historical knowledge," 13, 137
provincial archives, 95–97, 97n17
public archives. *See* archives
publications spéciales, 112, 112n78, 115, 116, *118–19*, *120*, 121–22
public opinion, 27, 74, 145–46, 146n17, 169–70, 174, 208, 325, 332, 336
publishing houses, 88, 144, 238–39, 246, 255, 262, 264, 266, 272, 314, 316–17

Qāhira, Al- (newspaper), 265
Qāsim, General, 277
Qāsimī, Jamāl al-Dīn al-, 25
Qaṣr al-ʿAynī hospital, 93
Qiṣṣat thawrat 23 yūliū (Ḥamrūsh), 323
qiyās, 24n12
Quddūs, Iḥsan ʿAbd al-, 263
Qurāni, Aḥmad Ḥusayn al-, *227*
Quṭb, Sayyid, 317

Radd rannān ʿala nabsh al-hadhayān (An Echoing Riposte to the Excavating of Nonsense, Zaydān), 40, 40n75
radio broadcasts, 146, 215, 254, 256, 261–62, 261n48, 269, 269n82
Raḍwān, Fatḥī, 262; and partisan historiography, 222, 226, 234–35; and revolutionary historiography, 249, 250n3, 251–52; and rewriting history, 302
Rāfiʿī, ʿAbd al-Raḥmān al-, 13–14, 32n47; 336; on ʿAbbās, 162–64; and ʿĀbdīn archive, 130, 134, 137, 164; and academic historians, 187, 187n7, 189, 191, 206, 213, 213n96; and Arab socialist historiography, 292, 292n43, 301–2, 302nn89,92; death of, 159n84, 213, 302–3; and de-Ottomanization, 71, 150; on Ibrāhīm, 160n90, 161; on Ismāʿīl, 164–71; on Muḥammad ʿAlī, 155, 155nn60,62, 156–57, 157n73, 158–59; National Corpus of, 150, 150nn33,34, 151n37, 221; and partisan historiography, 220–27, 223n16, 224n22, 225n26, 234–35; and revolutionary historiography, 249–55, 250nn7,8, 255n30, 260, 265–67, 265n67, 266n69, 276; vs. royal historiography, 142, 147–59, 149nn28,31, 150nn33,35, 151n37, 161–71, 164n106, 173–79, 178nn174,176, *182–83*, 184; on ʿUrābī revolt, 173–74, 173nn151,154, 174nn160,162
Raḥmān, ʿĀʾisha ʿAbd al-, 203
Rajabī, Aḥmad al-, 35
Ramaḍān, ʿAbd al-ʿAẓīm, 207, 233–35, 318, 318n18, 325–26
Ramaḍān, Muḥammad Rifʿat, *193*
rationality. *See* reasoning, modes of
Raymond, André, 331n73
Raz, Ronen, 113, 177
reading. *See* literacy
reasoning, modes of, 5, 7, 11, 13, 19, 21, 23–24, 24n12, 29, 113, 137, 337, 339
Recueil de la correspondance de Mohamed Aly, Khédive d'Égypte, 1807–1848 (Bey), 98
reforms, 10n28; and ʿĀbdīn archive, 129, 135; and academic historians, 190; agrarian, 190, 239, 243, 258, 258n44, 274–76, 282, 342; and authoritarian pluralism, 312–14, 321, 326; constitutional, 129, 169; and Cromer, 62, 78–79; educational, 313–14; and Islamic reformism, 17, 23–27; judicial, 12, 129, 169–70; and March 1968 Declaration, 312, 325; and Marxist historians, 241–43, 245; and Muḥammad ʿAlī, 33–34, 47, 61–62, 155–56, 190; and revolutionary historiography, 263; and royal vs. nationalist historiographies, 155–56, 156n70, 162, 163n103, 167, 169; of universities, 298–303
registries *(sijillāt)*, 92, 108, 108n65, 110–11, 110n74, 328
Reid, Donald, 114n82, 207
Rejwan, Nissim, 285–86
republican order, 12, 75, 86
respect des fonds (principle of provenance), 100–102, 107n59, 109–11, 127
respect pour l'ordre primitif (maintenance of original order), 100–102, 111
retrospective analysis, 41, 41n80, 43, 46
Return of Consciousness, The (al-Ḥakīm), 312
revelation, Islamic, 24
revisionist historiography, 1–2, 35n56, 161, 234–35; and Arab socialist historiography, 284–86, 292, 295, 297, 298–309; and authoritarian pluralism, 323–27, 331; and revolutionary historiography, 250, 250nn7,8, 267, 275
Revolution (1919), 12, 70, 86, 88, 88n86, 89, 91, 152, 171n142, 189, 323; and Arab socialist historiography, 284, 287, 290; and partisan historiography, 221–23, 223n16, 229, 244; and revolutionary historiography, 251, 253, 253n18, 255
Revolution (1952), 14, 75n32, 76, 258n44, 263; and academic historians, 197, 206–7, 212–13; and Arab socialist historiography, 296, 298, 308; and authoritarian pluralism, 323–28, 334; and partisan historiography, 224, 230, 232; and revolutionary historiography, 248, 250–53, 261–62, 266n69, 267, 276–77, 280; and royal vs. nationalist historiographies, 142, 148, 150, 150nn33,35, 174–75
Revolutionary Command Council (RCC), 283, 326
revolutionary events (1881–82), 21–22, 243, 251, 253
revolutionary historiography, 248–81, 248n1; and academic historians, 14, 249–50, 256,

revolutionary historiography *(continued)* 260, 263–65, 267–72, 270n85; and actualist philosophy of history, 257–60; and intellectual networks, 261–66, 262n52, 264n60; and Marxist historians, 249, 265, 272–78, 273n101, 281; and Pan-Arabism, 249, 254–57, 256nn32–37, 268
La révolution égyptienne (Ṣabrī), 86, 88
revolutions, popular, 22, 221, 254–55. *See* also ʿUrābī revolt; *entries beginning with* Revolution/revolutionary
Revue des Études Napoléoniennes, 115
rewriting of history. *See* revisionist historiography
RGS. *See* Royal Geographical Society (RGS)
Ridā, Rashīd, 25, 41, 64, 70, 80n51
al-Rifāʿī mosque, 93n4
Rifʿat, Muḥammad, 105n52, 147–48, 175, 179, *182*, 189, 208, 271
Risāla, Al-, 176, 180, 200
Risālat al-kalim al-thmān (Treatise on Eight Words, al-Marṣafī), 72–73
Risālat al-tawḥīd (Epistle of Divine Unity, ʿAbduh), 24
Rivlin, Helen, 109n70, 126–27, 295–96, 295n58
Rizq, Yunān Labīb, 310, 327
Robinson, Chase, 45
Royal Geographical Society (RGS), 93, 106, 111–12, 112n78, 115, 130, 158, 175, 175n165, 208, 210, 210n82, 299
Royal Historical Society, *183*, 207–14, 210nn82,83, 213n96. *See also* Egyptian Historical Society (EHS)
royal historiography, 71; on ʿAbbās, 162–64, 163n103; and ʿĀbdīn archive, 91–92, 104–5, 108–12, 114, 116–17, 122–36, 122n103, 133n141, 139–40; and academic historians, 188, 191, 194–96, 198, 208–11; and Arab socialist historiography, 295, 299, 303, 306; on Ibrāhīm, 159–62; on Ismāʿīl, 164–72, 165nn112,114, 166n117; on Muḥammad ʿAlī, 156–59; vs. partisan historiography, 219, 243–45; vs. popular-nationalists, 13, 146–50, 154, 156–79, 171n143, 178n176, *182–83*, 184; vs. revolutionary historiography, 248n1, 250; on ʿUrābī revolt, 172–74. *See also* monarchic authority; *names of royal historians*
royal project. *See* ʿĀbdīn project
Rüsen, Jören, 17
Rushdī, Aḥmad Ṣāliḥ, 242–43, 245
Rustum, Asad, *119*, 126, 161–62, 199–201, 216
Ṣabrī, Muḥammad, 7, 85–89, 85n72, 86n73, 256n33; and ʿĀbdīn archive, 134, 137; and revolutionary historiography, 254; vs. royal historiography, 147–48, 147n22, 152, 154, 154–55n59, 156, 161–62, 166, 166n115, 170, 173–74, 179, *182–83*
Ṣabrī, Mūsa, 307
Saʿd, Aḥmad Ṣādiq, 243
Saʿd al-Dīn, Ibrāhīm, 305
Sadat, Anwar, 15, 234, 311–14, 318, 323–27, 323n36, 329–30, 329n64, 332; assassination of, 314, 316, 326–27
Sadat, Jihan, 312
Saʿdist Party, 208, 208n75
Saʿd Pasha. *See* Zaghlūl, Saʿd
Saʿd Zaghlūl bayna al-yamīn wa-l-yasār (Saʿd Zaghlūl between Right and Left, al-Saʿīd), 237
Saffūf, Fu'ād, 165n114
Safran, Nadav, 305
Ṣafwat, Muḥammad Muṣṭafa, 205
Saʿīd, 82, 84, 98, 125, 161, 164, 167
Saʿīd, Aḥmad, 256
Saʿīd, Amīn, 249, 255, 255n30, 257, 268, 291
Saʿīd, Rifʿat al-, 237, 318
Saʿīd, Rushdī, 290n28
Ṣalāḥ al-Dīn, 32n46, 206
Ṣāliḥ, ʿAbbās, 307
Ṣāliḥ, Ilyās, 39–40, 40n75
Sālim, Ṣāliḥ, 261
Sāmī, Amīn, 81–85, 82nn55,56, 83n62, 85n69, 98, 122, 128
Sāmī, Muṣṭafa, 288
Sāmī Sharaf, 326
Sammān, ʿAbd Allāh al-, 318n18
Sammarco, Angelo: and ʿĀbdīn archive, 12, 114–15, 116, *118–19*, 121, 121n98, 125–26, 130–33, 136n154, 139; vs. popular-nationalists, 147n22, 163–66, 165n112, 168, 170, *182–83*
Sanhūrī, ʿAbd al-Razzāq al-, 298
Saraj, Sāmī, 126
Sarhank, Ismāʿīl, 7, 11, 43–47, 44n84, 77
Sarrūf, Yaʿqūb, 21
Sartre, Jean-Paul, 300
Sato, Masayuki, 337–38
Sayyid, Aḥmad Luṭfī al-, 335
Sayyid, Jalāl al-, 288, 290n28
scandal, politics of, 27, 285, 292, 330n67
School of Oriental and African Studies (SOAS) conference, 304–6
Schorske, Carl, 29

Schwartz, Hillel, 238
scientific inquiry, 3, 10, 12–13, 21, 23, 37–38, 78, 82–83, 324, 334, 337; and ʿĀbdīn archive, 13, 92, 100, 132–33, 132n137, 133n141, 136–37; and academic historians, 196–97, 200–202, 214–15, 218; and Arab socialist historiography, 284–85, 287–88, 291, 293, 302–4, 308–9, 309n125; and Marxist historians, 15, 241, 245–46, 249, 272–78, 284–85, 287–88; and royal vs. nationalist historiographies, 147, 162–63, 166, 181, 185
scientific socialism, 249, 272–78, 284–85, 287–88, 308–9, 309n125
Scott, Walter, 53, 57
Secretariat of the Propaganda and Socialist Thought, 292
secret societies, 26–27, 67
secularism, 4, 17, 20–21, 25, 29, 37, 70, 214, 316, 319–20, 322, 337, 340
self-congratulatory historiography, 14, 267, 279
self-reflection, 332–35
Selim, Samah, 36n
semantic field, 12, 65–66, 71–77
seriality (temporal notion), 43, 46
Shāfiʿī, Shuhdī ʿAṭiyya al-, 239, 273, 276, 308
Shafīq, Aḥmad, 81, 83–85, 83n64, 122, 260, 299
Shafīq, Muḥammad, 98
Shahdāwī, ʿAlī al-, 290
Shams al mushriqa, Al- (The Rising Sun, Kāmil), 45–47
Sharʿawī, ʿAlī, 87
Sharīʿa Courts, 92, 93n4
Sharīf Pasha government, 169
Sharqāwī, al-, 275
Shārūbīm, Mikhāʾīl, 7, 44–47, 77
Shaw, Stanford, 110, 110n74, 331n73
Shawkānī, Muḥammad Ibn ʿAlī al-, 25
Shawqī, Muḥammad, 261n49
Shayyāl, Jamāl al-Dīn al-, 6–8, 6n18, 8n25, 36, 60, 88, *193*, 305, 305n104
Shinnāwī, ʿAbd al-ʿAziz Muḥammad al-, *193*, 194n24, 198, 198n39, 264–65, 322
Shukrī, Muḥammad Fuʾād, *183*, 205, 205n65, 300
Ṣidqī, Ismāʿīl, 168, 180, 231–32, 240, 244, 292
silence, 2, 2n5, 6–7, 6n18, 261, 290, 338; and ʿĀbdīn archive, 13n, 92, 111, 121, 135, 140
Sivan, Emmanuel, 204n61
slander, 40, 165, 181
slavery/slave trade, 83n64, 111, 117, 167
Smiles, Samuel, 53, 53n121
SOAS conference. *See* School of Oriental and African Studies (SOAS) conference
socialist historiography, 14–15, 143, 207, 237, 240n84, 241, 244, 329; and Arab socialism, 278, 282–310; and National Charter, 283, 286–89, 292, 299; and political memoirs, 290, 292–94, 292n43, 296, 307–8; and rewriting of history, 284–86, 292, 295, 297, 298–309; and scientific socialism, 249, 272–78, 284–85, 287–88; and state documents, 289–98; theory of, 286–89. *See also* Marxist historiography
Société d'économie politique, de statistique, et de législation, 113
Society for the Revival of the Nation, 27
Society of the Muslim Brothers, The (Mitchell), 318, 318n20
socioeconomic factors, 92, 251, 274–77, 298, 307–8, 310, 327–29
Sommaire des archives turques du Caire (Deny), 106–7
Sonbol, Amira, 335
Sorbonne, 85, 86n73, 88
source material, 47n101, 71n17, 272, 275, 341; and ʿĀbdīn archive, 10, 92, 104, 121–22, 122n103, 128–30, 140; and academic historians, 194n23, 197–200, 197n33, 202, 207–8, 213, 215–16; and Arab socialist historiography, 284, 284n8, 292–94, 292n43, 296–97, 300, 304, 306, 308n119, 310; and authoritarian pluralism, 323–26, 328, 330–31, 333, 336; and chronicles, 44–45, 78, 82–84; manipulation of, 82–83, 128–30, 128n119, 132, 232–35; and partisan historiography, 225, 232–35; and royal vs. nationalist historiographies, 158–59, 163–64, 175, 184. *See also* archives; state documents
South/Southeast Asian historiography, 342–43
sovereignty, national, 51, 86, 168–70, 176, 178, 221, 297
sovereignty, popular, 12, 73, 75
Soviet Union, 246, 277–78, 283–84, 303, 309
space, perception of, 11, 30, 36, 48–52, 49nn106,109, 62, 82
Special Tribunal, 64–65
Spencerism, 19, 53
Spengler, Oswald, 89n90, 215
Stalin/Stalinism, 239, 242, 309
state documents, 36, 45; and ʿĀbdīn archive, 93–100, 98n22, 115; and academic historians, 197–98, 197n33, 213; and Arab socialist his-

state documents *(continued)*
toriography, 289–98, 300, 306; and authoritarian pluralism, 311, 323–27, 323n37, 329, 333, 335. *See also* source material
state-guidance *(tawjīh)*, 1, 263, 278, 303–4, 306–7, 324–26, 329
Stone, Elizabeth, 115n87
strikes, 68, 69n8, 74, 180
student demonstrations, 2, 221, 314
Study of History, A (Toynbee), 215, 269
subjectivity, 11, 30, 36, 46–48, 57, 61–62, 253
Sublime Porte, 122, 128
Sudan agreement (1899), 50, 68, 221
Suez Canal, 22, 68, 98, 121, 121n98, 155, 167, 219, 263–64; nationalization of (1956), 14, 252–53, 253n18, 255, 258, 258n44, 263–64, 272, 276n124
Suez Canal Company, 258, 263
superstructure, 241, 244–45
Surbūnī, al-, 86. *See also* Ṣabrī, Muḥammad
Syria: Egyptian occupation of (1831–48), 56, 97, 107, 116, 160, 160n88; unification with (1958), 258n44, 277, 326, 340
Syrian community, 7, 20–21, 25, 27, 39–40. *See also* Zaydān, Jurjī
Syrian nationalism, 254–55, 254n26

Ṭabarī, al-, 44
Tagher, Jacques, *119*, 128–30, 129nn120,125, 211n85
Ṭāhir, Muḥammad, 210
Ṭahṭāwī, Rifāʿa al-, 7, 43
Takwīn Miṣr (The Formation of Egypt, Ghurbāl), 216, 269
tamṣīr. See Egyptianization project
Ṭanāḥī, Ṭāhir al-, 163n103
Taqwīm al-Nīl (Almanac of the Nile, Sāmī), 82–84
Tārīkh al-tamaddun al-islāmī (History of Islamic Civilization, Zaydān), 54
Tārīkh Miṣr al-ḥadīth (A Modern History of Egypt, Zaydān), 37–39, 41, 41n80, 43, 47, 79
Tārīkh al-mufāwaḍāt (Ghurbāl), 206
Tārīkh bi-lā wathāʾiq (History without Sources, ʿAbduh), 325
Taṭawwur al-raʾsmāliyya wa kifāḥ al-ṭabaqāt fī Miṣr (The Development of Capitalism and Class Struggle in Egypt, Mursī), 243–44
Tawfīq, Khedive, 35, 83, 172, 174–75, 250n8
Tawfīq, Muḥammad, 95n8, *192*
tawḥīd (Islamic concept of), 24, 24n12
Taymūr, Aḥmad, 93, 106
Taymūr family, 93n5
textbooks, 148, 175, *182*, 190, 202n55, 226, 253–54, 259–60, 330, 336
textual hierarchy, 15, 184, 309, 311, 334, 336
Thābit, Karīm, 158, 158n80, *183*, *227*
Thawrat sanat 1919 (The 1919 Revolution, al-Rāfiʿī), 223
third-worldism, 229, 239, 256n36, 272, 282
Thompson, E. P., 331
time, perception of, 3, 11–12, 30, 36, 37–46, 61, 82, 110, 116, 260, 286, 337; and Zaydān, 41, 41n80, 43, 57, 59
Toledano, Ehud, 71–72, 71nn14,17, 162n97
torture, 265, 276, 312, 317
Toynbee, Arnold, 89n90, 147, 158, 187, 189–90, 208–9, 212, 215–16, 216–17nn108,110,111, 269–71, 291, 300
trade unionism, 74, 180, 315
translations, 52–53, 53n121, 87, 132, 209, 212; and ʿĀbdīn archive, 103–4, 105, 109–11, 126–30, 128n119, 164; manipulation of, 82–83, 128–30, 128n119, 132, 232–35; and Marxist historians, 239–41; and partisan historiography, 232–35, 239–41; and royal vs. nationalist historiographies, 151, 154n55, 160n89, 164, 165n114, 177, *182–83*
truthfulness, historical, 14, 39–40, 78, 84, 181, 184, 324–25, 339; and ʿĀbdīn archive, 132–34, 132n137, 137; and academic historians, 188, 196–201, 206, 214, 218; and Arab socialist historiography, 288–89, 303; and historical novels, 56–57; and partisan historiography, 233, 245, 247; and revolutionary historiography, 248–50, 260, 279–80
Ṭura prison, 317
Turkish elite, 71, 71n14, 81, 140
Turkish language, 25, 34, 80–81, 83, 85; and ʿĀbdīn archive, 106, 108n62, 109–10, 109n70; and royal vs. nationalist historiographies, 149, 171–72
Ṭūsūn, ʿUmar, Prince, 81, 88, 88n86, 147, 155, 160, 163n103, *182*, 199

UAR. *See* United Arab Republic (UAR)
ʿUbayd, Makram, 292
ʿUlaysh of al-Azhar, 24n13
ultranationalists, 67–69, 69n8, 76, 173n154, 234. *See also* National Party
ʿUmar b. al-Khaṭāb,, 206
ʿUmar Makram, 31n43, 154–55, 157, 251–53, 279, 334

'Umar Makram mosque, 252, 302
Umma Party, 67, 69–70, 73, 75
unions, 74, 180, 315
United Arab Republic (UAR), 254, 257, 282
universal value, 3, 10, 13n, 17, 133, 177, 209, 215, 338, 341
University of Alexandria, 198n39, 200, 202n55, 204, *204*, *205*
University of Chicago, 161, 199
University of Liverpool, 189, 205n65
upper class, 22, 237, 243, 313
'Urābī, Aḥmad, 172–74, 248n1, 251–52, 255n30
'Urābī revolt, 31, 35, 44, 72, 116, 170, 172–76, 221
Urabists, 21, 44
urban literates, 19, 228, 262
'Uthmān, 'Uways, *227*
'Uthmān, Ḥasan, 196, 200–202, 200n50, 202n55, 205, 208
utopianism, 15, 257, 278, 287
'Uwaynī, Muḥammad 'Alī, 126

Vatikiotis, P. J., 305
visual history, 38–39, 43, 51
Vitalis, Robert, 331n72
Von Ranke, Leopold, 28

wafd, 70
Wafd, 12, 14, 70, 77, 86, 88, 147, 168, 208–9, 208n75, 290; and authoritarian pluralism, 313, 318, 320, 323; and partisan historiography, 220, 223–30, 224n22, *227*, 232–34, 244; and revolutionary historiography, 250, 263, 265
Wallerstein, Immanuel, 331
waqā'i' al-miṣriyya, Al-, 95, 110
war (1948), 206, 212, 254n26
war (1956), 291
war (1967), 207, 234, 312, 324–25
war (October 1973), 311–13, 324
Wardānī, Ibrāhīm, 68
Ware, Lewis Beier, 40n75
war in Yemen, 257, 282, 312, 325
wasteland thesis, 8n25, 13n
waṭan, 79–80
Webb, Beatrice, 241
Webb, Sidney, 241
Western Historical Thinking: An Intercultural Debate, 17
Western historiographical model. *See* European/Western historiographical model
wheat subsidy riots (1977), 314, 329
White, Hayden, 62n158, 343
Widerszal, Ludwig, 115
Wiet, Gaston, 113, 210
women: and 'Ābdīn archive, 111, 115, 140; and authoritarian pluralism, 335, 335n88; emancipation of, 26; and nationalism, 171, 171n142, 223; and partisan historiography, 223, 228; Ṣabrī's views on, 86–87, 223. *See also* feminism
working class, 26, 28, 68, 74, 237, 244, 274–77, 290, 309, 313, 328
World War I, 69–70, 71n17, 72, 149, 189, 215, 223, 233–34, 254
World War II, 219, 221, 244

Yéghen, Foulad, *227*
Yemen war, 257, 282, 312, 325
Young Egypt, 230, 262
Young Turks revolution (1908), 80
Yūsuf, 'Alī, 27, 27n23
Yūsuf, Ḥasan, 180n178
Yūsuf, Sam'ān, 126, 132

Zaghlūl, Ṣafiyya, 228
Zaghlūl, Aḥmad Fatḥī, 65, 98
Zaghlūl, Sa'd, 14, 25, 68, 74, 74n26, 86, 249, 252, 317; and Arab socialist historiography, 287, 290, 292, 294, 307–8; and partisan historiography, 220, 223, 226–30, *227*, 232–35, 247
Al-Za'īm Aḥmad 'Urābī (al-Rāfi'ī), 174, 174n162
Zakī, 'Abd al-Raḥmān, 160
Zaky el-Ibrachy, Mohamed, *182*
Zaydān, Jurjī, 7, 20, 25, 74n26, *236*; debate over founder paradigm/thesis, 33, 33n51, 63–64; and de-Ottomanization, 78–80, 80n51, 83; and historical novels, 53–59, 59n, 89; and subjectivity, 47, 62; and time, perception of, 37–41, 40n75, 41nn78,80, 43; and visual history, 38–39, 43, 51
Zayni Barakat (al-Ghīṭāni), 312
Zayyāt, 'Abduh Ḥasan al-, *227*
Zionism, 270, 318
Ziyāda, Muṣṭafa, 196, 203, 208
Zubaida, Sami, 73

TEXT
10/12.5 Minion Pro
DISPLAY
Minion Pro
COMPOSITOR
BookMatters, Berkeley
INDEXER
Sharon Sweeney